Windows Server® 2008 PKI and Certificate Security

Brian Komar

PUBLISHED BY
Microsoft Press
A Division of Microsoft Corporation
One Microsoft Way
Redmond, Washington 98052-6399

Library of Congress Control Number: 2008920575

Printed and bound in the United States of America.

1 2 3 4 5 6 7 8 9   QWT   3 2 1 0 9 8

Distributed in Canada by H.B. Fenn and Company Ltd.

A CIP catalogue record for this book is available from the British Library.

Microsoft Press books are available through booksellers and distributors worldwide. For further information about international editions, contact your local Microsoft Corporation office or contact Microsoft Press International directly at fax (425) 936-7329. Visit our Web site at www.microsoft.com/mspress. Send comments to mspinput@microsoft.com.

Acquisitions Editor: Martin DelRe
Developmental Editor: Karen Szall
Project Editor: Denise Bankaitis
Editorial Production: Interactive Composition Corporation
Technical Reviewer: Paul Adare; Technical Review services provided by Content Master, a member of CM Group, Ltd.
Cover: Tom Draper Design

Body Part No. X14-60364

Contents at a Glance

Table of Contents

What do you think of this book? We want to hear from you!

Microsoft is interested in hearing your feedback so we can continually improve our books and learning resources for you. To participate in a brief online survey, please visit:

www.microsoft.com/learning/booksurvey/

Part II   Establishing a PKI

4   Preparing an Active Directory Environment **59**

5   Designing a Certification Authority Hierarchy **73**

What do you think of this book? We want to hear from you!

Microsoft is interested in hearing your feedback so we can continually improve our books and learning resources for you. To participate in a brief online survey, please visit:

www.microsoft.com/learning/booksurvey/

Acknowledgments

When you work on a book project, several people are involved in the writing process one way or another, and I am going to try my best to thank everyone who helped me through the research, envisioning, and writing of this book. If I did miss anyone, it is only because there were so many people who played a part in making this book a reality!

The first group of people that I want to thank is the PKI product and testing team, current members and past members, from Microsoft: David Cross, Vic Heller, Phil Hallin, Avi Ben-Menahem, Oded Ye Shekel, Jen Field, Kelvin Yiu, and Yogesh Mehta. All of you helped me get my head around several of the specifics of the Microsoft PKI and the new features of Windows Server 2008.

I especially want to thank Avi, Oded, Jen, and Carsten Kinder, who wrote many of the draft white papers that I used to research the topics for the second edition. Your white papers helped me learn the technologies and get my head around the the new nuances.

The second group of people that I have to thank are the clients that IdentIT Inc. has had the pleasure of working with over the last five years. Paul Adare and I have learned more than you can imagine by interacting with you and your networks.

A book is only as good as the project team that helps the author translate thoughts to words on a page. I want to specifically thank the following individuals:

- Martin DelRe, the product planner, for bringing the book proposal to Microsoft Press.

- Seth Scruggs, Chris Gregory, and Shawn Rabourn, for pushing me to proceed with a second edition.

- Denise Bankaitis, for keeping the project flowing (especially with my attempting to write parts of this book on every continent—again...).

- Paul Adare, for your outstanding technical review of the content. Although the reviews took me hours to incorporate, the book is much stronger because of your efforts and knowledge.

- The Trustworthy Computing Security Content Review Board (TwC SCRB), a Microsoft team that reviewed each and every chapter to provide the final check for technical accuracy and consistency with Microsoft product and technology messaging and strategies. The SCRB team members for this book were David Kennedy, Shawn Rabourn, Jonathan Stephens, Michiko Short, Elton Tucker, Ken Carr, Sanjay Pandit, Jose Luis Auricchio, Matthijs ten Seldam, Akshat Kesarwani, Edward Gomes, Lupe Brieno, Anders Brabæk, Mark Eden, and Monica Ene-Pietrosanu. A special thank-you to Ken, Shawn, and Jonathon for finding the time to review each and every chapter of this book.

- Sue McClung, for managing the vendor editorial team and keeping this book moving during the development process.

- Kenneth Jackson, for updating the enrollment script and creating a new version based on Certenroll.dll for Windows Vista clients.

- Ryan Hurst, for providing me information on the Online Certificate Status Protocol (OCSP) and agreeing to be quoted in the OCSP chapter.

Finally, I would like to thank you, the reader. If you bought the first edition of this book, your purchase helped convince Microsoft that this is a technology that needs to be documented and discussed for successful deployments. I have talked with many of you on public news groups and look forward to working with you in the future.

Foreword

The world of PKI, the deployments and the applications, have evolved significantly since Microsoft introduced user certificate enrollment in Windows XP and Windows Server 2003. Although we anticipated that we would change the world in how public key infrastructures were deployed and leveraged, little did we know how fast the market would change and the deployments flourish. When we set out with the Microsoft Windows 2000 release of the Microsoft PKI, we wanted to make PKI as easy and ubiquitous as TCP/IP, Web browsing, and Kerberos. To achieve that goal, we needed to accomplish two critical criteria:

- Simplify the configuration and management of certification authorities
- Eliminate the need for end users to see or understand PKI

Of course, every deployment and every application requirement is different—but the reality was the world needed an easy, cost–effective, and secure infrastructure to support the growing need for encryption, data integrity, and authentication capabilities in an increasingly hostile world. Five years later, when we look at our goals and the success to date, I am more than pleasantly surprised when I see the number of deployments and maturity of public key infrastructures in use. Not a week goes by that I don't hear about another customer that has issued millions of certificates for IPSec from a single Windows Server 2003 certificate server or an enterprise that has deployed a global smart card logon solution for all remote access and VPN users. What took months to set up and years to deploy in large numbers is now taking days and the deployments completed in the matter of a few months.

Yet, despite the maturity of PKI and the mass deployments, the technology continues to evolve and change with the security risks, attacks, and requirements of the time. Customer, consumers, and enterprises are becoming increasingly aware and demanding encryption and protection of data be applied and used whenever sensitive information is stored or transferred. This leads to increasing performance, reliability, and usability requirements in both the platform and applications. Windows Server 2008 includes the latest advancements in cryptographic algorithm strength, performance, and optimizations.

Windows Server 2008 provides the latest technology and updates to meet those ever-evolving needs and security requirements of the future. It not only provides support for the latest hash algorithms and asymmetric public key technologies and a modern revocation technology infrastructure, it also provides this capability on top of a modern agile cryptographic platform. What is unique in Windows Server 2008 is the introduction of Cryptography Next Generation (CNG), which enables independent hardware vendors, independent software vendors, and customers to use and plug in their own algorithms without waiting for a complete update or revision to the Windows platform. This is a significant step forward for the infrastructure to evolve dynamically as the security landscape changes unpredictably.

In addition to development and use of new algorithms, hashing techniques, and protocols, Windows Server 2008 introduces additional management and deployment enhancements such as native integration of the Simple Certificate Enrollment Protocol (SCEP), Microsoft Operations Manager (MOM) monitor and management pack, and inline revocation services that support Online Certificate Status Protocol (OCSP) clients. When you look at the number of enhancements and overall functionality in Windows Server 2008, you would agree the technology area is continuing to mature and innovate.

What's next for the future of PKI? If I were to be an oracle and predict the future, I would say that the industry will continue to see integration with card management systems, additional integration with identity management systems, and next generation deployment capabilities that are natively integrated into the latest Web service and wireless protocols. I think that you will see Windows Server 2008 as a preview of many of these integrations along with the release of other Microsoft products such as Identity Lifecycle Manager, System Center, and Forefront.

Why a second book on Microsoft PKI? Well, very frankly, the market demand for PKI and Active Directory Certificate Services demands it. As a whole, the market has not produced many PKI books, but I think Microsoft Press has found and hit a "sweet spot" in the industry— it focuses on real world deployments and IT professional needs, and of course, it is based on the most popular and widely deployed PKI globally: Active Directory Certificate Services.

Brian Komar has become a beacon and unique champion for the Microsoft PKI vision and solution around the world. He has a unique style and balance in his approach, which provides IT professionals and enterprises a pragmatic view of deployments while at the same time providing all the tricks, traps, and best practices to be aware of...before the deployment starts. Brian has built this database of knowledge, and subsequently represented in this book, through his long-term working relationship with the PKI product development team here in Redmond combined with numerous hands-on customer engagement and deployments using the Microsoft PKI solution.

This book is a "must have" for the Microsoft PKI administrator. It takes the best of the product team development knowledge, the best practices from our field consultants around the world (Microsoft Consulting Services), and our customer deployments to date and distills into a one-stop resource kit of knowledge that cannot be found in any other single source to my knowledge. The goal of the book helps to achieve the goal that we set out many years ago: Enable customers to deploy PKI to achieve their security and application protection requirements as easily as any other critical network infrastructure technology. I look forward to the day when PKI becomes a household word on the Internet just like "IP addresses." I think we are well on our way with people like Brian carrying the message.

December 2007

David B. Cross

Director of Program Management

Windows Security

Microsoft Corporation

Introduction

Welcome to *Windows Server 2008 PKI and Certificate Security*. This book provides detailed information about designing and implementing public key infrastructure (PKI) solutions with the Windows Server 2008 certification authority (CA). This book is based on the white papers and guidelines produced by the Microsoft PKI product team and on my experience working with Microsoft Consulting Services and my company's consulting engagements at customer sites over the past five years.

About This Book

Although you are welcome to read the book from cover to cover, it is divided into three self-contained parts. Each part contains chapters that build on the lessons and practices described within that part. Each chapter ends with a case study that enforces the critical concepts discussed in the chapter, allowing you to validate how well you understand the concepts of the chapter.

 Note   The answers for the case study questions are available in the appendix, "Case Study Questions and Answers" in both the print copy of the book and the eBook, which can be found on the *Windows Server 2008 PKI and Certificate Security* companion CD.

The three parts of this book are the following:

- **Part I, "Foundations of PKI"**   Part I provides an overview of cryptography and PKI concepts and culminates with one of the most important chapters in the book, Chapter 3, "Policies and PKI." Part I ensures that you understand the relationship between a PKI and your organization's security policies. Without strong policies and procedures, a PKI is simply a collection of application servers, rather than a mechanism for securing your network and its applications.

- **Part II, "Establishing a PKI"**   Part II provides a framework for designing and implementing a PKI within your organization, including detailed information on preparing your Active Directory Domain Services (AD DS) environment and designing and implementing your organization's CA hierarchy. Part II includes information on designing and implementing a CA hierarchy, designing certificate templates, planning deployment of certificates to users and computers, and disaster recovery recommendations. When you complete Part II, you will have a CA hierarchy that is ready to deploy certificates for any PKI-enabled application used by your organization. In addition, this section covers clustering a CA and implementing Online Certificate Status Protocols (OCSPs).

■ **Part III, "Deploying Application-Specific Solutions"**   Part III provides detailed information on deploying certificates for specific PKI-enabled applications. Each chapter in this section offers details on the types of certificates required for the specific application, recommendations on how to deploy the certificates to the required users and computers, and provides best practices for deploying each PKI-enabled application. New applications have been added in this second edition of the PKI book. The new applications include Microsoft Identity Lifecycle Manager (ILM) 2007, Document Signing, deploying certificates to domain controllers, and Network Device Enrollment Services (NDES). Also, major updates were performed on the chapters covering smart cards and implementing Secure Sockets Layer (SSL) for Web servers.

Note   Unfortunately, when you write a book, you must consider page count limits. Due to page count, I was unable to include chapters on deploying certificates for Network Access Protection (NAP) and Remote Desktop Protocol (RDP). I have included documentation on these two technologies on the *Windows Server 2008 PKI and Certificate Security* companion CD to provide you with at least some information on these technologies.

Windows Server 2008 PKI and Certificate Security Companion CD

The companion CD included with this book contains a variety of tools and scripts to help you deploy a Windows Server 2008 PKI and issue certificates to computers running Microsoft Windows 2000, Windows XP, Windows Server 2003, Windows Vista, and Windows Server 2008.

Note   The scripts are provided "as is" and serve as examples of how you can use scripts to configure your Windows Server 2008 PKI deployment.

To connect directly to the Microsoft Knowledge Base and enter a query regarding a question or issue you might have, go to *http://www.microsoft.com/learning/support/search.asp*. For issues related to the Windows operating system, please refer to the support information included with your product.

System Requirements

To use the scripts included on the companion CD-ROM, the following system requirements exist:

1. You can run the scripts included on the companion CD-ROM on a computer running Windows 2000, Windows XP, Windows Vista, Windows Server 2003, or Windows Server 2008. The specific operating system requirements are included in the chapter referencing the script.

2. You can deploy Certificate Services only on a computer running Windows Server 2003 or Windows Server 2008 Standard, Enterprise, and DataCenter editions.

3. A standalone certification authority (CA) in the CA hierarchy should be deployed on a computer running Windows Server 2003 or Windows Server 2008 Standard.

4. An issuing CA should be deployed on a computer running Windows Server 2003 or Windows Server 2008 Enterprise and DataCenter editions.

> **Find Additional Content Online**   As new or updated material that complements your book becomes available, it will be posted online on the Microsoft Press Online Windows Server and Client Web site. Based on the final build of Windows Server 2008, the type of material you might find includes updates to book content, articles, links to companion content, errata, sample chapters, and more. This Web site will be available soon at *www.microsoft.com/learning/books/online/serverclient*, and will be updated periodically.

> **Digital Content for Digital Book Readers:** If you bought a digital-only edition of this book, you can enjoy select content from the print edition's companion CD.
> Visit **http://go.microsoft.com/fwlink/?LinkId=113478** to get your downloadable content. This content is always up-to-date and available to all readers.

Part I
Foundations of PKI

Chapter 1

Cryptography Basics

This chapter will introduce the fundamentals of cryptography and provide a basic understanding of the type of encryption and signing that takes place in public key infrastructure (PKI)–enabled applications. This overview is not an in-depth look at cryptographic functions.

The chapter also introduces the new cryptographic options included in Windows Server 2008 and Windows Vista operating systems known as Cryptography Next Generation (CNG).

> **More Info**   For more information on cryptography, see *Cryptography and Network Security, Fourth Edition,* by William Stallings (Prentice Hall, 2006) or *Practical Cryptography,* by Niels Ferguson and Bruce Schneier (Wiley, 2003), which are referenced in the Additional Information section at the end of this chapter.

Encryption Types

Cryptography supports *symmetric encryption* and *asymmetric encryption* for cryptographic functions.

- **Symmetric encryption**   The same key is used for encryption and decryption. The key must be exchanged so that both the data sender and the recipient can access the plaintext data.

- **Asymmetric encryption**   Two mathematically related keys, a key pair consisting of a public key and a private key, are used in the encryption and decryption processes.

  - If the public key is used for encryption, the associated private key is used for decryption.

  - If the private key is used for encryption, the associated public key is used for decryption.

> **Note**   Only one person should hold the private key, but the public key can be distributed freely. The public key, as an attribute of a digital certificate, is often published in a network-accessible directory (such as Active Directory Domain Services, or AD DS) to allow easier access.

Algorithms and Keys

When data is encrypted, two inputs are required for encryption: an algorithm and a key.

- **Algorithm**   An *algorithm* defines how data is transformed when original plaintext data is converted into ciphertext and how the ciphertext is transformed back to the original plaintext data. Both the encryption and decryption processes must use the same algorithm.

- **Key**   A *key* is used as an input to the algorithm, along with the plaintext data, so that the algorithm can encrypt plaintext data into ciphertext or decrypt ciphertext back into plaintext data.

All applications determine how these inputs are distributed between the encoder and the decoder. Although it is not a security issue if an attacker identifies the algorithm used to encrypt the data, interception of the key is considered a security risk.

To enable encryption, a PKI-enabled application must do the following:

- **Identify the algorithms that are supported by the application.**   In some cases, the application must allow for algorithm negotiation so that the encoder and decoder can negotiate the strongest form of encryption.

- **Generate a key for use with the algorithm.**   In the best circumstances, the key is a one-time key—that is, it is used only for a single encryption and decryption process. When a key is reused many times, it becomes easier for attackers to determine the key, through a process called *differential cryptanalysis*. Differential cryptanalysis allows an attacker to determine the encryption key by supplying the encryption algorithm and several samples of ciphertext produced with the encryption key.

- **Determine a key distribution method.**   The key must be securely transmitted from the encoder to the decoder—that is, it must be protected against interception during this transmission and might have to be transmitted out-of-band (not on the network) or in an encrypted state.

Data Encryption

Encryption protects data against inspection by unauthorized people. This section will describe how symmetric encryption and asymmetric encryption processes work and how some applications combine symmetric and asymmetric processes.

Symmetric Encryption

As mentioned, symmetric encryption uses the same key for both encryption and decryption as shown in Figure 1-1. The algorithms associated with symmetric encryption are able to encrypt large amounts of data in little time thanks to the use of a single key and the fact that symmetric encryption algorithms are much simpler compared to asymmetric encryption algorithms.

> **Note**   Symmetric encryption is often referred to as *bulk encryption* because of its speed when encrypting large amounts of plaintext data.

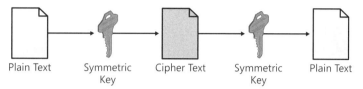

Plain Text   Symmetric   Cipher Text   Symmetric   Plain Text
                      Key   Key

Figure 1-1   The symmetric encryption process

When data is encrypted with a symmetric algorithm, the system generates a random symmetric key. The length of the key, typically expressed in the number of bits, is determined by the algorithm and the application using the symmetric algorithm.

Once the symmetric key is generated, the key is used to encrypt the plaintext data into an encrypted state, referred to as *ciphertext*. The ciphertext is then sent or made available to the data recipient.

> **Note**   The symmetric key must be securely transmitted to the recipient before the recipient can decrypt the ciphertext. The transmission of the symmetric key is the biggest security risk when using symmetric encryption algorithms. If the symmetric key is intercepted, attackers can decrypt all data encrypted with that key.

When a recipient receives the encrypted ciphertext and the symmetric key, he or she can use the symmetric key to decrypt the data back into its original plaintext format.

Symmetric Algorithms

Symmetric algorithms are among the most commonly used because of their ability to encrypt large amounts of data in little time. Symmetric algorithms used by PKI-enabled applications include:

> **Note**   This is not an exhaustive list of symmetric encryption protocols.

- **Data Encryption Standard (DES)**   An encryption algorithm that encrypts data with a 56-bit, randomly generated symmetric key.

- **Data Encryption Standard XORed (DESX)**   DESX is a stronger variation of the DES encryption algorithm. Instead of encrypting the plaintext directly, the plaintext is processed through an Exclusive Or (XOR) function with 64 bits of additional key material before the resulting data is encrypted with the DES algorithm. The output of the DES algorithm is also transformed with an XOR function with another 64 bits of key material. This helps protect the data against key search attacks based on the relatively short length of the DES 56-bit key.

- **Rivest's Cipher version 2 (RC2) (40 bit)**   A variable key-size block cipher with an initial block size of 64 bits that uses an additional string of 40 bits called a *salt*. The salt is appended to the encryption key, and this lengthened key is used to encrypt the message.

- **RC2 (128 bit)**   A variation on the RC2 (40-bit) cipher, where the salt length is increased to 88 bits.

- **RC4**   A variable key-size stream cipher with byte-oriented operations. The algorithm is based on the use of a random permutation and is commonly used for the encryption of traffic to and from secure Web sites using the Secure Sockets Layer (SSL) protocol.

- **Triple DES (3DES)**   A variation on the DES encryption algorithm in which DES encryption is applied three times to the plaintext. The plaintext is encrypted with key A, decrypted with key B, and encrypted again with key C. A common form of 3DES uses only two keys: The plaintext is encrypted with key A, decrypted with key B, and encrypted again with key A.

- **Advanced Encryption Standard (AES)**   Developed as a successor to DES, rather than using a 56-bit key, AES is able to use 128-bit, 192-bit, and 256-bit keys. AES uses the Rijndael algorithm and can encrypt data in one pass instead of three (as is the case with 3DES).

Note   AES was developed in response to a call for proposals by the National Institute of Standards and Technology (NIST) for encryption of unclassified data. Several algorithms were proposed, and the algorithm ultimately selected was the Rijndael algorithm. More information on AES is provided in the Additional Information section of this chapter.

Asymmetric Encryption

Asymmetric encryption increases the security of the encryption process by utilizing two separate but mathematically related keys known as a public key and a private key. The encryption process is more secure because the private key is possessed only by the user or computer that generates the key pair. The public key can be distributed to any person who wishes to send encrypted data to the private key holder.

Asymmetric encryption's use of two keys, one key for encryption and a related key for decryption, and the complexity of the asymmetric encryption algorithm make the encryption process much slower. Studies have shown that symmetric encryption is at least 100 times faster than asymmetric encryption when using software-based cryptography and can be as much as 10,000 times faster when using hardware-based cryptography.

When data is encrypted with asymmetric encryption, the key pair used is owned by the data recipient. The use of this key pair ensures that only the recipient has access to the necessary private key to decrypt the data, limiting data encryption to the recipient. (See Figure 1-2.)

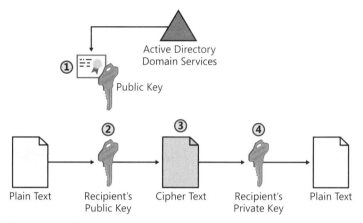

Figure 1-2   The asymmetric encryption process

1. The data sender obtains the recipient's public key. This can be sent to the data originator by the recipient or retrieved from a directory, such as AD DS.

2. The plaintext data is passed through an asymmetric encryption algorithm, using the recipient's public key as the encryption key. The encryption algorithm creates the encrypted ciphertext.

3. The ciphertext is sent or made available to the recipient. There is no need to send the key because the recipient already has the private key required to decrypt the ciphertext.

4. The recipient decrypts the ciphertext with his or her private key, and the resulting plaintext is the original plaintext created by the data originator.

Important   It is very rare for an application to use only an asymmetric encryption algorithm. Typically, the data is encrypted with a symmetric algorithm, and then only the symmetric encryption key is encrypted with the asymmetric encryption algorithm. This combination is discussed in the section "Combining Symmetric and Asymmetric Encryption," later in this chapter.

Asymmetric Signing Process

Asymmetric algorithms can be used to protect data from modification and prove the data creator's identity. In this scenario, the public and private key roles are reversed, requiring use of the originator's key pair.

> **Note**   Proof of the originator's identity is accomplished because only the originator has access to the private key of the key pair. Of course, this is subject to the method used to protect the originator's private key. A hardware-protected private key, such as a private key stored on a smart card, provides more assurance than a private key stored in the user's local certificate store.

Figure 1-3 shows how asymmetric signing proves the sender's identity and prevents the data from being modified.

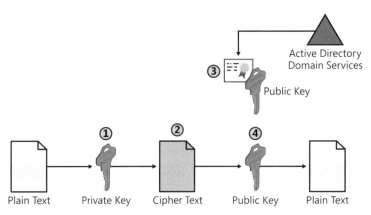

Figure 1-3   The asymmetric signing process

1. The plaintext data is passed through an asymmetric encryption algorithm, using the originator's private key as the encryption key. The result of the encryption algorithm is the encrypted ciphertext.

2. The ciphertext is sent or made available to the recipient.

3. The data recipient obtains the originator's public key. The public key can be sent with the ciphertext, or the recipient can obtain the public key from a trusted source, such as a directory.

4. The recipient decrypts the ciphertext with the originator's public key. The resulting plaintext is the original plaintext created by the data originator.

Decryption by the public key of the originator's key pair proves that the data was created by the originator. It also proves that the data was not modified in transit, because any modification results in a decryption process failure.

Asymmetric Algorithms

The following asymmetric algorithms are used in PKI-enabled applications when encrypting or digitally signing data.

■ **Diffie-Hellman Key Agreement**   This algorithm is not based on encryption and decryption but instead relies on mathematical functions that enable two parties to generate a shared secret key for exchanging information online confidentially. When the Diffie-Hellman key agreement is used between two hosts, the two hosts agree on a public value (v) and a large prime number (p). Each host chooses his or her own secret value and, using their three inputs, they arrive at a public value that can be exchanged. These two public values are used to calculate a shared secret key used by both hosts to encrypt data sent between them.

■ **Rivest Shamir Adleman (RSA)**   This algorithm can be used for encrypting and signing data. The encryption and signing processes are performed through a series of modular multiplications. The security of the RSA algorithm can be increased by using longer key lengths, such as 1,024 bits or more—the longer the key length, however, the slower the encryption or signing process.

> **Note**   Both Diffie-Hellman and RSA can be used for key exchange, allowing secure transmission or negotiation of a symmetric key between the data originator and recipient.

■ **Digital Signature Algorithm (DSA)**   This algorithm can be used only for signing data; it cannot be used for encryption. The DSA signing process is performed through a series of calculations based on a selected prime number. Although intended to have a maximum key size of 1,024 bits, longer key sizes are now supported.

Combining Symmetric and Asymmetric Encryption

In most applications, symmetric and asymmetric encryption are combined to take advantage of each method's strengths.

When symmetric and asymmetric encryption are combined:

■ Symmetric encryption is used to convert the plaintext to ciphertext. This takes advantage of the symmetric encryption speed.

■ Asymmetric encryption is used to exchange the symmetric key used for encryption. This takes advantage of the security of asymmetric encryption, ensuring that only the intended recipient can decrypt the symmetric key.

Figure 1-4 shows the process that takes place when symmetric and asymmetric encryption are combined:

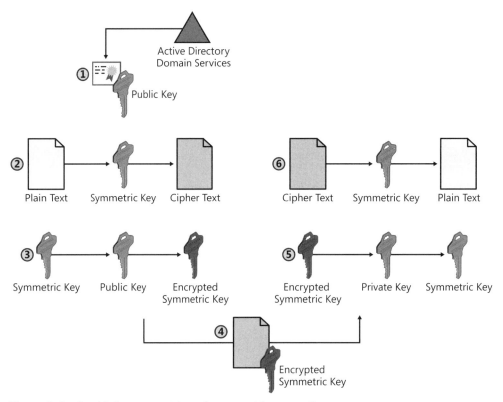

Figure 1-4   Combining symmetric and asymmetric encryption

1. The sender retrieves the recipient's public key. In an AD DS environment, the sender retrieves the public key from a trusted source, such as AD DS.

2. The sender generates a symmetric key and uses this key to encrypt the original data.

3. The symmetric key is encrypted with the recipient's public key to prevent the symmetric key from being intercepted during transmission.

4. The encrypted symmetric key and encrypted data are provided to the intended recipient.

5. The recipient uses his or her private key to decrypt the encrypted symmetric key.

6. The encrypted data is decrypted with the symmetric key, which results in the recipient obtaining the original data.

Digital Signing of Data

The goal of cryptography is three-fold: keep data secret, identify if data has been modified, and prove the source of the data. Although encryption can keep data secret and protect data against modification, only digital signing proves the source of the data in addition to protecting the data from modification. Digital signing protects data in the following ways:

- The digital signing process uses a hash algorithm to determine whether the original data has been modified in any way.

- A digital signature applied to the resulting message digest identifies who signed the message digest. This signing prevents users from denying they signed the message digest, as only they have access to the private key used to sign the message digest. The inability for signers to deny that a signature is theirs is known as *non-repudiation*.

The Hash Process

A hash algorithm takes a plaintext document as input and produces a mathematical result for the two inputs. This mathematical result is referred to as a *hash value*, *message digest*, *digest*, or *thumbprint*. If a single character is changed in the plaintext document, the resulting message digest has a value change for more than half of its digits. For example, if the resulting message digest is 128 bits in length, more than 64 bits change as a result of a single character change in the original plaintext document.

Note   It is technically possible for two data inputs to produce the same digest with a hash algorithm. Although possible, it is mathematically improbable that two data inputs will produce the same digest and be comprehendible.

Hash Algorithms

The following hash algorithms are commonly used in PKI-enabled applications to produce a hash value.

- **Message Digest 5 (MD5)**   This algorithm takes a message of any length and produces a 128-bit message digest.

- **Secure Hash Algorithm 1 (SHA1)**   This algorithm takes data that is less than 2^{64} bits in length and produces a 160-bit message digest.

Although the SHA1 algorithm is slightly slower than MD5, it is considered more difficult to find two data inputs that result in the same hash value when you use the SHA1 algorithm.

Note   It is recommended to use only SHA1 or the newer hash algorithms discussed in the section titled "Cryptography Next Generation (CNG)," later in this chapter.

Combining Asymmetric Signing and Hash Algorithms

Most applications that perform digital signing use a combination of asymmetric signing and hash algorithms. Whereas the hash algorithm provides a mechanism to determine whether the original message has been modified in any way, the addition of a digital signature protects the resulting digest from modification and proves that the digest was created by the originator of the data.

Figure 1-5 shows the interaction of asymmetric signing and hash algorithms in the digital signing process:

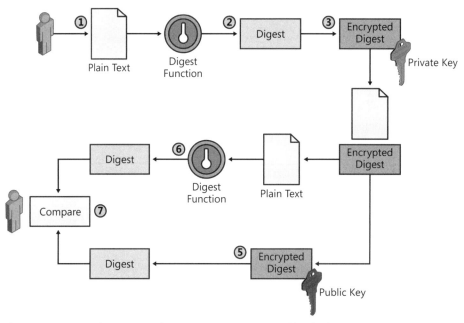

Figure 1-5   Digital signing with asymmetric signing and hash algorithms

1. The originator creates a plaintext data file.

2. The originator's software runs a hash algorithm against the plaintext message to create a message digest.

3. The digest is encrypted using the originator's private key.

4. The plaintext message and the encrypted digest are sent or made available to the recipient.

> **Note**   When using digital signing, no encryption is applied to the plaintext data. The plaintext can be modified, but modification invalidates the encrypted digest sent with the message.

5. The recipient decrypts the encrypted digest by using the sender's public key. The public key can be retrieved from a directory where the public key is stored (such as AD DS) or included with the signed data.

6. The recipient runs the same hash algorithm used by the sender to create his or her own digest of the message. This digest is created against the plaintext message received from the originator.

7. The two digests are compared. If the digests differ, the message or digest has been modified during transmission.

Cryptography Next Generation (CNG)

Cryptography Next Generation (CNG) is the replacement cryptography application programming interface (API) for the original Windows CryptoAPI. The new APIs will allow the use of newer, stronger encryption and signing algorithms when implementing cryptography.

Features of CNG

CNG has the following features that differentiate it from the legacy CryptoAPI:

- **Auditing** CNG increases auditing abilities to meet *Common Criteria* requirements. The events are captured by the Key Service Provider (KSP) in user mode and include:
  - ❑ Errors during testing of keys. The tests include verification, consistency, self-tests, and parity checks.
  - ❑ Failures during cryptographic operations. The operations include encryption, decryption, hashing, signature, verification, key exchange, and random number generation.
  - ❑ Generation, destruction, importing, and exporting of key pairs.
  - ❑ Reading and writing of persistent keys to and from the file system.

> **Tip** KSP audit logs are not generated automatically. You must use auditpol.exe to enable collection of all KSP auditing by running **auditpol/set/subcategory:"other system events"/success:enable/failure:enable.**

- **Certification and Compliance** CNG is targeting Federal Information Processing Standards (FIPS) 140-2 level 2 certification together with Common Criteria evaluation on selected platforms. Other platforms will meet FIPS 140-2 level 1 certification.

- **Cryptographic Agility** CNG will support *cryptographic agility,* or the ability to deploy new cryptographic algorithms for an existing protocol such as Transport Layer Security/Secure Sockets Layer (TLS/SSL) or to disable algorithms if a vulnerability is found with the specific algorithm. This modification to cryptographic operations required converting most standard cryptographic protocols (TLS/SSL, Secure Multipurpose Internet Mail Extensions, or S/MIME, Internet Protocol security, or IPsec, and Kerberos) to allow these protocols to take advantage of new algorithms available in CNG.

■ **Kernel Mode Support**   CNG supports cryptography in kernel mode. Kernel mode provides better performance for common cryptographic features such as TLS/SSL and IPsec. That being said, not all CNG functions can be called from kernel mode.

> **Note**   CNG does not support pluggable algorithms and providers in kernel mode. The only supported cryptographic algorithms available in kernel mode are those implementations provided by Microsoft through the kernel mode CNG APIs.

■ **Key Storage**   CNG provides a model for key storage that supports both legacy and CNG-capable applications. The key storage router, shown in Figure 1-6, conceals details for key access from both the application and the storage provider used.

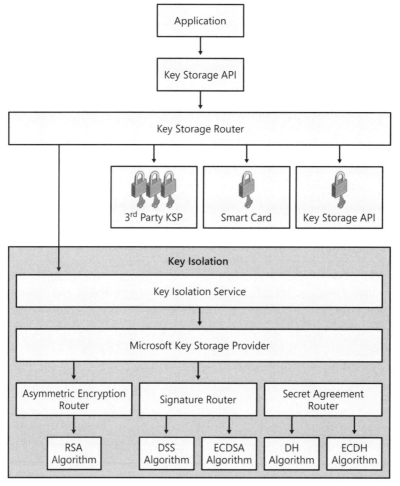

Figure 1-6   Key storage provider model

■ **Key Isolation**   CNG isolates long-lived keys so that they are never present in the application process. For example, CNG allows any computer with a Trusted Platform Module (TPM) to provide key isolation and key storage in TPM. The Local Security Authority (LSA) process is used as the key isolation process to maximize performance. The key isolation feature is not available on platforms prior to Windows Vista and Windows Server 2008. Also, only the Microsoft KSP is loaded in the key isolation service. Third-party key service providers are blocked from being loaded in the LSA process.

The Keys Have Moved

CNG also changes the default file system locations for the storage of cryptographic key materials. This change greatly simplifies the locations (removing the separate directory structures for RSA and DSS keys). In addition, CNG now supports Unicode characters for key container names, providing greater flexibility when generating RSA key pairs. The biggest change is the removal of the user's security identifier (SID) from the file path for key pairs. This change will ease the migration of key material when a user's account is moved between domains in a forest.

Table 1-1 summarizes the changes in the folder paths for various categories of key pairs:

Table 1-1   Changes in Crypto Folder Paths

Key type	CryptoAPI directories	CNG directory
User private	%APPDATA%\Microsoft\Crypto\RSA*User SID*\	%APPDATA%\Microsoft\Crypto\Keys
	%APPDATA%\Microsoft\Crypto\DSS*User SID*\	
Local system private	%ALLUSERSPROFILE%\Application Data\Microsoft\Crypto\RSA\S-1-5-18\	%ALLUSERSPROFILE%\Application Data\Microsoft\Crypto\SystemKeys
	%ALLUSERSPROFILE%\Application Data\Microsoft\Crypto\DSS\S-1-5-18\	
Local service private	%ALLUSERSPROFILE%\Application Data\Microsoft\Crypto\RSA\S-1-5-19\	%WINDIR%\ServiceProfiles\Local-Service
	%ALLUSERSPROFILE%\Application Data\Microsoft\Crypto\DSS\S-1-5-19\	
Network service private	%ALLUSERSPROFILE%\Application Data\Microsoft\Crypto\RSA\S-1-5-20\	%WINDIR%\ServiceProfiles\Network Service
	%ALLUSERSPROFILE%\Application Data\Microsoft\Crypto\DSS\S-1-5-20\	
Shared private	%ALLUSERSPROFILE%\Application Data\Microsoft\Crypto\RSA\MachineKeys	%ALLUSERSPROFILE%\Application Data\Microsoft\Crypto\Keys
	%ALLUSERSPROFILE%\Application Data\Microsoft\Crypto\DSS\MachineKeys	

■ **Legacy Support**   CNG provides support for the current set of algorithms in CryptoAPI 1.0 for legacy applications.

■ **Replaceable Random Number Generators**   Developers can replace the default random number generator for all cryptographic service providers when using CNG. Previously, it was not possible to redirect Microsoft Base Cryptographic Service Providers (CSPs) to another random number generator.

■ **Suite B Support**   This is probably the most recognized feature of CNG. In 2005, the United States National Security Agency (NSA) announced Suite B, a coordinated set of symmetric encryption, key exchange, digital signature, and hash algorithms, for United States government use. Suite B algorithms must be used for the protection of information designated as Top Secret, Secret, and Confidential Information.

What is special about Suite B algorithms is that they are publicly known, yet still considered very secure. This differs from previous "strong" algorithms that were unpublished to maintain secrecy.

■ **Thread Safety**   All functions within CNG are designed to support multithreaded/concurrent execution. Previously, a CryptoAPI function could operate only randomly in a multithreaded environment.

Algorithms Supported

Table 1-2 displays the default Suite B algorithms supported by Windows Vista and Windows Server 2008:

Table 1-2   Windows Vista and Windows Server 2008 Suite B Algorithms

Suite B algorithm	Description	Standard(s)
AES	The advanced encryption standard symmetric encryption algorithm.	FIPS 197
AES-GMAC*	The advanced encryption standard (AES) Galois message authentication code (GMAC) symmetric encryption algorithm.	SP800-38D
ECDH_P256	The 256-bit prime elliptic curve Diffie-Hellman key exchange algorithm.	SP800-56A
ECDH_P384	The 384-bit prime elliptic curve Diffie-Hellman key exchange algorithm.	SP800-56A
ECDH_P521	The 521-bit prime elliptic curve Diffie-Hellman key exchange algorithm.	SP800-56A
ECDSA_P256	The 256-bit prime elliptic curve digital signature algorithm (FIPS 186-2).	FIPS 186-2, X9.62
ECDSA_P384	The 384-bit prime elliptic curve digital signature algorithm (FIPS 186-2).	FIPS 186-2, X9.62

Table 1-2   Windows Vista and Windows Server 2008 Suite B Algorithms

Suite B algorithm	Description	Standard(s)
ECDSA_P521	The 521-bit prime elliptic curve digital signature algorithm (FIPS 186-2).	FIPS 186-2, X9.62
SHA256	The 256-bit secure hash algorithm.	FIPS 180-2, FIPS 198
SHA384	The 384-bit secure hash algorithm.	FIPS 180-2, FIPS 198
SHA512	The 512-bit secure hash algorithm.	FIPS 180-2, FIPS 198

* Only Windows Vista SP1 and Windows Server 2008 support this algorithm.

Supported Clients and Applications

CNG is not suitable for every operating system and every application. The following rules dictate when you can or cannot use CNG with your PKI deployment:

- The clients and servers must support CNG. CNG is supported only by Windows Vista and Windows Server 2008 clients and servers.

- You do *not* need to integrate with certification authorities (CAs) that do not support Suite B algorithms. For example, you want to issue an application's certificates from Microsoft Windows 2000, Windows Server 2003, and Windows Server 2008 CAs.

- The applications you implement must support Suite B algorithms. Even if the CA can issue and manage certificates that support Suite B types, the applications must be able to use the keys generated using Suite B algorithms and perform chain validation of the associated certificates.

Table 1-3 shows the certificate-enabled applications that can work with certificates that use CNG algorithms in Windows Vista and Windows Server 2008:

Table 1-3   Common Applications and CNG Support

Application name	Verify certificate chains with certificates using CNG algorithms	Use algorithms that are not supported by CryptoAPI
Encrypting File System (EFS)	Yes	No
IPsec	Yes	Yes
Kerberos	No	No
S/MIME	Microsoft Office Outlook 2003: no Microsoft Office Outlook 2007: yes	Outlook 2003: no Outlook 2007: yes
Smart card logon	No	No
SSL	Yes	Yes
Wireless	Yes	Yes

Case Study: Microsoft Applications and Their Encryption Algorithms

In this case study, you will research the encryption and hash algorithms supported by Encrypting File System (EFS). The research involves reviewing white papers available on the Internet (or the CD that accompanies this book if you do not have Internet connectivity):

Opening the EFS White Paper

Use the following procedure to open the "Encrypting File System in Windows XP and Windows Server 2003" white paper:

1. Insert the accompanying companion media in your CD-ROM drive.

2. Open Windows Explorer.

3. Open the folder X:\Case Studies\Chapter1\ (where X: is the letter of the CD-ROM drive).

4. In the X:\Case Studies\Chapter1 folder, double-click Encrypting File System in Windows XP and Windows Server 2003.htm.

> **Note** Alternatively, you can locate the "Encrypting File System in Windows XP and Windows Server 2003" white paper at *http://www.microsoft.com/technet/prodtechnol/ winxppro/deploy/cryptfs.mspx.*

5. On the Edit menu, click Find (on This Page).

6. In the Find dialog box, in the Find What box, type Default Encryption Algorithm, and then click Find Next.

7. In the Find dialog box, click Cancel.

Case Study Questions

1. Based on the encryption algorithms discussed in the "Default Encryption Algorithms" section of the white paper, does EFS use symmetric or asymmetric encryption?

2. What encryption algorithm is used to encrypt EFS data on a workstation running Windows 2000?

3. What encryption algorithms can be used to encrypt EFS data on Windows XP?

4. How does the application of Windows XP SP1 affect EFS encryption?

5. What Group Policy setting enables use of 3DES and AES encryption algorithms?

6. What asymmetric encryption algorithm is used to protect the FEK in EFS?

7. A developer in your organization has a laptop with a dual boot configuration of Microsoft Windows 2000 Professional and Windows XP Professional. Both operating systems have the latest service packs and security updates. The user's Outlook data file is encrypted, and the same EFS key pair is used in both operating systems to provide access to the Outlook data file.

   This morning, your developer was unable to access the Outlook data file when working in Windows 2000, but you are still able to create new encrypted files. Fearing that the Outlook data file was corrupt, she started Windows XP and was able to access the data file. What is the probable cause of this problem?

8. A project manager has read an article on Cryptography Next Generation and asks whether he can use AES-GMAC as the encryption algorithm for his EFS-encrypted files. What is the minimum operating system that he needs to run to support AES-GMAC?

9. Does EFS support the use of AES-GMAC for EFS encryption? What support does EFS provide for CNG algorithms and certificates that use CNG algorithms?

Additional Information

- Microsoft Official Curriculum, course 2821: "Designing and Managing a Windows Public Key Infrastructure" (*http://www.microsoft.com/learning/syllabi/en-us/ 2821Afinal.mspx*)

- *Cryptography and Network Security, Fourth Edition*, by William Stallings (Prentice Hall, 2006) (*http://www.prenhall.com/stallings/details8.html*)

- *Practical Cryptography*, by Niels Ferguson and Bruce Schneier (Wiley, 2003) (*http://www.wiley.com/WileyCDA/WileyTitle/productCd-0471223573.html*)

- "Cryptography and Microsoft Public Key Infrastructure" (*http://www.microsoft.com/ technet/security/guidance/cryptographyetc/cryptpki.mspx*)

- "Differential Cryptanalysis" (*http://en.wikipedia.org/wiki/Differential_cryptanalysis*)

- "Fact Sheet NSA Suite B Cryptography" (*http://www.nsa.gov/ia/industry/ crypto_suite_b.cfm*)

- "Specification for the Advanced Encryption Standard (AES)" (*http://csrc.nist.gov/ publications/fips/fips197/fips-197.pdf*)

- "Digital Signature Standard (DSS)" (Elliptic Curve Digital Signature Algorithm—FIPS 186-2 [using the curves with 256 and 384-bit prime moduli]) (*http://csrc.nist.gov/ publications/fips/fips186-2/fips186-2-change1.pdf*)

- "Recommendation for Pair-Wise Key Establishment Schemes Using Discrete Logarithm Cryptography" (NIST Special Publication 800-56A [using the curves with 256 and 384-bit prime moduli]) (*http://csrc.nist.gov/publications/nistpubs/800-56A/ SP800-56A_Revision1_Mar08-2007.pdf*)

- "Secure Hash Standard" (Secure Hash Algorithm—FIPS 180-2 [using SHA-256 and SHA-384]) (*http://csrc.nist.gov/publications/fips/fips180-2/fips180-2withchangenotice.pdf*)

- "Cryptography API: Next Generation" (*http://msdn2.microsoft.com/en-us/library/ aa376210.aspx*)

Chapter 2
Primer to PKI

This chapter provides an introduction to the building blocks of a public key infrastructure (PKI). This includes:

- Certificates
- Certification authorities (CAs)
- Certificate revocation lists (CRLs)

Certificates

Certificates provide the foundation of a public key infrastructure (PKI). Certificates are electronic representations of users, computers, network devices, or services, issued by a certification authority (CA), that are associated with a public and private key pair.

A certificate is a digitally signed collection of information generally 2–4 kilobytes (KB) in size. A certificate typically includes the following information:

- Information about the user, computer, or network device that holds the private key corresponding to the issued certificate. The user, computer, or network device is referred to as the subject of the certificate.
- Information about the issuing CA.
- The public key of the certificate's associated public and private key pair.
- The names of the encryption and/or digital signing algorithms supported by the certificate.
- A list of X.509 version 3 extensions included in the issued certificate.
- Information for determining the revocation status and validity of the certificate.

The CA must ensure the identity of the requestor before issuing a certificate. Identity validation can be based on the user's security credentials or might include a face-to-face or in-person interview to validate requestor identity. Once identity is confirmed, the CA issues the certificate and digitally signs the certificate with its private key. The signature certifies that the certificate was signed by the issuing CA and helps detect if changes are made to the certificate after issuance. Any change will result in the failure of the digital signature.

 Note It is nearly impossible for another user, computer, network device, or service to impersonate the subject of a certificate, because impersonation requires access to the certificate holder's private key. Impersonation is highly improbable if an attacker has access to the certificate only.

Three versions of digital certificates can be used in a PKI:

- X.509 version 1 certificates

- X.509 version 2 certificates

- X.509 version 3 certificates

X.509 Version 1

The X.509 version 1 certificate definition was defined in 1988. Its advanced age means you rarely see version 1 certificates in operation. The exceptions are some of the older root certificates and older Microsoft Exchange Key Management Service (KMS) deployments. The X.509 version 1 format defines the certificate fields, as shown in Figure 2-1.

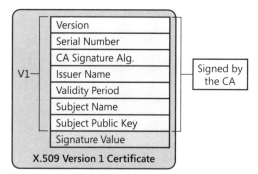

Figure 2-1   The X.509 version 1 certificate fields

An X.509 version 1 certificate contains the following fields:

- **Version**   Contains a value indicating that the certificate is an X.509 version 1 certificate.

- **Serial Number**   Provides a numeric identifier that is unique for each certificate issued by the CA.

- **CA Signature Algorithm**   The name of the algorithm the CA uses to sign the contents of a digital certificate. Figure 2-1 shows the fields included when creating the digital signature.

- **Issuer Name**   The distinguished name of the certificate's issuing CA. Typically, the distinguished name is represented in an X.500 or distinguished name format specified in the X.509 specification and Request for Comment (RFC) 3280, "Internet X 509 Public Key Infrastructure Certificate and Certificate Revocation List (CRL) Profile."

- **Validity Period**   The range of time for which the certificate is considered valid. In some implementations, the validity period is split into two fields: *Valid From* and *Valid To*.

- **Subject Name**   The name of the computer, user, network device, or service represented by the certificate. Typically, the subject name is represented in an X.500 or distinguished name format specified in the X.509 specification, but it can include other name formats, such as an RFC 822, "Standard for the Format of ARPA Internet Text Messages," e-mail name format.

- **Subject Public Key Info**   The public key of the certificate holder. The public key is provided to the CA in a certificate request and is included in the issued certificate. This field also contains the public key algorithm identifier, which indicates which public key algorithm is used to generate the key pair associated with the certificate.

- **Signature Value**   Contains the signature value that results from the CA signature algorithm used to sign the digital certificate.

In a version 1 certificate, the *Issuer Name* and *Subject Name* fields allow certificates to be organized into a chain of certificates that starts at the certificate issued to a user, computer, network device, or service and terminates with a root CA certificate.

> **Note**   Certificate chaining is fully discussed in Chapter 11, "Certificate Validation."

X.509 Version 2

Although the X.509 version 1 certificate format provides basic information about the certificate holder, the format offers little information about the certificate issuer. By including only the issuer, issuer name, CA signature algorithm, and signature value, the version 1 format does not have any provisions for CA renewal.

When a CA's certificate is renewed, two certificates possess the same *Issuer Name* field value. Likewise, it is possible for another organization to create a CA with the same issuer name. To address this, the X.509 version 2 certificate format was introduced in 1993. The version 2 format introduced two new fields to the certificate, as shown in Figure 2-2.

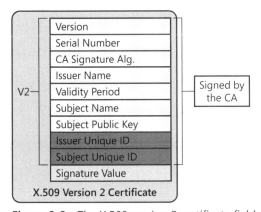

Figure 2-2   The X.509 version 2 certificate fields

The X.509 version 2 certificate format introduced the following fields:

- **Issuer Unique ID**   An optional field that contains a unique identifier, typically a hexadecimal string, for the issuing CA as defined by the issuing CA. When a CA renews its certificate, a new Issuer Unique ID is generated for that certificate version.

- **Subject Unique ID**   An optional field that contains a unique identifier, typically a hexadecimal string, for the certificate's subject as defined by the issuing CA. If the subject is also a CA, this unique identifier is placed in the Issuer Unique ID.

> **Note**   In addition to introducing the *Issuer Unique ID* and *Subject Unique ID* fields, the X.509 version 2 certificate's *Version* field changed to a value of 2 to indicate the version number.

The *Issuer Unique ID* and *Subject Unique ID* fields improved the certificate chaining process. The process now finds the CA certificate by matching the issuer name in the issued certificate to the subject name in the CA certificate and performs a second check by matching the Issuer Unique ID in the issued certificate with the Subject Unique ID of the CA certificate.

This additional level of matching allows a distinction between CA certificates when the CA renews a certificate. This method also allows for a distinction between CAs with the same subject name. (The likelihood of CA certificates with the same name increases when simple names are used–for example, *CN=Root CA* rather than *CN=Fabrikam Industries Inc. Corporate Root CA,O=Fabrikam,C=NL.*)

Although the addition of the Issuer Unique ID and Subject Unique ID aids in chain building, it's still possible for collisions to occur. A collision occurs when two certificates share the same *Subject Name* and *Subject Unique Identifier* fields.

> **Note**   Although the X.509 version 2 format improved on the version 1 format, the standard was not widely supported. In fact, RFC 3280, "Internet X.509 Public Key Infrastructure Certificate and Certificate Revocation List (CRL) Profile," recommends the omission of these X.590 version 2 fields.

X.509 Version 3

Released in 1996, the X.509 version 3 format introduced *extensions* to address the problems associated with matching the Issuer Unique ID with Subject Unique ID, as well as other certificate-validation issues. An X.509 version 3 certificate can contain one or more certificate extensions, as shown in Figure 2-3.

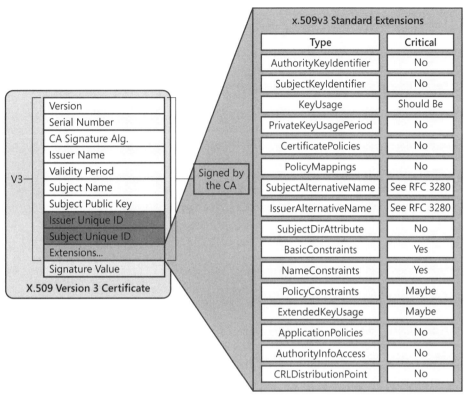

Figure 2-3   The X.509 version 3 certificate fields

Each extension in an X.509 version 3 certificate is composed of three parts:

■ **Extension Identifier**   An object identifier (OID) that indicates the format and definitions of the extension.

■ **Criticality Flag**   An indicator that signals whether the information in an extension is important. If an application cannot recognize the critical extension, or the extension contains no value, the certificate cannot be accepted or used. If the criticality flag is not set, an application can use the certificate even when the application does not recognize the extension.

■ **Extension Value**   The value assigned to the extension. The value varies depending on the specific extension.

In an X.509 version 3 certificate, the following certificate extensions can exist:

■ **Authority Key Identifier**   This extension can contain one of two values. The value can be either

  ❑ The subject of the CA and serial number of the CA certificate that issued the current certificate

  ❑ A hash of the public key of the CA certificate that issued the current certificate

■ **Subject Key Identifier**   This extension contains a hash of the current certificate's public key.

> **Note**   The use of the Authority Key Identifier and Subject Key Identifier in certificate chaining and validation is described in Chapter 11.

■ **Key Usage**   A CA, user, computer, network device, or service can have more than one certificate. The Key Usage extension defines the security services for which a certificate can be used. The options can be used in any combination and can include the following:

❑ **Digital Signature**   The public key can be used to verify signatures. This key is also used for client authentication and data-origin validation.

❑ **Non-Repudiation**   The public key can be used to validate the signer's identity, preventing a signer from denying that he or she signed an object.

❑ **Key Encipherment**   The public key can be used for key transport for processes, such as symmetric key exchange. This Key Usage value is used when an RSA key is used for key management.

❑ **Data Encipherment**   The public key can be used to directly encrypt data rather than exchanging a symmetric key for data encryption.

❑ **Key Agreement**   The public key can be used for key transport for processes such as symmetric key exchange. This value is used when a Diffie-Hellman key is used for key management.

❑ **Key Cert Sign**   The public key can be used to verify a certificate's signature.

❑ **CRL Sign**   The public key can be used to verify a CRL's signature.

❑ **Encipher Only**   This value is used in conjunction with the Key Agreement Key Usage extensions. The resulting symmetric key can be used only for data encryption.

❑ **Decipher Only**   This value is used in conjunction with the Key Agreement Key Usage extensions. The resulting symmetric key can be used only for data decryption.

■ **Private Key Usage Period**   This extension allows a different validity period to be defined for the private key of a key pair. The Private Key Usage Period can be set to a period shorter than the certificate's validity period. This gives the private key the ability to sign documents for a shorter period (say, one year), whereas the public key can be used to validate the signature for the certificate's entire five-year validity period.

■ **Certificate Policies**   This extension describes the policies and procedures used to validate a certificate's subject before the certificate is issued. Certificate policies are represented by OIDs. Optionally, a certificate policy can include a policy qualifier, which is typically a Uniform Resource Locator (URL) that describes, in text, the policies and procedures.

- **Policy Mappings**   This extension allows for policy-information translation between two organizations. For example, imagine that one organization defines a certificate policy named Management Signing, which is in certificates used for signing for large purchase orders. Another organization can have a certificate policy named Large Orders, which also is used to sign large purchase orders. Policy mapping allows the two certificate policies to be deemed equivalent.

> **Note**   Policy mapping typically requires that the participating organizations' legal departments inspect each certificate policy. The policies can be deemed equivalent only after the legal departments are satisfied.

- **Subject Alternative Name**   This extension provides a list of alternate names for the certificate's subject. Whereas the subject can include the subject name in an X.500 distinguished name format, the Subject Alternative Name allows for other representations, such as a User Principal Name (UPN), e-mail address, Internet Protocol (IP) address, or Domain Name System (DNS) name.

- **Issuer Alternative Name**   This extension provides a list of alternate names for the issuing CA. Though it is not typically implemented, the Issuer Alternative Name extension can contain the e-mail name associated with a CA.

> **Note**   The Subject Alternative Name and Issuer Alternative Name extensions can be either critical or noncritical. RFC 3280 states that if the *Subject* field is not empty, these extensions can be marked noncritical. If the *Subject* field is empty, these extensions must be marked critical to allow applications to inspect the contents of the Subject Alternative Name.

- **Subject Dir Attribute**   This extension can include any attributes from an organization's X.500 or Lightweight Directory Access Protocol (LDAP) directory. For example, the *country* attribute from a directory can be included in the Subject Dir Attribute extension. This extension can contain multiple attributes from the organization's directory. For each attribute, the OID and its corresponding value must be included.

- **Basic Constraints**   This extension allows a certificate to designate whether the certificate is issued to a CA or to a user, computer, network device, or service. Also, the Basic Constraints extension includes a path length constraint, which limits how many subordinate CAs can exist below a specific CA's issued certificate.

- **Name Constraints**   This extension allows an organization to designate which namespaces are allowed or disallowed in a CA-issued certificate. A separate name constraint must be defined for each namespace format used in certificates. For example, separate constraints are required for LDAP names versus e-mail names.

■ **Policy Constraints**   This extension can be included in CA certificates. The extension can prohibit policy mapping between CAs or require that each certificate in a certificate chain includes an explicit certificate policy OID.

■ **Enhanced Key Usage**   This extension indicates how a certificate's public key can be used. These are beyond the general purposes defined in the Key Usage extension. For example, OIDs exist for Client Authentication (1.3.6.1.5.5.7.3.2), Server Authentication (1.3.6.1.5.5.7.3.1), and Secure E-mail (1.3.6.1.5.5.7.3.4). When a certificate is presented to an application, an application can require the presence of an EnhancedKeyUsage OID specific to that application.

> **Note**   Enhanced Key Usage OIDs are also used when defining qualified subordination constraints. These constraints are discussed in Chapter 13, "Role Separation."

■ **CRL Distribution Points**   This extension contains one or more URLs where the issuing CA's base certificate revocation list (CRL) is published. If revocation checking is enabled, an application will use the URL to retrieve an updated version of the CRL. URLs can use Hypertext Transfer Protocol (HTTP), LDAP, or File.

■ **Authority Information Access**   This extension contains one or more URLs where the issuing CA's certificate is published. An application uses the URL when building a certificate chain to retrieve the CA certificate if it does not exist in the application's certificate cache.

■ **Inhibit Any Policy**   This extension is included in a CA certificate to inhibit the use of the All Issuance Policies OID (2.5.29.32.0) in subordinate CA certificates. This extension prevents the All Issuance Policies OID from being considered a match to a specific certificate policy OID in a subordinate CA certificate. The value of this extension defines the number of certificates that can appear below the CA certificate before the All Issuance Policies OID is not recognized.

■ **Freshest CRL**   This extension contains one or more URLs where the issuing CA's delta CRL is published. The delta CRL contains only the certificates revoked since the last base CRL was published. If revocation checking is enabled, an application will use the URL to retrieve an updated version of the delta CRL. URLs can use HTTP, LDAP, or File.

> **Note**   The use of base CRLs and delta CRLs is discussed in Chapter 11.

■ **Subject Information Access**   This extension contains information on how to access additional details about the certificate's subject. If the certificate is a CA certificate, the information can include particulars about the certificate validation services or the CA policy. If the certificate is issued to a user, computer, network device, or service, the extension can contain information about the services offered by the certificate subject and how to access those services.

> **Note**   In addition to introducing the extensions listed here, the X.509 version 3 certificate's *Version* field changed to a value of 3 to indicate the version number.

Certification Authorities

A certification authority (CA) is an essential component of the Microsoft PKI solution. In a Windows Server 2008 network, a CA is a Windows Server 2008 computer with Certificate Services installed. It performs the following tasks:

■ **Verifies the identity of a certificate requestor**   The CA must validate the requestor's identity before it can issue a certificate. Validation can range from ensuring that the requestor has the necessary permissions to ask for a specific type of certificate to having a certificate manager perform a face-to-face interview with the certificate requestor.

■ **Issues certificates to requestors**   After the requestor's identity is validated, the CA issues the requested type of certificate to the user, computer, network device, or service. The type of certificate requested determines the content of the issued certificate. For example, an Internet Protocol security (IPsec) certificate request results in a certificate that can be used only by a server or client to authenticate end points for IPsec communications.

■ **Manages certificate revocation**   The CA publishes a CRL at regularly scheduled intervals. The CRL contains a list of serial numbers of certificates that are revoked and the reason codes for each revocation.

In an enterprise PKI, more than one CA is typically implemented. The CAs are organized into a CA hierarchy consisting of a single root CA and several other subordinate CAs, as shown in Figure 2-4.

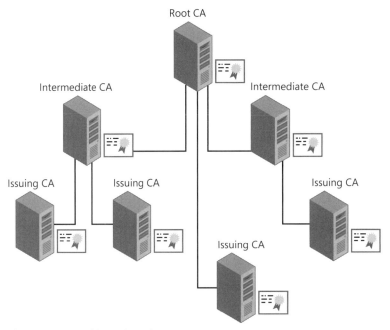

Figure 2-4   CA hierarchy roles

In Figure 2-4, the CAs are organized in a root CA hierarchy, which increases security and scalability of a CA hierarchy by allowing non-issuing CAs to be not attached to the network. If the root CA and second-tier CAs in a root CA hierarchy are not attached to the network, the offline CAs are protected from network-sourced attacks.

> **Note**   Do not assume that a root CA hierarchy always implements offline CAs. It is possible to deploy a root CA hierarchy without offline CAs, but it is not recommended because of security issues.

A root CA hierarchy allows the delegation of administration to different business units or divisions within an organization. Common-Criteria role separation allows the designation of CA management roles at each CA in the hierarchy, giving different administration groups the ability to manage one CA in the CA hierarchy but not others.

> **Note**   The root CA hierarchy is supported by all leading commercial CA vendors, including RSA, Thawte, and VeriSign. The root CA hierarchy is also supported by most applications and network devices, allowing for interoperability with a variety of applications and network devices.

Root CA

A *root CA* is the topmost CA in a CA hierarchy. In a PKI, the root CA acts as the trust point for certificates issued by CAs in the hierarchy. This means that if a certificate can be traced up through the CA hierarchy to a root CA that is trusted by a user, computer, network device, or service, the certificate is considered trusted.

A root CA is special in that its certificate is self-issued. This means that the certificate's *Issuer Name* and *Subject Name* fields contain the same distinguished name. The only way to verify whether a root certificate is valid is to include the root CA certificate in a trusted root store. The trusted root store contains the actual root CA certificate to designate that the certificate is trusted.

> **Note**   If a self-signed certificate is not included in the trusted root store, it is considered a nontrusted root CA.

The root CA can issue certificates to other CAs or to users, computers, network devices, or services on the network. When the root CA issues a certificate to another entity, the root CA certificate signs the certificate with its private key to protect against content modification and to indicate that the certificate was issued by the root CA.

> **Note**   Typically, the root CA issues certificates only to other CAs, not to users, computers, network devices, or services on the network.

Intermediate CA

An *intermediate CA* is a CA that is subordinate to another CA and issues certificates to other CAs in the CA hierarchy. The intermediate CA can exist at any level in the CA hierarchy except at the root CA level.

> **Note**   The CA that issues a certificate to another CA is often referred to as a *parent CA*. For example, a root CA that issues a certificate to an intermediate CA is referenced as the parent CA to the intermediate CA. The intermediate CA is also referred to as a *subordinate CA*, as it is directly subordinate to the parent CA in the hierarchy.

Policy CA

A special category of intermediate CA is a policy CA. A *policy CA* describes the policies and procedures an organization implements to validate certificate-holder identity and secure the CAs in the CA hierarchy. A policy CA issues certificates only to other CAs in the hierarchy. It is assumed that all CAs that are subordinate to a policy CA, whether directly subordinate or two or more levels below the policy CA, enforce the policies and procedures defined at the policy CA.

> **Note**   The policies and procedures are typically a combination of both logical controls (configuration settings at the policy CA) and qualitative controls (written policies that must be followed during operations).

If an organization must implement multiple policies and procedures when issuing certificates, multiple policy CAs must exist in the CA hierarchy, as shown in Figure 2-5.

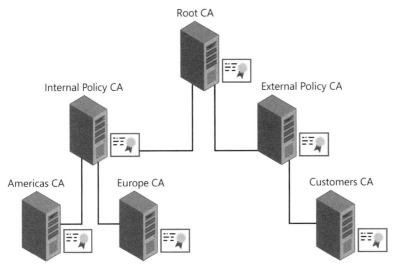

Figure 2-5   Policy CA example

In this example, two policy CAs exist in the CA hierarchy. The Internal Policy CA defines the policies and procedures used to validate the identity of the certificate requestor. The two issuing CAs (Americas CA and Europe CA), which are directly subordinate to the Internal Policy CA, must enforce the policies and procedures defined by the Internal Policy CA.

The External Policy CA defines the policies and procedures used to validate identity and secure the process of issuing certificates to nonemployees. The Customers CA, as a subordinate CA to the External Policy CA, must enforce the policies and procedures defined by the External Policy CA.

> **Note**   More than one policy or procedure can be defined at a policy CA, but it is also valid to implement one policy CA for each policy or procedure applied by the organization.

Issuing CA

An issuing CA issues certificates to users, computers, network devices, or services on the network. An issuing CA is typically located on the third tier of a CA hierarchy, but it can exist on the second level, as shown in Figure 2-4.

As mentioned, an issuing CA must enforce any policies and procedures defined by a policy CA that exists between the issuing CA and the root CA in the CA hierarchy. If an issuing CA is deployed at the second tier, it typically acts as both a policy CA and issuing CA and asserts its own policies and procedures.

Certificate Revocation Lists

In some cases, a CA must revoke a certificate before the certificate's validity period expires. When a certificate is revoked, the CA includes the serial number of the certificate and the reason for the revocation in the CRL.

 Note   A relying party should reject a certificate that is revoked.

Types of CRLs

Windows Server 2008 supports the issuance of two types of CRLs: base CRLs and delta CRLs.

A *base CRL* contains the serial numbers of all certificates revoked on a CA that are still time valid, as well as the reason for each revocation. A base CRL contains all time-valid revoked certificates signed by a CA's specific private key. If a CA's certificate is renewed with a new key pair, a new base CRL is generated that includes only revoked certificates signed with the CA's new private key.

A *delta CRL* contains only the serial numbers and revocation reasons for certificates revoked since the last base CRL was published. A delta CRL is implemented to provide more timely revocation information from a CA and to decrease the amount of data downloaded when retrieving a CRL. When a new base CRL is published, the revoked certificates in the delta CRL are added to the new base CRL. The next delta CRL will contain only certificates revoked since the new base CRL was published.

The delta CRL is much smaller than a base CRL because only the most recent revocations are included. The base CRL, which contains all revoked certificates, can be downloaded less frequently.

Note   If you implement delta CRLs, relying parties must still download the base CRL. It is the combination of the base CRL and the delta CRL that provides the complete information on all revoked certificates.

Important   Not all relying parties support delta CRLs. If a relying party does not support delta CRLs, the relying party will only inspect the base CRL to determine a certificate's revocation status.

Revocation Reasons

When a certificate is revoked, the CRL entry must contain further information about the revocation. The reason codes can include:

- **Key Compromise**   The private key associated with the certificate has been stolen or otherwise acquired by an unauthorized person, such as when a computer is stolen or a smart card is lost.

- **CA Compromise**   The private key of a CA has been compromised. This can occur when the computer running Certificate Services or the physical device that stores the CA's private key is stolen. If a CA's certificate is revoked, every certificate issued by the CA is also considered revoked because the CA that issued the certificates is no longer considered trustworthy.

- **Affiliation Changed**   The subject of the certificate, typically a user, is no longer affiliated with an organization.

- **Superseded**   The revoked certificate has been replaced by a new certificate. This can occur because of changes in the extensions in a certificate or the certificate's subject name changes.

- **Cessation Of Operation**   The certificate's subject has been decommissioned. This can take place when a Web server is replaced by a new Web server with a new name. Likewise, this can occur when a merger takes place and the previous DNS name is decommissioned, requiring replacement of all Web server certificates.

- **Certificate Hold**   A revocation where a certificate is determined to be temporarily revoked. This can occur when an employee takes a leave of absence. Certificate Hold is the only revocation reason that allows a certificate to be unrevoked.

Note   Although Certificate Hold allows a certificate to be unrevoked, use of the Certificate Hold reason code is not recommended because it can be difficult to determine if a certificate was valid at a specific time.

- **Remove From CRL** This reason is used when a certificate is unrevoked after being revoked with the Certificate Hold reason. Remove From CRL is used only in delta CRLs to indicate that a certificate revoked in the base CRL is unrevoked in the delta CRL.

- **Unspecified** If a certificate is revoked without providing a revocation reason, the unspecified reason is automatically included in the CRL.

> **Note** For more information about certificate revocation reason codes, see RFC 3280 (*http://www.faqs.org/rfcs/rfc3280.html*).

Online Certificate Status Protocol (OCSP)

Windows Server 2008 introduces an alternative to certificate revocation lists to determine whether a certificate is revoked. Rather than a client downloading a base CRL or delta CRL, the client (OCSP client) sends an HTTP-based certificate status request to a server (referred to as an OCSP responder). The client determines the OCSP responder's URL by inspecting the certificate's Authority Information Access extension. If the extension contains an OCSP responder URL and the client supports OCSP, the client can proceed with sending an OCSP request to the OCSP responder.

> **Note** OCSP is new to Windows Server 2008. The technology is not available in Windows Server 2003. Prior to Windows Server 2008, you had to implement third-party solutions to use OCSP with the Microsoft CA.

The responder communicates with the CA that issued the queried certificate to determine the revocation status and returns a digitally signed response indicating the certificate's status. The OCSP responder can communicate directly with the certification authority or inspect the CRLs issued by the CA to determine the revocation status of the requested certificate.

The advantage of OCSP is that the amount of data in the request and response is a fixed size. The number of certificates actually revoked by the certification authority does not affect the size of the OCSP responder's response. Additionally, the OCSP responder typically provides more up-to-date revocation information to the OCSP client.

The biggest issue faced when deploying OCSP is scalability of the OCSP responder. High availability is a must, requiring multiple servers in a Windows Load Balancing Service (WLBS) cluster or other load-balancing solution. The nodes in the cluster are often dispersed to major network hubs to allow timely responses to the OCSP clients.

OCSP Client

Windows Vista and Windows Server 2008 support the use of OCSP for certificate revocation status determination. The OCSP client meets RFC 2560–"X.509 Internet Public Key Infrastructure Online Certificate Status Protocol–OCSP" but also implements the recommendations in Standards Track RFC 5019–"The Lightweight Online Certificate Status Protocol (OCSP) Profile for High-Volume Environments" for optimization of OCSP in high-volume scenarios.

What Does RFC 5019 Support Add to OCSP?

The main reason for drafting RFC 5019 was to add functionality and performance to OCSP. Some of the major differences between the full profile (RFC 2560) and RFC 5019 include:

- The Lightweight OCSP Profile supports both the Hypertext Transfer Protocol (HTTP) and Hypertext Transfer Protocol Secure (HTTPS).

- Lightweight OCSP Profile responses must specify notBefore and notAfter dates, which are not required in the full profile.

- Signed requests are not supported in the Lightweight OCSP Profile. The client cannot create a signed request; if a signed request, which can be created by third-party OCSP clients, is sent to the Online Responder, an "Unauthorized" response is returned.

- With the Lightweight OCSP Profile, nonce (a unique identifier) is not supported in the request and is ignored in the response. However, the Online Responder supports the nonce extension and will return a response that includes the nonce extension if configured to do so.

Ryan Hurst

Co-author of RFC 5019

Online Responder Service

The Online Responder is a Microsoft Windows service (ocspsvc.exe) that runs on the OCSP server with Network Service privileges. The following operations are performed by the Online Responder service:

- **Manages OCSP configuration**   The Online Responder service attributes that can be configured include public interfaces, access control settings, audit settings, and Web proxy cache settings. The settings are stored in the registry of the OCSP server under HKEY_LOCAL_MACHINE\SYSTEM\CurrentControlSet\Services\OCSPSvc\Responder.

- **Retrieves and caches revocation information**   The Online Responder can retrieve and cache revocation information (such as base CRLs and delta CRLs) for future responses.

- **Signs OCSP responses**   When the OCSP server responds to an OCSP request, the Online Responder service signs the response with a pre-defined signing key.

- **Audits configuration changes**   You can audit any changes to the configuration of the Online Responder. The auditing configuration meets Common Criteria requirements for auditing.

Case Study: Inspecting an X.509 Certificate

In this case study, you will examine a sample certificate and answer questions related to the fields and extensions included in the certificate.

Opening the Certificate File

Use the following procedure to open the sample certificate file on the compact disc that accompanies this book.

1.   Insert the companion media in your CD-ROM drive.

2.   Open Windows Explorer.

3.   Open the folder CD:\Case Studies\Chapter2\.

4.   In the CD:\Case Studies\Chapter2 folder, double-click Samplecertificate.cer.

5.   In the Certificate dialog box, click the Details tab.

6.   From the resource materials for this chapter, open the Samplecertificate.cer file.

Case Study Questions

1.   What version is the certificate?

2.   What is the name of the issuing CA?

3.   What is the subject name of the certificate?

4.   Are any other names included in the certificate for the subject?

5.   What is the length of the public key associated with the certificate?

6.   What other X.509 extensions are included in the sample certificate?

7.   What extensions must you inspect to determine what forms of revocation checking are supported by the CA that issued the X.509 certificate?

8.   What forms of revocation checking are supported by the CA that issued the X.509 certificate?

9.   Where is the CRL published when revocation checking is performed against the certificate?

Additional Information

- Microsoft Official Curriculum, Course 2821: "Designing and Managing a Windows Public Key Infrastructure" (*http://www.microsoft.com/traincert/syllabi/2821afinal.asp*)

- RFC 3280–"Internet X.509 Public Key Infrastructure Certificate and Certificate Revocation List (CRL) Profile" (*http://www.faqs.org/rfcs/rfc3280.html*)

- RFC 2560–"X.509 Internet Public Key Infrastructure Online Certificate Status Protocol–OCSP" (*http://www.faqs.org/rfcs/rfc2560.html*)

- RFC 5019–"The Lightweight Online Certificate Status Protocol (OCSP) Profile for High-Volume Environments" (*http://tools.ietf.org/html/rfc5019*)

Chapter 3
Policies and PKI

A public key infrastructure (PKI) is only as secure as the policies and procedures that are implemented by an organization in conjunction with its PKI. Three policy documents directly affect the design of an organization's PKI:

- **Security policy** A *security policy* is a document that defines an organization's standards in regard to security. The policy usually includes the assets an organization considers valuable, potential threats to those assets, and, in general terms, measures that must be taken to protect these resources.

- **Certification policy** A *certification policy* (CP) is a document that describes the measures an organization will use to validate the identity of a certificate's subject and for what purposes a certificate following the certificate policy can be used. Validation might require a requestor-provided account and password submitted to the organization's directory, or photo identification and submission to a background check through a registration authority (RA) process.

- **Certification practice statement** A *certification practice statement* (CPS) is a public document that describes how a certification authority (CA) is managed by an organization to uphold its security and certificate policies. A CPS is published at a CA and describes the operation of the CA.

Security policies, certificate policies, and CPSs are typically created by members of an organization's legal, human resources, and information technology (IT) departments. The PKI design must enforce these policies.

> **Warning** Certificate policies and CPSs are used by other organizations to determine how well they trust certificates issued by an organization's CA hierarchy. You trust a certificate from another organization when you allow that certificate to be used on your network for signing or encryption purposes. Deploying a PKI without implementing certificate policies and CPSs can result in a PKI that causes your organization to be deemed untrustworthy by other organizations.

A dependency exists between the security policy, certificate policy, and CPS in a PKI, as shown in Figure 3-1. It operates as follows:

1. An organization first develops a security policy, defining the organization's security standards.

2. Next, a certificate policy is drafted to enforce and reflect the organization's security policy.

3. Finally, the CPS defines the CA's management procedures that enforce the certificate policy.

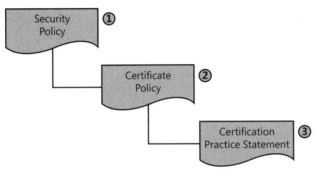

Figure 3-1   The dependency between the security policy, certificate policy, and certification practice statement (CPS)

Note   Security policies, certificate policies, and CPSs are typically legal documents that must be reviewed by an organization's legal department or legal representatives before publication to ensure that the documents are enforceable and do not misrepresent the organization's intent.

Security Policy

The design of a PKI starts with an inspection of the organization's security policy. A PKI designer uses a security policy to answer the following questions:

- **What data should be secured with certificates?**   Not all applications support certificate-based security. Typically, a security policy defines classes of data within the organization and measures that must be taken to protect that data when stored and when transmitted across a network. With a PKI in place, these measures can include the use of protocols such as Secure Sockets Layer (SSL) or Internet Protocol security (IPsec) to protect transmitted data and Encrypting File System (EFS) to protect stored data.

- **What measures must be taken to protect the private keys associated with a certificate?**   Measures can include storing the certificate on a smart card, protecting a CA's private key by implementing hardware security modules (HSMs), or preventing the export of a certificate's private key.

Defining Effective Security Policies

A security policy defines an organization's security standards. An organization typically has several security policy documents that provide comprehensive definitions of security issues, the risks and threats faced by the organization, and the measures that must be taken to protect the organization's data and assets.

> **Note**   An organization must do more than just define security policies. It must ensure that it deploys security solutions to enforce the security policies, and it must ensure that employees are aware of those security policies and their roles and responsibilities in maintaining security.

Once an organization defines its security policies, an initial assessment must be performed to identify measures that enforce those policies. Once these measures are identified, a *gap analysis* determines whether additional measures should be implemented to meet the defined security policies. After proper planning, the security policy implementation process can begin.

An organization should periodically review its security policies and the measures taken to enforce them to determine if modifications are necessary. Modifications might involve updating security policies or revising the processes and procedures that enforce them.

Resources for Developing Security Policies

Two of the most commonly used resources for defining a security policy are ISO 27002, "Code of Practice for Information Security Management," and RFC 2196, "The Site Security Handbook."

> **Note**   The International Standards Organization (ISO) recently renamed ISO 17799 and its predecessor British Standards (BS) 7799. The newly assigned numbers are ISO 27002 (formerly known as ISO 17799) and ISO 27001 (formerly known as BS 7799-2). The rename was initiated by ISO to align the standard under a common naming structure, the ISO 27000 series.

ISO 27002, available for purchase at *http://www.27000-toolkit.com*, provides detailed information and recommendations for developing enforceable security policies. Several Web sites provide security policy samples based on the intent and recommendations of ISO 27002.

RFC 2196, "Site Security Handbook," available at *http://www.ietf.org/rfc/rfc2196.txt*, is another guide for developing security policies. Although directed more toward computer security policies, the RFC describes several types of resources that should be covered in an overall security policy, as well as recommendations for securing those resources.

Effects of External Policies on Your PKI

As more and more organizations consider using certificates to authenticate, sign, or encrypt communications between their organization and other organizations, external policies are starting to influence your PKI design. To allow exchange and trust of certificates between your organization and a partner organization, you may need to meet the security policies defined in these common standards:

- **Qualified Certificates**   A *qualified certificate* (see RFC 3739, "Internet X.509 Public Key Infrastructure Qualified Certificates Profile") refers to a certificate issued in Europe that is defined to meet the requirements for the European Directive on Electronic Signatures. The primary purpose of a qualified certificate is to identify a person with a high level of assurance.

  A qualified certificate can optionally include biometric information, such as the digital image of the subject's written signature or a digital picture of the subject, to further validate the identity of the certificate subject.

- **Sarbanes-Oxley Act**   The Sarbanes-Oxley Act of 2002 (SOX) is a United States federal law that establishes reporting and operations standards for all U.S. public companies or public companies that do business in the United States. The act also covers issues such as auditor independence, corporate governance, internal control assessment, and enhanced financial disclosure. The act affects PKI deployments and policies regarding change control and auditing requirements and log maintenance. Likewise, PKI can assist an organization with SOX compliance by supporting initiatives for strong authentication, data encryption, and digital signing.

- **FIPS 201—Personal Identity Verification (PIV) of Federal Employees and Contractors**   FIPS 201 is a standard developed by the National Institute of Standards and Technology (NIST) to meet the deadlines set by President George W. Bush in Homeland Security Presidential Directive 12 (HSPD-12). FIPS 201 defines a standard for electronic identification for federal employees and contractors for both physical and logical access control.

  The standard is made up of two major sections.

    ❑ Part one describes the minimum requirements for a Federal personal identity verification system. The requirements include recommendations for personnel identity proofing, registration, and issuance.

    ❑ Part two provides detailed specifications on storing, processing, and retrieving identity credentials from a two-factor device to allow interoperability between different devices.

- **Federal Bridge Certification Authority (FBCA)**   The U.S. government has established a bridge CA to allow organizations participating in the FBCA to accept certificates issued to other participating organizations in the FBCA. The bridge CA acts as a hub between the relying parties allowing them to trust certificates issued to all participants in the bridge.

To participate in the bridge, an organization must meet the FBCA's certificate policy. To allow flexibility, the original FBCA has evolved into the Federal Public Key Infrastructure Architecture (FBKIA), which supports multiple policies and functions. The policies supported by the FPKIA include the FBCA, the Federal PKI Common Policy Framework (FCPF) CA, and the Citizen and Commerce Class Common (C4) CA.

> **Note**   Details on the FBCA can be found at *http://www.cio.gov/fbca/*.

■ **Certipath**   Certipath is another implementation of a bridge CA in the United States. The difference between Certipath and the FBCA is the scope of the bridge. Participants in the Certipath bridge are aerospace and defense industry companies such as Lockheed Martin, Northrop Grumman, and Boeing. In addition to providing trust between other Certipath bridge members, Certipath is also cross-certified with the FBCA. This cross-certification allows all Certipath members to interoperate with all FBCA participants in certificate-based applications.

Bridge CAs for Business-to-Business (B2B) Trust

As the co-author of the "Planning and Implementing Cross-Certification and Qualified Subordination Using Windows Server 2003" white paper for Microsoft (*http://www.microsoft.com/technet/prodtechnol/windowsserver2003/technologies/security/ws03qswp.mspx*), it is exciting to see theory come to life.

When David Cross and I drafted the white paper, we were putting on our visionary hats, discussing a future method of providing certificate trust between organizations. In the ensuing years, Certipath and the FBCA are now in operation and allowing bridge trust between organizations.

The biggest impact I see on customers is the certificate policy requirements for bridge CAs. In some cases, organizations have been forced to establish dedicated CA hierarchies to cross-certify with a bridge CA. Unfortunately, the main reason is that their current CA hierarchy would not pass compliance requirements for the bridge they wish to participate in.

The best advice I can give is that if you see the possibility of participating in the FBCA or another industry bridge, be sure to review the FBCA certificate policy (available at *http://www.cio.gov/fpkipa/documents/FBCA_CP_RFC3647.pdf*), and ensure that your PKI design meets these certificate policy requirements.

Defining PKI-Related Security Policies

Using ISO 27002 as a guide for developing security policies, you should consider updating or creating security policies for the following areas:

- **Organizational security**   Establish enforceable security policies for an organization. ISO 27002 is especially helpful when an organization does not have security policies in place prior to starting a PKI design.

- **Organizational security infrastructure**   Ensure the existence of security policies that recommend the implementation of a single organization-wide PKI. An organizational PKI is easier to manage than several project-based CAs. For example, an organization should not deploy separate CA implementations for a virtual private network (VPN), Secure/Multipurpose Internet Mail Extensions (S/MIME), and wireless projects. An enterprise PKI that provides certificates for all applications and services is preferred.

- **Asset classification and control**   Identify classes of assets that require public key encryption, digital signing, or other PKI-related technologies to ensure security. PKI-related security can be applied to both data storage and transmission.

- **Personnel security**   Include job descriptions and requirements for members of the PKI administration team in security policies. Requirements can include mandatory background checks for all administrators, tasks and procedures that must be followed, and any agreements or policies that administrators must sign when accepting their positions.

- **Physical and environmental security**   Ensure that the security policy includes requirements for physical security measures to protect CAs and their deployment in a PKI. Different security measures can be required for offline versus online CAs.

- **Communications and operations management**   Define managerial and operational roles for your PKI. These can include CA administrators, certificate managers, backup operators, auditors, certificate template designers, and key recovery agents.

- **Access control**   Define what measures will be taken to secure access to a CA. These measures might include manually approving Web-based enrollment requests or placing the physical CA in a server room with keycard access. Access control can dictate what forms of authentication are required to access data. For example, some asset classifications can require two-factor authentication (something you have and something you know) before access is permitted.

- **Change control process**   Establish what measures will be taken to maintain and modify a PKI after deployment.

- **Business continuity management**   Define measures that will ensure recovery of the PKI in the event of a disaster. These measures should include actions to be taken in advance of a catastrophe so that a CA can be recovered, what information must be documented about the CA configuration, and who will perform the recovery.

- **Compliance**   Provide recommendations to ensure that the implemented PKI enforces security policies that affect it. Nonconformance with security policies can devalue a PKI-issued certificate to the point that all certificates must be revoked and reissued to ensure compliance and trust of other organizations.

Certificate Policy

A certificate policy describes the measures taken to validate a certificate's subject prior to certificate issuance and the intended purposes of the certificate. For many organizations, it is the certificate-issuance policy that determines whether the presented certificate will be trusted.

For example, an organization is more likely to trust a certificate issued after a requestor presents photo identification than a certificate issued based on a user knowing an account and password combination.

Contents of a Certificate Policy

A certificate policy should include the following information:

- **How the user's identity is validated during certificate enrollment**   Is identity provided by an account and password combination or must requestors present themselves for face-to-face interviews? If interviews are required, what forms of identification must requestors present for validation?

- **The certificate's intended purpose**   Is the certificate used for authentication on the network or for signing purchase orders? If the certificate is used for signing purchase orders, is there a maximum value allowed? These questions should be addressed in the certificate policy.

- **The type of device in which the certificate's private key is stored**   Is the private key stored on the computer's local disk in the user's profile, or is the private key stored on a hardware device such as a smart card? Other measures, such as implementing strong private key protection or requiring a password to access the private key, can be included in this information.

- **The subject's responsibility for the private key associated with the certificate in the event that the private key is compromised or lost**   Is the user responsible for any actions performed using the acquired private key if the private key is compromised or a backup of the private key is lost? This decision can lead to preventing the archival or export of the private key associated with the certificate.

- **Revocation policies, procedures, and responsibilities**   Under what circumstances will your organization revoke an issued certificate before its validity period expires? This decision will determine what actions or events will lead to the revocation of a certificate, how the revocation process is initiated, and who performs the actual revocation procedure.

Certificate Policy Example

An excellent example of certificate policy is the X.509 Certificate Policy for the U.S. Department of Defense (DoD), available at *http://iase.disa.mil/pki/dod-cp-v90-final-9-feb-05-signed.pdf.*

The DoD defines five classes of certificates in its certificate policy document. The distinction between the various classes is based on the following variables:

- The measures taken to validate the subject's identity

- The value of transactions allowed for a certificate class

- The type of storage required for the private key material

A combination of these three variables leads to the following certificate classes:

- **DoD Class 1**   Users must provide a valid e-mail address for communications during the enrollment process. No other validation of the user's identity is performed.

- **DoD Class 2**   Users prove identity by providing a user name and password for an account in the organization's authoritative directory. Once a valid user name and password are provided, a certificate is issued. The certificate is typically stored on the hard drive of the computer where the certificate request is generated. A DoD Class 2 certificate can be used for:

  - ❑ Digital signatures for administrative data or day-to-day work on any network.

  - ❑ Key exchange for high-value data on an encrypted network or confidentiality of low-value information on nonencrypted networks.

- **DoD Class 3**   Users prove identity by providing at least one piece of official federal government photo identification or two credentials issued by other entities, with one of the documents being a photo ID (such as a driver's license). The private key associated with the certificate is still stored on the user's hard disk, but the increased subject validation allows the private key to be used for medium-value transactions on a public network.

- **DoD Class 3 Hardware**   A DoD Class 3 Hardware certificate uses the same subject validation process as a DoD Class 3 certificate. The difference is that the private key material and certificate are exported from the user's hard disk to a hardware token, such as a USB token. The movement of the private key to a hardware device increases the security of the private key.

> **Note**   Once the private key is successfully transferred to a hardware device, the private key should be deleted from the computer's hard drive to prevent unauthorized access.

- **DoD Class 4**   A DoD Class 4 certificate requires presentation of the same photo identification as the DoD Class 3 and DoD Class 3 Hardware certificates. The difference is that the private key pair is not generated on the local hard disk but on a hardware two-factor device such as a smart card. The increased security of the key pair associated with the certificate results in the certificate being valid for high-value transactions on public networks.

- **DoD Class 5**   Currently, there is no PKI that meets the subject-identification requirements for a DoD Class 5 certificate. In the future, a DoD Class 5 certificate will require biometric validation of the certificate's subject. This can include retinal scans, fingerprint matches, or even DNA matching. A DoD Class 5 certificate can be used to secure classified materials on public networks.

The DoD classifications do not assign actual values to low-value, medium-value, or high-value transactions. Rather than providing predetermined values that can become dated, general terms are used to allow value modification without requiring certificate policy modification.

Comparing Certificate Policies

Sometimes it is valuable to compare different available certificate policies when you are developing the certificate policies for your organization. As mentioned in the section "Federal Bridge Certification Authority (FBCA)" earlier in this chapter, the U.S. FBCA also defines a certificate policy.

When you compare the policies to the DoD certificate policies, you can see a definite similarity between the assurance levels.

The FBCA defines a Rudimentary assurance level that relies on the subscriber providing an e-mail address to receive a certificate. This is very close to the DoD Class 1 definition.

Likewise, the FBCA Low, Medium, and High assurance levels map pretty much one-to-one with the DoD Class 2, DoD Class 3, and DoD Class 4 definitions. This really should not come as a surprise, though. The DoD is one of the organizations participating in the Federal Bridge!

Certification Practice Statement (CPS)

A certification practice statement (CPS) defines the measures taken to secure CA operations and the management of CA-issued certificates. You can consider a CPS to be an agreement between the organization managing the CA and the people relying on the certificates issued by the CA.

By reviewing a CA's CPS—a public document that should be readily available to all participants— a relying party can determine whether the certificates issued by that CA meet its security requirements. The CPS can contain the following information:

■ How the CA will enforce the measures necessary to validate the certificate's subject, as required by the certificate policy

■ The liability of the organization in the event that an act of fraud is performed against the service protected by the certificate and the fault is found to be associated with the certificate

■ The circumstances under which a certificate can be revoked before its expiration

When a certificate is issued by a CA that follows a CPS, the CA's certificate (or that of its parent CA) can include a URL pointer to the CPS. If included in the CA's certificate, the CPS is viewed by clicking the Issuer Statement button on the General tab of the certificate, as shown in Figure 3-2.

Figure 3-2   A CA certificate that references a CPS

Note   When a CPS is included in a CA certificate, it is applicable to that CA and all subordinate CAs in the CA hierarchy. This means that the practices defined in the CPS must be implemented by that CA and all subordinate CAs.

RFC 3647, "Internet X.509 Public Key Infrastructure Certificate Policy and Certification Practices Framework," available at *http://www.ietf.org/rfc/rfc3647.txt*, recommends a standard CPS format to ensure compatibility between organizations and promote a stronger degree of trust of an organization's CPS by other companies. The RFC recommends the following nine sections:

- Introduction
- Publication and Repository Responsibilities
- Identification and Authentication (I&A)
- Certificate Life-Cycle Operational Requirements
- Facility, Management, and Operational Controls
- Technical Security Controls
- Certificate, CRL, and OCSP Profiles
- Compliance Audit and Other Assessment
- Other Business and Legal Matters

Note RFC 3647 recommends that the same format be used for both certificate policies and CPSs. The X.509 certificate policies for both the United States Department of Defense and the United States FBCA implement the nine sections discussed here. Differences between the certificate policy and the CPS are mainly related to the documents' focus. A certificate policy focuses on subject validation and is often compared between organizations to find similar policies, whereas a CPS describes the operations of the CA to enforce the implemented certificate policies.

CPS Section: Introduction

The introduction of a CPS provides an overview of the CA, as well as the types of users, computers, network devices, or services that will receive certificates. The introduction also includes information on certificate usage. This includes what types of applications can consume certificates issued under the CP or CPS and what types of applications are explicitly prohibited from consuming the CA's certificates. If a representative of another organization has any questions regarding the information published in the CPS, the introduction also provides contact information.

CPS Section: Publication and Repository Responsibilities

The Publication and Repository Responsibilities section contains details regarding who operates the components of the public key infrastructure. This section also describes the responsibilities for publishing the CP or CPS, whether the CP or CPS will be publicly available, whether portions of the CP or CPS will remain private, and descriptions of access controls on published information. The published information includes CPs, CPSs, certificates, certificate status information, and certificate revocation lists (CRLs).

CPS Section: Identification and Authentication

This section describes the name formats assigned and used in certificates issued by the CA. The section will also specify whether the names must be unique, meaningful, allow nicknames, and so on. The section's main focus is on the measures taken to validate a requestor's identity prior to certificate issuance. The section describes the certificate policy and assurance levels implemented at the CA and details identification procedures for:

■ **Initial registration for a certificate**   The measures taken to validate the identity of the certificate requestor.

■ **Renewal of a certificate**   Are the measures used for initial registration repeated when a certificate is renewed? In some cases, possession of an existing certificate and private key is sufficient proof of identity to receive a new certificate at renewal time.

■ **Requests for revocation**   When a certificate must be revoked, what measures will be taken to ensure that the requestor is authorized to request revocation of a certificate?

Note   A CA can implement more than one assurance level, so long as the CA's procedures and operations allow enforcement of each assurance level. To implement multiple assurance levels within a certificate policy, separate subsections can be defined, one for each assurance level.

CPS Section: Certificate Life-Cycle Operational Requirements

This section defines the operating procedures for CA management, issuance of certificates, and management of issued certificates. It is detailed in the description of the management tasks. Operating procedures described in this section can include the following:

■ **Certificate application**   The application process for each certificate policy supported by a CA should be described. Applications can range from the use of autoenrollment to distribute certificates automatically to users or computers, to a detailed procedure that pends certificate requests until the requestor's identity is proved through ID inspection and background checks.

■ **Certificate application processing**   Once the application is received by the registration authorities, the application must be processed. This section describes what must be done to ensure that the subscriber is who he says he is. The section can include what forms of identification are required, whether background checks are required, and whether there are time limits set on processing the application. The section may include recommendations on when to approve or deny a request.

■ **Certificate issuance**   Once the identity of a certificate requestor is validated, what is the procedure to issue the certificate? The process can range from simply issuing the certificate in the CA console to recording the certificate requestor's submitted identification in a separate database maintained by an RA.

- **Certificate acceptance**　When a certificate is issued to a computer or user, what procedures must be performed to install the certificate on the user's computer or a certificate-bearing device such as a smart card?

- **Key pair and certificate usage**　Once a certificate is issued, the parties involved in the usage of the certificate must understand when and how the certificate may be used. The section describes responsibilities for the certificate subscriber and relying parties when the certificate is used.

- **Certificate renewal**　When a certificate reaches its end of lifetime, the certificate can be renewed with the same key pair. The section provides details on when you can renew with the same key pair, who can initiate the request, and what measures must be taken to verify the subscriber's identity (these are typically less stringent than initial enrollment).

- **Certificate re-key**　Alternatively, when a certificate reaches its end of lifetime, the certificate can be renewed with a new key pair. The section provides details on when you must renew with a new key pair, who can initiate the request, and what measures must be taken to verify the subscriber's identity (these are typically the same as initial enrollment).

> **Note**　Setting a schedule for renewal and re-key is an important task in this section. For example, some some CPSs allow renewal without re-vetting only for a period of seven years for Medium assurance or DoD Class 3 certificates. The subscriber's identity during renewal is validated by the subscriber signing the request with his or her previous certificate (since the subscriber is the holder of the private key). In the seventh year, the subscriber must re-key and undergo the vetting process to re-establish his or her identity.

- **Certificate modification**　Sometimes, a certificate must be re-issued because of the subscriber's name change or change in administrative role. This section describes *when* you can modify a certificate and how the registration process proceeds for the modification of the certificate.

> **Note**　Technically, it is not a modification. You cannot modify a certificate because it is a signed object. Think of it more as a replacement of a certificate.

- **Certificate revocation and suspension**　Under which circumstances will the issuing party revoke or suspend an issued certificate? This section should detail the obligations of the certificate holder, as well as actions that can lead to certificate revocation. The section also includes information on what revocation mechanisms are supported by the CA. If CRLs are used, the section describes the publication schedule for the CRLs. If online revocation and status checking is implemented, the URL of the Web site is provided.

- **Certificate status services**　If the CA implements certificate status-checking services, this section provides operational characteristics of the services and the availability of the services.

- **End of subscription**   If a subscriber wishes to terminate her or his subscription, this section provides details on how the certificate is revoked. There may be multiple recommendations in this section detailing the different reasons that can require a subscriber to end his or her subscription. For example, an organization may choose to process the revocation request differently for an employee who is terminated than for an employee who retires.

- **Key escrow and recovery**   If the CA provides private key escrow services for an encryption certificate, this section describes the policies and practices governing the key archival and recovery procedures. The section typically references other policies and standards defined by the organization.

CPS Section: Facility, Management, and Operational Controls

This section describes physical, procedural, and personnel controls implemented at the CA for key generation, subject authentication, certificate issuance, certificate revocation, auditing, and archiving. These controls can range from limiting which personnel can physically access the CA to ensuring that an employee is assigned only a single PKI management role. For a relying party, these controls are critical in the decision to trust certificates because poor procedures can result in a PKI that is more easily compromised without the issuing organization recognizing the compromise.

This section also provides details on other controls implemented in the management of the PKI. These include:

- **Security audit procedures**   What actions are audited at the CA, and what managerial roles are capable of reviewing the audit logs for the CA?

- **Records archival**   What information is archived by the CA? This can include configuration information as well as information about encryption private keys archived in the CA database. This section should detail the process necessary to recover private key material. For example, if the roles of certificate manager and key recovery agent are separated, a description of the roles and responsibilities of each role should be provided so the certificate holder is aware that a single person cannot perform private key recovery.

- **Key changeover**   What is the lifetime of the CA's certificate, and how often is it renewed? This section should detail information about the certificate and its associated key pair. For example, is the key pair changed every time the CA's certificate is renewed or only when the original validity period of the CA certificate elapses?

- **Compromise and disaster recovery**   What measures are taken to protect the CA from compromise? Under what circumstances would you decommission the CA rather than restore the CA to the last known good configuration? For example, if the CA is compromised by a computer virus, will you restore the CA to a state before the viral infection and revoke the certificates issued after the viral attack or decommission the CA? If a CA fails, what measures are in place to ensure a quick recovery of the CA and its CA database?

- **CA or RA termination** What actions are taken when the CA or registration authority (RA) is removed from the network? This section can include information about the CA's expected lifetime.

CPS Section: Technical Security Controls

This section defines the security measures taken by the CA to protect its cryptographic keys and activation data. For example, is the key pair for the CA stored on the local machine profile on a two-factor device, such as a smart card, or on a FIPS 140-2 Level 2 or Level 3 hardware device, such as a hardware security module (HSM)? When a decision is made to trust another organization's certificates, the critical factor is often the security provided for the CA's private key.

This section can also include technical security control information regarding key generation, user validation, certificate revocation, archival of encryption private keys, and auditing.

 Warning The technical security control section should provide only high-level information to the reader and not serve as a guide to an attacker regarding potential weaknesses in the CA's configuration. For example, is it safe to disclose that the CA's key pair is stored on a FIPS 140-2 Level 2 or Level 3 HSM? It is not safe to describe the CA's management team members or provide specific vendor information about the HSM.

CPS Section: Certificate, CRL, and OCSP Profiles

This section is used to specify three types of information:

- **Information about the types of certificates issued by the CA** For example, are CA-issued certificates for user authentication, EFS, or code signing?
- **Information about CRL contents** This section should provide information about the version numbers supported for CRLs and what extensions are populated in the CRL objects.
- **OCSP profiles** This section should provide information on what versions of Online Certificate Status Protocol (OCSP) are used (for example, what RFCs are supported by the OCSP implementation) and what OCSP extensions are populated in issued certificates.

CPS Section: Compliance Audit and Other Assessment

This section is relevant if the CP or CPS is used by a CA that issues certificates that are consumed by entities outside of your organization. The section details what is checked during a compliance audit, how often the compliance audit must be performed, who will perform the audit (is the audit performed by internal audit or by a third party?), what actions must be taken if the CA fails the audit, and who is allowed to inspect the final audit report.

CPS Section: Other Business and Legal Matters

This section specifies general business and legal matters regarding the CP and CPS. The business matters include fees for services and the financial responsibilities of the participants in the PKI. The section also details legal matters, such as privacy of personal information recorded by the PKI, intellectual property rights, warranties, disclaimers, limitations on liabilities, and indemnities.

Finally, the section describes the practices for maintenance of the CPS. For example, what circumstances drive the modification of the CPS? If the CPS is modified, who approves the recommended changes? In addition, this section should specify how the modified CPS's contents are published and how the public is notified that the contents are modified.

Note   In some cases, the actual modifications are slight, such as a recommended rewording by an organization's legal department. In these cases, the URL referencing the CPS need not be changed, just the wording of the documents referenced by the URL.

What If My Current CP/CPS Is Based on RFC 2527?

Many of your organizations may have a CP or CPS based on RFC 2527 (the predecessor to RFC 3647). There is no immediate need to rewrite the CP or CPS to match the section names in RFC 3647. On the other hand, if you are in the process of drafting your CP or CPS now, I do recommend that what you write is based on the section names in RFC 3647.

Either way, RFC 3647 provides a great cheat sheet for you as you start your copy-and-paste adventure. Section 7, "Comparison to RFC 2527," provides a detailed table that shows the mappings between sections in RFC 2527 and RFC 3647. For example, in RFC 2527, compliance auditing is described in Section 2.7 and its subsections. In RFC 3647, the same subsections exist but are now recorded in Section 8. The table below summarizes the remapping of the sections regarding compliance auditing.

Section title	RFC 2527 section	RFC 3647 section
Compliance Audit	2.7	8.
Frequency of Entity Compliance Audit	2.7.1	8.1
Identity/Qualifications of Auditor	2.7.2	8.2
Auditor's Relationship to Audited Party	2.7.3	8.3
Topics Covered by Audit	2.7.4	8.4
Actions Taken as a Result of Deficiency	2.7.5	8.5
Communication of Results	2.7.6	8.6

Case Study: Planning Policy Documents

You are the head of security for Fabrikam, Inc., a large manufacturing company. Your IT department has several PKI-related initiatives planned for the next 18 months, and you are responsible for the drafting of all related policy documents.

Design Requirements

One of the applications planned by the IT department is the deployment of smart cards for both local and VPN authentication by all employees. During research for the smart card deployment, the IT department gathered the following information that will affect the policies you draft:

- Each employee will be issued a smart card on his or her first day with Fabrikam, Inc.

- Existing employees will receive their smart cards on an office-by-office basis. Members of the IT department will travel to each major regional office and deliver the smart cards to all employees in that region.

- Fabrikam has a high employee turnover. In any given month, as many as 1,000 employees leave Fabrikam and are replaced with roughly 1,200 new employees.

Case Study Questions

1. What is the relationship between a CPS, certificate policy, and security policy?

2. In what document would you define the methods used to identify the new hires when they start with Fabrikam?

3. Will the identification validation requirements for existing employees differ from those implemented for new employees of Fabrikam?

4. The high turnover of employees must be addressed in the CPS. Specifically, what sections must be updated to define the measures taken when an employee is terminated or resigns from Fabrikam?

5. You are considering modeling your certificate policies after the United States FBCA certificate policy. What certificate class would best match your deployment of smart cards?

Additional Information

- Microsoft Official Curriculum, course 2821: "Designing and Managing a Windows Public Key Infrastructure" (*www.microsoft.com/traincert/syllabi/2821afinal.asp*)

- ISO 27002–"Code of Practice for Information Security Management" (*http://www.27000-toolkit.com*)

- RFC 2196–"The Site Security Handbook" (*http://www.ietf.org/rfc/rfc2196.txt*)

- "X.509 Certificate Policy for the United States Department of Defense" (*http://iase.disa.mil/pki/dod-cp-v90-final-9-feb-05-signed.pdf*)

- RFC 2527–"Internet X.509 Public Key Infrastructure Certificate Policy and Certification Practices Framework" (*http://www.ietf.org/rfc/rfc2527.txt*)

- RFC 3647–"Internet X.509 Public Key Infrastructure Certificate Policy and Certification Practices Framework" (*http://www.ietf.org/rfc/rfc3647.txt*)

- The Information Security Policies/Computer Security Policies Directory (*http://www.information-security-policies-and-standards.com*)

- "Homeland Security Presidential Directive (HSPD)–12" (*http://csrc.nist.gov/policies/Presidential-Directive-Hspd-12.html*)

- "X.509 Certificate Policy for the Federal Bridge Certification Authority (FBCA)" (*http://www.cio.gov/fpkipa/documents/FBCA_CP_RFC3647.pdf*)

- "Planning and Implementing Cross-Certification and Qualified Subordination Using Windows Server 2003" (*http://www.microsoft.com/technet/prodtechnol/windowsserver2003/technologies/security/ws03qswp.mspx*)

- Certipath (*http://www.certipath.com/*)

- FIPS-201–"Personal Identity Verification (PIV) of Federal Employees and Contractors" (*http://csrc.nist.gov/publications/fips/fips201-1/FIPS-201-1-chng1.pdf*)

- RFC 3739–"Internet X.509 Public Key Infrastructure Qualified Certificates Profile" (*http://www.ietf.org/rfc/rfc3739.txt*)

Part II
Establishing a PKI

Chapter 4

Preparing an Active Directory Environment

When network administrators hear that their organization is going to deploy a Windows Server 2008 public key infrastructure (PKI), several questions typically come to mind:

- **Do I have to upgrade all domain controllers in my forest to Windows Server 2008?** The answer is no. A Windows Server 2008 PKI is not dependent upon Windows Server 2008 domain controllers. You can deploy a Windows Server 2008 PKI in a Microsoft Windows 2000 or Windows Server 2003 Active Directory directory service environment.

- **Do I have to upgrade my domain functional level or forest functional level to Windows Server 2008?** No again. A Windows Server 2008 PKI has no requirements for domain or forest functional levels.

- **What do I have to do to deploy a Windows Server 2008 PKI?** This chapter will describe the actions you must take to prepare Active Directory Domain Services (AD DS) to deploy a Windows Server 2008 PKI.

Analyzing the Active Directory Environment

Several preparations should be undertaken before installing a Windows Server 2008 enterprise certification authority (CA) in a Windows 2000 or Windows Server 2003 Active Directory environment. These preparations include:

- **Determining the number of forests in the environment** The number of forests will affect the number of enterprise CAs that you require in your Active Directory Certificate Services deployment. An enterprise CA can issue certificates only to users and computers with accounts in the same forest. If there are multiple forests that must consume certificates from the PKI, you must deploy at least one enterprise CA per forest.

- **Determining the number of domains in the forest** If there is more than one domain in the forest, one of the major design decisions is what domain will host the CAs. The selection of what domain will host the computer accounts of the CA computers will depend largely on whether your organization uses centralized or decentralized management. In a centralized model, the CAs will typically be placed in the same domain. In a decentralized environment, you may end up deploying CAs in multiple domains.

- **Determining the membership of the local Administrators groups for a member server** If you use software cryptographic providers to protect a CA's private key, all members of the CA's local Administrators group will have the ability to export the CA's private key. You should start identifying which domain or organizational unit in a domain will best limit the number of local Administrators. For example, an organization that has deployed an empty forest root may choose to deploy all enterprise CAs as members of the forest root domain to limit the number of local Administrators on the CA.

■ **Determining the schema version of the domain**   To implement Windows Server 2008 CAs and take advantage of all new features introduced for Active Directory Certificate Services, you must implement the latest version of the AD DS schema. The Windows Servers 2008 schema can be deployed in forests that contain Windows 2000, Windows Server 2003, or Windows Server 2008 domain controllers.

> **Note**   To apply the schema updates to a Windows 2000 domain controller, the domain controller must be upgraded to Windows 2000 Service Pack 4 or later. Windows Server 2003 does not have any minimum service pack level requirements. Details on upgrading the schema are found in the next section.

Upgrading the Schema

Microsoft Windows 2000 or Windows Server 2003 forests must have their schemas upgraded to the Windows Server 2008 schema to support the new features in a Windows Server 2008 PKI. These features include:

■ **Support for version 3 certificate templates**   The Windows Server 2008 schema includes the definition of the version 3 certificate template object. Version 3 certificate templates allow implementation of Cryptography Next Generation (CNG) algorithms in issued certificates.

■ **Addition of an online responder**   Windows Server 2008 introduces an Online Certificate Status Protocol (OCSP) responder service. This service allows up-to-date validation of subscriber certificates rather than using certificate revocation lists (CRLs).

■ **Network Device Enrollment Service**   Windows Server 2008 natively supports automated issuance of certificates to Cisco network devices using Simple Certificate Enrollment Protocol (SCEP). SCEP allows issuance of certificates to the network devices without having to create computer accounts for the devices in Active Directory.

■ **Native Support for Qualified Certificates**   Qualified Certificates, described in RFC 3739, "Internet X.509 Public Key Infrastructure Qualified Certificates Profile," allows issuance of certificates for a high level of assurance for use in electronic signatures. A qualified certificate can also include biometeric information regarding the certificate subscriber.

Identifying the Schema Operations Master

If your forest is a Windows 2000 or Windows Server 2003 forest, you must identify the schema operations master. The schema upgrade must take place at the schema operations master. To identify the schema operations master:

1. Open a command prompt.

2. At the command prompt, type **regsvr32 schmmgmt.dll**, and then press Enter.

3. In the RegSvr32 message box, click OK.

4. Open a new Microsoft Management Console (MMC) console.

5. From the File menu, click Add/Remove Snap-in.

6. In the Add/Remove Snap-in dialog box, click Add.

7. In the Add Standalone Snap-in dialog box, select Active Directory Schema, click Add, and then click Close.

8. In the Add/Remove Snap-in dialog box, click OK.

9. In the console tree, select Active Directory Schema, right-click Active Directory Schema, and then click Operations Master.

10. In the Change Schema Master dialog box, as shown in Figure 4-1, record the current schema master, and then click Close.

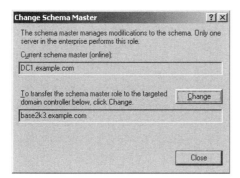

Figure 4-1   Determining the schema operations master in DC1.example.com

11. Close the MMC console without saving changes.

Performing the Schema Update

Once you have identified the schema operations master, log on at the console of the domain controller as a member of the Schema Admins and Enterprise Admins groups in the forest root domain, and the Domain Admins group for the domain that hosts the schema operations master. Then perform the following steps:

1. Insert the Windows Server 2008 DVD in the DVD drive.

2. Open a command prompt.

3. At a command prompt, type *X*: (where *X* is the drive letter of the DVD), and then press Enter.

4. At a command prompt, type **cd \sources\adprep**, and then press Enter.

5. At a command prompt, type **adprep /forestprep**, and then press Enter.

6. At the warning prompt, if you meet the minimum stated requirements, press C to continue with schema updates, as shown in Figure 4-2.

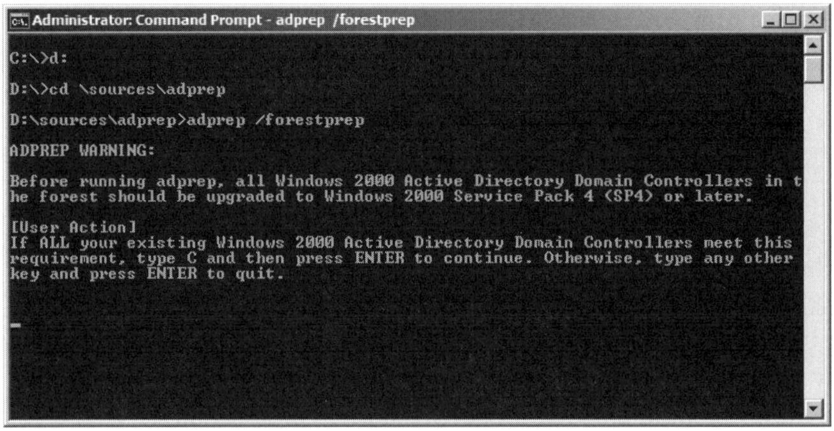

![Administrator: Command Prompt - adprep /forestprep window showing:
C:\>d:
D:\>cd \sources\adprep
D:\sources\adprep>adprep /forestprep
ADPREP WARNING:
Before running adprep, all Windows 2000 Active Directory Domain Controllers in the forest should be upgraded to Windows 2000 Service Pack 4 (SP4) or later.
[User Action]
If ALL your existing Windows 2000 Active Directory Domain Controllers meet this requirement, type C and then press ENTER to continue. Otherwise, type any other key and press ENTER to quit.]

Figure 4-2   Upgrading the Active Directory schema

Note   If you are upgrading the schema in a Windows 2000 Active Directory environment, the schema will upgrade from version 13 to version 44. In a Windows 2003 Active Directory environment, the schema will upgrade from version 30 to version 44. If you are running Windows Server 2003 R2, the upgrade will be from version 31 to version 44.

7. When the process completes, ensure that you receive the message that Adprep successfully updated the forest-wide information.

Note   If you want to view the actual modifications made to the schema in detail, you can look at the schema update LDAP Data Interchange Format (LDIF) files in the \source\adprep folder of the Windows Server 2008 CD. The files are named SCH##.ldf, where ## is a number between 14 and 44, representing the modifications made in each revision.

Once the update is complete, you must ensure that the modifications replicate fully to all domain controllers in the forest. You can view the replication status by using either the Replication Monitor (replmon.exe) graphical tool or the repadmin.exe command-line tool from Windows Support Tools.

Note   Read the documentation on each of these tools for information on how to best ensure that replication completes for the schema modifications.

After modification of the schema is replicated to all domain controllers in the forest, you can prepare each domain to benefit from the Windows Server 2008 schema extensions. To prepare each domain in the forest, use the following procedure:

1. Log on locally at the infrastructure master in the domain as a member of the Domain Admins group.

Tip   You can determine the infrastructure master for the domain in the Active Directory Users and Computers console.

2. Insert the Windows Server 2008 CD in the CD-ROM drive.

3. At a command prompt, type *X:* (where *X* is the drive letter of the CD-ROM), and then press ENTER.

4. At a command prompt, type **cd \sources\adprep**, and then press Enter.

5. At a command prompt, type **adprep /domainprep /gpprep**, and then press Enter.

Note   The adprep /domainprep /adprep /gpprep command both prepares the domain-wide information and adds cross-domain and resultant set of policy planning. The command modifies the file system and AD DS permissions on existing Group Policy Objects (GPOs).

6. Repeat the process for every domain in the forest.

Note   It is not necessary to run adprep /domainprep to install a Windows Server 2008 enterprise CA in the forest.

Modifying the Scope of the Cert Publishers Groups

The Cert Publishers group is a default group that exists in each domain in the AD DS forest. A domain's Cert Publishers group is assigned permission to read and write certificate information to the *userCertificate* attribute of user objects in that domain. Certificates published to these attributes are typically encryption certificates, which allow anyone to obtain the public key of a target's encryption certificate by querying AD DS.

The catch is that the scope of the Cert Publishers group is determined by the operating system of the initial domain controller for that domain.

- If the domain was created on a Windows 2000–based server (by running DCPromo.exe), the Cert Publishers group is a global group. This means that only computer accounts from the same domain can have membership in the Cert Publishers group.

- If the domain was created on a Windows Server 2003–based server or a Windows Server 2008–based server, the Cert Publishers group is a domain local group. This means that computer accounts from *any* domain can have membership in the Cert Publishers group.

If a CA issues a certificate to a user and is required to publish the certificate to the user's *userCertificate* attribute, the process will fail if the CA is not a member of the user's domain's Cert Publishers group.

> **Note**   If an enterprise CA does not have sufficient permissions to write a certificate to the *userCertificate* attribute, the following entry will appear in the application log of the CA:
>
> ```
> Event ID: 80
> Description:
> Certificate Services could not publish a Certificate for request # (where # is the
> request
> ID of the certificate request) to the following location on server dc.example.com:
> CN=brian.smith,OU=users,OU=Accounts,DC=east,DC=example,DC=com.
> Insufficient access rights to perform the operation. 0x80072098 (WIN32:8344).
> ```

For the next examples, let's assume that your forest is configured as shown in Figure 4-3.

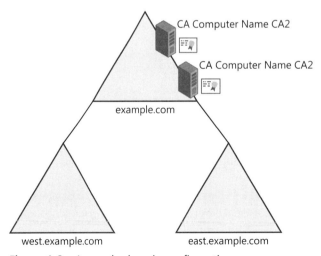

Figure 4-3   A sample domain configuration

There are two enterprise CAs in the forest, CA1 and CA2, and they are located in the Computers container of the example.com domain.

Cert Publishers Population When the Group Is a Domain Local Group

If the example.com, west.example.com, and east.example.com domains were created in Windows Server 2003 or Windows Server 2008, all you have to do is add the CA computer accounts from the example.com domain to the east.example.com and west.example.com Cert Publishers groups. There is no need to add the CA computer accounts to the Example\Cert Publishers group because this is an automatic group population when you install Active Directory Certificate Services.

The addition of the computer accounts to the east.example.com and west.example.com Cert Publishers group can be performed manually or by using a VBS script, as follows:

```
Set grp = GetObject("LDAP://CN=Cert Publishers,CN=Users,DC=west,DC=example,DC=com")
grp.SetInfogrp.add ("LDAP://CN=CA1,CN=Computers,DC=example,DC=com")
grp.SetInfogrp.add ("LDAP://CN=CA2,CN=Computers,DC=example,DC=com")
grp.SetInfo
Set grp = GetObject("LDAP://CN=Cert Publishers,CN=Users,DC=east,DC=example,DC=com")
grp.SetInfogrp.add ("LDAP://CN=CA1,CN=Computers,DC=example,DC=com")
grp.SetInfogrp.add ("LDAP://CN=CA2,CN=Computers,DC=example,DC=com")
grp.SetInfo
```

Cert Publishers Strategies If the Group Is a Global Group

If the domain was created in Windows 2000, there are two strategies:

■ Modify permissions to allow each CA's domain's Cert Publishers group read and write permissions to the *userCertificate* attribute for all other domains in the forest.

■ Change the scope of the Cert Publishers group to a domain local group and simply add the CA computer accounts to each domain's Cert Publishers group.

Modifying Permissions in Active Directory   Windows Knowledge Base Article 300532, "Windows 2000 Enterprise CAs Not Added to Certificate Publishers Group in Windows Server 2003 Domain," provides guidance on how to define permissions to allow the Cert Publishers group from one domain to publish certificates to a user's *userCertificate* attribute when the user's account exists in a *different* domain. The steps can be summarized as follows:

1. Assign the example.com domain's Cert Publishers group the Read userCertificate permission in all other domains in the forest.

2. Assign the example.com domain's Cert Publishers group the Write userCertificate permission in all other domains in the forest.

3. Assign the example.com domain's Cert Publishers group the Read userCertificate permission at the CN=adminsdholder,CN=system,*DomainName* container in all other domains in the forest.

4. Assign the example.com domain's Cert Publishers group the Write userCertificate permission at the CN=adminsdholder,CN=system,*DomainName* container in all other domains in the forest.

> **Note**   If CA computer accounts exist in multiple domains in the forest, you must modify the permissions assignments for a particular CA's domain's Cert Publishers group for all *other* domains in the forest.

You can script these permission assignments by using the dsacls.exe command from Windows Support Tools. As with the example where the domains were created in Windows Server 2003, it is assumed that the CA computer accounts (CA1 and CA2) exist in the Example.com domain:

```
:: Assign permissions to the east.example.com domain
dsacls "dc=east,dc=example,dc=com" /I:S /G "Example\Cert Publishers":RP;userCertificate,user
dsacls "dc=east,dc=example,dc=com" /I:S /G "Example\Cert Publishers":WP;userCertificate,user

:: Assign permissions to the west.example.com domain
dsacls "dc=west,dc=example,dc=com" /I:S /G "Example\Cert Publishers":RP;userCertificate,user
dsacls "dc=west,dc=example,dc=com" /I:S /G "Example\Cert Publishers":WP;userCertificate,user

:: Assign permissions to the Adminsdholder container in east.example.com
dsacls " cn=adminsdholder,cn=system,dc=east,dc=example,dc=com" /G "Example\Cert
Publishers":RP;userCertificate
dsacls " cn=adminsdholder,cn=system,dc=east,dc=example,dc=com" /G "Example\Cert
Publishers":WP;userCertificate

:: Assign permissions to the Adminsdholder container in west.example.com
dsacls " cn=adminsdholder,cn=system,dc=west,dc=example,dc=com" /G "Example\Cert
Publishers":RP;userCertificate
dsacls " cn=adminsdholder,cn=system,dc=west,dc=example,dc=com" /G "Example\Cert
Publishers":WP;userCertificate
```

> **Tip**   To use this script in your environment, simply modify the domain names to match the domain names in your forest. You must assign permissions to the CA's domain's Cert Publishers group to the domain and the AdminSDHolder container for all other domains in your forest.

Changing the Scope of the Cert Publishers group   What I have seen in practice is that you cannot easily predict what the scope of the Cert Publishers group will be without inspecting each domain in the forest. The scope is based only on what operating system the initial domain controller was running. If the domain was built using Windows 2000, the scope of Cert Publishers is a global group. If the domain was built using Windows Server 2003 or Windows Server 2008, the scope is domain local.

Typically, I have seen that only the forest root domain and any other initially deployed domains have a Cert Publishers group that is a global group. All the new domains (added in recent years) have a Cert Publishers group that is a domain local group.

This mixing of scope types added real complexity to modifying permissions. I realized that it is easier to change *all* Cert Publishers groups to be domain local groups. Once the groups were converted to domain local groups, the permissions problem was easy to solve. Just add the CA computer accounts to each domain's Cert Publishers group.

The catch was that you cannot change the scope from the Active Directory Users and Computers console. You can change the scope only through scripting. The script must do the following:

1.   Convert the Cert Publishers group from a global group to a universal group.

2.   Convert the Cert Publishers group from a universal group to a domain local group.

3.   Populate the group with all CA computer accounts in the forest.

Important   You cannot convert a group directly from a global group to a domain local group. This transition from global to universal to domain local is always required!

The script to do this is not very different from the script to populate the groups when the Cert Publishers group is a domain local group. The difference is in modifying the *groupType* attribute values. A universal group has a *groupType* attribute value of –2147483640, and a domain local group has a *groupType* attribute value of –2147483644.

In our Example.com domain scenario, the script would look like this:

```
Set grp = GetObject("LDAP://CN=Cert Publishers,CN=Users,DC=west,DC=example,DC=com")
grp.Put "groupType","-2147483640"
grp.SetInfo
grp.Put "groupType","-2147483644"
grp.SetInfo
grp.SetInfogrp.add ("LDAP://CN=CA1,CN=Computers,DC=example,DC=com")
grp.SetInfogrp.add ("LDAP://CN=CA2,CN=Computers,DC=example,DC=com")
grp.SetInfo
Set grp = GetObject("LDAP://CN=Cert Publishers,CN=Users,DC=east,DC=example,DC=com")
grp.Put "groupType","-2147483640"
grp.SetInfo
grp.Put "groupType","-2147483644"
grp.SetInfo
grp.SetInfogrp.add ("LDAP://CN=CA1,CN=Computers,DC=example,DC=com")
grp.SetInfogrp.add ("LDAP://CN=CA2,CN=Computers,DC=example,DC=com")
grp.SetInfo
grp.SetInfo
```

Tip   If a domain's Cert Publishers group is already a domain local group, simply remove the four *grp.Put "groupType"* and *group.setInfo* lines from the script for that specific domain.

Deploying Windows Server 2008 Enterprise CAs in Non–AD DS Environments

It is not possible to deploy Windows Server 2008 enterprise CAs in non–AD DS environments. An enterprise CA requires the existence of AD DS for storage of configuration information and certificate publishing as well as its security policy and authentication functionality. This does not mean that you cannot deploy a Windows Server 2008 PKI in a non–AD DS environment. It means only that every CA in the PKI hierarchy must be a standalone CA.

In a standalone CA environment, the contents of the certificates are defined in the actual certificate request files rather than using certificate templates in AD DS to define the content of issued certificates. In addition, all certificate requests are set to a pending status by default, requiring a certificate manager to approve or deny every certificate request submitted to the standalone CA.

> **Note**   Although you can change this default behavior to automatically issue certificates, it is not recommended. Without certificate templates, there is no authentication or validation system applied if a standalone CA automatically processes requests and issues certificates based on those requests.

Case Study: Preparing Active Directory Domain Services

You are the network administrator for Tailspin Toys, a toy manufacturing company. Your organization's forest consists of five domains: corp.tailspintoys.msft, amers.tailspintoys.msft, emea.tailspintoys.msft, wingtiptoys.msft, and apac.wingtiptoys.msft, as shown in Figure 4-4.

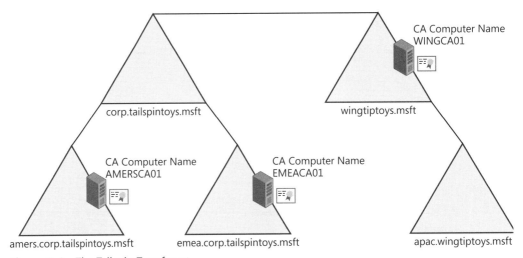

Figure 4-4   The Tailspin Toys forest

The corp.tailspintoys.msft domain is the forest root domain. The domain contains only domain controller and administrative user accounts. The two child domains below corp.tailspintoys.msft contain users and computer accounts for the specific region (Americas or Europe–Middle East).

- The corp.tailspintoys.msft and amers.corp.tailspintoys.msft domains are the original domains in the forest. They were originally deployed using Windows 2000 but were upgraded to Windows Server 2003 soon after the release of the product.

- The emea.corp.tailspintoys.msft child domain was added only two years ago when the organization expanded operations to France and Israel.

The wingtiptoys.msft and apac.wingtiptoys.msft domains came into being last year when the company acquired their competitor Wingtip Toys. The computers and users were migrated into new Windows Server 2003 domains in the corp.tailspintoys.msft forest.

- The wingtiptoys.msft domain contains users and computers based in North America.

- The apac.wingtiptoys.msft domain contains users and computers based in Asia and Australia.

You have deployed Windows Server 2003 enterprise CAs in three domains and are starting an e-mail encryption initiative. The project plan includes upgrading the CAs to run Windows Server 2008 to allow for certificates that support Cryptography Next Generation (CNG) encryption algorithms. When the project is completed, any CA in the forest must be able to issue the Secure/Multipurpose Internet Mail Extensions (S/MIME) CNG certificates to *any* user in the forest.

During the preliminary inspection of the existing environment, you notice that several of the CAs are reporting errors regarding publishing certificates. An example is provided below:

```
Certificate Services could not publish a Certificate for request # (where # is the request
ID of the certificate request) to the following location on server dc.example.com:
CN= Sidsel.Øby,OU=users,OU=Accounts,DC=emea,DC=corp,DC=tailspintoys,
DC=com.
Error Code 80: Insufficient access rights to perform the operation. 0x80072098 (WIN32:8344).
The details
```

On further inspection of the Cert Publishers group in each domain, the following group memberships were found:

Cert Publishers Group Memberships

Group	Membership
Corp\Cert Publishers	None
Amers\Cert Publishers	Amers\AMERSCA01
Emea\Cert Publishers	Emea\EMEACA01
Wingtiptoys\Cert Publishers	Wingtiptoys\WINGCA01
Apac\Cert Publishers	None

Network Details

Table 4-1 shows the current operation master roles to help you determine what configuration changes are required for AD DS before deploying a Windows Server 2008 PKI.

Table 4-1   Operation Master Assignments

Computer	Schema master	Domain naming master	RID master	PDC emulator	Infrastructure master
Corp\ROOTDC01		x			x
Corp\ROOTDC02	x		X	x	
Amers\NADC01		x	X	x	x
Amers\NADC02					
Emea\EUDC01		x		x	
Emea\EUDC02			X		x
WingtipToys\WTDC01		x			
WingtipToys\WTDC02			X	x	x
Apac\APDC01			X	x	
Apac\APDC02		x			X

Case Study Questions

Answer the following questions based on the Tailspin Toys scenario.

1. Is there a minimum service pack level required at each domain controller before applying the Windows Server 2008 schema modifications?

2. At what computer will you run adprep /forestprep? What group membership(s) is/are required?

3. What computer(s) will you use to run adprep /domainprep /gpprep? What group membership(s) is/are required? Is this command required to deploy Windows Server 2008 certification authorities?

4. What is causing the issuing CA to record the "Certificate Services could not publish a Certificate for request #" error for the certificate issued to Sidsel Øby?

5. What configuration change is required to remove the error condition?

6. Assuming no changes have been made to the default scope for each domain's Cert Publishers group, record in the following table the expected scope for each domain's Cert Publishers group.

Domain	Scope of Cert Publishers group
corp.tailspintoys.msft	
amers.corp.tailspintoys.msft	
emea.corp.tailspintoys.msft	
wingtiptoys.msft	
apac.wingtiptoys.msft	

7. Write a script to convert any Cert Publishers groups from global to domain local groups. The script must contain only the Cert Publishers groups that are *not* already domain local groups.

8. Write a script to correctly populate each domain's Cert Publishers group with all CA computer accounts in the forest.

Additional Information

■ Microsoft Official Curriculum, Course 2821: "Designing and Managing a Windows Public Key Infrastructure" (*http://www.microsoft.com/traincert/syllabi/2821afinal.asp*)

■ "Best Practices for Implementing a Microsoft Windows Server 2003 Public Key Infrastructure" (*http://www.microsoft.com/technet/prodtechnol/windowsserver2003/technologies/security/ws3pkibp.mspx*)

■ 219059–"Enterprise CA May Not Publish Certificates from Child Domain or Trusted Domain"

■ 300532–"Windows 2000 Enterprise CAs Not Added to Certificate Publishers Group in Windows Server 2003 Domain"

Note   The two articles above can be accessed through the Microsoft Knowledge Base. Go to *http://support.microsoft.com* and enter the article number in the Search The Knowledge Base text box.

Chapter 5

Designing a Certification Authority Hierarchy

Before deploying Windows Server 2008 Active Directory Certificate Services, an organization must spend time designing the certification authority (CA) hierarchy. Developing the correct structure involves investigating and processing related requirements for applications, security, business, technical, and external forces. Hierarchy elements covered in this chapter include:

- The number of tiers to use in a CA hierarchy
- How the CAs will be arranged into a CA hierarchy
- The types of certificates each CA will issue
- The types of CAs to be deployed at each tier
- Specifying where the CA computer accounts will exist in Active Directory Domain Services (AD DS)
- Security measures to protect the CAs
- Whether different certificate policies will be required

Determining the Number of Tiers in a CA Hierarchy

How many tiers to include in the CA hierarchy is a basic consideration addressed in the design process. It is also necessary to determine how many individual CAs will be required at each tier. Most CA hierarchies consist of two to four tiers; however, a single-tier CA can be appropriate in smaller organizations.

Single-Tier CA Hierarchy

Some organizations require only basic public key infrastructure (PKI) services. Typically, these are organizations with fewer than 300 user accounts in the directory service. Rather than deploying multiple CAs, a single CA is installed as an enterprise root CA.

The enterprise root CA is not removed from the network. Instead, the computer is a member of the domain and is always available to issue certificates to requesting computers, users, services, or networking devices.

> **Warning** If at all possible, install the enterprise root CA on a computer that is not a domain controller. The mix of a CA and a domain controller often results in issues in the future if you wish to move the CA to another computer.

A single-tier CA hierarchy is easy to manage because it involves administration of only a single CA. A problem with this design is the lack of redundancy. If the CA fails, Certificate Services will not be available to process incoming certificate requests, certificate renewals, or certificate revocation list publishing until the CA is restored to service.

Single-tier CA hierarchies generally are used only when simple administration is required, costs must be minimized, and the organization's security policy does not require the implementation of an offline root CA.

> **Warning**   If you choose this deployment model, ensure that you deploy a *single* enterprise root. Do not start deploying enterprise root CAs for each application that requires certificates. Deploying CAs in this manner typically leads to failed PKI deployments.

Two-Tier CA Hierarchy

A two-tier hierarchy comprises an offline root CA and one or more issuing CAs. The issuing CAs are a combination of policy CAs and issuing CAs. (See Chapter 2, "Primer to PKI," for a review of different CA types.) Figure 5-1 shows a two-tier CA hierarchy.

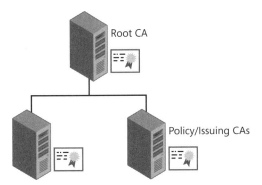

Figure 5-1   A two-tier CA hierarchy

To ensure security in a two-tier hierarchy, the root CA is deployed as a standalone root CA. This allows an organization to deploy the root CA offline—that is, the CA is detached from the network to protect the computer from all network-based attacks. In fact, the computer is *never* attached to the network for *any* of its lifetime in most deployments.

> **Note**   A standalone CA does not require domain membership, which allows the computer to never be connected to the organization's network for the purpose of communicating and maintaining a computer account in AD DS.

In a multi-tier CA hierarchy, it does not matter which second-tier CA issues the certificates to computers, users, services, or network devices. All that matters is that the certificate issued by the second-tier CA chains to a trusted root CA—the offline root CA in this configuration.

To enhance the availability of Certificate Services, two or more issuing CAs should exist at the second tier. This ensures that if one CA fails, Certificate Services will still be available on the other CAs. The number of issuing CAs depends on the organization's requirements. For example, you can deploy the same certificate templates at two CAs at the second tier to ensure that certificates are issued even if one of the CAs fails.

> **Note**   The design of issuing CAs is discussed in more detail later in this chapter in the section titled "Choosing an Architecture."

Three-Tier CA Hierarchy

A three-tier CA hierarchy provides the best security and flexibility. A three-tier CA hierarchy, as shown in Figure 5-2, consists of:

- An offline root CA installed as a standalone root CA
- One or more offline policy CAs installed as standalone subordinate CAs
- One or more issuing CAs installed as enterprise subordinate CAs or occasionally as subordinate standalone CAs

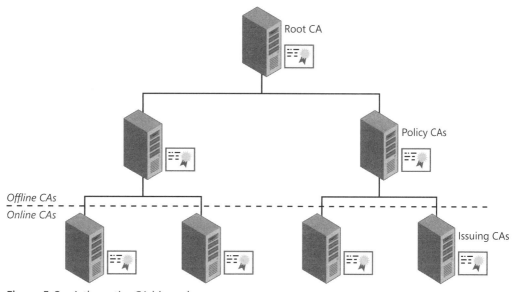

Figure 5-2   A three-tier CA hierarchy

A three-tier hierarchy is recommended in the following scenarios:

- Strong physical security of the CA hierarchy is mandated by the security policy. The offline deployment of the root and policy CA tiers protects computers from network-sourced attacks.

■ Certificates are issued under different assurance levels requiring different certificate policies. If you require different measures to validate a certificate subscriber, you may need separate policy CAs at the policy CA tier. For example, you may need different certification practice statements (CPSs) for subscribers that are employees of your organization and subscribers who are partners or customers of your organization. Each policy CA would implement its own CPS and related certificate policies and assurance levels.

■ Management of the CA hierarchy is split among different network administration teams—for example, one PKI management team manages the Europe CAs, while a separate team manages the Asia CAs. In this scenario, each team is responsible for defining the CPS for their policy CAs. (See Chapter 3, "Policies and Public Key Infrastructure (PKI)," for a review of defining the CPS.)

> **Note**   Remember that a CPS and its certificate policies (CPs) are effective at the CA where the CPS is defined in the CA certificate as well as at any CAs that are subordinate to that CA in the hierarchy.

Four-Tier CA Hierarchy

More than three tiers in the CA hierarchy might be required in some cases, but it is not recommended to deploy more than four layers. In a four-tier CA hierarchy, issuing CAs reside at both the third and fourth levels of the hierarchy. Figure 5-3 shows two regional CAs at the third level of the CA hierarchy and different CAs (for employees and contractors) at the fourth level.

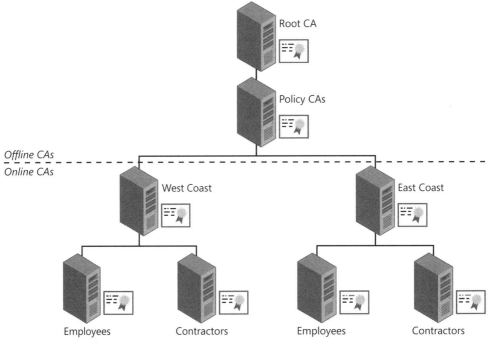

Figure 5-3   A four-tier CA hierarchy

Organizing Issuing CAs

The deployment model used for issuing CAs should be based on the following factors:

- **The number of certificates that will be issued**   The more certificates a CA hierarchy issues to users, computers, services, or network devices, the higher the number of issuing CAs required in the CA hierarchy. The higher number of issuing CAs provides redundancy so that the failure of a single CA does not prevent deployment of certificates.

- **Availability requirements in a wide area network environment**   In a wide area network (WAN) environment, there is a possibility of network outages. To mitigate the impact that a network outage would have on the ability of clients to communicate with a CA, CAs can be placed at major network hub sites. For example, Figure 5-4 shows a CA hierarchy in which issuing CAs are placed at a North American hub site, a European hub site, and an Asian hub site. If any othe intersite links fail, clients in the local site will still be able to request certificates.

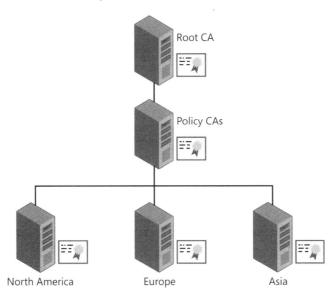

Figure 5-4   A CA hierarchy that distributes CAs by geographic hub sites

This geographic configuration might also require multiple policy CAs if different subject-identification processes or other PKI management processes are implemented for each region. For example, one CPS may apply to Asia and North America, but a separate CPS may be required for Europe. This causes a subtle change in the CA hierarchy, as shown in Figure 5-5.

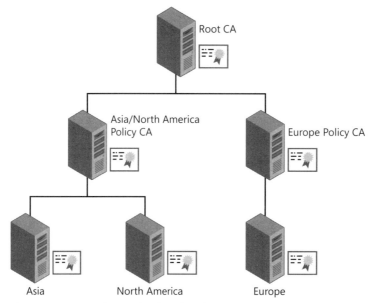

Figure 5-5   A CA hierarchy that distributes CAs by geographic hub sites

- ■ **The PKI management model**   Some companies use separate teams to manage projects for PKI-enabled applications. For example, one team manages all certificates related to virtual private networking, another team manages all certificates related to EFS, and a third team manages certificates related to secure e-mail. Figure 5-6 shows an example of a CA hierarchy based on decentralized certificate distribution.

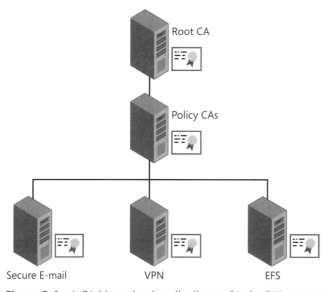

Figure 5-6   A CA hierarchy that distributes CAs by PKI management

In this example, separate CAs exist for each PKI-enabled project. The Secure E-mail CA issues the required certificates for Secure/Multipurpose Internet Mail Extensions (S/MIME); the VPN CA issues the required certificates for a virtual private network (VPN) solution; and the EFS CA issues the required certificates for EFS encryption.

■ **The structure of the company hosting the PKI**   In some cases, an organization is a member of a conglomerate of several organizations. For example, if A. Datum Corporation is a holding company that includes several autonomous but related companies, the CA hierarchy can include separate policy and issuing CAs for each company within the umbrella group, as shown in Figure 5-7.

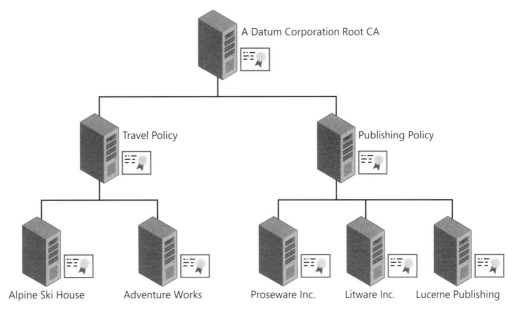

Figure 5-7   A CA hierarchy that distributes CAs by company structure

In this example, there are two policy CAs: one for the travel agency arm and one for the publication arm of A. Datum Corporation. Below the policy CAs, there are separate issuing CAs for each company within the A. Datum Corporation umbrella. The issuing CAs must enforce the policies and procedures defined at their respective policy CAs.

■ **Employee categories**   It is also common to have different CAs for each employee category within an organization. The creation of separate CAs for each employee category allows certificate management to be delegated to different groups. This architecture also allows different methods of subject identification for each employee category—for example:

   ■ **By citizenship**   Some United States military organizations, such as defense contractors, require delegation according to citizenship or nationality in which different subject-identification requirements exist for U.S. citizens, U.S. green card holders, and everyone else (referred to as *foreign nationals*). In this type of environment, a CA hierarchy is created that implements separate issuing CAs for each citizenship category.

■ **By employee type**   Some organizations classify employees according to organizational hiring status. For example, separate issuing CAs can be required for full-time employees, contractors, external consultants, and interns.

> **Note**   This is only a partial set of common factors.

Choosing an Architecture

There is no simple formula for choosing an architecture. Factors to consider when designing the CA hierarchy include:

■ **Organization distribution**   If an organization is geographically dispersed across continents or regions, a common CA hierarchy design places an issuing CA at major hub sites in the network topology to provide regional site availability.

■ **The management model**   The CA hierarchy can include fewer CAs in an organization with centralized management. In decentralized organizations, however, a common approach is to issue separate CAs for individual management teams. For example, in a project-based management scheme, separate CAs are used for each project team, as shown previously in Figure 5-6. Similarly, if an organization is comprised of several sectors, separate CA management can be defined by each sector in the organization, as shown previously in Figure 5-7.

■ **Industry regulations**   Industry regulations sometimes require specific management techniques. For example, a bank may have to follow industry regulations for private key protection for customer data on the network. These requirements may result in a separate set of certificate policies, requiring either a separate policy CA/issuing CA combination or a separate policy CA, in addition to associated issuing CAs.

Gathering Required Information

The process of gathering information will help you design your organization's CA hierarchy. You must collect the following data:

■ Application requirements

■ Security requirements

■ Technical requirements

■ Business requirements

■ External requirements

Identifying PKI-Enabled Applications

A PKI deployment is typically launched when an organization introduces one or more applications that are dependent on the existence of a PKI. This leads to defining requirements as to who will manage the applications, the number of users, the certificate distribution, and how certificates are used by the applications.

PKI-Enabled Applications

Applications and technologies that can trigger an organization to deploy a PKI include:

- **802.1X port-based authentication**   802.1X authentication allows only authenticated users or computers to access either an 802.11 wireless network or a wired Ethernet network. You can provide centralized user identification and authentication when implementing 802.1X authentication by using Remote Authentication Dial-In User Service (RADIUS) on the back end.

- **Digital signatures**   Certificates may be used for digital signing. Digital signatures secure Internet transactions by providing a method for verifying who sent the data and that content was not modified in transit. Depending on how a certificate is issued, digital signatures also provide nonrepudiation or content commitment. In other words, data signers cannot deny that they are the data senders because they are the only users with access to the certificate's private key.

- **Encrypting File System**   EFS encrypts data by using a combination of symmetric and asymmetric encryption methods.

- **Web authentication and encryption**   The distribution of Secure Sockets Layer (SSL) certificates to a Web server on either an intranet or the Internet allows a Web client to validate the Web server's identity and encrypt all data sent to and from the Web server. Optionally, client authentication certificates can be distributed to Web clients, allowing them to present a certificate as their form of authentication to the Web server. This provides mutual authentication of the Web client and the Web server.

- **Internet Protocol security**   Certificates can be used to authenticate the two endpoints in an Internet Protocol security (IPsec) association. Once authenticated, IPsec can be used to encrypt and digitally sign all communications between the two endpoints. Certificates do not play a part in the actual encryption and signing of IPsec-protected data—they are used only to authenticate the two endpoints.

- **Secure e-mail**   Secure e-mail provides confidential communication, data integrity, and nonrepudiation for e-mail messages. You can enhance e-mail security by using certificates to verify a sender's digital identity, the message's point of origin, and message authenticity, and to protect the confidentiality of messages by encrypting the message's content.

- **Smart card logon**   Smart card logon provides increased security by using two-factor authentication. To authenticate on the network, a user must have access to the smart card and know the personal identification number (PIN) for the smart card.

- **Code signing**   Code signing protects computers from installation of unauthorized controls, drivers, or applications. Applications that support code signing, such as Windows Internet Explorer, can be configured to prevent execution of unsigned controls.

- **Virtual private networks**   VPNs allow remote users to connect to a private network by using tunneling protocols, such as Point-to-Point Tunneling Protocol (PPTP), Layer 2 Tunneling Protocol (L2TP), or Secure Socket Tunneling Protocol (SSTP). Certificates increase the strength of user authentication and can provide authentication for IPsec if using L2TP with IPsec encryption.

Identifying Certificate Recipients

Once you have determined what PKI-enabled applications your organization is deploying and the certificate required by the applications, you must decide who must acquire the certificates. Typically, certificates are deployed to the following subjects:

- **Users**   A digital certificate uniquely identifies a user to a PKI-enabled application. A user can be assigned a single certificate that enables all applications or can receive application-specific certificates, such as an EFS encryption certificate that can be used for one purpose only. The certificates issued to the user are stored in the Current User certificate store.

- **Computers**   A digital certificate uniquely identifies the computer when a user or computer connects to the computer where the certificate is installed. The certificate becomes the computer's identifier and is stored in the Local Machine certificate store. If the Client Authentication object identifier (OID) is included in the certificate in either the Enhanced Key Usage (EKU) extension or the Application Policies extension, the computer certificate can be used by an application to initiate connections. If the Server Authentication OID is included in the certificate in the EKU or Application Policies extension, the certificate can be used to authenticate the computer's identity when a client application connects.

- **Network devices**   Several devices on a network allow the installation of certificates for client/server authentication. These devices include, but are not limited to, VPN appliances, firewalls, and routers. The actual process used to install a certificate on a network device is subject to the type of operating system and interfaces of the actual network device.

- **Services**   Some services require computer certificates for either authentication or encryption. Certificates are not actually issued to a service. Instead, the service certificate is stored either on the Local Machine store or in the user's profile of the associated service account. For example, if a certificate is installed for the World Wide Web (WWW) service of a Web server, the certificate is stored in the Local Machine store. On the other hand, the EFS recovery agent certificate for the EFS service is stored in the user profile of the designated EFS recovery agent.

> **Tip**   The easiest way to determine where to install a certificate for a service is to investigate what credentials the service uses to authenticate. If the service uses Local System, the certificate must be stored in the Local Machine store. If the service uses a user account and password, the certificate must be stored in that specific user's profile.

Determining Security Requirements

An organization should have a security policy that defines its security standards. This document (described in greater detail in Chapter 3) provides the security requirements for a PKI design. Some of the possible requirements include:

- **Physical security for offline CAs**   To increase the security of the root CA in a two-tier hierarchy and the root and policy CAs in a three-tier hierarchy, deploy the root and policy CAs as offline CAs, and store them in a physically secure location. In some organizations, only the hard disks are removed from the offline CAs and stored in a safe. This allows the offline CA computer's chassis to be used for other projects when the CA is not in use. Alternatively, you can simply keep the CA computers in a server room with restricted access.

- **Additional security for online CAs**   To secure an online CA, you can place the physical computer in a secure server room that requires controlled access, such as a PIN pad or keycard access. In addition, you should minimize services at an issuing CA. In other words, dedicate the computer as an issuing CA rather than installing the issuing CA on an existing domain controller.

> **Note**   If you are implementing a Windows Server 2008 server as an online certification authority, Certificate Services is the only service required. If you deploy the Certificate Services Web Enrollment pages on the same computer, however, a minimal installation of Internet Information Services (IIS) is also necessary. The required IIS components are automatically installed when you add the Certificate Services Web Enrollment role service.

- **Protection for the CA's private key**   An organization's security policy can require specific security measures for a CA's private key. For example, an organization might have to implement Federal Information Processing Standards (FIPS) 140-2 protection of the CA's private key to meet industry or organizational security requirements.

> **More Info**   FIPS 140-2, "Security Requirements for Cryptographic Modules," can be found at *http://csrc.nist.gov/publications/fips/fips140-2/fips1402.pdf.*

By default, the Microsoft CA implements a software cryptographic service provider (CSP), such as the Microsoft Strong Cryptographic Provider. A software CSP stores the CA's private key material on the computer's local hard disk. Although physical security measures can increase the protection of this key material, be aware that *any* member of the local Administrators group can export and reuse the private key material.

> **Note**   A CSP defines how a certificate's private key is protected and accessed. The CSP will determine where to generate the certificate's key pair when the certificate is requested and will implement mechanisms to protect access to the private key. For example, a CSP may require the input of a PIN to access a smart card's private key.

You can increase the security of the CA's private key by implementing one of the following two measures:

- ❑ **Using a smart card CSP**   A smart card CSP stores the CA's private key material on a two-factor authentication device. When the private key material is accessed, a user must type in the smart card's PIN.

- ❑ **Using a hardware security module**   A *hardware security module (HSM)* provides the strongest protection of a CA's private key by storing the private key on a physical security device. The HSM provides additional security measures to protect the private key from tampering and, in some cases, destroys the private key if an attack against the HSM occurs.

- ■ **Different issuance requirements for certificates**   An organization can issue certificates that require different issuance requirements. For example, some certificates are issued based on the user's account and password combination, whereas others are set to a pending state to allow validation of the user's identity through presentation of photo identification. To allow the validation of identity, separate issuing CAs or separate policy CAs can exist in the CA hierarchy.

Determining Technical Requirements

Technical requirements affect the structure of a CA hierarchy. Technical issues that should be considered during a PKI design process include:

- ■ Specifying PKI management roles

- ■ Minimizing risk of CA failure

- ■ Determining certificate validity periods

Specifying PKI Management Roles

Windows Server 2008 Active Directory Certificate Services allows you to specify PKI management roles for each CA. If technical requirements require you to delegate administration to a specific office or region, you can accomplish this by deploying a separate issuing CA and delegating management to users at that location.

Windows Server 2008 supports the definition of Common Criteria roles. Common Criteria includes the following roles for PKI management:

- **CA administrator**   This administrative role is responsible for managing the configuration of the CA computer, including defining the CA's property settings and certificate managers. A user is delegated this role through the assignment of the Manage CA permission at the CA.

- **Certificate Manager**   This administrative role, also known as the CA officer, is responsible for certificate management. Tasks include certificate revocation, issuance, and deletion. In addition, the certificate manager extracts archived private keys for recovery by a key recovery agent. A user is given this role through the assignment of the Issue and Manage Certificates permission at the CA.

- **Backup operator**   This administrative role is responsible for the backup and recovery of the CA database and CA configuration settings. A user is delegated this role through the assignment of the Back Up Files and Directories or the Restore Files and Directories user rights at the Group Policy Object (GPO) assigned to the CA or in the CA's local security policy.

- **Auditor**   This administrative role is responsible for specifying the events audited at the CA and for reviewing the security log for events related to PKI management and operations. A user is given this role through the assignment of the Manage Auditing and Security Log user right at the GPO assigned to the CA or in the CA's local security policy.

More Info   For more information on Common Criteria role separation, see the "Certificate Issuing and Management Components Protection Profile" at *http://www. commoncriteriaportal.org/public/files/ppfiles/PP_CIMCPP_SL1-4_V1.0.pdf.*

Note   The CA administrator and certificate manager roles are defined as CA permissions, whereas the backup operator and auditor roles are user rights and are not limited to Certificate Services. Rather, they are applicable to all applications running on the computer hosting Certificate Services.

You can specify separate CA administrators, CA officers (certificate managers), backup operators, and auditors for each CA in the hierarchy.

Warning   Windows Server 2008 Enterprise Edition allows you to enforce the Common Criteria roles through role separation. With the enforcement of role separation enabled, a user can hold only one of four roles. Individual users who hold two or more of these roles are blocked from all PKI-management activities.

Minimizing Risk of CA Failure

Your PKI hierarchy design can include measures to prevent the failure of Certificate Services, such as defining hardware specifications that prevent common forms of failure. For example, you can cluster a Windows Server 2008 issuing CA to provide high availability of Certificate Services for critical CAs. Alternatively, if your organization considers disk failure the biggest risk to Certificate Services, you can ensure that the CA database's disk partition is on a redundant array of independent disks (RAID) 5 or RAID 0+1 disk array to ensure the best performance and recoverability in the event of disk failure. Likewise, the CA log files can be placed on a RAID 1 mirror set to protect against disk failure. You can also ensure that disk partitions are large enough to store the volume of certificates for the expected certificate enrollment activity.

Hardware requirements are less demanding for an offline CA than for an online issuing CA. For example, Figure 5-8 shows two disk configurations that can be used to provide recoverability yet minimize the costs spent on hard disks for the offline CA.

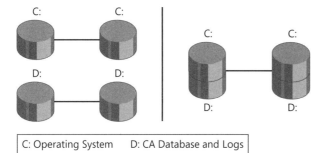

C: Operating System   D: CA Database and Logs

Figure 5-8   Disk configuration recommendations for offline CAs

In the configuration on the left, separate mirror sets are implemented for the operating system and the CA database and logs. This configuration separates all CA data from the operating system volume.

In the configuration on the right, one mirror set is installed at the offline CA with two partitions. The C: partition is dedicated to the operating system, and the D: partition is dedicated to the CA database and logs.

Note   The decision to use one or the other of these two configurations is often based on the number of disks supported by the server that hosts the offline CA or an organization's requirements for installing the operating system on a dedicated partition separate from application data such as the Certificate Services database and log files.

For an online CA, the disk activity performed by Certificate Services is far greater than that of an offline CA. It is recommended that a combination of RAID 1 mirrors and RAID 5 or RAID 0+1 volumes be used to store Certificate Services data, as shown in Figure 5-9.

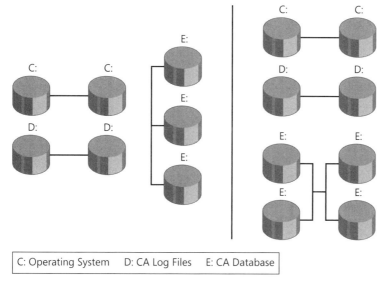

C: Operating System   D: CA Log Files   E: CA Database

Figure 5-9   Disk configuration recommendations for an online CA

On the left side, the disk configuration is shown using RAID 1 mirror sets for the C: drive for the operating system and for the D: drive for the CA database log files. The CA database is stored on a RAID 5 stripe set with parity. This configuration provides good performance for reading data from the CA database.

On the right side, the disk configuration is shown using the same RAID 1 mirror sets for the operating system and CA database log files. In this example, a RAID 0+1 set is used for the CA database. RAID 0+1 mirrors two RAID 0 stripe sets. RAID 0+1 provides higher input/output rates than RAID 5 and is often selected by organizations that foresee large volumes of certificate enrollment traffic on the CA database.

Determining Certificate Validity Periods

A certificate has a predefined validity period that comprises a start date and time and an end date and time. An issued certificate's validity period cannot be changed after certificate issuance. Determining the validity period at each tier of the CA hierarchy, including the validity period of the certificates issued to users, computers, services, or network devices, is a primary step when defining a CA hierarchy.

The recommended strategy for determining certificate validity periods is to start with the certificates issued to users, computers, services, or network devices by issuing CAs. The main point to remember is that a Microsoft CA cannot issue a certificate that exceeds the remaining lifetime on the CA certificate. Although allowed by the standards, this scenario can lead to certificates with remaining validity periods to expire when the issuing CA's certificate expires. You should ensure that the CA has enough remaining lifetime on its certificate to issue certificates with the required validity periods. A good rule of thumb is to make the CA certificate validity period at least twice as long as the maximum validity period of any CA-issued certificates. Figure 5-10 shows an example of a two-tier CA hierarchy that issues certificates with a maximum validity period of five years.

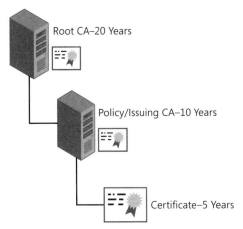

Root CA–20 Years

Policy/Issuing CA–10 Years

Certificate–5 Years

Figure 5-10 Determining CA validity periods

In this example, it is known that the maximum validity period for certificates issued by the policy/issuing CA is five years. To ensure that the remaining validity period of the policy/issuing CA does not affect the validity period of the issued certificates, you should double the validity period value of the policy/issuing CA certificate to 10 years.

In addition to doubling the validity period, you can also follow best practices and ensure that you renew the CA certificate at half of the remaining validity period. You can follow one of two strategies.

- The first strategy attempts to use a CA's private key for its entire lifetime. The first time you renew a CA certificate (after a period of five years in this scenario), you renew with the original key pair. After the next five years pass, you renew the CA certificate with a new key pair. This ensures that the same key pair is never used for a period longer than the intended original validity period of 10 years.

- The second strategy is to always renew a CA's certificate with a new key pair. After the initial five year period is completed, the CA renews its certificate with a new key pair. Likewise, at ten years, the CA again renews its certificate with a new key pair.

The validity period of the root CA certificate should also be double the validity period of the policy/issuing CA certificate. In this example, the validity period of the root CA certificate would be 20 years, double the 10-year validity period of the policy/issuing CA. As with the policy/issuing CA, you must choose between the two strategies for key renewal.

You should not go to extremes with the validity period. The longer a certificate's key pair is valid, the more time an attacker has to try to determine the value of the private key based on the public key and examples of the encryption performed by the private key. The possibility of determining the private key is even higher if the key length is shorter in length (1,024 bits) versus longer in length (4,096 bits). It is usually not recommended to implement a root CA with a validity period longer than 20 years.

> **More Info**   For recommendations on choosing a mix of validity periods, key lengths, and signing algorithms, please review the content at *http://www.keylength.com*.

Choosing Key Length

When you choose the key length for each CA in the CA hierarchy, the biggest restriction is the applications that will use the CA hierarchy for certificates. Some applications are known to not support keys larger than a certain value.

For example, a very common VPN appliance used in today's networks is the Cisco VPN 3000 series. These appliances are hard coded to not support a CA certificate with a key length greater than 2,048 bits. This is for *any* certificate in the CA hierarchy. So, if you deployed a CA hierarchy with a 4,096-bit key, no certificates from this hierarchy could be used with a Cisco VPN 3000 series device to negotiate an IPsec security association.

Other applications and devices that are known to have issues with CA certificates with key lengths greater than 2,048 bits include:

- **Nortel Contivity devices**   These devices cannot support any certificate in the chain with a key length greater than 2,048 bits. One solution that Nortel uses to get around this issue is to move the trust point to a subordinate CA. For example, suppose that you have a three-tiered CA hierarchy with a root key length of 4,096 bits and policy and issuing key lengths of 2,048 bits. You could still use certificates from this CA hierarchy by defining the trust point in the Nortel devices as the policy CA or the issuing CA.

- **Older Java applications**   Java applications developed in versions prior to Java Development Kit (JDK) version 1.5 support a maximum key length of only 2,048 bits for CA certificates. Recompiling the applications in version 1.5 solves this issue, as version 1.5 now supports 4,096-bit keys.

Determining Publication Points

The final technical requirement that must be met in your design is determining URLs for:

- Certificate revocation list (CRLs) retrieval

- CA certificate retrieval

- Online Certificate Status Protocol (OCSP) responses

> **More Info**   More details on certificate validation methods are found in Chapter 11, "Certificate Validation."

The certificate-chaining engine can use the URLs stored in the CRL Distribution Point (CDP) (if CRL checking is being used) and Authority Information Access (AIA) extensions (if OCSP is being used) to determine a certificate's revocation status.

> **Note**   An application can use other methods for building certificate chains and determining revocation lists. For example, some applications store the files on the local file system, whereas others can hard-code URLs for the CRL and CA certificate in their configuration.

At each CA in the hierarchy, you must define publication points for certificates issued by that CA. These publication points allow access to *that* CA's certificate and CRL. The following protocols can be used when defining publication points:

- **Hypertext Transfer Protocol (HTTP) URLs**   HTTP URLs are used for both internal and external publication points. The advantage of HTTP URLs is that there is little lag time between publication and availability. Once you publish an updated CRL or CA certificate to an HTTP URL, it is immediately available for download by PKI-enabled applications. In addition, HTTP URLs can typically be downloaded by clients behind firewalls and those who are not full AD DS clients, including those running an operating system earlier than Microsoft Windows 2000 and non-Microsoft clients.

- **Lightweight Directory Access Protocol (LDAP) URL**   A CA certificate or CRL that is published to an LDAP URL is by default published into the configuration naming context of AD DS. This means that the CRL or CA certificate is available at all domain controllers in the forest.

> **Note**   Although the default LDAP location references AD DS, you can publish a CA certificate or CRL to any LDAP directory, such as Active Directory Lightweight Directory Services.

There are two disadvantages to using the default LDAP URL location:

- ❑ It can take some time for CRLs or CA certificates to fully replicate to all domain controllers in the forest. The actual time depends on your network's replication latency, especially when the replication must take place between sites and not only between domain controllers in the same site.

- ❑ Non-support of the AD DS–related LDAP URLs can lead to delays in CRL or CA certificate retrieval. If the default LDAP URL is the first URL in the URL listing, a non–AD DS enabled client will time out for ten seconds before it moves on to the next available URL.

Note   When multiple URLs exist in the URL listing, the first URL in the listing is given 10 seconds to attempt to connect. Each subsequent CDP location will use a maximum of one half of the remaining time to connect to that specific CRL object before continuing to the next location. The maximum time allotted for retrieval is 20 seconds for Windows XP. The time spent attempting to connect to the LDAP URL depends on the order of the URL listing.

More Info   More information on choosing publication points can be found in the "Best Practices for Implementing a Microsoft Windows Server 2003 Public Key Infrastructure" document at *http://www.microsoft.com/technet/prodtechnol/windowsserver2003/technologies/ security/ws3pkibp.msp*. Even though this is a Windows Server 2003 white paper, the concepts still hold true for Windows Server 2008.

The decision as to which protocols to implement for CRL or CA certificate publication points depends on the frequency at which you publish CRLs, the protocols allowed to traverse network firewalls, and your network's operating systems. To ensure maximum availability, the URLs should be ordered so that the most common protocol used for CRL or CA certificate retrieval is listed first in the CDP extension. Other protocols are then listed in their order of usage.

More Info   Methods for defining CRL and CA certificate publication URLs are discussed in detail in Chapter 11.

Determining Business Requirements

Business requirements define an organization's goals. Typically, they define how an organization expects the PKI to improve its processes. For example, the following business requirements can affect a CA hierarchy design:

- **Minimizing PKI-associated costs**   When reviewing CA hierarchy designs, you might have to choose a CA hierarchy that deploys the fewest CAs. For example, some organizations combine the roles of policy CAs and issuing CAs into a single CA in the hierarchy, deploying a two-tier hierarchy rather than a three-tier hierarchy.

- **High availability of certificate issuance**   An organization can require that a CA be consistently available to ensure that no certificate requests fail due to a CA being down for any reason. To ensure that a CA is always available, you must implement clustering on the issuing CA that issues certificates based on the defined certificate template. If your up-time requirements are not as stringent, you may consider publishing the certificate template at more than one CA in the CA hierarchy, protecting against the failure of a single CA.

■ **Liability of PKI participants**   A CA hierarchy includes policy CAs that define the liability of the CA in the CPS. The liability should provide sufficient coverage for transactions that use CA-issued certificates. This liability definition must be reviewed by your organization's legal department to ensure that the definitions are legally correct and binding upon all participants in the PKI.

Determining External Requirements

Not all requirements are defined by an organization. In some cases, especially if you expect to use certificates in conjunction with other organizations, you might have to meet external requirements, such as those defined by other organizations or by the governments of countries in which your organization conducts business.

Examples of external requirements include:

■ **Enabling external organizations to recognize employee-used certificates**   Different solutions exist for this scenario. You can choose to not deploy an internal PKI and simply obtain certificates from commercial CAs, such as VeriSign or RSA. Alternatively, you can use cross-certification or qualified subordination to specify which external certificates you trust.

> **More Info**   Cross-certification and qualified subordination are discussed in detail in Chapter 16, "Creating Trust Between Organizations."

■ **Using your organization's certificate at partner organizations**   In some cases, the certificates issued by your CA hierarchy will be used by your employees for encryption or signing purposes at another organization. You might have to create custom certificates to meet the requirements of the other organization. One solution is to implement a CA hierarchy that defines separate internal and external policy CAs, as shown in Figure 5-11.

In this example, all certificates for use with partners are issued by the Partners CA. If different issuance policies are required for these certificates, the issuance policies are defined in the CPS deployed at the external policy CA.

■ **Industry or government legislation**   Several countries have legislation that affects the design of a CA hierarchy. For example, Canada enforces the Personal Information Protection and Electronic Documents Act. This act regulates the management of a customer's personal information when held by a private-sector company. The act requires that someone be accountable for compliance, and this person should be involved in the deployment and design of the CA hierarchy to ensure that all requirements of the act are enforced in the design.

> **More Info**   You can obtain a copy of Canada's Personal Information Protection and Electronic Documents Act at *http://laws.justice.gc.ca/en/p-8.6/91355.html*.

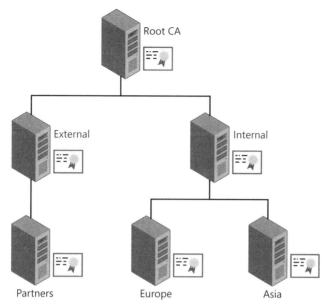

Figure 5-11   Implementing separate policy CAs for internal and external use

- **Certificates for nonemployees**   If you issue certificates to nonemployees, you must ensure that the CPS outlines nonemployee responsibilities and clearly defines the revocation policy in case you must revoke a certificate. Using a CA hierarchy such as the one defined previously in Figure 5-11, you can deploy a separate certificate policy that includes greater detail for external clients.

- **Validating certificates on external networks**   When designing the configuration of each CA, you must ensure that the CRL and CA certificate are published to externally accessible locations, such as a Web server in a perimeter network (also known as a screened subnet). This allows certificate validation to take place from the external network when using applications, such as extranet Web servers and VPN solutions when connections originate from the Internet.

Collecting AD DS Requirements

The last part of the design process is gathering AD DS requirements. These requirements include:

- Naming conventions for CA computers accounts, process/service accounts, group accounts, and Group Policy Objects (GPOs).

- Choosing which domain or domains will host the CA computer accounts.

- Defining an organizational unit (OU) structure for CA computer accounts, PKI management groups, and process/service accounts.

Naming Conventions

An organization typically has naming conventions for Active Directory objects. These conventions can include:

- **Computer accounts**   Many organization implement naming conventions that reflect server location, server role, and potentially room location information. This can be a dangerous naming convention for CA computer accounts because a CA computer account cannot be renamed, and its domain membership cannot be changed. In cases where site codes are included in the names, consider creating a pseudo site code such as INFR (for infrastructure) or PKI.

- **Process accounts**   When you configure a CA, you will typically configure scheduled tasks for day-to-day activities. The tasks can include monitoring scripts, CRL publication scripts, delta CRL publication scripts, and backup routines. Each of these scheduled tasks will require a process or service account for execution. You will have to name the process account based on the naming conventions of the customer. Commonly used conventions include adding prefixes such as p-*accountname* or s-*accountname*.

- **Group accounts**   When defining PKI management roles, you will typically use a combination of global groups, universal groups, and domain local groups. Commonly used naming conventions include prefixes for application type (for example PKI-) and suffixes for group type (adding a –U for universal groups or –G for global groups).

- **Group Policy Objects (GPOs)**   To ensure standardized application of PKI settings, you may deploy one or more GPOs. The GPOs can include designating trusted root certificates, installation restrictions for trusted root certificates, definition of Internet Explorer trusted sites, Encrypting File System (EFS) configuration settings, or audit settings for CA computers. Most organizations assign a prefix to the PKI-related GPOs so that it is easier to identify a PKI-related GPO. For example, you can prefix all PKI-related GPO settings with PKI-*GPOName*.

It does not matter which conventions are chosen for the naming standards. The key is to know the standards early in the design process so that you can choose names for your computer accounts, process accounts, group accounts, and GPOs.

Choosing Domains for CA Computer Accounts

The second AD DS design requirement is deciding which domain will host the CA computer account. In a single domain forest, this is an easy decision. But in a multiple domain forest, the main factor that should influence the decision is the number of members in the Domain Admins group. In many multiple domain models, a child domain will implement a rather large number of members in the Domain Admins group. It is best to choose a domain where the number is minimized. If your forest deploys an empty root domain, the root domain may be the best location because of the low number of user accounts in the domain.

> **Note**   Do not limit your focus to the Domain Admins group. You must consider all groups that can ultimately be a member of the local Administrators group on the CA computer. Remember that any member of the local Administrators group could modify the configuration of the CA and gain access to the CA's private key (if using a software-based cryptographic service provider).
>
> In one case, I observed a company that would have had over 230 members from the local Administrators group if they deployed a CA in a specific child domain. Needless to say, we decided against deploying a CA computer account in that domain.

Choosing an Organizational Unit Structure

The final AD DS design decision is where to place the CA computer account, PKI process accounts, and PKI management groups in the OU structure of a domain.

There is no set best practice; it really depends on your current OU structure. Figure 5-12 shows two common OU models for PKI management.

■ In the OU structure on the left, all PKI objects are stored under a common OU named PKI Objects. Below the PKI Objects OU, separate OUs are created for users, servers, and groups. The OU structure contains only objects related to PKI management.

■ In the OU structure on the right, separate OUs exist off the domain for different object types. Dedicated OUs for users, groups, and computers for PKI management are created under their object type OU.

In both cases, it is easy to find the PKI object or to delegate administrative rights to the OUs where they are located. If there are multiple domains in the forest, it is recommended to deploy the same OU structure in each domain. Of course, if there are no objects in the domain, you could choose to omit that OU from the structure. For example, if there are no CA computer accounts in a child domain, there is no need to create an OU for CA server objects in that child domain.

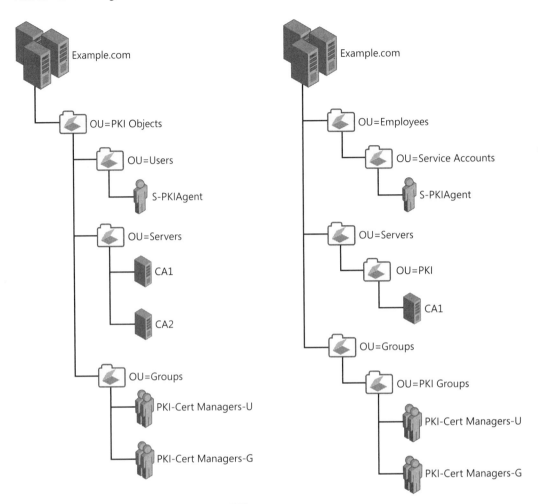

Figure 5-12   Common PKI management OU structures

Case Study: Identifying Requirements

In this case study, you will identify the technical and business requirements of Fabrikam, Inc. These requirements will determine the design of your CA hierarchy.

Fabrikam, Inc. plans to deploy several PKI-enabled applications, requiring the organization to deploy its own PKI. The design committee for the PKI has identified the following business requirements for the PKI-enabled applications:

- The corporate headquarters are in the United States, in Atlanta. All network services are managed from that location.

- Fabrikam, Inc. has international hub sites in Frankfurt, Singapore, and Lima. Several smaller offices connect to the nearest international hub on their continent, and each regional office has its own network services team responsible for network services implemented in that region.

- The international hub sites are connected to the Atlanta site by T3 lines.

- Smaller offices are connected to their nearest international hub with lines between 128 KB and 512 KB.

- The AD DS structure for Fabrikam is a single forest with four domains: fabrikam.com, americas.fabrikam.com, europe.fabrikam.com, and apac.fabrikam.com.

- Fabrikam.com is an empty forest root domain. Only default accounts exist in the forest root domain for forest-level administrative functions.

- Fabrikam implements a Service Level Agreement (SLA) that requires all critical network services to be available at all times. The PKI is a critical network service that must honor the SLA.

- Fabrikam places a high value on security, and the organization has a written security policy. The following sections in the security policy will influence the CA hierarchy's design:

    ❑ Enterprise servers are stored in secure network locations.

    ❑ Private keys for CAs must be protected from tampering and theft.

    ❑ Fabrikam implements a decentralized management structure, and the local administration staff performs management of enterprise servers.

- Fabrikam uses a Web-based factory tracking system. All communications must be protected from interception. In addition, all authentication must implement a two-factor methodology.

- The corporate Web site allows customers to input private information for record keeping. All private customer information must be protected from interception when input into the corporate Web site.

- Europe and Asia have implemented privacy laws that ensure that all information collected to identify a subscriber is protected against distribution against the wishes of the subscriber. Fabrikam collects information on the subscriber when issuing smart card certificates. The CA hierarchy must provide descriptions of how Fabrikam enforces these privacy laws.

Case Study Questions

1. How many tiers are required in the Fabrikam CA hierarchy?

2. What additional security measures are required for all CAs?

3. Are there any external requirements for the CA hierarchy?

4. Is role separation required in your CA hierarchy design? If so, how do you implement it?

5. How many policy CAs are required for the CA hierarchy?

6. What CA hierarchy design best fits the organization's requirements?

    a. A design based on certificate use

    b. A design based on geography

    c. A design based on company departments

    d. A design based on a combination of certificate use and geography

7. If offline CAs are implemented at the first and second levels of the CA hierarchy, where will you locate the offline CAs?

8. In what domain will the root CA's computer account exist?

9. In what domain will you place policy CA computer accounts?

10. In what domain will you place issuing CA computer accounts?

11. Based on the requirements presented in this case study, draw your proposed CA hierarchy for Fabrikam, Inc.

12. Assuming that your design resulted in a three-tier CA hierarchy and the maximum validity period of a certificate issued to users, computers, services, or network devices is five years, what is the validity period of the root CA certificates, the policy CA certificate(s), and the issuing CA certificates?

Additional Information

- "Guidance for Determining Key Lengths, Validity Periods, and Signing Algorithms" (*http://www.keylength.com*)

- FIPS 140-2–"Security Requirements for Cryptographic Modules" (*http://csrc.nist.gov/ publications/fips/fips140-2/fips1402.pdf*)

- "Certificate Issuing and Management Components Protection Profile" (*http://www.commoncriteriaportal.org/public/files/ppfiles/PP_CIMCPP_SL1-4_V1.0.pdf*)

- "Best Practices for Implementing a Microsoft Windows Server 2003 Public Key Infrastructure" (*http://www.microsoft.com/technet/prodtechnol/windowsserver2003/ technologies/security/ws3pkibp.mspx*)

- Canada's Personal Information Protection and Electronic Documents Act (*http://laws.justice.gc.ca/en/p-8.6/91355.html*)

Chapter 6
Implementing a CA Hierarchy

Once you've designed your CA hierarchy, it's time to install a certification authority (CA) hierarchy that follows the design. Implementation of a CA hierarchy always begins at the root CA and proceeds to the direct subordinates of the root CA. The process continues until all CAs in the hierarchy are installed.

This chapter provides detailed instructions for installing a CA hierarchy. The instructions can be used to build a hierarchy with a single CA or a hierarchy with two or more tiers.

The first section, "CA Configuration Files," is applicable to all CA hierarchy designs because it introduces the configuration and script files essential to ensuring that the CAs in your hierarchy are configured correctly. By using script files, you can ensure that desired settings are reproducible, provide documentation on each CA's configuration, and secure the ability to recover a CA's configuration in the event of a failure.

I'll use a three-tier CA hierarchy designed for Fabrikam, Inc. as the primary example in the chapter. (See Figure 6-1.)

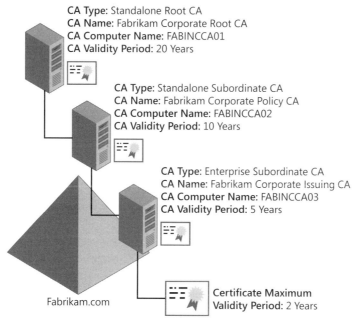

CA Type: Standalone Root CA
CA Name: Fabrikam Corporate Root CA
CA Computer Name: FABINCCA01
CA Validity Period: 20 Years

CA Type: Standalone Subordinate CA
CA Name: Fabrikam Corporate Policy CA
CA Computer Name: FABINCCA02
CA Validity Period: 10 Years

CA Type: Enterprise Subordinate CA
CA Name: Fabrikam Corporate Issuing CA
CA Computer Name: FABINCCA03
CA Validity Period: 5 Years

Fabrikam.com

**Certificate Maximum
Validity Period:** 2 Years

Figure 6-1   Fabrikam's three-tier CA hierarchy

This chapter will also discuss a single-tier CA, suitable for a smaller company—Margie's Travel in the example—a small travel company with only 147 users. (See Figure 6-2.)

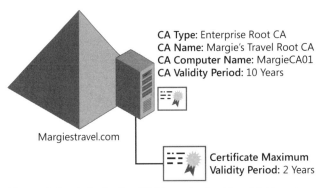

CA Type: Enterprise Root CA
CA Name: Margie's Travel Root CA
CA Computer Name: MargieCA01
CA Validity Period: 10 Years

Margiestravel.com

Certificate Maximum Validity Period: 2 Years

Figure 6-2   A single-tier CA hierarchy for Margie's Travel

CA Configuration Files

During the installation of each CA in the CA hierarchy, there are configuration files that are used to tailor each CA's configuration. These configuration scripts include:

- **CAPolicy.inf**   Provides Certificate Services configuration information, which is read during initial CA installation and whenever you renew a CA certificate.

- **Pre-installation configuration batch files**   When installing subordinate CAs in a multi-tier CA hierarchy, you must manually install your root CA certificate so that the subordinate CA considers the root CA to be a trusted root CA. In addition, you may have to install subordinate CA certificates and root and subordinate CA certificate revocation lists (CRLs) to allow revocation checking during the subordinate CA installation.

- **Post-installation configuration batch files**   Once Certificate Services is installed, you can complete configuration by scripting several Certutil.exe commands. The benefit of using the **certutil** commands in a batch file is that the configuration is reproducible, and it allows you to validate the configuration and fix any errors.

The following sections provide details and recommendations for each of the configuration file types.

CAPolicy.inf File

The CAPolicy.inf file defines settings specific to root CAs as well as settings that affect all CAs in the CA hierarchy. The CAPolicy.inf file provides the following information for a root CA:

- **Certificate revocation list (CRL) publication points**   When validating a certificate chain, the certificate chaining engine must validate every certificate in the chain. Rather than using the default CRL publication points, you can define custom revocation points based on your network's configuration. The actual order of the publication points is important because a client attempts to retrieve the CRL in the order specified in the CAPolicy.inf file.

- **CA certificate publication points**   The certificate chaining engine might have to download the root CA's certificate. This section of the CAPolicy.inf file defines the publication points for the root CA's certificate. The actual order of the publication points is important because a client attempts to retrieve the CA certificate in the order specified in the CAPolicy.inf file.

- **Enhanced Key Usage**   The CAPolicy.inf file can limit the application purposes of certificates issued by the CA. For example, if you limit the CA to issuing certificates for client authentication, server authentication, or secure e-mail, the CA cannot issue any certificates for the purpose of code signing.

- **The renewal configuration**   The CAPolicy.inf defines the renewal key length and validity period for the root CA's certificate. Typically, this section of the CAPolicy.inf file is configured to match the initial key length and validity period defined for the root CA. Matching the initial key length and validity period ensures that the designed settings are not modified when the CA's key pair is renewed.

> **Note**   You can designate the cryptographic service provider (CSP) used by the CA only at installation time. You cannot change the CSP by modifying the CAPolicy.inf file.

The CAPolicy.inf file is also used in the installation of subordinate CAs in the hierarchy. The following settings in the CAPolicy.inf file can be defined for both root and subordinate CAs:

- **Certification practice statement (CPS) information**   The CPS defines the operating procedures and practices employed at the CA as well as at subordinate CAs, which enforce the certificate policies implemented at the CAs. The CPS is typically applied at:

  - ❏ The root CA in a single-tier CA hierarchy.

  - ❏ The combination policy CA/issuing CA in a two-tier CA hierarchy.

  - ❏ The policy CAs in a three-tier CA hierarchy.

> **Note**   A CPS is considered to be effective for the CA in which the CPS is defined and for all subordinate CAs.

- **CRL publication interval**   The base CRL is published at the interval specified in the CAPolicy.inf file.

- **Delta CRL publication interval**   The delta CRL is published at the interval specified in the CAPolicy.inf file. If the interval is specified as a value of zero, the publication of delta CRLs is disabled at the CA.

■   **Basic constraints**   Limitations can be set on the number of certificates allowed below the CA in which the CAPolicy.inf file is defined. Basic constraints protect against complex hierarchies that implement long certificate chains. A basic constraint also indicates whether the certificate is issued to a CA or to an end entity other than a CA.

Creating the CAPolicy.inf File

By default, the CAPolicy.inf file does not exist when you install Windows Server 2008. You must manually create the file in the Microsoft Windows operating system folder (%Windir% folder). When you install Certificate Services, the operating system applies any settings defined in the CAPolicy.inf file.

> **Warning**   Be sure the file is named CAPolicy.inf and is stored in the %Windir% folder. It is a common mistake to create the file in Notepad and save the file as CAPolicy.inf.txt. To prevent this, change the file type to All Files from the default of Text Documents (*.txt).

Sample CAPolicy.inf Contents

You can implement specified settings when you create a CAPolicy.inf file, depending on which CA in the CA hierarchy you apply the file to. A template for the CAPolicy.inf file follows:

```
[Version]
Signature= "$Windows NT$"

[PolicyStatementExtension]
Policies = LegalPolicy
Critical = 0

[LegalPolicy]
OID = 1.3.6.1.4.1.311.21.43
Notice = "Legal policy statement text."
URL = "http://www.example.com/certdata/cps.asp"

[AuthorityInformationAccess]
Empty = true  ; Required only for Windows Server 2003
;URL = http://%1/Public/My CA.crt
;URL = file://\\%1\Public\My CA.crt
Critical = true

[CRLDistributionPoint]
Empty = true; Required only for Windows Server 2003
;URL = http://%1/Public/My CA.crl
;URL = file://\\%1\Public\My CA.crl
Critical = true

[EnhancedKeyUsageExtension]
OID = 1.3.6.1.4.1.311.21.6 ; szOID_KP_KEY_RECOVERY_AGENT
OID = 1.3.6.1.4.1.311.10.3.9 ; szOID_ROOT_LIST_SIGNER
OID = 1.3.6.1.4.1.311.10.3.1 ; szOID_KP_CTL_USAGE_SIGNING
Critical = false
```

```
[basicconstraintsextension]
pathlength = 3
critical=true

[certsrv_server]
renewalkeylength=2048
RenewalValidityPeriodUnits=20
RenewalValidityPeriod=years
CRLPeriod = days
CRLPeriodUnits = 2
CRLDeltaPeriod = hours
CRLDeltaPeriodUnits = 4
LoadDefaultTemplates=0
```

> **More Info**   A sample CAPolicy.inf file is included with the materials related to this chapter on the companion CD-ROM.

CAPolicy.inf File Sections

Within the CAPolicy.inf file, there are several predefined sections, each of which defines specific settings for Certificate Services. These sections and related decisions regarding their contents are outlined here. Also outlined is whether the section applies to root CA installations, subordinate CA installations, or to both root and subordinate CA installations.

[Version]   The [Version] section specifies that the INF file uses the Microsoft Windows NT format. This section must exist for both root and subordinate CA installations. It contains a single line:

```
Signature= "$Windows NT$"
```

[PolicyStatementExtension]   The [PolicyStatementExtension] section defines a CA's CPSs and certificate policies. This section's inclusion depends on the number of tiers in the CA hierarchy.

In a single-tier CA hierarchy, the [PolicyStatementExtension] and related [*PolicyName*] sections are defined at the root CA. In a two-tier CA hierarchy, you should include the [PolicyStatementExtension] and related [*PolicyName*] sections at each issuing CA in the hierarchy. In a three-tier CA hierarchy, the [PolicyStatementExtension] and related [*PolicyName*] sections are typically defined at the policy CAs on the second tier. If different CPSs are required, separate policy CAs are deployed in the CA hierarchy.

In the [PolicyStatementExtension] section, you define one or more subsections that will follow. Within the subsections, you define a minimum of three settings:

- **Object identifier (OID).**   An object identifier can be applied to each CPS. The OID is an identifier that is tied to the CPS or, if multiple policies are defined, to each CA's certificate policy.

> **Note** There is a practical limit to the number of certificate policies that can be included in a CA certificate. The Active Directory Domain Services (AD DS) schema allows only a maximum string length of 4,096 bytes for all CPS information, including OID, notification text, and URL. The total length of the certificate policy entries must be less than 4,096 bytes.

Where Do I Get an OID?

An OID is a unique sequence of numbers that identifies a specific directory object or attribute. You can define an OID for a CPS as either a public OID or a private OID.

If your organization plans to use PKI-enabled applications in conjunction with other organizations, you must obtain an OID from a public number-assignment company to ensure that your OID will be unique on the Internet. Sources for public OIDs include:

- **The Internet Assigned Numbers Authority (IANA)** This source issues free OIDs under the Private Enterprises arc. Every OID assigned by the IANA begins with the numbers 1.3.6.1.4.1, which represent iso(1).org(3).dod(6).internet(1).private(4).enterprise(1).

> **Note** An *arc* is the term used to reference a specific path in the global OID tree maintained by the International Organization for Standardization (ISO) and the International Telecommunication Union (ITU). This global OID tree is sometimes referred to as the joint ISO/ITU-T tree. For example, the Private Enterprises arc contains all OIDs that begin with 1.3.6.1.4.1.

- **The American National Standards Institute (ANSI)** This source issues OIDs for purchase under the United States organizations arc of the ANSI OID tree. Every OID assigned by the ANSI begins with the numbers 2.16.840.1, which represent joint-iso-itu-t(2).country(16).US(840).US company arc(1). Fees include acquisition fees for the OID arc and search fees to determine if your organization already owns an OID arc.

- **Other countries** Each country has its own OID-management organization. The easiest way to find the organization for a given country is to perform an Internet search with the search phrase *Country* (where *Country* is the name of the given country) and "Object Identifier." Here are some examples of the arcs available within the joint ISO/ITU-T tree:

  ❑ Canada: joint-iso-itu-t(2).country(16).canada(124)

  ❑ Netherlands: joint-iso-itu-t(2).country(16).netherlands(528)

❑   Switzerland: joint-iso-itu-t(2).country(16).switzerland(756)

❑   Thailand: joint-iso-itu-t(2).country(16).thailand(764)

You can also generate a private OID based on your forest's GUID within the Microsoft IANA-assigned tree. If you decide to use these OIDs, you will have an OID assigned from 1.3.6.1.4.1.311.21.8.*a.b.c.d.e*.1.402 (where *a.b.c.d.e* is a unique string of numbers based on your forest's GUID).

> **Note**   Use this private OID tree only if you do not foresee using the OIDs in conjunction with other organizations, and your organization is unwilling to obtain a free OID from the IANA. If you plan on using PKI-enabled applications within other organizations, obtain a free OID tree from the IANA, or buy a tree from the ANSI.

> **Tip**   You can obtain your forest's private OID by opening the Certificate Templates (certtmpl.msc) console as a member of the Enterprise Admins group. In the console tree, right-click Certificate Templates, and then click View Object Identifiers. In the resulting dialog box, choose the High Assurance Object Identifier, and then click the Copy Object Identifier button. Once you copy the OID, you can plug your forest's values into the placeholders *a.b.c.d.e* and remove any trailing digits.

■   **Notice**   The Notice line provides the text that appears when a user clicks the Issuer Statement button when the CA's certificate is displayed. The Issuer Statement is typically the title of the CPS and does not display any details about the CPS. Remember that you are limited to a total of 4,096 bytes of data in the Certificate Policies extension. Including the entire CPS in the Notice line will result in a very large CA certificate because the entire text of the CPS is included in the CA certificate.

■   **URLs**   Multiple URLs can be provided for the CPS. The URLs provide links to the actual text of the CPS. When you view the Notice text, clicking More Info opens a browser window that displays the content of the URL specified in the URL line. Typically, the URL is a Hypertext Transfer Protocol (HTTP) URL.

[AuthorityInformationAccess] and [CRLDistributionPoint]   The typical strategy for root CAs is to not publish CA certificate and CRL retrieval URLs in the root CA's certificate. By excluding the Authority Information Access (AIA) and CRL Distribution Point (CDP) extensions from the root CA certificate, you block the certificate chaining engine from checking the root CA certificate's revocation status. The root CA certificate is designated as trusted by adding the certificate to the trusted root CA store at client computers. Most applications do not check revocation status of the root CA certificate unless it contains a CDP extension. Removing the AIA and CDP extensions from the root CA certificate ensures that *all* applications bypass revocation checking on the root CA certificate.

In Windows Server 2003, you had to include the following lines in your CAPolicy.inf file to prevent the inclusion of the AIA and CDP extensions in the root CA certificate:

```
[AuthorityInformationAccess]
Empty = true

[CRLDistributionPoint]
Empty = true
```

> **Note**   Alternatively, you can exclude the Empty = true lines from each section. The inclusion of the [AuthorityInformationAccess] and [CrlDistributionPoint] sections in the CAPolicy.inf file will prevent the inclusion of the AIA and CDP extensions in the root CA certificate.

The [AuthorityInformationAccess] and [CRLDistributionPoint] sections specify the publication points for a root CA's certificate and CRL. These sections are disregarded by subordinate CAs because the CRL and CA certificate distribution points are defined in the configuration of the parent CA, not at subordinate CAs.

In Windows Server 2008, the default behavior is different. When you install a root CA, the default is to create a root CA certificate with no CDP and AIA extensions.

If you decide to define AIA and CDP URLs for the root CA certificate, you can use predefined variables rather than coding the actual URLs. Windows Server 2003 provides the variables shown in Table 6-1 for defining AIA and CDP URL paths.

Table 6-1   AIA and CDP Variable Definitions

Variable	Name	Description
%1	ServerDNSName	The CA computer's Domain Name System (DNS) name
%2	ServerShortName	The CA computer's NetBIOS name
%3	CA Name	The CA's logical name
%4	CertificateName	The name of the CA's certificate file
%5	Domain DN	Not used in the Windows Server 2003 PKI
%6	ConfigDN	The Lightweight Directory Access Protocol (LDAP) path of the forest's configuration naming context for the forest
%7	CATruncatedName	The CA's "sanitized" name
%8	CRLNameSuffix	The CRL's renewal extension
%9	DeltaCRLAllowed	Indicates whether delta CRLs are supported by the CA
%10	CDPObjectClass	Indicates that the object is a CDP object in AD DS
%11	CAObjectClass	Indicates that the object is a CA certificate object in AD DS

When variables are used in the CAPolicy.inf file, the installation of Certificate Services parses the file and replaces the variables with the actual names implemented by the CA. For example, if you do not define a [CRLDistributionPoint] section, a Windows Server 2003 root CA implements the following default paths for CRL publication:

■   %Windir%\System32\CertSrv\CertEnroll\%3%8%9.crl

- ldap:///CN=%7%8,CN=%2,CN=CDP,CN=Public Key Services, CN=Services,%6%10

- http://%1/CertEnroll/%3%8%9.crl

- file://\\%1\CertEnroll\%3%8%9.crl

Likewise, if you do not define an [AuthorityInformationAccess] section within a CAPolicy.inf file, a Windows Server 2003 root CA implements the following default paths for CA certificate publication:

- %Windir%\System32\CertSrv\CertEnroll\%1_%3%4.crt

- ldap:///CN=%7,CN=AIA,CN=Public Key Services,CN=Services,%6%11

- http://%1/CertEnroll/%1_%3%4.crt

- file://\\%1\CertEnroll\%1_%3%4.crt

> **Important**   The defaults have changed for Windows Server 2008. By default, the root CA certificate is created with no CDP or AIA extensions.

[EnhancedKeyUsageExtension]   This section is used to restrict the types of certificates a CA can issue.

For example, if you want to restrict a CA to issuing certificates for Client Authentication, Server Authentication, and Secure Email, you would define the [EnhancedKeyUsageExtension] as shown here:

```
[EnhancedKeyUsageExtension]
OID = 1.3.6.1.5.5.7.3.2  ; Client Authentication
OID = 1.3.6.1.5.5.7.3.1  ; Server Authentication
OID = 1.3.6.1.5.5.7.3.4  ; Secure Email
```

> **Note**   These are predefined OIDs defined by the IANA or by Microsoft. You can view the list of predefined OIDs in the Certificate Templates console using the same method you use to identify your forest's privately assigned OID tree.

[BasicConstraintsExtension]   The basic constraints section allows you to define path-length restrictions. A path-length restriction allows you to limit the depth of your CA hierarchy. For example, if you want to prevent the installation of an additional tier below the current CA, you can define the [BasicConstraintsExtension] extension as shown here:

```
[BasicConstraintsExtension]
pathlength = 0
```

> **Note**   All CA certificates have a basic constraints extension, even if you do not define the section in the CAPolicy.inf file. The basic constraints extension indicates whether the certificate is issued to a CA or to a user, computer, service, or network device. CA certificate identification allows the chaining engine to determine whether the certificate can be used to sign other certificates.

[certsrv_server]   The [certsrv_server] section has entries that apply to all CAs in the CA hierarchy. The following entries can be defined in this section:

- **RenewalKeyLength**   The requested length of the CA's private key and public key when the CA certificate is renewed. The value should match the value assigned to the CA's key length during initial installation, unless you decide to modify the length of the CA's certificate at renewal time.

- **RenewalValidityPeriod**   The validity period's unit of measurement. Accepted values are years, weeks, and days, though use of anything other than years is uncommon.

- **RenewalValidityPeriodUnits**   The specific number of units for the validity period. For example, if you configure a CA with a 15-year validity period, the RenewalValidityPeriod-Units value is 15.

> **Note**   You cannot set the initial CA key length and validity period in the CAPolicy.inf file. The value at installation is configured in the installation wizard for a root CA and is defined by the parent CA for all subordinate CAs. The CAPolicy.inf file specifies key length and validity period settings used when you renew the CA's certificate.

- **CRLPeriod**   The CRL publication interval's unit of measurement. The default value is days, but years, weeks, and hours are acceptable.

- **CRLPeriodUnits**   The specific number of units for the CRL publication interval. The default value is seven, but this value is typically changed based on the CA's design.

- **CRLOverlapUnits**   Works together with CRLOverlapPeriod to specify how long to extend the validity period of a base CRL beyond the specified base CRL publication interval. The CRLOverlapUnits is the specific number of units for the base CRL overlap.

- **CRLOverlapPeriod**   The base CRL overlap period's unit of measurement. The default is days, but years, weeks, minutes, and hours are acceptable.

- **CRLDeltaPeriod**   The unit of measurement for the delta CRL publication interval. The default unit or value is days, but years, weeks, and hours are acceptable.

- **CRLDeltaPeriodUnits**   The specific number of units for the delta CRL publication interval. The default value is 1, but this value is typically changed based on the CA's design.

- **CRLDeltaOverlapPeriod**   The delta CRL overlap period's unit of measurement. The default is minutes, but years, weeks, days, and hours are acceptable.

- **CRLDeltaOverlapUnits**   Works together with CRLDeltaOverlapPeriod to specify how long to extend the validity period of a delta CRL beyond the defined delta CRL publication interval. The CRLOverlapUnits is the specific number of units for the base CRL overlap.

- **ClockSkewMinutes**   A safety factor for clock synchronization issues. The base and delta CRL are published with a beginning time equal to the ClockSkewMinutes before the current time. The default value is 10 minutes. As an example, if the current time is 10:00, a new base or delta CRL will be published with an effective time of 09:50.

Windows Server 2008 introduces new options for the CAPolicy.inf file. These options include:

- **LoadDefaultTemplates**   The LoadDefaultTemplates option was introduced in Windows Server 2003 Service Pack 1. The setting prevents the publication of the default templates after installation of an enterprise CA if assigned a value of 0. In Windows Server 2008, the setting is applicable to *any* enterprise CA, whether the CA is a root CA or a subordinate CA.

- **DiscreteSignatureAlgorithm**   The DiscreteSignatureAlgorithm option, when assigned a value of 1, enables support for the PKCS#1 V2.1 signature format for both the CA certificate and CA certificate requests. If implemented on a root CA, the root CA will generate a root certificate that includes the PKCS#1 V2.1 signature format. If implemented on a subordinate CA, the subordinate CA will generate a certificate request that includes the PKCS#1 V2.1 signature format.

Note   Discrete signatures for RSA-based certificates are documented as part of the PKCS #1: RSA Cryptography Standard. For more information about the standard, see the RSA Web site at *http://www.rsasecurity.com/rsalabs/pkcs/pkcs-1/*.

What Are Discrete Signatures?

With the support of Cryptography Next Generation (CNG) and the new Suite B signature and encryption algorithms, it is necessary to include information about algorithms in both certificate and certificate requests. If this information is not included, an entity processing the certificate or certificate request may not be able to verify the signature of the object.

As shown in Figure 6-3, when a certificate or certificate request is signed, an initial hash is generated against the Subject, Public Key Algorithm, Public Key Length, Public Key, Request Attributes, and Certificate Extensions of the certificate or certificate request. Once the hash is generated, it is signed with the private key of the associated key pair by using an asymmetric algorithm.

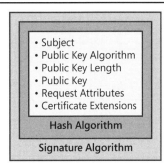

Figure 6-3   The combination of hash and signing algorithms

CNG introduces an increasing number of available algorithms. This results in an ever-growing list of possible combinations for hash and signature algorithms. For example, a certificate request might be hashed with a MD5 and signed with RSA but the issued certificate was hashed with SHA384 and signed with ECDSA_P256. Therefore, you must add information about the used algorithms into the certificate or request instead of maintaining a list of identifiers that translate the combinations.

Pre-Installation Scripts

In a CA hierarchy with two or more tiers, there are pre-installation scripts that must be executed to prepare the subordinate CA for installation. These pre-installation scripts include:

- Publish the root CA and all subordinate CA certificate and CRLs that exist between the new subordinate CA and the root CA to the local computer store.

- Publish the root CA and all subordinate CA certificate and CRLs that exist between the new subordinate CA and the root CA to AD DS.

Warning   If you do not install the certificates and CRLs before installation of the subordinate CA, you might receive an error message when you install the subordinate CA certificate stating that the CA cannot determine the revocation status of the CA certificate.

Publishing Certificates and CRLs to the Local Computer Store

You must be a member of the local Administrators group to add CRLs and certificates to the local computer store. The combination of certificates and CRLs that must be installed depends on where the target CA exists in the CA hierarchy:

- If the new CA is installed at the second tier of the hierarchy, you must install the root CA's certificate and CRL.

- If the new CA is at the third tier of the hierarchy or lower, you must install all CA certificates and CRLs in the certificate chain above the new CA.

To add a root CA's certificate to the trusted root CA store of the computer, you can use the following command:

```
certutil -addstore -f Root RootCACertificateFile.crt,
```

where *RootCACertificateFile* is the file name of the root CA's certificate file.

To add a root CA's CRL to the trusted root CA store, you can use the following command:

```
certutil -addstore -f Root RootCACRLFile.crl,
```

where *RootCACRLFile* is the file name of the root CA's CRL file.

To add a subordinate CA's certificate to the intermediate CA store, you can use the following command:

```
certutil -addstore -f CA SubCACertificateFile.crt,
```

where *SubCACertificateFile* is the file name of the subordinate CA's certificate file.

To add a subordinate CA's CRL to the intermediate CA store, you can use the following command:

```
certutil -addstore -f CA SubCACRLFile.crl,
```

where *SubCACRLFile* is the file name of the subordinate CA's CRL file.

Publishing Certificates and CRLs to AD DS

In addition to publishing the CA certificates and CRLs to the local machine store of subordinate CAs, you can publish CA certificates and CRLs for any offline CAs to AD DS. By publishing the CA certificates to AD DS, you ensure the automatic propagation of CA certificates and CRLs to all domain member computers running Microsoft Windows 2000 or later operating systems.

The published CA certificates and CRLs are automatically downloaded to the forest members running Windows 2000 or later through Group Policy. The processing of Group Policy triggers the autoenrollment mechanism, initiating the automatic download of any certificates or CRLs published in AD DS to the forest members. Figure 6-4 shows where the CA certificates and CRLs are published when they are published into AD DS.

In Figure 6-4, CA certificates are published into the following locations:

- All CA certificates are published into the CN=AIA,CN=Public Key Services,CN= Services,CN=Configuration,*ForestRootDomain* (where *ForestRootDomain* is the LDAP distinguished name of your organization's forest root domain) container.

- Root CA certificates are also published into the CN=Certification Authorities, CN=Public Key Services,CN=Services,CN=Configuration,*ForestRootDomain* container.

- Enterprise CA certificates are published into the CN=NTAuthCertificates,CN=Public Key Services,CN=Services,CN=Configuration,DC=*ForestRootDomain* object.

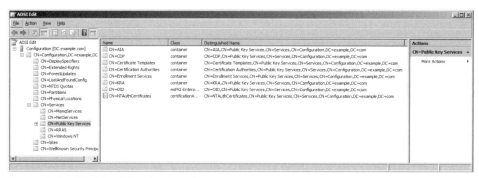

Figure 6-4   AD DS publication locations

Note   The AIA container and Certification Authorities container are used by the certificate chaining engine to acquire certificates for chain building. For example, subordinate CA certificates are included only in the AIA container, whereas root CA certificates are included in both the AIA and Certification Authorities container. The NTAuthCertificates container indicates CAs that can issue certificates used for smart card logon.

To publish a root CA certificate into AD DS, you can use the following command:

```
certutil -dspublish -f RootCACertificateFile.crt RootCA
```

where *RootCACertificateFile*.crt is the file name of the root CA's certificate file.

Note   If the CA certificate file's name contains spaces, you must delimit the file name with quotes. For example, the command line to publish the Fabrikam root CA certificate would be **certutil –dspublish –f "Fabrikam Corporate Root CA.crt" RootCA**.

To publish a subordinate CA's certificate to AD DS, you can use the following command:

```
certutil –dspublish -f SubCACertificateFile.crt SubCA
```

where *SubCACertificateFile*.crt is the file name of the subordinate CA''s certificate file.

Note   When the RootCA option is used with the **certutil –dspublish** command, the CA certificate is published to the both the AIA and Certification Authorities containers. If the SubCA option is used, the CA certificate is published only to the AIA container.

CRLs are published into unique containers within the CN=CDP,CN=Public Key Services, CN=Services,CN=Configuration,*ForestRootDomain* container. For example, the CRL for the server with the NetBIOS name FABINCCA01 is published within the CN=FABINCCA01, CN=CDP,CN=Public Key Services,CN=Services,CN=Configuration,*ForestRootDomain* container.

When adding a CA's CRL into AD DS, there is no difference between publishing a root CA and a subordinate CA CRL. To publish the CRL, use the following command:

```
certutil -dspublish -f CACRLFile.crl
```

where *CACRLFile* is the logical name of the root CA.

> **Note**   If publication fails, an error in the CRL might not contain sufficient LDAP information regarding the CRL publication location. You can force publication into AD DS by adding the CA's NetBIOS name to the publication command. For example, if the NetBIOS name of Fabrikam's root CA is FABINCCA01, the command to publish the Fabrikam root CA's CRL is **certutil –dspublish –f "Fabrikam Corporate Root CA.crl" FABINCCA01**.

Once the CA certificates and CRLs are published into AD DS, you can force their propagation at each client computer by using the Group Policy application to trigger the autoenrollment engine, resulting in the propagation of the certificates and CRLs to the client computer.

- At computers running Windows 2000, a user can type **secedit /refreshpolicy machine_policy /enforce**.

- At computers running Windows XP and later, a user can type **gpupdate /target:computer /force** and then type **certutil -pulse** to initiate autoenrollment requests.

Alternatively, publication also takes place the next time the computer restarts, forcing triggering of the autoenrollment engine or a wait period of 90 minutes with a randomized offset of plus or minus 30 minutes at client computers, the default interval for Group Policy application.

Post-Installation Scripts

Some of the configuration areas to include in the post-installation script are described in the next sections of this chapter.

> **Note**   Although reviewed separately in this chapter, the following sections of the chapter are combined into a single script file for post-installation configuration. This book does not show every possible configuration that uses the **certutil** command in a script.

Declaring the Configuration Naming Context

One of the first tasks required for a post-installation script file is to declare the forest's configuration naming context. The configuration naming context replicates to all domain controllers in the forest and contains the publication points for all CA certificates and CRLs. (See Figure 6-4, above.)

To define the configuration naming context for your forest, use the following **certutil** command, where *ForestRootDomain* is the LDAP distinguished name of your organization's forest. This command defines the variable %6:

```
certutil -setreg CA\DSConfigDN CN=Configuration,ForestRootDomain
```

Defining CRL Publication Intervals

A post-installation script is commonly used to ensure that CRL and delta CRL publication intervals are defined correctly. Although you can define these settings in the CAPolicy.inf file, adding the settings to a post-installation script ensures consistent application of the required settings. If you are unsure if settings are modified, you can re-run the post-installation script to reapply the correct settings.

> **Note**   Although the settings are replicated in both CAPolicy.inf and in the post-installation script, the settings in CAPolicy.inf are read only at installation and during renewal. The post-installation script can be executed at any time to reset CA configuration settings to the settings recorded in the script.

Adding the following entries to a post-installation script ensures that Certificate Services implements the desired publication intervals:

```
::Define CRL Publication Intervals
certutil -setreg CA\CRLPeriodUnits 26
certutil -setreg CA\CRLPeriod "Weeks"
certutil -setreg CA\CRLOverlapUnits 22
certutil -setreg CA\CRLOverlapPeriod "Weeks"
certutil -setreg CA\CRLDeltaPeriodUnits 0
certutil -setreg CA\CRLDeltaPeriod "days"
```

In this example, the CRL publication interval is set to every 26 weeks with a 2-week overlap, and the publication of delta CRLs is disabled with its interval set to zero days.

Defining Publication Points

One of the key tasks after installing Certificate Services is defining publication points for a CA's certificate and CRL. The publication points can be configured in the CA console in the CA's Properties dialog box. (See Figure 6-5.)

This dialog box allows you to choose between CDP URLs and AIA URLs. In both cases, you must also choose the URL path where the CRL or AIA will be referenced.

Table 6-2 shows the options available for CRL publication locations.

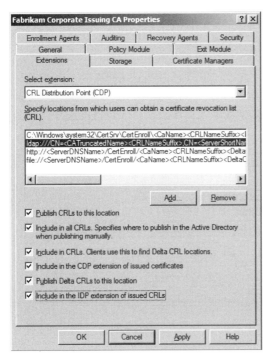

Figure 6-5   Defining CRL distribution points

Table 6-2   CRL Publication Options

Display name	Description	Label	Value
Publish CRLs to this location.	Identifies locations to which the CA should automatically publish the physical CRL files.	ServerPublish	1
Include in all issued certificates.	Place a URL for the base CRL in all certificates issued by the CA.	AddtoCertCDP	2
Include in CRLs. Clients use this to find delta CRL locations.	Places a URL for delta CRL retrieval in a base CRL. This publication point is stored in the freshest CRL extension of a CRL and is retrieved only during the CRL checking process.	AddtoFreshestCRL	4
Include in the CDP extension of CRLs.	Places a URL in the CDP extension of a CRL issued by the CA to allow the relying party certificate chaining engine to download the latest CRL version if the current version has expired.	AddtoCRLCDP	8
Publish delta CRLs to this location. Specifies where to publish in AD DS when publishing to LDAP URLs.	If the CA is configured to enable delta CRLs, the delta CRL files are automatically published to this location.	ServerPublish-Delta	64
Include in the IDP extension of issued CRLs	Used by non-Windows clients to determine the scope of the CRL. The scope can include end-entity certificates only, CA certificates only, attribute certificate only, or a limited set of reason codes.	Issuing-DistributionPoint	128

For each location, you can choose to enable any combination of check boxes by adding the numbers in the Value column. For example, if you want to enable the publication of CRLs and delta CRLs, a value of 65 will accomplish this.

Likewise, there are specific entries for CA certificate publication locations. When you enable these options, the URLs are placed in the AIA extension of issued certificates. Table 6-3 shows the values that are available for AIA publication URLs.

Table 6-3   AIA Publication Options

Display name	Description	Label	Value
Publish CRLs to this location	Identifies locations to which the CA should automatically or manually publish the physical CRL files	ServerPublish	1
Include in the AIA extension of issued certificates	Includes the URLs for the CA certificate in all issued certificates	AddtoCertCDP	2
Include in the Online Certificate Status Protocol (OCSP) extension	Includes the HTTP URL for the designated OCSP server in all issued certificates	AddtoCertOCSP	32

As with the CDP extensions, you can determine which check boxes to enable for each AIA extension by referencing the numbers in the Value column and adding the numbers.

Defining CRL Distribution Points   You can define a CA's CDP URLs by using the **certutil** command to edit the CRLPublicationURLs registry entry. The command allows you to designate one or more URLs as well as which CRL publication options are enabled for each URL.

For example, consider the following **certutil** command that defines the CDP extension:

```
certutil -setreg CA\CRLPublicationURLs
"1:%windir%\system32\CertSrv\CertEnroll\%%3%%8%%9.crl\n2:http://www.fabrikam.com/CertData/
%%3%%8%%9.crl\n10:ldap:///CN=%%7%%8,CN=%%2,CN=CDP,CN=Public Key
Services,CN=Services,%%6%%10"
```

This command defines three separate URLs. The URL order is important when implementing Windows clients because it specifies the order in which the certificate chaining engine searches URLs when retrieving an updated CRL version. Likewise, the number that precedes each URL represents the enabled options for each URL.

> **Note**   Each URL is separated by \n. This character combination is the line separation indicator used for multi-valued registry entries.

- **1:%windir%\system32\CertSrv\CertEnroll\%%3%%8%%9.crl**   This URL ensures that the CRL file is copied to the local file system every time the CRL is automatically or manually published.

- **2:http://www.fabrikam.com/CertData/%%3%%8%%9.crl**   This URL ensures that the URL *www.fabrikam.com/Certdata/%%3%%8%%9.crl* is included in the CDP extension of all issued certificates.

- **10:ldap:///CN=%%7%%8,CN=%%2,CN=CDP,CN=Public Key Services,CN=Services, %%6%%10**   This URL enables two values: 2 to designate the CRL's publication point in AD DS and 8 to include the CDP URL in all CA-issued certificates.

> **Note**   Notice that the variables used in the **certutil** commands are the same as those used in the CAPolicy.inf file. The only difference is that the variables are prefixed with %% rather than %. The additional % character is an escape character required by **certutil**.

Defining CA Certificate Distribution Points   As with the CDP extension, you can modify the AIA extension to designate CA-certificate publication points. This is accomplished by using the **certutil** command to modify the CACertPublicationURLs registry entry, as shown here:

```
::Modify the AIA Extension URLs
certutil -setreg CA\CACertPublicationURLs
"1:%windir%\system32\CertSrv\CertEnroll\%%1_%%3%%4.crt\n2:http://www.fabrikam.com/CertData/
%%1_%%3%%4.crt\n2:ldap:///CN=%%7,CN=AIA,CN=Public Key Services,CN=Services,%%6%%11"
```

This example places three entries in the registry value:

- **1:%windir%\system32\CertSrv\CertEnroll\%%1_%%3%%4.crt**   This entry ensures that the CA certificate is published to the local file system.

- **2:http://www.fabrikam.com/CertData/%%1_%%3%%4.crt**   This entry ensures that the HTTP URL is included in the AIA extension of all issued certificates.

- **2:ldap:///CN=%%7,CN=AIA,CN=Public Key Services,CN=Services,%%6%%11**   This entry ensures that the LDAP URL is included in the AIA extension of all issued certificates.

Defining Validity Periods for Issued Certificates

Another CA configuration option that can be defined with **certutil** is the maximum validity period for any CA-issued certificate. The manner in which the validity period for issued certificates is applied depends on whether the CA is a standalone CA or an enterprise CA.

In the case of a standalone CA, the specification of a validity period sets the validity period for all CA-issued certificates. In the case of an enterprise CA, the maximum validity period acts as a maximum value for any CA-issued certificates. An issued certificate is always assigned the lesser value of the remaining validity period of the CA certificate and the configured maximum validity period. In other words, if you specify the maximum validity period as four years, and the CA has only three years remaining in its certificate's validity period, the maximum validity period of a newly issued certificate is three years.

In the case of an enterprise CA, another variable enters the picture. Enterprise CAs issue certificates based on certificate templates. Each certificate template has its own configured validity period. The applied validity period for certificates issued by an enterprise CA is the minimum value of the CA certificate's remaining validity period, the CA's maximum validity period setting, and the certificate template's validity period.

To configure the maximum validity period for issued certificates, two **certutil** commands are required to modify the two related registry entries: ValidityPeriodUnits and ValidityPeriod. The following example shows the combination to set the maximum validity period to 10 years.

```
::Set Validity Period for Issued Certificates
certutil -setreg CA\ValidityPeriodUnits 10
certutil -setreg CA\ValidityPeriod "Years"
```

Enabling Auditing at the CA

You can enable auditing on a CA in Windows Server 2008 to provide an audit log for all Certificate Services management tasks. To enable auditing, you must ensure that both success and failure auditing is applied to either the Local Security Policy of an offline CA or a Group Policy Object (GPO) applied to the organizational unit (OU) containing the CA's computer account for an online CA. All Certificate Services auditing is reported to the security log in Event Viewer.

PKI Auditing Categories The following auditing categories can be enabled or disabled on a case-by-case basis:

- **Back up and restore the CA database** Any attempt to back up or restore the CA database is logged to the Windows security log.

- **Change CA configurations** Any attempt to modify CA configurations is logged. This can include attempts to define AIA and CDP URLs or a key recovery agent.

- **Change CA security settings** Any attempt to modify CA permissions is logged. This can include adding CA administrators or certificate managers.

- **Issue and manage certificate requests** Logs any attempt by a certificate manager to approve or deny certificate requests with subject approval pending.

- **Revoke certificates and publish CRLs** Logs any attempt by a certificate manager to revoke an issued certificate or by a CA administrator to publish an updated CRL.

- **Store and retrieve archived keys** Logs any attempt by the enrollment process to archive private keys in the CA database or by certificate managers to extract archived private keys from the CA database.

- **Start and stop Certificate Services** Any attempt by the CA administrator to start or stop Certificate Services is logged.

Note   To modify these settings in the properties of the CA, you must be assigned the Manage Auditing and Security Log user right at the CA.

PKI Auditing Details   Table 6-4 summarizes the security log entries related to Certificate Services auditing.

Table 6-4   **Certificate Services Event IDs**

Event ID	Event description
772	The certificate manager denied a pending certificate request.
773	Certificate Services received a resubmitted certificate request. This means that a certificate manager issued a certificate that was pending.
774	Certificate Services revoked a certificate.
775	Certificate Services received a request to publish the CRL.
776	Certificate Services published the CRL.
777	A certificate request extension changed.
778	One or more certificate request attributes changed.
779	Certificate Services received a request to shut down.
780	Certificate Services backup started.
781	Certificate Services backup completed.
782	Certificate Services restore started.
783	Certificate Services restore completed.
784	Certificate Services started.
785	Certificate Services stopped.
786	Security permissions for Certificate Services changed.
787	Certificate Services retrieved an archived key.
788	Certificate Services imported a certificate into its database.
789	The audit filter for Certificate Services changed.
790	Certificate Services received a certificate request.
791	Certificate Services approved a certificate request and issued a certificate.
792	Certificate Services denied a certificate request.
793	Certificate Services set the status of a certificate request to pending.
794	The certificate manager settings for Certificate Services changed.
795	A configuration entry changed in Certificate Services.
796	A property of Certificate Services changed.
797	Certificate Services archived a key.
798	Certificate Services imported and archived a key.
799	Certificate Services published the CA certificate to AD DS.
800	One or more rows have been deleted from the certificate database.
801	Role separation enforcement is enabled. If role separation enforcement is enabled, the event log entry will state Yes. If disabled, the event log entry will state No.

Once you have enabled object access auditing for successes and failures, the following lines in a post-installation script ensure that all auditing categories are enabled:

```
::Enable all auditing events for the CA
certutil -setreg CA\AuditFilter 127
```

CNG Auditing   To meet Common Criteria requirements, you can enable auditing in the Microsoft software key storage provider (KSP) to enable auditing of actions that happen in the CNG layer. These auditable actions include:

- Key and key-pair generation failures

- Key import and export actions

- Key destruction failures

- Writing and reading persistent keys from files

- Pair-wise consistency check failures

- Secret key validation failures

- Failures in encryption, decryption, hashing, signature, verification, key exchange, and random number generation

- Cryptographic self-test successes and failures

> **Note**   In general, if a key does not have a name, it is an *ephemeral* key. An ephemeral key does not persist, and the Microsoft KSP does not generate audit records for ephemeral keys.

When auditing is enabled for the Microsoft KSP, only audit records for events that occur in user mode in the Local Security Authority (LSA) process are included. No audit records are generated by kernel mode CNG operations.

Publishing an Updated CRL

Once all of the configuration changes are made to a CA, including the definition of CDP and AIA extensions, you must restart Certificate Services to enable the changes. Because the CDP extension allows you to modify the CRL location, it is advisable to copy the CRL to a floppy disk when configuring offline CAs. The following combination of commands enables the restart of Certificate Services, publishes an updated CRL, and copies the updated CRL to the floppy drive.

```
net stop certsvc & net start certsvc
Sleep 5
Echo Insert a Floppy disk in Drive A:
certutil -CRL
sleep 5
copy /y %windir%\system32\certsrv\certenroll\*.crl a:\
```

> **Note**   This script sample also utilizes the Sleep utility from the Windows Server 2003 Resource Kit. This command will pause a batch file for the indicated number of seconds—five seconds in this case. You may have to increase the sleep interval to a longer time frame depending on the size of your CA database and CRL. The sleep interval needs to be of a long enough duration to ensure that the CA has finished publishing the new CRL before the copy operation is attempted.

Implementing a Three-Tier CA Hierarchy

The following sections detail the implementation of a three-tier CA hierarchy.

Implementing an Offline Root CA

If you are implementing a multi-tier CA hierarchy, you should implement an offline root CA, which requires that Certificate Services be installed as a standalone root CA. This allows the computer to remain as a workgroup member so that the computer can be removed from the network for long periods of time.

> **Note**   You can use Windows Server 2008 Standard Edition for all offline CAs. Only online CAs can fully take advantage of the benefits of the features available in Windows Server 2008 Enterprise Edition.

Creating a CAPolicy.inf File

It is imperative that you implement a CAPolicy.inf file when installing the root CA in a multi-tier CA hierarchy. The CAPolicy.inf file is the only way to define specific configuration settings, such as renewal validity period and key length settings for the root CA certificate.

> **Note**   This example assumes that Fabrikam, Inc. has an existing AD DS deployment with a single domain named fabrikam.com. It does not matter if the domain is a Windows 2000, Windows Server 2003, or Windows Server 2008 domain, so long as the AD DS modifications discussed in Chapter 4, "Preparing an Active Directory Environment," are applied.

This CAPolicy.inf file for Fabrikam, Inc. makes the following assumptions:

- The root CA uses a key length of 2,048 bits.
- The validity period of the root CA certificate is 20 years.
- Base CRLs are published every 26 weeks with an overlap of 2 weeks.
- Delta CRLs are disabled.

■ The root CA does not contain a CDP or AIA extension to prevent revocation checking of the root CA certificate.

■ Discrete signatures must be enabled in the root CA certificate to allow the use of CNG algorithms for hash and certificate signing.

Based on these assumptions, the following CAPolicy.inf file can be installed in the %Windir% of the FABINCCA01 computer:

```
[Version]
Signature="$Windows NT$"

[certsrv_server]
renewalkeylength=2048
RenewalValidityPeriodUnits=20
RenewalValidityPeriod=years

CRLPeriod=weeks
CRLPeriodUnits=26
CRLOverlapPeriod=weeks
CRLOverlapUnits=2
CRLDeltaPeriodUnits=0
CRLDeltaPeriod=days

DiscreteSignatureAlgorithm=1
```

Note Because we are installing a Windows Server 2008 standalone root CA, there is no need to include [AuthorityInformationAccess] and [CRLDistributionPoint] sections with Empty=True lines. These are required only if installing a Windows Server 2003 standalone root CA.

Installing Certificate Services

Once the CAPolicy.inf file is installed, you can install Certificate Services on the root CA computer. The installation must be performed by a member of the local Administrators account on the CA computer, and the computer must not be a member of a domain. Domain membership would require the computer to be attached to the network.

The following assumptions are made about the root CA computer:

■ The naming of the computer uses the naming scheme previously shown in Figure 6-1.

■ The computer has two mirrored partitions—drive C: for the operating system and drive D: for the CA database and log files.

Note Internet Information Services (IIS) is not required for the installation of an offline root CA. The only certificate requests submitted to the root CA are for subordinate CA certificates, and these can be submitted by using the Certification Authority console.

To install the root CA, use the following procedure:

1. Log on as a member of the local Administrators group.

2. Ensure that the date and time on the root CA computer is correct.

3. Click Start, point to Administrative Tools, and then click Server Manager.

4. In the Roles Summary section, click Add Roles.

5. If the Before You Begin page appears, select the Skip This Page By Default check box, and then click Next.

6. On the Select Server Roles page, select the Active Directory Certificate Services check box, and when the role is populated, click Next.

7. On the Introduction to Active Directory Certificate Services page, click Next.

8. On the Select Role Services page, select the Certification Authority check box, and then click Next.

9. On the Specify Setup Type page, click Standalone, and then click Next.

10. On the Specify CA Type page, click Root CA, and then click Next.

11. On the Set Up Private Key page, click Create A New Private Key, and then click Next.

12. On the Configure Cryptography For CA page, set the following options, and then click Next.

    ❑ Select a cryptographic service provider (CSP): **RSA#Microsoft Software Key Storage Provider**

    ❑ Key character length: **2048**

    ❑ Select the hash algorithm for signing certificates issued by this CA: **sha256**

13. On the Configure CA Name page, provide the following information, and then click Next.

    ❑ Common name for this CA: **Fabrikam Corporate Root CA**

    ❑ Distinguished name suffix: **O=Fabrikam Inc.,C=US**

14. On the Set Validity Period page, change the validity period to 20 years, and then click Next.

15. On the Configure Certificate Database page, provide the following settings, and then click Next:

    ❑ Certificate database: **D:\CertDB**

    ❑ Certificate database log: **D:\CertLog**

16. After verifying the information on the Confirm Installation Selections page, click Install.

17. On the Installation Results page, review the information on the confirmation screen to verify that the installation was successful, and then click Close.

Post-Installation Configuration

Once the Root CA is installed, you must ensure that the root CA's registry settings are configured correctly. The following assumptions are made in regard to the Fabrikam network:

- All client and server computers are running Windows XP, Windows Vista, Windows Server 2003, or Windows Server 2008 and are members of the Fabrikam.com domain.

- There is a Web server named www.fabrikam.com. A virtual directory named Certdata contains CRL and AIA information for all CAs in the CA hierarchy. This Web server is accessible internally and externally.

- The subordinate CA below the root CA has a 10-year validity period.

- All auditing options must be enabled on the root CA.

- The root CA certificate and CRL are copied to a universal serial bus (USB) drive (assigned drive letter F:) to allow publication to AD DS and to the *www.fabrikam.com* Web server.

- Discrete Signatures must be supported and available for certificate requests submitted to the CA.

- Sleep.exe from the Windows Server 2003 Resource Kit is installed on the root CA computer.

You can use the following post-installation script to configure the root CA to implement these design assumptions and the assumptions stated earlier in this chapter:

```
::Declare Configuration NC
certutil -setreg CA\DSConfigDN CN=Configuration,DC=fabrikam,DC=com

::Define CRL Publication Intervals
certutil -setreg CA\CRLPeriodUnits 26
certutil -setreg CA\CRLPeriod "Weeks"
certutil -setreg CA\CRLDeltaPeriodUnits 0
certutil -setreg CA\CRLDeltaPeriod "Days"
certutil -setreg CA\CRLOverlapPeriod "Weeks"
certutil -setreg CA\CRLOverlapUnits 2

::Apply the required CDP Extension URLs
certutil -setreg CA\CRLPublicationURLs
"1:%windir%\system32\CertSrv\CertEnroll\%%3%%8%%9.crl\n10:ldap:///
CN=%%7%%8,CN=%%2,CN=CDP,CN=Public Key Services,CN=Services,%%6%%10\n
2:http://www.fabrikam.com/Certdata/ %%3%%8%%9.crl"

::Apply the required AIA Extension URLs
certutil -setreg CA\CACertPublicationURLs
"1:%windir%\system32\CertSrv\CertEnroll\%%1_%%3%%4.crt\n2:ldap:///CN=%%7,CN=AIA,CN=Public
Key Services,CN=Services,%%6%%11\n
2:http://www.fabrikam.com/CertData/%%1_%%3%%4.crt"

::Enable all auditing events for the Fabrikam Corporate Root CA
```

```
certutil -setreg CA\AuditFilter 127

::Set Validity Period for Issued Certificates
certutil -setreg CA\ValidityPeriodUnits 10
certutil -setreg CA\ValidityPeriod "Years"

:: Enable discrete signatures in subordinate CA certificates
Certutil -setreg CA\csp\DiscreteSignatureAlgorithm 1

::Restart Certificate Services
net stop certsvc & net start certsvc
sleep 5
certutil –crl
::Copy the Root CA certificates and CRLs to the USB Drive
Echo Insert the USB Drive in the USB slot
sleep 5
copy /y %windir%\system32\certsrv\certenroll\*.cr? F:\
```

Implementing an Offline Policy CA

Once the offline root CA is established, installation of the offline policy CA can begin with the certificate request submitted to the root CA so that the certificate chain is formed correctly.

Pre-Installation Configuration

Before installing Certificate Services on the policy CA, you must ensure that the policy CA machine account trusts the root CA. This is accomplished by manually installing the root CA certificate (stored on a USB drive) into the local computer's trusted root store. In addition, the root CA's CRL should be published to ensure that CRL checking is performed correctly.

The following script publishes the root CA certificate and CRL into the Local Machine Store (assuming that the USB drive is configured as the F: drive).

```
@echo off
F:
cd \
for %%c in (*.crt) do certutil -addstore -f Root "%%c"
for %%c in (*.crl) do certutil -addstore -f Root "%%c"
```

This batch file supports later revisions to the root CA certificate and will publish all versions of the root CA's certificate and CRL.

Creating a CAPolicy.inf File

Once the root CA's certificate and CRL are published in the local machine's Trusted Root Store, you must prepare a CAPolicy.inf file for the policy CA. The CAPolicy.inf file must define the CPS in a three-tier CA hierarchy. As mentioned previously, the CPS is defined by an OID, notice text, and a URL where the CPS is stored for retrieval.

The following assumptions apply to the Fabrikam, Inc. policy CA:

- It implements a single CPS, with the CPS published at *www.fabrikam.com/CPS/CPStatement.asp*.

- OID 1.3.6.1.4.1.311.509.3.1 is assigned to the CPS.

- The key length for the private key and public key is 2,048 bits.

- The validity period of the policy CA certificate is 10 years.

- Base CRLs are published every 26 weeks with a 2-week overlap.

- Delta CRLs are disabled.

- Discrete signatures must be enabled in the policy CA certificate to allow the use of CNG algorithms for hash and certificate signing.

- The policy CA will use the SHA256 hash algorithm.

Based on these assumptions, the following CAPolicy.inf file can be installed in the %Windir% of the Fabrikam, Inc. policy CA computer:

```
[Version]
Signature="$Windows NT$"

[PolicyStatementExtension]
Policies=FabrikamCPS

[FabrikamCPS]
OID=1.3.6.1.4.1.311.509.3.1
NOTICE=Fabrikam Industries Certification Practice Statement
URL=http://www.fabrikam.com/CPS/CPStatement.asp

[certsrv_server]
RenewalKeyLength=2048
RenewalValidityPeriodUnits=10
RenewalValidityPeriod=years

CRLPeriod=weeks
CRLPeriodUnits=26
CRLOverlapPeriod=weeks
CRLOverlapUnits=2
CRLDeltaPeriodUnits=0
CRLDeltaPeriod=days

DiscreteSignatureAlgorithm=1
```

Installing Certificate Services

After the CAPolicy.inf file is in place, you can install Certificate Services. Because the policy CA's certificate request is submitted to the root CA, the issuance of the subordinate CA certificate takes place at the root CA.

The following assumptions are made about the root CA computer:

- It uses the naming scheme shown previously in Figure 6-1.

- It has two mirrored partitions—drive C for the operating system and drive D for the CA database and log files.

> **Note** IIS is not required for the installation of an offline policy CA. The only certificate requests submitted to the policy CA are for subordinate CA certificates, and these can be submitted by using the Certification Authority console.

To start the process of installing Certificate Services, perform the following tasks at the policy CA:

1. Log on as a member of the local Administrators group.

2. Ensure that the date and time matches the date and time on the root CA computer.

3. Click Start, point to Administrative Tools, and then click Server Manager.

4. In the Roles Summary section, click Add Roles.

5. If the Before You Begin page appears, select the Skip This Page By Default check box, and then click Next.

6. On the Select Server Roles page, select the Active Directory Certificate Services check box, and when the role is populated, click Next.

7. On the Introduction To Active Directory Certificate Services page, click Next.

8. On the Select Role Services page, select the Certification Authority check box, and then click Next.

9. On the Specify Setup Type page, click Standalone, and then click Next.

10. On the Specify CA Type page, click Subordinate CA, and then click Next.

11. On the Set Up Private Key page, click Create A New Private Key, and then click Next.

12. On the Configure Cryptography For CA page, set the following options, and then click Next.

    ❑ Select a cryptographic service provider (CSP): **RSA#Microsoft Software Key Storage Provider**

    ❑ Key character length: **2048**

    ❑ Select the hash algorithm for signing certificates issued by this CA: **sha256**

13. On the Configure CA Name page, provide the following information, and then click Next.

    ❑ Common name for this CA: Fabrikam Corporate Policy CA

    ❑ Distinguished name suffix: O=Fabrikam Inc.,C=US

14. On the Request Certificate From A Parent CA page, click Save A Certificate Request to file, and manually send it later to a parent CA, accept the default file name, and then click Next.

15. On the Configure Certificate Database page, provide the following settings, and then click Next:

     ❑ Certificate database: **D:\CertDB**

     ❑ Certificate database log: **D:\CertLog**

16. After verifying the information on the Confirm Installation Selections page, click Install.

17. On the Installation Results page, note that the installation is incomplete, and then click Close.

18. Open C:\.

19. Copy the FABINCCA02_Fabrikam Corporate Policy CA.req file to the USB drive.

20. Remove the USB drive containing the certificate request file from the policy CA computer.

The USB drive must now be transported to the root CA computer to submit the certificate request and to copy the issued certificate back to the policy CA. While logged on at the root CA computer as a member of the local Administrators group, use the following process:

1. Insert the USB Drive containing the certificate request file into a USB port on the root CA computer.

2. From the Start menu, click Administrative Tools, and then click Certification Authority.

3. In the console tree, right-click Fabrikam Corporate Root CA, point to All Tasks, and then click Submit New Request.

4. In the Open Request File dialog box, in the File Name box, type **A:\FABINCCA02_Fabrikam Corporate Policy CA.req**, and then click Open.

5. In the console tree, expand Fabrikam Corporate Root CA, and then click Pending Requests.

6. In the details pane, right-click the certificate request, point to All Tasks, and then click Export Binary Data.

7. In the Export Binary Data dialog box, in the Columns That Contain Binary Data drop-down list, select Binary Request, and then click OK.

8. Review the request detail for accuracy:

    ❑ Verify that the subject name is Fabrikam Corporate Policy CA.

    ```
    Subject:
    CN=Fabrikam Corporate Policy CA
    O=Fabrikam Inc.
    C=US
    ```

    ❑ Ensure that the public key length is 2048 bits.

    ```
    Public Key Length: 2048 bits
    ```

❑ Ensure that the basic constraints indicate Subject Type=CA.

```
Basic Constraints
Subject type=CA
```

❑ Verify that the Certificate Policy statement is correctly configured with the Policy Identifier OID set to 1.3.6.1.4.1.1204.509.3.1, the Notice Text set to "Fabrikam Industries Certification Practice Statement," and the CPS qualifier set to *http://www.fabrikam.com/CPS/CPStatement.asp.*

```
Certificate Policies

[1] Certificate Policy:
Policy Identifier=1.3.6.1.4.1.1204.509.3.1
[1,1]Policy Qualifier Info:
Policy Qualifier Id=User Notice
Qualifier:
Notice Text=Fabrikam Industries Certification Practice Statement
[1,2]Policy Qualifier Info:
Policy Qualifier Id=CPS
Qualifier:
http://www.fabrikam.com/CPS/CPStatement.asp
```

❑ Verify that the Signature Algorithm is SHA256RSA.

```
Algorithm ObjectId: 1.2.840.113549.1.1.11 sha256RSA
```

❑ Verify that the signature matches the public key.

```
Signature matches Public Key
```

9. Close the Binary Request window.

10. In the details pane, right-click the pending SubCA certificate, point to All Tasks, and then click Issue.

11. In the console tree, click Issued Certificates.

12. In the details pane, double-click the issued certificate.

13. In the Certificate dialog box, click the Details tab.

14. On the Details tab, click Copy To File.

15. In the Certificate Export Wizard, click Next.

16. On the Export File Format page, click Cryptographic Message Syntax Standard–PKCS #7 Certificates (.P7B), select the Include All Certificates In The Certification Path If Possible check box, and then click Next.

17. On the File To Export page, in the File Name box, type **F:\policyca.p7b**, and then click Next.

18. On the Completing The Certificate Export Wizard page, click Finish.

19. In the Certificate Export Wizard message box, click OK.

20. In the Certificate dialog box, click OK.

21. Close the Certification Authority console.

22. Remove the USB drive containing the certificate request file.

Once the certificate is exported to the floppy disk, you must complete installation of the policy CA by installing the subordinate CA certificate at the policy CA. Use the following procedure:

1. Insert the USB Drive containing the PKCS#7 file into a USB port on the Policy CA computer.

2. From the Start menu, click Administrative Tools, and then click Certification Authority.

3. In the console tree, right-click Fabrikam Corporate Policy CA, point to All Tasks, and then click Install CA Certificate.

4. In the Select File To Complete CA Installation dialog box, in the File Name box, type **F:\policyca.p7b,** and then click Open.

5. In the console tree, right-click Fabrikam Corporate Policy CA, point to All Tasks, and then click Start Service.

> **Note**   At this point, Certificate Services starts and allows you to view and configure the policy CA. If the service does not start, the most common error is the revocation function being unable to check revocation status. This is typically because of forgetting to install the root CA certificate and CRL on the policy CA.

Post-Installation Configuration

Once the policy CA installation is complete, you must ensure that the policy CA's registry settings are configured correctly. The following assumptions are made regarding the Fabrikam network:

- All client and server computers are running Windows XP or later and are members of the Fabrikam.com domain.

- There is a Web server named *www.fabrikam.com*. A virtual directory named Certdata contains CRL and AIA information for all CAs in the CA hierarchy. This Web server is accessible internally and externally.

- The subordinate CA below the policy CA has a validity period of five years.

- All auditing options must be enabled on the policy CA.

- The policy CA certificate and CRL are copied to a floppy disk to allow publication to AD DS and to the *www.fabrikam.com* Web server.

- Sleep.exe from the Windows Server 2003 Resource Kit is installed on the policy CA computer.

- Discrete Signatures must be supported and available for certificate requests submitted to the CA.

To configure the policy CA to implement these design decisions and the assumptions stated previously, the following post-installation script can be used:

```
::Declare Configuration NC
certutil -setreg CA\DSConfigDN CN=Configuration,DC=fabrikam,DC=com

::Define CRL Publication Intervals
certutil -setreg CA\CRLPeriodUnits 26
certutil -setreg CA\CRLPeriod "Weeks"
certutil -setreg CA\CRLOverlapUnits 2
certutil -setreg CA\CRLOverlapPeriod "Weeks"
certutil -setreg CA\CRLDeltaPeriodUnits 0
certutil -setreg CA\CRLDeltaPeriod "Days"

::Apply the required CDP Extension URLs
certutil -setreg CA\CRLPublicationURLs
"1:%windir%\system32\CertSrv\CertEnroll\%%3%%8%%9.crl\n10:ldap:///
CN=%%7%%8,CN=%%2,CN=CDP,CN=Public Key Services,CN=Services,%%6%%10\n
2:http://www.fabrikam.com/Certdata/ %%3%%8%%9.crl"

::Apply the required AIA Extension URLs
certutil -setreg CA\CACertPublicationURLs
"1:%windir%\system32\CertSrv\CertEnroll\%%1_%%3%%4.crt\n2:ldap:///CN=%%7,CN=AIA,CN=Public
Key Services,CN=Services,%%6%%11\n
2:http://www.fabrikam.com/CertData/%%1_%%3%%4.crt"

::Enable all auditing events for the Fabrikam Corporate Policy CA
certutil -setreg CA\AuditFilter 127

::Set Validity Period for Issued Certificates
certutil -setreg CA\ValidityPeriodUnits 5
certutil -setreg CA\ValidityPeriod "Years"

:: Enable discrete signatures in subordinate CA certificates
Certutil -setreg CA\csp\DiscreteSignatureAlgorithm 1

::Restart Certificate Services
net stop certsvc & net start certsvc
sleep 5
certutil -crl
::Copy the policy CA certificates and CRLs to the USB Drive
Echo Insert the USB Drive in the USB slot
sleep 5
copy /y %windir%\system32\certsrv\certenroll\*.cr? f:\
```

Implementing an Online Issuing CA

The process for installing subordinate online CAs is slightly different than the process for installing subordinate offline CAs.

Pre-Installation Configuration

Before installing Certificate Services on the issuing CA, you must ensure that the issuing CA trusts the root CA and is able to download the policy CA certificate and CRL for certificate revocation checking.

This is accomplished by manually installing or publishing the root CA and policy CA certificates stored on a floppy disk to the following locations:

- **The local computer's Trusted Root Store and intermediate CA store**   This location is required if you are unable to publish the certificate into AD DS or to the HTTP URL referenced in the AIA and CDP extensions of certificates issued by the root or policy CA. This location is also required if the issuing CA is a standalone CA.

- **AD DS**   The root and policy CA certificate and CRLs can be published into AD DS. Publication into AD DS enables the automated download of the certificates to all Windows 2000, Windows XP, Windows Server 2003, Windows Vista, and Windows Server 2008 computers that are members of the forest.

- **HTTP URLs referenced in the AIA and CDP extensions**   The root and policy CA certificates and CRLs must be manually published to these locations to enable download of the CA certificates and CRLs to all clients using these URLs for chain building and revocation checking.

Installing Certificates Locally at the Issuing CA   If you have not published the root and policy CA certificates into AD DS or to the HTTP URLs included in the certificates issued by the root and policy CAs, you can manually install the certificates into the issuing CA's local machine store. This process is similar to the one used to install the root CA certificate and CRL at the policy CA. The difference is that both root and intermediate CA certificates are installed at an issuing CA.

> **Tip**   I still publish the root and policy CA certificates locally because of impatience. When you publish them to AD DS, you have to wait for replication and application of Group Policy before the issuing CA has knowledge of the certificates. Installing the certificate and CRL locally offers immediate recognition of the CA hierarchy.

The following script publishes the root CA certificate and CRL into the local machine store:

```
@echo off
a:
cd \
for %%c in ("FABINCCA01*.crt") do certutil -addstore -f Root "%%c"
```

```
for %%c in ("Fabrikam Corporate Root*.crl") do certutil -addstore -f Root "%%c"
for %%c in ("FABINCCA02*.crt") do certutil -addstore -f CA "%%c"
for %%c in ("Fabrikam Corporate Policy*.crl") do certutil -addstore -f CA "%%c"
```

This batch file supports later revisions to the root or policy CA certificates and publishes all versions of the root and policy CA certificates and CRLs.

Tip   When using this script in your environment, modify each line's search pattern to a pattern that uniquely describes the CA computer name for *.crt files and the CA logical name for *.crl files.

Publishing Certificates and CRLs into AD DS   The preferred method of publishing root and policy CA certificates and CRLs in a forest environment is to publish them into AD DS. When published into AD DS, the CA certificates and CRLs are published in the configuration naming context and are automatically downloaded to all forest members running Windows 2000, Windows XP, Windows Server 2003, Windows Vista, or Windows Server 2008 through autoenrollment.

To publish the root and policy CA certificates and CRLs, use the following script, which must be run by a member of the Enterprise Admins group:

```
@echo off
a:
cd \
for %%c in ("FABINCCA01*.crt") do certutil -dspublish -f "%%c" RootCA
for %%c in ("FABINCCA02*.crt") do certutil -dspublish -f "%%c" SubCA
for %%c in ("Fabrikam Corporate Root*.crl") do certutil -dspublish -f "%%c"
for %%c in ("Fabrikam Corporate Policy*.crl") do certutil -dspublish -f "%%c"
gpupdate /force
```

The next time Group Policy is applied to a computer that is a member of the forest, certificates will be automatically added to the trusted root or intermediate CA store of the local machine through the autoenrollment mechanism.

Tip   When using this script in your environment, modify each line's search pattern to a pattern that uniquely describes the CA computer name for *.crt files and the CA logical name for *.crl files.

Copying Certificates and CRLs to HTTP Publication Points   If you implement HTTP URLs in your offline CA CDP and AIA extensions, you must manually copy the files to the referenced location. The transfer mechanism entirely depends on the Web servers that host the CA certificates and CRLs. Some of the more commonly chosen mechanisms include: File Transfer Protocol (FTP), Robocopy (now part of the Windows Server 2008 operating system), Secure FTP, Remote Copy Protocol (RCP), and Trivial File Transfer Protocol (TFTP).

The actual commands that you use depend entirely on the method you choose to copy the files to the Web server or Web server cluster.

The following example shows how to use Robocopy to copy the root and Policy CA files to a Web server with the NetBIOS name FABWEB01 to a share named CertEnroll$. The batch file assumes that the necessary files are on the root of the USB Drive (F:).

```
@echo off
F:
net use \\FABWEB01.fabrikam.com
robocopy F: \\ FABWEB01.fabrikam.com\certenroll$ *.crt *.crl /R:5 /W:5 /V /
LOG:UpdateCrlLog.txt
net use \\FABWEB01.fabrikam.com /d
```

Creating a CAPolicy.inf File

Once the root and policy CA certificates and CRLs are downloaded to the local machine's trusted root store, you must prepare a CAPolicy.inf file for the issuing CA. The CAPolicy.inf file for an issuing CA must define certificate-renewal and CRL publication settings.

The following assumptions apply to the Fabrikam issuing CA:

- The key length for the private key and public key is 2,048 bits.

- The policy CA certificate's validity period is five years.

- Base CRLs are published every three days with an overlap of four hours.

- Delta CRLs are published every 12 hours.

- Discrete signatures must be enabled in the issuing CA certificate to allow the use of CNG algorithms for hash and certificate signing.

- The issuing CA will use the SHA256 hash algorithm.

- The CA will not have any certificate template available for enrollment initially.

Based on these assumptions, the following CAPolicy.inf file can be installed in the %Windir% of the Fabrikam, Inc. issuing CA computer:

```
[Version]
Signature="$Windows NT$"

[certsrv_server]
renewalkeylength=2048
RenewalValidityPeriodUnits=5
RenewalValidityPeriod=years

CRLPeriod=3
CRLPeriodUnits=days
CRLOverlapPeriod=4
CRLOverlapUnits=hours
CRLDeltaPeriod=12
CRLDeltaPeriodUnits=hours
```

```
DiscreteSignatureAlgorithm=1
LoadDefaultTemplates=0
```

What if I Am Deploying Only a Two-Tier Hierarchy?

If you are deploying a two-tier CA hierarchy, the major configuration change is the contents of the CAPolicy.inf file. In a two-tier CA hierarchy, the second tier is deployed as a combination policy and issuing CA. The CAPolicy.inf file must be changed to reflect this, as shown below. This example assumes that the same requirements exist for CPS publication.

```
[Version]
Signature="$Windows NT$"

[PolicyStatementExtension]
Policies=FabrikamCPS

[FabrikamCPS]
OID=1.3.6.1.4.1.311.509.3.1
NOTICE=Fabrikam Industries Certification Practice Statement
URL=http://www.fabrikam.com/CPS/CPStatement.asp

renewalkeylength=2048
RenewalValidityPeriodUnits=5
RenewalValidityPeriod=years

CRLPeriod=3
CRLPeriodUnits=days
CRLOverlapPeriod=4
CRLOverlapUnits=hours
CRLDeltaPeriod=12
CRLDeltaPeriodUnits=hours
DiscreteSignatureAlgorithm=1
LoadDefaultTemplates=0
```

This CAPolicy.inf file ensures that the CPS information is included in the issuing CA's certificate, but the file implements the CRL and CA certificate settings for an issuing CA.

Installing Certificate Services

Once the CAPolicy.inf file is in place, you can install Certificate Services. Because the issuing CA's certificate request is submitted to the policy CA, the issuance of the subordinate CA certificate occurs at the policy CA.

The following assumptions are made about the issuing CA computer:

- It uses the naming scheme shown previously in Figure 6-1.

- It has two mirrored partitions and a RAID 5 array—drive C: for the operating system, drive D: for the CA log files, and drive E:, a RAID 5 array, for the CA database.

To begin installing Certificate Services, ensure that you are logged on as a member of the Enterprise Admins group. In addition, ensure that the Enterprise Admins group is a member of the local Administrators group at the enterprise CA. Use the following procedure to install the enterprise CA:

> **Tip**   If installing a two-tier CA hierarchy, replace all instances of the policy CA with the root CA in the upcoming steps.

1. Ensure that the enterprise CA is a member of a domain in the forest.

2. Ensure that the date and time are correctly set.

3. Click Start, point to Administrative Tools, and then click Server Manager.

4. In the Roles Summary section, click Add Roles.

5. If the Before You Begin page appears, select the Skip This Page By Default check box, and then click Next.

6. On the Select Server Roles page, select the Active Directory Certificate Services check box, and when the role is populated, click Next.

7. On the Introduction To Active Directory Certificate Services page, click Next.

8. On the Select Role Services page, select the Certification Authority check box, and then select the Certification Authority Web Enrollment check box.

9. In the Add Roles Wizard dialog box, note that you must add the Web Server (IIS) role, and then click Add Required Role Services.

10. On the Select Role Services page, click Next.

11. On the Specify Setup Type page, click Enterprise, and then click Next.

12. On the Specify CA Type page, click Subordinate CA, and then click Next.

13. On the Set Up Private Key page, click Create A New Private Key, and then click Next.

14. On the Configure Cryptography For CA page, set the following options, and then click Next.

     ❑ Select a cryptographic service provider (CSP): **RSA#Microsoft Software Key Storage Provider**

     ❑ Key character length: **2048**

     ❑ Select the hash algorithm for signing certificates issued by this CA: **sha256**

15. On the Configure CA Name page, provide the following information, and then click Next.

     ❑ Common name for this CA: **Fabrikam Corporate Issuing CA**

     ❑ Distinguished name suffix: **O=Fabrikam Inc.,C=US**

16. On the Request Certificate From A Parent CA page, click Save a Certificate Request To File And Manually Send It Later To A Parent CA, accept the default file name, and then click Next.

17. On the Configure Certificate Database page, provide the following settings, and then click Next:

    ❑ Certificate database: **E:\CertDB**

    ❑ Certificate database log: **D:\CertLog**

18. On the Web Server (IIS) page, click Next.

19. On the Select Role Services page, accept the recommend role services, and then click Next.

20. After verifying the information on the Confirm Installation Selections page, click Install.

21. On the Installation Results page, note that the installation of Active Directory Certificate Services is incomplete whereas the installation of Web Server (IIS) is complete, and then click Close.

22. Open C:\.

23. Copy the FABINCCA03.fabrikam.com_Fabrikam Corporate Issuing CA.req file to the USB drive.

24. Remove the USB drive containing the certificate request file from the issuing CA computer.

The USB drive must now be transported to the policy CA computer to submit the certificate request and to copy the issued certificate back to the issuing CA. Use the following process at the policy CA logged on as a member of the local Administrators group:

1. Insert the USB Drive containing the certificate request file into a USB port on the root CA computer.

2. From the Start menu, click Administrative Tools, and then click Certification Authority.

3. In the console tree, right-click Fabrikam Corporate Policy CA, point to All Tasks, and then click Submit New Request.

4. In the Open Request File dialog box, in the File Name box, type **F:\FABINCCA03. fabrikam.com_Fabrikam Corporate Policy CA.req,** and then click Open.

5. In the console tree, expand Fabrikam Corporate Policy CA, and then click Pending Requests.

6. In the details pane, right-click the certificate request, point to All Tasks, and then click Export Binary Data.

7. In the Export Binary Data dialog box, in the Columns That Contain Binary Data drop-down list, select Binary Request, and then click OK.

8. Review the request detail for accuracy:

   ❑ Verify that the subject name is Fabrikam Corporate Issuing CA.

   ```
   Subject:
   CN=Fabrikam Corporate Issuing CA
   O=Fabrikam Inc.
   C=US
   ```

   ❑ Ensure that public key length is 2048 bits.

   ```
   Public Key Length: 2048 bits
   ```

   ❑ Ensure that the basic constraints indicate Subject Type=CA.

   ```
   Basic Constraints
   Subject type=CA
   ```

   ❑ Verify that the Signature Algorithm is SHA256RSA.

   ```
   Algorithm ObjectId: 1.2.840.113549.1.1.11 sha256RSA
   ```

   ❑ Verify that the signature matches the public key.

   ```
   Signature matches Public Key
   ```

9. Close the Binary Request window.

10. In the details pane, right-click the pending SubCA certificate, point to All Tasks, and then click Issue.

11. In the console tree, click Issued Certificates.

12. In the details pane, double-click the issued certificate.

13. In the Certificate dialog box, click the Details tab.

14. On the Details tab, click Copy To File.

15. In the Certificate Export Wizard, click Next.

16. On the Export File Format page, click Cryptographic Message Syntax Standard–PKCS #7 Certificates (.P7B), select the Include All Certificates In The Certification Path If Possible check box, and then click Next.

17. On the File To Export page, in the File Name box, type **F:\issuingca.p7b,** and then click Next.

18. On the Completing The Certificate Export Wizard page, click Finish.

19. In the Certificate Export Wizard message box, click OK.

20. In the Certificate dialog box, click OK.

21. Close the Certification Authority console.

22. Remove the USB drive containing the certificate request file.

Once the certificate is exported to the floppy disk, you must complete installation of the policy CA by installing the subordinate CA certificate at the issuing CA. Use the following procedure:

1. Insert the USB Drive containing the PKCS#7 file into a USB port on the issuing CA computer.

2. From the Start menu, click Administrative Tools, and then click Certification Authority.

3. In the console tree, right-click Fabrikam Corporate Issuing CA, point to All Tasks, and then click Install CA Certificate.

4. In the Select File To Complete CA Installation dialog box, in the File Name box, type **F:\issuingca.p7b,** and then click Open.

5. In the console tree, right-click Fabrikam Corporate Issuing CA, point to All Tasks, and then click Start Service.

> **Note**   At this point, Certificate Services starts and allows you to view and configure the issuing CA.

Post-Installation Configuration

Once the issuing CA is installed, you must ensure that the issuing CA's registry settings are configured correctly. The following assumptions are made regarding the Fabrikam network:

■ All client and server computers are running Windows 2000, Windows XP, or Windows Server 2003 and are members of the Fabrikam.com domain.

■ The issuing CA's certificate and CRL are published in AD DS, on the issuing CA's Web service, and at an externally accessible Web server.

■ There is a Web server named *www.fabrikam.com*. A virtual directory named Certdata contains CRL and AIA information for all CAs in the CA hierarchy. This Web server is accessible internally and externally.

■ The issuing CA issues certificates—with a maximum two-year validity period—to users, computers, services, and network devices.

■ The issuing CA certificate and CRL are copied to a floppy disk to allow publication to the *www.fabrikam.com* Web server.

■ All auditing options must be enabled on the issuing CA computer.

■ Discrete Signatures must be supported and available for certificate requests submitted to the CA.

■ Sleep.exe from the Windows Server 2003 Resource Kit is installed on the issuing CA computer.

■ CRL and CA certificate retrieval should take place in the following order:

  a. AD DS

  b. Externally accessible Web server

  c. The issuing CA's Web service

> **Note**   The order to use for CA certificate and CRL retrieval is discussed greater detail in Chapter 11, "Certificate Validation."

Use the following post-installation script to configure the issuing CA to implement these design decisions and the assumptions stated previously:

```
::Declare Configuration NC
certutil -setreg CA\DSConfigDN CN=Configuration,DC=fabrikam,DC=com

::Define CRL Publication Intervals
certutil -setreg CA\CRLPeriodUnits 3
certutil -setreg CA\CRLPeriod "Days"
certutil -setreg CA\CRLOverlapUnits 4
certutil -setreg CA\CRLOverlapPeriod "Hours"
certutil -setreg CA\CRLDeltaPeriodUnits 12
certutil -setreg CA\CRLDeltaPeriod "Hours"

::Apply the required CDP Extension URLS
certutil -setreg CA\CRLPublicationURLs
"65:%windir%\system32\CertSrv\CertEnroll\%%3%%8%%9.crl\n79:ldap:///
CN=%%7%%8,CN=%%2,CN=CDP,CN=Public Key
Services,CN=Services,%%6%%10\n6:http://www.fabrikam.com/CertData/%%3%%8%%9.crl\n6:
http://%%1/CertEnroll/%%3%%8%%9.crl "

::Apply the required AIA Extension URLS
certutil -setreg CA\CACertPublicationURLs
"1:%windir%\system32\CertSrv\CertEnroll\%%1_%%3%%4.crt\n3:ldap:///
CN=%%7,CN=AIA,CN=Public Key
Services,CN=Services,%%6%%11\n2:http://www.fabrikam.com/CertData/%%1_%%3%%4.crt\n2:
http://%%1/CertEnroll/%%1_%%3%%4.crt "

::Enable all auditing events for the Fabrikam Corporate Issuing CA
certutil -setreg CA\AuditFilter 127

:: Enable discrete signatures in issued certificates
Certutil -setreg CA\csp\DiscreteSignatureAlgorithm 1

::Set Maximum Validity Period for Issued Certificates
certutil -setreg CA\ValidityPeriodUnits 2
certutil -setreg CA\ValidityPeriod "Years"

::Restart Certificate Services
net stop certsvc & net start certsvc
sleep 5
```

```
certutil -crl
::Copy the issuing CA certificates and CRLs to the USB Drive assigned as F: drive
Echo Insert the USB token as F: drive
sleep 5
copy /y %windir%\system32\certsrv\certenroll\*.cr? f:\
```

Implementing an Enterprise Root CA

Some organizations do not require the security enhancements of a multi-tier CA hierarchy. They simply need a CA to issue certificates for the computers, users, services, and network devices on their network. There is no need for redundancy or to provide a high-assurance trust model.

In these circumstances, a CA hierarchy consisting of a single CA can be deployed. An example of this is the CA hierarchy for Margie's Travel shown previously in Figure 6-2.

> **Note**   It is always recommended to use Windows Server 2008 Enterprise Edition when installing an enterprise CA. Windows Server 2008 Enterprise Edition enables advanced features not available in Windows Server 2008 Standard Edition, such as the issuing of version 2 certificate templates, private key archival, and role separation enforcement.

Creating a CAPolicy.inf File

Even though you are deploying a single CA for the network, it is still recommended that you create a CAPolicy.inf file. The reason for this is to ensure that the configuration settings, which are defined only in the CAPolicy.inf file, are applied to the enterprise root CA.

> **Note**   This example of implementing an enterprise root CA assumes that Margie's Travel has an existing AD DS deployment with a single domain named margiestravel.com. It does not matter if the domain is a Windows 2000, Windows Server 2003, or Windows Server 2008 domain, as long as the AD DS modifications discussed in Chapter 4 are applied.

The CAPolicy.inf file for Margie's Travel makes the following assumptions:

- The root CA uses a key length of 2,048 bits.
- The validity period of the root CA certificate is 10 years.
- Base CRLs are published every two days.
- Delta CRLs are published every 12 hours.
- The root CA does not contain a CDP or AIA extension to prevent revocation checking of the root CA certificate.

- A CPS is not necessary.

- Default certificate templates should not be published at the CA.

Based on these assumptions, the following CAPolicy.inf file can be installed in the %Windir% of the MargieCA01 computer.

```
[Version]
Signature="$Windows NT$"

[certsrv_server]
renewalkeylength=2048
RenewalValidityPeriodUnits=10
RenewalValidityPeriod=years

CRLPeriod=days
CRLPeriodUnits=2
CRLDeltaPeriodUnits=12
CRLDeltaPeriod=hours

LoadDefaultTemplates=0
```

> **Note**   Because we are installing a Windows Server 2008 enterprise root CA, there is no need to include [AuthorityInformationAccess] and [CRLDistributionPoint] sections with Empty=True lines. These are required only if installing a Windows Server 2003 enterprise root CA.

Installing Active Directory Certificate Services

To install Windows Server 2008 Certificate Services as an enterprise CA, a user who is a member of both the Enterprise Admins group of the forest and the local Administrators group of the MargieCA01 computer must perform the install.

This installation procedure assumes that the naming conventions shown previously in Figure 6-2 and the assumptions made for the creation of the CAPolicy.inf file are still in effect. In addition, it is assumed that the enterprise CA will be installed on a computer with a single disk drive.

The following procedure performs the installation of the CA:

1. Log on as a member of the Enterprise Admins and local Administrators group.

2. Click Start, point to Administrative Tools, and then click Server Manager.

3. In the Roles Summary section, click Add Roles.

4. If the Before You Begin page appears, select the Skip This Page By Default check box, and then click Next.

5. On the Select Server Roles page, select the Active Directory Certificate Services check box, and when the role is populated, click Next.

6. On the Introduction to Active Directory Certificate Services page, read the items to Note, and then click Next.

7. On the Select Role Services page, select the Certification Authority and the Certification Authority Web Enrollment check boxes.

8. In the Add Role Services Required For Certification Authority Web Enrollment dialog box, click Add Required Role Services.

9. On the Select Role Services page, click Next.

10. On the Specify Setup Type page, click Enterprise, and then click Next.

11. On the Specify CA Type page, click Root CA, and then click Next.

12. On the Set Up Private Key page, click Create A New Private Key, and then click Next.

13. On the Configure Cryptography For CA pages, leave the default values (these meet our design requirements), and then click Next.

> **Note**   You can define a cryptographic service provider other than the default (RSA#Microsoft Software Key Storage Provider), key length greater or less than the default value of 2048, and a hashing algorithm supported by the selected CSP.

14. On the Configure CA Name page, provide the following information, and then click Next.

    ❑ Common Name for this CA: **Margie's Travel Root CA**

    ❑ Distinguished name suffix: **O=Margie's Travel,C=US**

15. On the Set Validity Period page, change the validity duration to 10 years, and then click Next.

16. On the Configure Certificate Database page, accept the default storage locations for the certificate database and the certificate database log, and then click Next.

17. On the Web Server (IIS) page, click Next.

18. On the Select Role Services page, accept the recommended role services, and click Next.

19. On the Confirm Installation Selections page, verify the presented information, and then click Install.

20. On the Installation Results page, ensure that status for both Active Directory Certificate Services and for Web Server (IIS) is Installation Succeeded, and then click Close.

Post-Installation Configuration

Once the installation of Certificate Services is complete, you should run a post-installation script to ensure that the correct settings are defined for the enterprise root CA.

To meet the objectives defined earlier for Margie's Travel and to apply the default CRL and AIA publication points, the following script can be used:

```
::Declare Configuration NC
certutil -setreg CA\DSConfigDN CN=Configuration,DC=margiestravel,DC=com

::Define CRL Publication Intervals
certutil -setreg CA\CRLPeriodUnits 2
certutil -setreg CA\CRLPeriod "Days"
certutil -setreg CA\CRLDeltaPeriodUnits 12
certutil -setreg CA\CRLDeltaPeriod "Hours"

::Apply the default CDP Extension URLs
certutil -setreg CA\CRLPublicationURLs
"65:%windir%\system32\CertSrv\CertEnroll\%%3%%8%%9.crl\n79:ldap:///
CN=%%7%%8,CN=%%2,CN=CDP,CN=Public Key Services,CN=Services,%%6%%10\n6:http://%%1/
CertEnroll/%%3%%8%%9.crl"

::Apply the default AIA Extension URLs
certutil -setreg CA\CACertPublicationURLs
"1:%windir%\system32\CertSrv\CertEnroll\%%1_%%3%%4.crt\n3:ldap:///CN=%%7,CN=AIA,CN=Public
Key Services,CN=Services,%%6%%11\n2:http://%%1/CertEnroll/
%%1_%%3%%4.crt"

::Enable all auditing events for the enterprise root CA
certutil -setreg CA\AuditFilter 127

::Set Validity Period for Issued Certificates
certutil -setreg CA\ValidityPeriodUnits 2
certutil -setreg CA\ValidityPeriod "Years"

::Restart Certificate Services
net stop certsvc & net start certsvc
sleep 5
certutil -crl
```

Enabling Auditing

In all of the deployment examples, the post-installation script enables all auditing events for Certificate Services. These auditing events depend on enabling success and failure auditing for Object Access. The configuration of this option depends mainly on whether the CA is an offline CA or an online CA:

- For an offline CA, the audit settings are defined in the Local Security Policy.

- For an online CA, the audit settings are typically enforced using a Group Policy Object (GPO) linked to the OU where the issuing CA accounts exist in AD DS.

Note   There is nothing wrong with enforcing the audit settings on an issuing CA in the local security policy. The risk is that a conflicting GPO would take precedence and potentially not enable the required audit settings.

1. If you wish to define CA audit settings by using Group Policy, perform the following steps:

    a. From Administrative Tools, open Active Directory Users And Computers.

    b. In the console tree, expand the OU structure, right-click the OU where the CA's computer account exists, and then click Properties.

    c. In the OU Properties dialog box, on the Group Policy tab, click New.

    d. Name the new Group Policy **CA Audit Settings**, and then click Edit.

    e. In the console tree, navigate to the following container: Computer Settings\Windows Settings\Security Settings\Local Policies\Audit Policy.

2. If you wish to define CA audit settings in the Local Security Policy console, perform the following steps:

    a. From Administrative Tools, open Active Directory Users And Computers.

    b. In the console tree, navigate to the following container: Security Settings\Local Policies\Audit Policy.

3. Enable the following auditing settings:

    ❑ Account Logon: **Success, Failure**

    ❑ Account Management: **Success, Failure**

    ❑ Directory Service **Access: Failure**

    ❑ Logon Events: **Success, Failure**

    ❑ Object Access: **Success, Failure**

    ❑ Policy Change: **Success, Failure**

    ❑ Privilege Use: **Failure**

    ❑ Process Tracking: **No auditing**

    ❑ System Events: **Success, Failure**

4. If defining a Group Policy Object, perform the following steps:

    a. Close the Group Policy Editor or the Local Security Policy console.

    b. In the OU Properties dialog box, click OK.

    c. Close Active Directory Users And Computers.

5. If defining a Local Security Policy, close the Local Security Policy console.

If you wish to enable KSP audit log events in the Windows Security log, a member of the local Administrators group must run the following command at each CA:

```
auditpol /set /subcategory:"other system events" /success:enable /failure:enable
```

It is recommended to then restart Certificate Services to ensure that the CNG audit settings are enforced.

Verifying Installation

Once you install the CA hierarchy—whether it is a single-tier or multi-tier hierarchy—you must ensure that the AIA and CDP URLs are configured correctly before you start issuing certificates.

If the URLs are configured incorrectly, the certificate chaining engine might encounter errors when it attempts to download CA certificates and CRLs from the referenced URLs. In addition, you cannot go back and edit issued certificates. As discussed in Chapter 2, "Primer to PKI," a certificate is a signed object and cannot be modified without invalidating the signature included in the thumbprint extension of the certificate.

The PKI Health Tool (PKIView.msc)—now included as part of the Certificate Services role installation—evaluates every URL included in the AIA and CDP extensions of the certificates in the CA hierarchy. The tool attempts to connect to each referenced URL and reports whether the certificate or CRL is reachable as well as whether the current version is reaching expiration.

You must run the PKI Health tool on a Windows Server 2008 computer that is a member of the forest. To use the tool, use the following procedure:

1. From the Start menu, click Run, type **pkiview.msc,** and then click OK.

2. In the console tree, click each CA in the hierarchy. In the details pane, review the status of each CRL and AIA location.

If a publication point is configured correctly, the status column will report a value of OK. If the publication point is configured incorrectly or if the CA certificate or CRL is not copied correctly to the publication point, the status column reports a status of Unable to Download. Finally, if the CA certificate or CRL is near expiration, the status column will report a value of Expiring.

Note   More details on using the PKI Health Tool are discussed in Chapter 8, "Verifying and Monitoring Your Microsoft PKI."

Case Study: Deploying a PKI

You are the network administrator for Fabrikam, Inc. Based on the design requirements, you have decided to deploy the CA hierarchy shown previously in Figure 6-1.

To assist you in configuring the CAPolicy.inf files, pre-installation batch files, and post-installation batch files, the following design requirements are provided:

- Root CA

  - The root CA must use a key length of 2,048 bits for its public and private key pair.

  - The root CA certificate must have a 20-year lifetime.

  - The root CA will publish its base CRL twice a year.

  - The root CA will not implement a delta CRL.

  - The root CA certificate will not include an AIA or CDP extension.

  - The root CA will issue subordinate CA certificates with a 10-year lifetime.

  - The root CA certificate and CRL are published in AD DS to allow automatic distribution to all Windows 2000 and later client computers.

  - The root CA must issue subordinate CA certificates that have an AIA extension with the first URL referencing the AD DS publication point and the second URL as *http://www.fabrikam.com/certdata/RootCACertificate* (where RootCACertificate is the default name of the Root CA's certificate file).

  - The root CA must issue subordinate CA certificates that have a CDP extension with the first URL referencing the AD DS publication point and the second URL as *http://www.fabrikam.com/certdata/RootCACRL* (where RootCACRL is the default name of the Root CA's CRL file).

- Policy CA

  - The certification practice statement (CPS) for the Fabrikam PKI is published at the URL *www.fabrikam.com/CPS/Fabrikampolicy.asp*.

  - The OID assigned to the Fabrikam CPS is 1.3.6.1.4.1.311.509.4.1.

- Issuing CA

  - The issuing CA will host the Certificate Services Web Enrollment pages.

  - The issuing CA will publish a base CRL daily and a delta CRL every eight hours.

Case Study Questions

The questions for this case study are divided into sections related to configuration of the Fabrikam Corporate Root CA, the Fabrikam Corporate Policy CA, and the Fabrikam Corporate Issuing CA.

Fabrikam Corporate Root CA

Answer the following questions relating to configuration of the Fabrikam Corporate Root CA based on the information provided in the design requirements:

1. How do you define the key length of 2,048 bits for the root CA during installation of the root CA?

2. How do you ensure that the key length will remain 2,048 bits when the root CA's certificate is renewed?

3. What entries are required in the CAPolicy.inf file to specify the required base CRL and delta CRL publication intervals?

4. How would you suppress the inclusion of an AIA and CDP extension in the root CA certificate on Windows Server 2008 Standard Edition?

5. After configuring the CAPolicy.inf file, you note that none of the settings are applied to the root CA when you install Certificate Services. You check and find that the file is located in the C:\temp folder. Why did the installation not apply the settings in the CAPolicy.inf file?

6. How do you configure the root CA to issue subordinate CA certificates with a lifetime of 10 years?

7. How do you define the location in Configuration naming context for publishing the root CA certificate and CRL to AD DS? (Assume that the forest root domain is the same as shown previously in Figure 6-1.)

8. What command is required to define the AIA publication URLs for the certificates issued by the root CA?

9. What command is required to define the CDP publication URLs for the certificates issued by the root CA?

Fabrikam Corporate Policy CA

Answer the following questions relating to configuration of the Fabrikam Corporate Policy CA based on the information provided in the design requirements:

1. On the first attempt to install the policy CA, you receive the error that the CA is unable to determine the revocation status for the policy CA certificate. What must you do to ensure that the policy CA recognizes the root CA certificate as a trusted root certificate and can determine the revocation status for the policy CA certificate?

2. What command do you use to add the root CA certificate as a trusted root CA certificate on the Fabrikam Corporate Policy CA, assuming that the name of the root CA certificate is FABINCCA01_Fabrikam Corporate Root CA.crt?

3. What command do you use to allow the policy CA to access the root CA CRL, assuming that the name of the root CA certificate is Fabrikam Corporate Root CA.crl?

4. How do you configure the CAPolicy.inf file on the policy CA to include the CPS and related OID?

Fabrikam Corporate Issuing CA

Answer the following questions relating to configuration of the Fabrikam Corporate Policy CA based on the information provided in the design requirements:

1. What commands do you use to ensure that the root CA and policy CA certificates are automatically added to the local machine store of all Windows 2000, Windows XP, and Windows Server 2003 domain members?

2. What commands do you use to ensure that the root CA and policy CA CRLs are automatically added to the local machine store of all Windows 2000, Windows XP, and Windows Server 2003 domain members?

3. On the first attempt to install the issuing CA, you receive the error that the CA is unable to determine the revocation status for the policy CA certificate. Assuming that you have successfully published the root and policy CA information to AD DS, what must you do to ensure that the issuing CA can determine the revocation status for the issuing CA certificate?

4. What are the minimum components of the World Wide Web Service required to install the Certificate Services Web Enrollment pages?

5. What commands are required at the issuing CA to publish the base CRL daily and the delta CRL every eight hours?

Additional Information

- Microsoft Official Curriculum, Course 2821: "Designing and Managing a Windows Public Key Infrastructure" (*http://www.microsoft.com/learning/syllabi/en-us/2821Afinal.mspx*)

- "Best Practices for Implementing a Microsoft Windows Server 2003 Public Key Infrastructure" (*http://technet2.microsoft.com/windowsserver/en/library/091cda67-79ec-481d-8a96-03e0be7374ed1033.mspx?mfr=true*)

- "Certificate Revocation and Status Checking" (*http://technet.microsoft.com/en-us/library/bb457027.aspx*)

- "Active Directory Certificate Server Enhancements in Windows Server Code Name 'Longhorn'" (*http://www.microsoft.com/downloads/details.aspx?familyid=9bf17231-d832-4ff9-8fb8-0539ba21ab95&displaylang=en*)

- 231182: "Certificate Authority Servers Cannot Be Renamed or Removed from Network"

- 555151: "How to Remove Manually Enterprise Windows Certificate Authority from Windows 2000/2003 Domain"

- 896733: "TechNet Support WebCast: Best Practices for Public Key Infrastructure: Steps to Build an Offline Root Certification Authority (Part 1 of 2)"

- 896737: "TechNet Support WebCast: Best Practices for Public Key Infrastructure: Setting Up an Offline Subordinate and an Online Enterprise Subordinate (Part 2 of 2)"

- 927169: "Custom Extensions in the CAPolicy.inf File Do Not Take Effect After You Renew the Root CA Certificate by Using a New Key"

Note The five articles above can be accessed through the Microsoft Knowledge Base. Go to *http://support.microsoft.com*, and enter the article number in the Search The Knowledge Base text box.

Chapter 7

Upgrading Your Existing Microsoft PKI

If you have an existing Microsoft Windows public key infrastructure (PKI) deployed, the process of migrating to Windows Server 2008 is different than implementing a new deployment (which is discussed in Chapter 6, "Implementing a CA Hierarchy").

This chapter looks at the supported scenarios for upgrading from a previous version of Certificate Services to Windows Server 2008 Active Directory Certificate Services. The chapter then provides details on performing the actual upgrade. The details include preparations before the in-place upgrade, the actual upgrade process, and post-upgrade decisions that must be made.

Supported Scenarios

First, you must determine whether your version of Windows Certificate Services can be upgraded to Windows Server 2008 directly. Additional migration steps are required if you previously deployed Windows Server 2003 certification authorities (CAs) using a 32-bit processor and want to deploy Windows Server 2008 on computers with 64-bit processors.

What Versions Can You Upgrade to Windows Server 2008?

The recommended method to upgrade to Windows Server 2008 Active Directory Certificate Services is to perform an in-place upgrade. Unfortunately, the in-place upgrade is not supported from all previous versions of Windows Certificate Services.

Table 7-1 provides the supported upgrade paths from previous versions of Certificate Services to Windows Server 2008 Active Directory Certificate Services.

Table 7-1 Upgrade Paths to Windows Server 2008

Windows version	Edition	Upgrade to Windows Server 2008		
		Standard Edition	Enterprise Edition	Datacenter Edition
Windows NT 4	All	No	No	No
Windows 2000	All	No	No	No
Windows Server 2003	Standard Edition (SP1 and later, R2)	Yes	Yes	No
	Enterprise Edition (SP1 and later, R2)	No	Yes	No
	Datacenter Edition	No	No	Yes
	Itanium-based Editions	No	No	No

As detailed in the table, the only version of Windows Certificate Services that supports a direct upgrade to Windows Server 2008 is Windows Server 2003 running on Service Pack 1 or later or on Windows Server 2003 R2. If you are running previous versions of Certificate Services, you must first upgrade to Windows Server 2003 with Service Pack 1 or later applied.

> **Note**   Alternatively, you could consider decommisioning the previous CAs if the deployment path is easier.

Finally, if you previously installed Certificate Services on Windows Server 2003 for Itanium-based systems, there is no upgrade path to Windows Server 2008. Active Directory Certificate Services is not supported on Windows Server 2008 for Itanium-based systems.

32-Bit to 64-Bit Considerations

The upgrade to Windows Server 2008 will not support upgrade between architectures. You will not be able to upgrade from a 32-bit version of Windows Server 2003 to a 64-bit version of Windows Server 2008.

There are three different methods to migrate from 32-bit CAs to 64-bit CAs in your CA Hierarchy:

- Deploying new CAs to replace the existing CAs
- Upgrading the existing CAs to Windows Server 2008 and then migrating the existing CA database, CA certificate, and key pair to a computer running the 64-bit edition of Windows Server 2008
- Migrating the Windows Server 2003 existing CA database, CA certificate, and key pair to a 64-bit Windows Server 2003 CA and then upgrading the 64-bit CA to Windows Server 2008

There probably will not be much demand to migrate existing root and policy CAs to 64-bit operating systems. The biggest benefit of the 64-bit version of Windows Server 2008 is the processing power. This level of processing power just isn't required for an offline CA.

> **Note**   In the future you may have to migrate offline CAs to 64-bit versions of the operating system. This can be because of an organization recommendation to move entirely to 64-bit server computers as the server standard or because of the lack of availability of 32-bit server hardware in the future.

Deploying New CAs to Replace the Existing CAs

The first strategy for migrating to 64-bit CAs is to deploy new CAs to replace the existing 32-bit CAs. Figure 7-1 shows the recommended implementation to replace the two existing 32-bit issuing CAs with 64-bit issuing CAs.

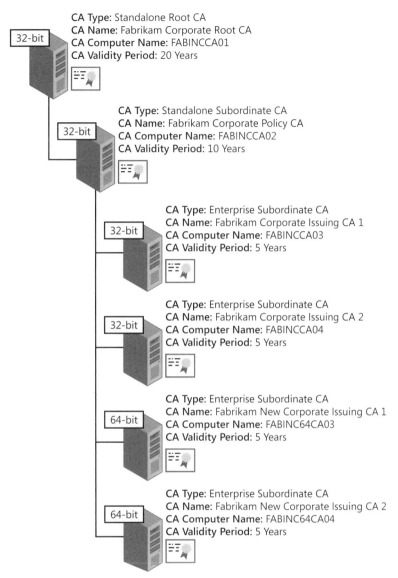

Figure 7-1   Migrating Fabrikam's issuing CAs to 64-bit CAs

In this example, the following procedures are performed:

- The new CAs, Fabrikam New Corporate Issuing CA 1 and Fabrikam New Corporate Issuing CA 2, are issued as subordinates below the existing Fabrikam Corporate Policy CA.

- The new CAs are deployed with new NetBIOS names: FABINC64CA03 and FABINC64CA04.

- All existing certificate templates available at Fabrikam Corporate Issuing CA1 and Fabrikam Corporate Issuing CA 2 are published at Fabrikam New Corporate Issuing CA 1 and Fabrikam New Corporate Issuing CA 2.

- All certificate templates are removed from the existing 32-bit issuing CAs, ensuring that the 32-bit CAs do not issue certificates to end entities.

- The existing 32-bit CAs continue to run, publishing updated certificate revocation lists (CRLs).

- If key archival is enabled at either of the 32-bit CAs, the private keys must be migrated to a 64-bit CA. The migration must allow foreign key import to allow import of archived certificates issued by a different CA.

> **Note**   For details on moving archived certificates between issuing CAs, see Chapter 18, "Archiving Encryption Keys."

Upgrading and Then Migrating

The second strategy is to upgrade the existing 32-bit CAs to the 32-bit version of Windows Server 2008. As discussed in the upcoming sections, the upgrade will maintain the existing CA database, CA certificate, CA key pair, and all archived encryption certificates.

Once the CA is upgraded to Windows Server 2008, you must:

- Back up the CA database by using **certutil –backupdb.**

- Export the CA's private key and CA certificate. The method will depend on the cryptographic service provider (CSP) used to protect the CA's private key.

- Back up the CA's configuration registry key (HKLM\System\CurrentControlSet\Services\CertSvc\).

- Back up the CAPolicy.inf file.

Once the backup is performed, remove the computer from the network (in the event that the migration fails). You can then build a new 64-bit CA to replace the existing 32-bit CA.

> **Important**   Do not remove or delete the 32-bit CA's computer account from Active Directory Domain Services (AD DS) if the CA is a domain member. To maintain permissions assigned to objects in AD DS, the CA computer account must not be deleted.

The CA must meet the following requirements:

- The CA must be running the same edition of Windows Server 2008 as the 32-bit CA.

- The CA must have the same NetBIOS name as the 32-bit CA.

- The CA must have the same domain or workgroup membership of the 32-bit CA.

Once the CA has been built and joined to the same domain or workgroup, you can then restore the CA key pair, CA database, CA registry settings, and the CAPolicy.inf file.

> **Note**   Details on performing the restoration are covered in Chapter 14, "Planning and Implementing Disaster Recovery."

Migrating and Then Upgrading

The final strategy is similar to the second strategy, but the order of the operations is switched. Rather than performing the upgrade to Windows Server 2008 on the 32-bit version of the CA, the CA is first migrated to the 64-bit version of Windows Server 2003. The migration and upgrade would use the following procedure:

1. Back up the CA key pair, the CA certificate, the CA database, CAPolicy.inf, and the CA registry settings on the existing 32-bit Windows Server 2003 CA.

2. Remove the 32-bit CA from the network.

3. Build a 64-bit version of the CA that maintains the 32-bit CA's NetBIOS name and domain membership.

4. Restore the CA key pair, the CA certificate, the CA database, CAPolicy.inf, and the CA registry settings to the 64-bit Windows Server 2003 CA.

5. Verify that the CA is operational.

6. Perform an in-place upgrade to upgrade the server computer to the 64-bit version of Windows Server 2008.

Performing the Upgrade

The actual upgrade process involves preparing AD DS, performing the in-place upgrade, updating the available certificate templates, and then choosing whether to implement the new Windows Server 2008 features and options.

Upgrading the Schema

Before you can upgrade your CAs to Windows Server 2008, you must ensure that the Active Directory schema is upgraded to the Windows Server 2008 version. The Windows Server 2008 schema update does not require you to migrate your domain controllers to Windows Server 2008.

As discussed in Chapter 4, "Preparing an Active Directory Domain Services Environment," the actual upgrade to the Windows Server 2008 schema involves the following steps:

1. Identify the schema operations master. The upgrade of the schema is performed on the schema operations master by a member of the forest's Schema Admins group.

2. Upgrade the schema from the Windows Server 2008 DVD by running **adprep /forestprep** from the \sources\adprep folder on the DVD.

3. Wait for the schema update to replicate to all domain controllers in the forest.

4. Optionally, at each domain's infrastructure master, run **adprep /domainprep /gpprep** from the \sources\adprep folder on the DVD to prepare each domain to use the schema extensions.

> **Note**   More detailed procedures for the schema update are available in Chapter 4.

Upgrading Certificate Templates

Windows Server 2008 adds two new default certificate templates to the existing 31 default certificate templates. The new certificate templates, OCSP Response Signing and Kerberos Authentication, are added to the Certificate Templates container when one of the following actions takes place:

■ The Certificate Templates console (certtmpl.msc) is opened for the first time after you have updated the schema to the Windows Server 2008 schema.

■ The first Windows Server 2008 CA is added to the forest. The installation of the CA automatically adds the two new certificate templates to the available certificate templates.

To add the new default templates, use the following procedure:

1. Add a computer running Windows Server 2008 to a domain in the forest.

2. Add the Enterprise Administrators group to the local Administrators group.

3. Log on to the computer running Windows Server 2008 as a member of the Enterprise Admins group.

4. From the Start menu, type **certtmpl.msc**, and then press Enter.

5. When the message in Figure 7-2 appears, click Yes to install the new certificate templates.

Figure 7-2   Installing the new Windows Server 2008 certificate templates

6. After the Certificate Templates console opens, verify that the OCSP Response Signing and Kerberos Authentication certificate templates appear in the list.

Performing the Upgrade

To perform an in-place upgrade to Windows Server 2008, use the following process:

1. If the CA is an issuing CA, ensure that the Enterprise Admins group is a member of the local Administrators group.

2. Log on to the Windows Server 2003 CA as a member of the Enterprise Admins group for issuing CAs and a member of the local Administrators group for offline CAs.

3. Ensure that you back up all critical Certificate Services files.

> **Note**   For details on the recommendations for backup, see Chapter 14.

4. Insert the Windows Server 2008 media in the DVD-ROM drive. Use Windows Server 2008 Standard to upgrade existing Windows Server 2003 Standard offline CAs and Windows Server 2008 Enterprise to upgrade existing enterprise CAs.

5. In the Install Windows dialog box, click Install Now.

6. On the Get Important Updates For Installation page, click Go Online To Get The Latest Updates For Installation (Recommended).

7. On the Type Your Product Key For Activation page, type your product key, select Automatically Activate Windows When I'm Online, and then click Next.

8. If the Select The Operating System You Want To Install page appears, select the full installation option, and then click Next.

> **Note**   The Select The Operating System You Want To Install page appears only if you have failed to input a valid product key. The product key determines the version of Windows Server 2008 that will be installed.

9. On the Please Read The License Terms page, read the licensing agreement, select the I Accept The License Terms check box, and then click Next.

10. On the Which Type of Installation Do You Want? page, click Upgrade.

11. On the Compatibility Report page, click Next. The actual copying of files and upgrade process is now performed.

    The computer will restart during the upgrade process.

12. When the upgrade is complete, log on as a member of the Enterprise Admins group.

13. From Administrative Tools, open Certification Authority.

14. Ensure that Active Directory Certificate Services is started and that all previously issued certificates are still listed in the console.

Post-Upgrade Operations

Once you have upgraded to Windows Server 2008 on your CA, you can choose to change the hash algorithm used by the Windows Server 2008 CA.

> **Note**   You can change the hash algorithm only for the provider. You cannot change the actual CSP or the asymmetric algorithm used by the CSP. The only way to change the CSP used by a CA is to replace the CA with a new Windows Server 2008 CA. The process would be similar to the process described earlier in this chapter regarding changing from a 32-bit operating system to a 64-bit operating system for the CA.

Changing the Hash Algorithm for a CryptoAPI Version 1 CSP

A legacy CSP can change the hash algorithm to only one of the supported hash algorithms. Typically a CryptoAPI version 1 (CAPI) CSP can choose only one of the following hash algorithms: SHA1, MD2, MD4, or MD5.

You can determine which hash algorithms are supported by your CA's CSP by using the following procedure:

1. Use the following command to determine the current CSP used by the CA:

   ```
   certutil –getreg ca\csp\Provider
   ```

2. In the resulting output, you will see the name of the current CSP:

   ```
   Provider REG_SZ = Microsoft Strong Cryptographic Provider
   ```

3. To determine the hash algorithms supported by the Microsoft Strong Cryptographic Provider, run the following command to capture the supported algorithms for all installed CSPs:

   ```
   certutil -v -csplist > csplist.txt
   ```

4. Open Csplist.txt in Notepad, and search for **Microsoft Strong Cryptographic Provider**. The listing will include all supported hash algorithms (where Algorithm Class = ALG_CLASS_HASH). For example, the settings for SHA1 would appear as:

   ```
   Provider Name: Microsoft Strong Cryptographic Provider

   SHA-1 (Secure Hash Algorithm (SHA-1))
   dwDefaultLen=160 dwMinLen=160 dwMaxLen=160
   CALG_SHA1
   Algorithm Class: 0x8000(4) ALG_CLASS_HASH
   Algorithm Type: 0x0(0) ALG_TYPE_ANY
   Algorithm Sub-id: 0x4(4) ALG_SID_SHA1
   ```

   The critical values for changing the algorithm are found in the Algorithm Class, Algorithm Type, and Algorithm Sub-id values. The sum of all three values is the hash algorithm ID that you have to put in the registry at the CA. So, to set the hash algorithm as SHA1, the value for the HashAlgorithm is 0x8004.

5.   To change the hash algorithm, type the following command at the command-line prompt:

```
certutil -setreg ca\csp\HashAlgorithm 0x8004
```

6.   Restart the CA to recognize the registry change.

Once restarted, the CA will use the newly designated hash algorithm to sign all issued certificates. If you have implemented this change on a root CA, the change will not be recognized in the root CA's certificate until you renew the root CA's certificate.

> **Important**   You can change only the HashAlgorithm. You must not change the provider or provider type. This will cause Certificate Services to fail.

Changing the Hash Algorithm for a CNG CSP

A Cryptography Next Generation (CNG) CSP can change the hash algorithm to one of the supported hash algorithms. A CNG CSP can choose one of the following hash algorithms: SHA1, MD2, MD4, MD5, SHA256, SHA384, or SHA512.

You can determine which hash algorithms are supported by your CA's CSP by using the following procedure:

1.   Use the following command to determine the current CSP used by the CA:

```
certutil -getreg ca\csp\Provider
```

2.   In the resulting output, you will see the name of the current CSP:

```
ProviderType REG_SZ =Microsoft Software Key Storage Provider
```

3.   To identify the current CNG hash algorithm, type the following command:

```
certutil -getreg ca\csp\CNGHashAlgorithm
```

The output will show one of the supported CNG hash algorithms: SHA1, MD2, MD4, MD5, SHA256, SHA384, SHA512, or AES-GMAC.

4.   To change the current CNG Algorithm (for example, to change to SHA384), type the following command:

```
certutil -setreg ca\csp\CNGHashAlgorithm sha384
```

5.   Restart the CA. Once restarted, all certificates issued by the CA will use sha384 as the hash algorithm (or whatever algorithm you designated as the new CNGHashAlgorithm).

> **Important**   You can change only the CNGHashAlgorithm. You must not change the provider, provider type, or CNGPublicKeyAlgorithm.

Implement Discrete Signatures

If a CA implements a CNG CSP, there are several combinations of hash algorithms and public key algorithms possible. Windows Server 2008 now supports the use of the PKCS #1 V2.1 signature format to designate which hash algorithms and public key algorithms are implemented by the CA.

You can designate the use of discrete signatures for:

- **CA Certificates and CA Certificate requests**   You force a root CA to generate a self-signed certificate using the PKCS #1 v2.1 signature format. To force a subordinate CA to generate a request that includes the #1 v2.1 signature format, you must add the Discrete-SignatureAlgorithm=1 line to the [certsrv_server] section of the CA's CAPolicy.inf file.

- **Certificate issued by a CA**   You force a CA to include discrete signatures in all certificate issued by the CA by running the following **certutil** commands at the CA:

```
certutil -setreg ca\csp\DiscreteSignatureAlgorithm 1
    net stop certsvc && net start certsvc
```

Case Study: Upgrading an Existing PKI

You are a consultant hired by Humongous Insurance to assist with their planned migration to Windows Server 2008 Active Directory Certificate Services. The current CA hierarchy is shown in Figure 7-3.

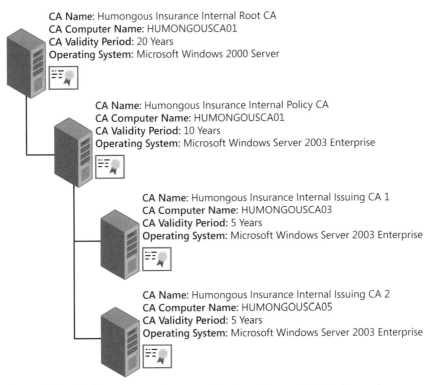

CA Name: Humongous Insurance Internal Root CA
CA Computer Name: HUMONGOUSCA01
CA Validity Period: 20 Years
Operating System: Microsoft Windows 2000 Server

CA Name: Humongous Insurance Internal Policy CA
CA Computer Name: HUMONGOUSCA01
CA Validity Period: 10 Years
Operating System: Microsoft Windows Server 2003 Enterprise

CA Name: Humongous Insurance Internal Issuing CA 1
CA Computer Name: HUMONGOUSCA03
CA Validity Period: 5 Years
Operating System: Microsoft Windows Server 2003 Enterprise

CA Name: Humongous Insurance Internal Issuing CA 2
CA Computer Name: HUMONGOUSCA05
CA Validity Period: 5 Years
Operating System: Microsoft Windows Server 2003 Enterprise

Figure 7-3   The Humongous Insurance Windows Server 2003 CA hierarchy

Humongous Insurance does not want to change the basic design of their CA hierarchy but does wish to take advantage of several new features available in Windows Server 2008.

To assist with the upgrade process, the following design requirements are provided:

- **Root CA**   The root CA must be upgraded from Windows 2000 Server to Windows Server 2008 Standard.

- The server currently uses MD5 as the signing hash algorithm. Humongous Insurance wishes to change the signing algorithm to SHA1 for all future certificates.

- The root CA certificate was originally signed with a 4,096-bit key. This key length has blocked the deployment of the Cisco VPN 3000 concentrator for VPN access. Humongous wishes to take this opportunity to reduce the key size to 2,048 bits.

- The base CRL for the root CA is published annually. No delta CRL is implemented for the CA.

- The root CA certificate must include a discrete signature.

- All subordinate CA certificates issued by the root CA must include a discrete signature.

- **Internal Policy CA**   The internal policy CA must be upgraded to Windows Server 2008.

- The Internal Policy CA certificate request must include a discrete signature.

- All subordinate CA certificates issued by the policy CA must include a discrete signature.

- **Internal Issuing CAs**   Humongous wishes to migrate the issuing CAs to the 64-bit version of Windows Server 2008.

- The issuing CAs issue all machine and user certificates for the forest.

- The longest validity period for any of the certificates issued by the internal issuing CAs is two years.

- For future applications, Humongous would like to implement CNG algorithms for the symmetric and asymmetric keys: SHA256 for the hash algorithm, and ECDSA P521 for the asymmetric keys.

Case Study Questions

The questions for this case study are divided into sections related to configuration of the Humongous Insurance Internal Root CA, the Humongous Insurance Internal Policy CA, and the Humongous Insurance Internal Issuing CAs.

Humongous Insurance Internal Root CA

Answer the following questions relating to configuration of the Humongous Insurance Internal Root CA based on the information provided in the design requirements:

1. Can you upgrade the root CA directly to Windows Server 2008?

2. How would you change the root CA's key length to 2,048 bits from the current 4,096 bits?

3. How would you configure the root CA certificate to include a discrete signature? Is any additional configuration required to include discrete signatures in all subordinate CA certificates issued by the root CA?

4. How would you change the root CA's hash algorithm from MD5 to SHA1?

Humongous Insurance Internal Policy CA

Answer the following questions relating to configuration of the Humongous Insurance Internal Policy CA based on the information provided in the design requirements:

1. To save money, Humongous Insurance would like to change the policy CA to Windows Server 2008 Standard rather than continue to use Windows Server 2008 Enterprise. Is this possible in an upgrade scenario?

2. If you can upgrade to Windows Server 2008 Standard, what would be the process?

3.   If you cannot change to Windows Server 2008 Standard doing an upgrade-in-place, what are your other options?

Humongous Insurance Internal Issuing CAs

Answer the following questions relating to configuration of the Humongous Insurance Internal Issuing CAs based on the information provided in the design requirements:

1. Can you perform an in-place upgrade to migrate the current issuing CAs from the 32-bit platform to the 64-bit platform?

2. If you cannot upgrade in place to 64-bit Windows, what process would you use to change the issuing CAs in the hierarchy to 64-bit Windows?

3. What measures could you take to reduce the amount of time you must support both the 32-bit and 64-bit issuing CAs?

4. What PKI management tasks must be maintained throughout the remaining lifetime of the 32-bit issuing CAs?

5. In the worst case scenario, how long would you have to maintain both the 32-bit and 64-bit CAs?

6. What measures can you take to further reduce the period for maintaining the 32-bit CAs?

Additional Information

- Microsoft Official Curriculum, Course 2821: "Designing and Managing a Windows Public Key Infrastructure" (*http://www.microsoft.com/learning/syllabi/en-us/2821Afinal.mspx*)

- "Best Practices for Implementing a Microsoft Windows Server 2003 Public Key Infrastructure" (*http://technet2.microsoft.com/windowsserver/en/library/091cda67-79ec-481d-8a96-03e0be7374ed1033.mspx?mfr=true*)

- "Certificate Revocation and Status Checking" (*http://technet.microsoft.com/en-us/library/bb457027.aspx*)

- "Active Directory Certificate Server Enhancements in Windows Server Code Name 'Longhorn'" (*http://www.microsoft.com/downloads/details.aspx?familyid=9bf17231-d832-4ff9-8fb8-0539ba21ab95&displaylang=en*)

Chapter 8

Verifying and Monitoring Your Microsoft PKI

Once you have completed the installation or upgrade of your Windows Server 2008 public key infrastructure (PKI), the process does not stop at this point. One of the first things you have to do is ensure that you have correctly configured all certification authorities (CAs) in the CA hierarchy. Any incorrect configuration settings must be identified and fixed before you start issuing certificates. Even after you have deployed your PKI, you must continue to monitor the PKI to identify proactively any issues that arise.

This chapter provides recommendations on what tools can verify your installation and what tools to use to monitor your PKI on an ongoing basis.

Verifying the Installation

Once you install the CA hierarchy—whether it is a single-tier or multi-tier hierarchy—you must ensure that clients can successfully download the certification authority (CA) certificates and the certificate revocation lists (CRLs) to perform revocation checking. The CA certificates are downloaded based on URL information in the Authority Information Access (AIA) extension of the issued certificates. Likewise, a CRL is downloaded based on URL information in the CRL Distribution Point (CDP) URLs in the issued certificates.

If the URLs are configured incorrectly, the certificate chaining engine might encounter errors when it attempts to download CA certificates and CRLs from the referenced URLs. In addition, you cannot go back and edit issued certificates. As discussed in Chapter 2, "Primer to PKI," a certificate is a signed object and cannot be modified without invalidating the signature included in the thumbprint extension of the certificate.

Two tools are commonly used to validate AIA and CDP extensions for your PKI:

- **PKI Health Tool** The PKI Health Tool (pkiview.msc) provides a graphical display of your internal CA hierarchies and provides information on each AIA and CDP URL defined in the CA hierarchy.

- **Certutil** The **certutil.exe** command-line tool includes the **–verify and –urlfetch** options, which allow you to determine the validity of an issued certificate.

The following sections provide details on using these tools to validate your CA hierarchy.

PKI Health Tool

The PKI Health Tool provides a graphical interface for troubleshooting PKI configuration issues. The tool, formerly a part of the Windows Server 2003 Resource Kit, is now included when you install the Active Directory Certificate Services Role on a computer running Windows Server 2008.

The console, shown in Figure 8-1, provides a graphical representation of each CA in the CA hierarchy. For each CA, the console tree shows the overall health for that specific CA. The details pane reports the status of each individual AIA and CDP extension supported by the specific CA.

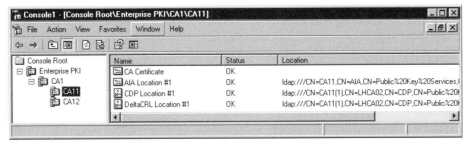

Figure 8-1   The PKI Health Tool pkiview.msc)

Installing the PKI Health Tool

By default, the PKI Health Tool is installed only on Windows Server 2008 CAs. You can make the tool available on a remote server by installing the Active Directory Certificate Services Tools on the remote server by using the following procedure:

1. Log on as a member of the local Administrators group.

2. From Administrative Tools, open Server Manager.

3. In the console tree, click Features.

4. In the details pane, in the Features Summary section, click Add Features.

5. On the Select Features page (see Figure 8-2), in the Features list, expand Remote Server Administration Tools, expand Active Directory Certificate Services Tools, select the Certification Authority Tools check box, and then click Next.

6. On the Confirm Installation Selections page, click Install.

7. On the Installation Results page, ensure that the status is Installation Succeeded, and then click Close.

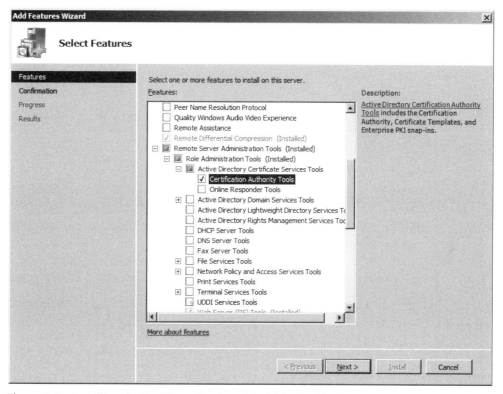

Figure 8-2   Installing the Certificate Services Administration Tools

Once the tool is installed, you can run the PKI Health Tool by running **pkiview.msc** from the Run dialog box.

> **Note**   In addition to the PKI Health Tool, the Certificate Templates console, the **certutil.exe** command-line tool, and the Certification Authority console are installed on the target computer.

Setting Global Options

When you open the PKI Health Tool, one of the first things you should do is configure the default display options (see Figure 8-3). The PKI Health Tool options are modified by right-clicking Enterprise PKI and then clicking Options.

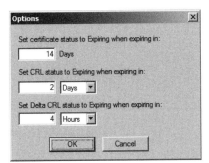

Figure 8-3   Setting PKI Health Tool options

In the options dialog box, you can set:

- **The expiring certificate indicator**   You can specify how many days before expiration of a certificate that the PKI Health Tool will indicate that a certificate is expiring. Consider using a much larger number than the default of 14 days. In fact, if you plan to issue certificates with a one-year validity period, you should use a notification of 365 days.

> **Note**   Remember that a CA cannot issue certificates beyond its remaining lifetime. If you left the default of 14 days, you could be issuing certificates with a 14-day validity period when you thought they would have a 1-year validity period.

- **The base CRL expiration indicator**   The base CRL indicator should be set to a value that reflects the base CRL publication interval. If you publish the base CRL at a weekly interval, consider keeping the default expiration interval of two days. If you publish the base CRL on a daily interval, consider a value of eight hours.

- **The delta CRL expiration indicator**   Like the base CRL setting, you must choose a delta CRL interval that reflects your delta CRL publication. If you publish a delta CRL every day, the default of every four hours may be the right value for you. If you publish the delta CRL every eight hours, consider a value of two hours for expiration notification.

Determining CA Certificate and CRL Access

The PKI Health Tool displays different icons to assist you in determining the health of each CA in the CA Hierarchy. The CA hierarchy shown in Figure 8-4 is an example of a poorly configured CA hierarchy.

The CA hierarchy displayed in the PKI Health Tool is built by enumerating the CAs by using the ICertConfig application programming interface (API). The CryptoAPI version 2 is then used to build the certificate chains.

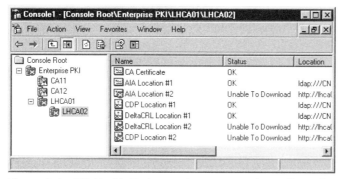

Figure 8-4   PKI Health Tool reporting on a poorly configured CA hierarchy

When you select a specific CA in the console tree, the details pane shows the expiration status of the CA certificate, the validation status of the certificate chain, the status and validity of each CA certificate in the AIA store, and the status and validity of each CRL in the CDP store. If an error is detected within the AIA or CDP stores, the PKI Health Tool will display different icons to describe the health state in the console tree:

- When the CA is being evaluated by the PKI Health Tool, a question mark appears over the CA icon in the console tree until the evaluation is complete.

- If, after the evaluation, a CA is in good working order, a green indicator appears over the CA icon.

- If a CA has a noncritical problem, such as when the CA certificate is entering the expiration notification window, a yellow indicator appears over the CA icon.

- If a CA has a critical error, a red indicator appears over the CA icon. A common example of a critical error is a CRL that has expired or an incorrect URL provided for a CDP or AIA location.

- If the CA cannot be contacted, a red X appears over the CA icon, and a CA Is Offline message appears in the details pane.

In addition, the details pane displays a message providing more details on the error. For each AIA and CDP URL, a status code appears regarding the status of that specific URL. The status codes include:

- **OK**   The CA certificate or CRL at the referenced URL is valid.

- **Expiring**   The CA certificate or CRL at the referenced URL is within the expiration period specified in the PKI Health Tool options.

- **Expired**   The CA certificate or CRL at the referenced URL is expired.

- **Unable to download**   The CA certificate or CRL could not be downloaded from the referenced URL.

For example, as shown previously in Figure 8-4, the selected LHCA02 server is in a critical condition because of the three Unable To Download errors reported for the HTTP AIA and CDP locations.

> **Note**   The PKI Health Tool determines the AIA and CRL distribution point locations for the offline CAs by inspecting the certificates issued by the offline CAs. For online CAs, the AIA and CDP locations are gathered by contacting the CA directly. This is a change in behavior from the Windows Server 2003 version of the PKI Health Tool. The Windows Server 2003 version inspected the most recent CA Exchange certificate to determine the AIA and CDP points for an issuing CA. This could lead to incorrect URL determination if the certificate was not deleted after changing an issuing CA's configuration.

The main goal is to ensure that there are *no* errors reported by the PKI Health Tool before you start issuing certificates to users, computers, and services on the network. If errors exist, the fixes can be easy, or they can be difficult.

What Do I Do if There Are Errors?

The measures that you take are entirely dependent on the errors reported by the PKI Health Tool. The actions can range from copying an updated CA certificate or CRL to the publication point to tearing down CAs and rebuilding.

The key is *where* the error is reported in the CA hierarchy. If the error is for an issuing CA, the fix is relatively simple. Fix the configuration issue, restart Certificate Services, and reissue any certificates that have the incorrect URLs in the certificates. If the error is for a root or policy CA, you will probably be required to redeploy all subordinate CAs below the incorrectly configured CA.

The actual remedy will depend on the actual cause of the error in the PKI Health Tool. For example, a configuration issue will take more effort to fix than a missing file at a publication point.

Examining Active Directory Certificate Stores

In addition to validating the status of your CA hierarchy, the PKI Health Tool provides a convenient way of examining each of the Active Directory certificate and CRL stores. The Manage AD Containers dialog box (shown in Figure 8-5) is viewed by right-clicking Enterprise PKI and then clicking Manage AD Containers.

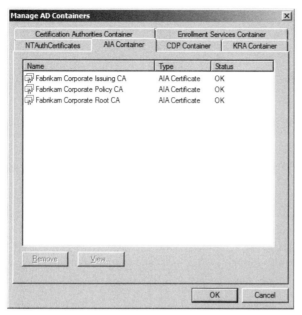

Figure 8-5 Managing AD Containers by using the PKI Health Tool

In the Manage AD Containers dialog box, you can view the contents of the following containers in the configuration naming context:

- **Certification Authorities Container**   Contains the CA certificates of all root CAs in your organization. The actual container is CN=Certification Authorities,CN=Public Key Services,CN=Services,CN=Configuration,*LDAPForestName* (where *LDAPForestName* is the Lightweight Directory Access Protocol [LDAP] distinguished name of your forest root domain).

- **Enrollment Services Container**   Contains all enterprise CA certificates for your organization. The actual container is CN=Enrollment Services,CN=Public Key Services, CN=Services,CN=Configuration,*LDAPForestName*.

- **KRA Container**   Contains all Key Recovery Agent (KRA) certificates published to Active Directory Domain Services (AD DS) that are available for key archival operations on enterprise CAs. The actual container is CN=KRA,CN=Public Key Services,CN= Services,CN=Configuration,*LDAPForestName*.

- **CDP Container**   Contains all base and delta CRLs for each CA in the CA hierarchy that publishes revocation information to AD DS. For each CA, a separate container is created, and all base and delta CRLs for that CA are located in that CA's container. For a CA named FABINCCA01, the actual container where the CRLs are stored is CN=*CANetBIOSName*,CN=KRA,CN=Public Key Services,CN=Services,CN= Configuration,*LDAPForestName* (where *CANetBIOSName* is the NetBIOS name of the CA computer account).

■ **AIA Container**   Contains all CA certificates for all CAs in the CA hierarchy. The actual container is CN=AIA,CN=Public Key Services,CN=Services,CN=Configuration, *LDAPForestName*.

> **Note**   A root CA certificate is published in both the Certification Authorities container and the AIA container.

■ **NTAuthCertificates**   The NT Authority certificate object contains all entries for all CAs that can issue certificates used for smart card authentication and for Remote Authentication Dial-In User Service (RADIUS) authentication. The NTAuthCertificates object is stored in AD DS as CN=NTAuthCertificates,CN=Public Key Services,CN= Services,CN=Configuration,*LDAPForestName*.

The Manage AD Containers dialog box can be used to examine the certificates and CRL published into AD DS, remove old certificates and CRLs from decommissioned CAs, and add NTAuth certificates into AD DS.

Certutil

A second tool that can be used to validate your CA hierarchy is the **certutil** command-line tool. Certutil.exe, included in the Active Directory Certificate Services Tools, allows a PKI administrator to manage a PKI from the command line. The specific commands that are used to validate the CA hierarchy are:

■ **Certutil –verify –urlfetch** allows you to check the validity of a specific certificate.

■ **Certutil –viewstore** allows you to determine whether a specific certificate is available in an Active Directory store.

The next sections will detail the specifics on each command and provide information on interpreting the output.

Checking the Validity of a Specific Certificate

One of the abilities of **certutil.exe** is to verify the validity of a given certificate through certificate chaining and CRL retrieval. By using the command **certutil –verify –urlfetch** *CertificateFileName*, you can verify the ability to retrieve CA certificates and CRLs for the entire certificate chain of the *CertificateFileName* file.

For example, if you were to verify the certificate brian.cer by typing **certutil –verify –urlfetch brian.cer**, the output would fetch each CDP and AIA URL in the certificate and report on the status of the URL.

Note   The **–urlfetch** option is the key entry. If you do not include the **–urlfetch** option, the chaining engine will use cached versions of CA certificates and CRLs. The **–urlfetch** option forces the client to download the CA certificates and CRLs from every defined AIA and CDP URL.

Certutil Success Examples   When you look at the output of the **certutil –verify –urlfetch** command, the output reports on every URL in every certificate in the certificate chain, from the examined certificate to the certificate chain's root CA.

If an LDAP URL is valid for a base CRL, the output appears like this:

```
Verified "Base CRL (36)" Time: 0

    [1.0] ldap:///CN=Fabrikam%20%Issuing%20CA,CN=IssuingCA,
CN=CDP,CN=Public%20Key%20Services,CN=Services,CN=Configuration,
DC=fabrikam,DC=com?certificateRevocationList?base?objectClass=
cRLDistributionPoint
```

Likewise, a validated HTTP URL for a base CRL appears like this:

```
Verified "Base CRL (36)" Time: 0
[0.0] http://www.fabrikam.com/CertData/Fabrikam%20Issuing%20CA.crl
```

Certutil Failure Examples   When the **certutil –verify –urlfetch** command fails to connect to one of the referenced URLs, the output will indicate the reason for the failure. For example, if the base CRL is unavailable at the defined location, **certutil** reports the following error:

```
Failed "CDP" Time: 0
  Error retrieving URL: Error 0x800701f6 (WIN32: 502)
  http://www.fabrikam.com/CertEnroll/Fabrikam%20Issuing%20CA.crl
```

A variation on this error could be an incorrectly typed URL or a URL location that is behind a firewall and not accessible to the computer performing the validation check. For example, if the person configuring the CA mistyped *fabrikam*.com as *fabirkam*.com (reversing the "r" and the "i"), the following error is reported:

```
    Error retrieving URL: The server name or address could not be resolved 0x80072ee7
(WIN32: 12007)
    http://www.fabirkam.com/CertEnroll/Fabrikam%20Issuing%20CA.crl
```

Finally, if **certutil** is able to build a chain, but it terminates in a non-trusted root, the output will report the following errors:

```
ChainContext.dwErrorStatus = CERT_TRUST_IS_UNTRUSTED_ROOT (0x20)

SimpleChain.dwErrorStatus = CERT_TRUST_IS_UNTRUSTED_ROOT (0x20)
```

> **Note**   These lines are *not* adjacent to each other in the output.

Certutil also provides a summary revocation status at the end of the output. In the following example, for one of the CA certificates, all of the CRL locations were unavailable or out of date, preventing successful validation of revocation status:

```
ERROR: Verifying leaf certificate revocation status returned. The revocation function was
unable to check revocation because the revocation server was offline. 0x80092013 (-2146885613)
CertUtil: The revocation function was unable to check revocation because the revocation
server was offline.
```

Viewing a Certificate Store

You can also use **certutil** to view the contents of a specific Active Directory Domain Services (AD DS) store or object. The command used is:

```
certutil -viewstore ObjectName
```

You can choose to view all certificates within a specific store. For example, to view all designated CA certificates published in the AIA container for the Fabrikam.com forest, you would use the following command:

```
certutil -viewstore "CN=AIA,CN=Public Key Services,CN=Services,CN=Configuration,
DC=Fabrikam,DC=com?cACertificate?one? objectClass=certificationAuthority"
```

The command will generate the dialog box (shown in Figure 8-6) that shows the root, policy, and issuing CA certificates. If any of the CA certificates were renewed, additional certificates would appear in the dialog box.

Figure 8-6   Viewing the AIA container by running **certutil –viewstore**

A similar command is used to view all of the CA certificates in the Certification Authorities container.

```
certutil -viewstore "CN=Certification Authorities,CN=Public Key Services,CN=Services,
CN=Configuration,DC=Fabrikam,DC=com?cACertificate?one? objectClass=certificationAuthority"
```

The command varies slightly when you view the NTAuthCertificates object. Because you are now viewing an object rather than the contents of an AD DS container, you do not add the object class data at the end of the command.

```
certutil -viewstore "CN=Certification Authorities,CN=Public Key Services,CN=Services,
CN=Configuration,DC=Fabrikam,DC=com"
```

A different **certutil** command option is required if you are inspecting the CDP container. You must:

- Use **certutil** with the **–store –enterprise** option flags.
- You must designate both the name if the issuing CA and the NetBIOS name of the CA computer account in the LDAP path. You must include the LDAP distinguished name of the CRL to view the CRL.
- The CRL object must be designated by adding **?certificateRevocationList?base?object-Class=cRLDistributionPoint** after the LDAP URL.

So to view the CRL for the Fabrikam root CA (FABINCCA01) named Fabrikam Corporate Root CA, you must use the following command:

```
certutil -store –enterprise "LDAP:///CN=Fabrikam Corporate Root CA,CN=FABINCCA01,CN=CDP,
CN=Public Key Services,CN=Services,CN=Configuration,DC=Fabrikam,DC=com?certificateRevocation
List?base?objectClass=cRLDistributionPoint"
```

The output will appear in the command prompt. For example, the output to the previous query would result in the following output:

```
================ CRL 0 ================
Issuer:
    CN=Fabrikam Corporate Root CA
    O=Fabrikam Inc.
    C=US
CA Version: V0.0
CRL Number: CRL Number=2
CRL Hash(sha1): 80 83 86 68 44 1e 3a 46 f5 12 13 1e 3d 63 f9 5b 67 9c 89 94
CertUtil: -store command completed successfully.
```

Ongoing Monitoring

Once you have deployed your PKI, you should monitor the CAs to ensure that they are continuing to operate in the expected manner. This section of the chapter looks at using both a custom script and the new Certificate Services Management Pack for Systems Center Operations Manager 2007.

CAMonitor.vbs Script

Microsoft has developed a CA monitoring script that allows an organization to monitor issuing CAs for critical issues. The script identifies critical issues before they cause failures in applications dependent on certificates.

> **Note**   The CA Monitor script is available for download at *http://www.microsoft.com/technet/ scriptcenter/solutions/camon.mspx*. A copy is also included on the companion CD.

The script works by creating events in the Windows Application log. In addition, the tool can send Simple Mail Transfer Protocol (SMTP) e-mail messages to configured distribution lists or e-mail aliases.

CA Monitoring Options

The CA monitoring script monitors for the following options:

- Verifies that the CA's Distributed Component Object Model (DCOM) interfaces are responding to requests submitted to the CA. If the DCOM interfaces are down, the CA cannot respond to client requests.

- Verifies that the CA's certificate is valid. This option tests the validity of the CA's entire certificate chain. If any certificate in the chain is invalid, an event is recorded in the event log. Optionally, an e-mail message can be distributed by using SMTP.

- Verifies that all CRL information for the CA's certificate chain is accessible and time valid. If a CRL is time invalid or not available, an event is recorded and distributed.

- Verifies that all Key Recovery Agent (KRA) certificates implemented at the CA are valid (not revoked or expired). If a KRA certificate is not valid, the CA is unable to issue any encryption certificates that enable key archival.

CA Monitor Notification Options

The CA monitoring script allows you to designate the notification options that are enabled. The available options include:

- Enabling or disabling event logging to the Windows Application log.

- Enabling or disabling SMTP or e-mail alerts.

- Specifying an SMTP mailing list. This designates the recipients of the SMTP alerts.

- Designating the SMTP server where the SMTP events are sent. The SMTP server must enable anonymous SMTP relays for the CA if the target e-mail addresses are not hosted on the designated SMTP server.

> **Tip**   Another option is to enable the local SMTP service on the CA computer but lock it down so that only the local host (127.0.0.1) is allowed to relay SMTP messages. This is more secure than enabling an anonymous SMTP relay on a separate server.

CA Monitoring Events to Include in an Event Monitoring Package

If you implement an event monitoring solution, such as Systems Center Operations Manager 2007, you can have the event monitor look for the occurrence of the events recorded by the CA monitoring script. The events are described in Table 8-1.

Table 8-1   CA Monitoring Script Events

Event ID	Event name	Description
1	Certificate Services service client remote procedure call (RPC) interface offline.	The Certificate Server is unable to receive client certificate request connection attempts.
2	Certificate Services service administration RPC interface offline.	The Certificate Server is unable to receive CA administration connection attempts, such as running the Certification Authority console on a remote computer.
10	CA Certificate expired.	The CA's certificate is no longer time valid.
11	CA Certificate remaining validity is less than one month.	The CA's certificate expiration date is within one month of the current date and time.
12	CA Certificate remaining validity is less than half its lifetime.	The CA's certificate expiration date is within one-half of the certificate's lifetime. Best practices recommend that the CA certificate renewal should be renewed at this point with a new key pair.
13	CA Certificate has been revoked.	The CA's certificate has been revoked by the parent CA.
20	CRL expired.	The CA's CRL is available at the CRL publication points, but it is now expired. This can indicate a failure in a CRL publication script or a missed CRL publication for an offline CA.

Table 8-1 CA Monitoring Script Events

Event ID	Event name	Description
21	CRL overdue.	The CA's CRL still has not yet expired, but the next update of the CRL has failed. CRL expiration is imminent. This is a critical error that could indicate failure of a hardware security module (HSM) or failure of Certificate Services.
22	CRL cannot be retrieved from AD DS.	The CA's CRL is not available in AD DS. The publication of the CRL has failed, and an expired version is not available.
23	CRL cannot be retrieved from Web server.	The CA's CRL is not available at the Web publication point. This could indicate a problem with the Web server itself because no expired CRL exists.
30	KRA Certificate expired.	A KRA certificate enabled at the CA is no longer time valid. Certificate requests that require key archival will fail.
31	KRA Certificate remaining validity is less than one month.	A KRA certificate enabled at the CA is within one month of expiration and should be renewed before its expiration.
32	KRA Certificate has been revoked.	A KRA certificate enabled at the CA has been revoked.
33	KRA Certificate is not trusted.	A KRA certificate enabled at the CA chains to a nontrusted root CA.

Note Even if a CA has multiple KRA certificates specified in its configuration, a single failed KRA certificate will prevent a CA from issuing *any* certificate that enables key archival. More details on KRA certificates are discussed in Chapter 18, "Archiving Encryption Keys."

Implementing the CA Monitoring Script

It is recommended to run the CA monitoring script in a manner that shadows the CRL publication implemented by the CA. If the CRL is published every eight hours, the CA monitoring script should also be executed every eight hours by using a scheduled task. The script should be executed at least 30 minutes after the execution of the CRL publication script to ensure that the CRLs are replicated successfully to the CRL distribution points.

It is recommended to implement a scheduled task at each issuing CA that executes a batch file with the following command line:

```
cscript camonitor.vbs /CAAlive /CACertOK /CACRLOK /KRAOK /SMTP /SMTPServer:mailDNS
/SMTPTo:CAManagementDL
```

where *mailDNS* is the Domain Name System (DNS) name of the SMTP server and *CAManagementDL* is a distribution list containing the e-mail addresses of all people who should receive the SMTP alerts.

> **Important**   The account that runs the script must be assigned the Manage CA permissions at the CA computer.

There really is no point running the CA monitoring script on an offline CA because the computer is not attached to the network, so therefore, the script cannot send any alerts to administrators.

Microsoft Operations Manager Certificate Services Management Pack

The Certificate Services Management Pack for System Center Operations Manager 2007 allows proactive monitoring of a computer holding the Active Directory Certificate Services role. The monitoring includes details on the Certificate Services role services, including certification authority, online responder, and network device enrollment services.

What's Included in the Certificate Services Management Pack

The Certificate Services management pack provides predefined processing rules and guidance for monitoring the performance and availability of Active Directory Certificate Services. Details are provided for the Certification Authority, Online Responder, and Network Device Enrollment Services role services.

The management pack includes:

- Event rules that generate either error or warning alerts for events that track the availability of Certificate Services.

- Performance rules that generate both performance charts and alerts for Certificate Services when counters reach critical levels.

> **Note**   The Certificate Services management pack adds 10 new Certification Authority counters, 8 new OCSP ISAPI counters, and 7 OCSP Server counters.

- Guidance specific to each event and performance rule that is generated by the management pack.

Operations Manager 2007 Computer Groups

Once installed in Operations Manager 2007, the following three new elements are introduced under the Computer Groups node:

- Windows Server 2008 Active Directory Certificate Services Certification Authorities. Contains all Operations Manager clients that meet the following search criteria:

```
AttributeValue(CertSrv Configuration Reg Key)AND MatchWildCard(AttributeValue
(Windows Current Version), "6.*")
```

- Windows Server 2008 Active Directory Certificate Services Online Responders. Contains all Operations Manager clients that meet the following search criteria:

  ```
  AttributeValue(OCSPSvc Reg Key)AND MatchWildCard(AttributeValue(Windows Current
  Version), "6.*")
  ```

- Windows Server 2008 Active Directory Certificate Services Network Device Enrollment Services. Contains all Operations Manager clients that meet the following search criteria:

  ```
  AttributeValue(MSCEP Reg Key)AND MatchWildCard(AttributeValue(Windows Current Version)
  , "6.*")
  ```

Certificate Services Management Pack Rule Groups and Rules

The Certificate Services management pack introduces a new folder under the Rule Groups named Active Directory Certificate Services 2008. Separate rules are provided for the Certification Authority, Online Responder, and Network Device Enrollment Services role services. Within each rule set, sub-rules are defined that provide details on subcomponents within a role service. For example, the Certification Authority rules provide individual rules on the CA database, CA service startup, and CA service status.

For each event rule, the Alert tab is configured to generate an alert with a predefined alert severity setting. The two possible alert severity levels are as follows:

- An *Error* event indicates a potential service outage or other critical system state that can prevent the use of the role service.

- A *Warning* event indicates that a potential future service outage or that quality of a service has deteriorated resulting in a loss of functionality.

For each rule, the Response tab is left blank, allowing the customer to designate the alert action that takes place if the rule is activated.

> **Note**   In addition, alert suppression is configured for each rule to prevent duplicate alerts from being recorded for domains and computers to prevent flooding of alerts for the same issue.

Using Views in Systems Center Operations Manager 2007

The Certificate Services management pack provides different views to allow a PKI administrator to quickly view the state of Certificate Services. Table 8-2 outlines the different categories of views available for PKI management.

Table 8-2   **Certificate Services Management Pack Views**

Category	Available views
Event Views	Windows Server 2008 Active Directory Certificate Services (folder)
	■ PKI Events (view)
	Certification Authorities (folder)
	■ CA Events (view)
	■ Network Device Enrollment Servers (folder)
	■ MSCEP Events (view)
	Online Responders (folder)
	■ OCSP Events (view)
Alert Views	Windows Server 2008 Active Directory Certificate Services (folder)
	■ PKI Alerts (view)
	Certificate Authorities (folder)
	■ CA Alerts (view)
	Network Device Enrollment Servers (folder)
	■ MSCEP Alerts (view)
	Online Responders (folder)
	■ OCSP Alerts(view)
State Views	Windows Server 2008 Active Directory Certificate Services (folder)
	■ PKI State (view)
	Certificate Authorities (folder)
	■ CA State (view)
	Network Device Enrollment Servers (folder)
	■ MSCEP State (view)
	Online Responders (folder)
	■ OCSP State (view)
Performance Views	■ PKI Performance
	■ CA Performance Data
	■ OCSP Performance Data

Note   For each view, the PKI Events/PKI Alerts/PKI States provides information from all Certificate Services role services: certification authorities, online responders, and NDES servers.

Deploying the Management Pack

To deploy the Certificate Services management pack, the following steps must be completed:

1. Using Systems Center Operations Manager 2007, configure firewall rules on each computer to be monitored.

2. Using Systems Center Operations Manager 2007, install the Operations Manager Agent on each computer to be monitored.

3. Using Systems Center Operations Manager 2007, import the Active Directory Certificate Services Management Pack in the administrative console.

4. Verify the monitoring configuration.

Configuring Firewall Rules   The Windows Firewall on management computers must be configured to allow communications from the Operations Manager server to the managed client. The following inbound rules must be enabled:

- TCP 135

- TCP and UDP 445

- TCP and UDP 1270

- TCP and UDP 137

- TCP and UDP 139

In addition, a firewall exception must be configured to allow the Operations Manager agent to communicate with the Systems Center Operations Manager 2007 server:

```
%Systemdrive%\A286B00A-C3DE-414F-A96A-2BD238948D88\MsMgmtAuxiliary.exe
```

Installing the Operations Manager Agent   After the firewall exceptions are configured on the managed client, the Operations Manager agent can be installed. The Operations Manager agent can be installed using the Operations Manager Administrator console's Install/Uninstall Agents wizard or installed manually at the managed client. In either case, the account performing the installation must be a member of the local Administrators group.

The installation requires the designation of a Operation Manager Agent Action account. To deploy the Operations Manager agent using the concept of least privilege, the account must have the following privileges:

- Member of the Local Users Group

- Member of the Local Performance Monitor Users group

- Manage auditing and security log privilege (SeSecurityPrivilege)

- Allow log on locally logon right (SeInteractiveLogonRight)

Importing the Management Pack   The Active Directory Certificate Services Management Pack is imported using the Operations Manager Administrator console. The .akm file is installed by right-clicking the Management Packs node in the console tree and running the Import/Export Management Packs Wizard.

Verifying Communications   After allowing the managed computers to establish initial communications computer running Systems Center Operations Manager 2007, you can view the status of the managed computers with the following procedure:

1. Open the Operations Manager Administrator console.

2. In the console tree, expand Administration, expand Computers, and then click Agent-Managed Computers.

3. In the details pane, view the Last Contacted column for each Certificate Services–managed computer.

4. Ensure that the Last Contacted column reports a time within the last five minutes.

Operations

Once you have deployed the Active Directory Certificate Services management pack, you must regularly review the alerts generated by the managed clients. Depending on your administrative duties, you can view PKI Alerts to view all alerts or look at specific alerts (Certification Authority, Online Responder, or Network Device Enrollment Services).

If an alert exists, look at the guidance provided for the alert, and act on the guidance.

Other Events to Monitor

In addition to the events monitored by the Certificate Services management pack for Systems Center Operations Manager 2007, there are other events that should be manually included in your confirmation. These events include:

- The events recorded by the CA monitoring script, discussed previously in Table 8-1.

- The events recorded by the audit configuration of the Certification Authority. There may be security events recorded to the Windows Security event log that are of interest and need to be acted upon.

To ensure that these actions are recorded in the CA's security event log, the CA must have both success and failure access enabled for object access. In addition, all check boxes on the Certification Authority's Auditing tab (see Figure 8-7) must be selected.

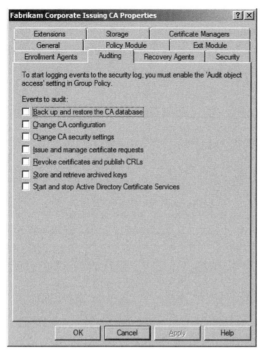

Figure 8-7   Available auditing options for a certification authority

Table 8-3 provides details on the events of interest that could appear when auditing is enabled for Certificate Services.

Table 8-3   CA Auditing Security Events

Event ID	Event description
772	The certificate manager denied a pending certificate request.
773	Certificate Services received a resubmitted pending certificate request.
774	Certificate Services revoked a certificate.
775	Certificate Services received a request to publish the CRL.
776	Certificate Services published the CRL.
777	A certificate request extension changed.
778	One or more certificate request attributes changed.
779	Certificate Services received a request to shut down.
780	Certificate Services backup started.
781	Certificate Services backup completed.
782	Certificate Services restore started.
783	Certificate Services restore completed.
784	Certificate Services started.
785	Certificate Services stopped.
786	Security permissions for Certificate Services changed.
787	Certificate Services retrieved an archived key.

Table 8-3   CA Auditing Security Events

Event ID	Event description
788	Certificate Services imported a certificate into its database.
789	The audit filter for Certificate Services changed.
790	Certificate Services received a certificate request.
791	Certificate Services approved a certificate request and issued a certificate.
792	Certificate Services denied a certificate request.
793	Certificate Services set the status of a certificate request to pending.
794	The certificate manager settings for Certificate Services changed.
795	A configuration entry changed in Certificate Services.
796	A property of Certificate Services changed.
797	Certificate Services archived a key.
798	Certificate Services imported and archived a key.
799	Certificate Services published the CA certificate to AD DS.
800	One or more rows have been deleted from the certificate database.
801	Role separation enforcement is enabled or disabled.

Case Study: Verifying a PKI Deployment

This case study will provide a review of verifying and monitoring a PKI deployment.

CA Hierarchy Details

You have just completed deploying the CA hierarchy for Fabrikam, Inc. Fabrikam implemented a three-tier CA hierarchy, as shown in Figure 8-8.

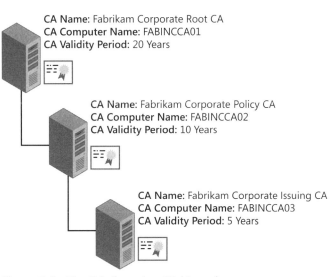

CA Name: Fabrikam Corporate Root CA
CA Computer Name: FABINCCA01
CA Validity Period: 20 Years

CA Name: Fabrikam Corporate Policy CA
CA Computer Name: FABINCCA02
CA Validity Period: 10 Years

CA Name: Fabrikam Corporate Issuing CA
CA Computer Name: FABINCCA03
CA Validity Period: 5 Years

Figure 8-8   The Fabrikam, Inc. CA hierarchy

Although the installation is complete, you have discovered that the CA hierarchy has an issue (see Figure 8-9) when you run the PKI Health Tool.

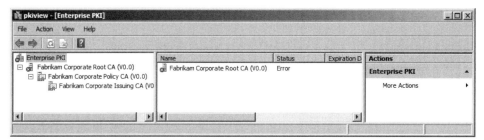

Figure 8-9   The PKI Health Tool for Fabrikam, Inc.

CA Hierarchy Verification Questions

1. Based on the PKI Health Tool display shown previously in Figure 8-9, which CA is incorrectly configured?

2. Figure 8-10 shows the details for the Fabrikam Corporate Root CA. Is the problem with an AIA or a CDP URL?

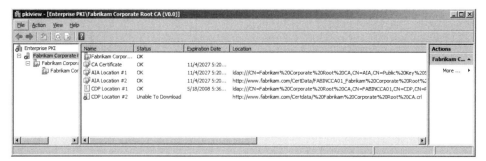

Figure 8-10   The PKI Health Tool details for the Fabrikam Corporate Root CA

3. What is wrong with the HTTP CDP URL?

4. Will this error prevent revocation checking from working for the Fabrikam CA hierarchy?

5. Which CA must be reconfigured to fix the error?

6. Assume that the root CA computer's post-configuration file contains the following line. What is wrong with the syntax of the line?

```
certutil -setreg CA\CRLPublicationURLs "1:%windir%\system32\CertSrv\CertEnroll\
%%3%%8%%9.crl \n10:ldap:///CN=%%7%%8,CN=%%2,CN=CDP,CN=Public Key Services,
CN=Services, %%6%%10\n2:http://www.fabrikam.com/CertData/  %%3%%8%%9.crl "
```

7. After the error is fixed, is there any further reconfiguration required?

Monitoring Requirements

Once the installation is verified and fixed, you must meet the following monitoring requirements:

- The organization does *not* use Systems Center Operations Manager 2007, nor do they intend to deploy Systems Center Operations Manager 2007 in the near future. They use a third-party monitoring product and wish to monitor Certificate Services with the existing monitoring package.

- Monitoring must report any operational issues with the CA hierarchy every day at 07:00 and 19:00 to provide information on issues twice a day.

- All Certification Authority auditing events must be enabled at the issuing CA.

Monitoring Questions

1. Can you use the Active Directory Certificate Services management pack with a third-party monitoring package?

2. How would you report on operational issues every day at 07:00 and 19:00?

3. What command would you execute to provide all monitoring tests and send the e-mail notification to PKIAdmins@fabrikam.com?

4. Are there any requirements for the SMTP Server designated in the monitoring scheduled task?

5. The Fabrikam Corporate Issuing CA's auditing configuration matches the settings shown previously in Figure 8-7, but none of the events described previously in Table 8-3 is reported in the Windows Security log. You know there are configuration issues, but no errors are reported. Why?

6. One morning your third-party monitoring software indicates that an Event ID 30 was recorded by the CAMonitor.vbs script at the Fabrikam Corporate Issuing CA. The CA is no longer able to issue custom EFS encryption certificates. What must be done to fix the problem?

7. A code-signing certificate issued last week was supposed to be valid for three years but is valid for only two years and five months. If you look back at the Fabrikam Corporate Issuing CA's application log, what event should you find that explains why the certificate is issued with a truncated validity period?

Additional Information

- "Best Practices for Implementing a Microsoft Windows Server 2003 Public Key Infrastructure" (*http://technet2.microsoft.com/windowsserver/en/library/091cda67-79ec-481d-8a96-03e0be7374ed1033.mspx?mfr=true*)

- "Certificate Revocation and Status Checking" (*http://technet.microsoft.com/en-us/library/bb457027.aspx*)

- "Active Directory Certificate Server Enhancements in Windows Server Code Name 'Longhorn'" (*http://www.microsoft.com/downloads/details.aspx?familyid=9bf17231-d832-4ff9-8fb8-0539ba21ab95&displaylang=en*)

- "Microsoft Operations Manager 2005 Operations Guide" (*http://go.microsoft.com/fwlink/?LinkId=33536*)

- "Managing a Windows Server 2003 Public Key Infrastructure" (*http://www.microsoft.com/technet/prodtechnol/windowsserver2003/technologies/security/mngpki.mspx*)

- Certification Authority Monitoring script (*http://www.microsoft.com/technet/scriptcenter/solutions/camon.mspx*)

Chapter 9
Securing a CA Hierarchy

A certification authority (CA) hierarchy is only as secure as the security measures that an organization takes to protect the CAs in the hierarchy. These measures can be categorized as:

- CA configuration measures
- Physical security measures

These measures can range from limiting which security groups can log on locally at the CA console to locating the CA computer in a secured location. Your security plan must include measures to protect each CA's private key from compromise.

CA Configuration Measures

CA configuration measures refer to the security measures involving the configuration of Certificate Services or the configuration of the Windows Server 2008 operating system.

Measures you can take to configure logical security for a CA include:

- **Minimizing server roles**   If at all possible, do not combine CAs with other server roles. For example, do not make the CA a domain controller, a network policy server, and a computer running Microsoft Exchange Server. The more roles taken on by the server, the harder it is to lock down the CA to prevent attacks.

- **Locking down the CA by using the Security Configuration Wizard**   The Security Configuration Wizard analyzes the roles and services installed on the CA and locks down the operating system to ensure that all known issues with the installed roles and services are mitigated. The wizard identifies all installed roles, disables unnecessary services, implements network security (if desired), and configures registry options that secure authentication mechanisms, previously set system settings, and default audit settings.

 Note   More information on using the Security Configuration Wizard can be found in the Security Configuration Deployment guide available at *http://go.microsoft.com/fwlink/?LinkID=45185*. Although written for Windows Server 2003 Service Pack 1, the content is still relevant to Windows Server 2008.

- **Enabling all auditing options in the properties of the Certification Authority**   By enabling all auditing options for the CA, you ensure that the Windows security log will contain all relevant security events related to Certificate Services operations.

Scripting the Configuration of Auditing Settings

The command **certutil -setreg CA\AuditFilter #** (where # is the sum of the values assigned to each audit setting on the Auditing tab) allows you to define what audit options are enabled at the CA. Figure 9-1 shows the Auditing properties tab of a CA as well as the values associated with each check box on the Auditing tab.

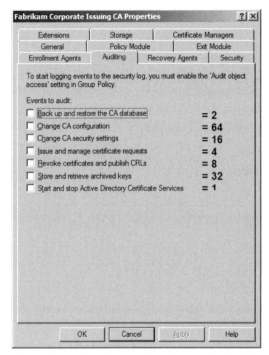

Figure 9-1   The values assigned to each check box on the Auditing tab of a CA's properties

For example, if you want to enable auditing for Backup And Restore The CA Database (2), Revoke Certificates And Publish CRLs (8), and Store And Retrieve Archived Keys (32), the sum of these options is 2+8+32, which is equal to 42. This means that to enable only these auditing options, you must run the command **certutil -setreg CA\AuditFilter 42**.

■ **Enabling BitLocker Disk Encryption**   BitLocker Disk Encryption (BDE) provides full volume encryption for the certification authority. An even more valuable benefit of it is that it protects against an attacker taking the hard disk and attempting to use the disk in another server. To best implement BDE on a CA, ensure that the CA has a Trusted Platform Module (TPM) version 1.2 chip on the motherboard. A TPM v 1.2 chip allows the protection of the Storage Root Key (SRK), which is used to decrypt the Volume Encryption Key (VEK), which protects the operating system volume.

How Does BDE Work?

BDE protects an NTFS volume through the use of two related encryption keys:

- The Volume Encryption Key (VEK) is used to encrypt the Microsoft Windows operating system volume.

- The Storage Root Key (SRK) is used to encrypt the VEK.

When the CA uses a TPM v 1.2 chip to protect the SRK, the process described in Figure 9-2 is used to decrypt the volume at boot time.

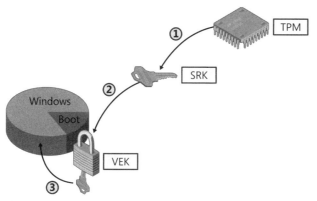

Figure 9-2   Protecting a CA hard drive with BDE

That process goes as follows:

1. The SRK is retrieved from the TPM chip.

> **Tip**   There are different methods available to secure access to the TPM chip. For an offline CA, consider implementing a personal identification number (PIN) for the TPM chip. For an issuing CA, it is better to simply protect the SRK with the TPM alone (no PIN) so that updates and patching can be performed without requiring administrator intervention to provide a PIN during reboot.

2. The encrypted VEK is accessed from the boot partition. The SRK is used to decrypt the VEK.

> **Note**   The boot partition is an unencrypted volume that contains the encrypted VEK, the master boot record (MBR), the Boot loader, and other small, unencrypted files related to the Windows boot process.

3. The VEK is used to decrypt the Windows volume, allowing the operating system to boot.

BDE is much stronger than the previous recommendation to implement BIOS startup passwords or Windows SYSKEY. The only risk you must mitigate is of losing the TPM owner's password or the BDE recovery key, so ensure that these are backed up. These files can be backed up to universal serial bus (USB) tokens for offline CAs (stored in safes) or to Active Directory Domain Services (AD DS) for issuing CAs that are domain members.

For more details on the use of BDE, see the BitLocker home page at *http://www.microsoft.com/technet/windowsvista/security/bitlockr.mspx.*

■ **Limiting membership in the local Administrators group**   If you implement the CA by using any of the software-based Microsoft cryptographic service providers (CSPs), the private key for the CA is stored in the local machine store. By default, all members of the local Administrators group can access the private key and export the private key to a PKCS #12 file. By limiting membership in the administrative groups, you can limit the number of users that could access the CA's private key.

> **Note**   Alternatively, storing the private key on a hardware security module (HSM) will prevent this type of security issue because the security mechanisms of the HSM will protect against a single local administrator gaining access to the CA's private key.

■ **Enforcing role separation**   Enforcing role separation ensures that a single person cannot hold multiple Common Criteria roles. A user can hold only one of the CA administrator, certificate manager, auditor, or backup operator roles. Assignment of two or more of these roles results in the user being blocked from *all* certificate management actions.

> **Note**   Common Criteria role separation is enforced by running **certutil –setreg CA\RoleSeparationEnabled 1** at a command prompt and then restarting Certificate Services. Remember that any user who is assigned two or more administrative roles will be blocked from all CA management activities from that point forward, unless you disable the enforcement of Common Criteria role separation by running **certutil –delreg CA\RoleSeparationEnabled** and then restarting Certificate Services.

Designing Physical Security Measures

In addition to logical security measures, you should implement several physical security measures to protect your CA computers.

■ **Store the offline CA computers in a physically secure room.**   Rather than keeping offline CA computers in the standard server room, consider storing them in a limited-access server room or in a safe. Allow only those with CA administration roles to enter the server room or open the safe, and record all attempts to access the server room. Alternatively, you could enforce physical access logs, where any access to the CA computers is logged.

- **Store the CA computers in a secured cage.**   Server cages are available that require users to enter a PIN code to open. Some models even track all attempts to access the server cage and allow retrieval of the access logs via serial connections.

- **Store offline CA-related hardware in a separate, secured location.**   Some companies remove the hard drives from the CA computers and store the hard drives in a remote safe, requiring an attacker to gain access to both the server hardware and the server drives before gaining access to an offline CA.

> **Note**   This methodology allows companies to still use the offline server computer for alternative uses when the CA is removed from the network. By installing a separate set of hard drives into the CA computer chassis, the hardware can be used for other purposes when the CA is removed from the network.

Securing the CA's Private Key

Your security measures also must protect a CA's private key. If an individual is able to obtain the CA's private key, it is possible for the user to build another CA computer with the same key pair, allowing impersonation of the CA and the ability to issue fraudulent certificates that are trusted by all users of your public key infrastructure (PKI). In the worst-case scenario, if the root CA private key is obtained, an attacker can build additional CAs that are trusted by the users and computers within your organization.

The measures you should take to protect your CA's private key depend on how the private key is stored. For a Windows Server 2008 CA, there are three possibilities:

- Store the private key in the local machine store of the CA computer.
- Store the private key on a two-factor device, such as a smart card.
- Store the private key on a hardware security module (HSM).

Private Key Stored in the Local Machine Store

If the CA's private key is stored in the local machine store of the CA computer, by default it is possible for *any* member of the local Administrators group to export the CA's private key to a PKCS #12 file. If the CA is a domain member, as is typical for online CAs, the local Administrators group of the CA computer will also include the Domain Admins group from the domain where the CA's computer account exists and could also contain the forest root domain's Enterprise Admins group. There is little you can do to protect a CA against these default groups.

> **Tip**   The main area of concern should be custom groups added to the local Administrators group. With one customer, we encountered an issuing CA where 265 individuals were local administrators because of nested group memberships.

The only way to protect the private key in this scenario is to attempt to limit membership in the local Administrators group. In addition, if your organization uses imaging software for server installations, changing the default Administrator account name and password from the default stored in the server image is recommended. This protects against access to the private key by anyone who gains knowledge of the default Administrator account name and password.

> **Warning**   Even if you implement Restricted Groups to limit membership in the local Administrators group, a member of Enterprise Admins or the domain's Domain Admins group can add his or her account to the local Administrators group. Limiting the membership of the local Administrators group ensures that the membership is initially restricted. Only by auditing membership and configuration changes can you detect if a rogue member of the Enterprise Admins or Domain Admins group is attempting to modify the security settings.

Private Keys Stored on Smart Cards

To increase the security of the private key, you can store the CA's private key on a two-factor device, such as a smart card. Moving the CA's private key to a smart card requires a CA administrator to have access to the smart card and know the smart card's PIN.

If you implement a smart card cryptographic service provider (CSP), you must select the Use Strong Private Key Protection Features Provided By The CSP check box in the Add Roles Wizard. (See Figure 9-3.) The Use Strong Private Key Protection Features Provided By The CSP option enables the display of the PIN entry dialog box for the smart card in the user's session when a machine-related private key is accessed.

You can further secure the implementation of a smart card for protecting the CA's private key by storing the CA's smart card in a secure location, such as a safe. By splitting the responsibilities of retrieving the smart card from the safe and knowing the smart card's PIN, you can ensure that at least two people are involved in starting Certificate Services at an online CA.

> **Note**   It is not recommended to implement a smart card for the CSP of an online CA, because the smart card must remain in the smart card reader of the CA computer at all times. Removing the smart card from the reader causes the computer to lose access to the private key material. This prevents Certificate Services from starting, new certificates from being issued, and updated certificate revocation lists (CRLs) from being published.

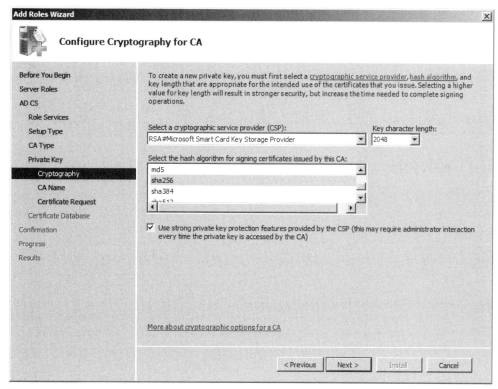

Figure 9-3   Allowing a smart card CSP to interact with the Windows desktop

Private Keys Stored on Hardware Security Modules

A hardware security module protects a CA's private key by moving all private key operations from the CA computer to a cryptographic device. The CA performs all cryptographic functions on a hardware security module (HSM), including key generation, certificate signing, and CRL signing.

Moving the key material from the CA to the HSM protects the key material from any attacks against the CA operating system. In addition, an HSM increases the protection of the private key by allowing an organization to require the involvement of several administrative personnel to access the CA's private key. For example, you can configure the HSM to require that four of nine administrators be present for an offline CA to publish an updated CRL or issue a new subordinate CA certificate. This requirement that a quorum of administrators be present is commonly referred to as an "M of N" or "K of N" scheme.

> **Note**   As with a smart card CSP, you must use strong private key protection features so that the operators of the HSM are prompted to authorize all private key usage by the HSM (during an interactive logon session).

Hardware Security Modules

Hardware security modules allow you to increase the protection of the CA's private key to meet Federal Information Processing Standard (FIPS) 140-2 level 2 and level 3 security. A FIPS 140-2 level 3 device protects the CA's private key by providing two features:

■ The cryptographic device is tamper evident. The cryptographic store within an HSM is typically coated with an epoxy layer, so that any attempts to access the cryptographic store is indicated in the epoxy layer.

■ If an attempt to compromise the cryptographic store on the HSM takes place, the data stored on the cryptographic store—namely the private key—is destroyed, which protects the private key from compromise.

> **Note**   The FIPS 140-2 document that defines the security requirements for cryptographic modules can be found at *http://csrc.nist.gov/publications/fips/fips140-2/fips1402.pdf.*

> **Note**   FIPS 140-2 level 4 devices now exist. A FIPS 140-2 level 4 device adds physical security to the HSM by providing a physical envelope of protection around the cryptographic module.

Categories of HSMs

In general, you can separate HSMs into two categories: dedicated HSMs and network-attached HSMs.

Dedicated HSMs

A dedicated HSM is directly attached to a CA through either a Small Computer System Interface (SCSI) card or a proprietary Peripheral Component Interconnect (PCI) or Peripheral Component Interconnect Extended (PCI-X) card inserted into the CA computer. (See Figure 9-4.)

CA   Dedicated HSM

Figure 9-4   A dedicated HSM

All communications with the CA computer are performed through the dedicated connection, and the private key material never leaves the protective space of the dedicated HSM. To allow communications with the HSM, a proprietary CSP must be installed on the CA computer. If required, device drivers for the PCI HSM or the PCI or PCI-X interface card must be installed also on the CA computer to allow communications between the CA computer and the HSM.

Network-Attached HSMs

Network-attached HSMs are another alternative for cryptographic security for CAs. Rather than implementing a dedicated HSM at each CA in the hierarchy, two or more CAs can share the same HSM. (See Figure 9-5.)

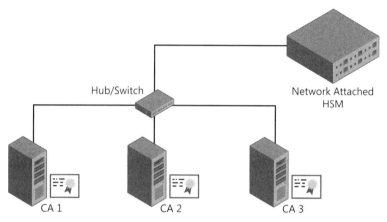

Figure 9-5   A network-attached HSM

As with a dedicated HSM, all cryptographic operations occur within the HSM, and the results are transmitted to the CA from the HSM. To protect communications between the CA and the HSM, the network channel is protected through both encryption and authorization. In other words, all communications are encrypted between the CA and the HSM. In addition, CAs authorize the HSM through unique hashes, certificates, or serial numbers and authorize the clients through certificates, IP addresses, or hashes.

You cannot implement an unlimited number of clients with a single network-attached HSM. The maximum number of client CAs is determined by the model of the network-attached HSM and the license agreement purchased by your organization.

> **Note**   The HSM and the CA computer do not have to be on the same network segment. The HSM and CA computer can be separated by routers and even firewalls as long as the required ports for communications are opened between the HSM and the CA computers.

HSM Deployment Methods

Several options exist for deploying HSMs in a CA hierarchy. This section reviews some of the more common designs and discusses the advantages and disadvantages of each design.

Dedicated HSMs on Each CA

The most basic deployment method for HSMs is to implement a dedicated HSM on each CA in the CA hierarchy. (See Figure 9-6.)

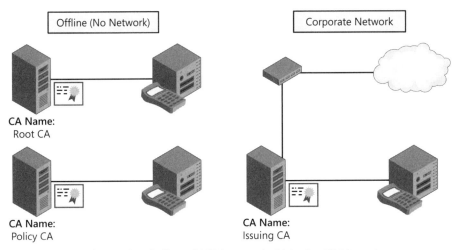

Figure 9-6   Implementing dedicated HSMs at each CA in the CA hierarchy

Implementing dedicated HSMs at each CA in the CA hierarchy allows for deployment of different FIPS 140-2 security levels at each CA. For example, if an organization's security policy requires FIPS 140-2 level 3 security for offline CAs and FIPS 140-2 level 2 security for online CAs, the required HSMs can be purchased on a CA-by-CA basis depending on the CA's role in the hierarchy.

The advantage of implementing dedicated HSMs at each CA in the CA hierarchy configuration is that each CA has its own HSM. The failure of a single HSM will affect only a single CA, not multiple CAs. The disadvantage is cost. If your hierarchy has five CAs, you are looking at purchasing at least five HSMs, one for each CA.

Note   You might require additional HSMs for redundancy. Alternatively, you could choose to share security worlds or domains between offline CAs and utilize the same HSM on each offline CA to reduce costs.

Network-Attached HSMs Shared by All CAs

With network-attached HSMs, it is now possible for an organization to deploy a single HSM for the entire network or at each location that hosts CA computers, sharing the HSM between multiple CAs. As shown previously in Figure 9-5, multiple CAs can share the network-attached HSM. Communications take place over the corporate network.

> **Note** The CAs do not have to be on the same subnet as the HSM. As long as packets are able to pass freely between the CAs and the HSM, through any routers or firewalls in between, connectivity can take place between multiple network segments.

The obvious advantage of implementing a single network-attached HSM is that you reduce the hardware costs associated with HSMs. Although you may think that a network-attached HSM is a bad idea for offline CAs because it requires them to be connected to the corporate network, there is a workaround.

Network-attached HSMs typically ship with two network interfaces. You can configure the network-attached HSM to have one network interface on a private network, where the offline CAs communicate with the network-attached HSM. The second network interface can be connected to the corporate network, allowing connectivity for all online CAs. Figure 9-7 shows this type of deployment.

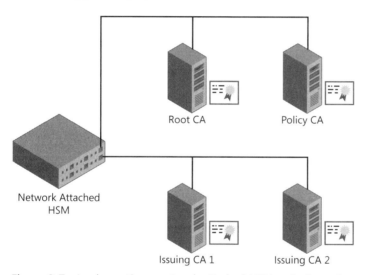

Figure 9-7 Implementing a network-attached HSM on both a private network and the corporate network

As you can see, the root CA and policy CA are not exposed to the corporate network. Network-attached HSMs do not enable routing, so traffic cannot be routed to the private network from the corporate network, allowing access to the offline CAs.

Dedicated HSMs on Offline CAs, Network-Attached HSMs on Online CAs

If an organization's security policy will not allow offline CAs to be connected to *any* network (private or corporate), you can deploy a combination of dedicated and network-attached HSMs. (See Figure 9-8.)

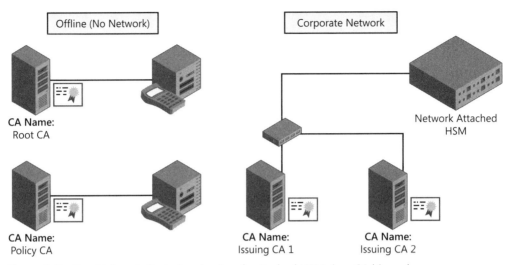

Figure 9-8   Combining dedicated and network-attached HSMs in a CA hierarchy

When you combine dedicated and network-attached HSMs, the offline CAs implement dedicated HSMs and are never attached to any form of network. The online CAs are connected to a network-attached HSM on the corporate network.

The advantage of this configuration is that physical access is required to use the offline CAs. Likewise, if an online CA is compromised, it does not allow an attacker to compromise an offline CA.

Preventing the HSM from Being a Single Point of Failure

One of the issues with deploying HSMs with the models described thus far in the chapter is that each HSM is a single point of failure. It is possible to deploy HSMs so that high availability is attained.

For dedicated HSMs, you can install an additional PCI HSM at an offline CA. The additional HSM will allow the offline CA to use either of the two internal HSMs to access the offline CA's private key.

> **Important**   This is not typically done with offline CAs. You should be able to replace a failed dedicated HSM on an offline CA with plenty of time available to publish an updated revocation list. An additional HSM would typically be used only when using dedicated HSMs for online CAs.

For network-attached HSMs, all vendors allow you to configure communications between multiple network-attached HSMs allowing operations to continue if one of the network-attached HSMs fails, as shown in Figure 9-9.

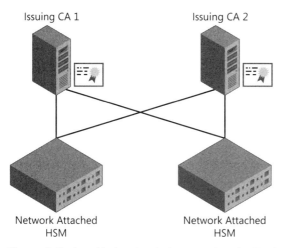

Figure 9-9   Load balancing between network-attached HSMs

In Figure 9-9, Issuing CA 1 is configured to communicate with both the local network-attached HSM and to the remote network-attached HSM. Issuing CA 1 is configured to use the local network-attached HSM as its primary HSM and the remote network-attached HSM as its secondary HSM. If either of the network-attached HSMs fail, the CA will continue to operate because it will use the functioning HSM for key operations. In a similar fashion, Issuing CA 2 will use its local network-attached HSM as its primary HSM and the remote network-attached HSM as its secondary HSM.

With most vendors, the network-attached HSMs and client software are intelligent enough to fail back to the original configuration once the failed HSM is replaced.

Choosing an HSM

At the time of the writing of this book, all HSMs are still undergoing evaluation for Windows Server 2008 certification. Table 9-1 provides details on vendors currently working with Windows Server 2003 and provides information on their dedicated and network-attached HSM solutions.

When making purchasing decisions, be sure to ask where the vendor stands with Windows Server 2008 certification, their support for Cryptography Next Generation (CNG), what FIPS 140-2 certifications their HSMs have achieved, and evaluation options for testing on your network.

Table 9-1   Windows Server 2003 HSMs

Vendor	HSM name	HSM type
SafeNet	Luna CA^3	Dedicated PCI
SafeNet	Luna SA	Network-attached
nCipher	nShield	Dedicated PCI
nCipher	netHSM	Network-attached
Utimaco	SafeGuard CryptoServer CS10	Dedicated PCI
Utimaco	SafeGuard CryptoServer CS50	Network-attached
Algorithmic Research	PrivateServer HSM	Network-attached
AEP	AEP Keyper	Network-attached

Case Study: Planning HSM Deployment

In this case study, you will plan the physical and logical security of the CAs for your organization's CA hierarchy.

Scenario

You are the security services manager for City Power and Light. Your organization has planned a three-tier CA hierarchy, shown in Figure 9-10.

The CA hierarchy implements both an offline root CA and an offline policy CA to allow flexibility in the future if City Power and Light starts to issue certificates to its customers.

To provide high availability of Certificate Services, issuing CAs are deployed at Atlanta, Georgia for the East Coast and at La Jolla, California for the West Coast. The network management model specifies separate managers for the certificates issued to infrastructure components, such as computers and network devices, and the certificates issued to City Power and Light employees.

The security policies of City Power and Light include the following:

- All CA computers in the CA hierarchy must implement FIPS 140-2 level 3 protection for the CA key material.

- The root and policy CA are maintained at the City Power and Light head office in Chicago.

- Offline CA computers must *never* be attached to the network. All interaction with the issuing CAs in the CA hierarchy must be performed through the use of removable media.

- Any operations of the offline CAs must involve the approval of three of the five network managers of City Power and Light. This includes the installation of the CA hierarchy and the issuance of subordinate CA certificates and CRLs.

- Online CAs must audit all security events at the CA except the starting and stopping of Certificate Services. For offline CAs, all security events must be audited at the CA.

- To allow ongoing issuance of certificates in the event of component failure, issuing CAs must not have a single point of failure.

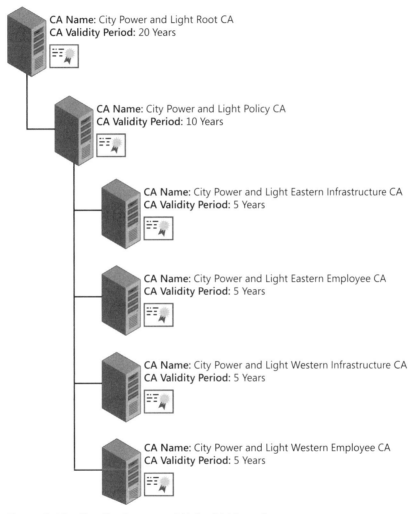

Figure 9-10   The City Power and Light CA hierarchy

Case Study Questions

1. If you were to script the configuration of auditing settings for the offline CAs, what command would you include in the script to meet the auditing requirements?

2. What command is required to meet the audit setting requirements for the online CAs?

3. Can you meet the security requirements for the CA hierarchy by implementing either a software-based CSP or a smart-card CSP? Why or why not?

4. Can you use dedicated HSMs at each CA in the hierarchy and meet the design requirements? What are the drawbacks to this approach if it is possible?

5. Can you use network-attached HSMs at each CA in the CA hierarchy and meet the design requirements? What are the drawbacks to this approach if it is possible?

6. If you wanted to implement network-attached HSMs for the issuing CAs in the CA hierarchy, how many network-attached HSMs would you recommend to City Power and Light?

Additional Information

- Microsoft Official Curriculum, Course 2821: "Designing and Managing a Windows Public Key Infrastructure" (*http://www.microsoft.com/traincert/syllabi/2821afinal.asp*)

- "Microsoft Windows Security Resource Kit" (*http://www.microsoft.com/mspress/books/6418.asp*)

- "Deploying Certificate Services on Windows 2000 and Windows Server 2003 with the Chrysalis-ITS Luna CA3 Hardware Security Module" (*http://www.microsoft.com/windows2000/techinfo/planning/chrysalis.asp*)

- "Microsoft Windows Server 2003 PKI and Deploying the nCipher nShield Hardware Security Module" (*http://www.ncipher.com/resources/downloads/files/white_papers/win2003_nshield_wp.pdf*)

- "Security Configuration Wizard Deployment Guide" (*http://go.microsoft.com/fwlink/?LinkID=45185*)

- "Windows Server 2003 PKI Operations Guide" (*http://www.microsoft.com/technet/prodtechnol/windowsserver2003/technologies/security/ws03pkog.mspx*)

- BitLocker Home Page (*http://www.microsoft.com/technet/windowsvista/security/bitlockr.mspx*)

- BitLocker Blog (*http://blogs.technet.com/bitlocker*)

- "Security Requirements for Cryptographic Modules" (*http://csrc.nist.gov/publications/fips/fips140-2/fips1402.pdf*)

- nCipher nShield Hardware Security Module (*http://www.ncipher.com/uploads/resources/nshield0806.pdf*)

- nCipher netHSM (*http://www.ncipher.com/uploads/resources/nethsm.pdf*)

- SafeNet Luna CA[3] (*http://www.safenet-inc.com/Library/3/Luna_CA3_PB.pdf*)

- SafeNet Luna SA (*http://www.safenet-inc.com/library/3/Luna_SA.pdf*)

- Utimaco SafeGuard CryptoServer CS10 (*http://americas.utimaco.com/ safeguard_cryptoserver/CS10.html*)

- Utimaco SafeGuard CryptoServer CS50 (*http://americas.utimaco.com/ safeguard_cryptoserver/CS50.html*)

- Algorithmic Research PrivateServer (*http://www.arx.com/documents/ PrivateServer-Brochure.pdf*)

- AEP Keyper (*http://www.alttech.com/files/products/aep/DataSheets/Keyper_Datasheet.pdf*)

Chapter 10
Certificate Revocation

Certificate revocation is necessary when you must terminate a certificate's usage before the validity period expires. When a certificate is revoked, a certificate manager must select the certificate to revoke in the Certification Microsoft Management Console (MMC) console as well as provide a reason for revocation. The serial number of the certificate is then stored in the CA's database with a reason code specifying why the certificate was revoked, which can then be used to publish a certificate revocation list (CRL).

> **Note** To revoke a certificate, a user must be assigned the Issue and Manage Certificates permission at the certification authority (CA) that issued the certificate. In addition, if certificate manager restrictions are implemented, the certificate manager must be allowed to manage the target user or a group containing the user, and the certificate must be based on a certificate template the certificate manager is allowed to revoke for that target user or group.

When Do You Revoke Certificates?

A certificate is revoked when a certificate's use must be terminated before its validity period expires. The choice to revoke involves knowing the available revocation reasons, mapping the revocation reasons to your organization's revocation policy, and then performing the revocation.

Revocation Reasons

The following revocation reasons are available when you revoke a certificate:

- **AffiliationChanged** An individual is terminated, resigns, or dies, or the computer account to which the certificate was issued is no longer in use. This revocation reason can also be used if a person changes roles within an organization and no longer requires the use of the certificate associated with that person's previous role. For example, an employee could move from the purchasing department and no longer require a certificate used to authorize purchase requests.

- **CACompromise** You suspect that a CA's private key is compromised and potentially in the possession of an unauthorized individual. If a CA's private key is revoked, all certificates below that CA in the CA hierarchy are considered revoked.

- **CertificateHold** A temporary revocation that indicates a CA will not validate a certificate at that specific time.

> **Tip**   Although CertificateHold allows a certificate to be unrevoked, use of the CertificateHold reason code is not recommended, because it becomes difficult to determine whether a certificate was valid at a specific time.

- **CessationOfOperation**   A server or workstation is decommissioned, and all certificates issued to the server are no longer required. This revocation reason can also be used when you decommission a CA.

> **Tip**   You cannot decommission a CA if any of the certificates issued by the CA are still in use. Even if you do not plan to issue any additional certificates, the CA must still publish CRL information at regular intervals for revocation checking purposes if you plan to use the existing certificates.

- **KeyCompromise**   You suspect that the private key associated with a certificate is compromised. For example, if a laptop belonging to a user in your organization is stolen, it is quite possible that any private keys stored on the laptop are compromised.
- **RemoveFromCRL**   If you revoke a certificate by using CertificateHold, you can unrevoke the certificate. The unrevoking process still lists the certificate in the CRL, but the certificate also appears in a delta CRL with the revocation code set to RemoveFromCRL. When the next base CRL is published, the CA removes the certificate from all forms of the CRL. If delta CRLs are not implemented, the certificate is simply removed from the next base CRL.
- **Superseded**   A new certificate must be issued if an issued certificate is replaced for any reason with a new updated certificate. For example, if you update a certificate template and reissue certificates, you could revoke the previous certificate with this reason code.
- **Unspecified**   You can revoke a certificate without providing a specific revocation code. Using Unspecified is not recommended, however, because it does not provide an audit trail identifying the reason a certificate was revoked.

Revocation Policy

A certificate manager should not arbitrarily revoke certificates based on whims. Instead, the best practice is to define the organization's revocation policy. Table 10-1 describes the sections of an RFC-3647–based Certification Practice Statement that define an organization's revocation policy.

Table 10-1   Defining a Revocation Policy

Section	Section title	Description
4.9.1	Circumstances for Revocation	Describes the circumstances under which a certificate issued by the managed CA must be revoked. The section should also detail the revocation reason that is applied under the specific circumstance.
4.9.2	Who Can Request Revocation	Identifies the individuals who request the revocation processing and who perform the actual revocation request.
4.9.3	Procedure for Revocation Request	Defines the workflow that must be followed during revocation request processing.
4.9.4	Revocation Request Grace Period	States whether a lag can occur between the trigger for the revocation event and the request for revocation.
4.9.5	Time Within Which CA Must Process the Revocation Request	Specifies how much time is allowed between receipt of the revocation request and processing the revocation request.
4.9.6	Revocation Checking Requirement for Relying Parties	States whether an application must enforce strong CRL checking in cases in which certificate revocation checking is enforced each time the relying party evaluates a certificate.
4.9.7	CRL Issuance Frequency	Defines the update schedule for both base CRLs and delta CRLs.
4.9.8	Maximum Latency for CRLs	Specifies the maximum time allowed between CRL update and availability of the CRL at the specified CRL Distribution Points.
4.9.9	Online Revocation/Status Checking Availability	If Online Certificate Status Protocol (OCSP) checking is available, specifies the Uniform Resource Locators that will host the OCSP responder.
4.9.10	Online Revocation Checking Requirements	Defines requirements for configuring the OCSP responder.
4.9.11	Other Forms of Revocation Advertisements Available	States whether revocation information is available in formats other than base CRLs, delta CRLs, or OCSP responders.
4.9.12	Special Requirements re Key Compromise	Provides details on the actions that must take place when a certificate is revoked because of a key compromise.
4.9.13	Circumstances for Suspension	Specifies the circumstances under which a certificate is revoked with the Certificate Hold revocation reason code.
4.9.14	Who Can Request Suspension	Specifies who can submit a request for suspending a certificate.
4.9.15	Procedure for Suspension Request	Provides details on the workflow requirements for performing a suspension request.
4.9.16	Limits on Suspension Period	Provides details on how long a certificate can remain in a suspended state before the certificate is reinstated or permanently revoked.

Performing Revocation

To revoke a certificate, a user must be designated as a certificate manager. You designate a user as a certificate manager by assigning the user or a group containing the user the Issue and Manage Certificates permission at the issuing CA. The permission assignment is performed by a CA Administrator, which is a user assigned the Manage CA permissions. You can verify the permissions assignment by using the following process:

1.   Log on to the CA computer.

2.   From Administrative Tools, open the Certification Authority console.

3.   In the console tree, right-click *CAName* (where *CAName* is the logical name of the CA), and then click Properties.

4.   In the *CAName* Properties dialog box, select the Security tab to ensure that the user account or a group that the user is a member of is assigned the Issue and Manage Certificates permission.

> **Note**   If you want to assign a new user or security group the certificate manager role to allow them to revoke certificates, assign the user or security group the Issue and Manage Certificates permission.

Once you assign the necessary permissions, the following procedure revokes a certificate:

1.   From Administrative Tools, open the Certification Authority console.

2.   In the console tree, expand *CAName*, and then click Issued Certificates.

3.   In the details pane, find the certificate that you need to revoke, right-click the certificate, point to All Tasks, and then click Revoke Certificate.

4.   In the Certificate Revocation dialog box, in the Reason Code drop-down list, select the appropriate reason code, and then click Yes.

Methods of Identifying Revoked Certificates

The Windows Server 2008 public key infrastructure (PKI) provides three ways to determine if a certificate has been revoked:

■   **Base CRL**   Contains the serial numbers of certificates revoked by the CA that are signed with the CA's private key. If you renew a CA's certificate with a new key pair, the CA maintains two separate CRLs—one for each key pair maintained by the CA. Base CRLs are recognized by all versions of the Microsoft Windows operating system.

■   **Delta CRL**   Contains only the serial numbers of certificates revoked by the CA since the last base CRL publication. Again, if the CA's certificate is renewed with a new key pair, separate delta CRLS are maintained for each CA key pair. Delta CRLs allow you to publish revocation information quicker and allow smaller updates to be downloaded by client computers.

- **Online Certificate Status Protocol (OCSP)**   Provides a responder service that can either connect directly to a CA database or inspect the base and delta CRLs published by the CA to determine revocation status of a specific certificate.

Problems with CRLs

CRLs have historically been the primary method for determining the revocation status of a specific certificate. Although widely supported, there are some known issues with using only CRLs to determine a certificate's revocation status.

Latency

The primary issue with CRLs is that there is latency in identifying that a certificate has been revoked. Once you have revoked a certificate, the revocation is not recognized by relying parties until the next publication of a CRL. The availability is determined by the CRL publication schedule. For example, if you publish an updated base CRL at 07:00 daily, a certificate revoked at 08:00 will not be recognized as a revoked certificate until the next day's publication takes place.

Caching of CRLs

When a client computer checks the revocation status of a certificate, it first checks for the desired base CRL or delta CRL in the CryptoAPI cache. If the base CRL or delta CRL is found, the CRL is checked to determine if the CRL is time-valid. Like certificates, a CRL has a validity period specified by the CRL publication interval. If a time-valid CRL is found in the CryptoAPI cache, that version of the CRL is used for revocation checking, even if an updated version of the CRL has been published manually. The use of the cached version of the CRL is done for performance reasons, to prevent excess network traffic. In addition, the use of a cached CRL follows the recommendations in RFC 3280 to acquire an updated CRL only when the previous CRL expires.

 Warning   Microsoft does not support designs that manually delete the cached version of a CRL from the CryptoAPI cache.

 Warning   The process described here follows the definition of CRL usage described in RFC 3280, "Internet X.509 Public Key Infrastructure Certificate and Certificate Revocation List (CRL) Profile," available at *http://www.ietf.org/rfc/rfc3280.txt*.

Support for Delta CRLs

Delta CRLs provide timelier recognition of revocation by publishing a limited revocation list. Only certificates that have been revoked since the last base CRL was published are included in the delta CRL.

Delta CRLs are not supported by all versions of Windows operating systems. Initially, only Windows XP and Windows Server 2003 supported delta CRLs when the Windows Server 2003 PKI shipped. In 2004, the patch MS04-11 changed the chaining engine for Windows 2000 clients, enabling them to support the use of delta CRLs. Delta CRLs are now supported on Windows 2000, Windows XP, Windows Server 2003, Windows Vista, and Windows Server 2008.

> **Note** It is safe to assume that delta CRLs will be supported by future versions of the Windows operating system as well.

For non-Windows systems, you must read the documentation provided with the operating systems to determine whether they or applications running on those operating systems support delta CRLs.

> **Important** If you implement delta CRLs, both the associated base CRL and a time-valid delta CRL must be available to the client to perform a valid revocation check. If the base CRL is not available, the delta CRL alone cannot provide the required revocation information, and revocation checking will fail.

Online Certificate Status Protocol (OCSP)

OCSP allows more timely and structured determination of revocation status for a specific certificate. Rather than having the client download a CRL that contains all certificates revoked by the CA, the client sends a revocation status request to a responder service. The responder service provides revocation status for *just* that certificate, allowing the client to make a revocation decision based on the response.

The advantages of OCSP include:

- **More timely revocation information** An OCSP responder can be configured to either directly query the CA database to determine or download CRLs at prescribed intervals rather than the normal publication schedule. Both methods provide a more timely determination of when a certificate is revoked by the CA.

- **Known traffic patterns and sizes** The OCSP request and response packets are HTTP packets of known size. The actual number of certificates revoked by the CA is irrelevant to the requesting client. The client receives revocation status information regarding only the certificate specified in the request.

■ **A trusted response**   An OCSP response is digitally signed to allow the client to determine if the response is trustworthy. If the signature fails inspection, the response is disregarded.

Microsoft's Implementation of OCSP

Windows Server 2008 introduces Microsoft's first implementation of OCSP.

OCSP Components

The OCSP solution is composed of the components shown in Figure 10-1.

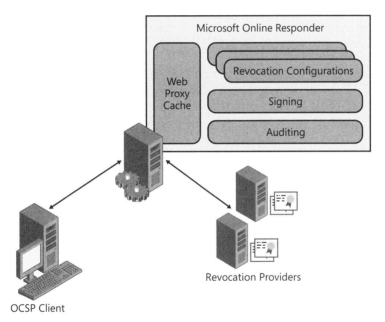

Figure 10-1   Microsoft OCSP components

■ **OCSP client**   The OCSP client, integrated with Windows Vista and Windows Server 2008, allows validation of certificates using OCSP. The OCSP client is based on RFC 5019, "The Lightweight Online Certificate Status Protocol (OCSP) Profile." An OCSP client will, by default, always use OCSP to validate the revocation status of a certificate if both OCSP and CRL information are included in the validated certificate.

Important   Windows versions prior to Windows Vista do not natively support OCSP. If you wish to use OCSP with Windows XP or Windows 2000, you must look at acquiring third-party OCSP providers, such as Tumbleweed.

Why Use Lightweight OCSP?

The specification of the OCSP profile for high-volume environments (RFC 5019) was motivated by a number of things, one of the most significant being that at the time no browser had revocation checking of server certificates enabled. This was primarily because of the fact that existing solutions were too fragile and did not perform well enough to meet the requirements of an Internet scale deployment.

When used with the TLS Extensions RFC (RFC 3546), RFC 5019 helps address these problems by:

- Enabling a Web server to act as an intermediary cache and proxy for the revocation information the client of the server needs to validate the servers certificate.

- Specifying how an OCSP responder should tag its responses so that they do not get cached by intermediary HTTP proxies (such as Microsoft Internet Security and Acceleration Server [ISA]) beyond the validity period of the OCSP responses themselves.

- Specifying a minimalistic profile of the OCSP protocol that has a greater likelihood of being supported by all clients as well as reducing the size of the average OCSP response.

- Clarifying how clients should both generate OCSP requests that result in cacheable responses as well as validate those responses in a secure fashion.

These changes should enable the ubiquitous deployment of revocation checking in the browser. Windows Internet Explorer 7 on Windows Vista already supports these techniques, and support within OpenSSL and Mozilla are already underway.

Ryan M. Hurst

Co-Author of RFC 5019

- **Microsoft Online Responder service**   The Online Responder is a Windows service (ocspsvc.exe) that runs with Network Service privileges. It manages the Online Responder configuration, retrieves and caches revocation information, signs responses, and audits configuration changes.

- **Web proxy cache**   The Web proxy cache represents the service interface for the Online Responder. The Web proxy cache is implemented as an Internet Server Application Programming Interface (ISAPI) extension and performs two major functions. First, it decodes requests from Abstract Syntax Notation One (ASN.1) syntax to extract the certificate serial number to be validated. Second, once a request is processed, the response is cached. By default, the cache item validity period is set to the remaining CRL validity period from which the response was generated. In addition, the IIS HTTP.SYS library performs caching for 120 seconds. If multiple requests are received by the Online Responder in that time period, the response is served with the cached response.

- **Revocation configuration**   A revocation configuration specifies how the Online Responder service responds to a certificate status request for a specific CA. Each revocation configuration contains the CA certificate, a signing certificate for the OCSP responses, and specific configuration information for the revocation provider.

> **Note**   An Online Responder can have multiple revocation configurations. Typically, one is configured for each revocation provider supported by the Online Responder.

- **Signing**   The Online Responder can sign OCSP responses by using the issuing CA key or a delegated signing key. A delegated signing certificate, the more common deployment, has a short validity period, includes the id-pkix-ocsp-nocheck extension (prevents revocation checking on the signing certificate), does not include CRL distribution point and authority information access extensions, and includes the id-kp-OCSP-Signing Enhanced Key Usage (EKU). All responses from the Online Responder are signed with the designated OCSP signing certificate for the revocation provider.

- **Auditing**   To comply with Common Criteria requirements for secure certificate issuance systems and to provide a secure platform, the Online Responder allows auditing of stopping and starting the Online Responder service, changes to the Online Responder configuration, changes to the Online Responder security settings, and details on all requests processed by the Online Responder service.

- **Revocation Providers**   Revocation providers retrieve and cache revocation information for use by the Online Responder service. When the Online Responder service receives an OCSP request, the revocation configuration determines which revocation provider will report on the status of the requested certificate serial number. The Online Responder service sends the serial number to the revocation provider, and the provider returns the status of the certificate to the Online Responder service.

> **Note**   Although the revocation providers were designed for extensibility to allow custom providers to be developed and used by the Online Responder, the Windows Server 2008 Online Responder provides only a default CRL-based revocation provider and does not allow new providers to be added.

The OCSP Process

When an application calls CryptoAPI 2.0 to verify a certificate that specifies locations to Online Responders in the Authority Information Access (AIA) extension, the process shown in Figure 10-2 is performed.

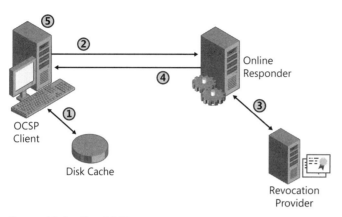

Figure 10-2   The OCSP process

1.   The OCSP client searches the local CryptoAPI 2.0 in-memory and disk cache to find a
     time-valid, cached OCSP response.

> **Note**   The disk cache is located at: C:\Users*UserName*\AppData\LocalLow\
> Microsoft\CryptnetUrlCache.

2.   If no acceptable cached response can be found, a request is sent by using the *HTTP GET*
     method to the Online Responder designated in the AIA extension. If the Online
     Responder does not support the *GET* method, CryptoAPI 2.0 will retry the request by
     using the *HTTP POST* method.

3.   The Online Responder, using the revocation configuration, queries the revocation
     provider to determine the revocation status of the submitted certificate serial number.

4.   The Online Responder creates and sends a signed OCSP response back to the OCSP client.

5.   The signature on the response, including the delegated OCSP signer certificate, is verified.

> **Note**   If the certificate contains the id-pkix-ocsp-nocheck extension, identified by the object
> identifier 1.3.6.1.5.5.7.48.1.5, CryptoAPI will not verify the revocation status of the delegated
> OCSP signer certificate.

If multiple Online Responder URLs exist in the AIA extension, the process is repeated for each
Online Responder designated in the AIA extension until the revocation status is determined.

Implementing the Microsoft Online Responder

Ideally, the Microsoft Online Responder is installed after Certificate Services is deployed but before any client certificates are issued by Certificate Services. The following sections walk you through the process of installing and configuring the Microsoft Online Responder.

Installing the Online Responder Service

The Online Responder service is installed by adding the Active Directory Certificate Services Role to the target server and designating the Online Certificate Status Protocol role service. The following procedure provides the details for installing the service:

1. Ensure that you are logged on as a member of the local Administrators group.

2. From Administrative Tools, open Server Manager.

3. In the Roles Summary section, click Add Roles.

4. On the Select Server Roles page, select Active Directory Certificate Services, and then click Next.

5. On the Introduction To Active Directory Certificate Services page, click Next.

6. On the Select Role Services page, select only the Online Responder check box.

7. In the Add Roles Wizard dialog box, you will be notified that you must add the Web Server (IIS) role services. Click Add Required Role Services.

8. On the Select Role Services page, click Next.

9. On the Web Server (IIS) page, click Next.

10. On the Select Role Services page, accept the recommended IIS settings, and then click Next.

11. On the Confirm Installation Selections page, click Install.

12. On the Installation Results page, click Close.

13. Close Server Manager.

Configuring the CAs

Once the Online Responder is installed, you must configure the CA to include the Online Responder's URL in the AIA extension of issued certificates. The following procedure adds the default OCSP URL to the AIA extension for a CA:

1. Log on as a user assigned the Manage CA permissions.

2. From Administrative Tools, open Certification Authority.

3. In the console tree, right-click *CAName*, and then click Properties.

4. In the *CAName* Properties dialog box, on the Extensions tab (see Figure 10-3), in the Select Extension drop-down list, select Authority Information Access (AIA), and then click Add.

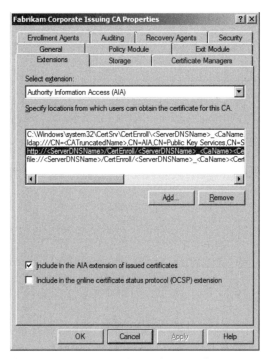

Figure 10-3   Viewing the Authority Information Access URLs

5. In the Add Location dialog box, in the Location box, type the URL of the Online Responder (see Figure 10-4), and then click OK.

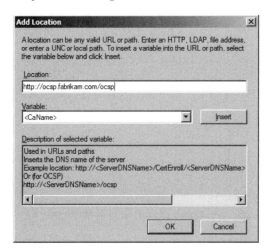

Figure 10-4   Adding a URL for the Online Responder

> **Note**   The default virtual directory for the Online Responder is /ocsp. Typically, you will add a URL in the format *http://DNSName/ocsp*; for example, *http://ocsp.fabrikam.com/ocsp*.

6. On the Extensions tab, select the added Online Responder URL, select the Include In The AIA Extension Of Issued Certificates and Include In The Online Certificate Status Protocol (OCSP) Extension check boxes, and then click OK.

7. In the Certification Authority dialog box, click Yes to restart Certificate Services.

As discussed in Chapter 6, "Impementing a CA Hierarcyy," you can also configure the OCSP URLs at a command prompt. The following command sets both CA Certificate and OCSP URLs for the designated CA:

```
::Modify the AIA Extension URLs
certutil -setreg CA\CACertPublicationURLs
"1:%windir%\system32\CertSrv\CertEnroll\%%1_%%3%%4.crt\n2:
http://www.fabrikam.com/CertData/%%1_%%3%%4.crt\n2:ldap:///CN=%%7,CN=AIA,
CN=Public Key Services,CN=Services,%%6%%11\n34:http://ocsp.fabrikam.com/ocsp"
```

To designate that the URL is included in the AIA extension and is published as an OCSP extension, a value of 34 is assigned. The value is based on the URL being included in the AIA extension (a value of 2) and being included in the OCSP extension (a value of 32).

Configuring the OCSP Response Signing Certificate Template

Once the CA is configured to include the Online Responder's URL in the AIA extension, a certificate template must be designed and deployed that is used by the Online Responder to sign the OCSP responses.

Designing the Template   Windows Server 2008 includes a new version 3 certificate template, OCSP Response Signing. This default template is preconfigured with all required extensions and attributes:

- The certificate is valid for only two weeks and is renewed two days before expiration.

- The certificate template adds Read permission to the Network Service account to allow access to the private key.

- The certificate template does not include AIA and CDP extensions.

- The certificate template implements the OCSP No Revocation Checking extensions (1.3.6.1.5.5.7.48.1.5), preventing revocation checking against the OCSP signing certificate.

The only modification required to the certificate template is to the Security tab to assign each Online Responder computer account the Read and Enroll permissions on the certificate template. Assign the permissions by using the Certificate Templates console (Certtmpl.msc).

> **Important**   Do not assign the autoenroll permission to the Online Responder computer accounts. An Online Responder will request multiple OCSP Response Signing certificates (one per revocation provider). The default autoenrollment protocol would renew only one of the OCSP Response Signing certificates and archive the rest, rendering them unusable.

Once the certificate template is modified, make the certificate template available for enrollment at a Windows Server 2008 enterprise CA by using the following procedure:

1. Log on as a user with the Manage CA permissions.

2. From Administrative Tools, open Certification Authority.

3. In the console tree, right-click Certificate Templates, point to New, and then click Certificate Template To Issue.

4. In the Available Templates list, select OCSP Response Signing, and then click OK.

5. Close the Certification Authority console.

Enrollment   The Online Responder service runs with Network Service privileges rather than Local System privileges. The restricted permissions prevent access to computer private keys by default.

The OCSP Response Signing certificate template allows access to the private key by selecting the Add Read Permission to Network Service on the private key check box in the certificate template as shown in Figure 10-5.

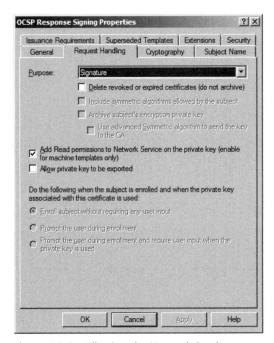

Figure 10-5   Allowing the Network Service account to access the OCSP Response Signing private key

If you choose to deploy a custom OCSP Response Signing certificate from a Windows Server 2003 enterprise CA, you must manually authorize the Network Service account to have access to the private keys. The following procedure enables the Network Service access to the private keys:

1. Log on as a member of the Administrators group.

2. Open a Certificates console focused on the Local Computer.

3. In the console tree, expand Certificates (Local Computer), expand Personal, and then click Certificates.

4. In the details pane, ensure that you have manually enrolled a certificate based on the custom OCSP Response Signing certificate template.

5. In the details pane, right-click the certificate based on the custom OCSP Response Signing certificate template, point to All Tasks, and then click Manage Private Keys.

6. In the Permissions dialog box, add Network Service, and assign Read permissions.

7. In the Permissions dialog box, click OK.

Renewal   Enrollment and renewal of the OCSP Response Signing certificate is controlled in the Revocation Configuration settings for the specific CA. By selecting the Auto-Enroll for an OCSP Signing Certificate check box, the OCSP Responder will automatically enroll and renew its OCSP signing certificate per the renewal settings in the certificate template.

There is one caveat to the autoenrollment of the OCSP Response Signing certificate. As shown in Figure 10-6, problems can arise in the period between the renewal of the CA certificate and the expiration of the previous version of the CA certificate.

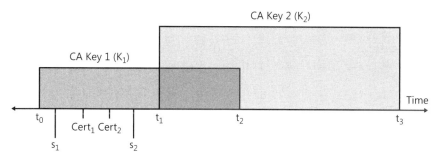

Figure 10-6   Renewing the OCSP Response Signing certificate

The problem arises because the same CA key that was used to sign issued certificates must be used to sign the OCSP Response Signing certificates. Once the CA renews its CA key (at time t_1), all new certificates issued by the CA are signed with the new CA private key (key K_2). If the OCSP client receives an OCSP response signed by K_2, the validation will fail. The response must be signed by the same private key used to sign the validated certificate.

To overcome this limitation, the Windows Server 2008–based CA was updated to allow the renewal of OCSP Response Signing certificates by using existing keys. The following procedure must be performed to allow the renewal of OCSP Response Signing certificates using existing CA keys:

1. On the CA computer, open a command prompt.

2. At the command prompt, type **certutil -setreg ca\UseDefinedCACertInRequest 1**, and then press Enter.

3. Restart Certificate Services.

> **Note**   This option is *not* enabled by default.

Configuring the Online Responder

Once you have configured the OCSP Response Signing certificate template, you can configure the Online Responder service. This involves defining Web proxy settings, audit settings, and security settings. All configuration is performed on the Online Responder Management console. Use the following procedure:

1. Log on as a member of the local Administrators group (by default, only local Administrators can manage the Online Responder).

2. From Administrative Tools, open Online Responder Management.

3. In the console tree, right-click Online Responder (*DNSName*), and then click Properties.

The Online Responder Properties dialog box appears, allowing you to manage the configuration of the Online Responder.

Web Proxy Settings   The Web Proxy tab (see Figure 10-7) allows you to configure the number of Web proxy threads and the maximum number of cached entries.

- **Web Proxy Threads**   Specifies how many threads of execution are allocated by the Online Responder ISAPI extension to handle OCSP client requests. Increasing the number of threads will allow more concurrent requests to be processed but uses more server memory. Likewise, reducing the number of threads will use less memory but will reduce the number of clients that can be processed concurrently.

- **Cached Entries**   Specifies the number of entries that may be cached in memory. The recommended size is between 1,000 and 10,000 entries. If you set the cache size to be too small, it will result in more cache faults. This increases the load on the Online Responder service because it must now perform lookup and signing operations against the revocation providers. Of course, the larger the number of entries, the more memory resources are used on the server.

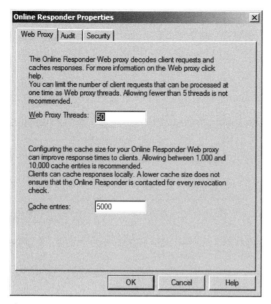

Figure 10-7   Web Proxy tab settings

> **Tip**   If the CA certificate is used to sign the responses, each cache entry will be roughly 200 bytes. If a delegated signer certificate (such as the OCSP Response Signing certificate) is used, each cache entry will be roughly 2 KB (based on the assumption that the key size of the signing certificate is 1,024 bytes).

Audit Settings   Determines what events are captured to the Windows Security log related to the Online Responder service (see Figure 10-8).

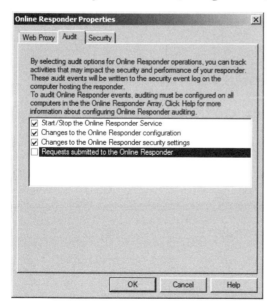

Figure 10-8   Online Responder audit settings

The events that can be audited include:

- **Start/Stop the Online Responder Service**   Records when the Online Responder service is stopped, started, or restarted.

- **Changes to the Online Responder configuration**   Records all configuration setting changes, including changes to the audit settings.

- **Changes to the Online Responder security settings**   Records all changes to the discretionary access control list (DACL) for the Online Responder.

- **Requests submitted to the Online Responder**   Records all requests processed by the Online Responder service that require the Online Responder to sign the response. Cached responses are not included in the log.

> **Warning**   Enable this audio option only when troubleshooting OCSP issues. Auditing all requests creates undue stress on the Online Responder service.

As with Certificate Services auditing, you must also enable Success and Failure auditing for Object Access on the Online Responder computer to record these auditing events.

Security Settings   The security settings for the Online Responder (see Figure 10-9) include three permission options that can be set for users and services to allow or deny access to the request and administration interfaces.

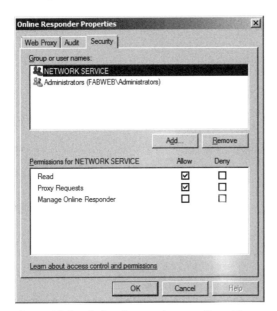

Figure 10-9   Online Responder security settings

- **Read**   Allows the assigned security principal to read the configuration of the Online Responder

- **Manage Online Responder**   Provides the ability to perform administrative tasks, such as creating and managing revocation configurations, and to modify the Online Responder's global settings by using the IOCSPAdmin interface

- **Proxy Requests**   Allows the Online Responder Web proxy component to submit requests for certificate status to the Online Responder service through the IOCSP-RequestD request interface

> **Note**   The IOCSPRequestD interface is not used by applications that submit the OCSP request.

Managing Revocation Configurations

Revocation configurations define the settings for signing OCSP responses for a specific CA. The following rules must be applied when creating revocation configurations.

- A separate revocation configuration should be created for each CA that includes an Online Responder authority information access extension in issued certificates referencing the local Online Responder.

- When you renew a CA with a new key pair, you must create a separate revocation configuration for the new key pair.

The Revocation Configuration view allows creating, modifying, and deleting revocation configurations.

Creating a Revocation Configuration   A revocation configuration must be created for each CA that implements an Online Responder authority information access extension referencing the local Online Responder. To create a new revocation configuration, use the following procedure:

1. Log on as a user assigned the Manage Online Responder permission.

2. From Administrative Tools, open Online Responder Management.

3. In the console tree, expand Online Responder: *DNSName*, and then click Revocation Configuration.

4. In the console tree, right-click Revocation Configuration, and then click Add Revocation Configuration.

5. On the Getting Started With Adding A Revocation Configuration page, click Next.

6. On the Name The Revocation Configuration page, in the Name box, type a name for the revocation configuration, and then click Next.

7. On the Select CA Certificate Location page, select one of the following options, and then click Next.

❑ **Select A Certificate For An Existing Enterprise CA**   Use this option if the CA is an enterprise CA in the forest. The certificate is retrieved from Active Directory Domain Services (AD DS).

❑ **Select A Certificate From The Local Certificate Store**   Use this option if the certificate is manually installed on the Online Responder. The certificate is retrieved from the local certificate store.

❑ **Import Certificate From A File**   The certificate is imported from a file.

8. On the Choose CA Certificate page, the options will depend on how you selected the CA certificate location. Once the CA certificate is selected, click Next.

❑ If you selected the enterprise CA option, you can browse by CA name or by querying AD DS for all available CA certificates.

❑ If you selected the local certificate store, you can browse the local certificate store to select the CA certificate.

❑ If you selected Import Certificate From A File, you will browse the local file system for the CA certificate.

> **Tip**   Once your selection is made, you can verify the CA certificate by clicking the *Certificate Name* link.

9. On the Select Signing Certificate page (see Figure 10-10), you can choose between automatic or manual enrollment of the OCSP signing certificate. Alternatively, you can choose to use the CA certificate for the revocation configuration.

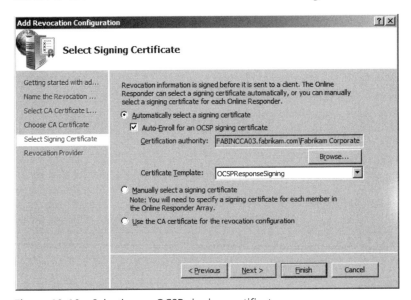

Figure 10-10   Selecting an OCSP signing certificate

If you choose to automatically enroll the certificate, the wizard will automatically populate the Certification Authority and Certificate Template fields if you use the default version 3 certificate template. If you have created a custom certificate template, you must designate the CA and the certificate template information.

> **Important**   When you enable autoenrollment, the enrolled certificates are stored in the Online Responder service's certificate store, not the local computer's certificate store. To view the certificate, you must create a custom Certificates console focused on the Online Responder service service account.

10. On the Select Signing Certificate page, click Next.

11. On the Revocation Provider page, click Finish.

Modifying a Revocation Configuration   Once you have created a revocation configuration, you can modify its properties. To modify the configuration, use the following procedure:

1. Log on as a user assigned the Manage Online Responder permission.

2. From Administrative Tools, open Online Responder Management.

3. In the console tree, expand Online Responder: DNSName, and then click Revocation Configuration.

4. In the details pane, right-click the revocation configuration, and then click Edit Properties.

5. The resulting dialog box provides three tabs that can be configured.

■   **Local CRL**   The Local CRL tab allows you to create a listing of revoked certificates at the Online Responder that are not included in the CA's CRL. The listing is useful when the CA is unavailable, but it is not usually recommended to implement a local CRL. If a certificate is included in the local CRL but not in the CA's CRL, the certificate is considered revoked in the response issued to the client.

■   **Revocation Provider**   The Revocation Provider tab allows you to configure the specific provider settings. When you click the Provider button, the dialog box shown in Figure 10-11 appears.

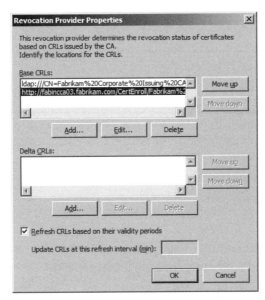

Figure 10-11   Setting Revocation Provider properties

The dialog box allows you to manually choose the order in which base CRL and delta CRL URLs are retrieved. The default order is based on the order provided in the issuing CA's configuration.

In addition, you can also specify CRL refresh rates. The default setting is to refresh CRLs based on the validity periods. To obtain more up-to-date revocation information, you can configure the update as frequently as every five minutes.

■ **Signing**   The Signing tab (see Figure 10-12) allows you to configure:

❑ **Hash Algorithm**   Choose which algorithm is used when signing OCSP responses.

❑ **Credentials**   You can choose whether to prompt for credentials during crypto-graphic operations. If you protect the OCSP Response Signing certificate with a hardware security module (HSM), and the HSM requires user input for the signing process, you must clear this check box.

❑ **Allow NONCE Requests**   If enabled, an OCSP request that includes the nonce extension (a unique identifier in the OCSP request) will result in the Online Responder ignoring a cached OCSP. Instead, the Online Responder will formulate a new response that includes the nonce provided in the request.

> **Warning**   If the Allow NONCE Requests option is disabled and a nonce request is received by the Online Responder, the request is rejected with an *unauthorized* error.

■ **Use Any Valid OCSP Signing Certificate**   Enables the OCSP responder to sign a response with any valid existing certificate that includes the OCSP Signing EKU extension. If this check box is selected, Windows Vista and Windows Server 2008 OCSP requests will fail.

■ **Online Responder Identifier** RFC 2560 requires that the Online Responder include identifying information in the OCSP Response. You can choose between using the key hash or subject of the signing certificate.

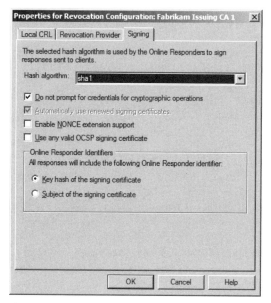

Figure 10-12 Choosing OCSP signing options

Deleting A Revocation Configuration If you wish to delete a revocation configuration, you must use the Online Responder Management console. You may wish to delete the revocation configuration if:

■ The CA referenced in the revocation configuration is deprecated.

■ The CA certificate referenced in the revocation configuration expires.

■ The revocation configuration is incorrect and will be more easily fixed by running the wizard than editing the properties of the revocation configuration.

To delete the revocation configuration, use the following procedure:

1. Log on as a user assigned the Manage Online Responder permission.

2. From Administrative Tools, open Online Responder Management.

3. In the console tree, expand Online Responder: *DNSName*, and then click Revocation Configuration.

4. In the details pane, right-click the revocation configuration, and then click Delete.

5. In the Online Revocation Services Message dialog box, click Yes to confirm the deletion.

Providing High Availability for the Online Responder

To provide high availability, many organizations will consider deploying the Online Responder in a clustered configuration, as shown in Figure 10-13.

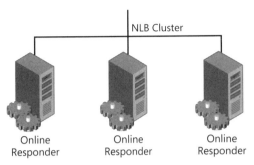

Figure 10-13   Deploying a clustered Online Responder

In this configuration, the OCSP URL referenced in the CA's AIA extension will resolve to the NLB cluster's IP address, not to the individual nodes in the array.

> **Note**   You do not have to use Online Certificate services. Clustering can be achieved using any available software or hardware load balancers that exist in the market.

Before being added to an array, each member must have the Online Responder installed. You can configure Web Proxy cache and auditing and security settings prior to adding to the array. There is no need to define revocation configuration, because this information is populated after the member is added to the array.

Adding Members

Once each member is individually configured to respond to OCSP requests, you can then add the members to an array. To add the members to an array, use the following procedure:

1. Log on as a user assigned the Manage Online Responder permission.

2. From Administrative Tools, open Online Responder Management.

3. In the console tree, right-click Array Configuration, and then click Add Array Member.

4. In the Select Computer box, type or browse for the Online Responder computer, and then click OK.

The selected computer will now appear as an array member.

Designating an Array Controller

Once you have added all members to the array, you must designate one of the array members as the array controller. The array controller becomes the authoritative source for all OCSP configuration settings. If the revocation configuration settings of the other array members differs from the array controller, the settings defined at the array controller are applied to the other array members.

To assign the array controller, use the following procedure:

1. Log on as a user assigned the Manage Online Responder permission.

2. From Administrative Tools, open Online Responder Management.

3. In the console tree, expand Array Configuration, and then select the Online Responder you wish to designate as the array controller.

4. In the Select Computer box, type or browse for the Online Responder computer, and then click OK.

5. In the console tree, right-click the selected Online Responder, and then click Set As Array Controller.

The revocation provider information is now updated at all other array members to match the array controller's configuration settings.

Backup and Restoration

To ensure that recovery is available in the event an Online Responder fails, you must ensure that you have backups of the following information:

■   Revocation configuration. A backup of the revocation configuration allows quick restoration of all revocation settings without re-creating all revocation configurations.

■   If you choose to deploy the OCSP Response Signing certificate from a Windows Server 2003 CA rather than a Windows Server 2008 CA, you must ensure that all signing keys and certificates are backed up.

If you have defined an array, the only member of the array that must be backed up is the Online Responder array controller. The configuration of the array controller is replicated to all other members of the array.

Two different strategies exist for backing up the array controller:

■   To back up the complete Online Responder revocation configuration, you should perform a full system state backup using the Windows Backup utility or a third-party backup utility that supports system state backups.

■   To back up only the revocation configurations settings, you can use the registry editor to back up the HKEY_LOCAL_MACHINE\SYSTEM\CurrentControlSet\ Services\OCSPSvc\Responder registry key.

> **Note** The system state backup includes all signing certificates used by the array members.

Case Study: Planning Revocation

This case study will test your knowledge of available revocation methods.

Design Requirements

You are responsible for designing the revocation policy and strategy for your organization. Your organization, Northwind Traders, is implementing a three-tier CA hierarchy, as shown in Figure 10-14.

The following requirements for your network influence your decision on where to publish the CA certificate and CRLs for your CA hierarchy:

■ Management is concerned that when a certificate is revoked, inconsistent actions are taking place. For example, there are concerns that certificates are revoked with incorrect revocation reasons or certificates are not being revoked when they should be.

■ Northwind Traders implements an AD DS forest with a single domain named *corp.nwtraders.com* on the production network.

■ The client computers run Windows Vista Enterprise.

■ All servers run Windows Server 2003 and Windows Server 2008.

■ Both issuing CAs are running Windows Server 2008 Enterprise Edition.

■ Some Web servers run BSD UNIX with Apache Web servers.

■ A third-party OCSP client is installed on non-Windows servers and clients.

■ All access to Web servers is authenticated by using certificate-based authentication.

■ Northwind Traders wishes to deploy OCSP for revocation checking wherever possible.

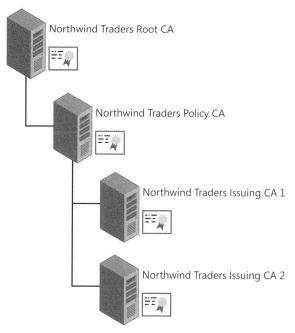

Figure 10-14 The Northwind Traders CA hierarchy

Case Study Questions

1. Management has specified the following circumstances when a certificate must be revoked. Complete the following table to provide recommendations on what revocation reason should be applied if a certificate is revoked under matching circumstances.

Revocation circumstance	Revocation reason applied
An employee voluntarily resigns.	
An employee is terminated.	
A computer is stolen.	
A Certification Authority is compromised.	
A smart card or other two-factor device is lost or misplaced.	
A certificate template is updated, requiring redeployment of certificates.	

2. What revocation checking method would you use for the offline CAs in the CA hierarchy?

3. Can you configure the issuing CAs to use only OCSP, or must you provide both OCSP and CRL support for revocation checking?

4. What certificate template would you use for OCSP Response Signing?

5. How many revocation configurations must be defined for the Northwind Traders network?

6. Assume that you have created a three-node Online Responder array to process the OCSP requests. Where would you define the revocation configuration?

7. For the purposes of disaster recovery, how would you back up the Online Responder configuration?

Additional Information

■ "Certificate Revocation and Status Checking" (*http://technet.microsoft.com/en-us/ library/bb457027.aspx*)

■ "Installing, Configuring, and Troubleshooting Microsoft Online Responder" (*http://go.microsoft.com/fwlink/?LinkId=101269*)

■ "AD CS: Online Certificate Status Protocol Support" (*http://technet2.microsoft.com/ windowsserver2008/en/library/99d1f392-6bcd-4ccf-94ee-640fc100ba5-f1033.mspx?mfr=true*)

■ "Active Directory Certificate Server Enhancements in Windows Server Code Name 'Longhorn'" (*http://www.microsoft.com/downloads/details.aspx?FamilyID=9bf17231-d832-4ff9-8fb8-0539ba21ab95&displaylang=en*)

■ RFC 2560–"X.509 Internet Public Key Infrastructure Online Certificate Status Protocol – OCSP" (*http://www.ietf.org/rfc/rfc2560.txt*)

■ "Summary of Changes to the CryptoAPI Certificate Chain Validation Logic in Q835732 on Windows 2000 Service Pack 2 or Later Versions" (*http://support.microsoft.com/kb/ 887195*)

■ RFC 3280–"Internet X.509 Public Key Infrastructure Certificate and Certificate Revocation List (CRL) Profile" (*http://www.ietf.org/rfc/rfc3280.txt*)

■ RFC 3546–"Transport Layer Security (TLS) Extensions" (*http://www.ietf.org/rfc/ rfc3546.txt*)

■ RFC 3647–"Internet X.509 Public Key Infrastructure Certificate Policy and Certification Practices Framework" (*http://www.ietf.org/rfc/rfc3647.txt*)

■ RFC 5019–"The Lightweight Online Certificate Status Protocol (OCSP) Profile" (*http://www.ietf.org/rfc/rfc5019.txt*)

Chapter 11
Certificate Validation

Certificate validation ensures that the certificate's information is authentic, the certificate can be used only for its intended purposes, and the certificate is trusted. The certificate is also verified to be time-valid and not revoked.

The Windows operating system automatically performs certificate validation and repeats the validation process for each certificate in a certificate chain until it reaches the root certification authority (CA). The certificate chaining engine within Windows performs the validation testing.

 More Info For more information on certificate revocation list (CRL) checking and certificate validation, see "Certificate Revocation and Status Checking," available at *http://technet.microsoft.com/en-us/library/bb457027.aspx*.

Certificate Validation Process

When a certificate is presented to an application, the application must use the certificate chaining engine to determine the certificate's validity. Only after the certificate chain is successfully validated can the application trust the certificate and the identity represented by the certificate. Three distinct but interrelated processes are used to determine a certificate's validity:

- **Certificate discovery** To build certificate chains, the certificate chaining engine must collect the issuing CA certificate and all CA certificates up to the root CA certificate. CA certificates are collected from the CryptoAPI cache, Group Policy, or Enterprise Policy, or, as a last resort, downloaded from Authority Information Access (AIA) Uniform Resource Locators (URLs) in issued certificates. Once a certificate is downloaded from a location other than the CryptoAPI cache, it is added to the user's CryptoAPI cache for faster retrieval.

- **Path validation** When the certificate chaining engine validates a certificate, it does not stop at the presented certificate. Each certificate in the certificate chain must be validated until a self-signed root certificate is reached. Validation tests can include verifying authenticode signatures, determining whether the issuing CA certificate is included in the NTAuth store, or the inclusion of specific application or certificate policy object identifiers (OIDs). If one certificate fails the validity test, it is possible that the entire chain will be deemed invalid and not used by the calling application.

■ **Revocation checking**   Once the certificate chain is built, the certificate chaining engine checks the revocation status of each certificate in the chain. Clients running Microsoft Windows 2000 (with security update MS04-11 applied) and Windows XP or later check revocation as the chain is built. Windows 2000, Windows XP, and Windows Server 2003 can perform revocation checking only by inspecting certificate revocation lists (CRLs). Windows Vista and Windows Server 2008 clients can also check revocation status by querying an Online Certificate Status Protocol (OCSP) responder.

> **Note**   If a certificate contains both OCSP and CRL checking extensions, Windows Vista and Windows Server 2008 clients will use OCSP by default to determine revocation status.

Certificate Validity Checks

When a certificate is presented to an application, the certificate chaining engine tests the following components:

■ **Certificate contents**   A certificate must have information in all required X.509 standard fields. If any required fields are missing or are populated incorrectly, the certificate is considered invalid.

> **Note**   An invalid certificate will not be used by the certificate chaining engine when building certificate chains. The certificate chaining engine excludes all invalid certificates found during the certificate discovery process.

■ **Certificate format**   A certificate must conform to a valid X.509 standard for digital certificates. The certificate chaining engine rejects a certificate that does not follow X.509 version 1, version 2, or version 3 formats.

■ **Critical extensions**   If the certificate contains any X.509 version 3 certificate extensions that are marked as critical, the chaining engine will identify the critical extensions to the calling application. If the calling application does not understand the critical extension or if the critical extension does not contain valid data, the application will consider the certificate invalid.

■ **Policy validation**   If the application that calls the certificate chaining engine expects a specific application policy or certificate policy object identifiers (OIDs) in the certificate, and the required OIDs are not contained within the certificates in the CA chain, the certificate chaining engine considers the certificate invalid.

■ **Revocation check**   The certificate chaining engine calls any installed revocation providers to ensure that the certificate's serial number is not in the issuing CA's CRL. If the certificate is in the CRL listing, the certificate is considered invalid. This revocation check is performed for each certificate in the certificate chain below the root CA certificate. Whether or not revocation checking is performed is dependent on the application.

- **Root check**   The certificate chain assembled by the certificate chaining engine must chain to a trusted root CA or be included in a certificate trust list (CTL) manually configured by the organization or downloaded from Windows Update. If the chain terminates at a nontrusted root CA or does not chain to a self-signed root CA certificate, the presented certificate is considered invalid.

- **Signature check**   When a CA issues a certificate, the CA's private key digitally signs the issued certificate's contents. If the contents are modified or corrupted, the digital signature validation fails, resulting in an invalid certificate.

- **Time validity**   The current date and time must fall within the presented certificate's validity period. If the current time falls outside of the validity period, the certificate chaining engine considers the certificate invalid. This includes using a certificate before its start date or after its expiry date.

> **Note**   The exception to this rule involves Code Signing certificates. When signing an application with a Code Signing certificate, you can use a time stamping service which will indicate to the relying party that the certificate was time valid at the moment the application was signed. The relying party will then accept the Code Signing certificate even though it may no longer be time valid.

Revocation Checking Methods

The certificate chaining engine will use either OCSP or CRLs to determine the revocation status of a presented certificate. The use of OCSP or CRL checking is determined by the following inputs:

- **The contents of the presented certificate**   If the certificate contains an OCSP URL in the Authority Information Access (AIA) extension, OCSP will be used to determine the revocation status. If the presented certificate does not contain an OCSP URL in the AIA extension but does contain URLs in the CRL Distribution Point (CDP) extension, the operating system will use CRL inspection to determine the revocation status of the certificate.

- **The operating system**   Of the available Microsoft operating systems, only Windows Vista and Windows Server 2008 support OCSP revocation checking natively. If a certificate contains revocation information for both OCSP and CRLs, a prior operating system client will resort to CRLs for revocation checking. If a certificate contains only an OCSP responder URL in the AIA extension, and a client does not support OCSP, revocation checking will fail.

> **Note**   Windows XP and Windows 2000 *can* support OCSP if a third-party OCSP client is installed. For example, the Tumbleweed client enables OCSP revocation checking on Windows 2000 and Windows XP clients. The catch is that you must purchase a license for every client computer that is enabled for OCSP checking. The Windows Vista and Windows Server 2008 OCSP client is built into the operating system.

Changing the Default Validation Behavior

You can change the default revocation checking behavior in Windows Vista through Group Policy Objects (GPOs) and registry settings on the Windows Vista clients.

Changing Revocation Checking Behavior

To change the default revocation checkings for Windows Vista and Windows Server 2008, edit the Certificate Path Validation Settings GPO by using the following procedure:

1. Log on as a user able to create and link GPOs.

2. From Administrative Tools, open the Group Policy Management console.

3. Create a new GPO.

4. Edit the GPO.

5. In the console tree, expand Computer Configuration, expand Windows Settings, expand security Settings, and then click Public Key Policies.

6. In the details pane, double-click Certificate Path Validation Settings.

7. In the Certificate Path Validation Settings Properties dialog box, on the Revocation tab (see Figure 11-1), you can select the following check boxes:

   ❑ **Always Prefer Certificate Revocation List (CRL) Over Online Certificate Status Protocol (OCSP) Responses**   This changes the default behavior to attempt CRL checking before OCSP checking.

   ❑ **Allow CRL And OCSP Responses To Be Valid Longer Than Their Lifetime**   This setting extends the validity period of a cached CRL or OCSP response by the designated time interval. This is used only when a CA fails and updated revocation information cannot be published.

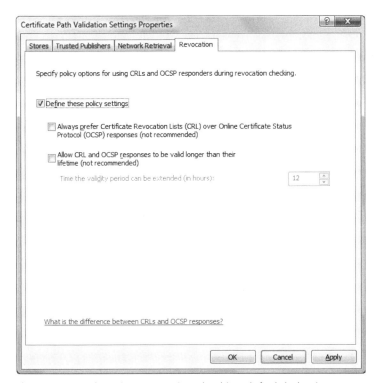

Figure 11-1 Changing revocation checking default behavior

Changing CRL Caching Behavior

By default, both downloaded CRLs and OCSP responses are cached by a Windows client. If a time-valid version of the CRL or OCSP response exists in the cache, the client will use the cached version rather than downloading an updated CRL or submitting a new OCSP request.

You can clear the cache on a Windows Vista or Windows Server 2008 client by modifying the ChainCacheResynchFiletime registry value. The ChainCacheResynchFiletime value specifies the date and time to clear the in-memory cache.

Note The registry key for changing the ChainCacheResynchFiletime value is HKEY_LOCAL_MACHINE\SOFTWARE\Microsoft\Cryptography\OID\EncodingType 0\ CertDllCreateCertificateChainEngine\Config.

Table 11-1 shows some examples of **certutil** commands that clear the in-memory cache.

Table 11-1 Modifying the ChainCacheResynchFiletime Value

Command	Purpose
certutil –setreg chain\ChainCacheResyncFiletime @now	Immediately clears the in-memory cache.
certutil –setreg chain\ChainCacheResyncFiletime @now+3:1	Clears the in-memory cache in 3 days and 1 hour.
certutil –getreg chain\ChainCacheResyncFiletime	Shows the current value of the ChainCache-ResyncFiletime registry value.
certutil –delreg chain\ChainCacheResyncFiletime	Deletes the ChainCacheResyncFiletime registry value.

Building Certificate Chains

The certificate chaining engine builds chains by inspecting specific extensions in a presented certificate. There are different processes the certificate chaining engine uses to determine the issuing CA's correct certificate. The actual selection is based on the current certificate's attributes. Specifically, the certificate chaining engine examines a combination of the following certificate fields and X.509 version 3 certificate extensions:

- **Authority Key Identifier (AKI) extension** The matching method the certificate chaining engine performs is based on the contents of the AKI extension. When using the Windows Server 2008 PKI, the AKI extension can contain:

  - ❑ The subject and serial number of the issuing CA's certificate.

  - ❑ The hash of the issuing CA's public key.

  - ❑ Nothing, or is not present in the evaluated certificate.

- **Issuer field** If an AKI extension is not present, the certificate chaining engine determines the issuing CA's name from the evaluated certificate's Issuer field.

- **Subject field of the issuing CA certificate** The subject is used to identify the issuing CA certificate. If the AKI contains the subject and the serial number of the issuing CA certificate, the CA certificate with the same serial number and subject is selected.

- **Serial Number field of the issuing CA certificate** If the AKI contains the subject and the serial number of the issuing CA certificate, the CA certificate with the same serial number and subject is selected.

- **Subject Key Identifier (SKI) extension of the issuing CA certificate** If the AKI contains the hash of the issuing CA's public key, the CA certificate's SKI contains a matching hash value.

These fields are used by the certificate chaining engine to build certificate chains. Based on the contents of the evaluated certificate's AIA extension, the chaining engine builds the certificate chain by using an exact match, key match, or name match.

Exact Match

In the event that an evaluated certificate contains the issuing CA's subject name and serial number, the certificate chaining engine uses an exact match, also known as a *key and name match*, to find the issuing CA's certificate. The chaining engine searches for a CA certificate with the subject name and the serial number specified in the evaluated certificate's AKI extension. (See Figure 11-2.)

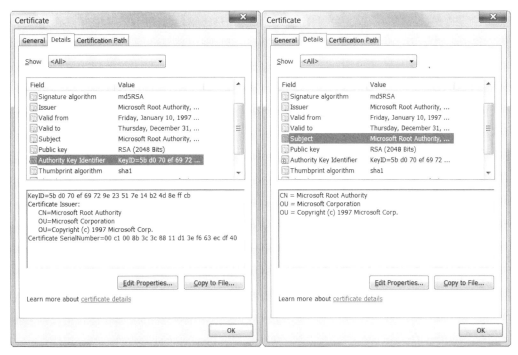

Figure 11-2   An exact match

The left certificate's AKI extension contains the subject and serial number of the issuing CA's certificate. Note that the certificate on the right has a matching serial number and subject name.

Note   A single match can happen only in the case of an exact match. Any time you renew a CA's certificate, the new certificate has a different serial number.

Key Match

If an evaluated certificate's AKI extension contains only the hash of the issuing CA's public key, the certificate chaining engine searches for CA certificates that have a matching value in each CA certificate's SKI extension. (See Figure 11-3.)

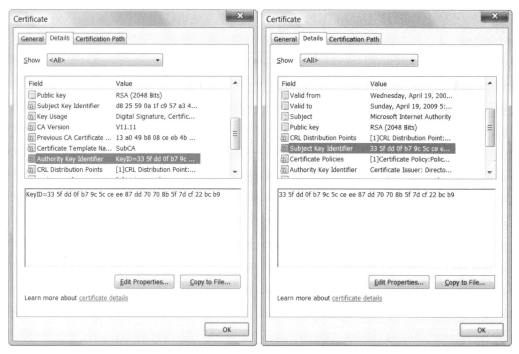

Figure 11-3   A key match

In the certificate on the left, the AKI extension contains the hash of the issuing CA's public key. In the issuing CA certificate on the right, the same public key hash exists in the SKI extension. For the match to be successful, the two hashes must be calculated using the same hash algorithm. Even if the issuing CA certificate does not have an SKI extension, a key match is still possible if the hash algorithm used to calculate the hash of the public key is SHA-1, the default hash algorithm used by the Microsoft CA and CryptoAPI. If other hash algorithms are used, the resulting hash of the public key must exist in both the evaluated certificate's AKI extension and the CA certificate's SKI extension.

> **Note**   There can be multiple matches when key matching is used to build a certificate chain. This scenario, known as *ambiguous chaining*, occurs when the CA certificate is renewed with the same key pair. Both versions of the CA certificate contain the same value in the SKI extension.

Name Match

If no information exists in the AKI, or if the AKI does not exist in the evaluated certificate, the certificate chaining engine uses a name match to find the issuing CA's certificate. To perform name matching, the certificate chaining engine matches the contents of the evaluated certificate's Issuer field to the Subject field of the issuing CA's certificate. (See Figure 11-4.)

> **Note**   The name matching process is case sensitive.

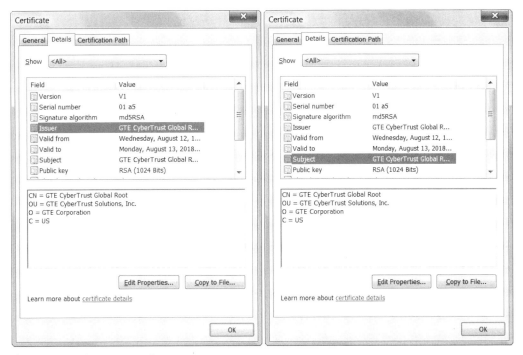

Figure 11-4   A name match

The left certificate's Issuer field contains the same subject name as the right certificate's Subject field.

> **Note**   There can be multiple matches when name matching is used to build a certificate chain. This scenario occurs when the CA certificate is renewed with either the same key pair or a new key pair. When the CA certificate is renewed, the subject of the CA certificate does not change.

Designing PKI Object Publication

To enable certificate validation, you must ensure that a CA's certificate and CRL are available for download by the certificate chaining engine. This is done by confirming that the certificate and CRL are available by using the desired protocols from the desired locations and are published at the required intervals.

Choosing Publication Protocols

Determining the protocols used for CA certificate and CRL retrieval is the first step in choosing publication points. The following protocols are available the Windows Server 2003 and Windows Server 2008 PKIs:

■ **HTTP**   The Hypertext Transfer Protocol (HTTP) provides the most flexibility. Almost all client computers have a Web browser installed that allows access to HTTP URLs. The HTTP protocol is also useful when computers that are not a member of the forest require access to the CA certificate or CRL. The CA certificate and CRL also can be published to a Web cluster to provide redundancy and high availability.

> **Note**   You must never implement Secure Sockets Layer (SSL) protection for the Web server hosting the CA certificate or CRL publication points. The use of SSL can cause recursion of revocation checks. To download the updated version of the CRL, you must check the CRL to ensure that the certificate that signed the CRL is valid. The Windows operating systems will not attempt to download CA certificates and CRLs published to HTTPS URLs since the release of the MS04-11 patch to prevent recursion during revocation checking.

■ **LDAP**   The Lightweight Directory Access Protocol (LDAP) provides high availability by publishing the CA certificate and CRL to the Active Directory Domain Services (AD DS) configuration naming context. LDAP URLs can be accessed by any forest members that can resolve them. This includes Windows 2000 and later and computers running Microsoft Windows 98, Windows Millennium Edition, and Windows NT Workstation 4.0 with the Directory Services Client installed.

> **Note**   If an explicit X.500 distinguished name is used in the LDAP URL, AD DS must contain an explicit referral to the object.

> **Note**   LDAP URLs can be accessed by operating systems other than Windows if the LDAP URL is modified to include the Domain Name System (DNS) name of the LDAP server in the LDAP URL. For example, rather than publishing the CDP URL as LDAP:///CN=*CAName*,CN=*CAComputer*,CN=CDP,CN=Public Key Services, CN=Services,CN=Configuration,DC=*ForestRootDomain*, you would publish the CDP URL as LDAP://*LDAPServer*/CN=*CAName*,CN=*CAComputer*, CN=CDP,CN=Public Key Services,CN=Services,CN=Configuration, DC=*ForestRootDomain*. In addition, if published in AD DS, the permissions of the CN=CDP,CN=Public Key Services, CN=Services, CN=Configuration,DC=*ForestRootDomain* container must be modified to allow anonymous access. If using Active Directory Lightweight Directory Services (AD LDS), formerly known as Active Directory Application Mode, or ADAM, you must ensure that anonymous access is enabled to the referenced URLs.

> **Note** With the release of Windows Vista Service Pack 1, support for Common Internet File System (CIFS) or Server Message Blocks (SMBs) through a File URL was dropped for AIA and CDP retrieval.

You can implement more than one publication protocol. When you set the publication points, the order in which they appear on the CA's Extensions tab is the order in which the client computers search the URLs.

Choosing Publication Points

Once you choose the publication protocols, you must choose *where* to publish the CA certificates and CRLs. The location decision includes the physical servers where you publish the files and the location of the servers on the corporate network: intranet or extranet.

Use the following rules when choosing publication points:

- If most computers are running Windows 2000 or later and are members of the forest, you should include an LDAP URL that references the Active Directory configuration naming context. This location is published to all domain controllers in the forest and ensures availability and fault tolerance.

- If you have several non-forest computers or third-party operating systems such as UNIX, you should include Web server publication points for HTTP URLs.

- If certificates are to be evaluated from the external network, the CA certificate and CDP must be published to an externally accessible location, such as a Web server or LDAP server in the perimeter network of the network.

- File publication points typically are not used for CA certificate and CRL retrieval. File publication points are more common for publishing CA certificates and CRL information to remote servers.

- The URL order is determined by the types of network clients. The order should be set so that the majority of clients can retrieve the CA certificate or CRL from the first URL in the listing. If a client cannot retrieve the CA certificate or CRL from the first URL, the client times out in an attempt to connect and then proceeds through the next URLs in the listing.

> **Note** The URL order is not necessarily important to all operating systems. Some UNIX systems will use their own methods to determine in what order URLs are fetched when multiple URLs exist in the CDP extension.

- Delta CRLs are published more frequently than base CRLs. You may not want to publish delta CRLs to LDAP locations because of Active Directory Domain Services (AD DS) replication latency. Instead, publish delta CRLs to HTTP locations. The AD DS replication interval must allow the delta CRL to be replicated before the prior delta CRL expires if you plan to publish the delta CRL to AD DS.

> **Note**   Delta CRLs can be published to a stand-alone LDAP server, such as Active Directory Lightweight Directory Services (AD LDS), because replication is not an issue with this form of LDAP server.

■ OCSP URLs must be hosted on highly available resources. If the OCSP responder is unavailable when an OCSP client submits a query, revocation checking will fail.

CDP URL Ordering Issues

When you implement multiple URLs in a CDP extension, the order of the URLs is very important. If you do not choose the correct order, a client will spend a specific amount of time attempting to connect to each URL in the listing before attempting to use the next URL in the listing. The default behavior for a Windows client is as follows:

■ The maximum timeout for all CRL retrievals is 20 seconds. If a download did start, the download will continue after the 20-second interval, perhaps resulting in a success the next time a connection is attempted.

■ The first CDP location is given a maximum of 10 seconds to succeed. If the CRL cannot be downloaded in the 10-second interval, the certificate chaining engine will proceed to the next URL in the listing. You should ensure that the first listing in the URL list can be accessed by the greatest number of computers. For example, if several computers are not members of the forest, or use other operating systems such as UNIX, consider moving the default first entry of LDAP:///CN=*CAName*,CN= *CAComputer*,CN=CDP,CN=Public Key Services,CN=Services,CN=Configuration, DC=*ForestRootDomain* to a lower placement in the URL listing.

■ Subsequent CDP locations each will use a maximum of one half of the remaining time to retrieve a specific CRL object before continuing to the next location.

■ Each location download is attempted in sequential order. If CryptoAPI is unable to retrieve a CRL for any reason during the allotted maximum timeout interval, such as invalid path or access denied, an error of "revocation offline" will be returned to the application.

Careful planning of the publication locations will prevent timeout errors from affecting certificate revocation status checking.

Choosing Publication Intervals

When you configure a CA, one of the design decisions is how frequently to publish the base CRL and, if necessary, the delta CRL. Before discussing these decision points, it is useful to review the interaction of base and delta CRLs, as shown in Figure 11-5.

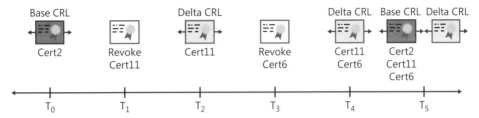

Figure 11-5   Base and delta CRL publication

1. In Figure 11-5, the initial base CRL is published at time T_0 and includes one revoked certificate, Cert2.

2. At time T_1, Cert11 is revoked with a revocation reason of *AffiliationChanged*.

3. At time T_2, when the delta CRL is published, the delta CRL only contains one entry, Cert11.

4. At time T_3, Cert6 is revoked with a revocation reason of *Superseded*.

5. At time T_4, when the next version of the delta CRL is published, the delta CRL contains both Cert6 and Cert11.

6. At time T_5, when the next version of the base CRL is published, the base CRL contains three certificates: Cert2, Cert6, and Cert11. In addition, a blank delta CRL is published with no entries in the delta CRL.

The decision on publication intervals is based on the answers provided to the following questions:

■ **What is the maximum period your organization is willing to accept a revoked certificate as valid?**   If you use the default publication intervals, the base CRL is published weekly and the delta CRL is published daily. You must reset these publication intervals to meet the risk level of your organization.

> **Note**   Remember that if you have Windows Vista and Windows Server 2008 clients, you can also use OCSP to receive more timely revocation information. The Online Responder can implement a revocation configuration that checks the CA as frequently as every five minutes to determine if any new certificates have been revoked.

- **What operating systems are running on your organization's network?** If your client computers run Windows 2000 or earlier versions, you must set short base CRL publication intervals so computers have up-to-date information. Only operating systems running Windows 2000 with MS04-11 applied and later support delta CRLs. If you are running other operating systems, such as UNIX, you must determine whether these operating systems support delta CRLs.

- **How much network traffic is associated with CRL retrieval?** The more frequently you publish the base CRL, the more often clients download the base CRL, which increases the network traffic associated with CRL retrieval. Publishing the CRL less frequently reduces the network traffic associated with CRL publication.

- **How large is the delta CRL?** Publishing several delta CRLs between each base CRL publication can result in large delta CRLs. The goal of delta CRLs is to reduce the size of downloaded CRLs, in addition to making more frequent updates. In this case, consider reducing the publication interval for base CRLs or publishing delta CRLs less frequently.

- **How often are certificates revoked?** The number of certificates revoked within a period greatly influences the publication interval for both base and delta CRLs. You must set publication intervals so that revoked certificates are recognized as soon as possible. You must balance the interval against the network load resulting from CRL download traffic.

- **What is the AD DS replication latency on your network?** The delta CRL and base CRL publication intervals are limited by the replication latency of AD DS. Because the replication latency can be as high as eight hours, setting CRL publication to an interval of less than eight hours can result in the CRL being unavailable until AD DS replication is completed. Replication latency results in the failure of the path-validation process.

> **Important**   Remember that a client computer, by default, will cache all revocation information. If a time-valid version of a CRL or delta CRL is found in the cache, the cached version is used for revocation checking. This is true even if a new CRL is published that includes the certificate being validated. The certificate is not recognized as revoked until the cached version of the base or delta CRL expires and a new CRL is downloaded.

Troubleshooting Certificate Validation

The misconfiguration of CA certificate and CRL publication points is the most common error in a PKI. If the publication points are referenced incorrectly, it can result in certificate validation errors, CA failures, issuance failures, logon failures, and more.

Note   If the certificate chaining engine cannot find an updated CRL as referenced in the CDP extension of a certificate, the chaining engine invalidates the certificate with a revocation status: "Cannot determine the revocation status of the certificate," also known as the *revocation unknown status code*. This revocation status is considered by most applications to be the equivalent of a revoked certificate when strong CRL checking is enabled, because it is safer to reject the certificate than to accept a revoked certificate.

CAPI Diagnostics

When revocation checking fails, it is often difficult to determine the cause of the failure. CryptoAPI 2.0 (CAPI2) diagnostics allows detailed troubleshooting of PKI-related problems for Windows Vista and Windows Server 2008 clients. During PKI-related operations, certificate chain building and revocation checking messages are logged in the Event Viewer.

Enabling CAPI2 Diagnostics

CAPI2 diagnostics logs events that generally correspond to the CAPI2 APIs that are being called. In addition to the parameters and results of these APIs, it also logs details such as all network retrieval attempts, HTTP errors, and proxy events. If you see problems related to CAPI2 in your application, use this feature to reproduce the problem. You can enable this feature from the Event Viewer. To enable the CAPI2 diagnostics, use the following procedure:

1. From Administrative Tools, open Event Viewer.

2. In the console tree, expand Applications And Services Logs, expand Microsoft, expand Windows, expand CAPI2, and then click Operational.

3. Right-click Operational, and then click Save Event As.

4. In the Save As dialog box, in the File Name box, type a name for the log, and then in the Save As Type drop-down list, select between standard event log format (.evtx) or XML format (*.xml).

Tip   If data is present in the logs, it is always recommended to clear the logs before starting your data collection.

CAPI Monitoring Overview

Before you start CAPI2 monitoring, it is a good idea to get the basics down.

CAPI2 Events   When a task is performed, events are logged in CAPI2 diagnostics. The events often correspond to the specific APIs that are called during the performance of the tasks. Some of the common certificate path validation events that are recorded are included in Table 11-2.

Table 11-2   Certificate Path Validation Events

Event	Description
CertGetCertificateChain	Displays the results of building a certificate chain.
CertVerifyRevocation	Displays the results of revocation checking.
CertVerifyCertificateChainPolicy	Shows the results of an application evaluating a certificate chain according to pre-defined policies in Windows.
CertOpenStore	Shows the results of opening certificate stores.
CryptRetrieveObjectByUrlCache	Shows the results of retrieving an object from the disk cache.
CryptRetrieveObjectByUrlWire	Logs details about retrieval of objects over the network. Objects can include CA certificates, CRLs, or OCSP responses.
CertRejectedRevocationInfo	Contains detailed error information when Windows obtained invalid revocation information.
X509Objects	Contains details of all objects processed as part of certificate path validation.

CAPI2 Event Correlation   When CAPI2 diagnostics records events, the events are recorded in a hierarchical format. If a top-level API (such as CertGetCertificateChain) calls other events, the called events are nested under the calling event.

For example, if you were validating a certificate in a two-tier CA hierarchy, you might see the following nesting of events:

```
CertVerifyRevocationStart
    CryptRetrieveObjectByUrlWireStart
    CryptRetrieveObjectByUrlWire
CertVerifyRevocation
CertVerifyRevocationStart
    CryptRetrieveObjectByUrlWireStart
    CryptRetrieveObjectByUrlWire
CertVerifyRevocation
CertGetCertificateChain
CertVerifyCertifcateChainPolicy
X509Objects
```

Common Errors

The following sections provide details on common errors recorded in the CAPI Logs.

Path Validation Errors   When issues are encountered validating a certificate chain, there are some common errors that may be reported by CAPI2 diagnostics. Table 11-3 provides details on these common errors.

Network Retrieval Errors   Many PKI problems can be related to network retrieval issues. This can be because of incorrect URLs in certificate extensions or failure to publish an

Table 11-3   Path Validation Errors

ErrorStatus flag	Description
CERT_TRUST_IS_NOT_TIME_VALID	The end entity certificate or one of the certificates in the chain is expired. More information about the certificate and its validity dates can be found in the X509Objects event.
CERT_TRUST_IS_NOT_SIGNATURE_VALID	The signature for the end entity certificate or one of the certificates in the chain cannot be verified.
CERT_TRUST_IS_REVOKED	The end entity certificate or one of the certificates in the chain is revoked. The revocation reason is available in the event data.
CERT_TRUST_IS_NOT_VALID_FOR_USAGE	The certificate is used for a purpose that is different from its Enhanced Key Usage (EKU). EKU and the application usage information can be obtained from the CertGetCertificateChain error event.
CERT_TRUST_IS_UNTRUSTED_ROOT	The certificate chain is built up to a nontrusted root CA.
CERT_TRUST_IS_CYCLIC	The certificate chain is cyclic. This is the case when a certificate in the chain was issued by a CA that is subordinate to the CA.
CERT_TRUST_IS_REVOCATION_UNKNOWN	The revocation status of the end entity certificate or one of the certificates in the certificate chain is unknown.
CERT_TRUST_IS_OFFLINE_REVOCATION	The revocation status of the end entity certificate or one of the certificates in the certificate chain is either offline or out of date.
CERT_TRUST_IS_PARTIAL_CHAIN	Certificate path discovery failure results in an incomplete certificate chain.

updated CRL to a listed CDP location. Table 11-4 includes details on some of the more common errors.

Table 11-4   Network Retrieval Errors

ErrorStatus flag	Description
HTTP Errors	
Object Not Found	The CA certificate is not present at the location referenced in the AIA extension, or the CRL is not present at the location referenced in the CDP extension. An HTTP 404 status code is returned in the *httpStatusCode* field.
Access Denied	An authentication failure has occurred at the server. Typically this occurs when anonymous authentication is not enabled for CRL or CA certificate retrieval. An HTTP 401 status code is returned in the *httpStatusCode* field.

Table 11-4 Network Retrieval Errors

ErrorStatus flag	Description
Method Not Allowed By The Web Server	The HTTP method used to request the data from the server is not allowed. An HTTP 405 error is returned in the *httpStatusCode* field.
Proxy Authentication Required	An authentication failure has occurred at the designated proxy server. An HTTP 407 status code is returned in the *httpStatusCode* field. Also look for the action name HTTP_STATUS_PROXY_AUTH_REQ in the CryptRetrieveObjectByUrlWire event if the proxy server does not support Windows Integrated authentication.
Timeout Errors	
Object Is Too Large	If a CRL grows to be too large in size, the CRL may not be downloaded within the timeout period. If the retrieval does not complete, a Network-RetrievalTimeout error is recorded. A background retrieval begins, and when complete, a Pending-NetworkRetrievalComplete action is logged for the CryptRetrieveObjectByUrlWire event.
Request Timed Out	A request can also time out if the server is not online, the DNS server times out, or the proxy server does not respond. In this case, the background retrieval thread also fails.
Proxy Server Issues	
Incorrectly Configured Proxy Server	The incorrect proxy server is configured (incorrect DNS name or nonresponding server). Look for a BadProxy action in the CryptRetrieveObjectby-UrlWire event data.
No Proxy Server Configured When One Should Be Configured	If a proxy server is required on the network, ensure that the CryptRetrieveObjectByUrlWire event does not include the action NoProxy.
LDAP Errors	
Path Parsing Issues	If CAPI2 cannot parse an LDAP URL, a CrackLdapUrl error is logged in the CryptRetrieveObjectbyUrl error event.
Other Network Retrieval Errors	
Failed To Retrieve The Contents Of Object	If a download object, such as a CRL, is corrupted, the action Call_CryptQueryObject in the CryptRetrieve-ObjectByUrlWire event will return extended error information.
Failed To Connect To The Server	If the server hosting the object is not online, an incorrect URL is specified, or the URL points to an incorrect IP address, the error ERROR_WINHTTP_CANNOT_CONNECT may be reported by the CryptRetrieveObjectByUrl API.

Table 11-4   **Network Retrieval Errors**

ErrorStatus flag	Description
Protocol Not Supported	If the protocol specified in the URL is not supported, a result value of "2" is reported in the CryptRetrieve-ObjectByUrlWire event. This can occur if, for example, an FTP URL is designated in the CDP or AIA extension.
Repeat Network Retrieval Failures	If an offline server is accessed too often during revocation checking, the CertRejectedRevocationInfo error event is recorded with an action CanRetrieve-fromNetwork.

Dealing with Timeout Issues

If the size of your CRL has grown to the point that you are often encountering timeouts during CRL retrieval, you can use Group Policy to increase the retrieval timeout for all clients.

In the GPO, expand Computer Configuration, expand Windows Settings, expand Security Settings, and then select Public Key Policies. In the details section, double-click Certificate Path Validation Settings. On the Network Retrieval tab (see Figure 11-6), you can increase the Default URL retrieval timeout from the default time of 15 seconds. In addition, you can also increase the cumulative retrieval timeout from the default of 20 seconds.

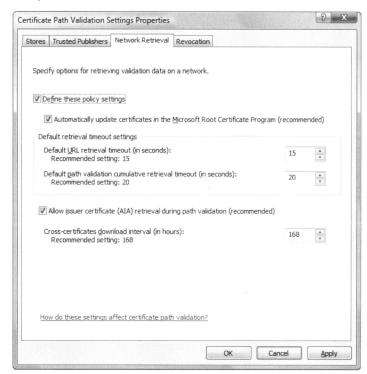

Figure 11-6   Modifying the default URL retrieval timeout

Again, increase these settings only if your clients consistently receive timeouts during CRL retrieval.

Revocation Check Failures   If a certificate fails the revocation checking process, different errors can be reported (depending on the reason for the revocation checking failure).

- If the CertGetCertificateChain event contains the ErrorStatus flag CERT_TRUST_REVOCATION_STATUS_UNKNOWN, the revocation check failed. Possible reasons for the failure include the following:

  - ❏ **CRL Is Expired**   The action CheckTimeValidity is reported in the CertRejected-RevocationInfo event. You can also identify the expiration of the CRL by examining the corresponding X509Objects event. You must find the CertificateRevocation-List element with the same file reference as the one logged in the CertRejected-RevocationInfo event.

  - ❏ **CRL Signature Is Invalid**   If the signature of the CRL cannot be verified, a Cert-RejectedRevocationInfo error event is logged with the action name IsCrlSignature-Valid.

  - ❏ **OCSP Response Cannot Be Validated**   If an OCSP response cannot be validated because the signature is not valid, the action IsResponseSignatureValid is logged in the CertRejectedRevocationInfo error event. If the signing certificate does not contain the correct OID, a CertRejectedRevocationInfo error event with an action element of IsUnsupportedResponseOID is logged. Finally, if no OID exists in the signing certificate, a CertRejectedRevocationInfo error event with an action element of IsMissingResponseOID is logged.

  - ❏ **Unauthorized OCSP Signer**   If the OCSP response signing certificate does not include the OCSP Signing EKU, the action GetOCSPSignerCertificate in the Cert-RejectedRevocationInfo event will record the failure. The error may also report a time-invalid certificate.

  - ❏ **Decoding Of OCSP Response Failed**   If an OCS response cannot be successfully decoded, a CertRejectedRevocationInfo error is recorded with the action Call_CryptDecodeObject_OCSP_RESPONSE, Call_CryptDecodeObject_OCSP_BASIC_SIGNED_RESPONSE, or Call_CryptDecodeObject_OCSP_BASIC_RESPONSE, depending on where the decoding failed.

  - ❏ **CRL Or OCSP Response Has Unsupported Critical Extension**   If the CRL or OCSP Response contains an unrecognized critical extension, the log will contain either a CertRejectedRevocationInfo error event with the action IsCrlCriticalExtension-Supported, if the error happens with a CRL, or an action IsResponseCritical-ExtensionSupported, if the OCSP response contains an unsupported critical extension.

❏ **OCSP Response Status Is Not Successful**   If the responseStatus is not successful, a CertRejectedRevocationInfo event with action name CheckResponseStatus is logged with a Malformed request, InternalError, TryLater, SigRequired, or Unauthorized value responseStatus.

❏ **Certificate Does Not Contain Revocation Information**   If a non-root certificate does not include a CDP or OCSP download location in the AIA extension, a CertRejectedRevocationInfo error event with the action GetCrlOrOcspUrls is recorded with the extended error Cannot Find Object Or Property.

■ If the retrieval of revocation information fails, the CertGetCertificateChain event contains an ErrorStatus flag of CERT_TRUST_IS_OFFLINE_REVOCATION.

Certificate Path Discovery Errors   When a certificate is validated, certificate path discovery builds a certificate chain for validation. If a certificate chain cannot be built, errors are recorded indicating why the chain failed to assemble.

■ Look for CertAIAUrlRetrievalWire errors, and look at the details for any typos or other configuration issues.

■ Look for the error status flag CERT_TRUST_IS_PARTIAL_CHAIN if the chaining engine cannot build a chain up to a trusted root CA. This error can be caused by incorrect AIA extensions or non-inclusion of the chain's root CA in the trusted root store of the computer performing the validation.

Chain Policy Errors   In some cases, the validation fails because of policy errors in the chain. The errors can range from the validated certificate not containing a required EKU to the subject of an SSL certificate not containing the DNS name referenced in the target URL. In both cases look for the CertVerifyCertificateChainPolicy events, and look at the Result attribute for warning events.

Case Study: Choosing Publication Points

This case study will test your knowledge of choosing CRL and CA certificate publication points.

Design Requirements

You are responsible for setting the CA certificate and CRL publication points for your CA hierarchy. Your organization, Northwind Traders, is implementing a three-tier CA hierarchy, as shown in Figure 11-7.

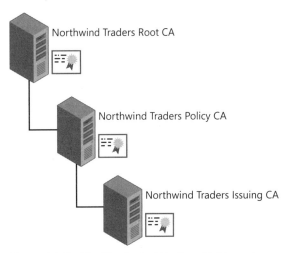

Figure 11-7   The Northwind Traders CA hierarchy

The following requirements for your network influence your decision on where to publish the CA certificate and CRLs for your CA hierarchy:

- Northwind Traders implements an AD DS forest with a single domain named corp.nwtraders.com on the production network.

- Externally accessible Windows 2003 Web servers are located in a perimeter network and are not members of the corp.nwtraders.com domain.

- The client computers run Windows XP Professional and Windows Vista Business.

- Some Web servers run BSD UNIX with Apache Web servers.

- All access to Web servers is authenticated by using certificate-based authentication.

- The Northwind Traders security policy requires that all applications implement strong CRL checking.

Case Study Questions

1. What URLs do you include in the Northwind Traders root CA certificate for the AIA and CDP extensions?

2. Are there any network design issues that prevent you from implementing an LDAP URL as the first URL in the list of available URLs for CA certificates and CRLs?

3. What form of URL should you implement as the first URL in CDP and AIA URL listings?

4. What protocol, by default, provides redundancy and high availability in an AD DS environment?

Troubleshooting Exercise

This exercise allows you to investigate a CAPI2 diagnostics log to determine why an error message is returned to a client when the client connects to a Web server.

1. Ensure that you are logged on at a computer running Windows Vista or Windows Server 2008 as a member of the local Administrators group.

2. From Administrative Tools, open Event Viewer.

3. From the Action menu, select Section and then select Open Saved Log.

4. Open cd:\Case Studies\Chapter11\Chap11CaseStudy.evtx.

5. In the Open Saved Log dialog box, accept the default name, and then click OK.

Now that you have the event log open, answer the following questions based on the log entries.

1. What is the reason for the Verify Chain Policy error event?

2. What object information is included in the X509 Objects event located between the two error events?

3. Was revocation and CA certificate information downloaded from URLs or retrieved from cache?

Additional Information

- "Certificate Revocation and Status Checking" (*http://technet.microsoft.com/en-us/library/bb457027.aspx*)

- "Installing, Configuring, and Troubleshooting Microsoft Online Responder" (*http://go.microsoft.com/fwlink/?LinkId=101269*)

- "AD CS: Online Certificate Status Protocol Support" (*http://technet2.microsoft.com/windowsserver2008/en/library/99d1f392-6bcd-4ccf-94ee-640fc100ba5f1033.mspx?mfr=true*)

- "Active Directory Certificate Server Enhancements in Windows Server Code Name 'Longhorn'" (*http://www.microsoft.com/downloads/details.aspx?FamilyID=9bf17231-d832-4ff9-8fb8-0539ba21ab95&displaylang=en*)

- RFC 2560–"X.509 Internet Public Key Infrastructure Online Certificate Status Protocol – OCSP" (*http://www.ietf.org/rfc/rfc2560.txt*)

- RFC 3280–"Internet X.509 Public Key Infrastructure Certificate and Certificate Revocation List (CRL) Profile" (*http://www.ietf.org/rfc/rfc3280.txt*)

- RFC 3546–"Transport Layer Security (TLS) Extensions" (*http://www.ietf.org/rfc/rfc3546.txt*)

- RFC 3647–"Internet X.509 Public Key Infrastructure Certificate Policy and Certification Practices Framework" (*http://www.ietf.org/rfc/rfc3647.txt*)

- RFC 5019–"The Lightweight Online Certificate Status Protocol (OCSP) Profile (*http://www.ietf.org/rfc/rfc5019.txt*)

Chapter 12
Designing Certificate Templates

Certificate templates are used by Active Directory Certificate Services (AD CS) to define the contents of certificates issued by enterprise certification authorities (CAs). The Certificate Templates console is an easy-to-use interface for creating and customizing certificate templates.

> **Note** For more detailed information on modifying and creating certificate templates, see "Implementing and Administering Certificate Templates" at *http://www.microsoft.com/downloads/details.aspx?FamilyID=3c670732-c971-4c65-be9c-c0ebc3749e24&displaylang=en*.

Certificate Template Versions

Windows Server 2008 supports three versions of certificate templates: version 1, version 2, and version 3. All certificate templates are stored as objects in Active Directory Domain Services (AD DS) and are stored in the Configuration naming context in the following location: CN=Certificate Templates,CN=Public Key Services,CN=Services,CN=Configuration,*ForestRootDomain* (where *ForestRootDomain* is the Lightweight Directory Access Protocol (LDAP) distinguished name of the forest root domain). By storing certificate templates in the Configuration naming context, forest-wide availability is ensured because the Configuration naming context is replicated to every domain controller in the forest.

Certificate templates can be modified by a user with the necessary permissions at any computer where the Certificate Templates console is installed.

Version 1 Certificate Templates

Version 1 certificate templates were introduced with Microsoft Windows 2000 Certificate Services. These same version 1 certificate templates are available for Windows Server 2003 Enterprise CAs and Windows Server 2008 Enterprise CAs; just as in Windows 2000. As with Windows 2000, you cannot modify any attributes of version 1 certificate templates except for the permissions assignments.

When you install an Enterprise CA or launch the Certificate Templates console for the first time, the following version 1 certificate templates are automatically installed in AD DS:

- **Administrator** Allows a holder to perform trust list signing, send secure e-mail, encrypt and decrypt files protected by the Encrypting File System (EFS), and perform user authentication.

- **Authenticated Session**   Enables a holder to use a certificate for user authentication.

- **Basic EFS**   Allows a user to use a certificate for encrypting and decrypting files.

> **Note**   If this certificate template is not available, and no version 2 certificate templates are distributed to users automatically, a user who encrypts a file using EFS will generate a self-signed EFS certificate. For more details on EFS, see Chapter 20, "Encrypting File System."

- **CEP Encryption**   Permits a holder to act as a registration authority (RA) for Simple Certificate Enrollment Protocol (SCEP) requests from Cisco network equipment.

> **Note**   The CEP Encryption certificate template requires that the Network Device Enrollment Services (NDES) feature role be installed on a server. Details on NDES are discussed in Chapter 27, "Network Device Enrollment Service."

- **Code Signing**   Permits a holder to digitally sign software.

- **Computer**   Allows a computer to authenticate to other computers and users on the network.

- **Domain Controller**   Allows a domain controller to authenticate to other computers and users on the network.

- **EFS Recovery Agent**   Allows a holder to recover files previously encrypted with EFS if the holder is designated as a data recovery agent for the file.

- **Enrollment Agent**   Allows a holder to request certificates, such as smart card certificates, on behalf of other users.

- **Enrollment Agent (Computer)**   Allows a computer account to request certificates on behalf of another subject.

> **Note**   This certificate is required if you deploy the Exchange 5.5 or Exchange 2000 Key Management Service (KMS), to allow the server to request e-mail certificates on behalf of any user.

- **Exchange Enrollment Agent (Offline request)**   Allows a computer hosting the Exchange Key Management Service (KMS) to request certificates on behalf of Exchange e-mail encryption users.

- **Exchange Signature Only**   Allows a holder to send digitally signed Secure/Multipurpose Internet Mail Extensions (S/MIME) e-mail messages.

- **Exchange User**   Allows a holder to receive and decrypt encrypted S/MIME e-mail messages.

- **IPsec**   Allows computers to digitally sign, encrypt, and decrypt network communications that use Internet Protocol security (IPsec).

- **IPsec (Offline request)**   Allows computers that are not members of the forest to participate in IPsec communications.

- **Root Certification Authority**   Allows a computer to function as the root CA of a CA hierarchy.

- **Router (Offline request)**   Allows a router to request certificates from a CA that holds a Certificate Enrollment Protocol (CEP) encryption certificate by using SCEP.

- **Smartcard Logon**   Allows a holder to authenticate with the network by using a smart card.

- **Smartcard User**   Allows a holder to authenticate with the network and send and receive digitally signed and encrypted e-mail messages by using a smart card.

- **Subordinate Certification Authority**   Permits a computer to function as a subordinate CA in a CA hierarchy.

- **Trust List Signing**   Allows a holder to digitally sign a certificate trust list.

- **User**   Permits a holder to send digitally signed or encrypted e-mail and authenticate with the network by using certificate-based authentication.

- **User Signature Only**   Allows a holder to authenticate with the network by using certificate-based authentication.

- **Web Server**   Allows a Web server to implement Secure Sockets Layer (SSL) security. The certificate proves the identity of the Web server and is used to encrypt communications between a Web client and the Web server.

Version 2 Certificate Templates

Version 2 certificate templates extend the abilities of version 1 certificate templates and are fully customizable. You can define any attribute within version 2 certificate templates, whereas version 1 certificate templates allow only permission modification. Windows Server 2008 ships with several version 2 certificate templates and allows new templates to be created by duplicating existing version 1 or version 2 templates.

> **Note**   Certificates based on version 2 templates can be issued only by Enterprise CAs running on the Enterprise or Datacenter edition of Windows Server 2003 and Windows Server 2008.

The following list describes the default version 2 certificate templates installed in AD DS when you open the Certificate Templates console for the first time or install a Windows Server 2003 Enterprise CA.

- **CA Exchange**   Allows a computer to encrypt private key material sent to the CA for key archival. The certificate is issued only to a CA that enables archival of private keys.

- **Cross Certification Authority**   Permits your organization to define qualified subordination constraints when issuing certificates to CAs outside of your organization's CA hierarchy.

- **Directory Email Replication**   Allows domain controllers to use secure Simple Mail Transfer Protocol (SMTP) for replication.

- **Domain Controller Authentication**   Allows domain controllers to authenticate with users and computers in the forest by using certificates.

- **Key Recovery Agent**   Allows a CA to implement key archival and recovery. The Key Recovery Agent certificate is used to encrypt and decrypt the certificate and private key in the CA database.

- **Kerberos Authentication**   An enhancement to the previous Domain Controller Authentication template that provides better assurance that the owner and presenter of the certificate template is truly a domain controller.

> **Note**   Details on issuing certificates to domain controllers are discussed in Chapter 26, "Deploying Certificates to Domain Controllers."

- **RAS and IAS Server**   Allows Remote Access Service (RAS) and Internet Authentication Service (IAS) servers to mutually authenticate with remote clients.

- **Workstation Authentication**   Allows computers to mutually authenticate with other computers and users on the network.

> **Note**   Users with computers running Windows 2000 can request only version 2 certificate templates through the Certificate Services Web Enrollment pages or through custom scripts by using the Certificate Enrollment control. A user at a computer running Windows XP or later can also use the Certificate Enrollment wizard or autoenrollment.

Version 3 Certificate Templates

Version 3 certificate templates allow the use of Cryptography Next Generation (CNG) definitions within the certificate template. You can configure the use of CNG encryption and hash algorithms, such as Elliptic Curve Cryptography (ECC), for:

- Certificate requests

- Issued certificates
- Protecting private keys during key exchange and key archival operations

Only Windows Server 2008 Enterprise CA computers running Enterprise or Datacenter editions can issue certificates based on version 3 certificate templates.

The only default version 3 certificate template is the OCSP Response Signing certificate template. This certificate template allows an Online Responder based on the Online Certificate Status Protocol (OCSP) to sign responses to clients requesting revocation information.

> **Note**   Details on OCSP and the OCSP Response Signing certificate template are discussed in Chapter 10, "Certificate Revocation."

Enrolling Certificates Based on Certificate Templates

For all versions of certificate templates, the ability to enroll a certificate based on a certificate template is set in the discretionary access control list (DACL) associated with a specific certificate template. If users have both Read and Enroll permissions assigned to their user accounts or to groups in which their user accounts have membership, they can request certificates based on the certificate template. Likewise, if the user is assigned the Read, Enroll, and Autoenroll permissions for a version 2 or version 3 certificate template, the certificate can be deployed to the user automatically through Group Policy.

Default Certificate Templates

When you install an enterprise CA, a default set of certificate templates is made available for client enrollment. The default list of certificate templates is dependent on the operating system version installed on the enterprise CA.

Table 12-1 shows the default templates made available at both Windows Server 2003 and Windows Server 2008 Enterprise CAs running Enterprise or Datacenter editions.

> **Important**   An Enterprise CA running on the Standard Edition of Windows Server 2003 or Windows Server 2008 can issue certificates based only on version 1 certificate templates. This is a common problem encountered by companies because they do not realize that the Standard edition cannot issue version 2 or version 3 certificate templates. The only way to issue version 2 or version 3 certificate templates is to perform an upgrade in place to the Enterprise Edition for your version of the operating system.

Table 12-1 Default Certificate Templates for Issuance

Template name	Windows Server 2003	Windows Server 2008
Administrator	✓	✓
Basic EFS	✓	✓
Computer	✓	✓
Directory E-mail Replication		✓
Domain Controller	✓	✓
Domain Controller Authentication	✓	
EFS Recovery Agent	✓	✓
Kerberos Authentication		✓
Subordinate Certification Authority	✓	✓
User	✓	✓
Web Server	✓	✓

You can prevent the loading of the default certificate templates on a Windows Server 2003 Enterprise root CA running Service Pack 1 or later or on any Windows Server 2008 Enterprise CA by adding the following lines to the CAPolicy.inf file before installing Active Directory Certificate Services.

```
[certsrv_server]
LoadDefaultTemplates=0
```

For Windows Server 2003 Enterprise subordinate CAs, there really is no way to prevent the availability of the default certificate templates during installation. You can immediately remove the default certificate templates by running the following post-installation script:

```
::Remove all default templates certificate templates.
certutil -SetCAtemplates -Administrator
certutil -SetCAtemplates -EFS
certutil -SetCAtemplates -Machine
certutil -SetCAtemplates -DirectoryEmailReplication
certutil -SetCAtemplates -DomainController
certutil -SetCAtemplates -DomainControllerAuthentication
certutil -SetCAtemplates -EFSRecovery
certutil -SetCAtemplates -SubCA
certutil -SetCAtemplates -User
certutil -SetCAtemplates -WebServer
```

Note You can also use this script sample to add certificate templates to a CA. For example, if you had a custom version 2 certificate template with a common name of ArchiveEFS, you could run **certutil –SetCAtemplates +ArchiveEFS** to publish the certificate template.

Modifying Certificate Templates

Creation and modification of certificate templates is an important step when deploying PKI-enabled applications. For each application, you must identify the required certificate templates and then customize them according to your PKI design document.

To modify a version 2 or version 3 certificate template, you must log on as a user that has Read and Write permissions for the certificate template. Once logged on, a user can use the Certificate Templates console (Certtmpl.msc) to modify existing certificate templates or create new version 2 or version 3 certificate templates.

The decision of whether to create a version 2 or version 3 certificate template is presented in the Duplicate Template dialog box (see Figure 12-1).

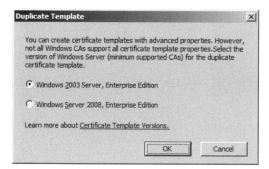

Figure 12-1   Choosing to create a version 2 or version 3 certificate template

- If you choose Windows Server 2003, Enterprise Edition, you create a version 2 certificate template.

- If you choose Windows Server 2008, Enterprise Edition, you create a version 3 certificate template.

Modifying Version 1 Certificate Template Permissions

Version 1 certificate templates allow you to modify only the permission settings for the certificate template. You cannot modify the contents of a version 1 certificate template. Figure 12-2 shows the Security tab for a version 1 certificate template.

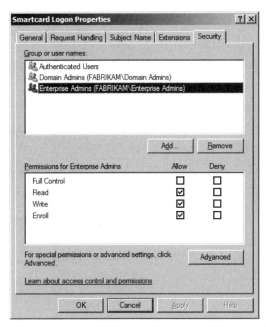

Figure 12-2   Modifying the Security tab for a version 1 certificate template

In the security template, you can add global or universal groups from AD DS and assign a combination of the following permissions:

- **Full Control**   Allows a permission holder to modify the permissions of the version 1 certificate template and to change the ownership of the certificate template.

- **Read**   Allows a permission holder to see the certificate template when enrolling for certificates. Read permission is required to enroll a certificate based on a version 1 certificate template and for a certificate server to find the certificate templates in AD DS.

- **Write**   Allows a permission holder to modify permissions of a version 1 certificate template.

- **Enroll**   Allows a permission holder to enroll for a certificate based on the certificate template. To enroll for a certificate, the security principal also must have Read permissions.

Modifying Version 2 and Version 3 Certificate Templates

Version 2 certificate templates allow users with Write permission to change any attribute. The following sections detail the modifications that can be made to version 2 certificate templates on a tab-by-tab basis.

Security Tab

As with version 1 certificate templates, a version 2 or version 3 certificate template's Security tab defines the permissions for a certificate template. (See Figure 12-3.)

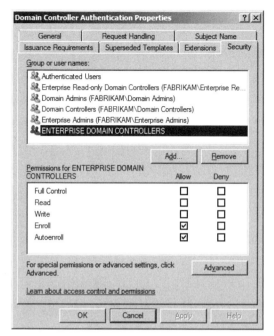

Figure 12-3   Modifying the Security tab for a version 2 or version 3 certificate template

For a version 2 or version 3 certificate template, the definition of the Write permission includes the ability to change *any* attribute of the certificate template, not just the permission of the certificate template.

The only additional permission for a version 2 certificate template is the Autoenroll permission. When a user or computer is assigned Read, Enroll, and Autoenroll permissions, it is possible to automatically distribute the certificate to the user or computer.

 Note   Autoenrollment is supported only for Windows XP or later.

General Tab

On the General tab (see Figure 12-4), you can configure the following attributes of the certificate template:

- **Template Display Name**   The display name of the version 2 certificate template shown in the console, in the Certificate Services Web Enrollment pages, or in the Certificate Services Enrollment wizard.

- **Template Name**   The name of the PKI-Certificate-Template object created in the CN=Certificate Templates,CN= Public Key Services,CN=Services,CN=Configuration, *ForestRootDomain* container.

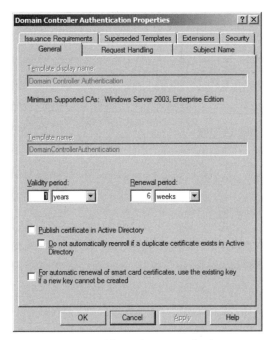

Figure 12-4   Modifying the General tab

- **Validity Period**   Specifies the certificate template's validity period.

- **Renewal Period**   Specifies the time before the validity period expires, which is when autoenrollment attempts to reenroll a certificate based on the certificate template.

> **Note**   There are default values specified for the renewal period that prevent you
> from setting too short a renewal period. For more details, see "Implementing and
> Administering Certificate Templates" at *http://www.microsoft.com/downloads/*
> *details.aspx?FamilyID=3c670732-c971-4c65-be9c-c0ebc3749e24&displaylang=en.*

- **Publish Certificate In Active Directory**   Allows you to publish the certificate into the userCertificate attribute of a user account object. This is typically enabled to allow users to access the associated public key of another user's encryption certificate.

- **Do Not Automatically ReEnroll If A Duplicate Certificate Exists In Active Directory**
  Prevents a user from enrolling multiple copies of a certificate based on the certificate template. If a version is already published in Active Directory, reenrollment is prevented during autoenrollment processes.

- **For Automatic Renewal Of Smart Card Certificates, Use The Existing Key If A New Key Cannot Be Created**   Prevents certificate enrollment failure if there is not enough private key space or public key space on a smart card to generate a new key pair during renewal. Allows renewal to reuse the existing key pair.

> **Note**   This setting is available only if you edit the certificate on a computer running Windows Vista or Windows Server 2008.

Request Handling Tab

The Request Handling tab differs between version 2 and version 3 certificate templates.

Version 2 Certificate Templates   On the Request Handling tab of a version 2 certificate template (see Figure 12-5), you can configure the following attributes of the certificate template.

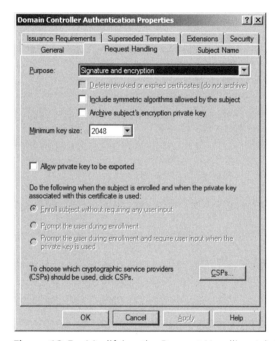

Figure 12-5   Modifying the Request Handling tab for a version 2 certificate template

- **Purpose**   Describes the overall purpose of the certificate template. Available choices are:
    - ❏ **Encryption**   The certificate's key pair can be used only to encrypt data.
    - ❏ **Signature**   The certificate's key pair can be used only to sign data or verify the signature applied to data.
    - ❏ **Signature And Encryption**   The certificate's key pair can be used for both encryption and digital signature applications.
    - ❏ **Signature And Smart Card Logon**   The certificate's key pair can be used only to sign data, verify the signature applied to data, or encrypt and decrypt data for

the purpose of Kerberos authentication. In addition, the key pair must be stored on a two-factor hardware device, such as a smart card.

> **Note** The Purpose setting determines what other settings are available or unavailable on the Request Handling tab. For example, the Archive Subject's Encryption Private Key check box is selected only if the certificate purpose is set to Encryption or Signature And Encryption.

■ **Delete Revoked Or Expired Certificates (Do Not Archive)** Deletes the subject's previous signing certificate from the local store if the previous certificate is expired or revoked when a newer version is obtained from the CA.

> **Note** This option is critical for conserving space on smart cards. When you enable this setting, the previous signing certificate is deleted from the smart card *after* the new smart card certificate is installed on the smart card.

■ **Include Symmetric Algorithms Allowed By The Subject** Ensures that supported symmetric encryption algorithms are included in the certificate for applications such as Microsoft Office Outlook.

■ **Archive Subject's Encryption Private Key** Enables archival of the certificate's private key in the CA database. To use this setting, key archival must be enabled at the CA.

■ **Minimum Key Size** Specifies the private or public key's minimum size in bits, as allowed by the cryptographic service provider (CSP). You cannot set a minimum key size above or below the values allowed by the CSP.

■ **Allow Private Key To Be Exported** Enables or disables the user's ability to export the certificate's private key.

■ **Do The Following When The Subject Is Enrolled And When The Private Key Associated With This Certificate Is Used** Specifies the level of user interaction required during the certificate enrollment process, if autoenrollment is used to deploy the certificate. The options are:

❑ **Enroll Subject Without Requiring Any User Input** The certificate enrollment occurs silently, without any notification to the user.

> **Note** You must set this option if you want to silently distribute certificates to users. If you wish to distribute computer certificates with autoenrollment, you must enable the option to not require any user input.

❑ **Prompt The User During Enrollment**   The user is notified that a certificate is available for autoenrollment. This option is typically enabled if a user action is required, such as selecting a certificate to sign the enrollment request or inserting a smart card in the smart card reader.

❑ **Prompt The User During Enrollment And Require User Input When The Private Key Is Used**   Enables strong private key protection, which requires that a user provide a password to access the private key material every time the private key is used.

■ **CSPs**   Allows you to specify the non-CNG cryptographic service providers (CSPs) that can be used when requesting a certificate based on the certificate template. You can choose to allow requests to use any CSP on the subject's computer or designate a specific CSP for the certificate template.

> **Note**   If you use a third-party CSP, you must install the CSP at the computer where you define the certificate template and at the computer(s) where enrollment occurs.

Version 3 Certificate Templates   For a version 3 certificate template, the Request Handling tab (see Figure 12-6) has minor differences from that of a version 2 certificate template.

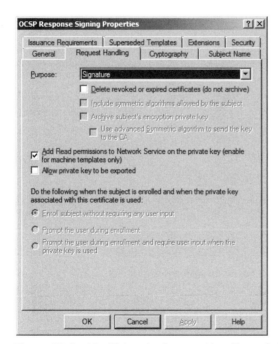

Figure 12-6   Modifying the Request Handling tab for a version 3 certificate template

■ All cryptography settings are moved to the Cryptography tab (discussed later in this section).

- A version 3 certificate template adds the Add Read Permissions To Network Service On The Private Key (Enable For Machine Templates Only) check box. Enabling this setting grants Read permissions to Network service to the private key in the local machine store. Services such as the Online Responder and Internet Information Services (IIS) require this permission to access the private key of the certificate.

- A version 3 certificate template adds the Use Advanced Symmetric Algorithm To Send The Key To The CA setting for encryption certificates. If enabled, AES-256 symmetric encryption is used to encrypt the private key during transport from the enrollment client to the CA. If not enabled, encryption falls back to 3DES encryption.

Cryptography Tab

The Cryptography tab (see Figure 12-7) is available only on version 3 certificate templates.

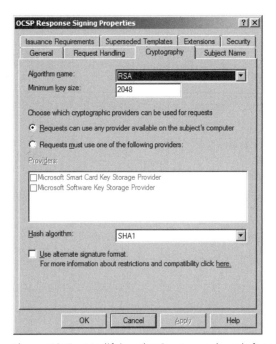

Figure 12-7   Modifying the Cryptography tab for a version 3 certificate template

The Cryptography tab contains the following settings:

- **Algorithm Name**   Introduces the ability to select an advanced algorithm for encryption, signing, or both as required by the purpose of the certificate template. By default, the following algorithms are available: DSA, ECDH_P256, ECDH_P384, ECDH_P521, ECDSA_P256, ECDSA_P384, ECDSA_P521, and RSA. Additional algorithms will appear if other custom CNG providers are installed.

> **Note**   Details and definitions of the available algorithms are found in Chapter 1, "Cryptography Basics."

- **Minimum Key Size**   You can specify the minimum key size for the certificates generated based on the certificate template. By default, the size is set to the minimum key length supported for the chosen algorithm. Any number can be entered.

- **Providers**   A dynamically generated list of all installed CNG providers. The list is populated based on key providers that can provide combination of requirements configured:

  - From the Cryptography tab, the selected algorithm name and minimum key size

  - From the Request Handling tab, the selected purpose and private key export options

  Only the CNG providers that can issue certificates that meet all four requirements are displayed.

- **Hash Algorithm**   Allows you to choose among the following hash algorithms: MD2, MD4, MD5, SHA1, SHA256, SHA384, and SHA512.

> **Note**   Details and definitions of the available hash algorithms are found in Chapter 1.

- **Use Alternate Signature Format**   Enables the use of discrete signatures in the certificate requests for certificates based on the version 3 certificate template. A PKCS#1 v2.1 format signature will be used in the certificate requests when the enrollment takes place using the Certificate Request wizard or autoenrollment. This setting does not enforce the discrete signature in the issued certificate, only in the request for the certificate.

> **Note**   Details on discrete signatures and issuing certificates with discrete signatures are discussed in Chapter 6, "Implementing a CA Hierarchy."

Subject Name Tab

The Subject Name tab defines what information is provided in the certificate request to build the issued certificate's subject name. (See Figure 12-8.) You must allow the subject information to be supplied in the certificate request or use information stored in the subject's Active Directory object when building the certificate request.

- **Supply In Request**   This option is commonly used when a certificate template is intended for users or computers that are not part of the forest—meaning that a user or computer account does not exist in AD DS. It is also used if the certificate request is generated programmatically or if the certificate template allows the requesting user to provide a name other than the user's own for the subject of the certificate. For example, a user requesting a Code Signing certificate may wish to assign the organization's name as the subject of the certificate rather than that user's own name.

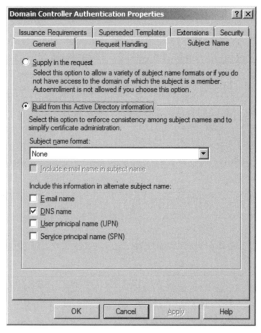

Figure 12-8 Modifying the Subject Name tab

> **Note** You cannot enable the option to supply the subject name in the request if you are using autoenrollment. Autoenrollment requires that the subject name be built from Active Directory information.

■ **Build From This Active Directory Information** If you choose to build the subject name from Active Directory information, you can choose what name formats from the requestor's Active Directory object are used in the subject name formation. Available choices are:

❏ **Subject Name Format** The subject name can contain either the object's common name or the object's fully distinguished name (the LDAP distinguished name) in AD DS. You can also choose to implement no value in the subject name.

> **Note** If you choose to implement no value in the subject name, you *must* include at least one alternate subject name format.

❏ **Include E-Mail Name In Subject Name** Includes the e-mail name in the subject name. The e-mail name is added to the front of the subject name, with a qualifier of E=e-mail name.

❑ **E-Mail Name**   Includes the user's e-mail name in the certificate's subject alternative name extension.

❑ **DNS Name**   Includes the computer's fully qualified Domain Name System (DNS) name in the certificate's subject alternative name extension.

❑ **User Principal Name (UPN)**   Includes the user's UPN in the certificate's subject alternative name extension.

❑ **Service Principal Name (SPN)**   Includes the computer's SPN in the certificate's subject alternative name extension.

Note   If you enable any of the alternative subject name settings, you must ensure that all users or computers that request the certificate have those fields populated in AD DS. For example, if a user requests a certificate that places the user's e-mail name in the subject alternative name extension, and the user does not have a defined e-mail name, the certificate request will fail.

Issuance Requirements Tab

The Issuance Requirements tab allows you to specify additional requirements to ensure the measures for validating a certificate requestor's identity. The tab also allows you to designate the measures required for reenrollment. (See Figure 12-9.)

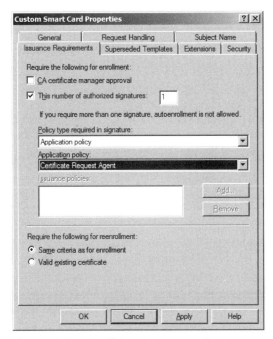

Figure 12-9   Modifying the Issuance Requirements tab

The following settings are available on the Issuance Requirements tab:

- **CA Certificate Manager Approval**   Places a certificate request in a pending state until a certificate manager issues or denies the request. This setting allows the certificate manager to perform any (manual) identification validation (that is specifies by an organization's certificate policy) to determine whether the certificate should be issued.

- **This Number Of Authorized Signatures**   Specifies how many digital signatures must be applied to the certificate request for approval. Once you specify the number of signatures required, you also must specify which application policy or issuance policy object identifiers (OIDs) are required in the signing certificate.

- **Policy Type Required In Signature**   Specifies whether a specific application policy OID, a specific issuance policy OID, or both are required.

> **Note**   Issuance policies are also known as *certificate policies*.

- ❑ **Application Policy**   Defines the specific application policy OID required in the signing certificate if an application policy is designated in the required signing certificate. For example, for an enrollment agent to request certificates on behalf of other users (place the target user's name in the subject name of the certificate), you must require the Certificate Request Agent application policy in the signature as shown previously in Figure 12-9.

- ❑ **Issuance Policy**   Specifies one or more issuance policy OIDs accepted in the signing certificate if an issuance policy is designated in the required signing certificate.

> **Important**   If you set complex signature requirements, such as requiring two or more signatures on a certificate request, you may have to create a custom workflow process, such as a custom Web enrollment page or a Microsoft Identity Lifecycle Manager (ILM) 2007 certificate management profile template, that will implement and enforce the required workflow to allow multiple signatures to be applied to the certificate request. Details on ILM 2007 certificate management are discussed in Chapter 17, "Identity Lifecycle Manager 2007 Certificate Management," and Chapter 21, "Deploying Smart Cards."

- **Require The Following For Reenrollment**   Allows you to designate whether the same identity validation procedures must be used for reenrollment. You can choose to implement the same validation procedures or simply allow reenrollment if the user holds a valid existing certificate. For example, when your organization initially distributes smart cards to its employees, it could require and enforce face-to-face interviews. Rather than have the employees participate in another face-to-face interview when the smart card certificate comes up for renewal, the employees can renew their certificate by proving that they have an existing certificate. This reduces the procedural overhead for certificate renewal.

Superseded Templates Tab

The Superseded Templates tab allows you to define updated certificate templates for previously defined version 1, version 2, or version 3 certificate templates. (See Figure 12-10.)

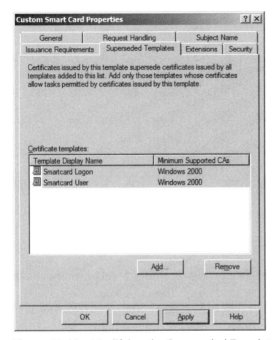

Figure 12-10   Modifying the Superseded Templates tab

By adding one or more certificate templates to the Superseded Templates tab, you can replace the existing certificate template(s) with an updated version 2 or version 3 certificate template. The updated template is automatically deployed by using certificate autoenrollment.

Note   When a certificate template is superseded, the original certificate is not removed from the user's certificate store. Instead, the certificate is marked as archived and suppressed from view in the Certificates console.

Extensions Tab

The Extensions tab allows you to define specific X.509 version 3 certificate extension settings. (See Figure 12-11.)

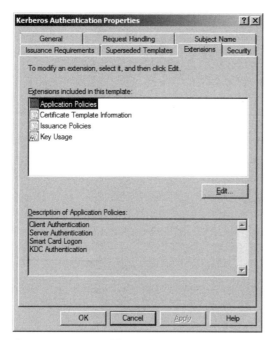

Figure 12-11   Modifying the Extensions tab

The following certificate extensions can be defined:

■ Application Policies   Define the specific applications for which a certificate can be used. Application policies are represented in a certificate by an OID that is defined for a given application. When the certificate is required, an application filters the available certificates to include only those with the necessary application policy OID.

> **Note**   The OIDs in the Application Policies extension are also duplicated in the Enhanced Key Usage (EKU) extension for older applications that do not recognize the Application Policies extension. The only difference is that you can enable the criticality flag for the Application Policies extension, but not for the EKU.

■ **Certificate Template Information**   Defines the display name of the certificate template, the automatically assigned OID for the certificate template, and the subject type. The available subject types are:

❑ Key recovery agent

❑ Directory e-mail replication

❑ Cross-certified certification authority

❑ Certification authority (CA)

❏   Computer

❏   User

> **Note**   You cannot edit the Certificate Template Information extension. You must ensure that the certificate template you duplicate has the required subject type.

- **Issuance Policies**   Also referred to as *certificate policies*, these define the measures taken to validate a certificate's subject. An OID is placed in the Issuance Policies extension, representing the implemented certificate policy, in addition to a URL that provides more information regarding the certificate policy.

- **Key Usage**   A certificate attribute that can further restrict how a certificate can be used. This allows the administrator to define a certificate's specific signing or encryption purposes.

  ❏   For signing certificates, you can further restrict certificates for Digital Signature, Signature Is A Proof Of Origin (Non-Repudiation), Certificate Signing, or CRL Signing.

  ❏   For encryption certificates, you can restrict certificates for key exchange without key encryption or key exchange with key encryption only.

> **Note**   The Key Usage extension is a critical extension. As shown previously in Figure 12-11, a critical extension has an exclamation point in the Extensions included in this template list.

The OCSP Response Signing version 3 certificate template includes a custom extension related to OCSP revocation checking (see Figure 12-12).

The OCSP No Revocation Checking extension (id-pkix-ocsp-nocheck) prevents revocation checking on certificates based on the OCSP Response Signing certificate template. OCSP response signing certificates are short-lived certificates (the default validity period is two weeks) that should not be checked for revocation. The certificate template does not include any AIA or CRL Distribution Point (CDP) extensions to even allow revocation checking.

> **Important**   The OCSP No Revocation Checking extension prevents revocation checking only if the certificate request contains the OCSP signing OID in the EKU and Application Policies extensions.

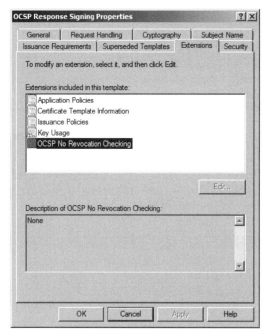

Figure 12-12   OCSP Response Signing enables the OCSP No Revocation Checking extension

Case Study: Certificate Template Design

You are responsible for designing certificate templates for your organization. The software development department has created several custom applications that require digital signing prior to network deployment. Digital signatures are required to meet the company's security policy regarding custom application security. The company uses a mix clients running Windows XP and Windows Vista and servers running Windows Server 2003 and Windows Server 2008.

Requirements

To meet the security policy, the manager of the security department has provided you with the following requirements:

- The code-signing certificate must be stored on a Gemalto .NET Base CSP smart card.

- Only members of the Code Signing group can request a code-signing certificate.

- All initial code-signing certificate requests are subject to the approval of the company's notary public.

- If you already have a code-signing certificate, you can reenroll without having to meet with the notary public again.
- The code-signing certificate must be valid for four years.
- The code-signing certificate must *never* reuse a previous key pair.
- The code-signing certificate must have a key length of 1,024 bits.

Case Study Questions

1. What MMC console do you use to perform certificate template management?

2. Does the default Code Signing certificate template meet the design requirements?

3. Can you modify the default Code Signing certificate template? If not, what would you do?

4. Should you create a version 2 or a version 3 certificate template?

5. In the following table, specify the settings on the General tab to meet the design requirements for your custom code-signing certificate template.

Attribute	Your recommended design
Template display name	
Template name	
Validity period	
Publish certificate in Active Directory	
Do not automatically reenroll if a duplicate certificate exists in Active Directory	
For automatic renewal of smart card certificates, use the existing key if a new key cannot be created	

6. In the following table, specify the settings on the Request Handling tab to meet the design requirements for the custom code-signing certificate template.

Attribute	Your recommended design
Purpose	
Allow private key to be exported	
Minimum key size	
Do the following when the subject is enrolled and when the private key associated with this certificate is used	
CSPs	

7. In the following table, specify the settings on the Issuance Requirements tab to meet the design requirements for the custom code-signing certificate template.

Attribute	Your recommended design
CA certificate manager approval	
This number of authorized signatures	
Require the following for reenrollment	

8. How must you configure the settings on the Superseded Templates tab to ensure that all certificates a CA issues for code signing use the version 2 certificate template?

9. What permission assignment modifications are required for the custom code signing certificate?

Best Practices for Certificate Template Design

When designing certificate templates, the following best practices should be employed:

- Determine whether a default version certificate template meets your business goals. A default template does not require any modifications other than permission assignment.

- If you need to change settings in a certificate template other than permissions, duplicate a template that is closest to the required template. This minimizes the number of changes required.

- If you replace an existing certificate template with an updated template, ensure that you add the previous template to the Superseded Templates tab.

- To enroll a certificate, a user or computer must be assigned Read and Enroll permissions, either directly or through group membership.

- To enroll a certificate with autoenrollment, a user or computer must be assigned Read, Enroll, and Autoenroll permissions.

- To modify a certificate template, a user must be assigned Write permissions.

- Determine whether you should deploy fewer certificates with multiple purposes or many certificates with specific purposes. The decision is based on the purposes you require and whether you foresee removing a purpose from a certificate holder.

- Do not create certificate templates that exceed the lifetime of the issuing CA or the values declared in the CA\ValidityPeriodUnits and CA\ValidityPeriod registry entries. A CA will issue the certificate with a lifetime equal to the lowest value of the three entries.

■ Use version 3 certificate templates only if the operating systems of the computers that will use the certificate template and the applications that will use the certificate templates support CNG algorithms. Currently, CNG–based algorithms are supported only on Windows Vista and Windows Server 2008. Table 12-2 summarizes common applications and their support for version 3 certificates.

Table 12-2   Application Support for Version 3 Certificates

Application name	Verify a certificate chain with version 3 certificates using CNG algorithms	Use algorithms that are not supported by CAPI (CSP)
EFS	Yes	No
IPsec	Yes	Yes
Kerberos	No	No
S/MIME	Microsoft Office Outlook 2003: no	Outlook 2003: no
	Outlook 2007: yes	Outlook 2007: yes
Smart Card Logon	No	No
SSL	Yes	Yes
Wireless	Yes	Yes

Additional Information

■ Microsoft Official Curriculum, Course 2821: "Designing and Managing a Windows Public Key Infrastructure" (*http://www.microsoft.com/traincert/syllabi/2821afinal.asp*)

■ "Implementing and Administering Certificate Templates" (*http://www.microsoft.com/downloads/details.aspx?FamilyID=3c670732-c971-4c65-be9c-c0ebc3749e24&displaylang=en*)

■ 283218: "A Certification Authority Cannot Use a Certificate Template"

■ 281260: "A Certificate Request That Uses a New Template Is Unsuccessful"

■ 313629: "A Custom Smart Card Template Is Unavailable on the Smart Card Enrollment Station"

■ 330238: "Users Cannot Enroll for a Certificate When the Include E-Mail Name in Subject Name Option Is Selected on the Template"

Note   The last four articles in the list above can be accessed through the Microsoft Knowledge Base. Go to *http://support.microsoft.com* and enter the article number in the Search the Knowledge Base text box.

Chapter 13
Role Separation

An important step in designing and implementing a public key infrastructure (PKI) is determining the groups or users who will manage it. To facilitate secure administration of Certificate Services, both the Windows Server 2003 Certificate Services and Windows Server 2008 Active Directory Certificate Services (AD CS) support Common Criteria role separation. Common Criteria role separation requires that PKI management be configured so that no single person has full control, thereby protecting an organization against a "malicious PKI administrator."

There are other roles that must be considered when designing and implementing your organization's PKI in addition to the roles defined in the Common Criteria protection profile. This chapter will discuss how to plan PKI management and implement role separation.

Note Because there is no difference in implementing Common Criteria role separation in Windows Server 2003 and Windows Server 2008, the rest of this chapter will refer to Windows Server 2008.

Common Criteria Roles

According to Common Criteria guidelines, no user can hold more than one PKI management role—and any user who does hold two or more PKI management roles must be blocked from all management functions.

Note You can assign multiple users the same role when defining role-holders. Enforcing Common Criteria role separation on a Windows Server 2008 certification authority (CA) ensures that *a single user cannot hold multiple roles, but multiple users can hold the same role.*

Common Criteria Levels

"Certificate Issuing and Management Components Family of Protection Profiles" is a standards document that defines requirements for the issuance, revocation, and management of X.509 certificates. Taking into consideration that different security levels are required for different organizations, the standards document describes four protection profiles. Each profile provides additional safety through increased security and assurance requirements for X.509 certificate distribution.

> **More Info**   Windows Server 2008 Certificate Services is designed to meet the role definitions listed in version 1.0 of "Certificate Issuing and Management Components Family of Protection Profiles," which can be found at *http://niap.bahialab.com/cc-scheme/pp/ PP_CIMC_SL1-4_V1.0.pdf.*

Security Level 1

Certificate Issuing and Management Components (CIMC) Security Level 1 defines the minimum level of certificate management security for environments in which threats against the PKI are considered to be low. It defines two PKI management roles:

- **CA administrator**   Responsible for account administration, key generation of the CA certificate's key pair, and auditing configuration

- **Certificate manager**   Responsible for certificate management. Management functions include issuing and revoking certificates

In addition to these two roles, the PKI must restrict access to only authorized PKI users and implement only cryptographic algorithms that are validated against Federal Information Processing Standards (FIPS) 140-1, "Security Requirements for Cryptographic Modules."

Security Level 2

CIMC Security Level 2 increases the level of certificate management security for environments in which the risks and consequences of data disclosure are not considered a significant issue. It also increases security by rejecting certificate requests by unauthorized users. All users must authenticate with the PKI before certificate issuance.

Security Level 2 uses the same two management roles as Security Level 1. The difference is that Level 2 requires increased auditing and cryptographic protection of audit logs and system backups. In addition, FIPS 140-1 Level 2 cryptographic modules are required for the protection of a CA's key pair.

Security Level 3

CIMC Security Level 3 further raises the security level and is intended for environments in which it is considered a moderate risk if data is disclosed or loss of data integrity. As compared to Security Level 2, CIMC Security Level 3 implements additional integrity controls to ensure that an unauthorized person cannot modify data. This includes protection against an unauthorized person who gains physical access to a CA.

Security Level 3 defines three PKI management roles:

- **CA administrator**   Responsible for account administration, key generation of the CA certificate's key pair, and auditing configuration.

> ## Choosing Auditing Behavior
>
> Windows Server 2003 Service Pack 1 and Windows Server 2008 allow you to choose which Common Criteria role can define audit settings. The default behavior in Windows Server 2003 and Windows Server 2008 is to allow the Auditor role to both define audit settings at the CA and to view and maintain the audit logs.
>
> With Windows Server 2003 Service Pack 1 or Windows Server 2008 installed, you can instead choose to have the CA administrator role define the audit settings at a specific CA. This is accomplished by having a local administrator run the following **certutil** command:
>
> **certutil -setreg CA\InterfaceFlags +IF_ENABLEADMINASAUDITOR**
>
> Once the command executes and Certificate Services is restarted, the task of defining the CA audit settings is allocated to the CA administrator role rather than the CA auditor role.

- **Certificate manager**   Responsible for certificate management. Management functions include issuing and revoking certificates.

- **Auditor**   Responsible for maintaining the CA audit logs.

Additional security measures include having at least two persons involved in the control and management of private keys, implementing FIPS 140-1 Level 3 protection of CA keys, and requiring digital signatures for all data transferred between the CA and the hardware security module (HSM).

Security Level 4

CIMC Security Level 4 provides the highest PKI security protection. It is intended for environments in which the consequences of data disclosure and loss of data integrity by either authorized or unauthorized users are significant to the organization.

Security Level 4 defines four PKI management roles:

- **CA administrator**   Responsible for account administration and key generation of the CA certificate's key pair

- **Certificate manager**   Responsible for certificate management, including functions such as issuing and revoking certificates

- **Auditor**   Responsible for maintaining and viewing the CA audit log entries in the Windows Security log

- **Backup operator**   Responsible for performing backups of PKI information

Security Level 4 requires signed third-party timestamping of audit logs to increase integrity. In addition, cryptographic modules at each CA must be validated to FIPS 140-1 Level 4.

> **Note**   The only cryptographic module rated at FIPS 140-1 Level 4 at the time of this book's publication is the AEP Keyper Enterprise (*http://www.aepnetworks.com/products/ key_management/keyper/ent_overview.aspx*). More FIPS 140-1 Level 4 devices should be available in the near future.

Windows Implementation of Common Criteria

Windows Server 2008 allows you to define PKI management roles in compliance with the four roles defined in CIMC Security Level 4. The Windows Server PKI management roles are:

- CA administrator
- Certificate manager
- Backup operator
- Auditor

The following sections detail information on Windows Server Common Criteria roles and how to implement each role.

> **Note**   AD CS does not require the user to have local administrative rights on the CA computer for day-to-day PKI management. The user must be assigned only the CA permissions or the user rights associated with one of the four Common Criteria roles.

> **Important**   The only tasks where administrative rights are required at a CA are the installation of a new CA or the renewal of a CA certificate. You must be a member of the local administrators to install AD CS and to generate key material in the local machine store. In addition, you must be a member of Enterprise Admins to install or renew an enterprise CA.

CA Administrator

A CA administrator configures and maintains the CA. A user assigned the CA administrator role can designate other CA administrators, assign certificate managers, and perform the following CA management tasks:

- **Configure extensions**   Define URLs for both CRL Distribution Points (CDPs) and Authority Information Access (AIA).
- **Configure policy and exit modules**   Policy and exit modules determine the actions a CA takes during certificate issuance. For example, the default policy module allows a CA

administrator to configure whether all certificate requests are pended or issued based on the user's credentials. An exit module allows you to define whether the certificate information is published to preconfigured file share locations.

Using Exit Modules

Exit modules can be used in many ways to enhance the functionality of a Windows Server 2008 CA. For example, Microsoft has deployed a custom exit module that performs a real-time, centralized logging function that tracks all issued certificates into a Microsoft SQL Server database. This functionality is discussed in the article "Microsoft IT Showcase: Deploying PKI Inside Microsoft," available at *http://www.microsoft.com/ downloads/details.aspx?FamilyId=46CA7043-0433-4140-853A-05F01430A30D&display-lang=en.*

In the default exit module for Certificate Services, you can enable additional functionality by enabling the Simple Mail Transfer Protocol (SMTP) functionality within the exit module. The SMTP functionality allows the CA to send SMTP e-mail messages to designated e-mail recipients when specific CA activities take place, such as the publication of a certificate revocation list (CRL), revocation of a certificate, or stopping and starting of Certificate Services. The SMTP exit module functionality is discussed in the "Windows Server 2003 PKI Operations Guide," available at *http://www.microsoft.com/down-loads/details.aspx?FamilyID=8e25369f-bc5a-4083-a42d-436bdb363e7e&DisplayLang=en.*

- **Define certificate manager restrictions**   Restrict each certificate manager to management of specific combinations of global groups and certificate templates.
- **Define enrollment agent restrictions**   Restrict each defined enrollment agent to management of specific combinations of global groups and certificate templates.
- **Define certificate managers**   Designate certificate managers to issue and deny certificate requests and to extract encrypted private keys from the CA database for key recovery.
- **Define key recovery agents**   Designate key recovery agent certificates at a CA for the archival and recovery of private keys at the CA database.
- **Define other CA administrators**   Designate CA administrators to perform CA management tasks.
- **Delete a single record in the CA database**   By using the **certutil –deleterow** command to delete the record associated with the certificate, you can remove specific certificate information from the CA database.
- **Enable, publish, or configure the CRL schedule**   Manage all aspects of publishing CRLs and delta CRLs at a CA.
- **Read the CA configuration information**   View the CA's current configuration and modify only those areas enabled for modification by CA administrators.

- **Stop and start Certificate Services**   Stop and start Certificate Services to apply registry changes.

> **Warning**   This does not prevent a local administrator from stopping and starting Certificate Services. This only allows a CA administrator to stop and start Certificate Services.

- **Configure audit parameters**   As mentioned earlier in the chapter, by running **certutil -setreg CA\InterfaceFlags +IF_ENABLEADMINASAUDITOR** you can allow a CA administrator to define audit settings at a CA rather than allow a CA auditor to configure these settings. A CA administrator can enable the following auditing settings for the CA in the Certification Authority console:

  - ❏ **Back Up And Restore The CA Database.**   Logs any attempt to back up or restore the CA database to the Windows Security log.

  - ❏ **Change CA Configurations**   Logs any attempt to modify CA configuration. This can include defining AIA and CDP URLs or defining a key recovery agent.

  - ❏ **Change CA Security Settings**   Logs any attempt to modify CA permissions. This can include adding CA administrators or certificate managers.

  - ❏ **Issue And Manage Certificate Requests**   Logs any attempt by a certificate manager to approve or deny certificate requests that are in a pending state.

  - ❏ **Revoke Certificates And Publish CRLs**   Logs any attempt by a certificate manager to revoke an issued certificate or by a CA administrator to publish an updated CRL.

  - ❏ **Store And Retrieve Archived Keys**   Logs any attempt during the enrollment process to archive private keys in the CA database or by certificate managers to extract archived private keys from the CA database.

  - ❏ **Start And Stop Certificate Services**   Logs any attempt by the CA administrator to start or stop Certificate Services.

> **Note**   To ensure that all events related to Certificate Services auditing are logged to the security log, ensure that both success and failure events are enabled for Object Access at the CA. The settings can be applied directly in the Local Security Settings or by applying a Group Policy Object (GPO) with the required auditing settings.

Certificate Manager

This role approves or denies certificate enrollment requests and revokes issued certificates. Specifically, a user assigned the certificate manager role can:

- **Issue or deny pending certificate requests**   At a standalone CA all certificate requests are pended by default until a certificate manager approves the certificate requests. Likewise, a certificate template can be defined so that a certificate manager must approve a certificate request before the CA issues the certificate.

- **Revoke issued certificates**   A certificate manager can revoke a certificate if the organization's revocation policy requires certificate revocation. For example, a certificate can be revoked if the private key is compromised. Certificate revocation terminates the certificate's validity prior to expiration.

- **Determine key recovery agents**   A certificate manager determines which defined key recovery agent can decrypt an archived private key from the CA database.

- **Extract archived private keys from the CA database**   A certificate manager can extract the archived private key from the CA database. The private key is extracted in a binary large object (BLOB) format, which is an encrypted PKCS #7 file that only the designated key recovery agent can decrypt.

> **Note**   A binary large object (BLOB) is a data type that can store any format of data in a binary format.

Auditor

An auditor can view the CA's Security event log to review auditing events related to Certificate Services.

Backup Operator

Performs backups of the CA database, the CA configuration, and the CA's private and public key pairs, known as a *key pair*.

> **Note**   If the CA's private and public key pair is stored on an HSM, backup operators can back up the CA key pair only if the HSM's security context allows this ability.

Assigning Common Criteria Roles

Once you determine which users should hold each Common Criteria role, you must define the role-holders. The definition is CA-specific, meaning that you can assign different role-holders at each CA in the hierarchy.

> **Tip**   Assign the permissions for Common Criteria role separation to either domain local groups (for domain member computers) or local groups within the local Security Account Management (SAM) database of each CA.

CA Manager

You can use the following procedure to define a CA administrator at a CA:

1. Open the Certification Authority console.

2. In the console tree, right-click *CAName*, and then click Properties.

3. On the Security tab, click Add, and then type the names of any users or domain local groups that will be CA administrators.

4. Assign the users or groups Manage CA permission, and then click OK.

Certificate Manager

You can use the following procedure to define a certificate manager at a CA:

1. Open the Certification Authority console.

2. In the console tree, right-click *CAName*, and then click Properties.

3. On the Security tab, click Add, and then type the names of any domain local groups that will be certificate managers.

4. Assign the users or groups Issue and Manage Certificates permission, and then click OK.

Auditor

You can use the following procedure to assign a user the role of auditor:

1. From Administrative Tools, open Local Security Policy.

2. In the console tree, expand Local Policies, and then click User Rights Assignment.

3. In the details pane, double-click Manage Auditing And Security Log.

4. Add the user accounts or groups that will perform auditing at the CA, and then click OK.

5. Close Local Security Policy.

 Warning   A CA auditor is assigned the auditor role systemwide. The user cannot be limited to viewing only Security event log entries related to Certificate Services. The user can view *all* entries in the Security event log.

Backup Operator

You can use the following procedure to assign a user or group the role of backup operator:

1. From Administrative Tools, open Local Security Policy.

2. In the console tree, expand Local Policies, and then click User Rights Assignment.

3. In the details pane, double-click Backup Files And Directories.

4. Add the user accounts or groups that will perform auditing at the CA, and then click OK.

5. In the details pane, double-click Restore Files And Directories.

6. Add the user accounts or groups that will perform auditing at the CA, and then click OK.

7. Close Local Security Policy.

> **Note**   Alternatively, you can choose to simply add the user account to the local Backup Operators group.

Implementing Certificate Manager Restrictions

Some organizations may require further restrictions on certificate manager activities. Rather than allow a certificate manager to issue or revoke *any* certificate issued by a CA, the organization may want a certificate manager to manage only a subset of all certificates.

AD CS allows a CA administrator to define restrictions for certificate managers. Not only can a certificate manager restriction limit a certificate manager to issuing or revoking certificates whose subject has membership in a specified security group (as previously implemented in Windows Server 2003), but now, you can further restrict the certificate manager to managing only certificates based on specific certificate templates.

For example, assume that the following groups are assigned the Issue and Manage Certificates permission:

- APACCertManagers
- EMEACertManagers
- EFSManagers

> **Important**   To define a certificate manager restriction for a specific user or group, the user or group must be explicitly defined in the Issue and Manage Certificates permission on the CA's security tab. You cannot define certificate manager restrictions for users or groups nested within a group assigned the Issue and Manage Certificates permission.

A CA administrator could then restrict which combinations of groups/computers/users and certificate templates each manager group can manage. For example, you could limit the APACCertManagers group to issuing certificates to or revoking certificates only of the members of the APACUsers and APACComputers groups. You could limit the EMEACertManagers group to issuing and revoking certificates issued to the EMEAUsers and EMEAComputers groups.

> **Important**   If a user account has membership in both the APACUsers and EMEAUsers groups, the certificate issued to that user can be managed by certificate managers in either the APACCertManagers or EMEACertManagers groups.

The new functionality allows you to define restrictions further. As shown in Figure 13-1, you can now restrict a certificate manager to a combination of certificate templates and to specific groups.

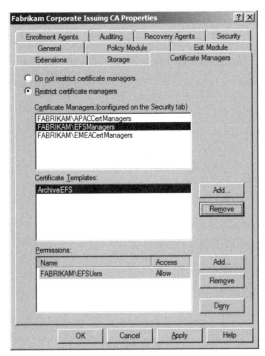

Figure 13-1   Restricting certificate managers

In the example, the EFSManagers group can manage certificates based only on the Archive EFS certificate template that is issued to members of the EFSUsers group. This new combination allows you to not only restrict the manager to members of a specific group but to a specific certificate template.

> **Note**   To implement certificate manager restrictions, the CA computer account must be included in the Pre–Windows 2000 Compatible Access group. Membership in this group allows the CA to determine the group memberships defined for the subject of a certificate.

Enforcing Common Criteria Role Separation

You can enforce Common Criteria role separation on the Windows Server 2003 Enterprise and Datacenter Editions and Windows Server 2008 Enterprise and Datacenter Editions. By enforcing role separation, AD CS blocks any user account that is assigned two or more Common Criteria roles from all Certificate Services management activities.

For example, if a user is assigned both the CA Administrator and Certificate Manager roles, the user cannot perform the tasks defined for either role.

To enforce Common Criteria role separation, a local administrator of the computer must configure the RoleSeparationEnabled registry value. This is done by performing the following procedure:

1. Type the following command at a command prompt:

   ```
   certutil -setreg CA\RoleSeparationEnabled 1
   ```

2. Restart AD CS.

If any users are assigned two or more roles, their administrative activities are blocked immediately.

> **Tip**   If you accidentally assign yourself two or more Common Criteria roles and block yourself from PKI management tasks, a local administrator must disable Common Criteria role separation by typing **certutil –delreg CA\RoleSeparationEnabled** and then restarting AD CS. With role separation disabled, a CA administrator or local administrator must fix the role assignments and reenable Common Criteria role separation.

Role Separation and CA Certificate Renewal

The one scenario where role separation hinders PKI management activities is the case of CA certificate renewal. When a CA's certificate is renewed, a user may have to hold different roles. The user:

- Must be a CA administrator to publish an updated CRL.

- Must be a local administrator to renew the CA certificate.

- Must be a member of the local Administrators group to access the local machine store of a software-based cryptographic service provider (CSP), such as the Microsoft Strong Cryptographic Service Provider v1.0.

- Must be a member of the *ForestRootDomain*\Domain Admins or Enterprise Admins group to allow creation of the CDP and CA certificate objects within the Configuration naming context.

  ❑ A new CDP object is created in the CN=*CAName*,CN=CDP,CN=Public Key Services,CN=Services,CN=Configuration,*ForestRootDomain* (where *CAName* is the NetBIOS name of the CA computer and *ForestRootDomain* is the Lightweight Directory Access Protocol (LDAP) distinguished name of the forest) container.

❑ A new CA certificate object is created in the AIA container (CN=AIA, CN=Public Key Services,CN=Services,CN=Configuration,*ForestRootDomain*).

❑ A new CA certificate object is added to the NTAuth store (CN=NTAuth-Certificates,CN=Public Key Services,CN=Services,CN=Configuration,*ForestRootDomain*).

❑ If the CA is an enterprise CA, a new CA certificate object is created in the Enrollment Services container (CN=Enrollment Services,CN=Public Key Services,CN=Services,CN=Configuration,*ForestRootDomain*).

If the CA is an enterprise root CA, a new CA certificate object is created in the Certification Authorities container (CN=Certification Authorities,CN=Public Key Services,CN=Services,CN=Configuration,*ForestRootDomain*).

To accomplish the task of CA certificate renewal, you must disable role separation temporarily during the CA certificate renewal process. Ensure that the account that performs the CA certificate renewal is a member of the Enterprise Admins group, is a member of the local Administrators group, and is assigned the Manage CA permission. Once the CA certificate renewal process is completed, role separation should be enforced.

Other PKI Management Roles

In addition to the Common Criteria roles, Windows Server 2008 can implement other roles in the PKI management structure, which are discussed in this section.

Local Administrator

The CA's local administrator is any member of the local Administrators group in the local accounts database of the CA computer. This typically includes the local Administrator account and the Domain Admins global group from the CA computer's domain. The membership can also contain the Enterprise Admins group from the forest root domain.

A local administrator can perform the following tasks at a Windows Server 2008 CA:

■ **All CA administrator tasks**   By default, the local Administrators group is assigned the Manage CA permission.

■ **All certificate manager tasks**   By default, the local Administrators group is assigned the Issue and Manage Certificates permission.

■ **Enable or disable Common Criteria role separation**   Members of the local Administrators group have the required permissions to make the necessary registry modifications to enable or disable Common Criteria role separation.

- **Install Certificate Services**   To install Certificate Services, the installer must be a member of the local Administrators group.

- **Renew a CA certificate**   To renew a CA certificate, the user must have access to the local machine's certificate store. By default, only members of the local Administrators group have the necessary access.

Enterprise Admins

By default, Enterprise Admins are able to create and modify objects stored in Active Directory Domain Services Configuration naming context. When you install an enterprise CA in your forest, a member of the Enterprise Admins group must perform the installation to ensure that the required objects are created in the Configuration naming context.

> **Note**   The user performing the installation must also be a member of the local Administrators group to install AD CS.

Enterprise Admins Tasks

A member of the Enterprise Admins group is able to perform the following PKI administration tasks:

- **Install an enterprise CA**   Only members of the Enterprise Admins group can create the required objects in the Configuration naming context when an enterprise CA is installed.

- **Modify and create certificate templates**   A member of the Enterprise Admins group can modify permissions of a version 1 certificate template and all properties of a version 2 or version 3 certificate template. In addition, members of the Enterprise Admins group can create new version 2 or version 3 certificate templates based on existing version 1, version 2, or version 3 certificate templates.

- **Publish CA certificates to Active Directory Domain Services**   A member of the Enterprise Admins group can publish the CA certificate for an offline CA, NTAuth certificates, and Cross Certification Authority certificates to the Configuration naming context.

- **Publish offline CA CRLs to Active Directory Domain Services**   A member of the Enterprise Admins group can publish the CRL for an offline CA to the Configuration naming context.

Certificate Template Manager

In some organizations, the task of managing certificate templates can be delegated to a custom group rather than be left to the Enterprise Admins group.

Certificate Template Manager Tasks

A certificate template manager is able to manage the properties of existing certificate templates. In addition, a certificate template manager is able to create, modify, or delete version 2 or version 3 certificate templates.

Assigning the Certificate Template Manager Role

Three separate tasks must be performed to assign the Certificate Template Manager role:

- Delegate permissions to the Certificate Templates container in the Configuration naming context to create new certificate templates.

- Delegate permissions to the OID container in the Configuration naming context to create new object identifiers (OIDs).

- Delegate permissions to every existing certificate template in the Certificate Templates container in the Configuration naming context.

Delegate Permissions for Creation of New Templates   You can delegate the permission to create new templates by assigning permissions to a custom universal group for the CN=Certificate Templates,CN=Public Key Services,CN=Services,CN=Configuration, *ForestRootDomain* container.

1. Log on as a member of the Enterprise Admins group or the forest root domain Domain Admins group.

2. Open the Active Directory Sites And Services console.

3. From the View menu, ensure that the Show Services Node setting is enabled.

4. In the console tree, expand Services, expand Public Key Services, and then click Certificate Templates.

5. In the console tree, right-click Certificate Templates, and then click Delegate Control.

6. In the Delegation Of Control wizard, click Next.

7. On the Users Or Groups page, click Add.

8. In the Select Users, Computers, Or Groups dialog box, type a user or group name, and then click OK.

9. On the Users Or Groups page, click Next.

10. On the Tasks To Delegate page, click Create A Custom Task To Delegate, and then click Next.

11. On the Active Directory Object Type page, click This Folder, Existing Objects In This Folder, and Creation Of New Objects In This Folder, and then click Next.

12. On the Permissions page, in the Permissions list, enable Full Control, and then click Next.

13. On the Completing The Delegation Of Control wizard page, click Finish.

Delegate Permissions for Creation of New OIDs   When a certificate template is created, an OID is generated to identify the certificate template. To create a new certificate template, a user must be delegated the permission to create new OIDs in the CN=OID,CN=Public Key Services,CN=Services,CN=Configuration,*ForestRootDomain* container.

1. Log on as a member of the Enterprise Admins group or the forest root domain Domain Admins group.

2. Open the Active Directory Sites And Services console.

3. On the View menu, ensure that the Show Services Node setting is enabled.

4. In the console tree, expand Services, expand Public Key Services, right-click OID, and then click Properties.

5. In the OID Properties dialog box, on the Security tab, click Advanced.

6. In the Advanced Security Settings For OID dialog box, click Add.

7. In the Select Users, Computers, Or Groups dialog box, type the names of the users or groups you want to delegate certificate management permissions to, and then click OK.

8. In the Permissions Entry For OID dialog box, in the Apply To drop-down list, select This Object And All Descendant Objects, select the Allow check box for Full Control, and then click OK.

9. In the Advanced Security Settings For OID dialog box, click OK.

10. In the OID Properties dialog box, click OK.

Delegate Permissions to Every Existing Certificate Template in the Certificate   Once you delegate permissions for creating and modifying new certificate templates, you must modify the permissions of the existing certificate templates.

You can run a script file to delegate certificate template permissions to a custom universal group. The script file must include the 34 default certificate templates and any other custom certificate templates that exist when the script is executed.

For each certificate template, the script must include the following line:

```
dsacls "CN=TemplateName,CN=Certificate Templates,CN=Public Key
Services,CN=Services,CN=Configuration,ForestRootDomain" /G
DomainName\GroupName:SDDTRCWDWOLCWPRPCCDCWSLO
```

For example, to delegate certificate template permissions for the EFS Recovery Agent certificate template in the example.com forest to a group named example\Template-Adminstrators, you would use the following command:

```
dsacls "CN=EFSRecovery,CN=Certificate Templates,CN=Public Key
Services,CN=Services,CN=Configuration,DC=example,DC=com" /G
example\TemplateAdministrators:SDDTRCWDWOLCWPRPCCDCWSLO
```

> **On the Disc**   A copy of this script is included on the accompanying CD-ROM. The script, DelegateTemplateModification.cmd, must be modified to replace the example\Template-Administrators group with the name of the custom universal group deployed in your forest.

Editing Existing Certificate Templates

If a delegated certificate template administrator attempts to edit an existing certificate template, the attempt will fail unless the certificate template administrator takes ownership of the certificate template. To take ownership, the certificate template administrator must:

1. Open the Certificate Templates console (Certtmpl.msc).

2. Right-click the existing certificate template, and then click Properties.

3. On the Security tab, click Advanced.

4. On the Owner tab, in the Change Owner To list, select the certificate template adminis-trator's user account name, and then click Apply.

5. In the Advanced Security Settings For TemplateName dialog box, click OK.

6. In the *TemplateName* Properties dialog box, click OK.

Enrollment Agent

An enrollment agent is able to request certificates on behalf of other users.

Enrollment Agent Tasks

The enrollment agent role is typically used to request smart card certificates on behalf of other users. An enrollment agent validates the smart card requestor's identity and then submits a smart card request on behalf of the requestor. The enrollment request differs from a normal enrollment request in that the enrollment agent signs the request with a certificate that has the Certificate Request Agent OID (1.3.6.1.4.1.311.20.2.1) in the certificate's Application Policies extension. The CA enforces that the certificate request must be signed by a certificate with the Certificate Request Agent OID if the subject provided in the certificate request does not match the identity of the account used to submit the certificate request.

Assigning the Enrollment Agent Role

To assign the enrollment agent role, a user must request a certificate with the Certificate Request Agent OID in the Application Policy or in the Enhanced Key Usage extension.

By default, the Enrollment Agent version 1 certificate template includes the necessary OID. A user becomes an enrollment agent by requesting and receiving a certificate based on the Enrollment Agent certificate template.

Note   The design decisions for deploying enrollment agent and smart card certificates are discussed in Chapter 21, "Deploying Smart Cards."

Key Recovery Agent

The key recovery agent role is responsible for recovering private keys archived in the CA database. Only the holders of the private key associated with the Key Recovery Agent certificate can recover the private keys once a certificate manager extracts the PKCS #7 BLOB file from the CA database.

Key Recovery Agent Tasks

A key recovery agent is responsible for decrypting a PKCS #7 BLOB file that contains an encrypted copy of the user's certificate and private key. The resulting decryption provides a PKCS #12 object (file) that can be imported by the user into his or her profile.

A key recovery agent is dependant on the certificate manager role to extract the encrypted PKCS#7 BLOB file from the CA database. The key recovery agent should not be assigned the certificate manager role to ensure that at least two people are involved in the key recovery process.

Warning   You should never assign a user both the certificate manager and key recovery agent roles. Even though Common Criteria role separation does not address key archival, allowing one user to hold both the certificate manager and key recovery agent roles allows that user to both extract and decrypt an archived private key from the CA database.

Assigning the Key Recovery Agent Role

To assign the key recovery agent role, a user must have a certificate with the Key Recovery Agent application policy OID. The default Key Recovery Agent version 2 certificate template includes this application policy OID and can be further secured by limiting the users and groups with enrollment permissions.

In addition, a CA must be configured to enable key recovery. This is done by designating one or more Key Recovery Agent certificates to act as the CA's key recovery agent. Only the holders of the private keys associated with the selected Key Recovery Agent certificates are able to decrypt the extracted PKCS #7 BLOBs.

> **Note** The design decisions for deploying key recovery agents and enabling key archival and recovery are discussed in Chapter 18, "Archiving Encryption Keys."

Case Study: Planning PKI Management Roles

In this case study, you will look at the definition of PKI Management roles.

Scenario

You are the security services manager for Tailspin Toys. Your organization implements a two-tier CA hierarchy, as shown in Figure 13-2.

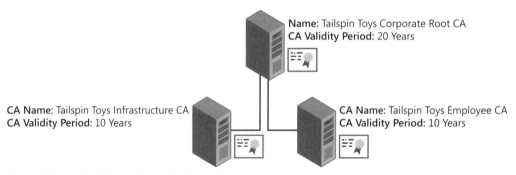

Name: Tailspin Toys Corporate Root CA
CA Validity Period: 20 Years

CA Name: Tailspin Toys Infrastructure CA
CA Validity Period: 10 Years

CA Name: Tailspin Toys Employee CA
CA Validity Period: 10 Years

Figure 13-2 The Tailspin Toys CA hierarchy

The CA hierarchy implements two issuing CAs:

- Tailspin Toys Infrastructure CA This CA issues certificates to domain controllers, servers, computers, and network devices.

- Tailspin Toys Employee CA This CA issues certificates to employees (users) of Tailspin Toys.

The issuing CAs are managed by two different teams: The network services team manages the Tailspin Toys Infrastructure CA, and the directory services team manages the Tailspin Toys Employee CA. Your team, security services, has the ability to manage both CAs.

Within each department, different users are assigned the PKI Common Criteria roles of CA Administrator and Certificate Manager. Backups are performed by a centralized backup services account. Auditing is performed by members of both the security services team and the internal audit department. The security policy of Tailspin Toys requires strong enforcement of Common Criteria role separation for PKI management.

Case Study Questions

1. The backup software implemented by Tailspin Toys uses a centralized backup services account. When reviewing the event logs, the backup operator notices that the backup fails every night on the two issuing CAs. On inspecting the event logs further, the backup software reports that the failed backup item is the System State backup. What is the likely cause of the error?

2. When inspecting the security permission assignments at the Tailspin Toys Infrastructure CA, you accidentally assign the CA Administrator group the Issue and Manage Certificates permission. When you try and fix the permissions assignment error, you find that access is denied. What must be done to fix the issue?

3. The certificate for the Tailspin Toys Employee CA is reaching the halfway point of its validity period and must be renewed. You are logged on to the CA as a CA Administrator but all attempts to renew the CA certificate fail. Who must perform the renewal of the CA certificate?

4. The Tailspin Toys Employee CA implements key archival for both Encrypting File System (EFS) certificates and e-mail encryption certificates. The security policy of your organization requires that all key recovery operations be performed by at least two employees. If you are assigned the Key Recovery Agent role, what Common Criteria role can you not hold, because this would break the security policy for key recovery?

5. Tailspin Toys implements several version 1 certificate templates at the Tailspin Toys Infrastructure CA. You have delegated the task of managing certificate templates to Andy, a member of the IT security team. Andy is able to create new version 2 and version 3 certificate templates but is unable to modify the permissions for any of the version 1 certificate templates deployed at the Tailspin Toys Infrastructure CA. Why is Andy unable to modify the version 1 certificate templates?

6. Tailspin Toys wishes to deploy a new enterprise subordinate CA named Tailspin Toys Contractor CA to issue certificates to contractors and vendors working on-site. When you attempt to install the enterprise CA, the options for both enterprise root CA and enterprise subordinate CA are unavailable. What group memberships are required to install an enterprise CA?

7. You have enabled auditing at all issuing CAs in the CA hierarchy. Today, you received a call from the audit department indicating that no events related to Certificate Services exist in the Windows Security log. You view the properties of each CA and find that the auditing is configured at each CA, as shown in Figure 13-3.

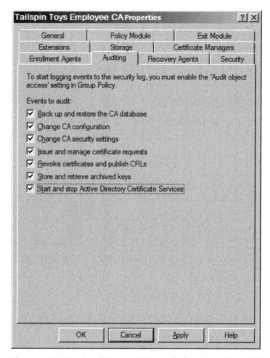

Figure 13-3   Auditing settings defined at the Tailspin Toys Employee CA

Why are there no audit entries related to Certificate Services?

Additional Information

- Microsoft Official Curriculum, Course 2821: "Designing and Managing a Windows Public Key Infrastructure" (*http://www.microsoft.com/learning/syllabi/en-us/2821Afinal.mspx*)

- "PKCS #7: Cryptographic Message Syntax Standard" (*ftp://ftp.rsasecurity.com/pub/pkcs/doc/pkcs-7.doc*)

- "Windows Server 2003 PKI Operations Guide" (*http://technet2.microsoft.com/windowsserver/en/library/e1d5a892-10e1-417c-be13-99d7147989a91033.mspx?mfr=true*)

- "Best Practices for Implementing a Microsoft Windows Server 2003 Public Key Infrastructure" (*http://technet2.microsoft.com/windowsserver/en/library/091cda67-79ec-481d-8a96-03e0be7374ed1033.mspx?mfr=true*)

- "PKI Enhancements in Windows XP Professional and Windows Server 2003" (*http://www.microsoft.com/technet/prodtechnol/winxppro/Plan/PKIEnh.asp*)

- "Active Directory Certificate Server Enhancements in Windows Server Code Name 'Longhorn'" white paper (*http://www.microsoft.com/downloads/details.aspx? familyid=9bf17231-d832-4ff9-8fb8-0539ba21ab95&displaylang=en*)

- "Microsoft IT Showcase: Deploying PKI Inside Microsoft" (*http://www.microsoft.com/ downloads/details.aspx?FamilyId=46CA7043-0433-4140-853A-05F01430A30D& displaylang=en*)

- "Certificate Issuing and Management Components Family of Protection Profiles" (*http://niap.bahialab.com/cc-scheme/pp/PP_CIMC_SL1-4_V1.0.pdf*)

Chapter 14

Planning and Implementing Disaster Recovery

When designing a public key infrastructure (PKI) for your organization, you must develop an effective disaster recovery plan to ensure that, in the event of failure of the computer hosting Certificate Services, you can recover in a timely manner with little effect to your organization.

Common reasons that make a disaster recovery plan necessary include:

- **Failed services**   If Certificate Services fails to start on the certification authority (CA) computer, no certificates can be issued, and certificate revocation lists (CRLs) cannot be published.

  Your disaster plan for recovery should include performing and testing either Microsoft Windows server backups or manual CA backups on a regular basis.

- **Hardware failure**   If the CA server hardware fails, the failure may prevent the server from booting, Certificate Services being unable to access its database or logs (because of a failed disk), or the CA being unable to access its private key because of a hardware security module (HSM) failure.

  Disaster plan options for recovering after hardware failure include:

  - Maintaining duplicate hardware (such as spare motherboards or spare computers)
  - Performing image backups with software (such as Symantec Ghost) to rebuild the CA in a timely manner on similar hardware
  - Implementing fault-tolerant RAID 1 or RAID 5 volumes to prevent CA failure caused by a single disk failure.
  - Implementing an active/passive cluster of Certificate Services.
  - Implementing fail-over HSMs.

- **Network infrastructure failure**   Disaster recovery plans must account for network infrastructure failures. If an application implements CRL checking, and network infrastructure failure prevents the application from accessing the most recent version of the CRL, the application will not validate the certificates presented to the application.

  Your disaster recovery should include methods of diagnosing network infrastructure failures and developing methods of publishing CRL information that are redundant to protect against network failure.

Developing Required Documentation

One of the most important tasks during the design and deployment of a PKI is to ensure that your network and configuration documentation is updated continually. When you are forced to implement your disaster recovery process, this documentation is the most important source of information regarding the previous Certificate Services configuration.

You should maintain the following documentation to ensure that you can apply all required configuration of Certificate Services successfully:

- **All certificate template definitions**   In the worst case, you might have to rebuild Active Directory Domain Services (AD DS), which requires the re-creation of all certificate templates. By documenting the individual settings for each certificate template on a tab-by-tab basis, you can easily re-create each certificate template.

- **All certificate templates published at the CA**   You can create a custom script file that implements **certutil -SetCAtemplates +<TemplateName>** to publish certificate templates and **certutil -SetCAtemplates -<TemplateName>** to remove certificate templates from the CA.

- **All permissions and user rights assignments**   CA permissions determine which users or groups hold the CA administrator Common Criteria role and the certificate manager Common Criteria role, which users or groups can read the CA configuration, and which users or groups can request certificates from the CA. In addition, the local security policy or domain-based Group Policy Objects (GPOs) applied to the CA's computer account determines the user rights applied to the computer account, including the Common Criteria backup operators and auditor role holders.

- **All names used for the CA**   Includes the CA's logical name, the NetBIOS name of the computer hosting Certificate Services, and the domain or workgroup membership. The certificate information is based on the CA's specific names and must be restored correctly.

- **All specific settings in the properties of the CA in the Certification Authority console**   Be sure to identify the certificates that are designated for key recovery, if implemented, as well as certificate manager and enrollment agent restrictions.

- **Any post-installation or pre-installation script files used to configure the CA**   For example, if you run a batch file consisting of **certutil** commands that define the CA's registry settings, you should store a copy of the batch file for documentation and recovery purposes. Likewise, you should keep a copy of a batch file that publishes the CA's CRL on an externally accessible Web server.

- **Audit Settings**   What audit settings are enabled for the CA.

- **CA data paths**   When you restore the CA, the previous file locations for the CA database, CA log files, and CA configuration information must be maintained to match the restored registry values.

- **CRL and Authority Information Access (AIA) publication points**   Once the CA is restored, you must publish an updated CRL and possibly, an updated CA certificate to the designated publication points. Ensure that no previous publication points are omitted. If using Online Certificate Status Protocol (OCSP), the OCSP URL must be added to the AIA extension.

- **Cryptographic service provider (CSP) used to protect the CA's private key**   The same CSP must be used to restore the previous key pair for the CA. The CSP might require additional software.

- **Key length of the CA's certificate**   If you are reinstalling the CA or renewing the CA certificate, you should maintain the same key length as originally deployed.

- **Logical disk-partitioning scheme for the CA computer**   When you restore Certificate Services configuration, the disk volumes must implement the same drive letters. Disk volumes can be different sizes or implement different RAID levels, but the drive letters and locations must remain the same for the CA database, CA logs, CA configuration folder (if implemented), and operating system.

- **Copy of the CAPolicy.inf file deployed in the %Windir% of the CA computer**   The CAPolicy.inf file must be in place when renewing the CA's certificate or in the case where the disaster recovery requires a reinstallation of the CA during the reinstallation process.

- **CA registry settings**   What registry settings are enabled at the CA. These can include custom CRL overlap settings and other performance-tuning settings that must be replicated in the event of disaster recovery.

Choosing a Backup Method

In addition to ensuring that your documentation is up-to-date, make certain that your organization performs regular CA computer backups. Certificate Services offers two backup methods: Windows server backups and manual backups.

Who Can Perform Backups of Certificate Services

If you implement Common Criteria role separation, choose carefully who can perform a Certificate Services backup. By definition, Common Criteria role separation prevents a user from performing the actions of two or more Common Criteria roles, which are CA administrator, certificate manager, auditor, and backup operator. If a user holds two or more roles, the Certificate Services backup fails.

If the user holds two or more roles, an error message appears stating: "CertUtil: The operation is denied. The user has multiple roles assigned and the CA is configured to enforce role separation." This indicates that Common Criteria role separation is preventing backup. You can overcome this error by disabling Common Criteria role separation, fixing the multiple role assignments, and reenabling Common Criteria role separation as discussed in Chapter 13, "Role Separation." In some cases, you can fix the issue by creating a dedicated backup account that holds only the backup role.

> **Note**   Holding multiple roles also causes *any* backup of Certificate Services to fail. This includes **Certutil.exe** backups and system state backups. The difference is that a system state backup will fail silently. The backup appears to succeed, but you cannot restore the Certificate Services database because role separation enforcement prevents a successful backup.

System State Backups

System state backup is the preferred method for backing up Certificate Services. A system state backup includes the following settings related to Certificate Services:

- **CA database**   Includes details on every certificate issued and revoked by the CA.
- **CA key pair**   The CA key pairs must be backed up to ensure that you can rebuild the CA using the same key pair. This also ensures that any certificates currently issued by the CA remain valid after the CA is restored. If the CA's certificate is renewed with a new key pair, the backup must include all versions of the CA key pair.

  If the CA implements a hardware security module (HSM), the backup of the CA's key pair can require third-party backup software. When an HSM is implemented, the CA's private key is removed from the CA computer and protected by the HSM device. This protection causes the system state to not include the CA's key pair in the backup set. The backup of the CA's key pair may require the use of HSM software or backup utilities.

- **All registry settings related to Certificate Services**   The installation and configuration of a CA includes changing several registry values. Inclusion of the registry in the backup set ensures that the registry settings are restorable.

The main advantage of system state backups is that all critical components of Certificate Services are included in a singe backup set.

Windows Server Backups

Windows server backup allows recovery of a server that has failed. A Windows server backup allows you to recover volumes, files, applications, and system state and to perform a bare-metal restoration of the server. After an initial backup is performed, incremental backups are performed to ensure that only files that have changed on the included volumes are included in the subsequent backups. If you perform a restoration, you can choose a backup and then select the specific items in the backup to restore.

The main advantage of Windows server backups is the fact that it is an all-in-one backup, which eliminates the need to restore multiple services, data sets, and registry settings.

Manual Backups

A manual backup of Certificate Services, a backup performed from the Certification Authority console or by using the **certutil** command, includes only the CA database and possibly the CA's key pair(s). A manual backup does not include the IIS metabase or any Certificate Services registry settings. These items must be backed up separately to ensure the full recovery of Certificate Services.

> **Note**   As with a system state backup, in a manual backup the CA's key pair cannot be backed up if the key pair is protected by an HSM. Details on how to exclude the key pair from the backup set when performing a manual backup are discussed later in this chapter in "Performing Manual Backups."

Performing a System State Backup

In Windows Server 2008, a system state backup is performed at a command prompt by using the **Wbadmin.exe** tool. This is a major change from Windows Server 2003 where a command-line system state backup was performed using the command line version of Microsoft NT Backup.

> **Important**   The previous form of backup used in Windows Server 2003, Windows NT Backup, is deprecated in Windows Server 2008. If you have upgraded from Windows Server 2003 and need to access Windows Server 2003 backups, you must download the Windows NT Backup—Restore utility at *http://go.microsoft.com/fwlink/?LinkId=82917*. You cannot restore system state backups created with Windows NT Backup by using **WBAdmin.**

Installing Windows Server Backup

Before you can run a system state backup, you must install the Windows Server Backup feature on the CA. By default, Windows server backup is not installed on a server. You must install Windows server backup through the Add Features Wizard. Use the following procedure:

1.   Log on as a member of the local Administrators group.

2.   From Administrative Tools, open Server Manager.

3.   In the console tree, click Features.

4.   In the Details pane, click Add Features.

5.   On the Select Features page, in the Features list, select Windows Server Backup Features.

6.   In the Add Features Wizard dialog box, click Add Required Features to add the Windows Recovery Disc feature.

7. On the Select Features page, click Next.

8. On the Confirm Installation Selections page, click Install.

9. Ensure that the installation completed successfully, and then click Finish.

> **Important**   After the installation is complete, ensure that the Volume Shadow Copy and Microsoft Software Shadow Copy Provider services' startup types set to Automatic and the services are started. The Windows Server Backup console will fail if the services are not enabled and running.

Performing a System State Backup

Once Windows Server Backup is installed, you can now perform a system state backup by using the **Wbadmin.exe** command-line utility. Use the following procedure:

1. Log on as a member of the Administrators group.

2. Open an Administrative Command Prompt.

3. At the command prompt, type the following command, and then press Enter:

```
wbadmin start systemstatebackup –backuptarget:DriveLetter
```

The command starts a system state backup to the root of the designated drive letter (for example D:).

Performing Windows Server Backups

To perform a Windows server backup, users can use Windows Server Backup, the backup software that ships with Windows Server 2008.

> **Note**   As with the **Wbadmin.exe** command-line utility, the Windows Server Backup feature must be enabled on the CA to perform a Windows server backup.

Creating a Scheduled Windows Server Backup

Windows Server Backup performs the backup to external universal serial bus (USB) or firewire disks, shared folders, local hard disks, or to optical drives such as DVD drives. Use the following procedure to perform a scheduled Windows server backup to an external disk location:

1. From Administrative Tools, open Windows Server Backup.

2. In the Actions bar, click Backup Schedule.

3. On the Getting Started page, click Next.

4. In the Windows Server Backup Warning dialog box

    ❑   Click Yes if this is the first backup of the server.

    ❑   Click No if this is not the first backup. Follow the instructions in the warning dialog box, and then click No.

5. On the Select Backup Configuration page, select Full Server (Recommended), and then click Next.

6. On the Specify Backup Time, choose from the following options, and then click Next.

    ❑   **Once A Day**   Designate a time for a once-a-day backup.

    ❑   **More Than Once A Day**   Add or remove specific times for the backup to be performed.

7. On the Select Destination Disk page, click Show All Available Disks.

> **Important**   The external disks must be attached *before* you run the Backup Schedule wizard.

8. In the Show All Available Disks page, select the disk you wish to use as the target of the backup operation, and then click OK.

9. On the Select Destination Disk page, select the available disk, and then click Next.

10. In the Windows Server Backup dialog box, click Yes to agree that all existing data on the disk will be deleted and that the entire disk will be dedicated for storing backups.

11. On the Label Destination Disk page, click Next.

12. On the Confirmation page, click Finish.

> **Note**   The disk is now formatted for use, and the backup schedule is created.

13. On the Summary page, click Close.

Backups will now execute based on the schedule you set in the wizard.

> **Note**   For more details on configuring Windows Server Backup, see the "Windows Server 2008 Backup and Recovery Step-by-Step Guide" at *http://technet2.microsoft.com/ windowsserver2008/en/library/40bdcbc9-ce96-4477-8df3-7a20d4bc42a51033.mspx?mfr=true*.

Performing a One-Time-Only Windows Server Backup

In some cases, you will want to create a one-time-only backup of the server. For example, you may create a backup to a DVD or to an external hard drive that is shipped off-site for remote storage.

To create a one-time backup of the server, use the following procedure:

1. From Administrative Tools, open Windows Server Backup.

2. In the Actions bar, click Backup Once.

3. On the Getting Started page, click Next.

4. On the Backup Options page, select from the following options, and then click Next.

   ❑ Use the same options used in the scheduled backups.

   ❑ Choose different options, including different destination locations or different items in the backup set.

5. On the Select Backup Configuration page, select Full Server (Recommended) or click Custom to exclude volumes from the backup set, and then click Next.

6. On the Specify Destination Location, select from the following options, and then click Next.

   ❑ **Local Drives**   Allows backup to attached external drives or to a DVD drive

   ❑ **Remote Shared Folder**   Allows backup to a shared folder on a remote target server

7. If you selected local drives, on the Select Backup Destination page, in the backup destination drop-down list, select *DriveLetter*, and then click Next.

   If you selected a remote shared folder, on the Specify Remote Folder page, type the Universal Naming Convention (UNC) path to the share folder, select the access control settings, and then click Next. Available access control settings include:

   ❑ **Do Not Inherit**   Provides credentials for the user allowed to access the completed backup for recovery operations

   ❑ **Inherit**   Allows anyone with access to the designated backup folder to access the completed backup for recovery operations

> **Note**   If you choose Do Not Inherit, you must provide the credentials for a user who has Write access to the designated shared folder.

8. On the Specify Advanced Option page, choose between a Volume Shadow Copy service (VSS) copy backup or a VSS full backup, and then click Next.

> **Note**   A VSS copy backup is recommended because it does not clear application log files.

9. On the Confirmation Disk page, ensure that the backup options are set correctly, and then click Backup.

> **Note**   If the destination is a DVD drive, the backup will span multiple DVD discs if the storage requirements are greater than the capacity of a single DVD disc.

10. On the Backup Progress page, click Close.

The backup will now process as a background task. When the backup is complete, you will be notified.

Performing Manual Backups

Manual backups can be performed from either the Certification Authority console or the command line by using the **certutil.exe** command. There is no technical difference between the results of the two backup methods; the only difference is in how you perform each backup.

> **Note**   Manual backups are recommended for organizations testing Certificate Services in a lab environment, to allow quick rollback if testing does not go as expected.

Using the Certification Authority Console

To perform a backup from the Certification Authority console, the user must be assigned the Backup Files And Directories user right—and not hold any other Common Criteria roles.

Use the following procedure to perform the backup:

1. From the Start menu, point to Administrative Tools, and then click Certification Authority.

2. In the console tree, ensure that Certificate Services is running.

3. In the console tree, right-click *CAName*, point to All Tasks, and then click Backup CA.

4. On the Welcome To The Certification Authority Backup Wizard page, click Next.

5. On the Items To Backup page, input the following options:

    ❑ **Private Key And CA Certificate**   Includes the CA's certificate and private key(s) in the backup set. Select this check box only if you are using a software CSP. If using a hardware CSP, leave this check box cleared.

    ❑ **Certificate Database And Certificate Database Log**   Always select this check box to ensure that you include the CA database and log files in the backup set.

❑ **Perform Incremental Backup**   This check box is not usually selected. Full backups of the CA database and log files are recommended instead.

❑ **Backup To This Location**   Select a folder on the local file system that does not contain any existing data.

6. If the Certification Authority Backup Wizard dialog box appears, click OK to create the location designated on the Items To Backup page.

7. If you choose to back up the private key and CA certificate, open the Select A Password page, type and confirm a password to protect the PKCS #12 file generated by the backup procedure, and then click Next.

8. On the Completing The Certification Authority Backup Wizard page, click Finish.

Once the backup is complete, open the folder designated in step 5. In the folder, there is a *.p12 file (the PKCS #12 backup of the CA's certificate and private key) and a subfolder named Database that contains the backup of the CA database and log files.

Certutil Commands

The **certutil** command allows you to automate the backup of the CA in a batch file. The batch file can be scheduled by using the Task Scheduler service.

If you are using a software CSP, ensure that the backup set includes both the CA database and the CA's key pair. To do this, use the following procedure:

1. Open a command prompt.

2. At the command prompt, type **net start certsvc** to ensure that Certificate Services is running.

3. Create a folder that will contain the results of the manual backup of the CA database— for example, C:\CABackup.

4. At the command prompt, type **certutil –backup C:\CABackup –p** *password*, and then press Enter.

> **Note**   If you are running the command in a Scheduled Task, you must provide the password at the command prompt. If you are performing a manual backup, it is recommended to provide the password during the backup process as shown below in steps 5 and 6.

5. At the command prompt, at the Enter New Password prompt, type a complex password, and then press Enter.

6. At the command prompt, at the Confirm New Password Prompt, type the same password again, and then press Enter.

7. When the backup is complete, ensure there are no error messages, and then close the command prompt.

You are providing a password to protect the PKCS #12 file containing the CA's key pair. To create a successful backup of the private key, you must be a local administrator of the computer; to create the backup of the CA database, you can hold only the Common Criteria role of backup operator. In other words, you can run this command successfully only if Common Criteria role separation is not enforced.

If Common Criteria role separation is enforced, you can separate the two backups by running two **certutil** commands.

To back up only the CA database, a backup operator can use the **–backupdb** option, as shown in the following procedure:

1. Open a command prompt.

2. At the command prompt, type **net start certsvc** to ensure that Certificate Services is running.

3. Create a folder that will contain the results of the manual backup of the CA database— for example, C:\CABackup.

4. At the command prompt, type **certutil –backupdb C:\CABackup,** and then press Enter.

5. When the backup is complete, ensure there are no error messages, and then close the command prompt.

Likewise, if you are a local administrator and want to back up only the CA's key pair, you can use the **-backupkey** option to back up the CA's private key and public key to a PKCS #12 file. Use the following procedure:

1. Open a command prompt.

2. At the command prompt, type **net start certsvc** to ensure that Certificate Services is running.

3. Create a folder that will contain the results of the manual backup of the CA database— for example, C:\CABackup.

4. At the command prompt, type **certutil –backupkey C:\CABackup,** and then press Enter.

5. At the command prompt, at the Enter New Password prompt, type a complex password, and then press Enter.

6. At the command prompt, at the Confirm New Password prompt, type the same password, and then press Enter.

7. When the backup is complete, ensure there are no error messages, and then close the command prompt.

HSM Backups

One method that protects a CA's private key material from being extracted from the local machine store by a member of the local Administrators group is to store the CA's key pair to an HSM. An HSM stores the key pair or a portion of the key material and all cryptographic operations in a secure *black box*. Because the key material is not stored on the CA, proprietary methods must be used to back up and restore the CA key material.

For example, if you implement a SafeNet Luna CA[3] or Luna SA HSM, the key material is backed up to Luna tokens. The backup process requires the participation of three *key holders*, where each key holder holds a separate PKI management role. The backup ensures that, in the event of HSM failure, the key material can be loaded onto a replacement HSM and, in the event of CA hardware failure, the replacement CA can be connected to the existing key material stored on the HSM.

Likewise, if you implement an nCipher HSM, the key material is protected by a combination of smart card tokens and Triple Data Encryption Standard (3DES) or Advanced Encryption Standard (AES) encrypted files stored on the CA or a remote file system server. The key pair is reassembled through the combination of a key pair split between a predefined number of operator cards and the encrypted data stored within the CA's C:\nfast\kmdata\local folder.

Restoration Procedures

The restoration procedure that you use depends on the type of backup you initially performed. The following sections detail the procedures for restoring from a system state backup, a Windows server backup, and a manual backup.

Determining Backup Versions

With system state and Windows server backups, you must first determine the versions of the backups that are available and what types of restorations are available for the backups.

To determine the versions of backups available, you can run the **wbadmin.exe** command-line utility. The command **wbadmin get versions** displays all available backups available for restoration and what type of restorations are available, as shown in the following output from the command:

```
wbadmin 1.0 - Backup command-line tool
(C) Copyright 2004 Microsoft Corp.

Backup time: 12/9/2007 5:19 PM
Backup target: Fixed Disk labeled Manual Backup(E:)
Version identifier: 12/09/2007-23:19
Can Recover: Volume(s), File(s), Application(s), Bare Metal Recovery, System State
```

```
Backup time: 12/9/2007 7:33 PM
Backup target: Fixed Disk labeled E:
Version identifier: 12/10/2007-01:33
Can Recover: Application(s), System State

Backup time: 12/9/2007 9:00 PM
Backup target: Fixed Disk labeled FABINCC 2007_12_09 11:30 DISK_01(\\?\Volume{c14bab36-a671-
11dc-bb2c-0003ff526e7d})
Version identifier: 12/10/2007-03:00
Can Recover: Volume(s), File(s), Application(s), Bare Metal Recovery, System State
```

> **Note**   In the **get versions** output, the first and third backups are Windows server backup. The second backup is a system state backup.

Restoring a System State Backup

To restore a system state backup, the recommended method is to use the **wbadmin.exe** command-line utility, as shown in the following procedure:

1.   Log on as a member of the Administrators group.

2.   Open an Administrative Command Prompt.

3.   At the command prompt, type the following command, and then press Enter:

    wbadmin start systemstaterecovery –version:*VersionIdentifier* **–backuptarget:** *DriveLetter* **–machine:***MachineName*

where:

- **-version:***VersionIdentifier*   The MM/DD/YYYY-HH:MM identifier of a backup returned by the **wbadmin get versions** output,

- **-backuptarget:***DriveLetter*   Specifies the storage location that contains the backup source for the recovery operation. Use when multiple drives contain backups of the CA.

- **-machine:***MachineName*   Specifies the name of the computer for the recovery operation. Use when multiple computers are backed up to the same location.

Restoring a Windows Server Backup

Windows Server Backup is used to restore an entire server. The restoration includes creating a Windows recovery disc and performing the restoration.

Creating a Windows Recovery Disc

To restore an entire server by using Windows Server Backup, you must first create a recovery disc. The recovery disc allows you to access the Windows Recovery Environment (Windows RE) and recover the operating system.

Note   Alternatively, you can boot from the Windows Setup disc and choose the Repair Your Computer option. The recovery disc allows you to boot directly into the Windows RE and secure access to the Windows Setup disc.

To create a recovery disc, use the following procedure:

1. Log on as a member of the local Administrators group.

2. From the Start menu, point to All Programs, point to Maintenance, and then click Create A Recovery Disc.

3. In the Create A Recovery Disc dialog box, select the target drive, insert a blank CD or DVD into the drive, and then click Create Disc.

4. If you do not have a Windows RE partition, you must insert the Windows Setup disc.

Note   Remove the target disc, replace it with the Setup disc, and then click Continue.

5. When the necessary files are ready for copying, remove the Setup disc, reinsert the target CD or DVD, and then click OK.

Restoring the Entire Server

To restore an entire server using Windows Server Backup, use the following procedure:

1. Insert the recovery disc into the CD or DVD drive, and then turn on the computer.

2. When the Install Windows Wizard appears, specify your language settings, and then click Next.

3. Click Repair Your Computer.

4. Setup will show either an existing Windows installation for recovery or provide an empty list (if recovering to new hardware). Select the existing Windows installation if it exists, and then click Next.

5. On the System Recovery Options page, click Windows Complete PC Restore.

6. In the Windows Complete PC Restore Wizard, select Use The Latest Available Backup (Recommended), and then click Next.

Note   If you choose to restore a different backup, you can select a different computer for the source of the backup. If you do choose a different computer, make sure that you are selecting the backup of the target server, not the backup of another server stored on the remote computer.

7.   On the Choose How To Restore The Backup page, perform the following optional tasks, and then click Next.

❑   Select the Format And Repartition Disks check box to delete existing partitions and reformat the destination disks to be the same as the backup. This enables the Exclude Disks button. Click this button, and then select the check boxes associated with any disks that you want to exclude from being formatted and partitioned. The disk that contains the backup that you are using is automatically excluded.

❑   Select the Only Restore System Disks check box to perform an operating system–only recovery.

❑   Click Install Drivers to install device drivers for the hardware that you are recovering to.

❑   Click Advanced to specify whether the computer will be restarted and the disks checked for errors immediate after the recovery.

8.   Confirm the details for the restoration, and then click Finish.

The restoration will proceed and return the computer to the state at the time of the backup operation.

Restoring a Manual Backup

If you performed a manual backup, you must reinstall Certificate Services, using the previous CA certificate and key pair to ensure that Certificate Services is using the same key pair for all signing operations, before restoring the manual backup.

Reinstalling Certificate Services

When you reinstall Certificate Services, the first step is to ensure that the CA certificate and private key are available to the CA.

■   For a software-based CSP, a local administrator of the computer can import a PKCS #12 into the local machine store. You can verify that the certificate is imported successfully by loading the Certificates MMC console focused on the local computer.

■   For a hardware-based CSP, such as an HSM, you must install the third-party CSP and utilities before you restore connectivity to the hardware device. Once you restore connectivity, the CA computer can communicate with the HSM and access the CA certificate and key pair.

Once the CA certificate and private key are loaded or accessible to the CA, use the following procedure to install Certificate Services using the previous CA certificate and private key:

1.   Log on as a member of the local Administrators group. If the CA is an enterprise CA, ensure you are also a member of the Enterprise Admins group.

2. Ensure that CAPolicy.inf is restored to the %Windir% folder.

3. Click Start, point to Administrative Tools, and then click Server Manager.

4. In the Roles Summary section, click Add Roles.

5. On the Select Server Roles page, select the Active Directory Certificate Services check box, and then when the role is populated, click Next.

6. On the Introduction To Active Directory Certificate Services page, read the items to Note, and then click Next.

7. On the Select Role Services page, select the Certification Authority and the Certification Authority Web Enrollment check boxes.

8. In the Add Role Services Required For Certification Authority Web Enrollment dialog box, click Add Required Role Services.

9. On the Select Role Services page, click Next.

10. On the Specify Setup Type page, click Stand-alone or Enterprise, and then click Next.

11. On the Specify CA Type page, click Root CA or Subordinate CA, and then click Next.

12. On the Set Up Private Key page, click Use Existing Private Key, select the Select A Certificate And Use Its Associated Private Key check box, and then click Next.

> **Note**   The cryptographic service provider (CSP) is automatically set to the CSP used to generate the existing private key.

13. On the Configure CA Name page, select the existing CA certificate, and then click Next.

14. On the Configure Certificate Database page, set the storage locations to the same database and log locations used by the original CA (same drive letters), and then click Next.

15. On the Web Server (IIS) page, click Next.

16. On the Select Role Services page, accept the recommended role services, and then click Next.

17. On the Confirm Installation Selections page, verify the presented information, and then click Install.

18. On the Installation Results page, ensure that status for both Active Directory Certificate Services and for Web Server (IIS) is Installation succeeded, and then click Close.

If Certificate Services starts, you can proceed to restoring the last System State or manual backup.

Restoring Manual Backups

A manual backup, whether it was created with **certutil** or the Certification Authority console, can be restored by using the Certification Authority console, using the following procedure:

1. From the Start menu, point to Administrative Tools, and then click Certification Authority.

2. In the console tree, click *CAName*.

3. In the console tree, right-click *CAName*, point to All Tasks, and then click Restore CA.

4. In the Certification Authority Restore Wizard, click OK to stop Certificate Services during the restore procedure.

5. On the Welcome To The Certification Authority Restore Wizard page, click Next.

6. On the Items To Restore page, select the Certificate Database And Certificate Database Log check box. If required, select the Certificate Key and CA Certificate check boxes, and then click Browse.

7. In the Browse For Folder dialog box, select the folder that contains the manual backup files, and then click OK.

8. On the Items To Restore page, click Next.

9. On the Completing The Certification Authority Restore Wizard, click Finish.

10. In the Certification Authority Restore Wizard dialog box, click Yes.

11. Verify that Certificate Services starts successfully.

Note   You can also use **certutil** rather than the Certification Authority console to restore the CA backup.

Evaluating Backup Methods

Although it is generally recommended to implement Windows server backups when planning for CA disaster recovery, there are circumstances where it is preferable to perform a manual backup. For example, if you replace a server, a system state backup (included in the Windows server backup) may not start.

No matter which method you ultimately choose for protecting your CA, ensure that you perform regular CA backups.

■ **For online CAs, perform full backups of the CA database nightly.**   This ensures that in the event of failure, the worst-case scenario is that you restore to the state at the time of the last full backup.

■ **For offline CAs, perform full backups each time you access the offline CA.**   This occurs whenever you publish a new CRL, renew a CA's certificate, or issue new subordinate CA certificates.

> **Note**   If you restore the previous night's full backup, the CA is not aware of any certificates issued between recovery time and backup time if the log file directory is unavailable. The certificates issued in this time frame *are* valid. The caveat is that you cannot revoke these certificates, because they do not appear in the Certification Authority console. WISeKey provides a product named CertifyID Guardian that records details on all certificates issued by the CA to a SQL database. If the CA fails, CertifyID Guardian allows the CA to be restored to its state at the time of failure. Alternatively, Identity Lifecycle Manager 2007 Certificate Management also records all certificates issued by the CA to its own SQL database. The difference is that the recovery of certificates issued since the last backup of the CA is a manual process.

The following sections describe some scenarios for disaster recovery of a CA and provide recommendations on how to perform CA backup.

Hardware Failure

If your CA suffers from hardware failure, the action you take depends on the nature of the hardware failure. If you can replace the failed hardware without affecting the operating system or disk files, you can simply replace the hardware and start the CA. If the failed hardware stores the CA database, the CA logs, or the CA key pair, you can reduce the risk of failure by storing the data on hardware RAID volumes. These hardware configurations prevent the failure of disks because of a single disk failure. Likewise, if your private key is stored on an HSM, maintaining backups of the HSM and providing redundant hardware can minimize CA downtime.

Certificate Services Failure

If Certificate Services fails, back up the folders containing the CA database and logs and the CA key pair. On the first restoration attempt, try removing and reinstalling Certificate Services using the existing key pair. The CA reinstallation attempts to use the existing files in the CA database and log folders. If this attempt fails, reinstall and restore from the latest backup set.

> **Note**   Ensure that you have included the registry in the backup by including the System State in the backup set or by manually backing up the HKEY_LOCAL_MACHINE\System\ CurrentControlSet\Services\CertSvc\Configuration*CAName* registry key.

Server Replacement

If the server hosting Certificate Services fails because of one or more hardware failures, you may have to replace the server hosting Certificate Services.

> **Note**   This procedure assumes that you perform nightly manual backups of the CA and have access to these backups for the replacement process. The backup must include: the CA's private key or the HSM files that will allow you to regain access to the HSM-protected private key, the most recent backup of the CA database, the CA Policy.inf file, a backup of the CA configuration files, and a registry dump of the CA's registry key (HKEY_LOCAL_MACHINE\System\ CurrentControlSet\Services\CertSvc\Configuration*CAName*).

Use the following process to move Certificate Services to a replacement server:

1. Build the replacement computer with the same disk partitioning as the original CA.

2. Ensure that the computer name is the same as the server being replaced.

3. If the Domain Name System (DNS) entries are static entries, ensure that the Internet Protocol (IP) address information for the new computer is the same as used on the computer being replaced.

4. If the computer is replacing an enterprise CA, join the new computer to the same domain as the computer being replaced.

5. Ensure that you copy all configuration files and previous backup files for the failed CA to the local disk of the replacement CA.

6. Copy the original CAPolicy.inf file to the %Windir% folder.

7. Reinstall Certificate Services using the existing key pair saved from the backup files copied to the CA in step 5.

8. Restore the registry file copied in step 5 of this procedure.

9. Restore the manual backup of the CA database.

10. Verify that Certificate Services starts successfully.

> **Important**   The recovery method described in this procedure is dependent on your performing a regular backup of the CA computer. The backup can be a scheduled task that runs a batch file that includes the items used during the restoration process (registry keys, configuration files, CA database, and CA private keys).

Availability Options

In many cases, you can prevent catastrophic failure of Certificate Services by planning for availability. Availability options that are discussed in this section include:

- CRL re-signing
- HSM Fail Over
- Clustering Certificate Services

CRL Re-Signing

If a CA is unavailable, it is easy to see that the CA is unable to issue any certificates until the CA is repaired or restored. What is not as evident is that soon afterward, all previously issued certificates will fail revocation checking. When the CA's base CRL or delta CRL expires, relying parties will be unable to validate *any* of the certificates issued by the failed CA.

To ensure continued use of certificate-based applications, it is critical to extend the lifetime of the most recent base CRL and delta CRL issued by the CA before it failed.

To re-sign a CRL, you must perform the following tasks on another computer:

1. Import the CA certificate.

   ❏ If the certificate and private key are software-based, you can import the PKCS #12 file by simply double-clicking the file and running the Certificate Import wizard.

   ❏ If the certificate and private key are protected by an HSM, you must first add the Distinguished Encoding Rules (DER)–encoded or Base64 certificate file (.cer) by running the Certificate Import wizard. Once the certificate is imported, ensure that the computer has connectivity to the HSM, and then run **certutil –repairstore My** "*SerialNumber*" **–csp** "*CSPName*". In this command, the serial number is the serial number of the CA certificate delimited with double quotes, and the CSP is the display name of the CSP used to protect the CA's private key delimited with double quotes.

2. Copy the previous versions of the base CRL and delta CRL to a temporary folder.

3. Open a command prompt and make the temporary folder the current folder.

4. At the command prompt, type **certutil –sign *CAName*.crl failed.crl *DD:HH***, and then press Enter. For example, to sign a CRL named Fabrikam Issuing CA 1.crl for a period of five days, type **certutil –sign "Fabrikam Issuing CA 1.crl" failed.crl 5:00**.

5. In the Certificate List dialog box, select the *CAName* certificate, and then click OK.

6. At the command prompt, type **certutil –sign "CAName+.crl" failed+.crl *DD:HH***, and then press Enter.

> **Tip**   Consider implementing the same validity period for both the base CRL and delta CRL. Designate a validity period that allows enough time to recover the failed CA.

7. In the Certificate List dialog box, select the CAName certificate, and then click OK.

Once you have re-signed the CRLs, two newly signed files exist: failed.crl and failed+.crl. These files must now be renamed to match the original file names and then copied to the locations designated in the CRL distribution point (CDP).

> **Note**   For Hypertext Transfer Protocol (HTTP) Uniform Resource Locators (URLs), copy the re-signed CRL files using whatever copy protocol you normally use to transfer CRLs to the Web server. For Lightweight Directory Access Protocol (LDAP) URLs, use **certutil –dspublish** to copy the updated CRLs to AD DS.

HSM Fail Over

As discussed in Chapter 9, "Securing a CA Hierarchy," you can have a CA communicate with two or more network-attached or dedicated HSMs to prevent the failure of Certificate Services in event that a single HSM fails.

If one of the HSMs fails, the CA is still able to access its private key through the remaining available HSM.

Clustering Certificate Services

Windows Server 2008 introduces a new method for providing high availability to Certificate Services: Failover Clustering. With Failover Clustering you can create an Active/Passive cluster for Certificate Services. An Active/Passive cluster is one in which only a single node in the cluster, the Active node, is being used. In the event that the Active node fails, the service, in this case Certificate Services, will fail over to the second, or Passive, node, which then becomes the Active node, and the service continues to function. When the original, failed, node is repaired and is brought back online, it becomes the Passive node. The failure of one node in the cluster does not prevent access to the CA nor to the CA database, CRL, or CA certificate and private key.

CA Clustering Guidelines

Windows Server 2008 Certificate Services clustering allows high availability of Certificate Services. There are specific scenarios that are supported for Certificate Services clustering:

- Clustering is supported only for the Active Directory Certificate Services service. Other Certificate Service role services, such as Web Enrollment, Online Responder, and Network Device Enrollment Service (NDES) are not supported.

- Failover Clustering is supported only on Windows Server 2008 Enterprise and Datacenter editions.

- The cluster must be a two-node cluster. A cluster with three or more nodes is not supported.

- The cluster must be configured as an Active/Passive cluster. Certificate Services can be active on only one node of the cluster at any one time. If the active node fails, the other node will become active, and Certificate services will fail over to the other node for all further operations.

■ The clustered nodes must store the CA database and the CA log file database on shared storage using iSCSI or Shared Bus. The storage must be available to both nodes in the cluster.

> **Note**   You can use Windows Virtual Server to test your clustered environment, but you must use an iSCSI virtualization product. The default shared Small Computer System Interface (SCSI) drivers available in Virtual Server are no longer supported for clustering in Windows Server 2008.

Preparing the CA Cluster Environment

Before you set up the Certificate Services cluster, you must prepare the cluster environment. This includes:

■ Installing Windows Server 2008 on both nodes of the cluster. You must install Windows Server 2008 Enterprise or Datacenter to support Failover Clustering.

■ Creating and configuring the witness disk for the cluster service.

■ Creating and configuring the shared storage for the CA Database and Log files. The shared storage must be available to both nodes in the cluster. Ensure that the CA shared storage is sufficient for all future certificate issuance. When planning storage space, use 64 KB per certificate to allow for storage of the certificate request and an archived private key (if implemented).

■ If using an HSM, ensure that both nodes in the cluster connect to the same HSM, and if necessary, the same partition on the HSM.

■ Identifying the names that will be implemented by the cluster. These names include:

❏ **Cluster node names**   Each node in the cluster will have a unique computer name. The computer accounts must be assigned permissions to write to the CA objects in the AIA container, the CA object in the Enrollment Services container, and the key recovery agent (KRA) object in the Enrollment Services container.

❏ **Cluster name**   The Certificate Services cluster has a logical name assigned that is used to manage the cluster. Certificate Services has no dependencies on the cluster name.

❏ **Service name**   This is the DNS name used by Certificate Services. The DNS name is included in the Certificate Services configuration string (for example, ca.fabrikam.com\Fabrikam Issuing CA). The service name is used in the CA Name container located below the CDP container.

> **Note**   You can query the service name by running **certutil –caconfig dns.**

❑   **CA name**   This is the logical name assigned to the CA when Certificate Services is installed. The CA name is used in the following objects: the CA name container below the AIA container, the CDP object name below the CDP\Service Name container, the CA name object in the Certification Authorities container, the CA name object in the Enrollment Services container, and the CA name object in the KRA container.

Note   All of the containers are located in the configuration naming context in the CN=Services,CN=Public Key Service container.

For the following sections, the procedures will deploy the clustered CA shown in Figure 14-1.

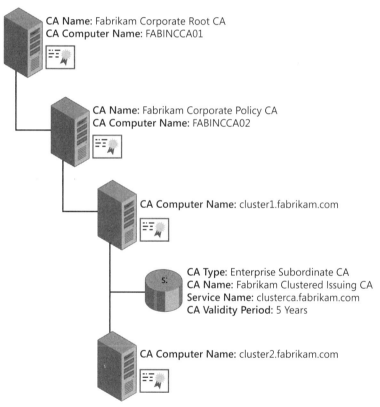

Figure 14-1   Deploying a clustered CA in the Fabrikam CA hierarchy

The CA will implement the following names:

■   **Cluster node 1**: cluster1.fabrikam.com

■   **Cluster node 2**: cluster2.fabrikam.com

■   **Cluster name**: CACluster

- **Service name**: clusterca.fabrikam.com
- **CA name**: Fabrikam Clustered Issuing CA

Installing the First Node of the CA Cluster

Once you have established the names to be used by the Certificate Services cluster, you can start installing the first node of the CA cluster.

> **Note**   The following process assumes that you are installing a clustered subordinate enterprise CA.

Ensure that Prerequisites Are Met   Before installation, you must make sure that the Prerequisite configuration is in place for the first node of the CA cluster.

- Ensure that the enterprise CA is a member of a domain in the forest.
- Ensure that the date and time are correctly set.
- If an HSM is being used, ensure that communications with the HSM are working.
- Ensure that the shared disks are available to the first node in the cluster. You can do this through the following procedure:

    a.   From Administrative Tools, open Server Manager.

    b.   In the console tree, expand Storage, and then click Disk Management.

    c.   In the details pane, ensure that the shared disks are online and assigned a drive letter (S: is the drive letter assigned to the CA shared disk in our example, and Q: is the witness disk).

Installing Certificate Services   Once you have verified the prerequisites, you can install Certificate Services by using the following procedure:

1.   Ensure that you are logged on as a member of Enterprise Admins and that the Server Manager console is running.

> **Tip**   Consider creating a CAPolicy.inf file that implements the LoadDefaultTemplates=0 option in the [certsrv_server] section. For details, see Chapter 6, "Implementing a CA Hierarchy."

2.   In the console tree, click Roles.

3.   In the Roles Summary section, click Add Roles.

4.   If the Before You Begin page appears, click Skip This Page By Default, and then click Next.

5. On the Select Server Roles page, select the Active Directory Certificate Services check box, and then when the role is populated, click Next.

6. On the Introduction To Active Directory Certificate Services page, click Next.

7. On the Select Role Services page, select only the Certification Authority check box, and then click Next.

> **Important** Only the Certification Authority role service can be clustered.

8. On the Specify Setup Type page, click Enterprise, and then click Next.

9. On the Specify CA Type page, click Subordinate CA, and then click Next.

10. On the Set Up Private Key page, click Create A New Private Key, and then click Next.

11. On the Configure Cryptography For CA page, set the following options, and then click Next.

    ❑ Select A Cryptographic Service Provider (CSP): **Choose the HSM provider's CSP.**

    ❑ Key Character Length: **Choose a key length supported by all certificate-based applications in use on the network.**

    ❑ Select The Hash Algorithm For Signing Certificates Issued By This CA: **Select a hash algorithm supported by all certificate-based applications in use on the network.**

12. On the Configure CA Name page, provide the following information, and then click Next.

    ❑ Common Name For This CA: **Fabrikam Clustered Issuing CA**

    ❑ Distinguished Name Suffix: **O=Fabrikam Inc.,C=US**

> **Important** The common name is the CA Name defined for the clustered CA, as discussed earlier in the chapter.

13. On the Request Certificate From A Parent CA page, click Save A Certificate Request To File And Manually Send It Later To A Parent CA, accept the default file name, and then click Next.

14. On the Configure Certificate Database page, designate certificate database and certificate database log locations on the shared volume (S: drive), and then click Next:

    ❑ Certificate Database: **S:\CertDB**

    ❑ Certificate Database Log: **S:\CertLog**

15. After verifying the information on the Confirm Installation Selections page, click Install.

16. On the Installation Results page, note that the installation of Active Directory Certificate Services is incomplete, and then click Close.

17. In Windows Explorer, open C:\.

18. Copy the cluster1.fabrikam.com_Fabrikam Clustered Issuing CA.req file to a USB drive or other external media device.

19. Remove the USB drive containing the certificate request file from the issuing CA.

The USB drive must now be transported to the policy CA computer to submit the certificate request and to copy the issued certificate back to the issuing CA. Use the following process at the policy CA logged on as a member of the local Administrators group:

1. Insert the USB Drive containing the certificate request file in a USB port on the policy CA.

2. From Administrative Tools, open click Certification Authority.

3. In the console tree, right-click Fabrikam Corporate Policy CA, point to All Tasks, and then click Submit New Request.

4. In the Open Request File dialog box, in the File Name box, type **USB:\cluster1 .fabrikam.com_Fabrikam Clustered Issuing CA.req** (where *USB* is the drive letter assigned to the USB drive), and then click Open.

5. In the console tree, expand Fabrikam Corporate Policy CA, and then click Pending Requests.

6. In the details pane, right-click the pending certificate request, point to All Tasks, and then click Issue.

> **Note**   Normally, you would review the submitted request for accuracy before issuing the certificate.

7. In the console tree, click Issued Certificates.

8. In the details pane, double-click the issued certificate.

9. In the Certificate dialog box, click the Details tab.

10. On the Details tab, click Copy To File.

11. In the Certificate Export Wizard, click Next.

12. On the Export File Format page, click Cryptographic Message Syntax Standard—PKCS #7 Certificates (.P7B), select the Include All Certificates In The Certification Path If Possible check box, and then click Next.

13. On the File To Export page, in the File name box, type **USB:\clusteredca.p7b,** and then click Next.

14.   On the Completing The Certificate Export Wizard page, click Finish.

15.   In the Certificate Export Wizard message box, click OK.

16.   In the Certificate dialog box, click OK.

17.   Close the Certification Authority console.

18.   Remove the USB drive containing the certificate request file.

Once the certificate is exported to the USB drive, you must complete installation of the clustered CA by installing the subordinate CA certificate at the first node of the CA cluster. Use the following procedure:

1.   Insert the USB Drive containing the PKCS #7 file in a USB port on the first node of the cluster.

2.   From the Start menu, click Administrative Tools, and then click Certification Authority.

3.   In the console tree, right-click Fabrikam Clustered Issuing CA, point to All Tasks, and then click Start Service.

4.   In the Microsoft Active Directory Certificate Services dialog box, click Yes to install the CA certificate.

5.   In the Select File To Complete CA Installation dialog box, in the File name box, type *USB*:**clusteredca.p7b**.

At this point, Certificate Services starts and allows you to view and configure the clustered CA.

Making the CA's Certificate and Private Key Available to the Second Node   The CA's certificate and private key need to be available to the second node in the cluster. If you are using a software-based CSP, use the following procedure:

> **Note**   If you are using an HSM, you will need to follow the HSM vendor's instructions on how to make the private key available to the second node in the cluster.

1.   From Administrative Tools, open Certification Authority.

2.   In the console tree, right-click Fabrikam Clustered Issuing CA, point to All Tasks, and then click Back Up CA.

3.   On the Welcome To The Certification Authority Backup Wizard page, click Next.

4.   On the Items To Back Up page, enable Private Key And CA Certificate, and then in the Backup To This Location box, type the name of a folder on the local file system that does not contain any existing data.

5.   If the Certification Authority Backup Wizard dialog box appears, click OK to create the location designated on the Items To Back Up page.

6.   On the Select A Password page, type and confirm a password to protect the PKCS #12 file generated by the backup procedure, and then click Next.

7.   On the Completing The Certification Authority Backup Wizard page, click Finish.

Once the backup is complete, open the folder designated in step 4. In the folder, there is a *.p12 file (the PKCS #12 backup of the CA's certificate and private key).

Preparing for the Installation of the Second Node   Before you can install the second node of the cluster, you must release the shared storage from the first node. Use the following procedure:

1.   Ensure that you are in the Certification Authority console.

2.   In the console tree, right-click Fabrikam Clustered Issuing CA, point to All Tasks, and then click Stop Service.

3.   Close the Certification Authority console.

Once you have stopped Certificate Services, you can now detach the shared storage from the first node of the cluster. Use the following procedure:

1.   From Administrative Tools, open Server Manager.

2.   In the console tree, expand Storage, and then click Disk Management.

3.   Right-click the shared storage disk, and then click Offline.

4.   Close all open windows, and then log off.

> **Important**   If you are using an HSM, you may have to stop the Windows service associated with the HSM to release the HSM for use by the second node.

Installing the Second Node of the CA Cluster

Once the first node of the cluster has released the shared storage, you can now install the second node of the cluster.

Ensure Availability of the Shared Components   The first step is to ensure that the shared disks are available to the second node of the cluster. Use the following procedure:

1.   From Administrative Tools, open Server Manager.

2.   In the console tree, expand Storage, and then click Disk Management.

3.   In the details pane, right-click the shared disk, and then click Online.

4.   In the details pane, right-click the shared disk, and then click Change Drive Letters And Paths.

5. In the Change Drive Letter And Paths For New Volume dialog box, click Add.

6. In the Add Drive Letter Or Path dialog box, in the Assign The Following Drive Letter drop-down list, select the same drive letter used for the shared drive on the first node of the cluster (S: in this example), and then click OK.

7. Close Server Manager.

> **Important**   If you are using an HSM, make sure that the second node of the cluster can successfully communicate with the HSM. For example, if you are using an nCipher HSM, ensure that the **enquiry** command reports the HSM as operational.

Providing Access to the CA Certificate and Private Key   Once you have access to the shared disk and the HSM (if necessary), you can now access the CA certificate and private key from the first node of the CA. The exact steps you take depend on whether the clustered CA's private key is protected with a software-based CSP or an HSM-based CSP.

■ If the certificate and private key is software-based, you can import the PKCS #12 file by running the Certificate Import wizard in a custom Certificates console focused on the local computer.

■ If the certificate and private key is protected by an HSM, you must:

a. Add the DER-encoded or Base64 certificate file (.cer) by running the Certificate Import wizard in a custom Certificates console focused on the local computer.

b. Once the certificate is imported, ensure that the computer has connectivity to the HSM, and then run **certutil −repairstore My** "*SerialNumber*" **−csp** "*CSPName*" (where *SerialNumber* is the serial number of the CA certificate delimited with double quotes and the *CSPName* is the display name of the CSP used to protect the CA's private key delimited with double quotes).

> **Tip**   You can verify that the certificate import is successful by viewing the CA certificate in the Certificates console focused on the local computer. If the import is successful, the General tab will show the text You Have A Private Key That Corresponds To This Certificate.

Installing Certificate Services on the Second Node   Once you have successfully provided access to the CA certificate and private key, you can log on as a member of the Enterprise Admins group and install the Certificate Services role on the second node of the cluster. Use the following procedure:

1. From Administrative Tools, open Server Manager.

2. In the console tree, click Roles.

3. In the details pane, in the Roles Summary section, click Add Roles.

4. On the Select Server Roles page, click Active Directory Certificate Services, and then when the role is populated, click Next.

5. On the Introduction To Active Directory Certificate Services page, click Next.

6. On the Select Role Services page, select only the Certification Authority check box, and then click Next.

7. On the Specify Setup Type page, click Enterprise, and then click Next.

8. On the Specify CA Type page, click Subordinate CA, and then click Next.

9. On the Set Up Private Key page, click Use Existing Private Key, click Select A Certificate And Use Its Associated Private Key, and then click Next.

10. On the Select Existing Certificate page, select the certificate imported from the first node of the cluster, and then click Next.

> **Note**   If the certificate and its private key are protected by an HSM, ensure that you select the Use Strong Private Key Protection Features Provided By The CSP check box.

11. On the Configure Certificate Database page, designate certificate database and certificate database log locations on the shared volume (S: drive), and then click Next:

   ❑ Certificate Database: **S:\CertDB**

   ❑ Certificate Database Log: **S:\CertLog**

> **Important**   Ensure that the paths match the database and database log paths implemented at the first node of the cluster.

12. In the warning dialog boxes that appear, click Yes to overwrite the existing database, and click Yes to overwrite the existing database log file.

13. After verifying the information on the Confirm Installation Selections page, click Install.

14. On the Installation Results page, ensure that the installation is successful, and then click Close.

15. Close all open windows.

16. From Administrative Tools, open Certification Authority.

17. Ensure that Certificate Services is started.

18. Close the Certification Authority console.

Configuring the CA Cluster

Now that both nodes of the cluster are installed, you can configure the CA cluster. This process includes:

- Installing Failover Clustering
- Validating a Failover Cluster configuration
- Creating a Failover Cluster
- Configuring the Failover Cluster
- Modifying the CRL Distribution Point for the cluster
- Creating CRL objects for the cluster
- Modifying the CA configuration in AD DS
- Modifying the DNS name for the cluster in AD DS

Installing Failover Clustering   To install the Failover Clustering feature, perform the following procedure on both nodes of the cluster:

1. Log on as a member of the local Administrators group at the CA.
2. From Administrative Tools, open Server Manager.
3. In the console tree, click Features.
4. In the details pane, in the Features Summary section, click Add Features.
5. On the Select Features page, in the Features list, select Failover Clustering, and then click Next.
6. On the Confirm Installation Selections page, click Install.
7. On the Installation Results page, ensure that the installation succeeded, and then click Close.

Validating a Failover Cluster Configuration   Once the Failover Clustering Feature is installed, you should validate the cluster configuration. To validate your configuration, use the following procedure:

1. From Administrative Tools, open Failover Cluster Management.
2. In the Actions pane, click Validate A Configuration.
3. On the Before You Begin page, click Next.
4. On the Select Servers Or A Cluster page, in the Enter Name box, type the computer name of the first cluster node (**cluster1.fabrikam.com**), and then click Add.
5. On the Select Servers Or A Cluster page, in the Enter Name box, type the computer name of the second cluster node (**cluster2.fabrikam.com**), and then click Add.

6. On the Select Servers Or A Cluster page, click Next.

7. On the Testing Options page, click Run All Tests (Recommended), and then click Next.

8. On the Confirmation page, review the tests selected for execution, and then click Next.

9. On the Summary page (see Figure 14-2), ensure that the tests completed successfully. If any errors occur, click View Report and determine what must be done to fix the errors.

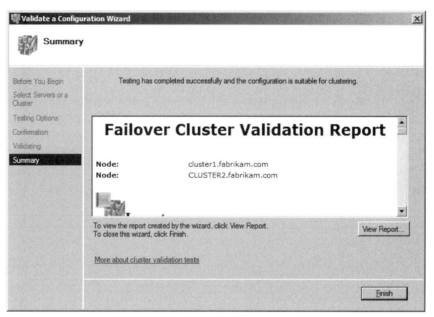

Figure 14-2 Completing the cluster validation testing

10. On the Summary page, click Finish.

Creating a Failover Cluster Once you have validated the Failover Clustering configuration, you can then create the failover cluster. Use the following procedure:

> **Note** This procedure will begin on the second node of the cluster because of the fact that the shared storage is currently active on the second node.

1. Ensure that you are still in the Failover Cluster Management console.

2. In the Actions pane, click Create A Cluster.

3. On the Before You Begin page, click Next.

4. On the Select Servers page, in the Enter Server Name box, type the computer name of the first cluster node (**cluster1.fabrikam.com**), and then click Add.

5. On the Select Servers page, in the Enter Server Name box, type the computer name of the second cluster node (**cluster2.fabrikam.com**), and then click Add.

6. On the Select Servers page, click Next.

7. On the Access Point For Administering The Cluster page, in the Cluster Name box, type **cacluster**, designate a cluster IP address, and then click Next.

8. On the Confirmation page, review the cluster name, each node for the cluster, and the cluster IP address. If they are all correct, click Next.

9. On the Summary page, verify the cluster creation report, and then click Finish.

Configuring the Failover Cluster   Once you have created the failover cluster, you must configure the cluster as an active/passive cluster. The following steps accomplish this configuration:

1. In the Failover Cluster Management console, in the console tree, right-click Services And Applications, and then click Configure A Service Or Application.

2. On the Before You Begin page, click Next.

3. On the Select Service Or Application page, in the list of services and applications, select Generic Service, and then click Next.

4. On the Select Service page, from the list of services, select Active Directory Certificate Services, and then click Next.

5. On the Client Access Point page, in the Name box, type *service short name* (in our example, the service short name is *clusterca*), in the Address box, designate the IP address of the cluster, and then click Next.

> **Note**   This is the DNS name used to reference the cluster CA in the configuration string for the CA.

6. On the Select Storage page, select the shared storage disk (drive S:), and then click Next.

7. On the Replicate Registry Settings page, click the Add button.

8. In the Registry Key dialog box, in the Root registry key box, type **SYSTEM\ CurrentControlSet\Services\CertSvc**, and then click OK.

9. On the Replicate Registry Settings page, click Next.

10. On the Confirmation page, review the configured settings, and then click Next.

11. On the Summary page, click Finish to complete the installation.

12. In the console tree, under Services And Applications, select clusterca.

13. In the details pane (see Figure 14-3), ensure that ClusterCA is online, ensure that shared volume (S: drive) is available, and that all other resources are Online.

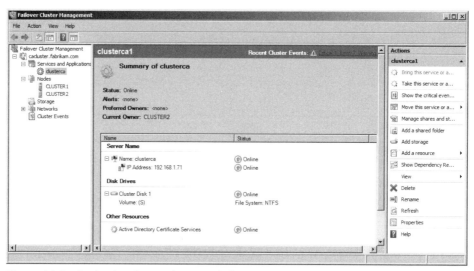

Figure 14-3   Reviewing the newly created cluster

If you have installed a service to access the network HSM, it is recommended to create a dependency between the CA and the network HSM service. To configure such a dependency, follow these optional steps:

1. In the Failover Cluster Management snap-in, in the console tree, click Services And Applications.

2. In the details pane, right-click the service name (cluseterCA), point to Add A Resource, and then click Generic Service.

3. On the Select Service page, click the HSM's associated service, and then click Next.

4. On the Confirmation page, verify the selected HSM service, and then click Next.

5. On the Summary page, click Finish.

6. In the console tree, expand Services And Applications, and then click *Service Name*.

7. In the details pane, right-click Active Directory Certificate Services, and then click Properties.

8. On the Dependencies tab, click Insert.

9. In the Resource drop-down list, select the HSM service, and then click OK.

Finally, you must ensure that the correct shared disk is designated as the disk witness. You can do this by running the following procedure:

1. Ensure that you are in the Failover Cluster Management console.

2. In the console tree, right-click *ClusterName*, point to More Actions, and then click Configure Cluster Quorum Settings.

3. On the Before You Begin page, click Next.

4. On the Select Quorum Configuration page, select Node And Disk Majority, and then click Next.

5. On the Configure Storage Witness page (see Figure 14-4), ensure that the witness shared drive is selected (not the CA database and log shared drive), and then click Next.

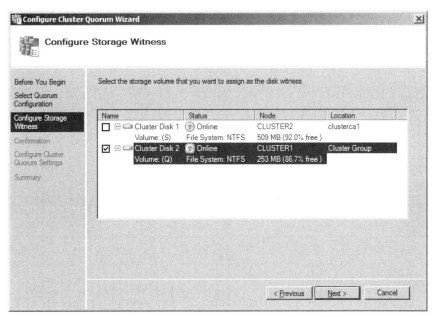

Figure 14-4   Selecting the Storage Witness drive

6. On the Confirmation page, ensure that the correct storage is selected, and then click Next.

7. On the Summary page, click Finish.

Now that the cluster is configured and ready for use, you must adjust the CA configuration settings.

> **Note**   The configuration settings are performed at the active node of the cluster.

Modifying the CRL Distribution Point for the Cluster   The CA's NetBIOS name is used as part of both the CDP and AIA URLs. You must change the CA's NetBIOS name to the NetBIOS name registered with the cluster. The following procedure accomplishes this:

1. Log on at the active cluster node as a member of the local Administrators group.

2. From the Start menu, run the Registry Edito (Regedt32.exe).

3. In the console tree, expand HKEY_LOCAL_MACHINE\System\CurrentControlSet\ Services\CertSvc\Configuration*CAName*.

4. In the details pane, double-click CRLPublicationURLs.

5. In the Edit Multi-String dialog box, identify each LDAP URL. You must change the LDAP URL from the default value of:

```
79:ldap:///CN=%7%8,CN=%2,CN=CDP,CN=Public Key Services,CN=Services,%6%10
```

You must change the %2 entry to the service short name specified in step 5 of the section "Configuring the Failover Cluster." In our example, the value would be changed to:

```
79:ldap:///CN=%7%8,CN=clusterca,CN=CDP,CN=Public Key Services,CN=Services,%6%10
```

6. In the Edit Multi-String dialog box, click OK.

7. Open a command prompt.

8. At the command prompt, type **net stop certsvc && net start certsvc**, and then press Enter.

9. At the command prompt, type **certutil –crl**, and then press Enter.

> **Note**   Although you receive a Remote Procedure Call (RPC) Server Is Unavailable error, an updated CRL was published to the local file system. The updated CRL contains the updated path for the LDAP path for the CRL.

Creating CRL Objects for the Cluster   The new CRL container (based on the cluster short name) must now be created in AD DS. At this point, the default permissions do not allow the clustered CA to automatically publish the CRL to AD DS. To enable automatic publication, you must create the sub-container below the CDP container by manually publishing the CRL to AD DS. Use the following procedure:

1. Ensure that you are logged on as a member of the Enterprise Admins group.

2. Open a command prompt.

3. Make %WINDIR%\System32\CertSrv\CertEnroll the current directory.

4. At the command prompt, type **certutil –f –dspublish "Fabrikam Clustered Issuing CA.crl"** and then press Enter.

5. Ensure that the command is successful.

6. If delta CRL publishing is enabled, at the command prompt, type **certutil –f –dspublish "Fabrikam Clustered Issuing CA+.crl"** and then press Enter.

7. You can verify the creation of the containers by running the **certutil –crl** command again. There should be no errors this time.

> **Important**   You must run the **certutil –dspublish** commands with the **–f** option to force the creation of the new container based on the cluster's short name below the CDP container.

Modifying the CA Configuration in Active Directory (AD DS)   To allow either node of the cluster to update the CA certificate and CRL objects in the directory, you must modify the permissions to allow either node of the cluster to modify the objects.

To allow either node of the cluster to update the CA certificate in the AIA container, use the following procedure:

1. Ensure that you are logged on as a member of the Enterprise Admins group.

2. In the Active Directory Sites And Services console, from the View menu, ensure that Show Services Node is enabled.

3. In the console tree, expand Services, expand Public Key Services, and then click AIA.

4. In the details pane, right-click the CA certificate for the clustered CA, and then click Properties.

5. In the *CAName* Properties dialog box, on the Security tab, click Add.

6. In the Select Users, Computers, Or Groups dialog box, click Object Types.

7. In the Object Types dialog box, click Computers, and then click OK.

8. In the Select Users, Computers, Or Groups dialog box, in the Enter The Object Names To Select box, type the computer name of the second cluster node, and then click OK.

9. On the Security tab, click the first node of the cluster, and ensure that the computer account is assigned Full Control permissions.

10. On the Security tab, click the second node of the cluster, and ensure that the computer account is assigned Full Control permissions.

11. In the *CAName* Properties dialog box, click OK.

12. Do not exit the Active Directory Sites And Services console.

The second container that requires permission modifications is the Enrollment Services container. Both nodes also have to be permitted on the Enrollment Services container. Use the following procedure:

1. Ensure that you are still in the Active Directory Sites And Services console.

2. In the console tree, expand Services, expand Public Key Services, and then click Enrollment Services.

3. In the details pane, right-click the CA certificate for the clustered CA, and then click Properties.

4. In the *CAName* Properties dialog box, on the Security tab, click Add.

5. In the Select Users, Computers, Or Groups dialog box, click Object Types.

6. In the Object Types dialog box, click Computers, and then click OK.

7. In the Select Users, Computers, Or Groups dialog box, in the Enter The Object Names To Select box, type the computer name of the second cluster node, and then click OK.

8. On the Security tab, click the first node of the cluster, and ensure that the computer account is assigned Full Control permissions.

9. On the Security tab, click the second node of the cluster, and ensure that the computer account is assigned Full Control permissions.

10. In the *CAName* Properties dialog box, click OK.

11. Do not exit the Active Directory Sites And Services console.

The final container that requires permission changes is the KRA container. As with the AIA and the Enrollment Services container, you must assign each node's computer account Full Control permissions on the CA certificate in the KRA container. Use the following procedure:

1. Ensure that you are still in the Active Directory Sites And Services console.

2. In the console tree, expand Services, expand Public Key Services, and then click KRA.

3. In the details pane, right-click the CA certificate for the clustered CA, and then click Properties.

4. In the *CAName* Properties dialog box, on the Security tab, click Add.

5. In the Select Users, Computers, Or Groups dialog box, click Object Types.

6. In the Object Types dialog box, click Computers, and then click OK.

7. In the Select Users, Computers, Or Groups dialog box, in the Enter The Object Names To Select box, type the computer name of the second cluster node, and then click OK.

8. On the Security tab, click the first node of the cluster, and ensure that the computer account is assigned Full Control permissions.

9. On the Security tab, click the second node of the cluster, and ensure that the computer account is assigned Full Control permissions.

10. In the *CAName* Properties dialog box, click OK.

11. Close the Active Directory Sites And Services console.

Modifying the DNS Name for the Cluster in Active Directory Domain Services (AD DS)

The final modification required for the cluster is to modify the DNS name referenced in the CA object in the Enrollment Services container. Because of the way a cluster is built, the first node of the cluster put its own fully qualified domain name (FQDN) in the DNS host name of the Enrollment Services object.

To change the FQDN, you must use the ADSI Edit console. Use the following procedure:

1. Ensure that you are logged on as a member of the Enterprise Admins group at a domain controller.

2. From the Start menu, run Adsiedit.msc, and then press Enter.

3. In the console tree, right-click ADSI Edit, and then click Connect To.

4. In the Connection Settings dialog box, in the Select A Well Known Naming Context drop-down list, select Configuration, and then click OK.

5. In the console tree, expand Configuration, expand CN=Configuration,*ForestRootDN*, expand CN=Services, expand CN=Public Key Services, and then click CN=Enrollment Services.

6. In the details pane, right-click the clustered CA certificate, and then click Properties.

7. In the CN=*ObjectName* Properties dialog box, in the Attributes list, select dNSHost-Name, and then click Edit.

8. In the String Attribute Editor dialog box, in the Value box, type the service name assigned to the cluster (in our example, use the name **clusterca.fabrikam.com**), and then click OK.

9. In the CN=*ObjectName* Properties dialog box, click OK.

10. Close the ADSI Edit console.

The cluster is now ready for use and will automatically publish updated CRL and CA certificate objects.

Testing CA Cluster Failover

Once you have configured the CA cluster, it is advisable to test failover in a controlled setting. You can do this by performing the following procedure:

1. Log on as a member of the local Administrators group on the active node of the cluster.

2. From Administrative Tools, open Failover Cluster Management.

3. In the console tree, expand ClusterName, expand Services and Applications, and then click *ServiceName*.

4. In the details pane, ensure that the Current Owner is set to the node that you are logged in to.

> **Tip**   If the other node is the current owner, log on to the other node as a member of the local Administrators group and repeat steps 1–4.

5. Open a command prompt.

6. At the command prompt, type **certutil –config** "*ServiceName\CAName*" **–ping**, and then press Enter.

> **Note**   This command ensures that the CA client interface is responding to requests on the clustered CA service name. In our example, the command would be **certutil -config "clusterca.fabrikam.com\Fabrikam Clustered Issuing CA" -ping.**

7. At the command prompt, type **certutil –config** "*ServiceName\CAName*" **–pingadmin**, and then press Enter.

> **Note**   This command ensures that the CA management interface is responding to requests on the clustered CA service name. In our example, the command would be **certutil -config "clusterca.fabrikam.com\Fabrikam Clustered Issuing CA" -pingadmin**.

8. Close the command prompt.

9. In the Failover Cluster Management console, in the console tree, right-click *ServiceName*, point to Move This Service Or Application To Another Node, and then click 1.- Move to node *NodeName*.

10. In the Please Confirm Action dialog box, click Move *ServiceName* to *NodeName*.

> **Note**   The resources will move through different states: Offline Pending, Offline, Online Pending, and Online. It does take about a minute for the service to fail over completely to the other node in the cluster.

11. When the services report an Online Status, switch back to the command prompt.

12. At the command prompt, type **certutil –config** "*ServiceName\CAName*" **–ping**, and then press Enter.

13. At the command prompt, type **certutil –config** "*ServiceName\CAName*" **–pingadmin**, and then press Enter.

Once you have verified the successful failover between the cluster nodes, you are ready to start issuing certificates from the clustered CA.

Case Study: Replacing Server Hardware

You manage the team responsible for the day-to-day operations of the CAs in the Fabrikam, Inc. network. Fabrikam has a three-tier CA hierarchy, as shown in Figure 14-5.

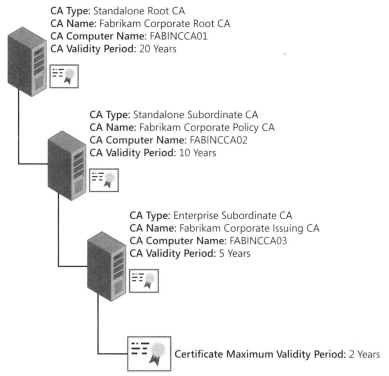

CA Type: Standalone Root CA
CA Name: Fabrikam Corporate Root CA
CA Computer Name: FABINCCA01
CA Validity Period: 20 Years

CA Type: Standalone Subordinate CA
CA Name: Fabrikam Corporate Policy CA
CA Computer Name: FABINCCA02
CA Validity Period: 10 Years

CA Type: Enterprise Subordinate CA
CA Name: Fabrikam Corporate Issuing CA
CA Computer Name: FABINCCA03
CA Validity Period: 5 Years

Certificate Maximum Validity Period: 2 Years

Figure 14-5   The Fabrikam, Inc. CA hierarchy

Scenario

The server hosting the Fabrikam Corporate Root CA is five years old and must be replaced because of server hardware errors detected when you attempted to start the server this morning. You must replace the old server hardware with the new server hardware in the next week because the CRL for the Fabrikam Corporate Root CA expires in seven days.

Before starting the hardware replacement, you gather the following details about the current root CA.

- The root CA computer has two drive partitions:
  - Drive C contains the Windows Server 2008 Standard operating system in a folder named C:\winnt.
  - Drive D contains the Windows Server 2003 Certificate Services database (D:\CertDB), the database logs (D:\CertLogs), and the shared folder (D:\CAConfig).
- The NetBIOS name of the computer is FABINCCA01.

- The last full backup of the offline root CA was a system state backup performed at the last CRL update 25 weeks ago.

- The root CA uses an HSM. You have the original media for the support software for the HSM.

You must replace the hardware for the root CA without interrupting Certificate Services on the network.

Case Study Questions

1. When you perform the installation of the replacement root CA computer, can you use the default installation folder for Windows Server 2008?

   No. The original CA was installed in the folder C:\winnt. The replacement computer must use the same folder for installation.

2. Can you assign the replacement CA computer the NetBIOS name FABINCCA01A to designate this as the second instance of the root CA computer? Why or why not?

   No. You cannot change the name of the computer when you replace the CA computer hardware. The CRL Distribution Point (CDP) in AD DS includes the CA computer name in the publication path.

3. Which registry key should you back up on the original CA computer to reduce the replacement CA computer configuration?

   HKLM\System\CurrentControlSet\Services\CertSVc\Configuration*CAName*, where *CAName* is the logical name of the CA.

4. What type of backup should you perform on the original root CA computer before you start the installation of the replacement CA computer—a system state backup or a manual backup?

   Assuming that the replacement hardware has advanced greatly in the last five years, it's most likely you would perform a manual backup of the CA database and log files. Due to hardware differences, a system state backup can result in the failure of the replacement computer.

5. What software must be installed on the replacement CA computer before you start the installation of Certificate Services? Why?

   The HSM support software must be installed on the replacement CA computer to allow the replacement computer to communicate with the HSM and access the certificate and key material on the HSM.

6. How does this installation of Certificate Services differ from the original installation of Certificate Services?

   You must choose to use an existing certificate by choosing the HSM's CSP and the certificate with the original name of the CA computer.

7. Once the installation of Certificate Services is complete, what must be done to allow the CA to recognize the certificates issued by the CA on the previous computer?

   Assuming you performed a manual backup before replacing the hardware, you must restore the CA database and log files to the original locations using the Certificate Services Restore Wizard.

8. What should be done to the original hardware before it is returned to the leasing company?

   The hard drives from the original hardware should be erased and degaussed to ensure that no data can be accessed from the original hardware. The use of the HSM reduces the risks, because the private key material never existed on the hard drive—only on the HSM.

9. Do you have to republish the root CA certificate in AD DS once the hardware replacement is complete?

   No. The replacement CA is still using the same certificate and private key. There is no need to republish the same certificate.

Additional Information

- Microsoft Official Curriculum, Course 2821: "Designing and Managing a Windows Public Key Infrastructure" (*http://www.microsoft.com/traincert/syllabi/2821afinal.asp*)
- "Deploying PKI Inside Microsoft" (*http://www.microsoft.com/technet/itsolutions/msit/security/deppkiin.mspx*)
- "Windows Server 2003 PKI Operations Guide" (*http://www.microsoft.com/technet/prodtechnol/windowsserver2003/technologies/security/ws03pkog.mspx*)
- Windows NT Backup–Restore Utility for Windows Server 2008 (*http://go.microsoft.com/fwlink/?LinkId=82917*)
- WBAdmin backup command-line utility (*http://technet2.microsoft.com/windowsserver2008/en/library/4b0b3f32-d21f-4861-84bb-b2eadbf1e7b81033.mspx?mfr=true*)
- "Windows Server 2008 Backup and Recovery Step-by-Step Guide" (*http://technet2.microsoft.com/windowsserver2008/en/library/40bdcbc9-ce96-4477-8df3-7a20d4bc42a51033.mspx?mfr=true*)
- "Using Microsoft Virtual Server 2005 to Create and Configure a Two-Node Microsoft Windows Server 2003 Cluster" (*http://www.microsoft.com/technet/prodtechnol/virtualserver/deploy/cvs2005.mspx*)
- "How to Configure the Node and Disk Majority Quorum" (*http://technet.microsoft.com/en-us/library/bb629541.aspx*)
- "Microsoft Windows Clustering: Storage Area Networks" (*http://www.microsoft.com/windows.netserver/techinfo/overview/san.mspx*)

- WISeKey CertifyID Guardian (*http://www.wisekey.com/Products/cid/guardian.htm*)

- Identity Lifecycle Manager 2007 Certificate Management (*http://www.microsoft.com/ilm*)

- 231182: "Certificate Authority Servers Cannot Be Renamed or Removed from Network"

- 298138: "How To: Move a Certification Authority to Another Server"

- 811944: "Computer Does Not Start After You Use Windows Backup to Restore the System State"

Note   The last three articles in the above list can be accessed through the Microsoft Knowledge Base. Go to *http://support.microsoft.com*, and enter the article number in the Search The Knowledge Base text box.

Chapter 15
Issuing Certificates

Having created the required certificate templates, the next step is to determine how to get the certificates to the desired computers, users, or network devices.

A certificate request involves actions performed at the computer where the certificate request is generated and at the certification authority (CA) that issues the certificate to the requestor.

When a certificate request is initiated, the process shown in Figure 15-1 takes place.

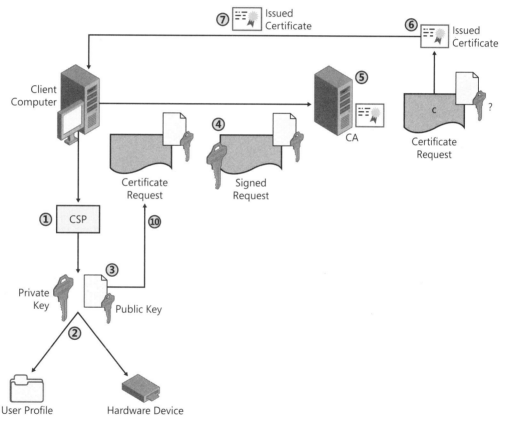

Figure 15-1   The certificate enrollment process

1. When the user generates a request for a certificate, the client computer asks the cryptographic service provider (CSP) designated by the certificate template or selected by the user to generate a key pair.

2. The CSP generates a key pair based on the key length designated in the certificate template or selected by the user. If the CSP is software-based, the key pair is generated in the user's profile. If the CSP is for hardware, such as a smart card, the key pair is generated on the hardware device.

> **Note**   The private key generated by a software CSP is protected by the Data Protection Application Programming Interface (DPAPI).

3. The public key of the key pair, along with any other information required by the certificate template or configured by the user, are added to the certificate request.

4. The certificate request is signed by the private key of the key pair and is sent to the CA.

5. The CA issues the requested certificate, denies the request, or causes the request to be pending until a certificate manager manually approves or denies it.

6. The certificate is generated at the CA. It includes the subject information either provided in the certificate request or built from information in Active Directory Domain Services (AD DS), as well as the public key of the key pair. The certificate is then signed with the CA's signing certificate, and the resulting hash is placed in the certificate's thumbprint extension.

7. The issued certificate is returned to the user and then loaded into the required store in the user's profile or on the hardware device. The certificate is now associated with the private key of the key pair and is ready to use.

Certificate Enrollment Methods

Windows Server 2008 Certificate Services provides several methods for enabling certificate enrollment. The methods range from manual methods that are initiated by a user performing the certificate request to automatic methods where the certificate request is initiated by Group Policy or a login script. The available certificate enrollment methods include:

■ **Certificate Services Web Enrollment pages**   Certificate Services Web Enrollment pages allow a user to request both user and computer certificates from a Web browser. Certificate Services Web Enrollment pages allow the requestor to ask for specific certificate templates from an enterprise CA, submit certificate request files from a network device or another operating system, and check on pending certificate requests.

> **Note**   Certificate Services Web Enrollment pages can be loaded on the Windows Server 2008 CA or onto a front-end Web server. The following requirements must be met: the Web server is a member of the same forest as the CA; the computer account for the Web server is trusted for delegation; and the Web server is running Internet Information Services (IIS) 7.0 on Windows Server 2008 Standard Edition, Windows Server 2008 Enterprise Edition, or Windows Server 2008 Datacenter Edition.

- **Certificate Enrollment wizard**   This wizard permits a user to request certificates from an enterprise CA by selecting the enterprise CA and the certificate template, as well as defining additional settings, such as key length and CSP. The wizard can be launched from the Certificates Microsoft Management Console (MMC) console.

> **Note**   The Certificate Enrollment wizard is greatly revamped in Windows Vista and Windows Server 2008. Many of the tasks that were previously relegated to the Certificate Services Web Enrollment pages, such as smart card requests and pended requests, are now available in the Certificate Enrollment wizard.

- **Automatic Certificate Request Settings (ACRS)**   This Group Policy setting allows the automatic deployment of version 1 computer certificates to computer accounts in the forest. The computer account must be in the domain or organizational unit (OU) where the Automatic Certificate Request Settings is defined. In addition, the computer account must belong to a group that is assigned the Read and Enroll permissions for the version 1 certificate template.

- **Autoenrollment settings**   This combination of version 2 and version 3 certificate templates and Group Policy settings allows automatic deployment of certificates to users and computers. All computers or user accounts within the domain or OU where the Autoenrollment Settings Group Policy setting is applied automatically receive any published version 2 or version 3 certificate templates to which the user or computer account is assigned Read, Enroll, and Autoenroll permissions. Autoenrollment can be used for initial certificate deployment as well as for certificate renewal.

> **Note**   For user and computer autoenrollment, the client computer must be running Windows XP or later. Microsoft Windows 2000 client computers do not recognize the Autoenrollment Settings Group Policy setting.

- **Certreq.exe**   This command-line tool allows a user to create, submit, retrieve, and accept certificate requests sent to a Windows Server 2008 CA. The requests can be sent to both standalone and enterprise CAs.

- **Custom scripting**   In some cases, such as when you want to automate user certificate enrollment at Windows 2000 client computers, you must create custom scripts. These scripts can use the CryptoAPI, CryptoAPI COM control (CAPICOM), and the Certificate Enrollment Control (Xenroll.dll or Certenroll.dll) to automate enrollment at a Windows 2000 computer.

> **Note**   Custom scripting is not relegated to Windows 2000 clients. The scripts can be run from any supported Windows client.

- **Network Device Enrollment Service (NDES)**   NDES is a new Certificate Services role service that enables enrollment through Simple Certificate Enrollment Protocol (SCEP). SCEP is a Cisco proprietary protocol that allows Cisco Internetwork Operating System (IOS) devices to contact a CA, obtain Internet Protocol security (IPsec) certificates, and install trusted root certificates.

> **Note**   NDES configuration and implementation is discussed in Chapter 27, "Network Device Enrollment Service."

- **Registration authorities**   Registration authorities, such as Microsoft Identity Lifecycle Manager (ILM) 2007 Certificate Management, allow custom workflows to be defined for certificate life-cycle management tasks. A registration authority ensures that any required data collection and approvals are collected before a certificate management task is processed.

> **Note**   Details on ILM 2007 Certificate Management are discussed in Chapter 17, "Identity Lifecycle Manager 2007 Certificate Management."

Choosing an Enrollment Method

For each PKI-enabled application, you must choose the best way to deploy certificates to users, computers, and network devices. In most cases, you'll have a primary method and a secondary method.

Choosing Among Manual Enrollment Methods

Manual enrollment is not well suited for mass certificate deployment because of the amount of time an organization must spend training personnel to use such a method. Table 15-1 shows the available manual enrollment methods for each version of certificate templates on client computers running Windows 2000, Windows XP, Windows Server 2003, Windows Vista, and Windows Server 2008.

Table 15-1   Manual Enrollment Methods

Enrollment method	Certificates MMC	Web enrollment
Manual enrollment on a Windows 2000 workstation.	V1 template: Yes	V1 template: Yes
	V2 template: No	V2 template: Yes
	V3 template: No	V3 template: No
Manual enrollment on a Windows XP or Windows Server 2003 workstation.	V1 template: Yes	V1 template: Yes
	V2 template: Yes	V2 template: Yes
	V3 template: No	V3 template: No

Table 15-1   Manual Enrollment Methods

Enrollment method	Certificates MMC	Web enrollment
Manual enrollment on a Windows Vista or Windows Server 2008 workstation.	V1 template: Yes V2 template: Yes V3 template: Yes	V1 template: Yes V2 template: Yes V3 template: Yes
Request a certificate template that is pended for certificate manager approval (Windows 2000, Windows XP, or Windows Server 2003).	V2 template: No V3 template: No	V2 template: Yes V3 template: No
Request a certificate template that is pended for certificate manager approval (Windows Vista or Windows Server 2008).	V2 template: Yes V3 template: Yes	V2 template: Yes V3 template: Yes

Choosing Among Automatic Enrollment Methods

Autoenrollment lowers the cost of a PKI by reducing the time and effort required to deploy certificates. Table 15-2 shows the automatic enrollment methods available for common deployment scenarios.

Table 15-2   Automatic Enrollment Methods

Enrollment method	ACRS	Autoenrollment settings	Scripting
Automatic deployment of certificates to computers	V1 template: Yes V2 template: No V3 template: No	V1 template: No V2 template: Yes V3 template: Yes	V1 template: Yes V2 template: Yes V3 template: Yes
Automatic deployment of certificates to users	V1 template: No V2 template: No V3 template: No	V1 template: No V2 template: Yes V3 template: Yes	V1 template: Yes V2 template: Yes V3 template: Yes
Automatic renewal of expired certificates to computers	V1 template: Yes V2 template: No V3 template: No	V1 template: No V2 template: Yes V3 template: Yes	V1 template: Yes V2 template: Yes V3 template: Yes
Automatic renewal of expired certificates to users	V1 template: No V2 template: No V3 template: No	V1 template: No V2 template: Yes V3 template: Yes	V1 template: Yes V2 template: Yes V3 template: Yes

Publishing Certificate Templates for Enrollment

Before enrolling a certificate manually, automatically, or through a scripting method, you must ensure that the certificate templates are available for enrollment at a CA. This process is known as *publishing the certificate template at the CA.*

The following procedure publishes a certificate template:

1. Log on at the CA computer as a user assigned the Manage CA permission.

2. From Administrative Tools, open the Certification Authority console.

3. In the console tree, expand *CAName* (where *CAName* is the logical name of the CA), and then click Certificate Templates.

4. In the console tree, right-click Certificate Templates, point to New, and then click Certificate Template To Issue.

5. In the Enable Certificate Templates dialog box, select one or more certificate templates not currently published at the CA, and then click OK.

Operating System Version Constraints

An enterprise CA cannot necessarily issue all defined certificate templates. The available certificate templates are constrained by both the version of the operating system and the edition of the operating system.

- Version 3 certificate templates can be issued only by Windows Server 2008 Enterprise Edition or Windows Server 2008 Datacenter Edition CAs.

- Version 2 certificate templates can be issued by Windows Server 2003 or Windows Server 2008 Enterprise Edition or Datacenter Edition CAs.

- For both Windows Server 2003 and Windows Server 2008, the enterprise CAs must be running either the Enterprise edition or Datacenter edition of the operating system. If the enterprise CA is installed on the Standard edition, only version 1 certificate templates are available for enrollment.

This is one of the most common mistakes made when deploying enterprise CAs. If you did install the enterprise CA on the Standard edition, you can perform an in-place upgrade to upgrade the server to the Enterprise edition.

Once you add the certificates, they are available for enrollment. The list of published certificate templates is defined on a CA-by-CA basis, allowing the availability of different certificate templates at each enterprise CA in the CA hierarchy.

If you want to remove a certificate template, select the certificate template or templates in the details pane, and then press Delete. After you have confirmed the deletion, the certificate templates are no longer available for enrollment. Note that this only prevents the certificate template from being used for enrollment at the CA and does not actually delete the certificate template object from Active Directory Domain Services.

Scripting the Publishing of Certificate Templates

Alternatively, you can use the **certutil** command to add or remove certificate templates to or from a CA. For example, to remove the User certificate template from a CA, you can run the following command at a command prompt or from a script:

```
certutil -SetCAtemplates -User
```

Likewise, you can also add certificate templates, such as the Key Recovery Agent certificate template, to the CA by using the following command:

```
certutil -setCAtemplates +KeyRecoveryAgent
```

The template name that you use is the object name, not the display name of the certificate template.

Performing Manual Enrollment

The sections that follow detail the procedures for requesting certificates from a Windows Server 2008 CA. If Certificate Services installation includes the Certificate Services Web Enrollment role service, IIS 7.0 is installed and configured as required for Web enrollment.

Requesting Certificates by Running the Certificate Enrollment Wizard

Another method of manually requesting a certificate is to use the Certificate Enrollment wizard. The Certificate Enrollment wizard can be used by Windows 2000, Windows XP, and Windows Server 2003 domain members when requesting certificates from an enterprise CA.

Note   The Certificate Enrollment wizard does not show the same certificates when run in different operating systems. A client computer running Windows 2000 shows only the available version 1 certificate templates. Windows XP and Windows Server 2003 clients show all the available version 1 and version 2 certificate templates, and Windows Vista and Windows Server 2008 clients show all version 1, version 2, and version 3 certificate templates.

Preparing the Certificates Console

The Certificate Enrollment wizard is launched from the Certificates MMC console focused on the current user, a service, or the local machine. The following procedure allows you to request a certificate by running the Certificate Enrollment wizard:

1. Open an empty MMC console.

2. On the File menu, click Add/Remove Snap-in.

> **Note**   If you are using Windows 2000, use the Console menu instead of the File menu.

3. In the Add/Remove Snap-in dialog box, click Add.

4. In the Add Standalone Snap-in dialog box, in the Available Standalone Snap-ins list, select Certificates, and then click Add.

5. In the Certificates Snap-in dialog box, click My User Account to request a user certificate, Service Account to request a certificate for a specific service, or Computer Account to request a computer certificate.

> **Note**   Service Account and Computer Account are available only if you are a member of the local Administrators group.

6. Select one of the following options:

   ❏ **Computer Account**   In the Select Computer dialog box, click Local Computer (The Computer This Console Is Running On), and then click Finish.

   ❏ **Service Account**   In the Select Computer dialog box, click Local Computer (The Computer This Console Is Running On), click Next, select the service you wish to manage, and then click Finish.

   ❏ **User Account**   Just click Finish.

7. In the Add Standalone Snap-in dialog box, click Close.

8. In the Add/Remove Snap-in dialog box, click OK.

> **Tip**   If you are using Windows XP or later, you can run certmgr.msc to launch the Certificates console focused on the current user.

Requesting a Certificate by Using the Certificates Console

Once you load the Certificates console, you can request a certificate by using the Certificate Enrollment wizard. Use the following procedure to request a certificate:

1. In the console tree, expand Personal, and then click Certificates. If the Certificates node does not appear, this user, computer, or service does not currently have any certificates issued.

2. In the console tree, right-click the Personal or Certificates folder, point to All Tasks, and then click Request New Certificate.

3. In the Certificate Enrollment wizard, click Next.

4. On the Request Certificates page (see Figure 15-2), a list of the certificate templates available for enrollment is displayed. The list is limited to the certificate templates for which either the current user or local machine have Read and Enroll permissions. On this page you can:

   ❑ Perform additional actions, such as providing the subject name, by clicking Details for the selected certificate template.

   ❑ Select to enroll more than one certificate template at one time by selecting multiple check boxes.

   ❑ Display all templates to determine why an expected certificate template is not available for enrollment.

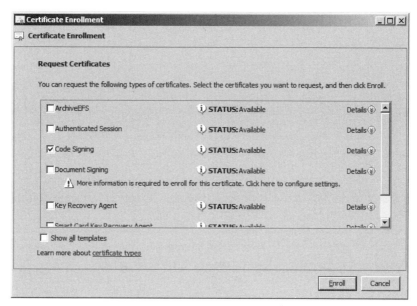

Figure 15-2   Choosing a certificate template

   Once you select the certificate template(s), click Enroll.

5. On the Certificate Installation Results page, ensure that the Status is Succeeded, and then click Finish.

6. If the certificate request is successful, the certificate appears in the details pane.

Providing a Custom Subject

If the request requires input of a custom subject, when you edit the properties of the request (see Figure 15-3), you can provide the Subject and Subject Alternative Names for the request.

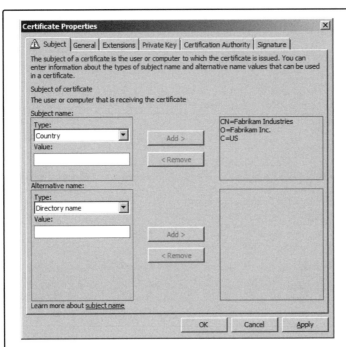

Figure 15-3 Providing a custom subject name

For each name, you can select the name attribute (such as common name or country), provide a value, and then click Add. In Figure 15-3, the subject was configured to be CN=Fabrikam Industries, O=Fabrikam Inc., C=US.

Using Web Enrollment to Request a Certificate

Use the following procedure to request a certificate from the Certificate Services Web Enrollment pages:

1. Open Windows Internet Explorer.

2. In Internet Explorer, open the URL *http://CertServerDNS/certsrv* (where *CertServerDNS* is the Domain Name System (DNS) name of the Windows Server 2008 CA).

> **Note** The Certificate Server's DNS name should be added to the Local intranet zone at all computers. If the Web site is not added to one of these zones, users are prompted for their user name and password.

3. On the Welcome page, click the Request A Certificate link.

4. On the Advanced Certificate Request page (see Figure 15-4), click the Create And Submit A Request To This CA link.

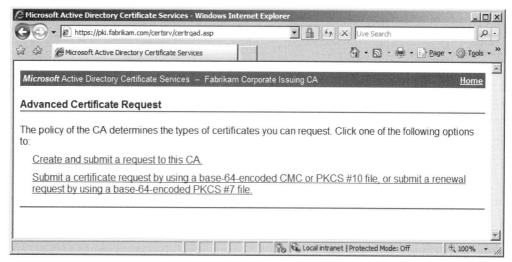

Figure 15-4   The Advanced Certificate Request page

5. On the Advanced Certificate Request page, you can choose the following options for the certificate request:

❑ **Certificate Template**   Lists the certificate templates for which the user is assigned Read and Enroll permissions.

❑ **Key Set**   Allows you to choose between generating a new key set or using the existing key set.

❑ **CSP**   Allows you to select a CSP installed on the client computer to use for the certificate request.

❑ **Key Size**   The length of the key pair generated for the certificate request.

❑ **Container Name**   The key container where the certificate's key pair is stored.

❑ **Export Options**   Allows you to request that the certificate's private key be exportable.

❑ **Strong Key Protection**   Requires a password each time the certificate's private key is accessed.

❑ **Request Format**   You can choose between Certificate Management Protocol using Cryptographic Message Syntax (CMC) or Public Key Cryptography Standards (PKCS) #10 request formats. CMC is required for digitally signed requests and key archival requests.

❑ **Friendly Name**   A logical name assigned to the certificate. This name is not part of the certificate. Rather, it is the logical display name when the certificate is viewed with Microsoft tools; the friendly name can be changed without invalidating the signature applied to the certificate.

> **Note**   The default values shown on the Advanced Certificate Request page are based on the values specified in the certificate template.

6. Once all options are set, click Submit on the Advanced Certificate Request page.

7. In the Web Access Confirmation dialog box, allow the Web site to request a certificate on your behalf by clicking Yes.

8. On the Certificate Issued page, click the Install This Certificate link.

9. In the Web Access Confirmation dialog box, accept that the Web site is adding a certificate to your computer by clicking Yes.

10. Ensure that the Certificate Installed page appears indicating that the certificate has installed successfully.

11. Close Internet Explorer.

> **Important**   If you are attempting to request a certificate from a Windows Server 2003 enterprise CA from a Windows Vista client, you must update the Web Enrollment pages on the Windows Server 2003 CA. Windows Vista and Windows Server 2008 clients use CertEnroll for Web enrollment, not XEnroll. The deprecation of XEnroll in Windows Vista and Windows Server 2008 makes them unable to use the Web Enrollment pages on a Windows Server 2003 CA to request certificates unless the procedure described in Microsoft Knowledge Base article 922706: "How to Use Certificate Services Web Enrollment Pages Together with Windows Vista" is performed.

Completing a Pending Certificate Request

If CA Certificate Manager Approval in the certificate template is enabled on the Issuance Requirements tab, the certificate request becomes pending until a certificate manager performs requestor validation.

> **Note**   To issue the certificate, the certificate manager must right-click the certificate request in the Pending Requests container of the Certification Authority container, point to All Tasks, and then click Issue.

With Windows Vista, a pending enrollment request can be completed using either the Web Enrollment pages (if the request was initiated from the Web Enrollment pages) or from the Certificates console (no matter where the request was initiated).

If the certificate was requested by using the Web Enrollment pages, the Web Enrollment pages maintain a cookie to track the request. The original requestor can complete the request as follows:

1. Open Internet Explorer at the same computer where the original request was submitted.

2. In Internet Explorer, open the URL *http://CertServerDNS/certsrv* (where *CertServerDNS* is the DNS name of the Windows Server 2008 CA).

3. On the Welcome page, click the View The Status Of A Pending Certificate Request link.

4. On the View The Status Of A Pending Certificate Request page, click the link for the pending certificate.

> **Note**   The computer where the certificate request is performed must have cookies enabled. If cookies are not enabled, the View The Status Of A Pending Certificate Request page does not show any entries.

5. On the Certificate Issued page, click the Install This Certificate link.

6. In the Potential Scripting Violation dialog box, accept that the Web site is adding a certificate to your computer by clicking Yes.

7. Ensure that the Certificate Installed page appears indicating that the certificate has installed successfully.

8. Close Internet Explorer.

> **Note**   If cookies are disabled in Internet Explorer, you cannot retrieve a pending certificate request.

If you wish to complete the request by using the Certificates console, the following process is required:

1. Open the Certificates console.

2. In the console tree, right-click Certificates, point to All Tasks, and then click Automatically Enroll And Retrieve Certificates.

3. On the Before You Begin page, click Next.

4. On the Request Certificates page (see Figure 15-5), ensure that the pending request is selected, and then click Enroll.

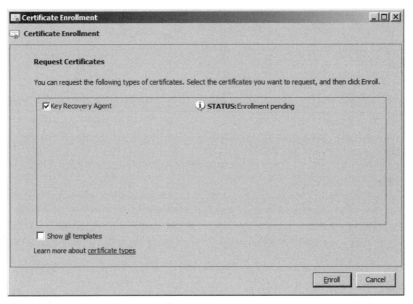

Figure 15-5   Processing a pending request

5. On the Certificate Installation Results page, ensure that the Status is Succeeded, and then click Finish.

Submitting a Certificate Request from Network Devices and Other Platforms

In some cases, the certificate request is generated at a network device or in another operating system, such as Linux. In these cases, the certificate request is commonly generated in a PKCS #10 format. Certificate Services Web Enrollment pages provide a facility to submit the PKCS #10 certificate request and issue a certificate based on the subject information and public key in the request.

Use the following procedure to request a certificate with a PKCS #10 file created by a network device or alternate operating system:

1. Open Internet Explorer.

2. In Internet Explorer, open the URL *http://CertServerDNS/certsrv* (where *CertServerDNS* is the DNS name of the Windows Server 2008 CA).

3. In the Welcome page, click the Request A Certificate link.

4. On the Request A Certificate page, click the Advanced Certificate Request link.

5. On the Advanced Certificate Request page, click the Submit A Certificate Request By Using A Base-64-Encoded CMC Or PKCS #10 File, Or Submit A Renewal Request By Using A Base-64-Encoded PKCS #7 File link.

Reviewing the Certificate Request

A certificate manager should not accept any PKCS #10 request file without first reviewing the certificate request's contents. The **certutil** command allows you to review the contents by running **certutil –dump** *request.req* (where *request.req* is the name of the PKCS #10 request file).

```
402.203.0: 0x80070057 (WIN32: 87): ..CertCli Version
PKCS10 Certificate Request:
Version: 1
Subject:
    CN=Andy Ruth

Public Key Algorithm:
    Algorithm ObjectId: 1.2.840.113549.1.1.1 RSA
    Algorithm Parameters:
    05 00
Public Key Length: 1024 bits
Public Key: UnusedBits = 0
    0000    30 81 89 02 81 81 00 bc    d6 cc 13 34 21 1e c9 dd
    0010    48 84 92 5b bf 7b 4e 1b    87 f8 3a 8e 9e 23 6c ce
    0020    5f 01 c5 3b 4a 01 5f b2    bb 67 3a 67 5f d7 76 15
    0030    78 f4 d8 f1 ba 3a b3 ab    56 69 bd e3 0d 39 22 f7
    0040    a4 18 96 61 c2 ee 12 b4    63 ba ee 04 cf ad fe d4
    0050    08 5e 95 51 44 3d 76 38    5c 00 77 c6 0e 7d 7b dd
    0060    96 58 70 8f 82 51 95 9b    75 be 45 a0 ea d3 a8 0a
    0070    52 5c 97 8e a4 c4 48 1a    4f 0f bd f9 20 a2 70 de
    0080    2f a9 22 6e a7 58 a5 02    03 01 00 01
Request Attributes: 4
  4 attributes:

  Attribute[0]: 1.3.6.1.4.1.311.13.2.3 (OS Version)
    Value[0][0]:
        5.1.2600.2

  Attribute[1]: 1.3.6.1.4.1.311.21.20 (Client Information)
    Value[1][0]:
    Unknown Attribute type
    Client Id: = 1
    XECI_XENROLL -- 1
    User:
    Machine: London.corp.microsoft.com
    Process: cscript

  Attribute[2]: 1.2.840.113549.1.9.14 (Certificate Extensions)
    Value[2][0]:
    Unknown Attribute type
Certificate Extensions: 5
    2.5.29.15: Flags = 1(Critical), Length = 4
    Key Usage
        Digital Signature, Non-Repudiation, Key Encipherment, Data Encipherment
(f0)
```

```
    1.2.840.113549.1.9.15: Flags = 0, Length = 37
    SMIME Capabilities
        [1]SMIME Capability
            Object ID=1.2.840.113549.3.2
            Parameters=02 02 00 80
        [2]SMIME Capability
            Object ID=1.2.840.113549.3.4
            Parameters=02 02 00 80
        [3]SMIME Capability
            Object ID=1.3.14.3.2.7
        [4]SMIME Capability
            Object ID=1.2.840.113549.3.7

    2.5.29.14: Flags = 0, Length = 16
    Subject Key Identifier
        7c 4e b0 7b ca b7 c1 66 a8 b5 c2 15 83 84 f2 7d a1 eb 43 ac

    2.5.29.37: Flags = 0, Length = c
    Enhanced Key Usage
        Client Authentication (1.3.6.1.5.5.7.3.2)

    1.3.6.1.4.1.311.20.2: Flags = 0, Length = 16
    Certificate Template Name
        ClientAuth


  Attribute[3]: 1.3.6.1.4.1.311.13.2.2 (Enrollment CSP)
    Value[3][0]:
    Unknown Attribute type
    CSP Provider Info
    KeySpec = 1
    Provider = Microsoft Enhanced Cryptographic Provider v1.0
    Signature: UnusedBits=0
    0000  9f f8 46 13 93 4c a4 79  bb 10 82 53 70 12 b9 8f
    0010  48 05 8b 76 07 c8 8c d1  db 78 71 e3 44 c3 a3 2b
    0020  c5 43 01 6d 15 1b c2 d3  aa 29 3f f5 3c 43 8a fa
    0030  e1 2d 6a 71 da 26 ff 97  a7 58 59 73 d8 db 8d 53
    0040  e7 25 3a bf 21 16 d5 1b  1c bc f7 1e 83 de 3e 92
    0050  0a f0 70 d0 b5 9a 11 79  44 7f d6 aa 4d 70 4d cd
    0060  25 83 9f 3a 3c 59 30 03  d0 05 24 1b 19 74 5e 24
    0070  76 7e 76 8f cb 39 14 48  66 19 84 45 d8 08 b0 0d
    0080  00 00 00 00 00 00 00 00
Signature Algorithm:
    Algorithm ObjectId: 1.2.840.113549.1.1.5 sha1RSA
    Algorithm Parameters:
    05 00
Signature: UnusedBits=0
    0000  31 84 ff 5d e4 0f 32 69  27 ca e4 fb 6a 34 f9 9c
    0010  53 6e ac d0 80 98 19 ba  d6 55 8f 9f 7b dd 2c 0e
    0020  32 a6 cc 18 0e 34 2f a3  dc 11 49 e3 54 69 08 ad
    0030  fa 15 8e 52 7b 16 b4 ad  98 bc 4f 0d 00 7a 20 29
    0040  a8 ac e2 c6 48 d6 c7 e7  dd 77 9a 0b 37 f9 ef 77
    0050  09 b1 28 01 f6 a1 40 12  2e a8 98 9d 16 b9 99 ff
    0060  8b b3 59 0d ac 50 ca 8a  1f d5 8c 38 ac 92 a8 71
    0070  28 f0 34 07 dc fb d2 68  4e ee d7 fc 5a 34 9b 11
```

```
Signature matches Public Key
Key Id Hash(sha1): 7c 4e b0 7b ca b7 c1 66 a8 b5 c2 15 83 84 f2 7d a1 eb 43 ac
CertUtil: -dump command completed successfully.
```

Before submitting the PKCS #10 request file to the CA, ensure that the subject information is correct, the correct key length and certificate template are selected, and the signature matches the public key. If these conditions are met, you can submit the certificate request to the CA.

6. On the Submit A Certificate Request Or Renewal Request page, right-click the Saved Request box, and then click Paste. Ensure that the Certificate Template drop-down list is set to the required certificate template, and then click Submit.

> **Note**   If the certificate is for a Secure Sockets Layer (SSL) accelerator or a third-party Web server, choose the Web Server certificate template.
>
> If the certificate request is generated by a Linux client for authentication, choose an authentication certificate template, such as Authenticated Session or a custom v2 certificate template.

7. On the Certificate Issued page, select Base-64 Encoded or DER Encoded, and then click the Download Certificate or Download Certificate Chain link.

8. In the File Download dialog box, click Save.

9. In the Save As dialog box, select a folder and file name for the certificate, and then click Save.

10. Close Internet Explorer.

The issued certificate now must be installed on the network device or on the other operating system. The process to select depends on the network device or operating system where the PKCS #10 request file was generated.

Performing Automatic Enrollment

The Windows Server 2008 PKI provides two methods for automatically deploying certificates to users and computers:

■ Automatic Certificate Request Settings

■ Autoenrollment Settings

The sections that follow discuss the best uses and implementation for each automated enrollment method.

Automatic Certificate Request Settings

Automatic Certificate Request Settings (ACRS) is an automated enrollment process to automatically distribute certificates, but the supported scenarios are limited:

- Certificates can be distributed to computers running Windows 2000 and later that are domain members.

- Only version 1 certificate templates can be distributed.

- Certificates cannot be distributed to user accounts.

Although limited, ACRS is useful for distributing Computer or IPsec certificates to all computers in a domain. To enable ACRS use the following procedure:

1. From Administrative Tools, open Active Directory Users And Computers.

2. In the console tree, right-click the domain or OU where you want to implement the Automatic Certificate Request Settings Group Policy setting, and then click Properties.

> **Note** You can also configure the ACRS Group Policy setting at a site by using the Active Directory Sites and Services console.

3. In the *DomainName* or *OUName* Properties dialog box, on the Group Policy tab, create and edit a new Group Policy Object (GPO), or link and edit an existing GPO.

4. In the Group Policy Object Editor, expand Computer Configuration, expand Windows Settings, expand Security Settings, expand Public Key Policies, and then click Automatic Certificate Request Settings.

5. In the console tree, right-click Automatic Certificate Request Settings, point to New, and then click Automatic Certificate Request.

6. In the Automatic Certificate Request Setup wizard, click Next.

7. In the Certificate Template page, in the list of available certificate templates, choose the version 1 certificate template for computers to you want to deploy automatically, and then click Next.

8. In the Automatic Certificate Request Setup wizard, click Finish.

Autoenrollment Settings

Autoenrollment Settings is a combination of Group Policy settings and version 2 or version 3 certificate templates. The combination allows the domain member client computer running Windows XP or later to enroll user or computer certificates automatically.

Note Autoenrollment Settings is not supported for a user with a client computer running Microsoft Windows 2000 Professional or Microsoft Windows 2000 Server. Only Windows XP and later domain members recognize the Autoenrollment Settings Group Policy setting.

Configuring Certificate Templates

Autoenrollment Settings require use of version 2 or version 3 certificate templates.

To enable autoenrollment in a version 2 or version 3 certificate template, make the following modifications to the certificate template:

■ **Security tab** Assign Read, Enroll, and Autoenroll permissions to the user, computer account, or group to which you want to deploy the certificate. If you use groups, assign the permissions to either global or universal groups.

Tip You should not assign certificate template permissions to a domain local group. The certificate template objects exist in the configuration naming context, which is replicated to all domain controllers in the forest. If you use a domain local group, the group is recognized only in the forest root domain.

■ **Request Handling tab** If a certificate template is enabled for autoenrollment, you must decide how the user interacts with the autoenrollment process. If you do not want any user involvement, choose Enroll Subject Without Requiring Any User Input. If you are using a smart card CSP, you require an ability to inform the user to insert the smart card into the smart card reader. To enable this interaction, choose Prompt The User During Enrollment.

Note You also must enable Prompt The User During Enrollment if you enable signing of the certificate request on the Issuance Requirements tab. Doing this allows the user to select the correct signing certificate before submitting the certificate request.

After autoenrollment has been enabled in the version 2 or version 3 certificate template, the certificate template is ready to be published at a CA for enrollment.

Configuring Group Policy

Once you configure the certificate templates to be deployed with autoenrollment, you must implement a Group Policy setting at the domain or OU where the user or computer account exists. In either case, you must modify the Autoenrollment Settings policy in the following Group Policy locations:

- **Computer autoenrollment**   Computer Configuration\Windows Settings\Security Settings\Public Key Policies\Autoenrollment Settings

- **User autoenrollment**   User Configuration\Windows Settings\Security Settings\Public Key Policies\Autoenrollment Settings

The same dialog box appears for both User and Computer autoenrollment when you double-click Autoenrollment Settings in the details pane. (See Figure 15-6.)

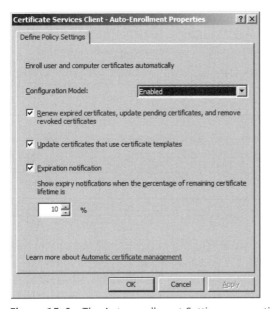

Figure 15-6   The Autoenrollment Settings properties dialog box

The options that must be enabled in the Autoenrollment Settings properties dialog box are:

- **Configuration Model**   You can choose to enable, disable, or not configure the Group Policy setting.

- **Renew Expired Certificates, Update Pending Certificates, And Remove Revoked Certificates**   Enables certificate autoenrollment for certificate renewal, issuance of pending certificates, and removal of revoked certificates from the subject's certificate store.

- **Update Certificates That Use Certificate Templates**   Enables autoenrollment for superseded certificate templates.

- **Expiration Notification**   Allows you to select the percentage of the remaining validity period at which expiration notifications will be sent to the users.

Note   The expiration notification settings are available only for user autoenrollment and are not available for computer autoenrollment.

Performing Scripted Enrollment

This section will look at the **certreq.exe** tool, which is included with computers running Windows XP and later, and the process of creating custom scripts based on the Certificate Enrollment Control for certificate deployment to users and computers.

Certreq.exe

The certreq.exe utility allows you to create batch files that can submit, retrieve, and accept certificate requests submitted to standalone and enterprise CAs. The primary switches used with the certreq.exe for certificate enrollment are:

- **Certreq –new *Policyfile.inf RequestFile.req*** Creates a certificate request file (*Request-File.req*) based on the inputs provided in the *Policyfile.inf* file. The format of the *Policyfile.inf* file is shown here:

```
[NewRequest]
    PrivateKeyArchive = FALSE
    KeyLength = 1024
    SMIME = TRUE
    Exportable = TRUE
    UserProtected = FALSE
    KeyContainer = "..."
    MachineKeySet = TRUE
    Silent = TRUE
    ProviderName = "Microsoft Enhanced Cryptographic Provider v1.0"
    ProviderType = 1
    UseExistingKeySet = TRUE
    RequestType = PKCS10
    KeyUsage = 0x80

[RequestAttributes]
CertificateTemplate=User
```

> **Note** There are additional settings that can be implemented in the *PolicyFile.inf* file, but the other settings are more likely to be required when you submit a certificate request to a standalone CA. When you submit the request to an enterprise CA, most of these additional settings are defined in the certificate template properties.

- **Certreq –submit –config *CADNSName\CALogicalName RequestFile.req*** Submits the certificate request file to the designated enterprise CA. The command returns the request ID of the submitted certificate request.

- **Certreq –retrieve -config *CADNSName\CALogicalName RequestID Certfile.cer*** Retrieves the issued certificate from the designated CA. The issued certificate is stored in the local file system in the designated *Certfile.cer*.

■ **Certreq –accept** *Certfile.cer*   Ties the returned certificate to the private key generated during the creation of the certificate request file. Once accepted, the certificate can be used for the intended encryption or signing operations.

Generating a Request by Using the Certificates Console

You can also use the Certificates console in Windows Vista or Windows Server 2008 to generate a custom request file. The Certificates console can create either a PKCS #10 or CMC request by using the following procedure:

1. Open the Certificates console focused on either the current user or the local machine.

2. In the console tree, right-click Personal, point to All Tasks, point to Advanced Operations, and then click Create Custom Request.

3. On the Before You Begin page, click Next.

4. On the Custom Request page (see Figure 15-7), choose whether to create a CNG key or Legacy key, choose whether to create a PKCS #10 or CMC Request, and then click Next.

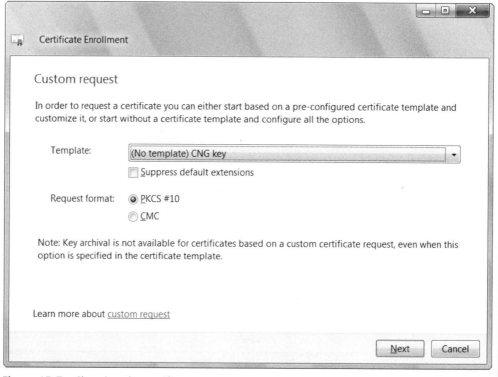

Figure 15-7   Choosing the certificate request format

5. On the Certificate Information page, click Details, and then click Properties to provide custom certificate attribute information.

6. In the Certificate Properties dialog box, you can now define the custom settings for the requested certificate. There are four tabs for information input:

   ❑ **General**   Specify the friendly name and a description for the certificate request.

   ❑ **Subject**   Specify the subject name and subject alternative name formats for the certificate request.

   ❑ **Extensions**   Specify key usage, extended key usage, basic constraints, symmetric algorithms, or custom X.509 version 3 extensions.

   ❑ **Private Key**   Specify the CSP, key options, and key type for the request.

7. Once all properties are specified, in the Certificate Properties dialog box, click OK.

8. On the Certificate Information page, click Next.

9. On the Where Do You Want To Save The Offline Request? page, type a full path for the file name, choose between a Base 64 or Binary format, and then click Finish.

The resulting request file can now be submitted at any certification authority for certificate issuance. If the CA is a Windows enterprise CA, you must designate the certificate template for the request during the submission. If the request is submitted to a standalone or third-party CA, the request is simply submitted without designating a certificate template.

Custom Scripting

Certreq.exe is more restricted on Windows 2000. For Windows 2000 clients, it is preferable to create custom scripts that automate the certificate request process. The scripts you develop use a combination of these development tools:

■ **CryptoAPI**   Provides a set of functions that allow applications to programmatically encrypt or digitally sign data.

■ **CAPICOM**   A reduced set of APIs that enables applications to encrypt or digitally sign data with far less code than CryptoAPI. In addition, CAPICOM uses the Component Object Model (COM), which allows scripting of CryptoAPI instructions.

> **Note**   CAPICOM requires Capicom.dll to be registered at all participating client computers.

■ **Certificate Enrollment Control**   Provides two COM interfaces to a DCOM server for generating certificate requests: the ICEnroll interface is primarily used by automation languages, such as Microsoft Visual Basic, whereas the IEnroll interface is primarily used when developing in C++.

> **Important**   Windows Vista changes the Certificate Enrollment Control to use Certenroll rather than XEnroll. If you connect a Windows Vista client to a Web page that still uses XEnroll, enrollment will fail. The pages or scripts must be updated to support CertEnroll for Windows Vista clients.

- **Certificate Request Control**   The Certificate Request Control is used to submit the certificate request generated by the Certificate Enrollment Control. The Certificate Request Control uses the ICertRequest2 COM interface to send the requests to the designated CA and receive the returned certificate.

> **More Info**   For more information on scripting using the Certificate Enrollment Control and the Certificate Request Control, see "Creating Certificate Requests Using the Certificate Enrollment Control and CryptoAPI," by David Hoyle, at *http://msdn.microsoft.com/security/ default.aspx?pull=/library/en-us/dncapi/html/certenrollment.asp*.

Sample Scripts

The actual coding of scripted solutions for certificate enrollment and certificate store queries is beyond the scope of this book. Two sample scripts are included on the CD accompanying this book, however. They are:

- **Ctool.vbs**   The **ctool.vbs** script utilizes CAPICOM to query the contents of a certificate store. The tool can list certificates in the designated certificate store that match the search criteria. The tool also can be used to add and remove certificates from the designated certificate store.

- **Enroll.vbs**   The **enroll.vbs** script utilizes both CAPICOM and the Certificate Enrollment Control to generate certificate requests and submit the requests to the designated CA.

Both scripts can be executed by running cscript ctool.vbs *options* or cscript enroll.vbs *options*. For a complete list of options, run cscript enroll.vbs /?.

Credential Roaming

Credential roaming is an enhancement to roaming profiles. Rather than roaming large amount of data (as invariably happens with roaming profiles), only certificate and Data Protection Application Programming Interface (DPAPI)–protected credential information is roamed between computers.

Windows XP Service Pack 2 clients with the Credential Roaming service update applied and Windows Vista clients can utilize credential roaming to ensure that software-based certificates are available at any domain member computer where the user logs in.

Credential roaming helps prevent the following:

- **Excess enrollment of signing certificates for users with multiple computers**   If a user logs on to more than one computer and is eligible to receive certificates through autoenrollment, the user will enroll a new certificate at each computer he or she logs on to. This results in excess growth of the CA database.

- **Encryption certificate issues**   If a user receives multiple encryption certificates, the user needs to have all available at a client to allow decryption of data. If the required encryption certificate is not available at the current computer, decryption attempts will fail.

- **Loss of certificates because of the deletion of a user's profile**   If an administrator deletes a user's profile because of profile corruption or slow logon times, credential roaming will restore the user's certificates when a new profile is created.

In these cases, CRS helps to prevent these problems. CRS stores the user's certificates as attributes of the user's Active Directory Domain Services (AD DS) user account. When the user logs on, the credential and certificate information stored in the user object is downloaded to the client. The download occurs *before* any autoenrollment requests are processed to ensure that duplicate certificates are not revoked.

When the user logs off, any new certificates are merged with the existing certificate in AD DS. This allows the propagation of encryption certificates between multiple computers. Once a user has logged on and logged off from every computer where he or she has encryption certificates, the certificates are now available at *every* computer where the user logs on.

What Is Included in the Roaming

Credential roaming supports a number of different items to roam for Windows XP, Windows Server 2003, Windows Vista, and Windows Server 2008 clients:

- DPAPI Master keys
- The DPAPI Preferred file (designating the current DPAPI master key)
- All certificates issued to the user
- Any current certificate requests for pending certificates
- Rivest Shamir Adleman (RSA) or Digital Signature Algorithm (DSA) keys

In Windows Vista and Windows Server 2008, additional items are included with credential roaming:

- Elliptic Curve Cryptography (ECC) keys
- Stored user names and passwords

How Does CRS Use Active Directory Domain Services?

When you implement CRS, information is populated into three Active Directory Domain Services (AD DS) attributes:

■ **ms-PKI-DPAPIMasterKeys**   A multi-valued attribute that contains master key files and information for DPAPI. All master key files must be maintained and roamed. They can never be removed, because they may be needed for future DPAPI decryption processes. The attribute also stores the current DPAPI master key as designated through the Preferred file (%APPDATA%\Microsoft\Protect\{userGUID}\Preferred).

■ **ms-PKI-AccountCredentials**   A multi-valued attribute that contains binary large object (BLOB) representations of encrypted credential objects. This includes the credential manager store objects, certificates, private keys, and certificate requests (for pending requests).

■ **ms-PKI-RoamingTimeStamp**   Contains the date and time of the latest change to the user object.

Requirements

To use credential roaming, the following requirements must be met:

■ Active Directory Domain Services must be running with the Windows Server 2008 schema installed.

■ Windows XP and Windows Server 2003 clients must apply the security update KB 907247: "Description of the Credential Roaming Service Update for Windows Server 2003 and for Windows."

■ Group Policy must be configured to enable Credential Roaming.

■ Credential Roaming settings must be configured in Group Policy.

Important   Rather than applying the Windows Server 2008 schema update, an interim schema update is included with KB 907247. This update just adds the necessary Active Directory attributes for Credential Roaming.

Group Policy Settings

To create a custom Group Policy Object (GPO) that configures Credential Roaming named PKI-Credential Roaming, use the following procedure:

1. Open the Group Policy Management console (GPMC.msc).

2. In the console tree, expand the forest node, right-click Domains, and then enable all domains in the forest.

3. In the console tree, select a target domain, right-click the domain, and then click Create A GPO In This Domain, And Link It Here.

4. In the New GPO dialog box, type **PKI-Credential Roaming**, and then click OK.

5. Right-click PKI-Credential Roaming, and then click Edit.

6. In the console tree, under User Configuration, expand Windows Settings, expand Security Settings, and then click Public Key Policies.

7. In the details pane, double-click Certificate Services Client – Credential Roaming.

8. In the Certificate Services Client – Credential Roaming Properties dialog box (see Figure 15-8), configure the following settings:

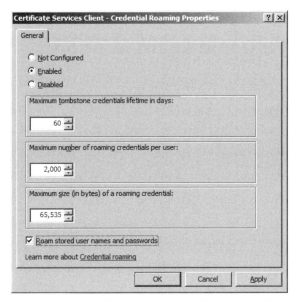

Figure 15-8 Configuring Credential Roaming settings

❑ **Enabled** Enables the Credential Roaming service

❑ **Maximum Tombstone Credentials Lifetime In Days** The length of time that a credential is tombstoned before expiration

❑ **Maximum Number Of Roaming Credentials Per User** The maximum number of credentials that are stored in Active Directory Domain Services for a single user

❑ **Maximum Size Of A Roaming Credential** The maximum amount of Active Directory storage allowed for a single user

❑ **Roam Stored User Names And Passwords** Stores any stored user names and passwords (for example, in Internet Explorer)

Important The roaming of user names and passwords is available only to Windows Vista clients.

9. In the Changing RUP Exclusion List dialog box, click OK to add the credential storage folders to the Roaming User Profile (RUP) exclusion list to prevent conflicts between the two services.

10. In the console tree, right-click PKI-Credential Roaming, and then click Properties.

11. On the General tab, select the Disable Computer Configuration Settings check box, and then click OK.

12. Close the Group Policy Management Editor.

13. Link the PKI-Credential Roaming GPO to all other domains in the forest.

Case Study: Selecting a Deployment Method

You are the PKI administrator for your organization, Lucerne Publishing. Lucerne Publishing has just deployed an enterprise PKI, with issuing CAs at each major hub on the network. The Lucerne Publishing CA hierarchy is shown in Figure 15-9.

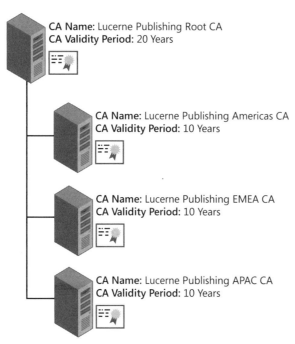

CA Name: Lucerne Publishing Root CA
CA Validity Period: 20 Years

CA Name: Lucerne Publishing Americas CA
CA Validity Period: 10 Years

CA Name: Lucerne Publishing EMEA CA
CA Validity Period: 10 Years

CA Name: Lucerne Publishing APAC CA
CA Validity Period: 10 Years

Figure 15-9   The Lucerne Publishing CA hierarchy

Lucerne Publishing deploys a single domain forest, LucernePublish.msft, with all client computers running Windows 2000, Windows XP, and Windows Vista configured as domain members.

Scenario

You identify several upcoming projects that require the deployment of certificates to users, computers, and network devices on the Lucerne Publishing network. You must recommend to management which enrollment method to use to deploy the certificates for each application.

The following projects require certificate deployment:

■ **Code signing**   Lucerne Publishing implements several Microsoft Office Excel spreadsheets that track a new book's development process. The spreadsheets use several macros that require lowering macro security to a medium level. By signing the macros, Lucerne Publishing can increase the macro security to the highest level. Code-signing certificates are to be issued only to the three members of the Quality Assurance team so that the macros are signed after extensive testing. The certificate template requires that the certificates be issued only after a face-to-face interview with the certificate manager.

■ **Encrypting File System (EFS) encryption**   An acquisition editor's laptop was recently stolen. The laptop contained information on the upcoming publishing schedule. Lucerne Publishing wants to protect all critical data on its laptops running Windows 2000, Windows XP, and Windows Vista by implementing EFS encryption. EFS certificates must be deployed to users automatically, and all recovery is to be performed by an EFS recovery agent. The same two EFS recovery agents are to be deployed at each issuing CA in the CA hierarchy.

■ **IPsec tunneling**   Each remote office connects to the corporate office by using IPsec tunnel mode. The remote offices use third-party virtual private network (VPN) devices, and the corporate office provides one computer running Windows Server 2008 as a tunnel termination point. The VPN devices support certificates and provide an option to generate a PKCS #10 certificate request for the device.

Case Study Questions

1. Assume that a custom version 2 certificate template is created for code signing that requires CA certificate manager approval. What enrollment method should you use for deploying the custom code-signing certificates to the three members of the Quality Assurance team if you perform the request from a Windows XP client computer?

2. If the user had a Windows Vista client, are other options available for enrollment?

3. Assume that a custom version 2 certificate template is created for EFS certificates. What options must be enabled in the certificate template to permit autoenrollment for all users in the Lucerne Publishing forest?

4. Where must you configure Group Policy to enable autoenrollment of the custom EFS certificate to all users in the LucernePublish.msft domain?

5. Does autoenrollment deploy custom EFS certificates to all users of laptops running Windows 2000, Windows XP, and Windows Vista? Why or why not?

6. What method of enrollment allows EFS certificates to be deployed to users of laptops running Windows 2000 without user intervention?

7. Assume that the default EFS Recovery Agent certificate template is modified so that only the two EFS recovery agents are assigned Read and Enroll permissions for the certificate template. What enrollment method(s) can they use to acquire their EFS Recovery Agent certificates?

8. Assuming that the default IPsec certificate is used for the IPsec tunnel mode project, do you use ACRS or Autoenrollment Settings to automate the deployment of IPsec certificates to computers running Windows Server 2008 at the corporate office?

9. What must be done to the IPsec certificate template and the Automatic Certificate Request Settings Group Policy setting to enable automatic enrollment of the IPsec certificates by computers running Windows Server 2008?

10. What must be done to the IPsec certificate template and the Autoenrollment Settings Group Policy setting to enable automatic enrollment of the IPsec certificates by computers running Windows Server 2008?

11. How do you deploy IPsec certificates to the third-party VPN devices at the remote offices?

Additional Information

- Microsoft Official Curriculum, Course 2821: "Designing and Managing a Windows Public Key Infrastructure" (*http://www.microsoft.com/traincert/syllabi/2821afinal.asp*)

- "Implementing and Administering Certificate Templates" (*http://www.microsoft.com/downloads/details.aspx?FamilyID=3c670732-c971-4c65-be9c-c0ebc3749e24&display-lang=en*)

- "Certificate Autoenrollment in Windows Server 2003" (*http://www.microsoft.com/technet/prodtechnol/windowsserver2003/technologies/security/autoenro.mspx*)

- "Windows Data Protection" (*http://msdn.microsoft.com/library/en-us/dnsecure/html/windataprotection-dpapi.asp*)

- "CAPICOM Reference" (*http://msdn.microsoft.com/library/en-us/security/Security/capicom_reference.asp*)

- "The Cryptography API, or How to Keep a Secret" (*http://msdn.microsoft.com/library/en-us/dncapi/html/msdn_cryptapi.asp*)

- "Certificate Enrollment Control" (*http://msdn.microsoft.com/library/en-us/security/security/certificate_enrollment_control.asp*)

- "Creating Certificate Requests Using the Certificate Enrollment Control and CryptoAPI" (*http://msdn.microsoft.com/security/default.aspx?pull=/library/en-us/dncapi/html/certenrollment.asp*)

- 249125: "Using Certificates for Windows 2000 and Cisco IOS VPN Interoperation"

- 309408: "Troubleshooting the Data Protection API (DPAPI)"

- 310389: "How To: Request a Certificate by Using the Certificates Snap-In in Windows 2000"

- 326474: "How To: Troubleshoot VPN with Extensible Authentication Protocol (EAP) Authentication"

- 330389: "Internet Explorer Stops Responding at 'Downloading ActiveX Control' Message When You Try to Use a Certificate Server"

- 907247: "Description of the Credential Roaming Service Update for Windows Server 2003 and for Windows"

- 922706: "How to Use Certificate Services Web Enrollment Pages Together with Windows Vista"

Note The seven articles above can be accessed through the Microsoft Knowledge Base. Go to *http://support.microsoft.com*, and type the article number in the Search The Knowledge Base text box.

Chapter 16
Creating Trust Between Organizations

When an organization implements its own public key infrastructure (PKI), the certificates typically are trusted by that organization only. With technologies such as code signing and secure e-mail that are used *between* organizations, it is often necessary for certificates to be trusted by other organizations.

This chapter introduces several methods for deciding which certificates issued externally will be trusted by your organization. The chapter focuses on using cross certification, wherein an organization defines trust criteria so that only certificates that meet the criteria will be trusted by your organization.

Methods of Creating Trust

When you implement a Windows Server 2008 public key infrastructure in an Active Directory Domain Services (AD DS) environment, several methods exist for creating trust between organizations, including:

- **Certificate trust lists (CTLs)**   A CTL is a signed list of hashes. Each hash in the list is a hash performed against a root CA's public keys. The CTL itself is signed by the holder of a Certificate Trust List Signing certificate. A CTL allows you to specify what certificate types, specifically what Extended Key Usages (EKUs) must exist in the certificate that your organization trusts. For example, your organization could choose to trust only certificates with the Client Authentication object identifier (OID) in the Enhanced Key Usage extension.

- **A common root CA**   If two organizations have CA hierarchies that share a common root CA, all certificates issued within the common CA hierarchy are trusted by both organizations. Alternatively, if two organizations must trust the certificates issued by the other organization, each organization can designate the other organization's root CA as a trusted root CA.

    Alternatively, the common root CA can be a commercial root CA. Commercial root CAs are typically trusted by all partner organizations (subject to their choosing to remove the commercial root CA from the root trust list). You can choose to directly purchase the individual certificates from the commercial provider or to implement a subordinate CA below the commercial root CA. In either case, certificates that chain to the commercial root CA will be trusted by other organizations.

- **Cross certification**   An organization can issue Cross Certification Authority certificates to a CA in another organization's CA hierarchy. After the certificate is issued, all certificates issued by this CA are trusted. If implemented with constraints, you can restrict which certificates are considered trusted from the partner organization. The constraints can restrict certificates based on namespace, certificate use, or issuance method.

- **Bridge CA**   This method allows multiple organizations to establish certificate trust. Every organization issues a certificate to a common bridge CA, which issues certificates to a CA in each organization's CA hierarchy.

These methods are discussed in greater detail in the sections that follow.

Certificate Trust Lists

A CTL is a Microsoft solution for trusting certificates from other organizations. This solution works with most Microsoft operating systems, but it is not extensible beyond Microsoft operating systems.

CTLs allow you to designate which foreign root CAs your organization trusts. You can then set restrictions on the root CA certificate, including specifying the length of time you trust certificates that chain to the root CA certificate and the Enhanced Key Usage OIDs that must be in a trusted certificate. If a certificate from a foreign CA hierarchy is presented with an Enhanced Key Usage OID that is not on the list, the certificate is not trusted.

CTLs are defined in Group Policy in the Computer Configuration\Windows Settings\Security Settings\Public Key Policies\Enterprise Trust container. The Group Policy Object (GPO) containing the defined CTL can be linked to any site, domain, or organizational unit (OU) in your AD DS, allowing the trust to be limited only to computer accounts where the GPO is applied.

> **Note**   CTLs can also be defined in the User Configuration\Windows Settings\Security Settings\Public Key Policies\Enterprise Trust container, but it is recommended to define CTLs in the Computer Configuration of GPO so that the CTLs are applied to all users of a computer.

The following procedure outlines the steps for defining a new CTL:

1. Log on to a domain for which you have administrative privileges to manage the GPO.

2. Open the GPO you want to edit.

3. In the console tree, expand Computer Configuration, expand Windows Settings, expand Security Settings, expand Public Key Policies, and then click Enterprise Trust.

4. On the Action menu, point to New, and then click Certificate Trust List.

5. On the Welcome To The Certificate Trust List Wizard page, click Next.

6. On the Certificate Trust List Purpose page (see Figure 16-1), type a Valid Duration period in months and days. In the Designate Purposes list, select all valid application policy OIDs from the listing, and then click Next.

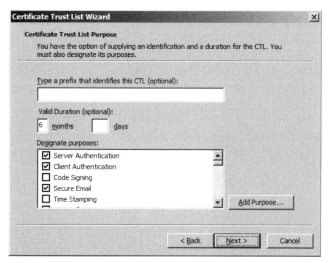

Figure 16-1   Defining the CTL duration and purpose

7. On the Certificates In The CTL page, add one or more root CA certificates from a file, and then click Next.

8. On the Signature Certificate page, click Select From Store, and then select a certificate with the Microsoft Trust List Signing application policy OID. After you select the certificate, click Next.

> **Note**   The Administrator certificate template includes the Microsoft Trust List Signing Enhanced Key Usage OID (1.3.6.1.4.1.311.10.3.1). Alternatively, a custom version 2 or version 3 certificate template can be created that enables the Microsoft Trust List Signing OID.

9. On the Timestamping page, you can choose whether to submit the CTL to a timestamping service. You must provide the correct URL and then click Next.

> **Note**   A timestamping service applies a date and time stamp to the CTL when it is signed with the Microsoft Trust List Signing certificate. This allows the certificate to be checked to see if it was valid at the time of signing, in case the signing certificate is later revoked.

10. On the Name And Description page, type a name and description for the CTL, and then click Next.

11. On the Completing The Certificate Trust List Wizard page, click Finish.

Common Root CAs

When a common root CA is implemented, it is used by two or more organizations as their organization's root CA. A common root CA allows an organization to trust any certificate issued by a CA that chains to the same common root CA. When a common root CA is used, all certificates are trusted—subject to any constraints defined in the subordinate CA certificates. This means that if the operator of the root CA issues subordinate CA certificates to a third organization, the two original organizations trust certificates that are issued by the third organization. A common root CA can be deployed with subordinate CAs existing at two or more separate organizations. (See Figure 16-2.)

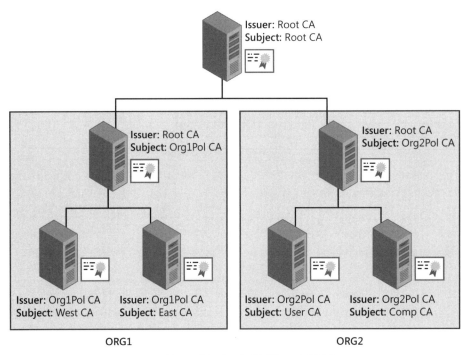

Figure 16-2   A common root CA used by both ORG1 and ORG2

In this example, both ORG1 and ORG2 have established policy CAs below the common root CA as well as issuing CAs that issue certificates to users, computers, and network devices in the organization.

The root CA need not necessarily be a root CA from a commercial vendor such as VeriSign or RSA. It also can be a root CA hosted by one of the two organizations. The merits of each configuration are discussed in greater detail in the sections that follow.

Commercial CAs

When an organization outsources root CA management to a commercial vendor, it is often for the following reasons:

- To increase the trust of the certificates issued by the organization

- To take advantage of the PKI expertise provided by the commercial vendor

When a root CA is hosted by a commercial vendor, the organization's CAs must follow the commercial CA organization's security policy and certificate policies. If an organization does not follow these policies, the commercial CA can revoke the immediate subordinate CA's certificate, resulting in all certificates being effectively revoked.

> **Note**   An organization can implement policy requirements that are more secure than the commercial CA's policies so long as none of the requirements in the policies conflict.

When you purchase a subordinate CA certificate from a commercial CA, you must pay for use and management of the trusted root. These costs can be quite high. Typically, you pay an annual fee for the subordinate CA certificate as well as a flat fee for a maximum number of annually issued certificates.

Umbrella Groups

As an alternative, some organizations establish a root CA hosted by one of the participating organizations. The participating organizations can then establish subordinate CAs below the common root CA. There still will be management costs for maintaining and operating the common root CA, but they can be shared between the participating organizations.

This configuration is often used by large organizations that own several sub-organizations. The parent organization can deploy a common root CA for all organizations within the umbrella group and then deploy separate CAs for each participating organization. The parent organization maintains control of the root CA in this configuration, but it is able to delegate PKI branch management to each organization within the umbrella group.

> **Note**   This configuration works well when mergers and acquisitions occur. With the root CA already created, CA hierarchy design can focus on the specific subordinate CA requirements for the merged organization.

Cross Certification

Cross certification allows you to issue a Cross Certification Authority certificate from a CA in your organization to a CA in another organization. The effect of the Cross Certification

Authority certificate is to "glue" the partner organization's CA structure below the CA that issues the Cross Certification Authority certificate. (See Figure 16-3.)

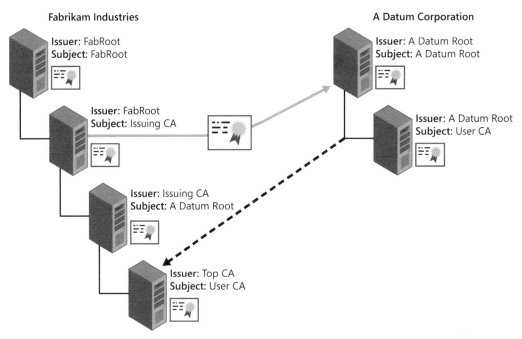

Figure 16-3   The effect of a Cross Certification Authority certificate

In this example, the IssuingCA of Fabrikam, Inc. issues a Cross Certification Authority certificate to the root CA of the A. Datum Corporation CA hierarchy. The effect of this Cross Certification Authority certificate is that the ADatumRootCA appears as a subordinate CA of the IssuingCA when the certificate is presented to a computer at Fabrikam, Inc. The Cross Certification Authority certificate glues the A. Datum Corporation CA hierarchy to the Fabrikam, Inc. CA hierarchy. The CA that is listed in the subject of the Cross Certification Authority certificate appears to be a subordinate CA of the CA that issued the Cross Certification Authority certificate.

> **Note**   If the Cross Certification Authority certificate is issued to the UserCA rather than to the ADatumRootCA, the UserCA appears to be directly subordinate to the IssuingCA when presented to a computer belonging to Fabrikam, Inc.

The advantage of cross certification is that you do not have to reissue any certificates to your organization's users. The partner organization simply chooses a CA in your CA hierarchy to receive the Cross Certification Authority certificate. All certificates that exist below that point in the hierarchy are considered trusted by the issuing organization.

Note   To define criteria for trusting specific certificates, the issuing organization must define conditions and constraints, which are implemented as extensions in the Cross Certification Authority certificate. These extensions filter out nonmatching certificates and trust only certificates that satisfy the specified conditions.

Important   Only Windows XP and later support Cross Certification Authority certificates. If you have computers on the network running Microsoft Windows 2000 or earlier, you must also implement CTLs to define the trust of another organization's certificates.

Bridge CAs

An alternative to cross certification is to implement a bridge CA. (See Figure 16-4.)

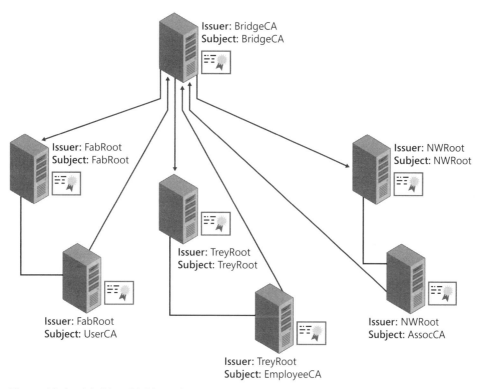

Figure 16-4   A bridge CA hierarchy

A bridge CA allows multiple organizations to recognize certificates issued by the CA hierarchies of the other organizations. The main component of the bridge CA hierarchy is the bridge CA itself. Every participating organization must issue a certificate to the bridge CA, which in turn issues a certificate to a CA in each CA hierarchy.

> **Note** Organizations typically issue the bridge CA its certificate from an issuing CA rather than an offline CA. This allows faster recognition of a certificate revocation if the organization leaves the bridge CA hierarchy. If the bridge CA certificate is issued from a root or offline policy CA, the certificate revocation list (CRL) cannot be published for a long period (usually three months to a year), whereas an issuing CA can publish its CRL on a daily or weekly basis.

As seen previously in Figure 16-4, three organizations are participating in a bridge CA hierarchy. If the certificates issued by Northwind Traders CA hierarchy (on the far right) are evaluated by a computer at Fabrikam, Inc., the certificate chain is built by the certificate chaining engine. (See Figure 16-5.)

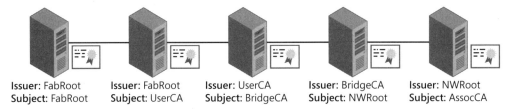

Issuer: FabRoot **Issuer:** FabRoot **Issuer:** UserCA **Issuer:** BridgeCA **Issuer:** NWRoot
Subject: FabRoot **Subject:** UserCA **Subject:** BridgeCA **Subject:** NWRoot **Subject:** AssocCA

Figure 16-5 Viewing a Northwind Traders certificate at Fabrikam, Inc.

In the certificate chain, note that the certificate issued to the BridgeCA was issued by the UserCA in the Fabrikam CA hierarchy. Likewise, the certificate issued to the NWRoot CA was issued by the bridge CA.

If the same certificate issued by the Northwind Traders CA hierarchy is evaluated by a computer in the Trey Research organization, a different certificate chain is built by the certificate chaining engine. (See Figure 16-6.)

Issuer: TreyRoot **Issuer:** TreyRoot **Issuer:** EmployeeCA **Issuer:** BridgeCA **Issuer:** NWRoot
Subject: TreyRoot **Subject:** EmployeeCA **Subject:** BridgeCA **Subject:** NWRoot **Subject:** AssocCA

Figure 16-6 Viewing a Northwind Traders certificate at Trey Research

This chain has the same TreyRoot CA as the root CA of the hierarchy. In this case, the BridgeCA certificate was issued by the Employee CA in the Trey Research hierarchy. In both cases, the certificates issued by the Northwind Traders CA hierarchy chain to the root CA of the organization evaluating the certificate.

Real-Life Bridge Certification Authority

I am asked frequently to describe *real* bridge CA deployments. IdentIT Inc., my consulting company, has integrated customer CAs into two bridge CA deployments.

The first bridge CA is the U.S. Federal Bridge Certification Authority, created to allow certificate recognition between all United States federal departments, even when different CA hierarchies issue the certificates. For more details on this deployment, see *http://www.cio.gov/fbca*.

The second bridge CA is the Certipath bridge CA. This bridge CA, originally designed for the international aerospace and defense community, is also cross-certified with the U.S. Federal Bridge Certification Authority. Details on Certipath can be found at *http://www.certipath.com*.

Cross certification also allows an organization to set conditions that must be met for certificates issued by another CA hierarchy to be considered trustworthy by your organization. The conditions apply to any certificate issued by the CA that issues the Cross Certification Authority certificate with constraint extensions, and potentially, CAs subordinate to that CA.

Note   In previous white papers and documentation, Cross Certification constraint and conditions were sometimes referred to as Qualified Subordination conditions. All of these refer to the same topic.

The following extensions related to Cross Certification constraints and conditions are available for inclusion in a Cross Certification Authority certificate:

- **Basic constraint**   Defines that the certificate is a certificate issued to a CA. This constraint also defines the maximum number of CAs from a partner's CA hierarchy that can be included in a certificate's certification path.

- **Name constraint**   Defines what namespaces are acceptable in certificates issued by a partner's CA hierarchy. The constraint can define both allowed and disallowed namespaces.

- **Application policies**   Defines the purposes that are allowed for certificates issued by a partner's CA hierarchy. For example, you can choose to trust only certificates whose purpose is client or server authentication.

Note   In certificates based on Microsoft certificate templates, the OIDs included in the Application Policies extension also exist in the Enhanced Key Usage extension if the certificate is based on a version 2 certificate template. If the certificate is based on a version 1 certificate template or does not include the Application Policies extension, cross certification will apply any application policy constraints to the OIDs defined in the Enhanced Key Usage extension.

- **Certificate policies**   Specifies the assurance level required for certificates issued by a partner's CA hierarchy. For example, your organization can decide to trust only certificates that the partner's CA hierarchy issues after face-to-face interviews.

The following sections provide more detailed information on each of the cross certification conditions that can be defined in a Cross Certification Authority certificate. The conditions are defined in one of two configuration files: Policy.inf or CAPolicy.inf. These constraints also can be applied to a subordinate CA certificate to apply cross certification conditions to certificates issued by the subordinate CA. Each solution requires a separate configuration file:

- **Policy.inf**   This text file defines cross certification conditions for Cross Certification Authority certificates.
- **CAPolicy.inf**   This text file defines cross certification conditions for root certification authority certificates.

Note   The syntax of the files is the same when defining cross certification conditions. The difference is how the file is read. Policy.inf is read when you generate the request for the Cross Certification Authority certificate by running the **Certreq.exe –policy** command. The CAPolicy.inf is read when you install Certificate Services on the root CA or renew the root CA certificate.

Name Constraints

Name constraints specify the namespaces that are allowed or disallowed in certificates issued by CAs subordinate to the CA that issues the Cross Certification Authority certificate. For example, if you wish to implement name constraints on a CA owned by A Datum Corporation, you can specify allowed namespaces for all forms of the Adatum.msft domain used in certificates you wish to recognize. This can include the following formats:

- DirectoryName: "DC=Adatum,DC=msft"
- E-mail = @adatum.msft
- UPN = .adatum.msft
- UPN = @adatum.msft

Note   You must specify each name format that can be used in a certificate issued by the partner organization. Omission of one of the name formats leads to certificate rejection, even if it should pass the defined name constraints. You can turn off the default behavior for name constraint validation for Windows XP SP2 and later by defining the HKEY_LOCAL_MACHINE\SOFTWARE\Policies\Microsoft\SystemCertificates\Root\ ProtectedRoots registry key to a value of 0x20 to disable name constraint enforcement for undefined name types.

Processing Name Constraints

When name constraints are defined, you can define both permitted and excluded namespaces. The following processing rules are used when multiple namespaces are defined:

- A certificate is accepted if all names in the certificate match the corresponding permitted name constraints.

- A certificate is rejected if any names in the certificate request match an excluded name constraint.

- If a namespace is defined in both a permitted and an excluded name constraint, the excluded name constraint takes precedence.

- If name constraints include only excluded namespaces, all other namespaces are implicitly permitted.

- If name constraints include only permitted namespaces, all other namespaces are implicitly excluded.

- Name constraints are applied to the Subject field and any existing Subject Alternative Name extensions.

Name Formats

Many name formats are allowed when defining name constraints for cross certification. Name formats can include:

- **Relative distinguished name**   Identifies the names of objects stored in directories, such as AD DS. The following entries are examples of relative distinguished names:
    - **DirectoryName= "DC=nwtraders,DC=msft"**   This entry includes all objects in the nwtraders.msft domain.
    - **DirectoryName= "OU=Marketing,DC=nwtraders,DC=msft"**   This entry includes all objects within the Marketing OU structure.

- **DNS name**   Identifies the Domain Name System (DNS) name of a computer or network device. This constraint is used for the evaluation of computer certificates only, because users are not assigned DNS names. The following entries are examples of relative distinguished names:
    - **DNS=www.nwtraders.msft**   Limits the DNS namespace to a single host, *www.nwtraders.msft*.
    - **DNS=.nwtraders.msft**   An entry that limits the DNS namespace to all hosts within the nwtraders.msft DNS domain. This includes *www.nwtraders.msft* and dc1.east.nwtraders.msft, because both names end with nwtraders.msft.

- **Uniform Resource Identifier (URI)**   Identifies resources on the Internet that use protocol identifiers such as Uniform Resource Locator (URL), File Transfer Protocol (FTP), and Hypertext Transfer Protocol (HTTP). The following entries are examples of URI names:

  ❑ **URL=http://www.nwtraders.msft**   Limits the acceptable certificates to only *www.nwtraders.msft* using the HTTP protocol.

  ❑ **URL=ftp://.nwtraders.msft**   Limits the namespace to all hosts within the nwtraders.msft DNS domain using the FTP protocol.

- **Email name**   Identifies acceptable e-mail names in a certificate's subject or Subject Alternative Name extension. The following entries are examples of e-mail names:

  ❑ **Email=@nwtraders.msft**   Matches any e-mail address that is part of the nwtraders.msft namespace.

  ❑ **Email=.nwtraders.msft**   Matches any e-mail address that is part of the nwtraders.msft namespace.

  ❑ **Email=komar@nwtraders.msft**   Matches any e-mail address that contains komar@nwtraders.msft. This matches both komar@nwtraders.msft and bkomar@nwtraders.msft.

- **User Principal Name (UPN)**   Like the E-mail name, the UPN constraint defines the acceptable UPNs within the certificate's Subject Alternative Name extension. UPN name formats are the same as the name formats for e-mail addresses. The following entries are examples of UPNs:

  ❑ **UPN=@nwtraders.msft**   Matches any UPN with the suffix of @nwtraders.msft.

  ❑ **UPN=.nwtraders.msft**   Matches any UPN with the suffix of nwtraders.msft, including east.nwtraders.msft and west.nwtraders.msft.

  ❑ **IP address**   Identifies the IP address of a computer or network device. This constraint allows you to choose either specific IP addresses or ranges of IP addresses. The following entries are examples of IP addresses:

  ❑ **IPADDRESS=192.168.3.0/255.255.255.0**   Matches any IP address in the 192.168.3.0 network, which encompasses IP addresses 192.168.3.0 through 192.168.1.255.

  ❑ **IPADDRESS=192.168.2.244/255.255.255.255**   Matches a specific IP address, 192.168.2.244.

Defining Name Constraints

When you enforce name constraints, an application will use a certificate only if each name in the certificate's subject or Subject Alternative Name matches at least one name constraint enforced in the Cross Certification Authority certificate. For example, if a certificate contains a Lightweight Directory Access Protocol (LDAP) distinguished name format in the subject and the UPN in the Subject Alternative Name, both names must match permitted name constraints. If one of the subject names does not match, an application will not use the certificate.

You implement name constraints by defining the permitted and excluded name constraints in the [NameConstraintsExtension] section of a Policy.inf file for Cross Certification Authority certificates or a CAPolicy.inf file for root certification authority certificates.

```
[NameConstraintsExtension]
Include = NameConstraintsPermitted
Exclude = NameConstraintsExcluded
Critical = True

[NameConstraintsPermitted]
DirectoryName = "DC=nwtraders, DC=msft"
email = @nwtraders.msft
UPN = .nwtraders.msft
UPN = @nwtraders.msft

[NameConstraintsExcluded]
DirectoryName = "DC=Contoso, DC=msft"
email = @contoso.msft
UPN = .contoso.msft
UPN = @contoso.msft
```

In this example, all name formats of the nwtraders.msft domain are permitted, but all name formats of contoso.msft are excluded. This is a common configuration for a Cross Certification Authority certificate issued by contoso.msft to nwtraders.msft. It ensures that Northwind Traders includes only its namespace in its certificates and prevents Northwind Traders from issuing certificates to Contoso's employees.

Basic Constraints

A basic constraint has two purposes within a certificate:

- Defines whether the certificate is issued to a CA or non-CA object. If the certificate is issued to a CA, the basic constraint allows the certificate to sign other certificates in a certificate chain.

- Allows you to limit the path length of a CA hierarchy below the CA where the basic constraint PathLength is defined.

You can define a basic constraint in a Cross Certification Authority certificate by adding a [BasicConstraintsExtension] section to the Policy.inf file. The [BasicConstraintsExtension] defines the maximum depth of a partner's CA hierarchy from which you accept certificates. For example, Figure 16-7 shows a CA hierarchy where a Cross Certification Authority certificate is issued to the PolicyCA in the CA hierarchy.

If a basic constraint is defined in the Cross Certification Authority certificate issued to the PolicyCA, where the path length is defined as one, only certificates issued by the Policy CA or

CAs that are one level below the PolicyCA are trusted. In Figure 16-7, this means that only certificates issued by the PolicyCA and IssuingCA are trusted. When this basic constraint is defined, the certificate issued to ScottC is trusted because it is issued by a CA that is one level below the PolicyCA. The certificate issued to RegionCA is not trusted, because it is a CA certificate. Likewise, any certificates issued by the RegionCA are not trusted.

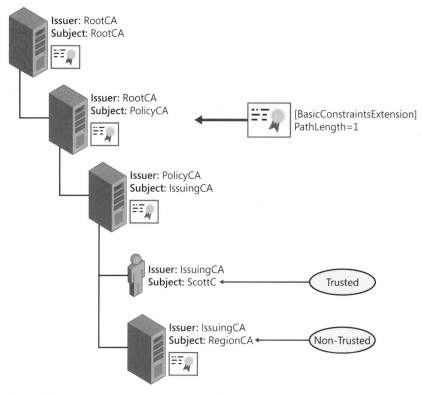

Figure 16-7   Implementing basic constraints

Note   When you implement basic constraints, you must be careful when you choose the CA to issue the Cross Certification Authority certificate. For example, if you want to trust certificates issued by CAs at the same level of the CA hierarchy, it is best to issue the Cross Certification Authority certificate to the parent CA of the two CAs with a path length of 1. If you want to trust only certificates issued by a specific CA, you can define a basic constraint with a path length value of 0.

Application Policies

Applications use application policy OIDs to determine whether a certificate can be used for a given purpose, such as authenticating a user, encrypting data, or signing a device driver. When an application receives signed information from a user, it reviews the certificate associated with the private key and verifies that the certificate contains the required application policy OID. Likewise, if the application queries the user's certificate store for an application to use for signing, the application filters the list to include only those certificates with the required application policy OIDs.

> **Note**   Application policies are a Microsoft proprietary extension that provide the same functionality as a certificate's Enhanced Key Usage (EKU) extension. Both application policies and EKUs indicate the purposes for which a certificate can be used and are represented by OIDs. If the Application Policy extension is not present in a certificate, an application or service examines the EKU extension for the required OIDs. Typically, a certificate has matching OID lists if the certificate includes both EKU and Application Policy extensions.

When defining cross certification conditions, you can limit the applications that can be used between organizations. Also, you can specifically limit the application policy OIDs that must be in the partner certificates you deem trustworthy.

By including a list of approved application policies in the cross certification conditions, you can specify that your organization trusts certificates issued by a partner's CA hierarchy that are intended only for code signing and client authentication. The listing of approved application policy OIDs is included in the issued Cross Certification Authority certificate.

Determining Application Policy OIDs

The following procedure obtains application policy OIDs in an AD DS environment:

1. Open the Certificate Templates console (Certtmpl.msc).
2. In the console tree, right-click Certificate Templates, and then click View Object Identifiers.
3. In the list of Available Object Identifiers, select the application policy OID you want to copy, and then click Copy Object Identifier.

The OID is then copied to the Windows clipboard and can be pasted into the Policy.inf file.

Defining Application Policies

When you issue a Cross Certification Authority certificate, you can configure a Policy.inf file to specify which application policy OIDs are permitted in partner-issued certificates. Likewise, you can define a CAPolicy.inf file to specify which application policy OIDs are permitted in root certification authority certificates.

To configure application policies in a Policy.inf or CAPolicy.inf file, create the following sections:

```
[ApplicationPolicyStatementExtension]
Policies = AppCodeSign, AppCTL, AppClientAuth
CRITICAL = FALSE
```

```
[AppCodeSign]
OID = 11.3.6.1.5.5.7.3.3 ; Code Signing

[AppCTL]
OID = 1.3.6.1.4.1.311.10.3.1; Trust List Signing

[AppClientAuth]
OID = 1.3.6.1.5.5.7.3.2 ; Client Authentication
```

Using Custom Application Policies

Some organizations define their own application policy OIDs for custom applications. Although most application policy OIDs are predefined and used universally, it may be necessary to define the mapping between your organization's application policy OID and a partner's application policy OID if custom application policies have been defined.

To configure the mapping, you must create a section that maps your organization's application policy OID to a similar application policy OID at the partner organization. This mapping has been defined in an [ApplicationPolicyMappingsExtension] section in the Policy.inf or CAPolicy.inf file. A sample is shown here:

```
[ApplicationPolicyMappingsExtension]
1.3.6.1.4.1.311.21.64 = 1.2.3.4.98
1.3.6.1.4.1.311.21.65 = 1.2.3.4.100
critical = true
```

Enabling the criticality flag enforces the requirement that an application processing this extension not trust the certificate that contains the extension unless the application understands the contents of the extension. (For more information on the criticality flag, review the definitions of X.509 version 3 certificates in Chapter 2, "Primer to PKI.")

Certificate Policies

Certificate policies, also known as issuance policies, can identify the methods taken to validate a subject's identity before certificate issuance. A certificate policy can also describe the protection level of the private key associated with a certificate. For example, a private key protected by a hardware security module (HSM) is considered more secure than one stored in the local machine store protected by the Data Protection Application Programming Interface (DPAPI). You can use cross certification to accept only certificates with specific certificate policy OIDs in the certificate policy extension.

Default Certificate Policies

When you deploy a Windows Server 2008 PKI in an AD DS environment, the initial installation of the updated certificate templates also creates six default certificate policies:

- **Low Assurance (1.3.6.1.4.1.311.21.8.a.b.c.1.400)**   Indicates that minimal effort is used to validate the certificate subject's identity. For example, the certificate can be issued if the requestor knows the user account's name and password.

- **Medium Assurance (1.3.6.1.4.1.311.21.8.a.b.c.1.401)**   Indicates that some effort is used to identify the certificate's subject. For example, the pending certificate can require a certificate manager to approve the request.

- **High Assurance (1.3.6.1.4.1.311.21.8.a.b.c.1.402)**   Indicates that additional measures are taken to identify the certificate's subject and protect the certificate's private key. For example, the same validation tests can be performed for both a medium and high assurance certificate, but a high assurance certificate's private key can be stored on a two-factor device, such as a smart card, whereas the medium assurance certificate's private key can be stored on the local disk subsystem.

> **Note**   The *a.b.c.* portion of the OID is a randomly generated numeric sequence that is random for each forest with the Windows Server 2003 or Windows Server 2008 schema extensions.

- **All Issuance policies (2.5.29.32.0)**   Allows the acceptance of any certificates that have any issuance policy OIDs. Typically, this OID is assigned only to certificates issued to CAs.

- **European Qualified Certificate (0.4.0.1862.1.1)**   The primary purpose of a certificate issued under the European qualified certificate issuance policy is to meet the legal framework defined in the European Directive on Electronic Signatures. Details on qualified certificates are available in Directive 1999/93/EC of the European Parliament and of the Council of 13 December 1999 on a Community framework for electronic signatures (*http://eurlex.europa.eu/LexUriServ/LexUriServ.do?uri=CELEX:31999L0093: EN:HTML*).

- **Secure Signature Creation Device Qualified Certificate (0.4.0.1862.1.4)**   Indicates a signature creation device that can create only unique signatures, that cannot be derived by reasonable means, and does not alter the signed electronic data during the signing process. For example, the Turkish definitions on the use of secure signature creation devices can be found in Article 6 of the Turkish Electronic Signature Law available at (*http://www.tk.gov.tr/eng/pdf/Electronic_Signature_Law.pdf*).

> **Note**   The low assurance, medium assurance, and high assurance OIDs are also included with Windows Server 2003. You can still create the issuance policies for European Qualified Certificate and Secure Signature Creation Device Qualified Certificate manually.

Custom Certificate Policies

In many cases, an organization creates its own custom OIDs for certificate policies. This allows the organization to define certificate policy OIDs in its organization's OID space rather than use the default Microsoft OIDs.

> **Note**   For more information on obtaining an OID tree for your organization, review Chapter 6, "Implementing a CA Hierarchy."

Custom certificate policies also allow an organization to programmatically define the exact issuance process and certificate usage. For example, an organization can create a certificate policy called *Notarized*, which is included in a digital signing certificate issued to the organization's notary publics. To receive a certificate with the Notarized certificate policy, a requestor's application must prove to a certificate manager that the requestor is a notary public. This could be accomplished by showing the certificate manager proof of his or her designation.

If you implement custom certificate policies, a partner company will not be using the same OID to represent a similar certificate policy. For example, a partner company can have a similar certificate policy named *Notaries Public*. In this case, the two companies must define a mapping between their OIDs to ensure that a certificate with the Notaries Public OID is recognized as equivalent to a certificate with the Notarized OID.

Implementing Certificate Policies

To implement certificate policies when defining cross certification conditions, you must map the certificate policy OIDs you require in a partner's certificates to OIDs that exist within your environment. The mappings are defined in the Policy.inf file so that the certificate policy mappings are included in the issued Cross Certification Authority certificate.

You can create the following sections in the Policy.inf file to define certificate policies:

```
[PolicyStatementExtension]
Policies = Notarized
CRITICAL = FALSE

[Notarized]
OID = 1.3.6.1.4.1.311.509.3.1
```

Note   Certificate policy extensions are recognized only by computers running Windows XP or later. If the extension is marked critical, the Cryptographic API (CryptoAPI) passes the extension to the application. It is the responsibility of the calling application to enforce the certificate policy OID requirement.

The example shows that a single certificate policy is defined, named Notarized, and it is assigned the 1.3.6.1.4.1.311.509.3.1 OID.

Note   This is a fabricated OID based on Microsoft's OID space. It is not an actual production OID. Microsoft owns the 1.3.6.1.4.1.311 OID tree.

Once you define your organization's certificate policies, you must map your OID to the partner's OID. For example, if the partner organization assigns the Notaries Public certificate policy with the 1.3.6.1.4.1.311.600.4.2 OID, you must specify that the Notaries Public certificate policy is equivalent to your organization's Notarized certificate policy.

The following example shows how certificate policy mapping is configured in a Policy.inf file:

```
[PolicyMappingsExtension]
1.3.6.1.4.1.311.509.3.1 = 1.3.6.1.4.1.311.600.4.2
```

This line states that the Notarized OID (1.3.6.1.4.1.311.509.3.1) is equivalent to the Notaries Public OID (1.3.6.1.4.1.311.600.4.2).

Best Practices

When planning cross certification conditions in either a Policy.inf or CAPolicy.inf file, follow these best practices:

- **Define only the required conditions.**   If you do not see a need for restricting certificate policies, do not set conditions on them.

- **Exclude your namespace in all name constraints.**   By excluding your namespace in the Cross Certification Authority certificate, you prevent the partner organization from issuing unauthorized certificates representing your users, computers, or network devices. This prevents a certificate issued by a partner to be used to represent one of your employees or resources.

- **Involve the legal department in negotiations with the partner organization.**   Cross certification opens your network to certificates issued by another organization. Your legal department might want to define compliance requirements, such as requiring audits to ensure that certificate policies are followed when issuing certificates for use in your organization.

■ **Issue separate Cross Certification Authority certificates for each purpose.**   If you must trust a partner's organization for multiple projects with different requirements, issue a separate Cross Certification Authority certificate for each project.

Implementing Cross Certification with Constraints

This section describes the steps involved in cross certifying your organization's CA hierarchy with a partner's CA hierarchy. The first step is to create a Cross Certification Signing certificate template. By default, there is no certificate template that satisfies the requirements for cross certification requests, so a custom version 2 certificate template must be created.

The certificate template must include the Qualified Subordination application policy OID (1.3.6.1.4.1.311.10.3.10). You can also enforce CA certificate manager approval and limit Read and Enroll permissions to designated users or groups.

> **Important**   The Qualified Subordination application policy OID must be included in the certificate template because the Cross Certification Authority certificate template requires that the requestor sign the certificate request with a certificate that contains the Qualified Subordination application policy OID.

Creating the Cross Certification Signing Certificate Template

The following procedure creates a version 2 certificate template that meets the Cross Certification Signing requirements:

1. Log on as a user assigned the permissions to create and modify certificate templates.

2. Open the Certificate Templates console (Certtmpl.msc).

3. In the details pane, right-click Enrollment Agent, and then click Duplicate Template.

4. In the Duplicate Template dialog box, select Windows Server 2003, Enterprise Edition, and then click OK.

5. In the Properties of New Template dialog box, on the General tab, in the Template Display Name box, type Cross Certification Signing, and then click OK.

6. In the details pane, double-click Cross Certification Signing.

7. In the Cross Certification Signing Properties dialog box, on the Extensions tab, in the Extensions Included In This Template list, select Application Policies, and then click Edit.

8. In the Edit Application Policies Extension dialog box, in the Application policies list, select Certificate Request Agent, and then click Remove.

9. In the Edit Application Policies Extension dialog box, click Add.

10. In the Add Application Policy dialog box, in the Application policies list, select Qualified Subordination, and then click OK.

11. In the Cross Certification Signing dialog box, on the Security tab, assign Read and Enroll permissions to a global or universal group that contains the users that will request the Cross Certification Signing certificate, and then click OK.

Publishing the Cross Certification Signing Certificate Template

Once you create the Cross Certification Signing certificate template, you must publish it at an enterprise CA so that it is available for enrollment. You also must publish the Cross Certification Authority certificate template. Both certificate templates are necessary to generate a Cross Certification Authority certificate with cross certification constraint extensions.

> **Note**   You might have to modify the Cross Certification Authority certificate template before publication. By default, only members of the forest root domain's Domain Admins and Enterprise Admins groups have Read and Enroll permissions. Unless the user accounts that will be issued the Cross Certification Signing certificates are members of these groups, the permissions of the Cross Certification Authority certificate template must be modified. You must assign these user accounts Read and Enroll permissions either directly or though a group membership.

To publish the Cross Certification Signing and Cross Certification Authority certificate templates, use the following procedure:

1. Ensure that you are logged on as a CA administrator.

2. Open the Certification Authority console.

3. In the Certification Authority console, in the console tree, expand *CAName* (where *CAName* is the logical name of your CA), and then click Certificate Templates.

4. In the console tree, right-click Certificate Templates, click New, and then click Certificate Template To Issue.

5. In the Enable Certificate Templates dialog box, select Cross Certification Signing and Cross Certification Authority, and then click OK.

6. In the details pane, verify that the Cross Certification Signing and Cross Certification Authority certificate templates appear.

Once the certificate templates are published, ensure that all designated users acquire the Cross Certification Signing certificate.

Implementing the Policy.inf File

The Policy.inf file defines the cross certification conditions in a Cross Certification Authority certificate request. The conditions include only those conditions required for establishing a relationship between your CA hierarchy and the partner's CA hierarchy.

The Policy.inf file:

- **Does not exist by default**   The Policy.inf file must be created and defined manually.

- **Can exist in any folder on the network**   Unlike CAPolicy.inf, the Policy.inf file must be accessible to the person generating the Cross Certification Authority certificate request file. This can include the local file system or a network share.

- **Does not have to be named Policy.inf**   Unlike CAPolicy.inf, the **certreq –policy** command allows you to designate the location and name of the Policy.inf file.

> **Tip**   Provide a descriptive name for the Policy.inf file so that its purpose is easily recognizable. For example, *NWTraders to Fabrikam for code signing*.inf is a much better name than Policy2.inf.

- **Is read during the processing of a Cross Certification Authority certificate request**   The Policy.inf file is read only during the execution of the **certreq –policy** command. The file is not read during the installation of Certificate Services or when a CA certificate is renewed.

> **Note**   A sample of the Policy.inf file is available in Appendix A of "Planning and Implementing Cross Certification and Qualified Subordination Using Windows Server 2003," available at *http://www.microsoft.com/technet/prodtechnol/ windowsserver2003/technologies/security/ ws03qswp.mspx.*

Acquiring a Partner's CA Certificate

Once you create the Policy.inf file, you must obtain the partner's CA certificate. This certificate represents the CA to which you are going to issue the Cross Certification Authority certificate.

The certificate is used to generate the Cross Certification Authority certificate's subject name. By using the CA's certificate to obtain the CA's name, the process is protected against a user making typographical errors during subject input. Using the CA's certificate also ensures that the Cross Certification Authority certificate preserves the subject name from the provided certificate.

Generating the Cross Certification Authority Certificate

The following elements are necessary to generate a Cross Certification Authority certificate:

- The Policy.inf file with all required cross certification conditions defined
- The CA certificate of the target CA in the partner's CA hierarchy
- A Cross Certification Signing certificate and private key stored in the current user's profile

Creating the Cross Certification Authority Request File

1. Copy the partner's CA certificate and Policy.inf file to a common folder.
2. At a command prompt, type **certutil –policy** to create the certificate request file that enforces all the cross certification conditions defined in the Policy.inf file.
3. In the Open Request File dialog box, in the Files Of Type box, select Certificate Files (*.cer, *.crt, *.der), select the target CA's certificate, and then click Open.
4. In the Open Inf File dialog box, select the configured Policy.inf file, and then click Open.
5. In the Certificate List dialog box, select your Cross Certification Signing certificate, and then click OK.
6. In the Save Request dialog box, in the File Name box, type a name for the Cross Certification Authority certificate request file, and then click Save.

Note   The Cross Certification Authority certificate request file is a Certificate Management Protocol using a Cryptographic Message Syntax (CMC) request file that contains all the defined cross certification extensions and is signed with the requestor's Cross Certification Signing certificate.

Submitting the Cross Certification Authority Request

Once the CMC certificate request file is generated, it must be submitted to an enterprise CA to request the Cross Certification Authority certificate. The Cross Certification Authority certificate template must be published at the CA where the request is submitted. Use the following procedure to submit the request:

1. Open the Certification Authority console.
2. In the console tree, right-click *CAName* (where *CAName* is the name of the enterprise CA), point to All Tasks, and then click Submit New Request.
3. In the Open Request File dialog box, select the request file you created in the previous process, and then click Open.
4. In the Save Certificate dialog box, indicate a name for the issued certificate file, and then click Save.

Publishing to Active Directory Domain Services

The certificate object is published automatically into the CN=AIA,CN=Public Key Services, CN=Services,CN=Configuration,*ForestRootDomain* container as a CrossCA object. The certificate is never distributed to the target CA in the other organization's CA hierarchy. Instead, it is downloaded via autoenrollment to all domain member computers so that the Cross Certification Authority certificate can be used to build certificate chains between the two CA hierarchies. This allows recognition of the partner CA's certificates that satisfy the cross certification conditions.

> **Note**   When the autoenrollment process is triggered by Winlogon or a Group Policy refresh interval, the operating system queries AD DS to download the appropriate certificate stores into the local store on the client machine, for example, root CA certificates, Cross Certification Authority certificates, and the NTAuth container.

When participating in a bridge CA hierarchy structure, the Cross Certification Authority certificates issued by the bridge CA must be manually published by each organization participating in the bridge CA hierarchy structure. This is because the bridge CA is not a member of your organization's forest and is unable to publish its issued Cross Certification Authority certificates into your forest automatically.

You can use the following **certutil.exe** command to manually publish a Cross Certification Authority certificate into AD DS:

```
certutil –f –dspublish <CrossCertFile.crt> CrossCA
```

Verifying Cross Certification Constraints

Once you publish the necessary Cross Certification Authority certificates to AD DS, you should verify their publication. The recommended verification method is the certutil command described here:

1. Open a command prompt.

2. At the command prompt, type **certutil -viewstore "CN=*CAName*, CN=AIA,CN=Public Key Services, CN=Services, CN=Configuration,*ForestRootDN*?crossCertificatePair** (where *CAName* is the name of the CA to which the Cross Certification Authority certificate is issued, and *ForestRootDN* is the LDAP distinguished name of the forest that issued the Cross Certification Authority certificate).

3. In the View Certificate Store dialog box, select the Cross Certification Authority certificate you want to view, and then click View Certificate.

4. In the Certificate dialog box, on the Certification Path tab, ensure that the certification path shows that the *CAName* certificate chains to your organization's root CA certificate.

This process should be repeated for each Cross Certification Authority certificate published in your organization's AD DS.

Case Study: Trusting Certificates from Another Forest

The software development group at The Phone Company, a large telecom provider in Europe, recently started to develop ActiveX controls for Web-based applications for internal projects. To download the ActiveX controls, they must be signed with a code-signing certificate.

The Phone Company implements two forests on its corporate network:

■ **test.thephonecompany.msft**   The test forest

■ **ad.thephonecompany.msft**   The production forest

All ActiveX controls must be created and tested in the certification forest before they are deployed to the production forest. Once application testing is complete, the plan is for the software development manager to sign the ActiveX control on behalf of The Phone Company, indicating that the ActiveX control is suitable for deployment on the production network.

You are the PKI manager. To better replicate the production network in a test environment, the same CA hierarchy structure is deployed in the certification forest and the production forest, as shown in Figure 16-8.

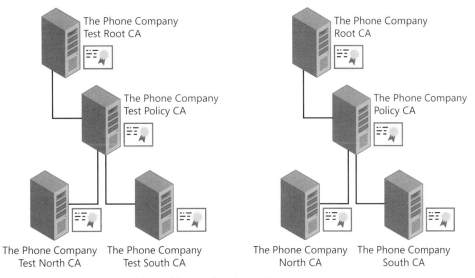

Figure 16-8   The two CA hierarchies at The Phone Company

Both CA hierarchies implement two issuing CAs to allow CAs to be placed at the London and Barcelona offices of The Phone Company. The offline CAs are stored at the company's Munich office. For both forests, the CAs are deployed at the actual locations rather than in a test lab.

The software development manager prepared the following requirements to enable code signing recognition between the forests:

- The ActiveX controls must be signed in the test forest only. The signing process must not be duplicated when the ActiveX control is deployed to the production forest. The same signature must be recognized in both the certification and production networks.

- The subject of the code-signing certificate issued to the manager has the following AD DS common name: CN=The Phone Company,OU=PKI Roles,DC=ad,DC=thephonecompany,DC=msft. Only the distinguished name is included in the code-signing certificate subject.

- The certificate is issued by The Phone Company South CA in the production network. The Phone Company North CA does not issue code-signing certificates.

- The code-signing certificate issued to the software development manager contains the following extensions:

    ❑ Enhanced Key Usage: code signing (1.3.6.1.5.5.7.3.3)

    ❑ Issuance policies: None

You must perform cross certification between the two CA hierarchies so that cross certification conditions allow the certification forest to trust only the manager's code-signing certificate. You must design the cross certification conditions to be as restrictive as possible so that no other code-signing certificates are accepted.

Case Study Questions

1. Which CA in the production hierarchy must be issued the Cross Certification Authority certificate to satisfy the design requirements?

2. What CA must be used to issue the Cross Certification Authority certificate on the test network to satisfy the design requirements?

3. If the Cross Certification Authority certificate is issued to the The Phone Company Policy CA, what lines must be included in the Policy.inf file to recognize certificates issued by the The Phone Company South CA?

4. If the Cross Certification Authority certificate is issued to the The Phone Company South CA, what lines must be included in the Policy.inf file to recognize certificates issued by the The Phone Company South CA?

5. What name constraints are required in the Policy.inf file to limit permitted certificates to the single certificate issued to the software development manager?

6. What application policy entries are required in the Policy.inf file to limit the certificates to only code-signing certificates?

7. Assuming that the Cross Certification Authority certificate is issued by the The Phone Company Test South CA to the The Phone Company South CA, how does the certificate chain for the manager's certificate look when viewed on a computer running Windows XP in the certification forest?

8. Assuming that the Cross Certification Authority certificate is issued by the The Phone Company Test South CA to the The Phone Company South CA, how does the certificate chain for the manager's certificate look when viewed on a computer running Windows Vista in the production forest?

Additional Information

- Microsoft Official Curriculum, Course 2821: "Designing and Managing a Windows Public Key Infrastructure" (*http://www.microsoft.com/traincert/syllabi/2821afinal.asp*)

- "Implementing and Administering Certificate Templates in Windows Server 2003" (*http://www.microsoft.com/technet/prodtechnol/windowsserver2003/technologies/security/ws03crtm.mspx*)

- RFC 3280–"Internet X.509 Public Key Infrastructure Certificate and Certificate Revocation List (CRL) Profile" (*http://www.ietf.org/rfc/rfc3280.txt*)

- "Qualified Subordination Overview" (*http://www.microsoft.com/resources/documentation/WindowsServ/2003/enterprise/proddocs/en-us/sag_CS_Using_QSub.asp*)

- "How to Perform Qualified Subordination" (*http://www.microsoft.com/resources/documentation/WindowsServ/2003/enterprise/proddocs/en-us/sag_cs_procs_qs.asp*)

- "Planning and Implementing Cross Certification and Qualified Subordination Using Windows Server 2003" (*http://www.microsoft.com/technet/prodtechnol/windowsserver2003/technologies/security/ws03qswp.mspx*)

- Turkish Electronic Signature Law available at (*http://www.tk.gov.tr/eng/pdf/Electronic_Signature_Law.pdf*)

- "Directive 1999/93/EC of the European Parliament and of the Council of 13 December 1999 on a Community Framework for Electronic Signatures" (*http://eurlex.europa.eu/LexUriServ/LexUriServ.do?uri=CELEX:31999L0093:EN:HTML*)

- "Community Framework for Electronic Signatures" (*http://europa.eu/scadplus/leg/en/lvb/l24118.htm*)

- "The Legal and Market Aspects of Electronic Signatures" (*http://www.secorvo.de/publikationen/electronic-sig-report.pdf*)

Part III
Deploying Application-Specific Solutions

Chapter 17

Identity Lifecycle Manager 2007 Certificate Management

In late 2005, Microsoft acquired a small Ottawa-based company named Alacris. The key software included in this acquisition was a registration authority then known as Alacris idNexus.

The product was initially rebranded as Certificate Lifecycle Manager (CLM). Just before its official launch in 2007, the product was merged with Microsoft Identity Integration Server (MIIS) 2003 to become a suite of products known as Microsoft Identity Lifecycle Manager 2007.

- The former MIIS product is now referred to as Identity Lifecycle Manager (ILM) 2007 Metadirectory Services.

- The former CLM product is now referred to as ILM 2007 Certificate Management.

- The new CLM Management agent allows certificates to be included in user account provisioning and deprovisioning actions.

In late 2007, an update to ILM 2007 Certificate Management, Feature Pack 1, was released. This update includes enabling Windows Vista clients to use CLM, enabling an offline update management policy for Microsoft Base Smart Card Cryptographic Provider smart cards, and providing language packs for multiple language support.

Note Soon after the publication of this book, the next version of ILM, known as ILM "2," will be released. At the time this book was being written, ILM "2" was in an early beta release and as such will not be discussed in this chapter.

This chapter provides a general overview of what ILM 2007 Certificate Management is, provides planning information for a deployment, provides implantation procedures, and walks you through using CLM to deploy Code Signing certificates.

For ease of reference, Identity Lifecycle Manager 2007 shall be referred to as CLM for the rest of the chapter.

Key Concepts

Before looking at how to deploy and manage certificates with ILM 2007 Certificate Management, it is a good idea to start with the basics. The following sections provide details on ILM 2007 Certificate Management fundamentals.

Profile Templates

The profile template (see Figure 17-1) is the core of CLM management activities. It provides a single administrative object that combines:

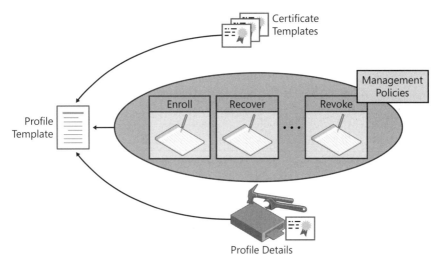

Figure 17-1 Profile template components

- **Certificate templates** Defines the content of a certificate based on that certificate template. A profile template can contain one or more related certificate templates to allow bulk enrollment of multiple certificates in a single management action.

- **Profile details** Provides details on whether the profile template is for software or smart card certificate deployment, how encryption certificates are generated, and which certificate templates are included in the profile template. For each certificate template included in the profile template, a single CA is designated for the issuance of certificates based on that certificate template.

- **Management policies** Define the workflows used for certificate management within the profile template for the entire life cycle of the profile template. The management policies specify who performs specific management tasks within each workflow.

CLM Roles

In a CLM deployment, the participants are broken down into one of two roles:

- **Certificate subscribers** Certificate subscribers are simply users that will be issued certificates by CLM. The certificates can be issued by a certificate manager or can be issued using self-service, where the certificate subscriber initiates and completes the certificate management task.

- **Certificate managers** Certificate managers are users that can initiate, approve, or execute certificate management tasks for other users or can configure the CLM application.

  Typically, the management of a certificate will occur within the CLM application Web portal. A certificate subscriber will connect to the CLM subscriber Web portal. A user who is a manager for *any* profile template will connect to the CLM manager Web portal by default.

Permissions

To allow definition of workflows for certificate management tasks, CLM implements its own set of custom permissions. These permissions specify the actions that a certificate manager can perform for a certificate subscriber. The custom permissions include:

- **CLM Audit** Allows the generation and display of CLM policy templates, setting management policies within a profile template, reviewing management policy settings, and generating CLM reports.

- **CLM Enrollment Agent** Allows certificate requests on behalf of another user.

- **CLM Request Enroll** Allows the initiation, execution, or completion of an enrollment request.

- **CLM Request Recover** Allows the initiation of encryption key recovery from the CA database.

- **CLM Request Renew** Allows the initiation, execution, or completion of a renewal request. The renewal request replaces a user certificate that is near its expiration date with a new certificate with a new validity period.

- **CLM Request Revoke** Allows certificate revocation before its expiration date. This can be necessary, for example, if a user's computer or smart card is lost or stolen.

- **CLM Request Unblock Smart Card** Allows a smart card's user personal identification number (PIN) to be reset, reestablishing access to the smart card's key material.

In addition to these seven permissions, an additional permission, CLM Enroll, is defined for the actual profile template object. The CLM Enroll permission allows the assigned user or group to enroll certificates based on the profile template.

> **Important**   A manager cannot initiate enrollment actions for a user unless both the manager *and* the subscriber are assigned the Read and CLM Enroll permissions on the profile template object.

Permission Assignment Locations

The trickiest part of CLM is understanding permission assignments and permission assignment locations. Many people consider the CLM permission model to be the most complex model implemented by a Windows–based product.

There are five separate permission assignment locations that determine the requesting user's actual authorization level when they perform an action in the CLM Web portal. The five permission assignment locations (see Figure 17-2) are:

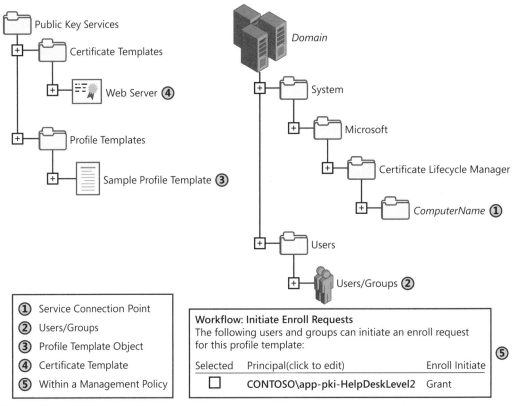

Figure 17-2   CLM permission assignment locations

1. **Service connection point (SCP)**   SCP permissions determine whether or not a user is assigned a management role within the CLM deployment. For example, if a user must initiate requests for other users, the user is assigned the CLM Request Enroll permission

at the SCP. The permission assignment means only that they *could* perform the management action if other permission assignments exist.

> **Important**   All users participating in the CLM environment must have Read permissions on the SCP to allow reading of the permission assignments.

2. **Users or groups**   A CLM permission assignment on a user or group identifies the target for a management action. For example, if you assigned a CLM manager CLM Request Enroll permission at the SCP, a second CLM Request Enroll permission on the Domain\West Users group would identify the group of users who could be a target of an enrollment request.

3. **Profile template object**   The profile template permissions determine if a user can read the profile template's contents (to execute management policy workflows within the profile template) or receive certificates based on the profile template's management policies. If a user is required to enroll certificates based on the profile template, the user must be assigned the CLM Enroll permission on the profile template. Likewise, a manager that initiates any requests that enroll certificates must *also* have the CLM Enroll permission on the profile template.

4. **Certificate templates**   The user or group that submits certificate requests to the certification authority (CA) must be assigned Read and Enroll permissions on all certificate templates within a profile template. Note that this is not always going to be the certificate subscriber.

5. **Within a management policy**   A user or group must be assigned the management role within the management policy. For example, if a user is tasked with approving enrollment requests, you must assign the user the privilege to approve enrollment requests within the Enroll management policy.

> **Important**   An incorrect permission assignment at any of the five locations will lead to a failure in the management policy workflow.

CLM Components

A CLM deployment contains many components, as shown in Figure 17-3.

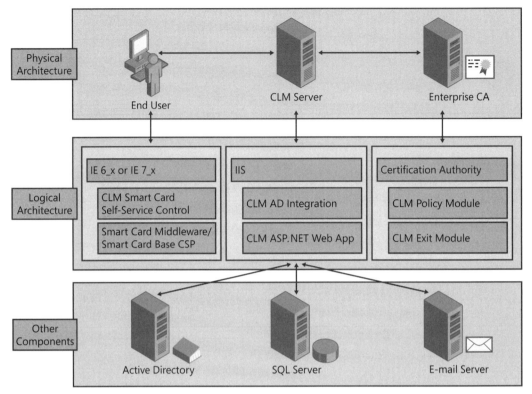

Figure 17-3   CLM components

The three primary components of a CLM deployment are:

■ **CLM Server**   CLM is a Microsoft ASP.NET application that requires both Internet Information Server (IIS) 6.0 and Microsoft .NET Framework 2.0. The CLM Server uses Microsoft SQL Server 2000 Service Pack 4 or SQL Server 2005 Service Pack 1 as its relational data store.

> **Note**   The SQL server hosting the CLM data store can be hosted on the local CLM server or hosted on a remote SQL Server.

The CLM server provides a Web interface for both management and user functions and is the focal point of a CLM system. The CLM server provides all required CLM functions. It communicates with:

❑ Active Directory Domain Services for authentication services

❑ SQL Server for configuration, storage, and reporting functions

❑ One or more CAs for certificate issuance and management

■ **CLM Certification Authority Modules**   The CLM Policy module and CLM Exit module must be installed and configured locally on each issuing CA server participating in the CLM deployment. The modules communicate with the CLM server, control CA behavior, and communicate with the SQL Server.

■ **Certificate Lifecycle Manager Client**   The Certificate Lifecycle Manager Client enables users and administrators to manage smart cards by allowing the CLM Web portal to manage the provided smart card. When deployed, the client must also have either a legacy smart card cryptographic service provider (CSP) and middleware installed or the Microsoft Base Smart Card CSP and the mini-driver for the vendor's smart card deployed.

> **Important**   The Certificate Lifecycle Manager Client is required only for smart card deployments. Details on using CLM for a smart card deployment are discussed in Chapter 21, "Deploying Smart Cards."

Planning an ILM 2007 Certificate Management Deployment

Before you deploy ILM 2007 Certificate Management, you must conduct planning, providing the following prerequisite information:

■ Determining which management policies are available and must be defined for a specific certificate deployment

■ Determining which registration model to use when defining a management policy

■ Determining the permissions required for the selected registration model

Management Policies

CLM management policies define the workflow, data collection, and principals who participate in the certificate-management process. Within a management policy, an administrator can specify:

■ **Who can initiate a request**   The initiator can be the user referenced in the issued certificate's subject or another user acting on behalf of the issued certificate's subject.

■ **Who must approve a request**   To increase the assurance level of a certificate, the request can be paused until one or more certificate managers approve the request.

■ **What data is collected during the workflow**   The administrator can define what data is collected, who performs data collection, and how the data is validated during collection.

- **Who will receive one-time passwords to complete a workflow and in which format the passwords are distributed** The administrator can define one-time passwords that are distributed to the subscriber, the subscriber's manager, or the request originator to complete a workflow. The configuration also includes the number of one-time passwords and the length and life span of the one-time passwords.

- **What documents are printed** The workflow may require instructions to be distributed to the certificate subscriber. These documents can be printed as part of the workflow.

Table 17-1 provides a list of the available management policies within CLM and specifies whether the management policy is available in software profile templates, smart card profile templates, or in both software and smart card profile templates.

Table 17-1   CLM Management Policies

Management policy	Software	Smart card	Purpose
Disable Policy		X	Allows disabling of all certificates on a smart card prior to their expiration date.
Duplicate Policy	X	X	Creates a duplicate of an existing profile. The original profile is referred to as the *primary profile*. All other copies are referred to as *duplicate profiles*.
Enroll Policy	X	X	Determines the workflow used for the initial enrollment of a certificate.
Offline Unblock Policy		X	Specifies who can perform an offline unblock of a user's smart card PIN where the subscriber provides a challenge string and the manager provides a response string, enabling the user to set a new PIN for the smart card.
Online Updates Policy	X	X	Allows updates to profiles when a certificate must be renewed, when certificate content changes, when certificate templates are added or removed from the profile template, and when applets must be added or removed from a smart card.
Recover on Behalf Policy	X	X	Allows a certificate manager to recover a profile assigned to another user. Used to allow an administrator to access data encrypted by another user during an investigation or after a user has left the company.
Recovery Policy	X		Allows the recovery of a profile in the event a user's profile is deleted. During the recovery workflow, new signing certificates are issued, and previous encryption certificates are recovered from the CA database.

Table 17-1 **CLM Management Policies**

Management policy	Software	Smart card	Purpose
Renew Policy	X	X	Defines the workflow for the renewal of certificates within a profile template when they reach their expiration date.
Replace Policy		X	Allows replacement of a smart card if the smart card is lost, damaged, or stolen. As with the Recovery Policy, the Replace Policy allows the recovery of encryption certificates and their private keys from the CA database, with new certificates replacing any existing signing certificates.
Retire Policy		X	Allows revocation of a certificate on a smart card and redeployment of the smart card to either the same user or to another user.
Revoke Policy	X		Allows revocation of all certificates contained in a profile. Optionally, you can provide either a static revocation reason or provide the revocation reason at the time of the revocation request.
Suspend and Reinstate Policy	X	X	Allows temporary revocation of a profile or smart card by using the Certificate Hold revocation reason. When a profile is reinstated, the certificate's serial number is removed from the CRL by adding the certificate to the delta CRL with a Remove from CRL reason.
Temporary Cards Policy		X	The temporary cards policy is used to either provide temporary access to the network for users without any existing certificates for a short period of time or to provide a short-term replacement smart card for a user who has misplaced or forgotten the smart card and requires network access.
Unblock Policy		X	Specifies who can perform an online unblock of a user's smart card PIN.

Registration Models

When you define a management policy, there are some common registration models that are used to define the workflows for certificate issuance. The most common registration models used are:

- Self-service
- Manager-initiated
- Centralized

The following sections provide details on each of the registration models.

> **Note** You can define a different registration model for *each* management policy within a profile template. You are not obligated to use the *same* registration model for *all* management policies within a profile template.

Self-Service Registration Model

A self-service registration has the subscriber both initiating and executing the request. In some scenarios, an organization may implement approvals in the management policy, requiring one or more managers to approve the request before the subscriber can execute it.

The self-service registration model is typically used for lower-security certificates, where knowledge of a user's account and password is sufficient proof of identity for certificate issuance. In this model, the following process is implemented:

1. The certificate subscriber initiates the request for the smart card certificate.

2. If data collection is enabled, the certificate subscriber provides any data required by the workflow.

3. If low to medium assurance is desired, the smart card request is left in a pending state until certificate manager approval.

4. Once approval is received, the certificate subscriber executes the smart card request.

Permission Requirements for the Self-Service Registration Model

When you implement a management policy using the self-service registration model, you must implement the required CLM permissions to allow the management policy to execute as designed.

Table 17-2 outlines the permission requirements at all five permission locations for implementing a self-service registration model.

Table 17-2 Permission Requirements for Self-Service Requests

Permission location	Permission assignment requirements
Service connection point	Assign the manager Read and CLM Audit permissions if approvals are required.
User or group	Assign the manager Read and CLM Audit permissions if approvals are required.
Profile template	Assign the subscriber Read permissions.
	Assign the subscriber CLM Enroll permissions if workflow requests certificates from a CA.

Table 17-2   Permission Requirements for Self-Service Requests

Permission location	Permission assignment requirements
Certificate template	Assign the subscriber Read and Enroll permissions if workflow requests certificates from a CA on each included certificate template.
Management policy	Enable the self-service option in the management policy's General Settings. Assign the manager approval in the management policy if approvals are required.

Manager-Initiated Registration Model

A manager-initiated registration model has the request started by a person other than the certificate subscriber. Control of the request is passed to the certificate subscriber through the use of one-time passwords so that the subscriber can complete the request.

> **Note**   A manager-initiated request typically raises the assurance level of a certificate request because of the required participation of one or more certificate managers during the request process.

In the manager-initiated registration model, the following process is implemented:

1.   A certificate manager initiates the request.

2.   A certificate manager responds to any data collection requests.

3.   If approvals are configured for the smart card request, a different certificate manager should approve the request. This ensures that two people are involved in the enrollment initiation process.

4.   Once approved, an e-mail message containing a one-time password (OTP) is sent to the certificate subscriber. Alternatively, a second OTP can be distributed to the certificate subscriber's manager or to the certificate manager originating the request. This second password must be securely transmitted to the certificate subscriber before the certificate subscriber can execute the request.

5.   The certificate subscriber inputs the distributed OTP(s) and then completes the request. For example, if the request is to unblock the subscriber's smart card PIN, the subscriber would place the smart card in the smart card reader and specify the new PIN for their smart card.

Permission Requirements for the Manager-Initiated Registration Model

When you implement a management policy using the manager-initiated registration model, you must implement the required CLM permissions to allow the management policy to execute as designed.

Table 17-3 outlines the permission requirements at all five permission locations for implementing a manager-initiated registration model.

Table 17-3   Permission Requirements for Manager-Initiated Requests

Location	Permission assignment requirements
Service connection point	Assign the manager Read and necessary CLM permissions.
User or group	Assign the manager Read and necessary CLM permissions.
Profile template	Assign the manager and subscriber Read permissions.
	Assign the subscriber CLM Enroll permissions if workflow requests certificates from a CA.
Certificate template	Assign the subscriber Read and Enroll permissions if workflow requests certificates from a CA.
Management policy	Assign the manager the Initiate privilege in the management policy.
	Assign the manager approval in the management policy if approvals are required.

Note   The actual permission assignments at the service connection point and on the target users or groups will depend on the management policy that you are defining. For example, if you are defining the Revoke or Disable management policies, you must assign the manager the Read and CLM Request Revoke permissions.

Centralized Registration Model

A centralized registration model removes the certificate subscriber from the execution of the management policy workflow. For example, during a centralized enrollment workflow, a user designated as the originator initiates the request, and an enrollment agent executes the request. The use of an enrollment agent is mandatory in a centralized registration model because only an enrollment agent can request certificates on behalf of other users.

Note   The originator and enrollment agent do not have to be the same person. In fact, an additional person who approves the requests submitted by the originator can be added to the workflow.

In the centralized registration model, the following process is implemented:

1. A request, originated by the smart card procurement system, is forwarded to the certificate manager.

2. The certificate manager, acting as an enrollment agent, executes the smart card request on behalf of the certificate subscriber. In most cases, the smart card is shipped with a randomized or server-assigned PIN so that only the user can unblock the PIN.

3. The smart card and either PIN unblock instructions or a PIN letter are sent to the certificate subscriber. If the smart card is shipped ready-to-use, a PIN letter can be sent to provide the smart card's initial PIN.

4. The certificate subscriber receives the smart card and either initiates an unblock request or uses the initial PIN provided in a PIN letter to access the smart card.

> **Note**   Although typically used for smart card deployments, a centralized model can be used for software certificates, with the certificate then being exported as a PKCS #12 and provided to the subscriber.

Permission Requirements for the Centralized Registration Model

When you implement a management policy using the centralized registration model, you must implement the required CLM permissions to allow the management policy to execute as designed.

Table 17-4 outlines the permission requirements at all five permission locations for implementing a centralized registration model.

Table 17-4   Permission Requirements for Centralized Requests

Location	Permission assignment requirements
Service connection point	Assign the manager Read and necessary CLM permissions.
	Ensure that permissions assigned to the manager include CLM Enrollment Agent.
User or group	Assign the manager Read and necessary CLM permissions.
	Ensure that permissions assigned to the manager include CLM Enrollment Agent.
Profile template	Assign the manager and subscriber Read and CLM Enroll permissions.
Certificate template	Assign the manager Read and Enroll permissions.
Management policy	Assign the manager the Initiate privilege in the management policy.
	Assign the manager the Enrollment Agent privilege in the management policy.

Deploying ILM 2007 Certificate Management

Once you have defined the registration models you wish to use for each management policy, you cannot proceed until you deploy the ILM 2007 Certificate Management. The deployment requires both installation and configuration of each of the required components, as follows.

Installation of Server

The installation of CLM requires:

- Ensuring that the hardware, software, and infrastructure meet the installation requirements
- Preparing the schema
- Performing the installation of the server software

The following sections provide details on each of these steps.

Installation Requirements

Before you install CLM, you must make sure that your environment meets the hardware, software, and infrastructure requirements.

Hardware Requirements   CLM can be run only on servers that meet the minimum hardware requirements. The hardware requirements are:

- CPU: 1.8 GHz Pentium 4 or AMD Opteron class recommended
- RAM: 1 gigabyte (GB) (2 GB or more recommended)
- Disk: 40 GB or larger

CLM can be run only on 32-bit hardware. There is no support for 64-bit Windows Server 2003.

From the Source

The Identity Lifecycle Manager (ILM) product team is committed to providing support for the Windows Server 2008 Certification Authority in the next version of ILM, code named ILM "2."

Angela Mills,

Product Unit Manager, Microsoft Identity Management Team

Software Requirements   CLM requires the following software to be installed and enabled prior to performing CLM installation:

- Windows Server 2003 Enterprise or Datacenter editions.
- Internet Information Services (IIS) 6.0 with ASP.NET.
- .NET Framework 2.0.
- The ASP.NET v2.0.50727 extension must be enabled in IIS 6.0.

Infrastructure Requirements   In addition to one or more CLM servers, a CLM deployment requires the following infrastructure components:

- **Active Directory Domain Services**   CLM requires you to extend the Active Directory schema prior to performing CLM installation. The schema update adds two new object classes, *ms-Clm-Profile-Template* and *ms-Clm-Service-Connection-Point,* and adds a new string attribute, *ms-Clm-Data,* which contains the profile template Extensible Markup Language (XML) definition string. In addition, the schema update adds the following extended permissions:

  - ms-Clm-Audit (displayName: CLM Audit)
  - ms-Clm-Enroll (displayName: CLM Request Enroll)
  - ms-Clm-Recover (displayName: CLM Request Recover)
  - ms-Clm-Renew (displayName: CLM Request Renew)
  - ms-Clm-Revoke (displayName: CLM Request Revoke)
  - ms-Clm-SmartCard (displayName: CLM Request Unblock Smart Card)
  - ms-Clm-Enrollment-Agent (displayName: CLM Enrollment Agent)
  - ms-Clm-Subscriber-Enroll (displayName: CLM Enroll)

- **Database server**   CLM requires SQL Server 2000 with Service Pack 4 or later or SQL Server 2005 with Service Pack 1 or later. SQL Server can be installed on the same server as CLM or on a separate server and can use either Windows Integrated or Mixed Mode authentication.

- **Certification authority**   One or more Windows Server 2003 enterprise CAs must be installed in your environment prior to installing CLM. The CAs must be running Windows Server 2003 Enterprise Edition or later and must be either an enterprise root CA or an enterprise subordinate CA.

- **SMTP Server**   To allow CLM to deliver notifications and one-time passwords, a Simple Mail Transfer Protocol (SMTP) server must be available that allows anonymous SMTP relaying.

> **Note**   You can download an evaluation version of Identity Lifecycle Manager 2007 Feature Pack 1 from *http://www.microsoft.com/downloads/details.aspx?FamilyId=EE7233D8-B3C9-4BF5-A232-7ABC58C9940A&displaylang=en.*

Preparing the Schema

To prepare the schema, you must log on as a member of both the Enterprise Admins and the Schema Admins groups. Once logged on, you can prepare the schema by using the following procedure:

1. Log on at the schema operations master.

2. Extract the contents of the ILM 2007 Feature Pack 1 download to C:\ilm_CD.

3. Open the C:\ilm_CD\CLM\Schema folder.

4. Double-click the ModifySchema.vbs file to update the schema.

5. When the schema update is complete, in the Success message box, click OK.

6. Close any open windows.

Performing the Installation

Once you have prepared the schema, you can now install the CLM software on the CLM server. The installation must be performed by a member of the local Administrators group by using the following procedure:

1. Extract the contents of the ILM 2007 Feature Pack 1 download to C:\ilm_CD.

2. Ensure that IIS is installed and includes ASP.NET as part of the installation.

3. Ensure that the .NET Framework 2.0 is installed.

4. Open the C:\ilm_CD\CLM folder.

5. Double-click CLM.MSI to begin the installation process.

6. On the Welcome To The Installation Wizard page, click Next.

7. On the Certificate Lifecycle Manager License Agreement page, click I Accept The Terms In The License Agreement, and then click Next.

8. On the Product Key page, type your product key, and then click Next.

9. If you did not provide a license key, in the Certificate Lifecycle Manager Installation program Information message box, click OK to accept the 180-day evaluation period notice.

10. On the Custom Setup page, verify that CLM System Files and Web Files are selected for installation and that CLM CA Files is not selected, and then click Next.

 Note   This procedure assumes that the CA is installed on a separate computer.

11. On the Virtual Web Folder page, in the Virtual Folder text box, verify that Clm appears, and then click Next.

12. On the Ready To Install Certificate Lifecycle Manager page, click Install.

13. When the installation is complete, on the Certificate Lifecycle Manager Installation Complete page, deselect the Launch Certificate Lifecycle Manager check box, and then click Finish.

Configuration of Server

Once you have installed the CLM software on the CLM server, you must now run the CLM Configuration wizard to configure your environment. Figure 17-4 shows the servers and clients that are used for the example deployment.

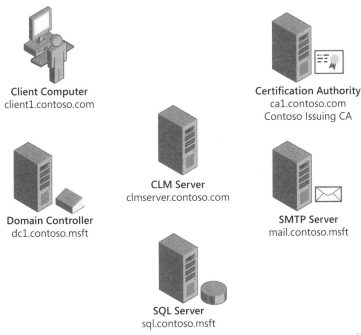

Figure 17-4   CLM example deployment

Agent Accounts

Before you configure the CLM server, you may have to prepare the six agent accounts used by the CLM server.

> **Note**   The CLM Configuration wizard can create the accounts for you in the directory, but many organizations will want to prepare the accounts beforehand, providing names that match the naming rules of the organization and assigning specific passwords to the agent accounts.

The six agent accounts that are required by the CLM server are:

- **CLM Agent**   Used by the CLM server to sign data, encrypt data collection items, and revoke certificates at the CA. The default account name is clmAgent.

- **Authorization Agent** Used by the CLM server to determine access rights and privileges for users and groups. The default account name for the Authorization Agent is clm-AuthAgent.

- **Key Recovery Agent** Used by the CLM server to recover archived private keys from the CA database. The default account name for the Key Recovery Agent is clmKRAgent.

- **CA Manager Agent** Used by the CLM server to conduct actions against the CA, such as publishing an updated certificate revocation list (CRL). The default account name for the CA Manager Agent is clmCAMngr.

- **Web Pool Agent** Used by CLM to run the Web application in IIS and is assigned as the identity for the CLM application pool. The account is also used as the identity for all operations with the SQL database. The default account name for the Web Pool Agent is clmWebPool.

- **Enrollment Agent** Used by the CLM server to request smart card certificates on behalf of another user account. The enrollment agent signs all requests with its Enrollment Agent certificate before submitting the requests to the configured CA. The default account name for the Enrollment Agent is clmEnrollAgent.

Agent Certificates

During the configuration of CLM, three of the agent accounts are issued certificates for CLM operations. Table 17-5 provides details on the default certificates issued to the three agent accounts.

Table 17-5 CLM Agent Account Certificates

Agent account	Required certificate
clmKRAgent	The default certificate template used to issue this certificate is the KeyRecovery-Agent certificate template. You can use the default or create a custom v2 certificate template based on the KeyRecoveryAgent certificate template.
clmAgent	This certificate is used for signing certificate requests within the CLM environment as well as for encrypting PINs, one-time passwords, and data collected during workflows. The default certificate template is the User certificate template, but it is recommended to create a version 2 certificate template based on the User certificate template that removes the Encrypting File System and Secure Email application policies.
clmEnrollAgent	This certificate is used when requesting certificates on behalf of other users. The default certificate template used to issue this certificate is the EnrollmentAgent certificate template.

For all three certificate templates, it is recommended to modify the default permissions to allow the associated agent account the Read and Enroll certificate template permissions.

Using a Hardware Security Module

If your deployment includes the use of a hardware security module (HSM) to protect CA key material, you must designate the HSM's CSP for use by the CLM Configuration wizard. The following procedure accomplishes this:

1. Open C:\Program Files\Microsoft Certificate Lifecycle Manager\Bin\ Microsoft.Clm.Config.exe.config with Notepad.exe.

2. Look for the Microsoft.Clm.Config.CspName value definition line.

3. Change the CSP name from Microsoft Enhanced RSA and AES Cryptographic Provider to your HSM vendor's CSP display name.

4. Ensure that the CLM server computer can successfully communicate with the HSM.

5. Execute the CLM Configuration wizard.

You do not have to modify the three certificate templates to use the HSM's CSP. The CLM Configuration wizard ignores the CSP settings in the three certificate templates and hard-codes the certificate requests to use the CSP designated in the Microsoft.Clm.Config.exe.config file.

SQL Server Authentication

The CLM server uses a SQL database to store its configuration information and collected registration data. To communicate with the CA, different accounts must be assigned SQL management roles.

CLM defines two SQL management roles when you run the CLM Configuration wizard:

- The ClmApp role is used by the CLM application to execute predefined stored procedures. The role is assigned SQL execute permissions on all stored procedures within the CLM database except for external procedures. In addition, the role is explicitly denied Select, Insert, Update, Delete, and Declare Referential Integrity (DRI) permissions on the CLM database tables. The ClmApp role is assigned to:
  - ❑ The CLM Web Pool account to execute CLM stored procedures
  - ❑ CA computer account(s) to execute CLM stored procedures when connecting to the CLM database with the CLM Exit Module or CLM Policy Module
  - ❑ Custom accounts used by the Provision API or Notification API to execute CLM stored procedures
- The ClmExternalAPI role is used by the CLM application to execute predefined stored procedures. The stored procedures write and modify data only in the ExternalRequests table. The role is assigned to any accounts used to execute scripts that implement the CLM External SQL API.

SMTP Server

To send OTP messages and other notification messages to CLM users, the CLM server must have connectivity to an SMTP server that allows anonymous relay of e-mail messages. It is recommended to implement the SMTP service on the local CLM server and restrict anonymous relay to the local host address (127.0.0.1) to enable SMTP message notifications.

The following procedure enables anonymous SMTP relay for the local CLM server:

1. From the Administrative Tools menu, open Internet Information Services (IIS) Manager.

2. In the console tree, expand CLMSERVER, right-click Default SMTP Virtual Server, and then click Properties.

3. In the Default SMTP Virtual Server Properties dialog box, on the Access tab, click Relay.

4. In the Relay Restrictions dialog box, click Add.

5. Verify that Single Computer is selected, in the IP Address text box, type **127.0.0.1**, and then click OK.

6. In the Relay Restrictions dialog box, deselect the Allow All Computers Which Successfully Authenticate To Relay, Regardless Of The List Above check box, and then click OK.

7. In the Default SMTP Virtual Server Properties dialog box, click OK.

Running the CLM Configuration Wizard

Once you have prepared the environment, you can now run the CLM Configuration wizard at the CLM servus, using the following procedure:

1. From the Microsoft Certificate Lifecycle Manager menu, click Configuration Wizard.

2. On the Welcome To The Configuration Wizard page, click Next.

3. On the CA Configuration page, verify the following, and then click Next:

    ❑ Certification Authority: **Contoso Issuing CA**

    ❑ Server: **ca1.contoso.com**

4. On the Set Up The SQL Server Database page, in the Name Of The SQL Server text box, type **sql.contoso.com**, verify that Use My Credentials To Create The Database Option is selected, and then click Next.

5. On the Database Settings page, verify the following, and then click Next:

    ❑ Database name: **CLM**

    ❑ Specify a location for the database file To use the default SQL Server location, leave this blank

    ❑ SQL integrated authentication

6. On the Set Up Active Directory page, verify that the suggested service connection point URL is cn=clmserver,cn= Certificate Lifecycle Manager,cn=Microsoft, cn=System,DC=contoso,DC=com, and then click Next.

7. On the Agents – Microsoft CLM page, select the Use The CLM Default Settings check box, and then click Next.

8. On the Set Up Server Certificates page, set the following options, and leave all other settings at their default values:

   ❑ Certificate Template To Be Used For The Recovery Agent Key Recovery Agent Certificate: **KeyRecoveryAgent**

   ❑ Certificate Template To Be Used For The CLM Agent Signing Certificate: **User**

   ❑ Certificate Template To Use For The Enrollment Agent Certificate: **EnrollmentAgent**

> **Note** If you created custom certificate templates, designate the custom certificate templates rather than the default certificate templates listed above. The certificate templates *must* be available for enrollment at the certification authority designated in step 3 of this procedure.

9. On the Set Up Server Certificates page, click Next.

10. On the Set Up E-mail Server, Document Printing page, accept the default values by clicking Next.

11. On the Ready To Configure page, verify that the actions to be performed are correct, and then click Configure.

12. In the Configuration Wizard – Microsoft Certificate Lifecycle Manager dialog box, click OK to confirm that SSL is not configured.

13. When the dialog box states Certificate Lifecycle Manager Was Configured Successfully, click Finish.

After you complete the configuration of the CLM Service, there are some additional configuration settings that must be performed. These include:

- Verifying that the SMTP Service is started

- Enabling Kerberos delegation of the clmWebPool account

- Verifying the clmWebPool Service Principal Names (SPNs)

Verifying the SMTP Service When you run the CLM Configuration wizard, the restart of IIS Service sometimes omits restarting the SMTP service. You can restart the SMTP Service by running **net start smtpsvc** at a command prompt.

Enabling Kerberos Delegation of the clmWebPool Account   The clmWebPool account is used to impersonate subscribers and managers that connect to the CLM Web portal. The impersonation is enabled by using Kerberos delegation. To enable Kerberos delegation, the clmWebPool account must be trusted for delegation. To enable Kerberos delegation, use the following procedure:

1. Log on at a domain controller or a computer with domain controller utilities loaded.

2. From the Administrative Tools menu, open Active Directory Users And Computers.

3. In Active Directory Users And Computers, on the View menu, ensure that Advanced Features is enabled.

4. In the console tree, click Users, and then in the details pane, double-click clmWebPool.

> **Note**   If you used a custom clmWebPool account, you may be choosing a different account name and probably a different container or organizational unit.

5. In the clmWebPool Properties dialog box, on the Delegation tab, verify that Trust This User For Delegation To Any Service (Kerberos Only) is selected, and then click OK.

6. Close Active Directory Users And Computers.

Verifying the clmWebPool Service Principal Names   The clmWebPool account must register an SPN that matches the URL that users will use to connect to the CLM Server. For example if you wish the users to connect to **http://clm.contoso.com/clm** rather than **http://clmserver.contoso.com/clm**, you must register the clm.contoso.com SPN on the clmserver computer account.

You can add the name by using the SETSPN utility, as shown in the following procedure:

1. Open a command prompt.

2. At the command prompt, type **setspn –a HTTP/clm.contoso.com Contoso\clmWebPool,** and then press Enter.

3. At the command prompt, type **setspn –l,** and then press Enter.

4. Ensure that the output shows the following names:

    ❑ HTTP/clm.contoso.com

    ❑ HTTP/CLMSERVER.contoso.com

    ❑ HTTP/CLMSERVER

> **Note**   The three names are the custom name you added in step 2, the default DNS name, and the default NetBIOS name of the CLM server.

5. Close the command prompt.

> **Important**   Make sure that the clm.contoso.com DNS resource record is created to allow resolution of the clm.contoso.com Web site.

Enabling the Certificate Lifecycle Manager Service

An optional service that is included with CLM is the Certificate Lifecycle Manager service. The service is installed but not enabled during the installation and configuration of CLM.

Certificate Lifecycle Manager Service Functionality   This service runs on the CLM server and provides the following functions:

- **Certificate renewal notification**   Allows CLM to automatically issue a renewal request for certificates that are within the certificate template's specified renewal time.

- **Disabling temporary smart cards**   CLM permits the issuance of temporary smart cards if a smart card is left at home. The Certificate Lifecycle Manager Service enables automatic disabling of these temporary smart cards or their associated primary cards.

- **External API processing**   The CLM External SQL API allows custom applications to submit CLM requests through external processes.

- **Online updates**   The Online Updates function is similar to the Certificate Renewal function in that it can be used to update certificates before they expire, if the certificate content changes, if the certificate templates included in a profile change, or if an applet is added or removed from a profile template.

- **Custom plug-ins**   The Certificate Lifecycle Manager Service can also be used to process custom plug-ins developed by customers.

Certificate Lifecycle Manager Service Configuration   Once you have completed the installation of CLM, you can enable the Certificate Lifecycle Manager service by performing the following tasks.

To configure the Certificate Lifecycle Manager service, you must perform the following tasks:

1. Create a new domain user account with a non-expiring, complex password.

2. Configure the Certificate Lifecycle Manager Service to use this user account for processing.

3. Grant the user account the following user rights:

    - Act as part of the operating system
    - Generate security audits
    - Replace a process level token

4. Add the account to the CLM server's local Administrators and IIS_WPG groups.

5. If using SQL integrated authentication, assign the user account the clmApp role for the CLM database.

6. Configure the Certificate Lifecycle Manager Service to start automatically.

7. If the Certificate Lifecycle Manager Service is running, restart it.

8. Grant the necessary CLM Extended Permissions to the Certificate Lifecycle Manager Service's service account to perform tasks within each required workflow.

> **Note**   For example, to have the Certificate Lifecycle Manager Service initiate a renewal workflow, the associated service account must be assigned the CLM Request Renew and CLM Request Enroll permissions on both the service connection point and on the target group containing the subscribers. The service account must also have the Read and CLM Enroll permissions on the profile template and be specified as a Renew Initiator in the actual renew policy of the profile template.

CA Component Installation

Once you have installed and configured the CLM Server, you must install the custom policy and exit modules at each CA computer that will issue certificates managed by CLM.

> **Note**   In our example, only one CA is used: – ca1.contoso.com. If there were multiple CAs, the following procedure must be executed once per CA.

To install the CLM custom modules, use the following procedure:

1. Extract the contents of the ILM 2007 Feature Pack 1 download to C:\ilm_CD.

2. Open the C:\ilm_CD\CLM folder.

3. Double-click CLM.MSI to begin the installation process.

4. On the Welcome To The Installation Wizard page, click Next.

5. On the Certificate Lifecycle Manager License Agreement page, click I Accept The Terms In The License Agreement, and then click Next.

6. On the Product Key page, type your product key, and then click Next.

7. If you did not provide a license key, in the Certificate Lifecycle Manager Installation Program Information message box, click OK to accept the 180-day evaluation period notice.

8. On the Custom Setup page, click the drop-down arrow next to Web Files, and then click This Feature Will Not Be Available.

9. On the Custom Setup Type page, click Next.

10. On the Ready To Install Certificate Lifecycle Manager page, click Install.

11. When the installation is complete, on the Certificate Lifecycle Manager Installation Complete page, click Finish.

CLM Policy Modules

The installation of the CLM Modules at a CA installs four custom policy modules for use in profile templates. Table 17-6 shows the four custom modules that are installed at the CA and the purpose of each module.

Table 17-6   Custom CLM Policy Modules

Module name	Description
Certificate SMimeCapabilities Module 1.0	Used to limit the available algorithms that can be used with Secure/Multipurpose Internet Mail Extensions (S/MIME) certificates
Certificate Subject Module 1.0	Used to insert a custom subject into a certificate's Subject field
SubjectAltName Module 1.1	Used to insert a custom subject alternative name (SAN) into a certificate
Support for non-Clm certificate requests	Used to register certificates issued to users outside of CLM, for example, autoenrollment or the IIS Certificate Request wizard

---

Once the CLM Modules are installed, you must configure the CLM Exit Module to connect to the SQL Server hosting the CLM database. This is accomplished in three separate procedures:

■ Creating a login account for the CA computer account at the SQL Server

■ Verifying the Service Principal Names of the SQL Server Service

■ Defining a connection string at the CA

Creating a SQL Login for the CA Computer Account

1. Ensure that you are logged on at the SQL Server as a member of the local Administrators group.

2. From the Microsoft SQL Server 2005 menu, open SQL Server Management Studio.

3. In the Connect To Server dialog box, accept the default authentication options, and then click Connect.

4. In the console tree, expand Security, and then click Logins.

5. Right-click Logins, and then click New Login.

6. In the Login – New dialog box, on the General page, provide the following information:

    ❑ Name: **contoso\ca1$**

    ❑ Authentication: **Windows Authentication**

    ❑ Default Database: **CLM**

7. On the User Mapping page, enable the CLM database, and then enable the clmApp And Public Roles.

8. In the Login – New dialog box, click OK.

9. Close Microsoft SQL Server Management Studio.

Verifying the SQL Service SPN

The authentication between the CA computer account and the SQL Server is a mutual authentication. For SQL Server to authenticate, the service account assigned to the SQL Server Service must have the **MSSQLSvc/*DNSName*:1433** name registered.

■   If the service runs as the Local System account, the name is registered by the computer running SQL Server's computer account. In our example, you would verify this by running **setspn –l Contoso\clmdc** at a command prompt and ensuring that the **MSSQLSvc/sql.contoso.com:1433** registration exists.

■   If the service runs as a specific user account, the name is registered by the user account designated in the properties of the service. In our example, you would verify this by running **setspn –l Contoso\SqlService** (assuming this is the name of the service account) at a command prompt and ensuring that the **MSSQLSvc/sql.contoso.com:1433** registration exists.

Defining a Connection String at the CA

Once you have verified that the CA computer account is granted a login at the SQL Server and that the SQL Server has the correct SPN registered, you can then define the connection string in the properties of the CLM Exit Module. To modify the connection string, use the following procedure:

1. Ensure that you log on to the CA computer as a member of the local Administrators group.

2. From the Administrative Tools menu, open Certification Authority.

3. In the console tree, right-click Contoso Issuing CA, and then click Properties.

4. In the Contoso Issuing CA Properties dialog box, on the Exit Module tab, select the Certificate Lifecycle Manager Exit Module, and then click Properties.

5. In the Configuration Properties dialog box, in the Specify Certificate Lifecycle Manager Database Connection String text box, type **Connect Timeout=15;Persist Security**

Info=True;Integrated Security=sspi;Initial Catalog=CLM;Data Source=sql. contoso.com; and then click OK.

> **Note**   The connection string assumes that the CLM server uses Windows Authentication to communicate with the computer running SQL Server.

6. In the Microsoft Certificate Lifecycle Manager message box, click OK to acknowledge that Certificate Services must be restarted.

7. In the Contoso Root CA Properties dialog box, click OK.

8. In the Certification Authority console, on the toolbar, click Stop This Service.

9. After Certificate Services has stopped, on the toolbar, click Start This Service.

10. From Administrative Tools, open Event Viewer.

11. In the console tree, select Certificate Lifecycle Manager.

12. Select the most recent event in the details pane.

13. Ensure that the event states that the Exit Module loaded using settings from SYSTEM\CurrentControlSet\Services\CertSvc\Configuration\Contoso Root CA\ ExitModules\Clm.Exit.

> **Warning**   One initial warning will exist. When you first install the CLM CA modules, there is no connection string set. If you have an error in your connection string or errors in either SQL Server or CLMDC SPNs, additional errors will exist.

14. Close all open windows.

At this point, the CLM server is ready to define profile templates and management policies for software certificate issuance.

> **Note**   If you are deploying smart cards with CLM, additional software must be installed at the client computers. The installation procedures are discussed in Chapter 21.

Deploying a Code Signing Certificate

The following example walks you through the configuration of a profile template for software-based Code Signing certificates. The example includes only two of the available management policies: Enroll and Revoke.

> **Note** Other management policies may be relevant for your organization. Only two are presented here for illustrative purposes.

Defining Certificate Template Permissions

To issue the Code Signing certificates, you must ensure that the Code Signing certificate template is available at the Contoso Issuing CA. Before you publish the certificate template, you must ensure that the target group (contoso\CodeSigners) is assigned the Read and Enroll permissions on the certificate template. This will allow the members of the group to enroll certificates based on the certificate template.

Creating a Profile Template

The first step in creating a profile template is to copy an existing profile template. CLM allows you only to copy existing profile template to create new profile templates. To create a profile template named "Code Signing Certificates," use the following procedure:

1. Open Windows Internet Explorer.

2. In Internet Explorer, open **http://clm.contoso.com/clm**.

3. Click the Microsoft Certificate Lifecycle Manager graphic.

4. On the Home page, in the Administration section, click Manage Profile Templates.

5. On the Profile Template Management page, in the Profile Template List section, select the check box next to CLM Sample Profile Template, and then click Copy A Selected Profile Template.

6. On the Duplicate Profile page, in the Profile Template Name section, in the New Profile Template Name box, type **Code Signing Certificates**, and then click OK.

7. Minimize Internet Explorer.

Defining Profile Template Details

Once you create the Code Signing Certificates profile template, you must configure the details of the profile template by using the following procedure:

1. In the left pane, in the Select A View section, ensure that Profile Details is selected.

2. On the Edit Profile Template [Code Signing Certificates] page, in the General Settings section, click Change General Settings.

3. On the Edit Profile Template [Code Signing Certificates] page, in the Name And Description section, in the Description box, type **Allows issuance and management of Code Signing certificates**.

4. On the Edit Profile Template [Code Signing Certificates] page, leave all other settings at their default value, and then at the bottom of the page, click OK.

5. On the Edit Profile Template [Code Signing Certificates] page, in the Certificate Templates section, click Add New Certificate Template.

6. Make the following changes in the Edit Profile Template [Code Signing Certificates] page:

   ❑ Certificate Authorities: Enable **Contoso Issuing CA**

   ❑ Certificate Template: Enable **CodeSigning**

7. At the bottom of the Edit Profile Template [Code Signing Certificates] page, click Add.

8. In the Certificate Templates section, select the User check box, and then click Delete Selected Certificate Templates.

9. In the Microsoft Internet Explorer dialog box, click OK to delete the selected items.

This ensures that the profile template will issue certificates based only the Code Signing certificate template. The certificates will be issued by the Contoso Issuing CA.

Enrollment

Now that the profile template exists, you can start to define management policies. This example assumes that the manager-initiated workflow shown in Figure 17-5 is used for the Enroll management policy.

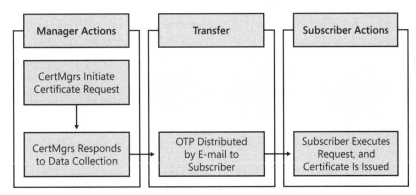

Figure 17-5   Enroll management policy workflow

In this example, the Code Signing certificate request is initiated by a member of the CertMgrs group. After initiating the action, the CertMgrs must respond to a data collection item. Once the data is collected, a one-time password is distributed to the subscriber. The subscriber inputs the one-time password into the CLM Subscriber portal, and then a certificate is issued to the subscriber.

Assigning Permissions   To enable the enrollment workflow described, we must assign the necessary permissions. Table 17-7 shows the permissions required for the enrollment workflow.

Table 17-7   Enroll Policy Permissions

Location	Permission assignment requirements
Service Connection Point	Assign the Contoso\CertMgrs group Read and CLM Request Enroll permissions.
User or Group	Assign the Contoso\CertMgrs group Read and CLM Request Enroll Permissions on the Contoso\CodeSigners group.
Profile Template	Assign the Contoso\CertMgrs and the Contoso\CodeSigners groups Read permissions and CLM Enroll permissions on the Code Signing Certificates profile template.
Certificate Template	Assign the Contoso\CodeSigners group Read and Enroll permissions on the Code Signing certificate template.

Defining the Management Policy   The last permission assignment requires configuring the Enroll policy for the profile template. Configuration of the Enroll policy starts with the general settings. This includes setting whether self-service is enabled, how many approvals are required, and whether the user is limited to a specific number of active profiles.

1. In the left pane, in the Select A View Section, click Enroll Policy.

2. On the Edit Profile Template [Code Signing Certificates] page, in the Workflow: General section, click Change General Settings.

3. Make the following changes on the Edit Profile Template [Code Signing Certificates] page:

   ❑ Enable Policy: **Enabled**

   ❑ Use Self Serve: **Disabled**

   ❑ Require Enrollment Agent: **Disabled**

   ❑ Allow Comments To Be Collected: **Disabled**

   ❑ Allow Request Priority To Be Collected: **Disabled**

   ❑ Default Request Priority: **0**

   ❑ Number Of Approvals: **0**

   ❑ Number Of Active Or Suspended Profiles/Smart Cards Allowed: **Set Value: 1**

4. At the bottom of the Edit Profile Template [Code Signing Certificates] page, click OK.

Once you have configured the general settings, you can now start configuring the workflow. The first step is to specify who can initiate the enrollment request. As shown previously in

Figure 17-5, the enrollment request is initiated by members of the Contoso\CertMgrs group. Use the following procedure:

1. In the Workflow: Initiate Enroll Requests section, click Add New Principal For Enroll Request Initiation.

2. On the Edit Profile Template [Code Signing Certificates] page, in the Permission section, click Lookup.

3. In the Microsoft Certificate Lifecycle Manager 2007 – Webpage Dialog dialog box, in the Name box, type **CertMgrs**, and then click Search.

4. In the returned listing of groups and users, click CONTOSO\CertMgrs.

5. In the Permission section, ensure that the Enroll Initiate Permission drop-down list is set to Grant, and then click OK.

6. In the Workflow: Initiate Enroll Requests section, select the check box next to NT AUTHORITY\SYSTEM, and then click Delete Principals For Enroll Request Initiation.

> **Note**   The NT AUTHORITY\SYSTEM account can be deleted with no issues because it is only a placeholder account.

7. In the Microsoft Internet Explorer dialog box, click OK to confirm the deletion.

If the workflow requires data collection, you must now specify the actual data collection items. For each data collection item, you must define what the data collection item is, its data type, who collects the data, and how the data is validated. In our example, we will record the employee's badge number (a numeric value). Use the following procedure:

1. On the Edit Profile Template [Code Signing Certificates] page, in the Data Collection section, select the check box next to Sample Data Item, and then click Delete Data Collection Items.

2. In the Microsoft Internet Explorer dialog box, click OK to confirm the deletion.

> **Note**   Sample Data Item is an example of a data collection item and should always be deleted.

3. In the Data Collection section, click Add New Data Collection Item.

4. In the Data Item Name And Type section, apply the following settings:

   ❑ Name: **Employee Badge Number**

   ❑ Description: **Number is located on the back of the employee badge**

   ❑ Type: **Numeric**

❏ Default Value: **Disabled**

❏ Required: **Enabled**

5. In the Data Item Originator section, select Certificate Manager.

6. In the Data Item Validation section, select Data Type.

7. In the Data Item Storage section, apply the following settings:

❏ Store Data In: **Database**

❏ Encrypted: **Enabled**

8. At the bottom of the page, click OK to save any changes.

Our workflow transfers control of the workflow to the certificate subscriber by using a one-time password. In our example, a single one-time password is sent by e-mail to the subscriber. To define a one-time password, use the following procedure:

1. On the Edit Profile Template [Code Signing Certificates] page, in the One-Time Password section, click Change Password Provider Settings.

2. In the Password Provider section, ensure that Default Password Provider is selected and that the Number Of One Time Passwords box has a value of 1, and then click OK.

3. On the Edit Profile Template [Code Signing Certificates] page, in the Passwords Distribution section, click Display On Screen.

4. On the Edit Profile Template [Code Signing Certificates] page, in the One-Time Password Distribution section, do the following:

❏ In the Distribution Method drop-down list, select Email Subscriber.

❏ In the Mail From box, type **CLMAdmin@contoso.com.**

❏ In the Mail Subject box, type **Your Code Signing Certificate.**

❏ In the Mail Body box, type the following:

```
Dear {User!givenName},
Please input the following one-time password into the CLM portal
(http://clm.contoso.com/clm) to complete enrollment for your Code Signing
certificate:
{Secret1}
Regards,
Help Desk Support
```

5. At the bottom of the page, click OK to save any changes.

Revoke Policy

This example assumes that the workflow shown in Figure 17-6 is used for the Revoke management policy:

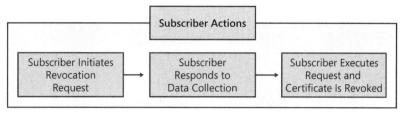

Figure 17-6   Revoke management policy workflow

The Revoke management policy will allow a self-service registration model. The subscriber will connect to the CLM Subscriber Web portal, initiate the Revoke request, and respond to a data collection item, and then CLM will revoke the certificate.

Assigning Permissions   To enable the enrollment workflow described, we must assign the necessary permissions. Table 17-8 shows the permissions required for the revocation workflow.

Table 17-8   Revoke Policy Permissions

Location	Permission assignment requirements
Service Connection Point	No permission assignments are required for a self-service workflow.
User or Group	No permission assignments are required for a self-service workflow.
Profile Template	Assign the Contoso\CodeSigners groups Read permissions on the Code Signing Certificates profile template.
Certificate Template	No permission assignments are required for the revoke workflow.

Defining the Management Policy   The last permission assignment requires configuring the Revoke policy for the profile template. Configuration of the Revoke policy starts with the general settings. This includes setting whether self-service is enabled, how many approvals are required, and whether the user is limited to a specific number of active profiles. Use the following procedure:

1. In the left pane, in the Select A View section, click Revoke Policy.

2. On the Edit Profile Template [Code Signing Certificates] page, in the Workflow: General section, click Change General Settings.

3. Ensure that the following options are set on the Edit Profile Template [Code Signing Certificates] page:

    ❑   Enable Policy: **Enabled**

    ❑   Use Self Serve: **Enabled**

    ❑   Allow Comments To Be Collected: **Disabled**

    ❑   Allow Request Priority To Be Collected: **Disabled**

❑   Default Request Priority: **0**

❑   Number Of Approvals: **0**

4.   At the bottom of the Edit Profile Template [Code Signing Certificates] page, click OK.

For the Revoke policy, you must specify how CLM will revoke the certificate. This includes specifying the revocation reason and choosing whether to publish a base CRL, a delta CRL, or both a base and delta CRL.

1.   On the Edit Profile Template [Code Signing Certificates] page, in the Workflow: Revocation settings section, click Change Revocation Settings.

2.   Configure the settings in the Workflow Options For Revocation section as follows:

❑   Revocation Delay: **Use a fixed revocation delay [hours] = 0**

❑   Revocation Reason: **Set the revocation reason when the request is completed**

❑   Publish Base Certificate Revocation List (CRL): **Disabled**

❑   Publish Delta CRL: **Enabled**

3.   In the Workflow Options For Revocation section, click OK.

Because we are configuring only self-service for the revocation requests, we must delete the default assignment to NT AUTHORITY\SYSTEM. Use the following procedure:

1.   On the Edit Profile Template [Code Signing Certificates] page, in the Workflow: Initiate Revoke Requests section, select the check box next to NT AUTHORITY\SYSTEM, and then click Delete Principals For Revoke Request Initiation.

2.   In the Microsoft Internet Explorer dialog box, click OK to confirm the deletion.

You must now define the data collection item. In this workflow, we will record a text reason why the certificate is being revoked. Use the following procedure:

1.   On the Edit Profile Template [Code Signing Certificates] page, in the Data Collection section, select the check box next to Sample Data Item, and then click Delete Data Collection Items.

2.   In the Microsoft Internet Explorer dialog box, click OK to confirm the deletion.

3.   In the Data Collection section, click Add New Data Collection Item.

4.   In the Data Item Name And Type section, apply the following settings:

❑   Name: **Revocation Circumstances**

❑   Description: **Input why the Code Signing certificate was revoked**

❑   Type: **String**

❑   Default Value: **Change in job function**

❑   Required: **Enabled**

5. In the Data Item Originator section, select User.

6. In the Data Item Validation section, select Data type.

7. In the Data Item Storage section, apply the following settings:

    ❏ Store Data In: **Database**

    ❏ Encrypted: **Disabled**

8. At the bottom of the page, click OK to save any changes.

Finally, we must disable the use of one-time passwords. A self-service workflow does not require a transfer of control, because the request is both initiated and completed by the subscriber. Use the following procedure:

1. On the Edit Profile Template [Code Signing Certificates] page, in the One-Time Passwords section, click Change Password Provider Settings.

2. On the Edit Profile Template [Code Signing Certificates] page, in the Password Provider section, click Default Password Provider, and then in the Number Of One-Time Passwords (Password Provider Data) box, type **0**, and then click OK.

3. Close all open windows.

Executing the Management Policies

Now that the two management policies are set, you can test the execution of the management policies. To execute the enrollment policy, the following group memberships are assumed:

- Manager1 is a member of the CertMgrs group.

- Subscriber1 is a member of the CodeSigning group.

Performing an Enrollment

To perform the initial enrollment of a Code Signing certificate, Manager1 must log on at any workstation and perform the following procedure:

1. Open Windows Internet Explorer.

2. In Windows Internet Explorer, open *http://clm.contoso.com/clm*.

3. If the Microsoft Phishing Filter dialog box appears, select Turn On Automatic Phishing Filter (Recommended), and then click OK.

4. Click the Microsoft Certificate Lifecycle Manager Feature Pack 1 graphic.

5. On the Home page, in the Common Tasks section, click Enroll A User For A New Set Of Certificates Or A Smart Card.

6. On the Search for Users page, in the Search Criteria For Users section, in the Name box, type **Subscriber1**, and then press Enter.

7. On the Search For Users page, click Subscriber1.

8. If the Profile Selection: All page appears, select the Code Signing Certificates profile template, and then click Next.

9. On the Manager-Initiated Enroll page, in the Data Collection section, in the Employee Badge Number box, type **2468**, and then click OK.

10. On the Request Status page, ensure that the Request Status is Approved, and then click OK.

11. Close all open windows, and then log off.

> **Note** It really does not matter which computer is used by Manager1 to initiate the request.

Once the request is initiated, Subscriber1 will receive an e-mail message from the CLMAdmin@contoso.com account. When the message is received, Subscriber1 must perform the following tasks:

1. In the inbox of Subscriber1's e-mail application, open the message from: CLMAdmin@contoso.msft.

2. In the message, select the one-time secret, and then from the Edit menu, click Copy.

3. In the message, click the *http://clm.contoso.com/clm* link.

4. If the Microsoft Phishing Filter dialog box appears, select Turn On Automatic Phishing Filter (Recommended), and then click OK.

5. In Internet Explorer, click the Microsoft Certificate Lifecycle Manager Feature Pack 1 graphic.

6. On the Home page, in the Common Tasks section, click Complete A Request With One-Time Passwords.

7. On the One-Time Password validation page, in the Enter Passwords section, right-click the One-Time Password 1 box, click Paste, and then click Next.

> **Tip** You can suppress the second password box (if you require only one one-time password) by changing the URL in the e-mail message to *http://clm.contoso.com/clm/content/sm/auth/Authorization.aspx?PasswordCount=1.*

8. In the Potential Scripting Violation dialog box, click Yes to submit the certificate request.

9. In the Potential Scripting Violation dialog box, click Yes to install the certificate.

> **Note** The previous two dialog boxes have slightly different names if connecting from a client computer running Windows Vista.

10. On the Installing Certificates page, in the Certificate Installation section, verify that the Success column contains a check mark, and then click Next.

11. Verify that the request status is Completed and that the profile status is Active.

The Code Signing certificate is now available for use by Subscriber1.

Performing a Revocation

Now assume that Subscriber 1 has taken a new job within the organization. The new job no longer requires him or her to sign code for publication, so Subscriber 1 must now revoke the certificate.

To revoke the certificate, the following procedure is used:

1. Log on as Subscriber1.

2. Open Windows Internet Explorer.

3. In Windows Internet Explorer, open *http://clm.contoso.com/clm*.

4. On the Home page, in the View My Information section, click Show Details Of My Certificate.

5. On the User Details page, in the Certificate Profiles section, click Code Signing Certificates.

6. On the Profile page, in the Profile Details section, click Revoke This Profile.

7. On the Revoke Certificate Profile page, in the Data Collection section, accept the default revocation circumstances entry, and then click Next.

8. On the Revocation Details page, in the Reason For Revocation drop-down list, select Cessation Of Operations, and then click Next.

9. On the Request Complete page, ensure that the request status is completed and the profile's status is disabled.

10. Close Windows Internet Explorer.

Case Study: Contoso, Ltd.

Contoso, Ltd. has discovered that the current system of deploying Key Recovery Agent certificates is breaking down and certificates are issued that do not meet the requirements described in their Certificate Policy.

The Certificate Policy states:

Key Recovery Agent certificates must be issued using a medium assurance certificate policy. The medium assurance certificate policy requires that the designated subscriber meet the registration authority in a face-to face meeting. During the meeting, the subscriber must present one form of national or state photo identification. After the identification is presented, the subscriber shall receive his or her certificate. For renewals, the Key Recovery Agent needs only access to the previous certificate's private key.

To ensure that all future Key Recovery Agent certificates are issued to enforce the medium assurance certificate policy, Contoso has purchased a copy of Identity Lifecycle Manager 2007. A consultant assists Contoso with designing and deploying a profile template for Key Recovery Agent certificates.

Proposed Solution

The consultant proposes creating a profile template with the Enroll policy using the workflow shown in Figure 17-7.

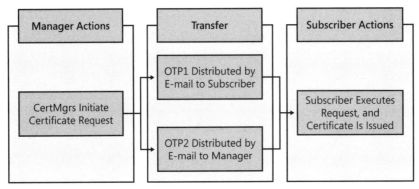

Figure 17-7 Proposed enrollment policy workflow

For renewals, the workflow shown in Figure 17-8 is proposed.

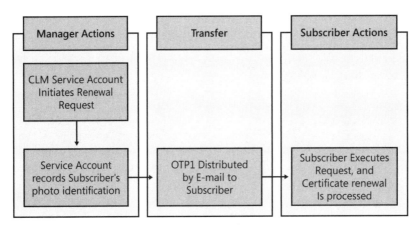

Figure 17-8 Proposed renewal policy workflow

Case Study Questions

1. Does the proposed enrollment workflow enforce the defined certificate policy for enrollment?

2. How would you modify the enrollment workflow to meet the defined certificate policy?

3. In Table 17-9, specify the permission assignments required to perform the enroll policy workflow.

Table 17-9   Enroll Policy Permissions

Location	Permission assignment requirements
Service connection point	Assign the Contoso\CertMgrs group _____ and _____ permissions.
User or Group	Assign the Contoso\CertMgrs group _____ and _____ Permissions on the Contoso\KRAs group.
Profile Template	Assign the _____ group and the _____ group _____ and _____ permissions on the Key Recovery Agent profile template.
Certificate Template	Assign the _____ group _____ and _____ permissions on the Key Recovery Agent certificate template.

4. Are there any issues with the defined renewal workflow?

5. Are there any issues with the proposed renewal request workflow? What must be done to fix the workflow?

6. Is it possible to send one one-time password to the subscriber and a second one-time password to the manager?

7. How many one-time passwords must be entered by the subscriber to complete the renewal request?

Best Practices

- **Only assign certificate manager permissions at the Service Connection Point.**   If a user is assigned any of the custom CLM permissions at the Service Connection Point, that user is connected to the CLM manager portal.

- **Assign CLM permissions to universal or global security groups.**   Profile templates and certificate templates are stored in the configuration-naming context. Because the objects are replicated to all domain controllers in the forest, only global or universal group memberships are recognized.

■ **Review CLM permissions at all five permission locations.**   The CLM permission model is very complex. A mistake at any one of the five permission locations can result in a workflow failure.

■ **Choose the registration model for each management policy based on your organization's certificate policies.**   Each management policy can implement a distinct registration model. Choose the best registration model for each management policy, ensuring that the selected registration model enforces your organization's policies.

■ **Use integrated authentication rather than native authentication when connecting to the CLM SQL data store.**   SQL integrated authentication ensures that the credentials used to connect to the SQL database are protected from inspection. In addition, integrated authentication enforces mutual authentication of the SQL client and the SQL server.

■ **Disable a management policy if it is not required for your deployment.**   By default, management policies are enabled for self-service. Leaving the default settings can result in unexpected execution of management policies.

■ **Test your proposed workflows in a test network before deploying in production.**   Because of the complexity of the CLM permission model, it is always recommended to test your settings in a test environment. If changes are required, the changes do not affect your production deployment.

Additional Information

■ RFC 3647–"Internet X.509 Public Key Infrastructure Certificate Policy and Certification Practices Framework" (*http://www.ietf.org/rfc/rfc3647.txt*)

■ Identity Lifecycle Manager 2007 Web site (*http://www.microsoft.com/ilm*)

■ "Installing and Configuring CLM 2007 on a Server" (*http://technet2.microsoft.com/ ILM/en/library/423113e7-9ac7-4009-a708-156f25afecc11033.mspx?mfr=true*)

■ Microsoft Certificate Lifecycle Manager 2007 (CLM 2007) Technical Library (*http://technet2.microsoft.com/ILM/en/library/a4d5346d-418c-497c-bbab-ff49e94e982b1033.mspx?mfr=true e*)

Chapter 18

Archiving Encryption Keys

You can archive the private keys for encryption certificates at either a Windows Server 2003 or Windows Server 2008 enterprise certification authority (CA) to allow recovery of the private key if a user's private key is lost or corrupted. This functionality is available at a Windows Server 2003 or Windows Server 2008 enterprise CA running on the Enterprise or Datacenter edition.

An organization should specify key archival and recovery in its security policy. If an organization does not specify that it allows key archival and recovery, it is almost impossible for the organization to implement key archival and recovery, because there are no guidelines for the implementation. If the security policy allows key archival, the policy must state when it is permissible for a certificate's private key to be recovered from the CA database.

An organization's security policy typically lists the following reasons for allowing key recovery:

- **A user profile is deleted.** When an encryption private key is stored in a user's profile folder, the private key is lost if anyone deletes that specific profile. Many organizations use profile deletion to fix problems with user logon. For example, if the desktop fails or takes a long time to appear, many organizations prescribe deleting the user's profile and generating a new profile. This results in deletion of the user's private key material.

- **A hard disk is corrupted.** The corruption of a hard disk can cause users to lose access to their profiles. This can mean a total loss of access or loss of access to the private key material within the user profile.

- **The operating system is reinstalled.** When the operating system is reinstalled, access to the previous user profiles is lost, including any private keys stored in the user's profile.

- **A computer is stolen or lost.** When a computer is stolen or lost, access to the private key material in the user profile is lost or compromised.

- **A smart card fails.** If a smart card fails, the encryption private keys stored on the smart card are lost. If the smart card cryptographic service provider (CSP) supports key archival (through the enabling of the **crypt_archivable** flag), the private key is archived at the issuing CA. The private key may be recovered to a replacement smart card.

Note Smart card failure may still allow access to the certificates on the smart card. For example, if the smart card is also used for building access, failure of the building access component may require the replacement of the smart card.

A difference among the reasons listed, however, is that a computer theft or loss can mean that the user's private key is compromised and, therefore, the certificate associated with the private key should be revoked. There is no reason to revoke the certificate for the other reasons in this list, because the user's private key is not compromised.

Roles in Key Archival

When you enable key archival at a Windows Server 2003 or Windows Server 2008 enterprise CA, the key recovery process has two management roles:

- **Certificate manager**   The certificate manager Common Criteria role is responsible for extracting the encrypted private key from the CA database in a binary large object (BLOB) file format. The certificate manager also determines which key recovery agent (KRA) can decrypt each encrypted private key.

- **Key recovery agent**   The key recovery agent is responsible for decrypting the private key from the BLOB file extracted by the certificate manager. Once the key recovery agent extracts the private key, the resulting PKCS #12 file must be distributed to the original user.

Although it is recommended that you assign separate people to the certificate manager and key recovery agent roles, a single person can hold both. Because the key recovery agent role is not a required or defined Common Criteria role, there are no operating system restrictions on one user holding both roles. Your organization's security policy for data recovery must determine whether these two roles must be held by separate employees.

The Key Archival Process

When a certificate template specifies key archival, the private key associated with a certificate request must be securely transmitted from the requesting client computer to the CA for archival in the CA database. When the client requests a certificate that has key archival enabled, the process shown in Figure 18-1 takes place.

1.   The client queries the CN=Enrollment Services,CN=Public Key Services, CN=Services,CN=Configuration,DC=*ForestRootDomain* container to find an enterprise CA.

2.   The client makes an authenticated Distributed Component Object Model (DCOM) connection to the selected enterprise CA and requests its CA Exchange certificate.

3.   The CA sends the CA Exchange certificate to the client computer.

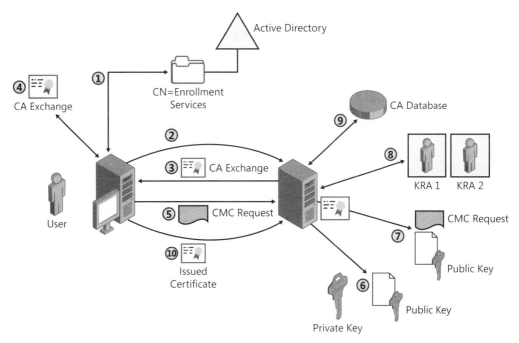

Figure 18-1   The key archival process

Cryptography Next Generation and CA Exchange Certificates

With Windows Server 2008, you can specify a Cryptography Next Generation (CNG) provider and cryptographic algorithm when generating CA Exchange certificates. The provider and algorithm are defined in the following registry values:

- HKEY_LOCAL_MACHINE\System\CurrentControlSet\Services\CertSvc\Configuration*CAName*\EncryptionCSP\Provider

- HKEY_LOCAL_MACHINE\System\CurrentControlSet\Services\CertSvc\Configuration*CAName*\EncryptionCSP\KeySize

- HKEY_LOCAL_MACHINE\System\CurrentControlSet\Services\CertSvc\Configuration*CAName*\EncryptionCSP\ProviderType (0 for a CAPI CSP and 1 for a CNG provider)

- HKEY_LOCAL_MACHINE\System\CurrentControlSet\Services\CertSvc\Configuration*CAName*\EncryptionCSP\EncryptionAlgorithm

If the CA Exchange certificate template is available at an issuing CA, the certificate template is used for all other settings other than the four defined in the above registry entries. If the validity period and overlap periods differ in the registry, the registry entries are automatically changed to match the certificate template.

You can enforce the use of the CA Exchange certificate template (rather than autogenerating a CA Exchange certificate) by running the following command to set the appropriate registry flag:

```
Certutil -setreg CA\CRLFlags +CRLF_USE_XCHG_CERT_TEMPLATE
```

If the CA certificate is not available, the generation attempt will fail. Also ensure that the CA's computer account has Read and Enroll permissions assigned for the CA Exchange certificate.

4. The client performs the following tests on the CA Exchange certificate:

   ❑ Verifies that the CA Exchange certificate is signed by the CA's signing certificate. This ensures that the private key is being sent to the correct CA and only the intended CA can decrypt the private key.

   ❑ Performs a certificate validation and revocation status check on the CA Exchange certificate.

5. The client encrypts the private key corresponding to the request with the CA Exchange certificate's public key, builds a Certificate Management Message over the Cryptographic Message Syntax (CMC) request, and sends a CMC full PKI request to the CA.

> **Note**   If the user is using Windows Vista or Windows Server 2008, the private key may be encrypted using Advanced Encryption Standard (AES). This option is available only if a version 3 certificate template implements the "Use Advanced Symmetric Algorithm To Send The Key To The CA" option, and the certificate template is issued by a Windows Server 2008 enterprise CA.

6. The CA verifies that the encrypted private key is the matched key to the public key in the CMC request.

7. The CA validates the signature on the request with the public key in the request to ensure that the contents of the request are not modified.

8. The CA encrypts the user request's private key with a random Triple DES (3DES) or Advanced Encryption Standard (AES) symmetric key and then encrypts the symmetric key with one or more Key Recovery Agent certificate public keys defined in the CA's properties.

Using AES for Key Archival

AES is used only for symmetric key for key archival if the Windows Server 2008 CA is configured to use a CNG key provider that supports AES, and the following registry settings are enabled at the CA:

■   `Certutil -setreg CA\EncryptionCSP\CNGEncryptionAlgorithm AES`

> ■ `Certutil -setreg CA\EncryptionCSP\SymmetricKeySize 256`
>
> Once the settings are configured, you must then restart Certificate Services.
>
> If you enable AES, the key length can be set to 128, 192, or 256 bits. Also, key recovery operations must be performed only at a computer running Windows Vista or Windows Server 2008. Computers running Windows XP do not support AES algorithms by default AES support was added in Windows XP SP1.

9. The CA saves the encrypted key BLOB—which contains the encrypted private key and the symmetric key encrypted with one or more Key Recovery Agent certificate's public keys—to the CA database.

10. The CA processes the certificate request normally and responds to the client with a CMC, full PKI response containing the certificate issued to the requestor.

The result of this process is that the client receives a certificate signed by the issuing CA, and the certificate and the associated private key are archived in the CA database. Because of the encryption, only a designated key recovery agent can decrypt the private key material stored in the CA database.

The Key Recovery Process

When a user loses access to his or her encryption private key because of any of the reasons given in this chapter, the key recovery process proceeds in the following steps:

1. A certificate manager for the CA that issued the certificate determines the certificate's serial number, which uniquely identifies an issued certificate and finds the certificate and private key in the database.

2. The certificate manager extracts the encrypted private key and certificate from the CA database. The BLOB file is encrypted with the public key of one or more Key Recovery Agent certificates.

3. The certificate manager transfers the BLOB file to the key recovery agent. Because the BLOB file is encrypted so that only a specified key recovery agent can recover the encrypted certificate and private key, no additional security is required.

4. The key recovery agent recovers the private key and certificate from the encrypted BLOB file at a secure workstation also known as the recovery workstation. The private key and certificate are stored in a PKCS #12 file and are protected with a password assigned by a key recovery agent.

> **Important**   If the option to use AES encryption to protect the archived private key is enabled, the recovery must take place at a computer running Windows Vista.

5. The key recovery agent supplies the PKCS #12 file and the password to the user, who then imports the certificate and private key into his or her certificate store by using the Certificate Import Wizard.

Requirements for Key Archival

The following conditions must be met to enable key archival at a Windows Server 2003 or Windows Server 2008 CA:

■   One or more users must acquire a certificate with the Key Recovery Agent application policy or the Enhanced Key Usage (EKU) object identifier (OID). This certificate allows the private key holder to decrypt private key material stored in the CA database. By default, the Key Recovery Agent certificate template requires certificate manager approval for issuance to ensure that only authorized personnel receive the Key Recovery Agent certificate.

■   The CA must be configured and enabled for key archival. In the CA's properties, you must designate one or more Key Recovery Agent certificates that the CA must use to encrypt the private keys archived in the CA database. If at least one Key Recovery Agent certificate is designated, key archival is enabled at the CA (once Certificate Services is restarted).

> **Important**   All designated Key Recovery Agent certificates must be valid. If any of the Key Recovery Agent certificates is revoked or fail any certificate validation test, key archival is not possible at the CA, and certificate requests that require key archival will fail.

■   A certificate template is enabled for key archival. A certificate template must select the Archive Subject's Encryption Private Key check box to enable key archival. In addition, the certificate template may require private key export and be published at a CA that enabled key archival.

> **Note**   Private key export is required only if the certificate is requested from a script running on client computer running Microsoft Windows 2000. Only computers running Windows XP and later recognize that a certificate template with key archival enabled allows export of the private key during the initial certificate request. Computers running Windows 2000 must have key export enabled to allow the private key to be included in the certificate request.

■   The CSP must support key export or **crypt_archivable** flag for key generation. If the CSP does not allow key export or archiving of the private key, a certificate request using the CSP will fail if the certificate template attempts to archive the private key. The CSP will not allow the private key to be sent to the CA.

> **Important**   Both software and smart card CSPs can support the **crypt_archivable** flag. It is a common misconception that a smart card CSP cannot support key archival and recovery.

Defining Key Recovery Agents

To define a key recovery agent, you must ensure that a Key Recovery Agent certificate is issued to the designated user. You can choose between deploying a software-based or a smart card–based Key Recovery Agent certificate.

Deploying a Software-Based Key Recovery Agent Certificate

The default Key Recovery Agent certificate template requires that certificate issuance be validated by a certificate manager. The process described in the next section assumes that this requirement does not change.

> **Note**   The holder of the private key associated with the Key Recovery Agent certificate is, ultimately, the key recovery agent. In that respect, the subject name of the certificate is inconsequential.

Requesting the Key Recovery Agent Certificate   The following processes assume that the certificate template has the default settings, though the permissions are set to allow a custom global or universal group Read and Enroll permissions.

To request the Key Recovery Agent certificate, use the following process:

1. Log on to the domain with an account assigned Read and Enroll permissions for the Key Recovery Agent certificate template.

2. Open Windows Internet Explorer.

> **Note**   You must use Windows Internet Explorer for the certificate request because the Certificate Enrollment Wizard in Windows 2000 and Windows XP does support pended requests. The Certificate Services Web Enrollment pages provide content to allow you to check the status of a pending certificate request. The link is maintained through a cookie issued at the requesting computer.

3. In Internet Explorer, open the URL *http://CertSrvDNS/certsrv* (where *CertSrvDNS* is the Domain Name System (DNS) name of the CA issuing the Key Recovery Agent certificates).

4. On the Welcome page, click the Request A Certificate link.

5. On the Advanced Certificate Request page, click the Create And Submit A Request To This CA link.

6. On the Advanced Certificate Request page, in the Certificate Template drop-down list, select Key Recovery Agent.

7. On the Advanced Certificate Request page, in the Friendly Name box, type Key Recovery Agent, and then click Submit.

8. In the warning dialog box, allow the Web site to request a certificate on your behalf by clicking Yes.

> **Note**   The title of the warning dialog box differs between Windows Vista and earlier versions of the Windows operating system.

9. On the Certificate Pending page, ensure that the Web page states that the request ID is in a pending state.

10. Close Windows Internet Explorer.

> **Note**   You do not have to use Web enrollment from a computer running Windows Vista. The updated Certificate Enrollment Wizard allows processing of pended requests.

Issuing the Pending Certificate   Once the certificate request is pending, the key recovery agent must have his or her identity validated by a certificate manager. The method used to identify the key recovery agent depends on your organization's certificate policies. With the requestor's identity validated, a certificate manager can issue the Key Recovery Agent certificate by using the following process:

1. Log on to the issuing CA as a user assigned the Issue and Manage Certificates permission.

2. Open the Certification Authority console.

3. Expand the certification authority name, and then click Pending Requests.

4. Ensure that the Key Recovery Agent certificate requestor has met the defined certificate policy, right-click the pending certificate request in the details pane, point to All Tasks, and then click Issue.

5. Close the Certification Authority console.

This process must be repeated for all pending Key Recovery Agent certificates. When the certificate is issued, the CA publishes the certificate to the CN=KRA,CN=Public Key Services, CN=Services,CN=Configuration,DC=*ForestRootDomain* container. Publication in this container allows the Key Recovery Agent certificate to be added to the configuration of an enterprise CA in the forest, enabling key archival.

Installing and Exporting the Key Recovery Agent Certificates   Once a certificate is issued, the Key Recovery Agent certificate requestor must complete the installation. If you requested the Key Recovery Agent certificate by using the Certificate Services Web Enrollment pages, you complete the installation by performing the following process:

1. Open Windows Internet Explorer at the same computer where the original request was submitted.

> **Important**   The private key material, as well as the cookie that has information about the pending certificate request, exist only at this computer. If you implemented a smart card CSP for the Key Recovery Agent certificate template, you also must have the smart card used to generate the certificate request.

2. In Windows Internet Explorer, open the URL *http://CertSrvDNS/certsrv* (where *CertSrvDNS* is the Domain Name System name of the certification authority issuing the Key Recovery Agent certificates).

3. On the Welcome page, click the View The Status Of A Pending Certificate Request link.

4. On the View The Status Of A Pending Certificate Request page, click the (*Date* and *Time*) link.

5. On the Certificate Issued page, click the Install This Certificate link.

6. In the warning dialog box, accept that the Web site is adding a certificate to your computer by clicking Yes.

> **Note**   The title of the warning dialog box differs between Windows Vista and earlier versions of the Windows operating system.

7. Ensure that the Certificate Installed page appears, indicating that the certificate has been installed successfully.

8. Close Windows Internet Explorer.

If you requested the certificate on Windows Vista using the Certificate Request wizard, certificate autoenrollment will automatically detect when the pending certificate is issued and install the certificate on the client computer.

> **Note**   You can invoke the autoenrollment by running **GPUpdate /force** at the client computer after the pending certificate is issued by a certificate manager.

Exporting the Certificate and Private Key   Once you successfully enroll the Key Recovery Agent certificate, it is recommended that you export the certificate and private key to a PKCS #12 file and remove the key material from the hard drive of the computer where the request was performed. This process allows key recovery to take place at any computer where the private key is imported. It also ensures that the private key no longer remains on the computer where the request was performed.

To export the certificate and private key, ensure you are logged on as the user who requested the Key Recovery Agent certificate, and use the following process:

1. From the Start menu, click Run, type **certmgr.msc,** and then click OK.

2. In the console tree, expand Personal, and then click Certificates.

3. In the details pane, right-click the Key Recovery Agent certificate, point to All Tasks, and then click Export.

4. On the Welcome To The Certificate Export Wizard page, click Next.

5. On the Export Private Key page, click Yes, Export the Private Key, and then click Next.

6. On the Export File Format page, click Personal Information Exchange–PKCS #12, and then select the following check boxes for Windows 2000 or Windows XP:

   ❑ Include All Certificates In The Certification Path, If Possible

   ❑ Enable Strong Protection

   ❑ Delete The Private Key If The Export Is Successful

   For Windows Vista, the check boxes that must be selected are:

   ❑ Include All Certificates In The Certification Path, If Possible

   ❑ Delete The Private Key If The Export Is Successful

   ❑ Export All Extended Properties

7. On the Export File Format page, click Next.

8. On the Password page, type and confirm a password to secure the PKCS #12 file, and then click Next.

> **Tip**   Use a complex password to protect the PKCS #12 file. In some organizations, this password is given to a person other than the PKCS #12 file holder. This ensures that two people are required to access the Key Recovery Agent certificate and private key.

9. On the File To Export page, type a location to export the file to (preferably removable media, such as a floppy disk or USB drive), and then click Next.

10. On the Completing The Certificate Export Wizard page, click Finish.

11. In the Certificate Export Wizard message box, click OK.

12. Close the Certificates console, remove the floppy disk or USB drive from the computer, and log off from the network.

This process must be repeated for all defined key recovery agents.

Deploying a Smart Card–Based Key Recovery Agent Certificate

Many organizations try to increase the assurance level of the Key Recovery Agent certificates by issuing the certificates on smart cards. The smart cards increase security by:

- Removing the requirement to delete the key recovery agent's profile from a computer after performing key recovery.

- Storing the private key on a two-factor device. You can access the Key Recovery Agent private key only if you have access to the smart card and have knowledge of the personal identification number (PIN) protecting the smart card.

In addition, the smart card makes it easier to perform recovery at any computer that has a smart card reader and the smart card CSP installed.

Creating a Combined Login and Recovery Certificate Template   It is recommended to create a custom certificate template when deploying a smart card–based Key Recovery Agent certificate. The combined certificate template will allow both authentication to the network and key recovery capabilities.

The following settings must be enabled in the custom certificate template:

- On the Request Handling tab, change the purpose to Signature and Encryption, do not allow the private key to be exported (the certificate is on a smart card), and prompt the user during enrollment to allow them to input their smart card PIN.

- Set the CSP to be your vendor's smart card CSP. You may have to pre-install the vendor's smart card CSP to allow you to designate the CSP in the certificate template.

- On the Subject tab, ensure that the User Principal Name (UPN) is enabled. The authenticating domain controller identifies the user's account by looking up the UPN in the global catalog.

- On the Application Policies tab, enable Client Authentication, Key Recovery Agent, and Smart Card Logon for the Application Policy extension.

- On the Security tab, assign a custom group containing all key recovery agents the Read, Enroll, and Autoenroll permissions.

If you implement a version 3 certificate template, you can use a CNG algorithm for asymmetric and hashing operations. Implementing a CNG algorithm ensures that all operations that use the certificate utilize CNG during their operations.

> **Note**   To implement a smart card with a version 3 certificate template, you must designate the Microsoft Smart Card Key Storage Provider on the Cryptography tab.

Requesting a Custom Key Recovery Agent Certificate   The new Certificate Request wizard in Windows Vista allows you to request a pending certificate by using the wizard rather than the Certificate Services Web enrollment pages.

To request a Key Recovery Agent certificate from Windows Vista, use the following procedure:

1. Open Certmgr.msc.

2. If User Account Control is enabled, click Yes to load the console.

3. In the Certificate console, in the console tree, right-click Personal, point to All Tasks, and then click Request New Certificate.

4. On the Before You Begin page, click Next.

5. On the Request Certificates page, in the list of certificates, enable the custom Key Recovery Agent certificate template, and then click Enroll.

6. When prompted, in the Windows Security dialog box, type the PIN for your smart card.

7. On the Certificate Installation Results, the status is reported as Enrollment Pending.

> **Note**   A certificate manager must issue the pending certificate. Your certificate policy may require the Key Recovery Agent to show photo identification and provide other identification data before the certificate is issued.

Installating the Key Recovery Agent Certificate   Once the certificate is issued, you can complete the enrollment process in the Certificates console.

1. Open the Certificates console (Certmgr.msc).

2. In the console tree, right-click Certificates – Current User, point to All Tasks, and then click Automatically Enroll And Retrieve Certificates.

3. On the Before You Begin page, click Next.

4. On the Request Certificates page, select the check box for all pending certificate requests, and then click Enroll.

5. In the Windows Security dialog box, type the PIN for your smart card, and then click OK.

6. On the Certificate Installation page, ensure that the status is Succeeded, and then click Finish.

Enabling a CA for Key Archival

Once the Key Recovery Agent certificates are published to Active Directory Domain Services (AD DS), you can enable key archival on an enterprise CA–by–enterprise CA basis.

> **Note**   The CA must be an enterprise CA running on the Enterprise or Datacenter edition of Windows Server 2003 or Windows Server 2008. Key archival is not supported on the Standard Edition.

The following procedure enables key archival at an enterprise CA:

1. Log on at the enterprise CA as a user assigned the Manage CA permissions (known as a CA Admin).

2. On the Start menu, click Administrative Tools, and then click Certification Authority.

3. In the console tree, right-click the *CA name,* and then click Properties.

4. In the *CA name* Properties dialog box, click the Recovery Agents tab. (See Figure 18-2.)

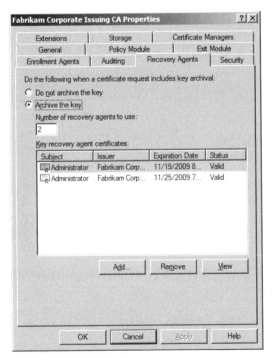

Figure 18-2   The Recovery Agents tab

5. On the Recovery Agents tab, click Archive The Key, in the Number Of Recovery Agents To Use box, type **1**, and then click the Add button.

6. In the Key Recovery Agent Selection dialog box, select one or more Key Recovery Agent certificates, and then click OK.

Choosing the Number of Key Recovery Agents

On the Recovery Agents tab, you typically set the Number of Recovery Agents To Use box to be the same value as the number of Key Recovery Agent certificates added to the CA. If you specify the value to be lower than the total number of Key Recovery Agent certificates, Certificate Services randomly selects the number of designated certificates from the pool of available certificates for each encryption procedure.

This adds complexity to the encryption process, however, and is considered excessive in most cases. Instead, consider setting the Number of Recovery Agents To Use box to be the same value as the number of Key Recovery Agent certificates added. In fact, if you implement Microsoft Identity Lifecycle Manager (ILM) 2007 Certificate Management, you must designate a value equal to the total number of Key Recovery Agent certificates loaded. Designating a matching number ensures that the ILM 2007 Certificate Management Key Recovery Agent agent account is *always* selected as a KRA when archival takes place.

---

7. In the *CA name* Properties dialog box, click Apply.

> **Note**   When you click the Apply button, the CA performs a certificate validation test against each designated Key Recovery Agent certificate. If any certificate fails the validation test, the failure is designated once you restart Certificate Services.

8. In the Certification Authority dialog box, click Yes to restart certificate services.

9. On the Recovery Agents tab, ensure each added Key Recovery Agent certificate's status is reported as Valid, and then click OK.

> **Warning**   You might have to close and reopen the *CA name* Properties dialog box to see the change in certificate status.

10. Close the Certification Authority console.

The CA is enabled for key archival and can now issue certificates based on certificate templates that enable key archival.

Enabling Key Archival in a Certificate Template

Once the CA is enabled for archival, you can create and publish certificate templates that enable key archival. To enable key archival in a certificate template, the first thing that you must do is set the purpose of the certificate template to either *Encryption* or *Signature and Encryption*. Key archival is possible for certificate templates only with these purposes. In fact, if the certificate template's purpose is Signature or Signature and Smart Card Logon, it is not possible to enable key archival for the certificate template.

Once you configure the purpose of the certificate template as Encryption or Signature and Encryption, the following properties must be configured on the Request Handling tab of the certificate template (see Figure 18-3).

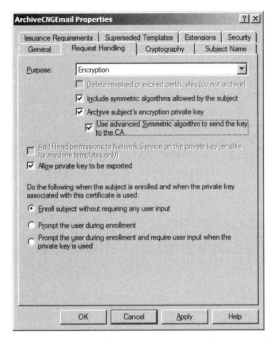

Figure 18-3   Enabling AES to protect the private key during transport to the CA

Note   If you enable this certificate template, make sure that the certificate template is enabled only at Windows Server 2008 enterprise CAs. The CA utilizing the Key Recovery Agent certificate must support AES for encryption and decryption.

- **Archive Subject's Encryption Private Key**   Enable this setting.

- **Allow Private Key To Be Exported**   Enable this setting if you want to allow manual export of the certificate's private key by the holder of the private key. This option is also required if the certificate will be requested by Windows 2000 clients by using the Certificate Services Web Enrollment pages.

- **Use Advanced Symmetric Algorithm To Send The Key To The CA**   If you implement a version 3 certificate template, enabling this setting requires the client to use AES to encrypt the private key during the transmission to the CA. If enabled, both the client and the CA must support AES encryption; otherwise enrollment will fail.

- **CSP**   Select a CSP that enables key export. If the CSP does not enable the **crypt_archivable** flag, the CSP will not support key export. If you enable a version 3 certificate template, the CSP is designated on the Cryptography tab.

Performing Key Recovery

When a private key must be recovered from a CA, the certificate manager and key recovery agent must work together to extract the encrypted BLOB from the CA database, decrypt the private key from the encrypted BLOB, and distribute the PKCS #12 file to the original user.

Using Certutil to Perform Key Recovery

This process can be performed at a command prompt by running the certutil.exe utility.

> **Note**   The Key Recovery Tool used in Windows Server 2003 is no longer available. The tool can still be used to recover certificates archived at Windows Server 2003 enterprise CAs but is not supported for Windows Server 2008 CAs.

The **certutil.exe** command is used by both the certificate manager and the key recovery agent when key recovery is performed at a command prompt.

1. The certificate manager first determines the serial number of the affected certificate by viewing the properties of the certificate in the Certification Authority console.

> **Note**   If the serial number cannot be determined, the certificate manager can still search on the user's UPN or account name.

2. Once the serial number is known, the certificate manager can extract the encrypted BLOB file by running **certutil -getkey** *SearchToken OutputBlob* at a command prompt on the CA computer. *SearchToken* can be the serial number of the certificate, the Common Name of the certificate, the Thumbprint of the certificate, the certificate requestor's user account name (domain\username), or the requestor's User Principal Name (UPN) (user@domain.com). *OutputBlob* is a file name for the output file.

   If you designate a user name or common name, and more than one archived certificate exists at the CA, rather than creating an OutputBlob file, the output will present a list of all certificates and their serial numbers with archived private keys at the CA. The command can then be reexecuted against each serial number.

   ```
   Serial Number: 1464be10000000000007
   Subject: CN=Sample User, CN=Users, DC=fabrikam, DC=com
   NotBefore: 1/13/2007 11:51 AM
   NotAfter: 1/13/2008 11:51 AM
   Template: ArchiveEFS
   Cert Hash(sha1): a2 7f 77 bc 2f 7b eb 26 bd 3e ed 43 b8 2a 24 04 2e 55 b8 64

   Serial Number: 1464fcbc000000000008

   Subject: CN= Sample User, CN=Users, DC=fabrikam, DC=com
   ```

```
NotBefore: 1/16/2007 12:51 PM
NotAfter: 1/13/2009 12:51 PM
Template: KeyA, KeyArchival
Cert Hash(sha1): 21 bd 88 2c 2a 84 0c e5 57 7b 2a bf f0 43 4b b3 ed bf 02 5a
```

3.   The key recovery agent can then log on and use the **certutil -recoverkey** *OutputBlob PKCS#12File* command to recover the private key from the BLOB file into a PKCS #12 file. This process defines the file name and sets a password on the PKCS #12 file.

Now the resulting PKCS #12 file can be transported to the user and then imported by the user at his or her computer, allowing access to the private key at the computer.

> **Important**   If the KRA certificate was generated using an advanced CryptoAPI Next Gener-
> ation (CNG) algorithm, such as Elliptic Curve Cryptography (ECC), you must specify the
> provider by including the **-CSP** flag in the recovery command, for example: **certutil –csp
> "Microsoft Software Key Storage Provider" –recoverkey** *OutputBlob* **user.pfx.**

Once the key recovery agent recovers the private key, the private key must be imported back into the original user's profile at his or her computer.

To import the private key, the key recovery agent must provide the user with the PKCS #12 file and the password required to import the file. To ensure that an attacker cannot easily gain access to both the PKCS #12 file and its associated password, these two pieces of information should be transmitted to the original user separately. For example, the key recovery agent can send the PKCS #12 file to the user by e-mail and send the associated password to the user's voice mailbox.

Once the user receives both the PKCS #12 and the associated password, the following process imports the private key into the user's profile:

1.   Ensure that the user associated with the private key is logged on at his or her computer.

2.   The user must double-click the provided PKCS #12 file.

3.   On the Certificate Import Wizard page, click Next.

4.   On the File To Import page, click Next.

5.   On the Password page, in the Password box, type the password provided by the key recovery agent.

6.   Click Mark This Key As Exportable. This allows you to back up or transport your keys at a later time. Then click Next.

7.   On the Certificate Store page, click Automatically Select The Certificate Store Based On The Type Of Certificate, and then click Next.

8.   On the Completing The Certificate Import Wizard page, click Finish.

9.   In the Certificate Import Wizard message box, click OK.

Performing Key Recovery with ILM 2007 Certificate Management

Alternatively, ILM 2007 Certificate Management can be used to create a recover or replace workflow. (The recover workflow is used for a software-based profile template, and the replace workflow is used for a smart card–based encryption profile template.)

The most common registration model used for key recovery is the delegated registration model. Figure 18-4 shows the workflow that could be created with ILM 2007 Certificate Management for key recovery.

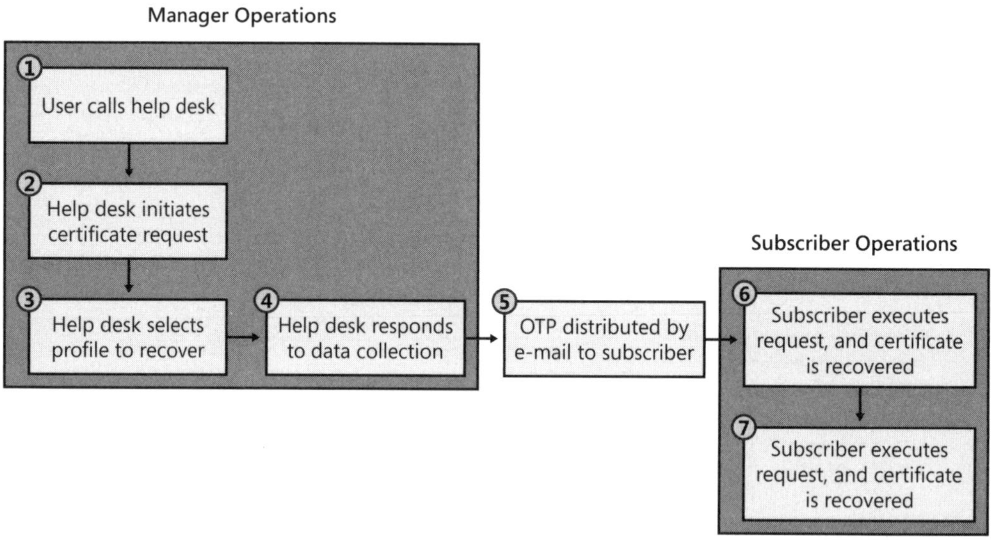

Figure 18-4   An ILM 2007 recovery workflow for encryption certificates

1.   The recover or replace request starts when the user calls the help desk to report that he or she is unable to access an encrypted file.

2.   The help desk employee searches for the user's smart card or software profile and initiates a recover or replace request.

3.   The help desk employee inputs the user's name and selects the profile that must be recovered or replaced.

4.   The help desk employee inputs a data collection item, such as the reason why the recover operation is taking place.

5.   A one-time password is sent by e-mail to the subscriber.

6.   The subscriber connects to the ILM 2007 Certificate Management subscriber portal and clicks the link to complete a request with One-Time Passwords.

7.   The subscriber executes the request by providing a password to protect the private key, downloads the certificate and private key, and, providing the protection password, imports the certificate.

When the request is executed, two ILM 2007 Certificate Management agent accounts are involved in the process:

- The clmAgent account acts as a certificate manager, extracting the encrypted BLOB for each archived certificate from the CA database.

- The clmKRAgent account acts as the key recovery agent, decrypting the encrypted BLOB file and creating the PKCS #12 file to be downloaded by the subscriber.

> **Important**   If you implement ILM 2007 Certificate Management for key recovery operations, the issuing CA must be configured so that the number of key recovery agents used for recovery operations equals the total number of designated Key Recovery Agent certificates. You *cannot* configure the CA to use round robin selection because this could prevent the clmKRAgent certificate from being able to recover all archived private keys.

Case Study: Lucerne Publishing

You manage the CAs for Lucerne Publishing. Lucerne Publishing is a global publishing company that has implemented a two-tier CA hierarchy, as shown in Figure 18-5.

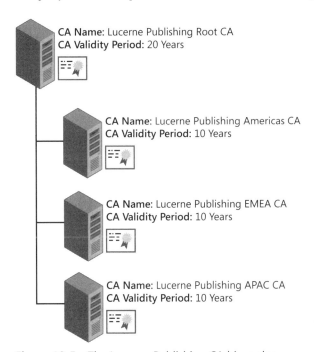

Figure 18-5   The Lucerne Publishing CA hierarchy

Scenario

Lucerne Publishing is planning to deploy encryption certificates that will require key archival at a Windows Server 2008 enterprise CA. Applications that could be considered for key archival include the Encrypting File System (EFS) and Secure E-mail using Secure/Multipurpose Internet Mail Extensions (S/MIME).

The following design requirements have been identified for encryption certificates:

- Key recovery must be possible for both a centralized key recovery agent and a regional key recovery agent.

- The centralized Key Recovery Agent certificate and private key will be located at the corporate office in Chicago, USA.

- The regional Key Recovery Agent certificates will be located at the major network hub site for that specific region. The regional hub sites are:

  - ❑ EMEA: Frankfurt, Germany

  - ❑ APAC: Kuala Lumpur, Malaysia

  - ❑ Americas: Winnipeg, Canada

- Common Criteria role separation is enforced at all issuing CAs.

- All key recovery operations must involve at least two persons.

Case Study Questions

1. At what CAs in the CA hierarchy must you enable key archival? How many key recovery agents must be defined at each CA?

2. What operating system must be installed on the issuing CAs to allow key archival?

3. Can you combine the key recovery agent role with the roles of CA administrator, certificate manager, auditor, or backup operator? Why or why not?

4. What Common Criteria role is blocked from being a key recovery agent because of the design requirements?

5. What certificate template must be available to allow secure transmission of the requestor's private key to the issuing CA?

6. What **certutil** command is used by a certificate manager to extract the encrypted BLOB from the CA database?

7. What **certutil** command is used by a key recovery agent to decrypt the PKCS #12 file within the encrypted BLOB file?

8. What risk is there to allowing the key recovery agent to send the PKCS #12 file and password to the user in the same e-mail message?

9. What risk is there to archiving a certificate template with the purpose of Signature and Encryption?

10. If ILM 2007 Certificate Management was used to recover the EFS and S/MIME certificates, what account would act as the certificate manager in the key recovery process?

11. If ILM 2007 Certificate Management was used to recover the EFS and S/MIME certificates, what account would act as the key recovery agent in the key recovery process?

12. Assuming that ILM 2007 will use certificates issued only by the Lucerne Publishing Americas CA, how many Key Recovery Agent certificates would be designated at the Americas CA? How many recovery agents must be used for each archival operation?

Best Practices

- **Determine whether a certificate needs to be revoked before initiating the key recovery process.**   You have to revoke the associated certificate only if the private key is compromised—for example, if the private key is located on a stolen laptop. There is no need to revoke the associated certificate if the private key was lost because of the deletion of a user's profile or the rebuild of a computer.

- **Develop a secure method for transporting private keys to the original owner.**   After the key recovery agent retrieves the PKCS #12 file, he or she must securely transfer the file and its associated password to the original owner of the private key. Never send the two together. For example, consider sending the PKCS #12 file by e-mail, and leave the password in the user's voice mailbox or send the password to the user's manager.

- **Do not archive private keys for high-value certificates.**   If a certificate is used to encrypt high-value data, in some circumstances it is better to lose access to the encrypted data rather than allow private key recovery.

- **Do not archive private keys used for digital signing.**   Do not enable key archival for certificates with the Signature and Encryption purpose. Access to this private key can lead to impersonation for signing operations.

- **Do not combine the certificate manager and key recovery agent roles.**   Require that two people be involved in the recovery process to prevent a single person from recovering a user's private key.

- **Limit the number of CAs enabled for key archival.**   Do not archive keys for users at many CAs in the CA hierarchy, because recovery operations become confusing.

- **Enable the CA to audit the storage and retrieval of archived keys.**   This ensures that all retrieval of archived private keys is captured in the Windows Security Log.

- **Never leave the Key Recovery Agent certificate and private key in a user's profile.**   Once you complete any key recovery operation, log off the network and delete the profile directory of the user account used to perform the key recovery operation. This prevents leaving additional copies of the Key Recovery Agent certificate and private key on the network.

■ **Protect the Key Recovery Agent certificate and private key by using a smart card or other two-factor device.**   A smart card protects the Key Recovery Agent certificate's private key with two-factor authentication. The key recovery agent must have access to the smart card and must know the PIN of the smart card. A smart card also prevents the Key Recovery Agent certificate's private key from ever being stored on the local file system of the computer.

■ **Implement ILM 2007 Certificate Management to enforce recovery workflows.**   ILM 2007 Certificate Management allows you to enforce a predefined workflow for recover operation. The workflow must ensure that the identity of the certificate subscriber is verified before the recovery operation is performed.

Additional Information

■ Microsoft Official Curriculum, Course 2821: "Designing and Managing a Windows Public Key Infrastructure" (*http://www.microsoft.com/traincert/syllabi/2821afinal.asp*)

■ "Key Archival and Management in Windows Server 2003" (*http://www.microsoft.com/ technet/prodtechnol/windowsserver2003/technologies/security/kyacws03.mspx*)

■ "Implementing and Administering Certificate Templates in Windows Server 2003" (*http://www.microsoft.com/technet/prodtechnol/windowsserver2003/technologies/ security/ws03crtm.mspx*)

■ "Implementing and Administering Certificate Templates in Windows Server 2008" (*http://go.microsoft.com/fwlink/?LinkID=92522*)

■ "Key Archival and Recovery in Windows Server 2008" (*http://go.microsoft.com/fwlink/ ?LinkID=92523*)

Chapter 19

Implementing SSL Encryption for Web Servers

Web browsing on the Internet or on local intranets is one of the most commonly used applications within an organization. By default, the Hypertext Transfer Protocol (HTTP) does not employ data encryption for transfers between the Web server and the Web client.

With a Web Server certificate installed at the Web server, however, the Web server can implement Secure Sockets Layer (SSL), an encryption protocol. SSL implementation at the Web server accomplishes two things:

- The client's Web browser validates the Web server's identity by performing certificate validation on the Web Server certificate.

- Data is encrypted as it is transferred between the Web server and the client's Web browser.

This chapter discusses design decisions and details for implementing SSL at Web servers. Additional topics include using certificate-based authentication for Web clients and issuing Web Server certificates to third-party Web servers and Web accelerators.

 Note Implementing SSL encryption for other protocols, such as Post Office Protocol version 3 (POP3) or Internet Message Access Protocol version 4 (IMAP4), will be covered in Chapter 22, "Secure E-Mail."

How SSL Works

When a Web client connects to an SSL-secured Web server, in basic terms, the following process validates the Web server's identity and encrypts data:

1. An SSL connection attempt begins when a user types or clicks a Uniform Resource Locator (URL) that begins with Hypertext Transfer Protocol Secure (HTTPS–HTTP with SSL encryption).

2. When the connection is established, the Web server transmits its Web Server certificate to the Web browser.

3. To authenticate the Web server, the Web browser performs certificate validation (as described in Chapter 11, "Certificate Validation") with the following tests:

   ❑ Ensures that the Web Server certificate chains to a trusted root certification authority (CA)

   ❑ Ensures that the Domain Name System (DNS) name in the certificate's subject matches the DNS name in the HTTPS URL

   ❑ Ensures that the Web Server certificate is time-valid

   ❑ Ensures that the Web Server certificate has not been revoked

---

Enabling Strong Certificate Revocation List (CRL) Checking in Internet Explorer

The test for certificate revocation is performed only when CRL checking is enabled in the Web browser. Prior to Windows Internet Explorer 7.0, CRL checking was disabled for SSL connections. To verify that strong CRL checking is enabled, use the following procedure:

1. Open Internet Explorer.

2. From the Tools menu, click Internet Options.

3. In the Internet Options dialog box, on the Advanced tab, select the Check for Server Certificate Revocation check box.

4. In the Internet Options dialog box, click OK.

You must restart the computer for certificate revocation checking to take effect.

> **Warning** Enabling strong CRL checking can cause failures when connecting to SSL-protected Web sites if the CRLs cannot be downloaded in a timely manner. For example, if the user has a slow Internet connection, a large CRL may not download in a timely manner, resulting in a revocation checking error.

---

4. If the Web Server certificate fails any of these tests, the behavior depends on the version of Internet Explorer used. For Microsoft Internet Explorer version 6.0 and earlier, the user is prompted to proceed with the dialog box shown in Figure 19-1.

> **Note** In Figure 19-1, the Web Server certificate does not chain to a trusted root CA, and the certificate's subject does not match the DNS name used by the Web client. Even though the validation tests fail, the user can still implement SSL encryption between the Web client and the Web server by clicking Yes.

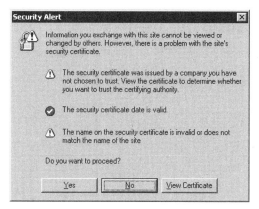

Figure 19-1   In Internet Explorer 6.0, the user must select whether to continue if the Web server's certificate fails validation testing.

Internet Explorer 7.0 changes the behavior greatly. Rather than a simple dialog box, where a user is tempted to click the Yes button, the warning is far more visual, as shown in Figure 19-2.

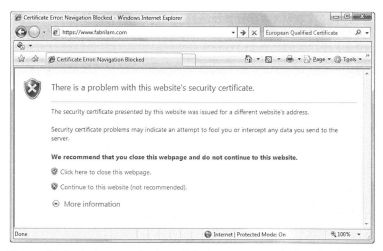

Figure 19-2   In Internet Explorer 7.0, the recommended option is to not proceed to the Web site.

As you can see, it is recommended to not connect to the *https://www.fabrikam.com* Web site.

5. If the Web Server certificate passes all tests, the Web browser extracts the certificate's associated public key.

6. The Web browser creates a pre-master secret, which is a string of randomly created bits whose length is determined by a negotiation between the Web browser and the Web server.

7. The Web browser encrypts the pre-master secret with the Web server's public key and sends the encrypted pre-master secret to the Web server.

8. The Web server decrypts the pre-master secret with its private key.

9. Depending on the cryptographic service provider (CSP) installed at the Web server, a Diffie-Hellman or a Rivest Shamir Adleman (RSA) negotiation allows the Web server and Web client to use the pre-master key to generate a symmetric session key using the same symmetric encryption algorithm.

10. The symmetric session key is used by the Web server and the Web client to encrypt data transmitted between the two. The session key is used until either the Web client or the Web server terminates the HTTPS session.

> **Tip**   When you are connected to a Web server using SSL, the Web browser displays a lock or key icon in the status bar for Internet Explorer 6.0 and to the right of the address bar in Internet Explorer 7.0, indicating that SSL is enabled for the session. You can view the properties of the Web server's certificate by double-clicking the lock or key icon.

Certificate Requirements for SSL

When you implement SSL, you must identify the certificates that are necessary for enabling SSL encryption between the Web client and the Web server. Two types of certificates can be used:

- **Web server certificate**   A Web Server certificate is mandatory when implementing SSL for a Web server. The Web Server certificate provides encryption of the pre-master secret when it is sent from the Web client to the Web server. In addition, the Web server certificate allows the Web client to validate the Web server's identity, ensuring that the Web server is not an attacker's Web server impersonating the target Web server. The Web server certificate must include the Server Authentication object identifier (OID) in the Enhanced Key Usage extension.

- **Web client certificate**   When a Web site requires authentication to identify the actual user connecting to the Web site, the Web client can use certificate-based authentication. Certificate-based authentication is not required for SSL connections, but it does increase the security of the user's credentials. The Web client certificate must include the Client Authentication OID in the Enhanced Key Usage extension.

Choosing a Web Server Certificate Provider

When you implement SSL at a Web server, you must determine where you will obtain the Web Server certificate. The decision is most often based on whether the clients connecting to the Web server are internal or external. Internal clients are employees or partners of your organization who might or might not have computer accounts within your network. An external client is typically a customer that does business with you but does not have a user or computer account on your network.

An organization typically chooses to issue Web Server certificates from a private CA when:

■ The organization must enforce its security policies and certificate policies. A certificate obtained from a commercial CA requires an organization to follow the guidelines set in the commercial CA's certification practice statement (CPS).

■ The organization wants to reduce the costs associated with issuing certificates to intranet Web servers, which accept connections only from employees or other trusted partners. In these circumstances, an organization can require employees or partners to trust the root CA of the organization's CA hierarchy. This eliminates the need to purchase Web Server certificates from a commercial organization only for internal use.

An organization typically chooses to acquire the Web Server certificates from a commercial CA when:

■ The organization has not deployed an internal public key infrastructure (PKI). By outsourcing PKI management to a commercial CA, an organization eliminates the costs associated with designing, implementing, and managing CAs and certificates for the deployment of Web Server certificates.

■ The organization uses the Web site to sell goods and services over the Internet, and the commercial CA can provide transaction liability insurance for commerce-based Web sites.

■ A commercial CA is recognized by most consumers and is included in the Trusted Root Certification Authority store for most organizations.

■ The organization wishes to deploy an Extended Validation (EV) certificate. EV certificates cause Internet Explorer's address bar to turn green indicating that the commercial provider has spent additional resources and time verifying that the person that acquired the site's SSL certificate actually represents the organization represented in the URL. Because of the additional background checking, additional charges are associated with EV certificates.

Placement of Web Server Certificates

When an organization implements SSL, the organization must choose where to deploy the Web Server certificates. The deployment location depends on the network configuration implemented by the organization. Certificate placement for common Web server deployment scenarios is discussed in the next sections.

Single Web Server

When SSL is implemented for a single Web server, the Web Server certificate must be deployed at the Web server. (See Figure 19-3.)

Figure 19-3   Deploying a Web Server certificate to a single Web server

In this scenario, the Web Server certificate must be deployed at the Web server computer. This allows the client computer to validate the Web server's identity and use the Web Server certificate's public key to encrypt the pre-master secret key when sending it to the Web server.

Clustered Web Servers

A common Web server deployment tactic is to arrange a Web site in a clustered configuration. In a clustered configuration, either a common disk exists between multiple servers, or the servers host a common Web site through a Network Load Balancing (NLB) cluster. In either case, when users connect to a specific URL, they are redirected to any one of the cluster nodes. (See Figure 19-4.)

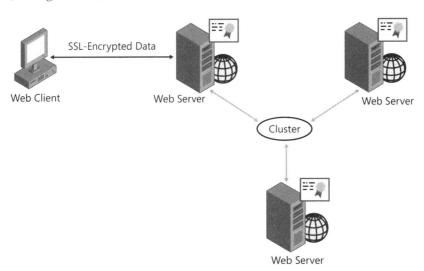

Figure 19-4   Deploying a Web Server certificate to a clustered Web server

When you implement SSL in a clustered configuration, each Web server in the cluster must have its own Web Server certificate. The only requirement is that the Web Server certificate's subject name is the DNS name used by Web clients to connect to the Web site.

> **Important**   A common misconception is that the same certificate and private key pair must be deployed at each Web server in the cluster. Each node in the cluster does require its own certificate, but it is not necessary to deploy the same certificate and key pair at each node in the cluster. If a node in the cluster fails, all Web clients connected to that node must re-establish connections to another node in the cluster. Remember that this is a new SSL connection, which requires that a new symmetric session key be negotiated between the Web client and the Web server. In fact, if you purchase your Web Server certificates from a commercial organization, such as VeriSign or RSA, you might be required to purchase separate Web Server certificates for each node.

Web Server Protected by ISA Server with Server Publishing

Microsoft Internet Security and Acceleration (ISA) Server with server publishing allows you to host a Web site behind a firewall. When you implement server publishing, all traffic that connects to the ISA Server's SSL listening port (TCP port 443) is redirected to the Web server protected by the ISA Server. (See Figure 19-5.)

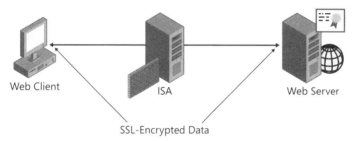

Figure 19-5   Deploying a Web Server certificate when using ISA Server publishing

In this configuration, the Web Server certificate must be installed at the Web server. The DNS name in the certificate's subject must match the DNS name used by Web clients to connect to the ISA Server's external interface. In other words, the DNS name must resolve to an Internet Protocol (IP) address bound to the ISA Server's external interface.

> **Tip**   You can also use this configuration with many industry-standard firewalls, such as Cisco PIX or Checkpoint Firewall-1, which implement port mapping to redirect inbound traffic to a server behind a firewall.

This configuration allows an organization to satisfy the technical requirement of implementing end-to-end encryption of data transmitted between the Web client and the Web server.

Web Server Protected by ISA Server with Web Publishing

ISA provides an alternate method of transmitting data to a Web server protected by a firewall. When you implement Web publishing, the data received by the ISA Server is decrypted and inspected by application filters. These application filters, such as URLScan, inspect Web traffic for worm attacks or other Web-based attacks against a Web server.

When you implement Web publishing, two certificate deployment scenarios are possible:

- Implementing end-to-end SSL
- Implementing SSL between the Web client and the computer running ISA Server

Implementing End-to-End SSL

In the first scenario, ISA Server implements SSL between the Web client and the computer running ISA Server as well as between the computer running ISA Server and the Web server. (See Figure 19-6.)

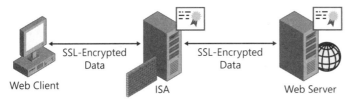

Figure 19-6   Deploying Web Server certificates when using ISA Web publishing with SSL on all connections

In this configuration, Web Server certificates must be installed at both the computer running ISA Server and at the Web server. Two separate SSL connections occur:

- The first SSL connection is between the Web client and the ISA Server. The subject of the Web Server certificate installed at the ISA Server must contain the DNS name used by the Web client to connect to the Web server, and the DNS name must resolve to the external IP address of the computer running ISA Server.

- The second SSL connection is between computer running ISA Server and the Web server. The subject of the Web Server certificate installed on the Web server must contain the DNS name or IP address indicated in the Web publishing rule at the computer running ISA Server.

Note   If your company has an SLA for performance, such as servicing 1,000 transactions per second, you can consider implementing SSL acceleration cards at the Web server and the computer running ISA Server. Otherwise, any acceleration gains made by connecting to the computer running ISA Server are lost when data is reencrypted and transmitted to the back-end Web server.

Implementing SSL Between the Web Client and Computer Running ISA Server

In the second scenario, SSL is implemented only between the Web client and computer running ISA Server. (See Figure 19-7.)

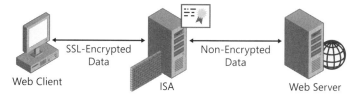

Figure 19-7   Deploying Web Server certificates when using ISA Web publishing with SSL only between the Web client and the computer running ISA Server

In this configuration, a Web Server certificate must be installed only on the computer running ISA Server. Once the application filter of the computer running ISA Server inspects the incoming HTTPS stream, the data is redirected as HTTP to the back-end Web server.

> **Note**   This scenario allows network intrusion detection systems such as Snort to inspect all data as it is transmitted to the Web server's network.

In this scenario, the subject of the Web Server certificate installed at the computer running ISA Server must contain the DNS name used by the Web client to connect to the Web server, and the DNS name must resolve to the external IP address of the computer running ISA Server.

Choosing a Certificate Template

If your organization chooses to proceed with deploying Web Server certificates to internal Web servers, the default Web Server certificate template meets the needs of most companies. Typically, the only change that must be performed is to modify certificate template permissions to enable Read and Enroll permissions at a custom universal or global group that contains Web server administration user accounts.

> **Important**   Although you can create a version 2 certificate template based on the Web Server certificate template to enable modification of application policies or certificate policies, this prevents the automated submission of the certificate request from Internet Information Services (IIS). Instead, you must generate a request file and then submit the request file to the CA, designating the custom version 2 certificate template during the submission.

Issuing Web Server Certificates

The process of requesting and issuing a Web Server certificate varies according to the type of device on which the certificate request is generated. When issuing certificates from an enterprise CA, options include:

- Issuing certificates to Web servers running IIS on domain-member computers for all domains in the forest.

- Issuing certificates to Web servers running IIS on non-domain member computers.

- Issuing certificates to third-party Web servers or hardware-based Web acceleration devices.

Issuing Web Server Certificates to Domain Members

When you issue a Web Server certificate to a domain member, the certificate request is submitted in the security context of the user performing the certificate request. The user performing the request must belong to a group assigned Read and Enroll permissions for the Web Server certificate template. In addition, the user must be a member of the local Administrators group on the Web server to allow him or her to write certificate information into the computer's local store.

Performing the Request for Windows 2000 Server and Windows Server 2003

Installation of the Web Server certificate in a domain environment is a two-step process for Microsoft Windows 2000 Server and Windows Server 2003:

1. Request and install the Web Server certificate at the Web server.

2. Configure the Web server to enable SSL encryption for a Web site or virtual server.

Requesting and Installing the Web Server Certificate   The Web Server Certificate Wizard is launched from the Internet Services Manager console in Windows 2000 and the Internet Information Services (IIS) Manager console in Windows Server 2003. The following process installs a Web Server certificate:

1. From the Start menu, point to Programs, point to Administrative Tools, and then if you are using Windows 2000, click Internet Services Manager; if you are using Windows Server 2003, click Internet Information Services (IIS) Manager.

2. In the console tree, expand *ServerName,* and then click Default Web Site.

3. Right-click Default Web Site, and then click Properties.

4. In the Default Web Site Properties dialog box, click the Directory Security tab.

5. On the Directory Security tab, in the Secure Communications section, click Server Certificate.

6. In the Web Server Certificate Wizard, click Next.

7. On the Server Certificate page, click Create A New Certificate, and then click Next.

8. On the Delayed Or Immediate Request page, click Send The Request Immediately To An Online Certification Authority, and then click Next.

> **Note**   By sending the request to an online CA, the enterprise CA decides whether to issue or deny the certificate request based on the permissions assigned to the Web Server certificate template.

9. On the Name And Security Settings page, in the Name box, type a description of the Web server, set the Bit Length to 1024, and then click Next.

> **Note**   In Windows Server 2003, you can choose which SChannel CSP to use for the Web Server certificate on the Name And Security Settings page.

10. If you are running Windows Server 2003 and you want to choose the CSP on the Available Providers page, select the CSP you want to implement, and then click Next.

> **Note**   The default providers for Web Server certificates include the Microsoft RSA/ Schannel Cryptographic Provider and the Microsoft Diffie-Hellman/SChannel Cryptographic Provider.

11. On the Organization Information page, type the organization and department name, and then click Next.

12. On the Your Site's Common Name page, in the Common Name box, type the ***DNSName*** of the Web site (where *DNSName* is the full DNS name of the Web site as typed by a Web client), and then click Next.

> **Note**   For example, use ***www.example.com*** rather than **webserver** when providing the common name for the certificate request.

13.   On the Geographical Information page, type the country, state, and city information, and then click Next.

14. If you are using IIS 6.0, on the SSL page, accept the default port of 443, and then click Next.

15. On the Choose A Certification Authority page, in the Certification Authorities drop-down list, select an available enterprise CA, and then click Next.

16. On the Certificate Request Submission page, verify the settings, and then click Next.

17. On the Completing The Web Server Certificate Wizard page, click Finish.

As you can see, there are only minute differences between the Web Server Certificate Wizard in Windows 2000 and Windows Server 2003. At the completion of this procedure, the Web Server certificate is installed in the local machine store and is available for use by IIS.

Enabling SSL at the IIS Web Server   Once you install the Web Server certificate, you can enable SSL protection for an entire Web site or for a virtual folder within a Web site. The following procedure describes the steps involved:

1. In the Internet Services Manager or Internet Information Services (IIS) Manager console tree, right-click the Web site or virtual directory where you want to enable SSL, and then click Properties.

2. In the Properties dialog box, click the Directory Security tab.

3. On the Directory Security tab, in the Secure Communications section, click the Edit button.

4. In the Secure Communications dialog box, select the Require Secure Channel (SSL) check box, select the Require 128-bit Encryption check box, and then click OK.

> **Note**   Selecting the 128-bit encryption check box is subject to international export laws. For example, the United States prohibits the export of strong encryption to embargoed countries. For details on U.S. export law changes, see "Revisions to Encryption Items," available at *http://frwebgate.access.gpo.gov/cgi-bin/getdoc.cgi?dbname=2000_register&docid=fr19oc00-5.*

5. In the Properties dialog box, click OK.

6. Close the Internet Services Manager or Internet Information Services (IIS) Manager console.

> **Note**   After you enable SSL, you should ensure that the Web site implements SSL, as required. To verify encryption, open the Web site using the URL *https://WebServerDNSName/vdir.* If 128-bit encryption is enabled, you can verify the encryption level in Internet Explorer by resting the mouse pointer over the lock icon on the window's bottom right corner. If you have enabled 128-bit encryption, the words *SSL Secured (128 Bit)* appear.

Performing the Request for Windows Server 2008

Windows Server 2008 revamps IIS and requires a different process for requesting Web Server certificates for domain-member computers. A three-step process is used as follows:

1. Request and install the Web Server certificate at the Web server.

2. Bind the certificate to a Web site.

3. Configure the Web server to enable SSL encryption for a Web site or virtual directory.

Requesting and Installing the Web Server Certificate   Windows Server 2008 has eliminated the original Web Server Certificate Wizard and instead has separate processes for domain request and offline requests. The following process uses a domain request to install a Web Server certificate:

1. From the Start menu, point to Administrative Tools, and then click Internet Information Services (IIS) Manager.

2. In the console tree, click *ServerName*.

3. In the details pane, double-click Server Certificates.

   A list of all currently installed certificates is listed in the Server Certificates pane (see Figure 19-8).

Figure 19-8   The IIS Server Certificates management screen

4. In the Actions section, click Create Domain Certificate.

5. On the Distinguished Name Properties page (see Figure 19-9), provide the following information, and then click Next.

   ❑ Common Name: **DNSName** of the Web site (where *DNSName* is the full DNS name of the Web site as typed by a Web client)

> **Tip**   For example, use **www.example.com** rather than **webserver** when providing the common name for the certificate request.

   ❑ Organization: The name of the organization represented in the Web site

   ❑ Organizational Unit: The department managing the Web server

   ❑ City/Locality: The city where the Web server is located

   ❑ State/Province: The state or province where the Web server is located

   ❑ Country/Region. The two-letter abbreviation for the country where the Web server is located

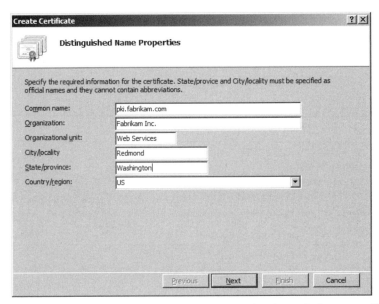

Figure 19-9   Configuring the name properties for the Web Server certificate

6.   On the Online Certification Authority page, click Select.

7.   In the Select Certification Authority page, select the target CA for the certificate submission, and then click OK.

8.   On the Online Certification Authority page, in the Friendly Name box, type a logical name for the certificate (for example, Certificate Services SSL), and then click Finish.

Binding the Web Server Certificate to the Web Site   Once you have requested the Web Server certificate, you must bind the certificate to a Web site. You can bind any of the available Web Server certificates listed in the Server Certificate pane.

To bind a Web Server certificate, use the following procedure:

1.   Ensure that you are in the Internet Information Services (IIS) Manager console.

2.   In the console tree, expand *ServerName*, expand sites, and then click the target site. For example, you can select the Default Web Site.

3.   Right-click the target site, and then click Edit Bindings.

4.   In the Site Bindings dialog box, determine if there is already a site binding for HTTPS.

     ❏   If there is a binding for HTTPS, select the HTTPS binding, and then click Edit.

     ❏   If there is no binding for HTTPS, click Add.

5.   In the Add Site Binding dialog box (see Figure 19-10), set the binding Type to HTTPS, assign either a specific IP address or all unassigned IP addresses, accept the default

port (443), and then in the SSL certificate drop-down list, select the certificate assigned the friendly name in the certificate request process, and then click OK.

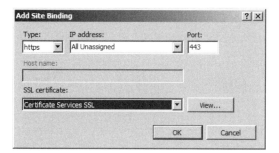

Figure 19-10   Binding the Web Server certificate to the Web site

> **Tip**   If you are unsure, you can view the certificate to confirm the subject name of the certificate.

6. In the Site Binding dialog box, click Close.

Enabling SSL   The final step is to enable SSL for the entire Web site, for an application, or for a virtual directory. Use the following procedure:

1. Ensure that you are in the Internet Information Services (IIS) Manager console.

2. In the console tree, expand *ServerName*, expand sites, and then click the target site or expand the site to select a specific application or virtual directory. For example, on a CA you can select the Certsrv application.

3. On the SiteName Home page, double-click SSL Settings.

4. On the SSL Settings dialog box, select the Require SSL check box, select the Require 128-bit SSL check box, and then in the Actions list, click Apply.

Issuing Web Server Certificates to Non-Forest Members

When you issue a Web Server certificate to a non-forest member, the certificate request cannot be submitted to the Windows Server 2008 CA directly. Instead, the certificate request must be saved to a PKCS #10 request file and then submitted to the CA by a member of the managing organization.

> **Note**   This process is the same as when you submit a Web Server certificate request to a commercial CA organization, such as VeriSign or RSA. The only difference is in the certificate issuance, which varies depending on the type of CA used by the commercial CA.

The installation of the Web Server certificate to a non-forest member is a four-step process, as follows:

1. Generate a Web Server certificate request at the Web server.

2. Submit the Web Server certificate request to the CA.

3. Install the issued Web Server certificate at the Web server.

4. Configure the Web server to enable SSL encryption for a Web site or virtual directory.

> **Note**   There is no difference in enabling SSL encryption at an IIS Web server when the certificate is installed on a forest member versus a non-forest member. For details on how to enable and verify SSL encryption, see the section "Enabling SSL at the IIS Web Server" earlier in this chapter.

This process can also be used if you wish to use a different certificate template than the default Web Server certificate template. Generating a request allows you to use a custom certificate template when you submit the request to the CA.

Generating the Web Server Certificate Request

The method used to generate the Web Server certificate request varies depending on the version of IIS you are using.

Generating a Request for Windows 2000 and Windows Server 2003   The Web Server Certificate Wizard is launched from the Internet Services Manager console in Windows 2000 and the Internet Information Services (IIS) Manager console in Windows Server 2003. The following process generates a Web Server certificate request file:

1. From the Start menu, point to Programs, point to Administrative Tools, and then if you are using Windows 2000, click Internet Services Manager; if you are using Windows Server 2003, click Internet Information Services (IIS) Manager.

2. In the console tree, expand *ServerName,* and then click Default Web Site.

3. Right-click Default Web Site, and then click Properties.

4. In the Default Web Site Properties dialog box, click the Directory Security tab.

5. On the Directory Security tab, in the Secure Communications section, click Server Certificate.

6. In the Web Server Certificate Wizard, click Next.

7. On the Server Certificate page, click Create A New Certificate, and then click Next.

8. On the Delayed Or Immediate Request page, click Prepare The Request Now, But Send It Later, and then click Next.

> **Note**   By generating the certificate request, you can submit the request to any CA, whether it is a Microsoft enterprise CA, a Microsoft standalone CA, or a commercial CA. The PKCS #10 request format file is interoperable with any (standards compliant) CA.

9. On the Name And Security Settings page, in the Name box, type a description of the Web server, set the Bit Length to 1024, and then click Next.

> **Note**   In Windows Server 2003, you can choose the SChannel CSP for the Web Server certificate on the Name And Security Settings page.

10. If you are running Windows Server 2003 and you want to choose the CSP on the Available Providers page, select the CSP you want to implement, and then click Next.

11. On the Organization Information page, type the organization and department name, and then click Next:

   ❏ Organization: *Organization Name*

   ❏ Organizational unit: *Department Name*

12. On the Your Site's Common Name page, in the Common Name box, type the *DNSName* of the Web site (where *DNSName* is the full DNS name of the Web site as typed by a Web client), and then click Next.

13. On the Geographical Information page, type the country, state, and city names, and then click Next:

14. On the Certificate Request File Name page, in the File Name box, type a file path and name for the PKCS #10 request file, and then click Next.

15. On the Request File Summary page, verify the settings, and then click Next.

16. On the Completing The Web Server Certificate Wizard page, click Finish.

Generating a Request for Windows Server 2008   Windows Server 2008 modifies the way you generate offline requests. Use the following process to generate an offline Web Server certificate request:

1. From the Start menu, point to Administrative Tools, and then click Internet Information Services (IIS) Manager.

2. In the console tree, click *ServerName*.

3. In the details pane, double-click Server Certificates.

4. In the Actions section, click Create Certificate Request.

5. On the Distinguished Name Properties page (as previously shown in Figure 19-9), provide the naming information for the certificate, and then click Next.

> **Warning**   The most critical component of the name is the common name. Make sure that you input the *DNS* name that people will use to connect to the Web site. A mismatched name will lead to certificate warning errors during connection attempts.

6.   On the Cryptographic Service Provider page, choose an available SChannel CSP, specify the bit length for the certificate's keys, and then click Next.

7.   On the File Name page, provide a name for the request file, and then click Finish.

Submitting the Request File

The previous procedures result in a request file, which can be e-mailed to a commercial provider or submitted through a form on the provider's Web site for certificate issuance.

If the certificate is to be issued by a Windows Server 2003 or Windows Server 2003 enterprise CA updated with the Windows Server 2008 certificate enrollment pages, the following procedure issues and verifies the certificate:

> **Note**   If you are connecting from a client computer running Windows Vista or Windows Server 2008, you must update the Certificate Services Web Enrollment pages as discussed in Chapter 15, "Issuing Certificates." The default Windows Server 2003 Web Enrollment pages do not support CertEnroll requests.

1.   Retrieve the request file generated in the previous procedure.

2.   Log on at a computer running Windows as a user assigned Read and Enroll permissions for the Web Server certificate template.

3.   Open Internet Explorer.

4.   In Internet Explorer, open the URL *http://CADNSName/certsrv* (where *CADNSName* is the DNS name of the enterprise CA computer).

5.   On the Welcome page, click the Request A Certificate link.

6.   On the Advanced Certificate Request page, click the Submit A Certificate Request By Using A Base 64–Encoded CMC or PKCS #10 File, Or Submit A Renewal Request By Using A Base 64–Encoded PKCS #7 File link.

7.   On the Submit A Certificate Request Or Renewal Request page, provide the following information:

      ❑   Saved Request: Paste the request file's contents into the Base 64–Encoded Certificate Request box.

> **Note**   You can open the request file in Notepad, select all the file's contents by pressing Ctrl+A, and copy it to the clipboard by pressing Ctrl+C. The contents of the file can be copied into the Base 64–encoded certificate request by clicking in the box and pressing Ctrl+V.

- ❑ Certificate Template: Web Server or a custom certificate template.

- ❑ Additional Attributes: No input is required

8. On the Submit A Certificate Request Or Renewal Request page, click Submit.

9. On the Certificate Issued page, select Base 64–Encoded, and then click Download Certificate Chain.

10. In the File Download dialog box, click Save.

11. In the Save As dialog box, provide a file name, and then click Save.

> **Note**   The Download Certificate Chain link downloads the certificate chain for the Web Server certificate, including the root CA certificate and any intermediate CA certificates in the certificate chain. These certificates are necessary to add the root CA as a trusted root CA at the Web server and to install any intermediate CA certificates and the issuing CA certificate into the Intermediate Certification Authorities store.

12. Close Internet Explorer.

> **Tip**   To increase the security of the Web server request, you can configure a custom certificate template that requires CA Certificate Manager approval. The request is then pended until a certificate manager approves the request.

Installing the Web Server Certificate at the Web Server

Once you download the Web Server certificate chain, you must complete the installation of the certificate *and chain* at the Web server. The completion of the request differs based on whether the Web server is running Windows Server 2003 or Windows Server 2008.

Installing a Web Server Certificate on Windows 2000 or Windows Server 2003   The following procedure completes the Web Server certificate request on a Windows 2000 or Windows Server 2003 Web server:

1. From the Start menu, point to Programs, point to Administrative Tools, and then if you are using Windows 2000, click Internet Services Manager; if you are using Windows Server 2003, click Internet Information Services (IIS) Manager.

2. In the console tree, expand *ServerName,* and then click Default Web Site.

3. Right-click Default Web Site, and then click Properties.

4. In the Default Web Site Properties dialog box, click the Directory Security tab.

5. On the Directory Security tab, in the Secure Communications section, click Server Certificate.

6. In the Web Server Certificate Wizard, click Next.

7. On the Pending Certificate Request page, click Process The Pending Request And Install the Certificate, and then click Next.

8. On the Process A Pending Request page, in the Path And File Name box, type the path and file name to the CA certificate chain file (*.p7b), and then click Next.

9. If you are using IIS 6.0, on the SSL Port page, in the SSL Port This Web Site Should Use box, type **443**, and then click Next.

10. On the Certificate Summary page, review the details of the certificate, and then click Next.

11. On the Completing The Web Server Certificate Wizard page, click Finish.

> **Tip** By changing the defaults to designate the PKCS #7 file containing the Web server's certificate chain, you complete two steps in one. You install the Web Server certificate at the Web server, and you install all certificates in the certificate chain to the local machine store, allowing the Web server to trust the root CA certificate.

At this point, you can enable the Web site or a virtual directory within the Web site for SSL protection, as discussed earlier in the chapter.

Installing a Web Server Certificate on Windows Server 2008 The following procedure completes the Web Server certificate request on a Windows Server 2008 Web server:

1. From the Start menu, point to Administrative Tools, and then click Internet Information Services (IIS) Manager.

2. In the console tree, click *ServerName*.

3. In the details pane, double-click Server Certificates.

4. In the Default Web Site Properties dialog box, click the Directory Security tab.

5. In the Actions section, click Complete Certificate Request.

6. On the Specify Certificate Authority Response page, provide the PKCS #7 certificate chain file name, provide a friendly name for the certificate, and then click OK.

Tip   By changing the defaults to designate the PKCS #7 file containing the Web server's certificate chain, you complete two steps in one. You install the Web Server certificate at the Web server, and you install all certificates in the certificate chain to the local machine store, allowing the Web server to trust the root CA certificate.

At this point, you can bind the Web Server certificate to a Web site and then implement SSL protection, as discussed earlier in the chapter.

Issuing Web Server Certificates to Third-Party Web Servers and Web Acceleration Devices

In many organizations, Web servers other than IIS are used for Web applications. Although the Web servers are not Microsoft Web servers, there is nothing preventing the Web servers from receiving their Web Server certificate from a Windows Server 2008 CA.

When a Web Server certificate is required on a third-party Web server or a Web acceleration appliance, the same process is required to enable SSL at the Web server or appliance as for a non-domain member IIS server. To implement SSL at the Web server or appliance, you must:

1. Generate a key pair and Web Server certificate request at the third-party Web server or device using the tools provided by the third-party Web server or device.

2. Submit the Web Server certificate request to the Windows Server 2008 CA.

3. Install the issued Web Server certificate at the third-party Web server or device.

4. Enable SSL at the third-party Web server or device.

Note   For detailed information on the procedure for your Web server or network appliance, review the documentation for the server or appliance, focusing on generating certificate requests and installing certificates at the server or device.

Certificate-Based Authentication

In addition to implementing SSL encryption, a Web server can implement certificate-based authentication. Rather than typing credentials or simply being connected to a Web site anonymously, users select a certificate from their certificate store with the Client Authentication Enhanced Key Usage (EKU) for authentication. The certificate is associated to a user account in IIS's available account databases through a process known as *mapping*. There are two types of mappings:

■ **Explicit mapping**   The certificate is mapped directly in the properties of a user's Active Directory Domain Services (AD DS) account.

■ **Implicit mapping**   The certificate is mapped to a user account based on the information included in either the Subject or the Subject Alternate Name extension. For example, when AD DS mapping is implemented, the Subject Alternate Name must include the user principal name (UPN) name form.

> **Note**   Implicit mappings require that the certificate of the CA that issues the user's certificate be included in the NTAuth object in AD DS.

Whatever mapping method is used to associate the presented certificate with a user account, the user presenting the certificate must have access to the certificate's private key to prove his or her identity. Just having the access to the certificate is insufficient because the certificate is a public document. Possession of the private key proves that the user is the certificate's subject.

Defining Certificate Mapping

When you define certificate mapping, you can choose to implement either one-to-one mappings, where each certificate is directly mapped to a single user account, or many-to-one mappings, where a group of certificates with common attributes is mapped to a single user account.

One-to-One Mappings

In one-to-one certificate mappings, you are defining a direct relationship between a certificate and an account in AD DS. Once the Web server validates the presented certificate, the certificate's private key holder is identified as a user account mapped to the certificate. The user is granted any rights or permissions assigned to the associated account.

Many-to-One Mappings

In many-to-one mappings, multiple certificates are mapped to a single user account by rules specified in AD DS. If the certificate matches the rule set defined in AD DS, and a user holds the private key associated with the certificate, he or she is assigned the rights and permissions assigned to the associated account.

For example, your organization might have a partnership with Fabrikam, Inc. All users who require access to your organization's extranet Web site have received a client authentication certificate with a subject in the form OU=Employees,DC=Fabrikam,DC=com. When you define the many-to-one relationship, you specify that any certificate that has CN=*, OU=Employees,DC=Fabrikam,DC=com as its subject maps to a user account in your directory named Fabrikam User.

Note   When you define a many-to-one mapping, you cannot differentiate individual users connecting to your Web site. Auditing shows access only by user accounts included in the many-to-one mapping. If you require auditing of each person's access to a Web site, you must define one-to-one mappings.

Combining One-to-One and Many-to-One Mappings

If you define both one-to-one and many-to-one mappings, a one-to-one mapping takes precedence. This allows you to define one-to-one mappings for specific users you want to track when they connect to your Web site, yet it grants universal access to other users whose certificate matches a many-to-one mapping.

For example, if you define a one-to-one mapping for Andy Ruth (CN=Andy Ruth,OU=Employees, DC=fabrikam,DC=com) and a many-to-one mapping for anyone with a certificate issued by the CA whose subject is CN=Fabrikam Employees CA,OU=Employees,DC=fabrikam, DC=com, Andy's one-to-one mapping takes precedence, even though his certificate is a match for both mapping rules.

Performing Certificate-Based Authentication

IIS can use AD DS as its mapping directory. As mentioned earlier, the advantage of using AD DS is that the mapping is available on multiple Web servers (as long as they are members of the forest) and can be used by applications other than Web browsers.

The following steps enable IIS to use Active Directory mapping:

1.   Create a certificate template for user authentication.
2.   Define the mappings in AD DS.
3.   Enable IIS to use certificate mapping.
4.   Enable the directory service mapper.

Creating a Certificate Template

The first step in setting up a certificate mapping in AD DS is to design a certificate template that allows a user to authenticate in a Web browser. The user certificate must meet the following requirements:

- The certificate must be a signing certificate that implements the Digital Signature key usage.
- The certificate must include the Client Authentication (1.3.6.1.5.5.7.3.2) object identifier (OID).

> **Note**   The default Authenticated Session certificate template satisfies these requirements without providing additional capabilities. If you want to create a custom authentication certificate template, it is recommended that you duplicate the Authenticated Session certificate template and make any further customizations. Alternatively, if you want to use a smart card for authentication, the Smart Card Login certificate template meets these requirements.

Defining the Mapping in Active Directory Domain Services

You might have to define certificate mapping in AD DS. The decision on whether to define mapping is often based on the answers to the following questions:

- **Is the certificate issued by an enterprise CA in your forest?**   If so, the certificate contains the user's UPN in the Subject Alternative Name extension, and the CA's certificate is included in the NTAuth store of AD DS. This enables the ability to use implicit mappings.

- **Is the certificate issued by a foreign CA?**   If the CA is not from your forest, you must set up an explicit mapping to enable certificate-based authentication. In addition, you must add the foreign CA's certificate to the NTAuth store and ensure that the certificate's Subject or Subject Alternative Name contains the user's user principal name (UPN).

Enabling Implicit Certificate Mappings

If you intend to use a certificate based on the Authenticated Session or Smart Card Login certificate templates, you can implement implicit certificate mappings. For an implicit certificate mapping, you only have to ensure that the issuing CA is in the NTAuth store. You can verify this using the following procedure:

1. Log on as a member of the Enterprise Admins group at an enterprise CA on the network.

2. Open the PKI Health Tool (Pkiview.msc).

3. In the PKI Health Tool, in the console tree, right-click Enterprise PKI, and then click Manage AD Containers.

4. In the Manage AD Containers dialog box, on the NTAuthCertificates tab, ensure that the issuing CA's certificate appears. If the CA certificate does not appear, click Add.

5. In the Open dialog box, in the File Name box, type the file location of the issuing CA certificate, and then click Open.

6. In the Manage AD Containers dialog box, click OK.

7. Close the PKI Health Tool.

Enabling Explicit Mappings

To enable an explicit mapping in AD DS, the user holding the private key associated with a client authentication certificate must provide you with access to the certificate. He or she can do this by simply e-mailing the certificate to you or by copying the certificate to a removable device and providing access to you.

> **Note**   Even if you define an explicit mapping for a certificate, SChannel will attempt to perform an implicit mapping based on the certificate's subject before determining if an explicit mapping exists.

Once you obtain the certificate, you can define the explicit mapping in AD DS as follows:

1. Log on as a user who is delegated the permissions to modify the target user account.

2. Open Active Directory Users And Computers.

3. In the View menu, click Advanced Features.

4. In the console tree, navigate to the container or OU in which the user account you want to associate with the certificate exists. You might have to create this user account.

5. In the details pane, right-click the user account, and then click Name Mappings.

6. In the Security Identity Mapping dialog box, on the X.509 Certificates tab, click Add.

7. In the Add Certificate dialog box, in the File Name box, type the path and file name of the user's certificate file, and then click Open.

8. In the Add Certificate dialog box, verify the subject and issuer information. In this dialog box you can choose whether to implement a one-to-one or a many-to-one mapping:

    ❑ If you select the Use Subject For Alternate Security Identity check box, you are enabling a one-to-one mapping. The certificate must contain the designated subject information for the mapping to occur.

    ❑ If you deselect the Use Subject For Alternate Security Identity check box, you are enabling a many-to-one mapping. The certificate must contain the designated issuer information for the mapping to occur.

> **Note**   If you choose to implement a many-to-one mapping, a dialog box appears warning you that you cannot switch the mapping back to a one-to-one mapping without redefining the mapping. The subject information is lost once you deselect the Use Subject For Alternate Security Identity check box.

9. In the Security Identity Mapping dialog box, click OK.

> **Important**   Explicit mappings cannot be used for smart card logon. Smart card logon uses only an implicit mapping by mapping the UPN in the Subject Alternative Name of the certificate to the UPN of a user account in AD DS. Explicit mappings can be used for Web authentication, wireless authentication, and VPN authentication.

Once you have defined the certificate mappings in AD DS, you must enable certificate-based authentication in Internet Information Services (IIS).

Enabling Windows Server 2003 to Use Certificate Mapping

After defining all of the required certificate mappings, you must enable the IIS 6.0 server to enable certificate-based authentication by using the following procedure:

1. Open the Internet Information Services (IIS) Manager.

2. In the console tree, navigate to the Web site or virtual directory where you want to enable certificate-based authentication.

3. In the Properties dialog box, on the Directory Security tab, in the Secure Communications section, click Edit.

4. In the Secure Communications dialog box, ensure that the following settings are enabled to enforce certificate-based authentication:

    ❑ **Require secure channel (SSL): Enabled**   Certificate-based authentication is a mutual authentication between the client and the server. You must have SSL enabled to enable server authentication.

    ❑ **Require client certificates: Selected**   This option enforces certificate-based authentication. If you want to provide alternate methods of authentication, such as Windows Integrated Authentication, you can choose Accept Client Certificates instead.

    ❑ **Enable client certificate mapping: Enabled**   This option enables the Web site to perform certificate mapping.

5. In the Secure Communications dialog box, click OK

6. In the Properties dialog box, click OK.

> ## Preventing Other Forms of Authentication
> You can further restrict the Web site to disallow other forms of authentication. This is accomplished by disabling all other authentication methods for the Web site or virtual directory, as follows.
>
> 1. Open the Internet Information Services (IIS) Manager.

2. In the console tree, navigate to the Web site or virtual directory where you want to enable certificate mapping.

3. In the Properties dialog box, on the Directory Security tab, in the Anonymous Access And Authentication Control section, click Edit.

4. In the Authentication Methods dialog box, deselect all check boxes, and then click OK.

> **Note** This configuration disables all other forms of authentication. If certificate-based authentication fails, the user is no longer provided with an alternative authentication method.

5. In the Properties dialog box, click OK.

> **Note** In addition, you must configure the NTFS permissions on the folder where the Web content exists to limit access to groups in which there are authorized users. The permissions assigned must allow the user to perform the tasks required by the Web site.

Once you enable certificate mapping for the Web site or virtual directory, you must enable the Windows directory service mapper. The Windows directory service mapper enables the Web server to query AD DS to determine the certificate mapping. To do this, perform the following steps:

1. Open the Internet Information Services (IIS) Manager.

2. In the console tree, right-click Web Sites, and then click Properties.

3. In the Web Sites Properties dialog box, on the Directory Security tab, click Enable The Windows Directory Service Mapper, and then click OK.

4. Close Internet Information Services (IIS) Manager.

Enabling Windows Server 2008 to Use Certificate Mapping

Windows Server 2008 implements greater Web server security than previous versions of Windows. Rather than installing all forms of authentication supported by the Web server, you must select exactly what forms of authentication are supported when you configure role services. To ensure that client certificate mapping authentication is enabled on the Web server, use the following procedure:

1. Log on as a member of the local Administrators group.

2. From Administrative Tools, open Server Manager.

3. In the console tree, expand roles, and then click Web Server (IIS).

4. In the details pane, in the Role Services section, in the Security group, determine whether Client Certificate Mapping Authentication is installed. If it is installed, this task is complete; otherwise continue with step 5.

5. In the Role Services section, click Add Role Services.

6. On the Select Role Services page, in the Security section, select the Client Certificate Mapping Authentication check box, and then click Next.

7. On the Confirm Installation Selections page, click Install.

8. On the Installation Results page, ensure that the installation is successful, and then click Close.

Once client certificate mapping is installed, you must enable Active Directory Client Certification Authentication as a valid form of authentication for the Web server. This is accomplished by specifying the Authentication methods supported by the Web server, as shown in the following procedure:

1. Log on as a member of the local Administrators group.

2. From Administrative Tools, open Internet Information Services (IIS) Manager.

3. In the console tree, click *ServerName*.

4. In the details pane, in the IIS section, double-click Authentication.

5. In the details pane, right-click Active Directory Client Certification Authentication, and then click Enable.

This enables mapping of certificates to AD DS for all Web sites and virtual directories hosted on the Web server. Once you have enabled Active Directory certificate mapping, the last step is to enforce certificate-based authentication for the your Web site or virtual directory. As with the Windows Server 2003 example, the following procedure will disable all other forms of authentication:

1. Log on as a member of the local Administrators group.

2. From Administrative Tools, open Internet Information Services (IIS) Manager.

3. In the console tree, expand *ServerName*, expand Sites, and then select the site or virtual directory for which you wish to enforce certificate-based authentication.

4. In the details pane, double-click SSL Settings.

> **Note**   This procedure assumes that you have already assigned an SSL certificate to the Web site.

5. In the details pane, in the SSL Settings section, enable the following options to enforce certificate-based authentication.

    ❑ Require SSL: **Enabled**

    ❑ Require 128-bit SSL: **Enabled**

    ❑ Client certificates: **Require**

6. In the Actions pane, click Apply.

7. In the console tree, double-click the Web site or virtual directory you are securing.

8. In the details pane, double-click Authentication.

9. In the details pane, in the Authentication section, disable all forms of authentication available for the Web site.

> **Note**   As with Windows Server 2003, this enforces the requirement that only certificate-based authentication is supported. The Web server will *not* fall back to other forms of authentication.

10. Close the Internet Information Services (IIS) Manager console.

Connecting to the Web Site

Once you have enforced certificate-based authentication, it is recommended to test the Web site. Assuming that you have acquired a client authentication certificate, the following process is used to connect to the Web site:

1. Log on as a user authorized through NTFS permissions to connect to the Web site.

2. Open Internet Explorer.

> **Note**   Certificate-based authentication is *not* limited to Internet Explorer. I have used both Firefox and Mozilla on Linux systems to connect to a secured Web site with certificate-based authentication.

3. In the address bar, type the URL for the secure Web site.

4. In the Choose A Digital Certificate dialog box (see Figure 19-11), select an authentication certificate, and then click OK.

> **Note**   If more than one certificate appears, you must select a certificate that is valid for the one-to-one or many-to-one mapping defined in AD DS.

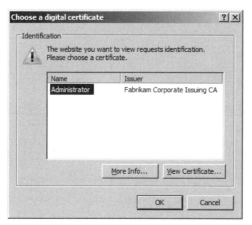

Figure 19-11   Selecting an authentication certificate in Internet Explorer

5.   The Web site opens, providing certificate-based authentication access to the Web site.

Controlling Certificate Selection Behavior

Internet Explorer allows you to specify what happens when only a single certificate (as shown previously in Figure 19-11) is available for authentication. Rather than presenting the certificate (the default behavior), you can configure Internet Explorer to automatically use the certificate if only one valid certificate is found, using the following procedure:

1.   Open Internet Explorer.

2.   From the Tools menu, select Internet Options.

3.   On the Security tab, select the Security Zone in which the Web Site exists, and then click Custom Level.

4.   In the Security Settings–*ZoneName* dialog box, change the Don't Prompt For Client Certificate Selection When No Certificates Or Only One Certificate Exists to Enable.

5.   In the Security Settings–*ZoneName* dialog box, click OK.

6.   In the Internet Options dialog box, click OK.

Enable this option only in the Local Intranet or Trusted Sites zones. It is never recommended to enable automatic certificate selection in the Internet or Restricted Sites zones.

Case Study: The Phone Company

You manage the IIS Server for The Phone Company, a large telephone company with major offices in Toronto, Amsterdam, and Dallas. The Phone Company has a two-tier CA hierarchy with an offline root CA, named The Phone Company Root CA, at the Dallas office and three second-tier issuing CAs at the Toronto, Amsterdam, and Dallas offices. The CAs are named:

- The Phone Company Canadian Issuing CA
- The Phone Company American Issuing CA
- The Phone Company Dutch Issuing CA

The offline root CA is a standalone root CA owned and managed by The Phone Company, and the issuing CAs are members of the thephone-company.com forest and are configured as enterprise subordinate CAs.

Scenario

The Phone Company has two new Web-based applications you must deploy in the next month, and SSL is identified as a requirement for both Web-based applications.

The Customer Billing System

The first Web-based application is a customer bill reporting system that must be available to all customers by viewing *www.thephone-company.com/billing*.

When customers connect to the Web page, they must enter their telephone number and assigned personal identification number (PIN) in a Web-based form to authenticate with the application. Once authenticated, customers can view their phone records for the past six months as well as make changes to their calling plans.

The computer that hosts the customer billing system Web site is at the Dallas office and is assigned the NetBIOS name DALTXIIS01. The DALTXIIS01 Web server is protected by a Cisco PIX. (See Figure 19-12.) All traffic received on TCP port 443, the SSL port, is redirected to the DALTXIIS01 server with no content inspection by the Cisco PIX firewall.

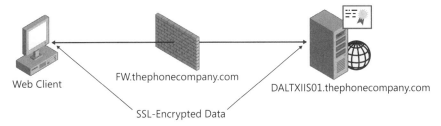

Figure 19-12   The customer billing application Web server network infrastructure

The Benefits Web Application

The second Web-based application is an internal application that allows The Phone Company's employees to review and modify their benefits.

To allow high-availability, the benefits Web site, *https://benefits.thephone-company.com*, is deployed using an NLB cluster with the three Web servers—DALTXIIS02, AMSNLIIS01, and TORONIIS01—located at the Dallas, Amsterdam, and Toronto offices. (See Figure 19-13.) The three Web servers are members of thephone-company.com domain.

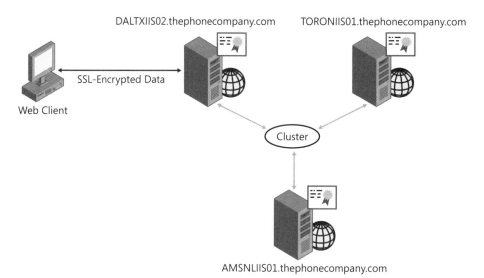

Figure 19-13   The customer billing application Web server network infrastructure

Only The Phone Company employees can access the benefits Web site. To provide enhanced password security, employees can access the Web site only by using their smart card certificate. Employees use their existing The Phone Company smart cards, based on the Smart Card User certificate template.

Case Study Questions

1. Which CA should issue the Web Server certificate for the customer billing system Web site?

2. Which CA should issue the Web Server certificate for the employee benefits Web site?

3. Where should the Web Server certificate(s) be deployed for the customer billing system Web site?

4. Where should the Web Server certificate(s) be deployed for the employee benefits Web site?

5. How do you implement certificate mapping for the customer billing Web site?

6. If you perform an implicit certificate mapping, what form of name must be included in the Subject or the Subject Alternative Name extension of the user certificate? Does the Smart Card User certificate template satisfy this condition?

7. What subject is required for the Web Server certificate for the customer billing system Web site?

8. What subjects are required for the Web Server certificate for the employee benefits Web site?

Best Practices

- **Implement Web Server certificates from a private CA if the Web server is an intranet server.**   An intranet server is accessed only by computers and users within your organization. It is possible to deploy the trusted root certificate to an organization's computers through enterprise policy, Group Policy, or CAPICOM scripts.

- Implement Web Server certificates from a commercial CA when:

  - ❏ **The Web server is on the Internet or on an extranet.**   If the Web server is accessed by non-organization–managed computers or users, you increase trust in your Web site by deploying a Web Server certificate from a commercial CA.

  - ❏ **The Web server is selling goods or services on the Internet.**   A commercial CA certificate can provide liability insurance for e-commerce transactions on the Web server.

- **Enable SSL for only those Web sites that require enhanced security.**   There is extra performance overhead involved in connecting to a Web server implementing SSL. Implement SSL only in cases where you must prove the Web server's identity or provide encryption to data transmitted between the Web server and the Web client.

- **Ensure that all Web clients trust the root CA certificate of the Web Server's certificate chain.**   If the Web Server certificate chains to a nontrusted root CA, users are warned that the certificate is not trusted, which can prevent them from connecting to the Web site.

- **Ensure that the Web Server certificate's subject matches the Web server's DNS name.**   If the subject name does not match the Web site's DNS name, the user is warned.

Additional Information

- Microsoft Official Curriculum, Course 2821: "Designing and Managing a Windows Public Key Infrastructure" (*http://www.microsoft.com/learning/syllabi/en-us/2821Afinal.mspx*)

- "Windows Server 2008 Security Resource Kit" (*http://www.microsoft.com/MSPress/books/11841.aspx*)

- "IIS 7.0 Portal Resources" (*http://www.iis.net/default.aspx?tabid=7*)

- Brett Hill's IIS Blog (*http://brettblog.com/*)

- "SSL Diagnostics Version 1.0" (*http://www.microsoft.com/downloads/details.aspx? FamilyId=CABEA1D0-5A10-41BC-83D4-06C814265282&displaylang=en*)

- "Configuring Server Certificates for SSL" (*http://www.microsoft.com/technet/prodtechnol/ WindowsServer2003/Library/IIS/ca7be648-02cb-4cf2-a7a5-56c507707114.mspx?mfr=true*)

- 308160 "How To: Configure Internet Information Services Web Authentication in Windows Server 2003"

- 313070: "How To: Configure Client Certificate Mappings in Internet Information Service 5.0"

- 324069: "How To: Set Up an HTTPS Service in IIS"

- 324276: "How To: Configure Internet Information Services Web Authentication in Windows Server 2003"

- 330211: "ActiveX Error Messages Using Certificate Enrollment Web Pages to Enroll a Smart Card in Internet Explorer"

- 310178 "How To: Install Imported Certificates on a Web Server in Windows Server 2003"

- 332077: "IIS 6.0: Computer Must Trust All Certification Authorities Trusted by Individual Sites"

- 813618: "Security Alert: The Name of the Security Certificate Is Invalid or Does Not Match the Name of the Site"

- 816794: "How To: Install Imported Certificates on a Web Server in Windows Server 2003"

Note   The last nine articles in the above list can be accessed through the Microsoft Knowledge Base. Go to *http://support.microsoft.com*, and enter the article number in the Search The Knowledge Base text box.

Chapter 20

Encrypting File System

Encrypting File System (EFS) provides a method to encrypt files on a local file system in Microsoft Windows 2000, Windows XP, Windows Vista, and Windows Server 2008. Whereas Windows 2000 and Windows XP were primarily used for local file encryption, the enhancement for EFS in Windows Vista and Windows Server 2008 will allow easy and consistent use of EFS on both local and remote locations.

This chapter will focus on the public key infrastructure (PKI) aspects of deploying EFS on your organization's network. There are many more design decisions that must be addressed before you enable EFS. For a larger discussion of those decisions, see the article "Encrypting File System in Windows XP and Windows Server 2003," available at *http://www.microsoft.com/technet/prodtechnol/winxppro/deploy/cryptfs.mspx.*

 Note This chapter will demonstrate how to distribute certificates based on custom version 2 templates with the required Encrypting File System object identifier (OID) to users so that the certificate exists in their certificate store when they attempt to encrypt their first file. This certificate is typically distributed through Autoenrollment Settings so that the certificate exists in the user's certificate store prior to file encryption.

EFS Processes

Before addressing the PKI-related design decisions for EFS, it's important to understand how EFS protects data on client computers running Windows 2000, Windows XP, or Windows Vista. This section looks at the following processes:

- How Windows chooses an EFS encryption certificate
- The EFS encryption process for a local file
- The EFS encryption process for files stored on a remote file server
- The EFS decryption process
- The EFS recovery process

How Windows Chooses an EFS Encryption Certificate

When a user performs the first file encryption using EFS, the following process takes place to designate or acquire an EFS-enabled certificate:

1. The user's registry is queried to determine whether a certificate is currently designated as the default EFS encryption certificate.

> **Note**   The actual registry value queried is *HKEY_CURRENT_USER\Software\Microsoft\ Windows NT\CurrentVersion\EFS\CurrentKeys\CertificateHash*. This registry value contains the contents of the thumbprint property of the designated EFS encryption certificate.

2. If a default certificate is not designated, EFS must determine whether the user has an acceptable certificate for EFS encryption (before encrypting a file), as follows:

    a. The user's certificate store is queried to determine whether a certificate exists with the Encrypting File System object identifier (OID): 1.3.6.1.4.1.311.10.3.4. If a certificate is found with this OID in the application policy or Enhanced Key Usage (EKU) extension, this certificate is designated as the EFS encryption certificate.

    b. If no certificate is found with the Encrypting File System OID, and the computer is a member of a domain, an automated request for an EFS certificate is sent, one at a time, to each enterprise CA in the forest. For Windows 2000 and Windows XP clients, the certificate requested is a Basic EFS certificate. For Windows Vista, you can designate the default certificate by using Group Policy. When the certificate is enrolled successfully, it is designated as the EFS encryption certificate in the user's registry.

    c. If the Basic EFS certificate template is not available at an enterprise CA, or the computer is not a member of a domain, EFS generates a self-signed certificate with the Encrypting File System OID. The self-signed certificate is issued by and to the user. It is then designated as the default EFS encryption certificate in the user's registry.

> **Note**   You can now prevent the generation of a self-signed certificate for Windows XP SP2 and Windows Vista. For Windows XP clients, you must obtain the security update described in Microsoft Knowledge Base article 912761: "Encrypting File System (EFS) Generates a Self-signed Certificate When You Try to Encrypt an EFS File on a Windows XP-based Computer." For a Windows Vista client, Group Policy allows you to prevent generation of self-signed certificates.

Local EFS Encryption

Once an EFS encryption certificate is designated, the EFS encryption process can begin. (See Figure 20-1.)

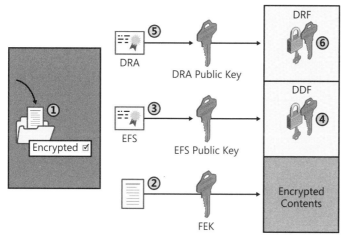

Figure 20-1   The EFS encryption process

1. A user must choose to encrypt a file. This can be done by enabling an individual file for EFS encryption or by creating a file in a folder that is enabled for EFS encryption.

2. The local security authority (LSA) on the computer generates a random encryption key, called a File Encryption Key (FEK), to encrypt the file. The symmetric encryption algorithm used by the FEK depends on the version of the computer's operating system:

    ❑   For Windows 2000, the Data Encryption Standard XORed (DESX) algorithm is used to encrypt the file.

    ❑   For Windows XP with no services packs, the Triple DES (3DES) algorithm can be used to encrypt the file, instead of DESX.

    ❑   For Windows XP Service pack 1 and Windows Vista, the Advanced Encryption Standard (AES) algorithm with a 256-bit key is used to encrypt the file.

> **Note**   For more information on how these encryption algorithms work, review Chapter 1: "Cryptography Basics."

3. The LSA retrieves the user's designated EFS certificate and obtains the user's public key from the certificate.

4. The LSA encrypts the FEK by using the Rivest Shamir Adleman (RSA) asymmetric encryption algorithm with the user's public key and places the encrypted FEK in the Data Decryption Field (DDF) in the file's metadata.

> **Note**   In Windows XP or Windows Vista, the DDF can contain multiple entries, allowing multiple users to share an encrypted file. In Windows 2000, it is possible to create only a single DDF through the user interface.

5. The LSA retrieves the certificate for each EFS recovery agent, also known as the data recovery agent (DRA), from the local computer configuration for workgroup members, or by determining the resultant set of policy for Active Directory Domain Services (AD DS) or domain members, and extracts each EFS recovery agent's public key.

6. The LSA encrypts the FEK by using the RSA encryption algorithm with the retrieved EFS recovery agent's public key and places the encrypted FEK in the Data Recovery Field (DRF) in the file's metadata.

> **Note**   If multiple EFS recovery agents are designated, multiple entries will be stored in the DRF, one for each defined EFS recovery agent.

Remote Encryption

The EFS encryption process changes when you attempt to encrypt a file on a remote server. The process used by Windows 2000 and Windows XP clients is different from the new process implemented for Windows Vista clients.

Remote EFS Encryption for Windows 2000 and Windows XP Clients

When you perform remote file encryption from a Windows 2000 or Windows XP client using Server Message Block (SMB) or Common Internet File System (CIFS), the file is encrypted at a remote file server in a share created on the file server. Encryption is performed by allowing the remote file server to impersonate the user.

> **Important**   The computer account of the remote file server must have the Trusted For Delegation option enabled for its computer object in AD DS. This allows the computer to impersonate *any* user through Kerberos delegation. For this reason, many organizations consider enabling the Trusted for Delegation option a huge security risk.

When the computer account impersonates a user, it loads a user profile for the user account on the local file system and follows the same process to determine whether an EFS certificate exists for the user account. A different EFS encryption certificate is implemented at each file server where EFS encryption is enabled. In fact, the remote EFS encryption certificates are different that the EFS certificate used for local EFS encryption.

> **Important**   The same process is used by a Windows Vista client when it connects to a share hosted on a server computer running Windows 2000 Server or Windows Server 2003.

An alternative to allowing EFS encryption on file servers is to implement Web-based Distributed Authoring and Versioning (WebDAV), or Web folders, at the remote file server.

Rather than connecting to the file server on TCP port 445 (or TCP port 139 for the older SMB protocol), the server allows connections through the Hypertext Transfer Protocol (HTTP) port, TCP port 80 (or TCP port 443 if Secure Sockets Layer [SSL] is implemented).

The benefit of using WebDAV is that a Windows XP client performs file encryption on the local computer rather than the remote file server. This provides better data protection as the file is transmitted from the client's computer to the remote file server.

When a Windows XP client connects to a WebDAV access point on a remote server, files are encrypted locally on the client and then sent to the WebDAV server as an encrypted file using an HTTP PUT command.

Likewise, when a Windows XP client connects to the WebDAV access point to open a previously encrypted file, the encrypted file is transmitted to the Windows XP client via an HTTP GET command and then decrypted locally on the client.

Remote Encryption Changes for Windows Vista

Windows Server 2008 changes the behavior for remote EFS encryption. The encryption process was modified to work the same way as remote WebDAV encryption in Windows Server 2003.

- Certificates and keys are stored on the client rather than generating profiles on the server.

- The file server no longer needs to be trusted for delegation. This setting is no longer required because the server no longer impersonates the user.

- The files are now transmitted as encrypted data to the remote file server.

- Users can share files between workstations if Credential Roaming Service is implemented

 Note   Credential Roaming Service is discussed in Chapter 15, "Issuing Certificates."

If a client is running Windows 2000 or Windows XP, it can perform remote encryption on a file server computer running Windows Server 2008, as long as the server is trusted for delegation. The Windows 2000 and Windows XP clients will continue to perform remote encryption as described earlier in this chapter.

EFS Decryption

When an EFS-encrypted file is opened by a user with access to the FEK in the DDF information, EFS decryption process takes place, as shown in Figure 20-2.

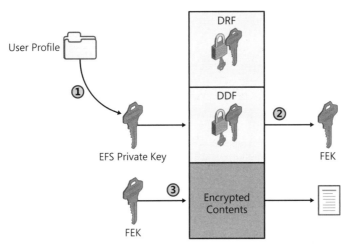

Figure 20-2   The EFS decryption process

1. When the user attempts to open the encrypted file, the LSA retrieves the private key of the certificate used to encrypt the FEK in the DDF. The private key is retrieved from the current user's personal store.

> **Note**   As long a user has access to a private key associated with the public key used to encrypt the FEK in a DDF, that user can open an EFS-encrypted file. The user's name does not have to match the user name stored in the subject of the certificate.

> **Note**   The user attempting to open the EFS encrypted file must be assigned the Read & Execute and Read NTFS permissions to open the file.

2. The LSA uses the private key from the user's store to decrypt the FEK from the DDF.

3. The LSA uses the FEK to decrypt the file.

The file is decrypted in memory so that the application accessing the file can read the unencrypted file. The version of the file stored on the hard drive remains encrypted.

EFS Data Recovery

When a designated EFS recovery agent attempts to access an EFS-encrypted file, a process similar to the EFS decryption process takes place. (See Figure 20-3.) The only difference is that the FEK is retrieved from the DRF rather than the DDF.

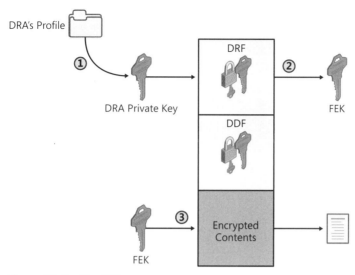

Figure 20-3   The EFS recovery process

When the recovery agent attempts to open the file:

1. The LSA retrieves the private key of the certificate used to encrypt the FEK in the DRF.

> **Note**   It does not matter if the name of the user does not match the subject name in the EFS certificate. As long as the user has access to a private key associated with the public key used to encrypt the FEK in a DDF, he or she can open the EFS-encrypted file.

> **Note**   The recovery agent's user name does *not* have to match the user name in the EFS Recovery Agent certificate's subject. The recovery agent only requires access to the Public Key Cryptography Standards (PKCS) #12 file containing the Recovery Agent's certificate and private key and import the certificate and private key into his or her user profile.

2. The LSA uses the private key from the EFS recovery agent's user store to decrypt the FEK from the DRF.

3. The LSA uses the FEK to decrypt the file.

One Application, Two Recovery Methods

In Windows Server 2003 PKI and Windows Server 2008 PKI deployments, EFS allows two methods to recover an EFS-encrypted file when a user no longer has access to his or her EFS-encryption private key:

- **Data recovery** An EFS recovery agent decrypts the file. Once the file is decrypted, the user can open the plaintext file and then reencrypt the file using a newly issued certificate with the Encrypting File System OID.

- **Key recovery** The user's original certificate and private key are recovered from the CA database and restored to the user's profile. Recovery of the user's certificate and private key allows the user to access the FEK stored in the DDF of the EFS-encrypted file, returning access to the file to the user.

The following sections discuss some of the design decisions an organization faces when choosing between data recovery and key recovery, or a mix of both.

Data Recovery

Data recovery allows a designated EFS recovery agent to decrypt all EFS-encrypted files on a computer. By default, the location of the default EFS recovery agent's certificate and private key is dependent on the domain membership of a computer. If the computer:

- **Is a member of a domain** The EFS recovery agent's certificate and private key are stored in the Administrator's profile of the first domain controller in a domain. When the first domain controller is promoted as a domain controller for the newly created domain, the local administrator's EFS Recovery Agent certificate is designated as the domain's EFS recovery agent.

- **Is a member of a workgroup** The EFS recovery agent's certificate and private key are stored in the user profile of the first member of the local Administrators group who logs on at the computer running Windows 2000. Typically, this is the local Administrator account, but it can be another account.

> **Caution** Deploying EFS in a workgroup environment is risky. The storage of the EFS recovery agent's key pair on the local file system makes the computer subject to alternate operating system attacks, such as the Nordahl attack, that attempt to gain access to the key pair through other operating systems. It is recommended to deploy Syskey.exe with the system set to require either a password or a disk with the system key password at startup before allowing access to the local hard disk. For more information on the system key, see Chapter 13, "Securing Mobile Computers," and Chapter 14, "Implementing Security for Domain Controllers," in 2nd Edition *Microsoft Windows Security Resource Kit*, by Ben Smith and Brian Komar (Microsoft Press, 2003).

A common misconception is that the Administrator account is the EFS recovery agent. Remember that EFS is a PKI-enabled application and has nothing to do with the user account. It depends only on who has the EFS Recovery Agent certificate's associated private key. You can lose access to the EFS recovery agent's private key in the following circumstances:

- If you remove, rebuild, or retire the first domain controller in a domain environment

- If you overwrite the Administrator's profile with a roaming profile created at another computer

- If you delete the Administrator's profile on the first domain controller in the domain or on the local computer in a workgroup

> **Important**   If you have overwritten or lost the EFS recovery agent's private key, you must designate a different EFS recovery agent to allow data recovery and update the EFS recovery agent information for each encrypted file. In Windows Vista, you can use the EFS Re-Key Wizard to update the EFS recovery agent information..

Defining EFS Recovery Agents

Defining an EFS recovery agent involves two steps:

1. Obtain a certificate with the File Recovery application policy OID.

2. Designate the certificate as the EFS recovery agent (in domain or local group policy).

Obtain an EFS Recovery Agent Certificate   This is the first step to ensure that the user assigned the EFS recovery agent role acquires an EFS Recovery Agent certificate. An EFS Recovery Agent certificate includes the File Recovery application policy OID (1.3.6.1.4.1.311.10.3.4.1). There are four ways this type of certificate can be obtained:

- Request a certificate based on the EFS Recovery Agent certificate template. You must modify the default template permissions to assign Read and Enroll permissions.

- Request a certificate based on a custom version 2 certificate template based on the EFS Recovery Agent certificate template. The advantage of a version 2 certificate template is that you can require CA certificate manager approval before issuance.

> **Note**   For Windows Vista and Windows Server 2008, you can store the EFS Recovery Agent certificate on a smart card. Windows 2000 and Windows XP are limited to software-based EFS Recovery Agent certificates.

- Use the `cipher /R:`*filename* command to generate a certificate file and a PKCS #12 file containing the private key on a computer running Windows XP or Windows Vista.

- In a Group Policy Object (GPO), right-click the *Computer Configuration\Windows Settings\Security Settings\Public Key Policies\Encrypting File System* policy, and then click Create Data Recovery Agent.

> **Note**   The Create Data Recovery Agent option requires that the EFS Recovery Agent certificate template be available for enrollment at an enterprise CA in the forest and that the user performing the procedure is assigned the Read and Enroll permissions for the EFS Recovery Agent certificate template.

Designate the EFS Recovery Agent   Once you issue the certificate with the File Recovery application policy OID, you must import the certificate, as follows:

- In a domain environment, you can import the EFS recovery agent's certificate into the *Computer Configuration\Windows Settings\Security Settings\Public Key Policies\Encrypting File System* policy of a GPO. The GPO must be linked to the organizational unit (OU) where the user's computer account, not the user account, exists. The certificate can be imported from either a Base-64 or DER-encoded certificate file, or from AD DS if the certificate template enables publication of the certificate file.

- In a workgroup environment, you can import the EFS recovery agent's certificate into the *Computer Configuration\Windows Settings\Security Settings\Public Key Policies\ Encrypting File System* policy (of the local computer). In this scenario, the EFS Recovery Agent certificate must be imported from a file.

> **Note**   If you generated the EFS Recovery Agent certificate by using the Create Data Recovery Agent option in Group Policy, you do not have to import the certificate. The EFS Recovery Agent certificate is automatically added to the GPO policy.

Choosing EFS Recovery Agents

If you work for a large organization, provide the private key associated with the EFS Recovery Agent certificate to the internal audit department. Members of the internal audit department can then import the certificate and private key, allowing them to open any file stored on the corporate network without intervention by network administrators when performing an audit. Removing control of the private key from the network administrator also prevents the network administrator from opening encrypted files.

Large organizations may also require more than one EFS recovery agent. In forests with multiple domains, an organization may implement a different EFS recovery agent for each domain. Rather than having disjoint EFS recovery agents, consider implementing two EFS recovery agents at each domain: one EFS recovery agent that is unique to the domain and another EFS recovery agent that is common to all domains in the forest. The common EFS recovery agent provides centralized recovery, and the unique EFS recovery agent provides decentralized recovery to the organization.

Securing the Private Keys

If you issued a software-based EFS Recovery Agent certificate, it is recommended that you remove the EFS recovery agent's private key from any user profile. This protects against an attacker attempting to log on as the EFS recovery agent and accessing the private key.

To remove the EFS Recovery Agent certificate and private key from the user's profile, you can export the certificate and private key and enable the options to Delete The Private Key If Export Is Successful and Enable Strong Private Key Protection. These options ensure that the private key is removed from the user's profile and that the PKCS #12 export file is protected with a password. Once removed, you should store the PKCS #12 on removable media and store the media in a secure location, such as a safe.

If you stored the EFS Recovery Agent certificate on a smart card, the private key never leaves the smart card chip. The smart card allows you to perform EFS recovery operations on any computer running Windows Vista or Windows Server 2008 with a smart card reader. When the recovery operation is complete, the smart card can be stored in a safe to provide physical security.

Key Recovery

You can enable key recovery for EFS encryption certificates. This allows the recovery of a lost EFS encryption private key without the intervention of an EFS recovery agent. A certificate manager extracts the encrypted private key from the CA database, and a key recovery agent decrypts the private key and distributes the resulting PKCS #12 file to the original user, allowing the original user to import the private key back into the user profile.

> **Note**   Enabling key recovery at an enterprise CA running on Windows Server 2008 Enterprise is covered in Chapter 18, "Archiving Encryption Keys."

Once your recovery methods are defined, you can start deploying EFS encryption certificates to users.

Implementing EFS

The deployment scenario that follows assumes that you implement key recovery and data recovery for an organization's EFS implementation. To deploy this solution, you must define the necessary certificate templates and plan how to deploy certificates to users.

Enabling and Disabling EFS

An organization might not want to allow EFS encryption on all client computers, preferring instead to enable EFS encryption for specific OUs or domains.

Enabling EFS

To enable EFS encryption on a computer running Windows 2000, you must ensure that an EFS recovery policy is implemented at the domain or OU containing the computer account that designates one or more EFS Recovery Agent certificates. Windows XP and Windows Vista can implement EFS encryption without designating an EFS recovery agent.

> **Note**   In a Windows 2000 domain, EFS is enabled by default. The EFS Recovery Agent certificate's private key is stored in the first administrator's profile on the first domain controller installed in the domain.

Disabling EFS

To disable EFS encryption on a computer running Windows 2000, you must implement an empty EFS recovery policy, where an EFS recovery policy is designated with no EFS Recovery Agent certificates.

> **Note**   Enabling an empty EFS recovery policy is different from implementing no EFS recovery policy. If no EFS recovery policy is implemented, the client computer implements the EFS encryption settings defined in the local security policy.

To disable EFS encryption on a computer running Windows XP or Windows Vista, you must configure Group Policy to block EFS encryption. This is accomplished with the following procedure:

1. Link a new GPO to the OU where the computer accounts of computers running Windows XP exist.

2. Open the GPO in the Group Policy Editor.

3. In the console tree, navigate to Computer Configuration\Windows Settings\Security Settings\Public Key Policies\Encrypting File System.

4. In the console tree, right-click Encrypting File System, and then click Properties.

5. If editing the policy for Windows XP or Windows Server 2003, in the Encrypting File System Properties dialog box, clear the Allow Users To Encrypt Files Using Encrypting File System (EFS) check box, and then click OK.

6. If editing the policy for Windows Vista or Windows Server 2008, in the Encrypting File System Properties dialog box, on the General tab, set File Encryption Using Encrypting File System to Don't Allow, and then click OK.

Certificate Templates for EFS Encryption

Three certificate templates are required when deploying an EFS encryption solution with both data recovery and key recovery:

- An EFS Recovery Agent certificate template
- A Key Recovery Agent certificate template
- An EFS user certificate template

The sections that follow describe the specific configuration recommendations for each certificate template.

EFS Recovery Agent Certificate Template

It is recommended that you create a version 2 certificate template based on the EFS Recovery Agent certificate template. The advantage of creating a version 2 certificate template is that you make the certificate request subject pending and require a certificate manager's approval to issue the certificate, increasing the assurance, or trust, of the EFS Recovery Agent certificate.

Table 20-1 shows the recommended settings for the version 2 EFS Recovery Agent certificate template.

Table 20-1   EFS Recovery Agent Certificate Template Settings

Tab	Actions
General	Template Display Name: *Company* EFS Recovery Agent
	Template Name: *Company*EFSRecoveryAgent
	Validity Period: Two years
	Publish Certificate In Active Directory: Enabled
Request Handling	No modifications
Subject Name	No modifications
Issuance Requirements	CA Certificate Manager Approval: Enabled
Superseded Templates	EFS Recovery Agent
Extensions	No modifications
Security	Assign a custom universal or global group Read and Enroll permissions. Remove the assignment of the Enroll permission from any other security principals.

Note   Publishing the certificate in AD DS allows an administrator to select the certificate from AD DS rather than having to import the EFS recovery agent's certificate from an export file.

Note   If a user already has an EFS Recovery Agent certificate in his or her user certificate store, the enrollment attempt of a *Company* EFS Recovery Agent certificate will result in the EFS Recovery Agent certificate being archived in the user certificate store.

If you are using Windows Vista clients, you can optionally change the cryptographic service provider (CSP) to a smart card–based CSP. Only Windows Vista and Windows Server 2008 clients can access the EFS Recovery Agent certificate and private key from a smart card.

Key Recovery Agent Certificate Template

The default version 2 certificate template implements all recommended settings for EFS key recovery. The only required modification for the Key Recovery Agent certificate template is to assign Read and Enroll permissions to a custom universal or global group. In addition, Read and Enroll permission should be removed from the Administrators, *ForestRoot-Domain*\Domain Admins, and *ForestRootDomain*\Enterprise Admins groups.

EFS User Certificate Template

It is recommended that you create a custom version 2 certificate template based on the default Basic EFS certificate template. The custom certificate template allows an organization to implement both private key archival and autoenrollment of certificates for users with client computers running Windows XP and Windows Vista. Table 20-2 shows the recommended settings for the custom certificate template.

Table 20-2   EFS User Certificate Template Settings

Tab	Actions
General	Template Display Name: *Company* EFS
	Template Name: *Company*EFS
	Validity Period: Two years
	Publish Certificate In Active Directory: Enabled
Request Handling	Purpose: Encryption
	Archive Subject's Encryption Private Key: Enabled
	Include Symmetric Algorithms Allowed By The Subject: Enabled
	Minimum Key Size: 1,024 bits
	Allow Private Key To Be Exported: Enabled
	Enroll Subject Without Requiring Any User Input: Enabled
Subject Name	No modifications
Issuance Requirements	No modifications
Superseded Templates	Basic EFS
Extensions	In the Application Policies listing, in addition to the Encrypting File System OID (1.3.6.1.4.1.311.10.3.4), you can create a custom OID based on the organization's OID space. This custom OID can be used in CryptoAPI COM control (CAPICOM) scripts to determine whether the certificate is a custom EFS certificate rather than a Basic EFS certificate or another default certificate template (such as the User certificate template that includes the Encrypting File System OID).
Security	The permissions assignment depends on who requires EFS encryption certificates. If all users require EFS encryption abilities, assign the Authenticated Users group Read, Enroll, and Autoenroll permissions.

By deploying the certificate (based on this template) to all users, you then have an EFS certificate with key archival enabled before they start encrypting files.

Important   You cannot protect the EFS certificate with strong private key protection. The EFS decryption and recovery processes are performed by the local security authority (LSA) in kernel mode. To input the password protecting the user certificate, the LSA would be required to be exposed to the desktop, which is a security risk. To prevent this security risk, exposure of the LSA to the desktop is not allowed. If you do implement strong private key protection for an EFS certificate, EFS will silently fail because the password dialog box is never exposed to the user.

If you are using Window Vista clients, you can optionally store the EFS certificate on a smart card. If you wish to store the EFS certificate on a smart card, you must enable a smart card–based CSP in the certificate template.

Certificate Enrollment

Once you design the three certificate templates, you must publish the certificate templates at one or more enterprise CAs in the forest. After the certificates are available for enrollment, the two methods that follow are recommended for issuing the certificates.

EFS Recovery Agent and Key Recovery Agent Certificates

It is recommended that you deploy EFS Recovery Agent and Key Recovery Agent certificates by using a registration authority, such as Microsoft Identity Lifecycle Manager (ILM) 2007 Certificate Management. ILM 2007 allows you to define specific workflows that must be followed to ensure that only authorized personnel are issued the EFS Recovery Agent and Key Recovery Agent certificates.

When defining profile templates for EFS Recovery Agent and Key Recovery Agent certificates, keep these best practices in mind:

- Include data collection in the enroll management policy to record the identity documents provided during the enrollment process.

- Design the enroll management policy to match the assurance level asserted in the certificate template.

- Design management policies for the entire life cycle of the certificates. Include enrollment, recovery, revocation, and renewal.

- If storing the certificates on smart cards, identify the registration model you are implementing to determine who submits the request to the CA and needs access to the blank smart card.

Note   Details on defining profile templates are covered in Chapter 17, "Identity Lifecycle Manager 2007 Certificate Management."

EFS User Certificates

The method you use to distribute the EFS User certificates to user accounts depends on the operating system:

- For Windows XP and Windows Vista clients, it is recommended that you deploy the EFS encryption certificates by using Autoenrollment Settings in Group Policy. This method triggers the users who have user accounts in the OU where the Autoenrollment Settings GPO is applied to acquire the certificates by using autoenrollment when the user logs on to the network.

- For Windows 2000 clients, users must manually enroll certificates through the Certificate Services Web Enrollment pages via the Advanced Certificate Request page. This page enables users to select the version 2 certificate template and enroll the certificate.

> **Important**   A user with a computer running Windows 2000 cannot use the Certificate Enrollment Wizard to enroll certificates based on version 2 certificate templates. The Certificates console, where the Certificate Enrollment Wizard is launched, displays only version 1 certificate templates on a computer running Windows 2000.

> **Note**   You can automate certificate enrollment by creating a custom enrollment script that uses the Certificate Enrollment Control. The custom script should use CAPICOM to determine whether the user already has a certificate with both the Encrypting File System application policy OID and the custom EFS application policy OID, as recommended previously in Table 20-2.

What's New in Windows Vista for EFS Management

Windows Vista introduces many new features for EFS (some of which have been discussed earlier in this chapter). The new features include:

- User EFS encryption certificates and keys can be stored on smart cards.

- EFS data recovery certificates and keys can be stored on smart cards.

- The Windows paging file can be encrypted using EFS with a key that is generated when the system starts up. This key is destroyed when the system shuts down.

- Data in the offline files cache is encrypted using the specific user's encryption keys, rather than a machine-based system key. This prevents one user from accessing another user's data in the offline files cache.

The biggest improvement in EFS is the ability to manage default settings with Group Policy. As shown in Figure 20-4, the new Group Policy settings allow you more detailed control of EFS policies.

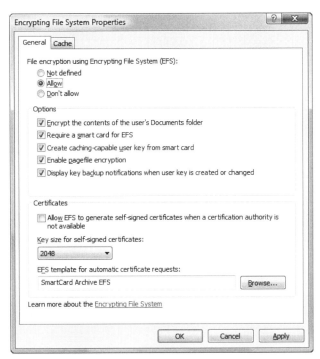

Figure 20-4   Defining EFS group policy settings

The Group Policy allows you to define the following options:

- As with Windows XP, you can choose to enable or disable EFS.

- You can choose to automatically encrypt the user's Documents folder.

- If you implement EFS keys on smart cards, the caching-capable user key option allows you to generate a cacheable key so that the smart card is not accessed each and every time a file is decrypted. The symmetric cacheable key is derived using the private key on the smart card. The cacheable master key is stored in software for the session and is used to encrypt and decrypt FEKs. The symmetric key can be derived only by using the smart card's private key.

- You can choose to automatically encrypt the page file.

- You can enable wizard protection to back up EFS encryption keys if the user generates a new EFS encryption key or the key is changed.

- You can disable the use of EFS self-signed certificates.

- If self-signed is enabled, you can define a minimum key length.

- You can change the default certificate template from Basic EFS to a custom version 2 certificate template.

The Group Policy also allows you to define key cache options (see Figure 20-5), to protect against attacks attempting to access encrypted files by accessing a cached key.

Figure 20-5   Defining EFS caching options

You can choose to set cache limits by:

- **Limiting a time-out**   Once the time-out occurs, you must generate a new master key based on the smart card's private key.

- **Clearing the cache when a user locks the workstation**   When the workstation is unlocked, the master key is regenerated by accessing the private key on the smart card.

- **Clearing the cache when the user removes the smart card**   The master key is regenerated only when the smart card is reinserted and the personal identification number (PIN) is provided to gain access to the smart card's private key to regenerate the master key.

> **Important**   EFS encryption is available only on Windows Vista Business Edition, Windows Vista Enterprise Edition, and Windows Vista Ultimate. EFS is unavailable in all other editions of Windows Vista.

Other EFS Management Tools

If you are deploying EFS, it is recommended to implement other EFS management tools to aid in a successful deployment. Some of the available tools and utilities include:

- **The Data Encryption Toolkit for Mobile PCs: Microsoft Encrypting File System Assistant**   The toolkit allows you to enforce your organization's data protection policy when protecting data with EFS. The tool allows you to specify the data that must be encrypted on a client workstation and helps you enforce these encryption policies.

- **EFS Certificate Configuration Updater**   This utility, developed by Mike Smith-Lonergan, allows you to update all existing EFS encrypted data on a client computer to use a new EFS certificate. This utility greatly assists in EFS deployments where some users have previously implemented EFS with self-signed or Basic EFS certificates and you want to move to a custom v2 certificate template that implements key archival.

- **Advanced EFS Data Recovery (AEFSDR)**   If a computer has been rebuilt and the user's previous user profile still exists on the hard disk, Advanced EFS Data Recovery allows you to recover the EFS encryption key. This tool is useful if self-signed or Basic EFS certificates were used to implement EFS and the user did not manually back up the EFS certificate and private key. The tool (and other competing tools) work by using the user's password to decrypt the Data Protection Application Programming Interface (DPAPI)–protected data in the user's previous user profile. You must have knowledge of the user password used at the time the user profile was in use. Without the user password or the user's previous user profile, it is not possible to recover the data by using an EFS data recovery tool.

Although this isn't an exhaustive list, these tools will greatly aid your EFS deployment.

Case Study: Lucerne Publishing

You manage the CAs for Lucerne Publishing, a global publishing company that has implemented a two-tier CA hierarchy, as shown in Figure 20-6.

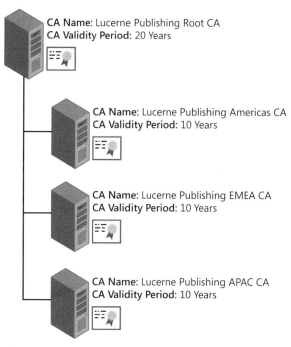

Figure 20-6   The Lucerne Publishing CA hierarchy

Scenario

Last year, a Lucerne Publishing acquisitions editor's laptop was stolen. One of the files on the laptop was a listing of proposed book titles on computer security. Within six months of the theft, a rival publishing company released titles based on the same topics.

To prevent a similar incident, Lucerne Publishing wants to enable EFS encryption on all laptops to ensure that sensitive data is protected.

Design Requirements

The following design requirements are provided to you:

■ Only the Lucerne Publishing Americas CA is enabled for key archival. Three key recovery agents are defined at the CA: one from Europe, one from Asia, and one from the Americas. The Lucerne Publishing Americas CA uses all three Key Recovery Agent certificates when archiving a private key. The users acting as key recovery agents are members of the Enterprise Admins group.

■ All notebook computers were recently upgraded to Windows Vista. The notebooks are all members of the lucernepublish.msft domain, and their computer accounts are in the organizational unit named OU=Notebooks,OU=Computer Accounts,DC=lucerne-publish,DC=msft.

- Lucerne Publishing implements both Windows XP Professional and Windows Vista Enterprise on the desktop computers.

- EFS encryption must be enabled for only notebook computers running Windows Vista. EFS encryption must be disabled on all other computers.

- The EFS encryption certificates must be deployed to all notebook users without user intervention. The private key of the EFS encryption certificate must be archived to allow key recovery operations.

- Smart cards are not in use at Lucerne Publishing.

- The internal audit department must be able to open any file stored on a Lucerne Publishing computer asset. If an EFS private key cannot be retrieved from the CA database, the internal audit provides the EFS Data Recovery key to a help desk technician to perform data recovery.

- If a user's profile is deleted, the first attempt to regain access to the EFS certificates must use key recovery. Data recovery is implemented only if key recovery fails to regain access to an EFS-encrypted file.

Proposed Solution

You assign Andy, a member of your department, the task of developing a solution that meets these design requirements. Andy proposes the following:

- The default EFS Recovery Agent and Key Recovery Agent certificate templates are used for the EFS project. The certificate templates are published only at the Lucerne Publishing Americas CA.

- Key recovery agents are defined at each issuing CA in the CA hierarchy. The key recovery agent for each region is designated as the only key recovery agent for that region's issuing CA.

- Permissions on the EFS Recovery Agent certificate template are modified to allow only members of the internal audit department Read and Enroll permissions. Three team members enroll the EFS Recovery Agent certificates, and the certificates are exported to Base64 export files to allow definition of EFS recovery agents.

- A GPO named EFS Recovery is linked to the organizational unit named OU=Notebooks,OU=Computer Accounts,DC=lucernepublish,DC=msft. The GPO designates the three EFS recovery certificates issued to the internal audit department as EFS recovery agents.

- The Default Domain Policy is modified to implement an empty EFS recovery agent policy.

- A version 2 certificate template is created that enables the following settings:

Tab	Actions
General	Template Display Name: Lucerne Publishing EFS
	Template Name: LucerneEFS
	Validity Period: Two years
	Publish Certificate In Active Directory: Enabled
Request Handling	Purpose: Encryption
	Archive Subject's Encryption Private Key: Enabled
	Include Symmetric Algorithms Allowed By The Subject: Enabled
	Minimum Key Size: 1,024 bits
	Allow Private Key To Be Exported: Enabled
	Enroll Subject Without Requiring Any User Input: Enabled
Subject Name	No modifications
Issuance Requirements	No modifications
Superseded Templates	Basic EFS
Extensions	Application Policies: Encrypting File System
Security	LucernePublish\Domain Users: Read, Enroll, and Autoenroll

- A GPO named EFS Autoenrollment is linked to the OU named OU=Notebooks, OU=Computer Accounts,DC=lucernepublish,DC=msft. The GPO enables all autoenrollment settings for computer accounts.

Case Study Questions

1. Does the default EFS Recovery Agent certificate template satisfy the design requirements for the Lucerne Publishing EFS project?

2. Does the default Key Recovery Agent certificate template satisfy the design requirements for the Lucerne Publishing EFS project?

3. Do the design requirements allow the EFS Recovery Agent and Key Recovery Agent certificate templates to be published only at the Lucerne Publishing Americas CA?

4. Does Andy's proposed solution meet the design requirements for designation of key recovery agents in the forest?

5. Is EFS encryption disabled for all computers running Windows XP not in the OU named OU=Notebooks,OU=Computer Accounts,DC=lucernepublish,DC=msft?

6. Does Andy's proposed design disable EFS encryption for computer accounts of computers running Windows XP and Windows Vista not in the OU named OU=Notebooks,OU=Computer Accounts,DC=lucernepublish,DC=msft?

7. Does the Lucerne Publishing EFS certificate template allow for autoenrollment by Windows Vista users?

8. Does the proposed EFS Autoenrollment GPO enable autoenrollment of the Lucerne Publishing EFS certificate template by users with computers running Windows XP?

Best Practices

- **When you deploy notebook computers, ensure that the notebooks are members of the organization's Active Directory Domain Services (AD DS).** Domain members are protected against disk attacks, such as the Nordahl attack, because the DRA's private key is not stored on the local disk of the notebook computer.

- **Enable the Store And Retrieve Archived Keys auditing option at a CA where key archival is enabled.** By enabling this auditing setting, you ensure that all key recovery operations are tracked in the CA's security event log.

- **Implement role separation of certificate managers and key recovery agents.** If you implement role separation, you ensure that a minimum of two people are involved in any key recovery process.

- **If an encryption certificate's private key is compromised, revoke the certificate before performing the key recovery operation.** By revoking the certificate, you ensure that the private key of the certificate can be used only to decrypt EFS-encrypted files. The certificate cannot be used to encrypt new files.

- **If implementing key recovery, ensure that the EFS-enabled certificate with private key archival is distributed to workstations *before* EFS encryption is performed.** By deploying a certificate with the Encrypting File System application policy OID, you ensure that the EFS-enabled certificate with private key archival is used for all EFS-encrypted data.

- **Implement a central recovery workstation for EFS data recovery if using a software-based CSP for the EFS recovery agent.** An EFS-encrypted file can be restored to the central recovery station by using a backup utility to back up encrypted files from the source workstation and then restoring those files to the central recovery machine. In this configuration, the DRA's private key can be stored on the recovery machine permanently or imported as required. This method prevents the DRA's private key from being exposed to the network from a typical workstation.

- **Implement Data Recovery Agent certificates from a CA.** Rather than using the default, self-signed EFS Recovery Agent certificate, implement a CA-issued certificate, which can be revoked or renewed and has a configurable expiration date.

- **Plan which folders on the workstation are enabled for encryption.** By encrypting common folders such as My Documents and temporary folders, you can ensure that any data saved in these folders is encrypted.

- **Store the Key Recovery Agent certificate and private key on a smart card or other hardware-based CSP.** This ensures that the key recovery agent's certificate is not susceptible to disk attacks.

- **Use Syskey in mode 2 with a boot floppy or mode 3 with a boot password for non-domain member computers.** Setting the system key (Syskey) to mode 2 or mode 3 prevents attacks that use an alternate operating system to access the EFS private key material stored on the local disk subsystem.

■ **If using Windows Vista, consider storing the EFS encryption and EFS Recovery Agent certif-icates on smart cards.**   Windows Vista allows you to implement the EFS encryption and EFS Recovery Agent certificates on smart cards. Smart cards provide stronger protection of the private keys and portability of the keys.

Additional Information

■ Microsoft Official Curriculum, Course 2821: "Designing and Managing a Windows Public Key Infrastructure" (*http://www.microsoft.com/traincert/syllabi/2821afinal.asp*)

■ *Microsoft Windows Security Resource Kit*, by Ben Smith and Brian Komar (Microsoft Press, 2003)

■ "Key Archival and Recovery in Windows Server 2008" (*http://go.microsoft.com/fwlink/ ?LinkID=92523*)

■ "Encrypting File System in Windows XP and Windows Server 2003" (*http://www.microsoft.com/technet/prodtechnol/winxppro/deploy/cryptfs.mspx*)

■ "The Windows Server 2003 Family Encrypting File System" (*http://www.msdn.microsoft.com/library/default.asp?url=/library/en-us/dnsecure/html/ WinNETSrvr-EncryptedFileSystem.asp*)

■ "Windows Data Protection" (*http://msdn.microsoft.com/library /en-us/dnsecure/html/ windataprotection-dpapi.asp*)

■ "Deploying EFS: Part 1" (*http://www.microsoft.com/technet/technetmag/issues/2007/ 02/SecurityWatch/default.aspx*)

■ "Deploying EFS: Part 2" (*http://www.microsoft.com/technet/technetmag/issues/2007/ 03/SecurityWatch/default.aspx*)

■ "Data Encryption Toolkit for Mobile PCs: Microsoft Encrypting File System Assistant" (*http://www.microsoft.com/technet/security/guidance/clientsecurity/dataencryption/ efsassistant/default.mspx*)

■ "EFS Certificate Configuration Updater" (*http://www.codeplex.com/EFSCertUpdater*)

■ "Advanced EFS Data Recovery Tool" (*http://www.elcomsoft.com/ aefsdr.html?r1=pr&r2=efs_vista3*)

■ 298009: "Cipher.exe Security Tool for the Encrypting File System"

■ 302093: "How To: Prevent Files from Being Encrypted When Copied to a Server"

■ 307877: "How To: Encrypt a File in Windows XP"

■ 308989: "How To: Encrypt a Folder in Windows XP"

■ 308991: "How To: Share Access to an Encrypted File in Windows XP"

■ 309408: "Troubleshooting the Data Protection API (DPAPI)"

- 313365: "How To: Configure a Domain EFS Recovery Policy in Windows 2000"

- 315672: "How To: Use Cipher.exe to Overwrite Deleted Data in Windows"

- 320166: "How To: Identify Encrypted Files in Windows XP"

- 324897: "How To: Manage the Encrypting File System in Windows Server 2003"

- 329741: "EFS Files Appear Corrupted When You Open Them"

- 814599: "How To: Use Cipher.exe to Overwrite Deleted Data in Windows Server 2003"

- 818200: "An Attacker with Physical Access to Your Computer May Be Able to Access Your Files and Other Data"

- 939391: "Error Message When You Try to Open an EFS-encrypted File in Windows XP or in Windows Server 2003 After the File Has Been Opened in Windows Vista: 'Access Is denied'"

- 912761: "Encrypting File System (EFS) Generates a Self-signed Certificate When You Try to Encrypt an EFS File on a Windows XP-based Computer"

 Note   The last 15 articles in the list can be accessed through the Microsoft Knowledge Base. Go to *http://support.microsoft.com*, and type the article number in the Search The Knowledge Base text box.

Chapter 21
Deploying Smart Cards

Many organizations are implementing two-factor authentication solutions to increase network security. Two-factor authentication increases security by requiring something you have, a smart card or other device with a smart card chip, such as a universal serial bus (USB) token, and something you know, such as the personal identification number (PIN) for the smart card or USB token.

To use a smart card, an organization must deploy the related hardware and software to each desktop.

- **Hardware** A smart card reader, as well as a smart card that is on the Microsoft Windows hardware compatibility list or includes drivers for Microsoft Windows 2000, Windows XP, or Windows Server 2003, Windows Vista, or Windows Server 2008 clients on your network. Alternatively, a USB token, which is a combination USB reader and card, can be used.

- **Software** A smart card cryptographic service provider (CSP) that allows the Microsoft cryptographic application programming interface (CryptoAPI) to interact with the smart card. In addition, the smart card may require middleware to perform advanced functions such as resetting PINs and loading application code.

Note In Windows Vista and Windows Server 2008, Microsoft introduces the Microsoft Base Smart Card Cryptographic provider. Similar to the Windows printer driver model, the base smart card CSP is a universal model where smart card vendors provide only a mini-driver to allow communications with their specific hardware. All cryptographic calls are made through a common CSP. The CSP is also available for Windows XP and Windows Server 2003 and can be downloaded from *http://www.microsoft.com/downloads/details.aspx?FamilyID=e8095fd5-c7e5-4bee-9577-2ea6b45b41c6*.

Using Smart Cards in an Active Directory Environment

All Active Directory environments since Windows 2000 support smart card authentication, which is an extension to Kerberos authentication. This means that a user can only authenticate with a smart card at Windows 2000 and later client computer that are domain members.

Smart Cards and Kerberos

Smart cards allow Kerberos authentication through Public Key Initialization (PKINIT) extensions to the Kerberos protocol. PKINIT extensions allow a public/private key pair to be used to authenticate users when they log on to the network.

Requirements for Smart Card Certificates

The requirements for smart card certificates vary depending on the client operating system being used.

Requirements Prior to Windows Vista

To use smart cards with Windows 2000, Windows XP, or Windows Server 2003 clients, the following requirements must be met:

- All domain controllers and computers in the forest must trust the root certification authority (CA) of the smart card certificate's certificate chain.

- The CA that issues the smart card certificate must be included in the Active Directory NT Authority (NTAuth) store. When a CA certificate is added to the NTAuth object in Active Directory (CN=NTAuthCertificates,CN=Public Key Services,CN=Services, CN=Configuration,DC=*ForestRootDomain*), the thumbprint of the CA's certificate is automatically distributed to all domain members running Windows 2000 and later in the HKEY_LOCAL_MACHINE\Software\Microsoft\EnterpriseCertificates\NTAuth\ Certificates registry key.

- The smart card certificate must contain the Smart Card Logon (1.3.6.1.4.1.311.20.2.2) and Client Authentication (1.3.6.1.5.5.7.3.2) object identifier (OID) in the Enhanced Key Usage (EKU) extension or in the Application Policies extension.

> **Important**   The Smart Card Logon and Client Authentication OIDs must be valid in the entire certificate chain.

- The smart card certificate must contain the user's user principal name (UPN) in the subject alternative name extension.

- The smart card certificate and private key must exist in the default slot of the smart card (also referred to as slot 0).

- The smart card logon certificates must have a Key Exchange (AT_KEYEXCHANGE) private key.

- The smart card certificate must include a certificate revocation list (CRL) distribution point extension.

■ All domain controllers must have a Domain Controller, Domain Controller Authentication, or Kerberos Authentication certificate installed. Smart card authentication requires mutual authentication of the user and the domain controller involved in the Kerberos authentication.

Both Windows Server 2003 and Windows Server 2008 enterprise CAs meet these requirements. Alternatively, a third-party CA can issue a smart card certificate, as long as the requirements are met.

> **Note** The requirements are detailed in Microsoft Knowledge Base Article 281245, "Guidelines for Enabling Smart Card Logon with Third-Party Certification Authorities."

Requirements for Windows Vista

For Windows Vista and Windows Server 2008 clients, the requirements for smart card logon have been greatly modified:

■ The CRL extension is no longer required in the smart card logon certificate.

■ The subject alternative name (SAN) does not have to include the UPN of the user. A manual mapping of a certificate to an account in Active Directory Domain Services (AD DS) is now supported.

> **Note** It is still recommended to include the UPN in the certificate because it allows an automatic mapping of the certificate to the user name through a global catalog lookup. If you do not include the UPN in the certificate, the certificate must be manually mapped to the specific user account in AD DS.

■ The EKU extension does not have to contain the Smart Card Logon OID.

> **Note** If you want to use the same certificate template for all supported versions of Windows, you would still include the smart card logon OID.

■ The smart card's certificate private key must be for digital signature but can be either Signature Only (AT_SIGNATURE) or Key Exchange (AT_KEYEXCHANGE).

■ The smart card certificate can exist in any available slot on the smart card.

Changes in Smart Card Logon Behavior

These changed requirements for Windows Vista and Windows Server 2008 allow changed smart card logon behavior.

■ Smart card logon is no longer initiated by the smart card insertion event. Smart card logon starts only when the user presses Ctrl+Alt+Delete.

- The support for certificates in any slot on the smart card allows the user to choose from multiple identities stored on the smart card. All valid smart card logon certificates are displayed as available authentication accounts.

- The CSP is accessed in the local security authority process (Lsass.exe) rather than the Winlogon process.

Although Windows Vista now supports Cryptography Next Generation (CNG), you cannot use Elliptical Curve Cryptography (ECC)–based certificates for smart card logon. Microsoft has decided to not support ECC-based PKINIT until a standard is approved by the Internet Engineering Task Force (IETF).

> **Note**   Information about the IETF Kerberos working group is available at *http://www.ietf.org/ html.charters/krb-wg-charter.html*.

Planning Smart Card Deployment

Planning a smart card deployment involves several interrelated steps, including:

- **Determining the assurance level required for smart card issuance**   A smart card increases protection for a certificate's private key. To compromise a smart card's private key, an attacker must obtain the smart card and know the associated PIN. As added protection, a smart card blocks access to the smart card's private key(s) after a designated number of PIN failures. The private key can be accessed only after the smart card is unlocked by using the smart card's administrative key or administrative PIN. You can increase the security of the smart card distribution by requiring face-to-face interviews during enrollment. This requires the user to meet with either the enrollment agent requesting the smart card certificate or with another person, sometimes referred to as a local registration authority (LRA), who verifies the user's identity.

> **Note**   To indicate that you have performed a face-to-face interview before issuing a smart card, you can add a custom certificate policy OID to the Issuance Policies extension that indicates the measures taken to validate the smart card holder's identity before issuance.

- **Identifying the required certificate templates**   To deploy smart card certificates by using face-to-face validation of the user's identity, your organization must provide certificates for the two roles in smart card deployment:
  - ❑ **Enrollment agent**   An enrollment agent must hold a certificate that allows him or her to request a smart card certificate on behalf of another user. This is made possible by including the Certificate Request Agent OID (1.3.6.1.4.1.311.20.2.1) in the Enhanced Key Usage or Application Policies extension of the certificate. This functionality is provided in the default version 1 Enrollment Agent certificate template.

> **Note**   If you choose to deploy smart card certificates by using Microsoft Identity Lifecycle Manager (ILM) 2007 Certificate Management, you do not have to issue Enrollment Agent certificates to users. Instead, the clmEnrollAgent agent account holds the certificate and signs the smart card certificate requests. The enrollment agent role holder in ILM 2007 Certificate Management initiates the enrollment and inserts the smart card in the reader but does not possess the Enrollment Agent certificate and private key.

❑ **Smart card authentication**   The smart card authentication certificate must include the Client Authentication (1.3.6.1.5.5.7.3.2) OIDs in the certificate's Enhanced Key Usage (EKU) or Application Policies extension for Windows Vista and Windows Server 2008 clients. For Windows 2000, Windows XP, and Windows Server 2003 clients, the certificate must also contain the Smart Card Logon (1.3.6.1.4.1.311.20.2.2) OID in the EKU extension.

> **Note**   Most organizations implement a custom version 2 certificate template based on either the Smart Card Logon or Smart Card User default version 1 certificate templates. Custom smart card authentication certificate templates allow an organization to enable autoenrollment for certificate renewal, add a certificate policy to describe the issuance method of the smart card certificate, add additional application policies to the smart card certificate, and enforce the use of a specific smart card CSP.

■ **Determining certificate distribution methods**   In a Windows Server 2003 or Windows Server 2008 Active Directory environment, two options exist for deploying the smart card certificates:

❑ Deploying smart cards with the native tools in Windows Vista

❑ Deploying smart cards with Identity Lifecycle Manager 2007 Certificate Management

The following sections provide details on these deployment options.

Deploying Smart Cards with Windows Vista

Windows Vista and Windows Server 2008 allow you to deploy smart card certificates using the native tools available in the core operating systems. To deploy smart card certificates in this environment, you must perform the following steps:

■ Designing an Enrollment Agent certificate template

■ Designing a smart card certificate template

■ Restricting the enrollment agents

■ Restricting the certificate managers

■ Performing the deployment process

Enrollment Agent Certificate Requirements

The default Enrollment Agent certificate template requires manual enrollment by the designated enrollment agent from the Certificates Microsoft Management Console (MMC) console. If you wish to increase the assurance level of the Enrollment Agent certificate, you can create a custom version 2 Enrollment Agent certificate template based on the version 1 Enrollment Agent certificate template. Table 21-1 lists the recommended modifications to the version 2 certificate template.

Table 21-1   Custom Enrollment Agent Certificate Template

Tab	Recommendations
General	Create a custom Template Display Name and Template Name, based on the organization name, that indicates that the certificate template is for enrollment agents. The validity period is typically no longer than one year.
Request Handling	If you wish to store the custom Enrollment Agent certificate on a smart card, change the CSP to the smart card vendor's CSP.
Subject Name	No modifications are required.
Issuance Requirements	Select the CA Certificate Manager Approval check box.
Superseded Templates	Designate the Enrollment Agent version 1 certificate template as a superseded template.
Extensions	Add a custom Issuance Policy that indicates that the certificate holder's identity is validated before issuance.
Security	Assign a custom universal group Read and Enroll permissions. Consider removing Enroll permissions for the Enterprise Admins and Domain Admins group from the forest root domain.

Once the required enrollment agents have obtained their Enrollment Agent certificates, consider removing the Enrollment Agent certificate templates from all CAs in the organization. To help prevent unauthorized certificate enrollment of Enrollment Agent certificates, publish the certificate template on a CA only when a new enrollment agent must be designated or when certificate renewal is required.

Tip   If you deploy the Enrollment Agent certificate on a smart card, consider adding a second smart card reader to the smart card enrollment station. If the enrollment station has only a single smart card reader, the enrollment agent must continually switch smart cards (the Enrollment Agent and the smart card authentication) during the enrollment process.

Smart Card Certificate Template Requirements

In the case of smart cards, it is recommended to create a custom version 2 certificate template based on either the default Smart Card Login or Smart Card User version 1 certificate templates. The version 2 certificate templates give you greater flexibility in the configuration of the certificate contents.

> **Important**   You cannot use a version 3 certificate template for a smart card logon certificate. Cryptography Next Generation (CNG) algorithms are not supported for smart card authentication.

Table 21-2 lists the recommended modifications to the version 2 certificate template.

Table 21-2   Custom Smart Card Certificate Template

Tab	Recommendations
General	Create a custom Template Display Name and Template Name, based on the organization name, that indicates that the certificate template is for smart card certificates. The validity period is typically no longer than one year.
Request Handling	Make the following changes on the Request Handling tab: ■ Change the Purpose drop-down list to Signature and Smart Card Logon to prevent the smart card from being used for encryption. Setting the purpose to Signature and Smart Card Logon ensures that the user is prompted during enrollment to input the smart card's PIN. ■ Increase the minimum key size to 1,024 bits if using smart cards with 8 KB or more storage space. ■ Specify the specific smart card CSP you want to use with the certificate template.
Subject Name	For ease of use, it is recommended to include the UPN in the subject alternative name extension. Enable the e-mail name options if you intend to use the smart card for Secure/Multipurpose Internet Mail Extensions (S/MIME) e-mail purposes.
Issuance Requirements	To enable enrollment by an enrollment agent, configure the certificate template to require one authorized signature, with the signing certificate containing the Certificate Request Agent OID. To allow the user to renew when the certificate nears expiration, set the Require The Following For Reenrollment setting to Valid Existing Certificate.
Superseded Templates	Add both the Smart Card User and Smart Card Login certificate templates, specifying that the custom version 2 certificate template is the organization's preferred version.
Extensions	For application policies, include the Smart Card Logon and Client Authentication. If you want to use the smart card for signing e-mail, include the Secure Email OID. In addition, add a custom application policy OID that indicates that the certificate is *YourOrganization's* smart card. This OID can be used in applications, such as Microsoft's Remote Authentication Dial-In User Service (RADIUS) server, to restrict certificate usage to only certificates with this custom OID. Add a custom certificate policy OID that specifies the process used for verifying the identity of the smart card certificate subscriber. The custom issuance policy OID can also include a Web Uniform Resource Locator (URL) reference that provides a text description of the process.

Table 21-2   **Custom Smart Card Certificate Template**

Tab	Recommendations
Security	Modify the permissions for the certificate template so that only a custom global or universal group that contains all enrollment agents has Read and Enroll permissions. Consider removing the Enroll permission assignment from the Enterprise Admins and forest root's Domain Admins groups.
	Add a custom global or universal group that contains all smart card users, and assign the group Read, Enroll, and Autoenroll permissions to allow renewals of the certificates.

This certificate template can be published at multiple CAs for fault tolerance and must be available at all times to allow an enrollment agent to create a smart card for any user at any time.

Restricting Enrollment Agents

Windows Server 2008 allows you to restrict enrollment agents so that they are limited in two ways:

- The enrollment agent can request certificates only for specific AD DS groups.
- For each designated AD DS group, the enrollment agent can request certificates based only on specific certificate templates.

These restrictions allow you to protect against a rogue enrollment agent requesting certificates for an unauthorized user or request unauthorized certificates for an authorized user. For example, enrollment agent restrictions can prevent an enrollment agent from requesting a combined code signing and smart card authentication certificate for an unauthorized user even if the enrollment agent is allowed to request a smart card authentication–only certificate for the authorized user.

For example, if you wanted to:

- Restrict the enrollment agents in the group Fabrikam\EnrollmentAgents to request certificates only for the group Fabrikam\SmartCardUsers, or
- Restrict the Fabrikam\SmartCardUsers group to receive certificates based only on the Fabrikam Smart Card certificate template,

you must configure the issuing CA to implement the settings shown in Figure 21-1 on the Restrict Enrollment Agent tab of the CA's Properties dialog box:

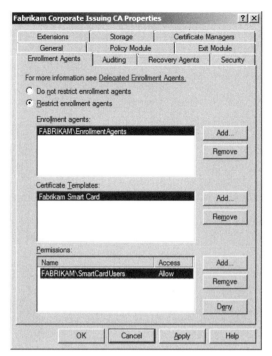

Figure 21-1   Enabling enrollment agent restrictions

Restricting Certificate Managers

If you implement the custom enrollment agent with a custom version 2 certificate template, you can enforce certificate manager restrictions on the issuing CA so that only a limited number of certificate managers are authorized to issue pending Enrollment Agent certificates.

> **Note**   The procedures for restricting certificate managers are covered in Chapter 13, "Role Separation," in the section "Implementing Certificate Manager Restrictions."

Deployment Procedures

The deployment procedures for the smart cards are separated into two processes:

1. The enrollment agent must acquire his or her Enrollment Agent certificate.

2. The enrollment agent must request a certificate for a smart card user.

Deploying the Enrollment Agent Certificate   To deploy the Enrollment Agent certificate, the enrollment process begins with the enrollment agent logging on and initiating the request from the Certificates console focused on the local user, as shown in the following procedure:

1. Log on to a computer running Windows Vista or Windows Server 2008 as a member of the designated enrollment agents group.

2. Open the Certificates console focused on the current user (Certmgr.msc).

3. Insert a blank smart card in the smart card reader.

4. In the console tree, right-click Personal, point to All Tasks, and then click Request New Certificate.

5. On the Before You Begin page, click Next.

6. On the Request Certificates page, select the check box for your custom Enrollment Agent certificate template, and then click Enroll.

7. In the Windows Security dialog box, in the PIN box, type the PIN for your smart card, and then click OK.

> **Note**   The PIN is required to generate the key pair for the custom Enrollment Agent certificate. Depending on the CSP used by your smart card, you may be presented with a custom PIN entry dialog box.

8. On the Certificate Installation Results page (see Figure 21-2), the certificate request enters a pending state until approved by a certificate manager.

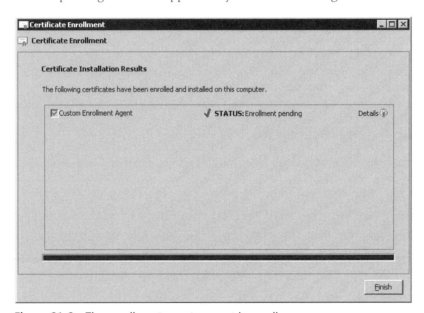

Figure 21-2   The enrollment agent request is pending.

9. On the Certificate Installation Results page, click Finish.

Once the certificate enters a pending state, a certificate manager must issue the pending certificate. Depending on the assurance level asserted in the Enrollment Agent certificate, this may require a face-to-face meeting and recording of identity information from the applicant. After the necessary data is collected and recorded, the certificate manager can issue the certificate, using the following procedure:

1. Log on as a user assigned the Issue and Manage Certificates permission at the CA.

2. From Administrative Tools, open Certification Authority.

3. In the console tree, click Pending Certificates.

4. In the details pane, right-click the custom Enrollment Agent certificate request, point to All Tasks, and then click Issue.

5. Close the Certification Authority console, and then log off.

Once the certificate is issued, the enrollment agent can complete the enrollment process, as shown in the following procedure:

1. Return to the workstation running Windows Vista or Windows Server 2008 where the custom Enrollment Agent certificate request was initiated, and then open the Certificates console.

2. Insert the smart card used for the custom Enrollment Agent certificate request into the smart card reader.

3. In the console tree, right-click Certificates – Current User, point to All Tasks, and then click Automatically Enroll And Retrieve Certificates.

4. On the Before You Begin page, click Next.

5. On the Request Certificates page, ensure that the check box for the pending certificate is selected, and then click Enroll.

6. If prompted, in the Windows Security dialog box, in the PIN box, type the PIN for your smart card, and then click OK.

> **Note**   If you have not removed the smart card from the smart card reader, you are not required to reenter the user PIN. You still have an active session with the smart card and its private information.

7. On the Certificate Installation Results page, ensure that the status is Succeeded, and then click Finish.

Deploying a Smart Card User Certificate   Once you have deployed the custom
Enrollment Agent certificate to the enrollment agent, the enrollment agent can start requesting
certificates for smart card users. As mentioned earlier, an enrollment agent with Windows
Vista uses the Certificates MMC console. Use the following procedure:

> **Note**   The use of the Certificates MMC console is the biggest change in behavior from
> previous versions of Windows. Prior to Windows Vista, you had to request a smart card
> certificate by using the Certificate Services Enrollment Web Pages. Windows Server 2008
> removes the smart card enrollment pages from the Certificate Services Enrollment Web pages
> and supports only requests that use the Certificates console.

1.   Open the Certificates console focused on the current user.

2.   In the console tree, right-click Personal, point to All Tasks, point to Advanced
     Operations, and then click Enroll On Behalf Of.

3.   On the Before You Begin page, click Next.

4.   On the Select Enrollment Agent Certificate page, click Browse.

5.   In the Select Certificate dialog box, select your Enrollment Agent certificate, and then
     click OK.

6.   On the Select Enrollment Agent Certificate page, ensure that your user name appears for
     the Signing certificate, and then click Next.

7.   When the Insert Smart Card dialog box appears, insert your enrollment agent smart
     card, and then click OK.

8.   In the Enter PIN dialog box, in the PIN box, type the smart card's PIN, and then
     click OK.

9.   On the Request Certificates page, click the Fabrikam Smart Card certificate, and then
     click Next.

10. On the Select A User page, click Browse.

11. In the Select User dialog box, in the Enter The Object Name To Select box, type the user
     name for the smart card recipient, and then click OK.

12. On the Select A User page, ensure that the user's name appears, and then click Enroll.

13. When the Insert Smart Card dialog box appears, insert a blank smart card for the user in
     the second smart card reader. The enrollment process starts immediately.

14. When the "Enter PIN. Enrolling For The User Certificate" dialog box appears, in the PIN
     box, type the PIN for the smart card, and then click OK. The key pair for the user's
     certificate is generated.

15. On the Certificate Installation Results page, ensure that the status is Succeeded, and
     then click Close.

> **Tip**   It is not recommended to use a single smart card reader on the workstation if you store the Enrollment Agent certificate on a smart card. The continual switching of smart cards is confusing and actually very frustrating to the user.

Issues with the Default Deployment Model

These are the issues with the default deployment model all related to assurance level enforcement:

- Workflows must be created outside of the default tools. There are no mechanisms for recording the certificate subscriber's identity information. You must build workflow tools to ensure that the enrollment agent records the required information *before* issuing the smart card to the user.

- The enrollment agent has knowledge of the user's PIN. If the user is not present or does not take control of the smart card to change the user PIN, the enrollment agent has a period of time where he or she can use the smart card to impersonate the subscriber.

- If the Enrollment Agent certificate is stored on a smart card, the process is very confusing if the workstation has only a single smart card reader. The process requires switching between the enrollment agent and user smart card during the enrollment process.

- Without the enforcement of enrollment agent restrictions, an enrollment agent could request a certificate for an unauthorized user or for an unauthorized certificate template.

- There are no default PIN management tools. Custom development is required to develop PIN reset tools.

- There are no default smart card printing tools. You must acquire separate software and hardware to implement smart card printing.

Deploying Smart Cards by Using ILM 2007 Certificate Management

Many of the issues identified with the default tools are mitigated by implementing the smart card management process by using Microsoft Lifecycle Manager 2007 Certificate Management.

The following sections provide details on deploying and managing smart card certificates by using ILM 2007 Certificate Management.

Additional Installation Requirements

Before you start deploying smart cards by using ILM 2007 Certificate Management (also referred to as CLM), there is additional software that must be deployed:

- Smart card CSPs and middleware
- Smart card self-service control

In addition, if smart card printing is required, you must deploy a smart card printing station. This requires:

- Datacard ID Works Enterprise Edition 5.1
- Bulk issuance tool
- A Datacard smart card printer

Supported Cards and Middleware   CLM does not support *all* smart card and token vendors in today's marketplace. Only smart card middleware and smart cards that have been tested for by the Microsoft product group are included on the supported list. The following vendor middleware is supported for CLM Feature Pack 1:

- Axalto Client Software (ACS) v 5.3
- AET SafeSign v2.3
- Aladdin eToken RTE 4.5
- Gemplus GemSafe v5.1
- Siemens HiPath Security Card API v3.2
- Microsoft Base Smart Card CSP version 5

Important   This list of vendors will *not* increase. Only the initial list of providers supported in CLM will continue to be supported in future versions of the product. If you have a smart card that is from another vendor, the vendor must support one of the CSPs in the list above or provide a smart card based on the Microsoft Base Smart Card CSP.

Base Smart Card CSP

The Microsoft Base Smart Card CSP applies the Windows printing model to smart card deployments. In the past, a smart card vendor had to provide their own CSP for the Windows operating system. The vendor had to provide all functionality in their CSP including interaction with the Smart Card Resource Manager and interfacing with the CryptoAPI.

The Microsoft Base Smart Card CSP changes this architecture by implementing common functions, such as hashing, symmetric and public key operations, PIN entry, and PIN caching, in a common CSP. To use the base smart card CSP, a vendor must provide a mini-driver (sometimes referred to as a *card module*). A vendor's mini-driver provides a common interface used by the Base Smart Card CSP.

When a vendor develops a base CSP smart card and mini-driver, they are submitted to the Microsoft Smart Card Certification Center (SCCC). Once certified, the smart card and mini-driver receive the Designed for Windows Logo for smart cards and are added as an available optional download in Windows Update.

> **Note**   A full list of the certified smart cards and mini-drivers is available at *http://test.catalog.update.microsoft.com/v7/site/Search.aspx?q=umdf.*

Default settings for the Microsoft Base Smart Card CSP can be found in the HKEY_LOCAL_MACHINE\SOFTWARE\Microsoft\Cryptography\Defaults\Provider\Microsoft Base Smart Card Crypto Provider registry key. Settings that can be configured include:

- **DefaultPrivateKeyLenBits (DWORD)**   Length of the private key generated on the base CSP smart card. Default value is 1,024 bits (-0x400).

- **RequireOnCardPrivateKeyGen (DWORD)**   If set to the default value, a private key generated on the host can be imported to the base CSP smart card. Use the default value only if the smart card does not support on-card key generation or if key archival is required. Default value is 0 (0x0).

- **TransactionTimeoutMilliseconds (DWORD)**   The timeout for holding transactions to the base CSP smart card. Default value is 1.5 seconds (0x5dc1500).

- **AllowPrivateSignatureKeyImport (DWORD)**   Allows importing of signature keys to the base CSP smart card. Default value is 0 (0x0).

- **AllowPrivateExchangeKeyImport (DWORD)**   Allows importing of exchange keys to the base CSP smart card. Default value is 0 (0x0).

The two most commonly set values are the AllowPrivateSignatureKeyImport and AllowPrivateExchangeKeyImport to allow key archival and recovery with base CSP smart cards.

Certificate Lifecycle Manager Client   The Certificate Lifecycle Manager Client includes the smart card self-service control. The self-service control interacts with the smart card CSPs and middleware to allow management of the smart cards in CLM. The self-service control reads the smart card on insertion to determine the smart card vendor and the smart card's serial number. The combination of the vendor and serial number acts as an identifier for the smart card in the ILM 2007 CLM system.

> **Important**   The CLM Web portal must be associated with the Trusted Sites security zone in Windows Internet Explorer. In addition, the Trusted Sites settings can be modified to allow pass-through authentication of the current user's credentials to allow integrated authentication with the site. If the site is not in the Trusted Sites zone, a warning will appear at the client identifying that the site must be added to the Trusted Sites zone.

To install the Certificate Lifecycle Manager Client, use the following procedure:

1. Extract the contents of the ILM 2007 Feature Pack 1 download to C:\ilm_CD.

2. Open C:\ilm_CD\CLMClient\ClmClient.msi.

3. On the Welcome To The Installation Wizard page, click Next.

4. On the Certificate Lifecycle Manager Client License Agreement page, click I Accept The Terms In The License Agreement, and then click Next

5. On the Setup Type page, click Complete, and then click Next.

6. On the Ready To Install Certificate Lifecycle Manager Client page, click Install.

7. When the installation is completed, click Finish.

Smart Card Printing Station   If you implement a smart card printing station, there is default software and hardware that must be configured at the smart card printing station. Although a smart card printing station is not required in order to deploy smart cards with CLM, if you implement a station, you must properly configure it.

To perform smart card printing with CLM, specific requirements must be met. By default, only three printers are supported for use with the Bulk Issuance Client:

- **Datacard SP35**   Designed for low-volume to mid-volume one-sided card printing.

- **Datacard SP55**   Designed for mid-volume, one-sided or two-sided card printing.

- **Datacard SP75**   Designed for mid-volume to high-volume one-sided or two-sided card printing.

Once you have acquired a supported printer, the following prerequisite software must be installed.

- **Microsoft .NET Framework 2.0**   The Microsoft .NET Framework must be installed on the smart card printing station.

- **Smart card CSP and related software**   You must install the smart card CSP and support software for your smart cards. If using a legacy smart card, you must install the CSP and PKCS #11 middleware. For a base CSP smart card, you must install the Microsoft Base Smart Card CSP and the vendor's mini-driver.

- **Certificate Lifecycle Manager Client**   The Certificate Lifecycle Manager Client is used during smart card enrollment and to read the smart card serial number.

- **Datacard ID Works 5.1 Enterprise Identification Software**   The enterprise version of Datacard ID Works 5.1 must be installed at the smart card printing station. The Bulk Issuance Client uses the ID Works software to integrate CLM and Active Directory attributes on the printed smart cards.

> **Important**   Although version 6.0 of ID Works is now available, only version 5.1 is supported for use with CLM Feature Pack 1.

- **CLM Bulk Issuance Client**   Allows bulk printing of smart cards and installs application plug-ins for interaction with ID Works.

Creating a Profile Template

The first step in creating a smart card profile template is to copy an existing smart card profile template. To create a profile template named Smart Card Certificates, use the following procedure:

1. Open Internet Explorer.

2. In Internet Explorer, open *http://clm.contoso.com/clm.*

3. Click the Microsoft Certificate Lifecycle Manager graphic.

4. On the Home page, in the Administration section, click Manage Profile Templates.

5. On the Profile Template Management page, in the Profile Template List section, select the check box next to CLM Sample Smart Card Profile Template, and then click Copy A Selected Profile Template.

6. On the Duplicate Profile page, in the Profile Template Name section, in the New Profile Template Name box, type **Smart Card Certificates**, and then click OK.

7. Minimize Internet Explorer.

Configuring Profile Template Details   Once you create the Smart Card Certificates profile template, you must configure the details of the profile template, using the following procedure:

1. In the left pane, in the Select A View section, ensure that Profile Details is selected.

2. On the Edit Profile Template [Contoso Smart Card Certificates] page, in the General Settings section, click Change General Settings.

3. On the Edit Profile Template [Contoso Smart Card Certificates] page, in the Name And Description section, in the Description box, type Allows Issuance And Management Of Smart Card Certificates.

4. On the Edit Profile Template [Contoso Smart Card Certificates] page, leave all other settings at their default value, and then at the bottom of the page, click OK.

5. On the Edit Profile Template [Contoso Smart Card Certificates] page, in the Certificate Templates section, click Add New Certificate Template.

6. Make the following changes on the Edit Profile Template [Contoso Smart Card Certificates] page:

   ❑ Certificate Authorities: Enable Contoso Issuing CA

   ❑ Certificate Template: Enable ContosoSmartCard

7. At the bottom of the Edit Profile Template [Contoso Smart Card Certificates] page, click Add.

8. In the Certificate Templates section, select the User check box, and then click Delete Selected Certificate Templates.

9. In the Microsoft Internet Explorer dialog box, click OK to delete the selected items.

This ensures that the profile template will issue certificates based only on the Contoso Smart Card certificate template. The certificates will be issued by the Contoso Issuing CA.

Configuring Smart Card Details   For a smart card profile template, in addition to defining the certificate templates included in the profile template, you must configure the default settings for smart cards managed by the profile template. The settings, applied to all management policies within a profile template, include:

- **Provider name**   Specifies the middleware used to communicate with the deployed smart cards. When you select the provider name, a provider ID is automatically set.

- **Processing information**   Configures several options for processing smart cards. These include:

  - **Initialize new card prior to use**   Erases all existing data from the smart card before issuance.

  - **Reuse retired card**   Allows a card that is in a retired state to be deployed to either the same user or to another user.

  - **Use secure key injection**   Transfers key material from the host computer to the smart card over an encrypted channel. This option is not supported by all vendors' smart cards.

  - **Install certificate authority certificates**   If enabled, installs all CA certificates in the chain to the smart card for propagation purposes.

  - **Certificate label text**   Specifies a logical label applied to a certificate on the smart card.

  - **Maximum number of certificates**   Specifies the maximum number of certificates that can be stored on the smart card before the smart card is full.

- **Microsoft Smart Card Base CSP options**   Allows you to diversify the Admin key. Diversification ensures that the Admin key is changed every time that the Admin key is used to unblock or manage a target smart card. If enabled, you can specify which initialization provider to use and the initialization provider data.

- **Administrative PINs**   Legacy smart cards use administrative PINs rather than an Admin key. In this section, you can enable Administrative PIN rollover so that the Administrative PIN is not left at the default value. Like Admin key diversification, the Administrative PIN is changed each time the Administrative PIN is used for management functions. If enabled, you must specify the length, character set, and initial PIN value.

- **User PINs**   In this section, you can configure how the PIN is set on a new smart card. The choices include:

  - ❏ **Randomized**   A random PIN is set based on the specified user PIN length and character set. The PIN is not known nor can it be published.

  - ❏ **Server distributed**   A random PIN is set based on the specified user PIN length and character set. The PIN can be published in PIN letters for distribution to a subscriber.

  - ❏ **User provided**   The subscriber is prompted to input an initial PIN.

  - ❏ **Custom server distributed**   Allows the use of a custom PIN generator for publication of the PIN in a PIN letter.

- **Printing options**   Allows you to configure smart card printing settings. The settings include:

  - ❏ **Print project name**   The name of the ID Works print project.

  - ❏ **Card name**   The name of the card definition within the ID Works print project.

  - ❏ **Print project field mappings**   The mapping of AD DS or CLM attributes to ID Works variables for use in smart card printing.

Smart Card Enrollment Definition   Now that the profile template exists, you can start to define management policies. This example assumes that the manager-initiated workflow shown in Figure 21-3 is used for the Enroll management policy.

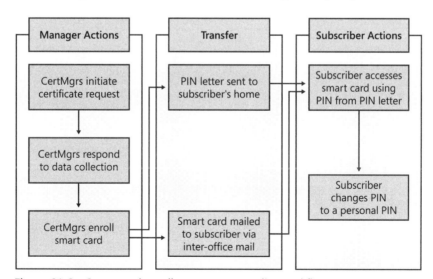

Figure 21-3   Smart card enroll management policy workflow

In this example, the Contoso Smart Card certificate request is initiated by a member of the CertMgrs group. After initiating the action, the CertMgrs must respond to a data collection item. Once the data is collected, the CertMgrs enroll the smart card. During the enrollment process, a server-assigned PIN is set on the smart card and printed in a PIN letter at a remote printer.

The smart card is distributed to the subscriber through inter-office mail, and the PIN letter is mailed to the subscriber's home. When the user has both the PIN letter and the smart card, he or she can then access the smart card with the initial PIN. The initial PIN can then be used to set a personal PIN on the smart card.

Assigning Permissions To enable the enrollment workflow described, we must assign the necessary permissions. Table 21-3 shows the permissions required for the enrollment workflow.

Table 21-3 Enroll Policy Permissions

Location	Permission assigning requirements
Service Connection Point	Assign the Contoso\CertMgrs group Read, CLM Request Enroll, and CLM Enrollment Agent permissions.
User or Group	Assign the Contoso\CertMgrs group Read and CLM Request Enroll, and CLM Enrollment Agent Permissions on the Contoso\Smart-CardUsers group.
Profile Template	Assign the Contoso\CertMgrs and the Contoso\SmartCardUsers groups Read permissions and CLM Enroll permissions on the Contoso Smart Card Certificates profile template.
Certificate Template	Assign the Contoso\CertMgrs group Read and Enroll permissions on the Contoso Smart Card certificate template.

Defining the Management Policy The last permission assignment requires defining the Enroll policy for the profile template. The configuration of the Enroll policy starts with defining the general settings, using the following procedure:

1. In the left pane, in the Select A View section, click Enroll Policy.

2. On the Edit Profile Template [Contoso Smart Card Certificates] page, in the Workflow: General section, click Change General Settings.

3. Make the following changes on the Edit Profile Template [Contoso Smart Card Certificates] page:

   ❑ Enable Policy: Enabled

   ❑ Use Self Serve: Disabled

   ❑ Require Enrollment Agent: Enabled

   ❑ Allow Comments To Be Collected: Disabled

   ❑ Allow Request Priority To Be Collected: Disabled

   ❑ Default Request Priority: 0

   ❑ Number Of Approvals: 0

   ❑ Number Of Active Or Suspended Profiles/Smart Cards Allowed: Set Value: Unlimited

4. At the bottom of the Edit Profile Template [Contoso Smart Card Certificates] page, click OK.

Once you have configured the general settings, you can now start defining the workflow. The first step is to specify who can initiate the enrollment request. As shown previously in Figure 21-3, the enrollment request is initiated by members of the Contoso\CertMgrs group. Use the following procedure:

1. In the Workflow: Initiate Enroll Requests section, click Add New Principal For Enroll Request Initiation.

2. On the Edit Profile Template [Contoso Smart Card Certificates] page, in the Permission section, click Lookup.

3. In the Microsoft Certificate Lifecycle Manager 2007–Webpage Dialog dialog box, in the Name box, type **certmgrs**, and then click Search.

4. In the returned listing of groups and users, click Contoso\CertMgrs.

5. In the Permission section, ensure that the Enroll Initiate Permission drop-down is set to Grant, and then click OK.

6. In the Workflow: Initiate Enroll Requests section, select the check box next to NT AUTHORITY\SYSTEM, and then click Delete Principals For Enroll Request Initiation.

> **Note** NT AUTHORITY\SYSTEM can be deleted with no issues because it is only a placeholder account.

7. In the Microsoft Internet Explorer dialog box, click OK to confirm the deletion.

In the example workflow, the Contoso\CertMgrs group also acts as the enrollment agent for the smart card issuance process. CLM implements the enrollment agent role differently than native Windows does. A CLM enrollment agent specifies which subscriber's name will be inserted in the subject of the smart card certificate but does not actually possess an Enrollment Agent certificate. Instead, the request is signed by the clmEnrollAgent agent account hosted on the CLM server. To designate the enrollment agent, use the following procedure:

1. In the Workflow: Enroll Agent For Enroll Requests section, click Add New Principal For Enrollment Agent.

2. On the Edit Profile Template [Contoso Smart Card Certificates] page, in the Permission section, click Lookup.

3. In the Microsoft Certificate Lifecycle Manager 2007–Webpage Dialog dialog box, in the Name box, type **certmgrs**, and then click Search.

4. In the returned listing of groups and users, click Contoso\CertMgrs.

5. In the Permission section, ensure that the Enrollment Agent Permission drop-down is set to Grant, and then click OK.

6. In the Workflow: Enroll Agent For Enroll Requests section, select the check box next to NT AUTHORITY\SYSTEM, and then click Delete Principals For Enrollment Agent.

7. In the Microsoft Internet Explorer dialog box, click OK to confirm the deletion.

If the workflow requires data collection, you must now specify the actual data collection items. For each data collection item, you must specify what the data collection item is, its data type, who collects the data, and how the data is validated. In our example, we will record the employee's badge number (a numeric value) using the following procedure:

1. On the Edit Profile Template [Contoso Smart Card Certificates] page, in the Data Collection section, select the check box next to Sample Data Item, and then click Delete Data Collection Items.

2. In the Microsoft Internet Explorer dialog box, click OK to confirm the deletion.

> **Note**   Sample Data Item is an example of a data collection item and should always be deleted.

3. In the Data Collection section, click Add New Data Collection Item.

4. In the Data Item Name And Type section, apply the following settings:
   - ❑ Name: Employee Badge Number
   - ❑ Description: Number is located on the back of the employee badge
   - ❑ Type: Number
   - ❑ Default Value: Disabled
   - ❑ Required: Enabled

5. In the Data Item Originator section, select Certificate Manager.

6. In the Data Item Validation section, select Data Type.

7. In the Data Item Storage section, apply the following settings:
   - ❑ Store Data In: Database
   - ❑ Encrypted: Enabled

8. At the bottom of the page, click OK to save any changes.

Our defined workflow distributes the PIN to the user through the use of a PIN letter. The PIN letter is implemented through document printing. The PIN letter can be created in Microsoft Office Word by typing the following text:

Dear {User!givenName}

The PIN for your new smart card with serial number {SCSerialNumber} is {SCPIN}.

You can change the PIN by using the Change PIN application in the Microsoft Certificate Lifecycle Manager menu option on your computer.

Regards,

The Contoso Smart Card Team

The document must be saved as a Web Page, Filter (*.htm) document in the C:\Program Files\Microsoft Certificate Lifecycle Manager\Print Documents folder. Once the document is created and saved in the correct location, you can designate the document in the profile template by using the following procedure:

1. In the Document Printing section, click Add New Documents To Print.

2. In the Printed Document Information section, type the following information:

   ❑ Name: **PIN Letter**

   ❑ Description: User **PIN Letter**

   ❑ Document Path: **PinLetter.htm**

   ❑ Mime Type: **application/msword**

3. In the Document Print Location, select Print On Client, and then click OK.

> **Note**   The Print On Client option sets printing to occur on the default printer on the local client computer. To ensure a higher assurance level, the document could be printed on the server, but this requires configuring the clmAgent account for printing and Distributed Component Object Model (DCOM) access.

Processing the Smart Card Enrollment   Once you have set up the enroll policy for the profile template, you can now start the enrollment of smart cards using the following procedure:

1. Log on as a member of the Contoso\CertMgrs group.

2. Open Internet Explorer.

3. Open *http://clm.contoso.com/clm.*

4. Ensure that the site is in the Trusted Sites security zone, and then click the ILM 2007 Feature Pack 1 logo.

5. On the Home page, in the Common Tasks section, click Enroll A User For A New Set Of Certificates Or A Smart Card.

6.   On the Search For Users page, in the Search Criteria For Users section, in the Name box, type the user name of the subscriber, and then click Search.

7.   On the Search For Users page, in the Search Results section, click the subscriber's user name.

> **Note**   You will have to select the user's name only if there are multiple matches to the search string typed in the Name box in step 6.

8.   On the Data Collection page, in the Employee Badge Number box, type **2467**, and then click OK.

9.   On the Request Status page, click Execute.

10. On the Assigning Smart Card To User page, validate the information, insert the new smart card in the smart card reader, and then click Assign.

11. If multiple smart card readers exist on the workstation, in the Insert Smart Card dialog box, select the target smart card reader, and then click OK.

12. The Smart Card Self-Service control will now appear and provide status on the smart card enrollment.

13. On the Print Documents page, in the Print Documents On Your Computer page, click PIN Letter.

14. In the File Download dialog box, click Open.

15. Print the document on the remote printer, and then mail the PIN letter to the user.

> **Note**   If you were using the CLM Bulk Issuance client to print the smart cards, the PIN letter would print automatically without user intervention. In this configuration, the PIN letter is sent to a remote printer without the member of the Contoso\CertMgrs group having an opportunity to view the PIN.

16. On the Print Documents page, click Finish.

The subscriber will now receive the smart card and the PIN letter at two different locations. The sending of the PIN letter to a separate location from the smart card increases the assurance level of the smart card.

Once received, the user can change his or her PIN by using the following procedure:

1.   Log on as the subscriber using the smart card and the PIN provided in the PIN letter.

2.   From the Microsoft Certificate Lifecycle Manager menu, click Change PIN.

3. In the CLM Smart Card Client PIN Entry dialog box (see Figure 21-4), type the following information:

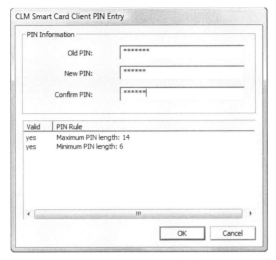

Figure 21-4   The CLM smart card change PIN tool

❑ Old PIN: Input the PIN from the PIN letter

❑ New PIN: Input a new subscriber PIN

❑ Confirm PIN: Reinput the new subscriber PIN

4. In the CLM Smart Card Client PIN Entry dialog box, click OK.

5. If the PIN change is successful, the application will close without any prompts to the user.

Other Smart Card Lifecycle Management Options

The real benefit of CLM is the ability to manage the smart card through its entire life cycle. Because of space considerations, this chapter will look only at the topic of unblocking PINs, but CLM can be used to define workflows for replacing smart cards, disabling smart cards, suspending smart cards, and issuing temporary smart cards.

Unblocking PINs   The most common management task once smart cards are issued in the organization is providing a means to unblock the user PINs when a user either forgets his or her PIN or incorrectly inputs it numerous times resulting in the blocking of the smart card.

CLM Feature Pack 1 supports two methods of unblocking smart cards:

■ Online unblocks

■ Offline unblocks

> **Important**   Offline unblocks are available only if you are using a smart card that uses the Microsoft Base Smart Card Cryptographic Provider. The offline unblock is based on the challenge/response mechanisms included in the CSP and cannot be used for legacy smart cards.

Online Unblock   During an online unblock, the client computer must have network connectivity to the CLM server. The online unblock will use one of two methods to unblock the user's smart card:

- For legacy smart cards, the Admin PIN for the smart card is used to allow the user to reset the user PIN on the smart card.

- For base CSP smart cards, the Admin key is used to allow the user to reset the user PIN on the smart card.

Typically, an online unblock is performed using a manager-initiated registration policy. The manager initiates the unblock process, and then a one-time password is provided to the user (either sent through e-mail or read to the user over the phone by the certificate manager).

The user provides the one-time password and then completes the unblock workflow by providing and confirming a new user PIN for the smart card.

To allow a manager-initiated workflow, the permissions shown in Table 21-4 must be assigned:

Table 21-4   Enroll Policy Permissions

Location	Permission assignment requirements
Service Connection Point	Assign the Contoso\CertMgrs group Read and CLM Request Unblock Smart Card permissions.
User or Group	Assign the Contoso\CertMgrs group Read and CLM Request Unblock Smart Card Permissions on the Contoso\SmartCardUsers group.
Profile Template	Assign the Contoso\CertMgrs and the Contoso\SmartCardUsers groups Read permissions on the Contoso Smart Card Certificates profile template.
Certificate Template	No certificate template permissions are required for an unblock workflow.
Within the Unblock Management Policy	Assign the Contoso\CertMgrs group the Initiate Unblock permission.
	Define a single one-time password (OTP) that is sent by e-mail to the user.

Offline Unblock   The problem with the online unblock is that it assumes that the user has network connectivity to the CLM Web portal. If the user is not connected to the network, the online unblock does not work.

To allow unblocking of a smart card when network connectivity is not available, CLM Feature Pack 1 introduces the Offline Unblock management policy. Offline unblock allows users to unblock their smart card *without* connecting to the network.

The permission assignments are the same for both the online unblock and the offline unblock at all permission locations except for within the management policy. In the management policy, you have to specify only the security group that is allowed to initiate offline unblocks.

When the user calls the certificate manager to initiate the unblock, the user provides a challenge string to the certificate manager. The challenge string is generated in one of two ways:

- On a client computer running Windows XP or Windows Server 2003, the client can generate a challenge string by using Pintool.exe as shown in Figure 21-5. In the figure, the challenge string is generated after the user inserts his or her smart card in the smart card reader and then clicks Unblock.

Figure 21-5   Generating a challenge string with PinTool.exe

- On a computer running Windows Vista, you can enable the Allow Integrated Unblock screen to be displayed at the time of logon Group Policy option (described later in this chapter). This option enables the Unblock screen to appear (see Figure 21-6) when you choose the Change Password option from the CTRL-ALT-DEL screen.

Figure 21-6   Windows Vista integrated unblock

Note   You can also copy Pintool.exe from a computer running Windows XP or Windows Server 2003 to one running Windows Vista or Windows Server 2008.

The certificate manager will type the provided challenge string into the CLM Manager portal. The portal will generate the matching response string to the certificate manager. When provided to the user, the user inputs the response string and then types and confirms a new PIN for the smart card.

Managing Issued Smart Cards

In addition to deploying smart cards to the users in your organization, security settings in Active Directory Domain Services (AD DS) and other services further increase network security. They include:

- Requiring smart cards for interactive logon
- Requiring smart cards for logon at specific computers
- Requiring smart cards for remote access logon
- Configuring smart card removal behavior
- Configuring smart card default settings

Requiring Smart Cards for Interactive Logon

You can require a user to use a smart card for interactive logon by enabling the Smart Card Is Required For Interactive Logon option on the Account tab of the user's object in AD DS. This method gives you flexibility in that you can enforce smart card use on a user-by-user basis.

Warning   Do not enable the Smart Card Is Required For Interactive Logon and the User Must Change Password At Next Logon options for a user account. When you enable the Smart Card Is Required For Interactive Logon option in a Windows Server 2003 or Windows Server 2008 environment, the operating system takes over user password management. The operating system assigns a maximum-length password that is equivalent to 255 characters and ensures that the password meets complexity requirements, effectively blocking the user from logging on to the network by using a password.

Important   When you enforce smart card logon in your domain, you must ensure the validity and availability of the CRL Distribution Point (CDP) and Authority Information Access (AIA) URLs in the smart card certificates and all CA certificates in the certification chain. The domain controller accepting the smart card authentication attempt will perform a revocation check on the smart card certificate during the logon process.

Requiring Smart Cards at Specific Computers

In some cases, it is more important to enforce smart card logon for a specific computer, rather than for a specific user. You can enforce smart card logon on computers by applying a Group Policy Object (GPO) that enables the Interactive Logon: Require Smart Card Security option.

Requiring Smart Cards for Remote Access

To enforce smart card authentication for remote access, you must configure a remote access policy at a remote access server or a RADIUS server to require Extensible Authentication Protocol–Transport Layer Security (EAP-TLS) authentication in the profile settings. When you enforce EAP-TLS authentication, you can elect to restrict client certificates to a smart card or other certificate. The only additional configuration required at the Routing and Remote Access server or the Network Policy Server (NPS) is designating the Server Authentication certificate used by the server for mutual authentication.

Configuring Smart Card Removal Behavior

You can also use Group Policy to specify the action that takes place when users remove their smart cards from a smart card reader. You do this by configuring the Interactive Login: Smart Card Removal Behavior Group Policy setting. This setting, configured in Computer Settings\Windows Settings\Security Settings\Local PoliciesSecurity Options, ensures that smart card removal behavior is consistent for all computer accounts in the organizational unit (OU) or domain where the Group Policy is applied.

In this Group Policy setting, you can configure the removal behavior one of four ways:

- **No Action**   The default setting. The removal of the smart card does not lock the workstation or log off the current user.

- **Lock Workstation**   The removal of the smart card causes the workstation to lock. The user must click Log On Interactively or provide the PIN for the smart card to unlock the workstation.

- **Force Logoff**   The user currently logged on is automatically logged off.

- **Disconnect From Remote Terminal Server Session**   Disconnects the terminal server session without logging off the user.

Configuring Smart Card Settings

Group Policy can also be used to configure default smart card usage settings. The settings, available in the Group Policy Management Editor at Computer Configuration\Administrative Templates\Windows Components\Smart Card, allow you to better manage the behavior of smart cards in a Windows Server 2008 and Windows Vista environment:

- **Allow certificates with no extended key usage certificate attribute**   Allows certificates without the smart card logon OID in the EKU extension to be used for smart card logon. If set to a value of 1, only smart card certificates with the smart card logon OID or certificates with no EKU extension are listed for logon.

- **Allow integrated Unblock screen to be displayed at the time of logon**   Allows unblock of base CSP smart cards from the Windows logon screen if set to a value of 1 (enabled). An incorrect PIN must be provided to show the Unblock screen.

- **Allow signature keys valid for Logon**   Enables any signature key–based certificates on a smart card to be enumerated and available for smart card logon.

- **Allow time invalid certificates**   Allows time invalid certificates to be presented for smart card logon at the client computer. Enabling this option does *not* guarantee that an expired smart card logon certificate can be used for logon. There is a dependency on whether the domain controllers will accept expired or not yet valid smart card logon certificates.

- **Turn on certificate propagation from smart card**   If enabled, all certificates on the smart card are propagated and available for use in applications such as Microsoft Office Outlook.

- **Configure root certificate cleanup**   Allows you to specify whether root certificates are not cleaned up, are cleaned on smart card removal, or are cleaned up when a user logs off the computer.

Important   This policy works in conjunction with HKEY_LOCAL_MACHINE\ SOFTWARE\Policies\Microsoft\SystemCertificates\Root\ProtectedRoots\Flags. If this is set (off by default), root certificates will be disabled for propagation, even from the smart card.

■ **Turn on root certificate propagation from smart card**   If enabled, root certificates included on the smart card are added to the trusted root store on the computer where the smart card is inserted.

> **Note**   This policy depends on the Turn On Certificate Propagation From Smart Card policy being enabled.

■ **Prevent plaintext PINs from being returned by Credential Manager**   If enabled, prevents plaintext PINs from being returned by Credential Manager. Ensure that you test the option with your smart cards because some vendors do not allow the use of plaintext PINS.

■ **Filter duplicate logon certificates**   If multiple certificates exist on a smart card that have the same UPN in the Subject Alternative Name extension and are based on the same certificate template with the same major version number, only one of the duplicate certificates is displayed at logon. The displayed certificate will be the certificate in the default slot of the smart card. If the none of the duplicates is in the default slot, the certificate with the expiration date furthest in the future is shown.

> **Note**   This setting is applied *after* the Allow Time Invalid Certificates policy to allow the display of time invalid certificates if necessary.

■ **Force the reading of all certificates from the smart card**   If enabled, all certificates available on the smart card are read in a single call to the smart card, regardless of the feature set of the smart card CSP. This can result in a significant impact on performance.

■ **Display string when smart card is blocked**   Enables a specific message to appear when the integrated Unblock screen is shown. You can add help desk contact information or procedural information to appear on the screen.

■ **Reverse the subject name stored in a certificate when displaying**   By default, both the UPN and the common name of the certificate are displayed to identify a smart card logon certificate. If the certificate does not contain a UPN, and a custom distinguished name is used on the certificate, you may need to customize how the subject name is displayed by enabling this policy.

■ **Allow user name hint**   If enabled, an optional field is displayed at the logon screen allowing a user to input their user name or domain\username to associate the selected certificate with the designated user name.

> **Note**   This option is required only if you choose to use smart card logon certificates that do not implement the user's UPN in the Subject Alternative Name.

Case Study: City Power and Light

You manage the team deploying public key infrastructure (PKI)–enabled applications for City Power and Light, the largest power producer in the region. The CA hierarchy deployed by City Power and Light is shown in Figure 21-7.

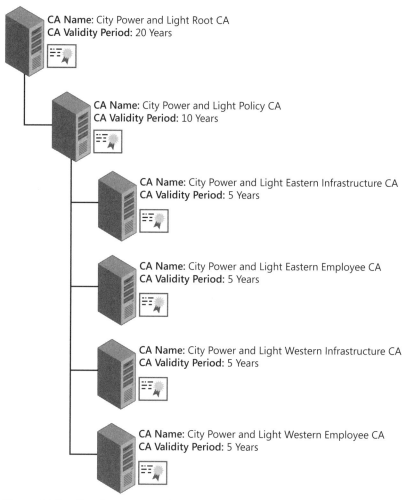

Figure 21-7   The City Power and Light CA hierarchy

City Power and Light wants to deploy smart cards to network administration staff so that smart cards, rather than accounts and passwords, are used for administrative authentication. The following design requirements have been identified for the administrator smart card deployment:

- All administrators will have two user accounts: one for day-to-day tasks and one for all network administrative tasks.

- Smart cards must be enforced for authenticating all administrative tasks. The smart cards will not be used for any purpose other than authentication.

- The company will use Gemalto .NET cards based on the Microsoft Base Smart Card CSP.

- Andy will be the only enrollment agent for all smart cards issued.

- The Enrollment Agent certificate issued to Andy must be authorized by the certificate manager at the Atlanta office where the City Power and Light Eastern Employee CA is located.

- All administrators must present their current City Power and Light employee badges for identity validation before smart card issuance.

- For new administrative hires, employee badges must be issued before Andy can issue administrative smart cards.

- Smart card certificates can be issued by the City Power and Light Eastern Employee CA or the City Power and Light Western Employee CA.

- For administrators, smart card logon will be enforced for both interactive and remote access logons.

- All administrators will be issued desktop computers running Windows Vista with an integrated smart card reader in the keyboard.

- City Power and Light wishes to use the default Windows Server 2008 tools for the smart card deployment

Case Study Questions

1. Can you use the default Enrollment Agent certificate template to satisfy the design requirements for City Power and Light? Why or why not?

2. If you create a custom certificate template for the enrollment agent, how do you enforce the requirement that only Andy receives a custom Enrollment Agent certificate?

3. How do you enforce the Atlanta certificate manager's authorization of the Enrollment Agent certificate issued to Andy?

4. Can you use the default Smart Card User certificate template for the administrative smart cards?

5. Do you have to use a custom certificate template to meet the design goals of City Power and Light?

6. How do you limit enrollment of the smart card certificate template to Andy?

7. Assuming that the administrators can log on from both servers and desktop workstations spread among any OU in the forest, how do you enforce smart cards for interactive logon for the Administrator accounts?

8. How do you enforce smart card authentication for remote access connections by the administrative staff?

9. If a project implements smart cards for regular user accounts, can the administrators use the same smart card for their user certificates?

10. Can you implement Elliptical Curve Cryptography (ECC) in a custom version 3 certificate template for the administrators?

11. What tool would Andy use for enrolling the user smart card certificates?

Best Practices

- **Add the Certificate Services Web Enrollment pages to the Local intranet or Trusted Sites security zone in Internet Explorer.**   This allows you to ensure that the zone has the correct ActiveX settings to enable download of the Smart Card Enrollment ActiveX control. If added to the Trusted Site zone, you must enable automatic passing of the current user's logon information.

- **Add the CLM Web portal URL to the Trusted Sites security zone in Internet Explorer.**   The Smart Card Self-Service Control is hard coded to require that the CLM Web portal be in the Trusted Sites zone. You must enable automatic passing of the current user's logon information.

- **Choose one smart card vendor for smart card deployment.**   This reduces the complexity of smart card management, allowing a single toolset to be used. If using ILM 2007 Certificate Management, a smart card based on the Microsoft Base Smart Card CSP allows you to switch vendors with minimal impact.

- **If using native Windows tools, create a custom version 2 certificate template for the enrollment agent.**   The custom certificate template can require certificate manager approval and use a smart card CSP. Both measures will increase the assurance level of the certificate.

- **Establish a smart card management system such as ILM 2007 Certificate Management before deploying smart card certificates.**   This ensures that your management system addresses the management of the smart cards for the entire life cycle of the smart card.

- **If using ILM 2007 to deploy smart card certificates in a centralized registration model, ensure that all certificate templates implement a requirement to sign the request with a certificate with the Certificate Request Agent OID.**   Failure to require the Certificate Request Agent OID for signing results in the enrollment agent's name being placed in the subject of the smart card certificate rather than the certificate subscriber's name.

- **Define workflows for all portions of the certificate life cycle in ILM 2007 Certificate Management.**   Do not limit your design to enrollment of the smart cards. You must ensure that you have planned management through all stages of the life cycle. Remember that you can use any of the available registration models for each of the individual management policies.

■ **Disable nonrequired management policies in a profile template.**   If you do not plan to offer one of the default management policies, disabling the management policy ensures that self-service requests cannot be performed.

■ **Implement Admin key diversification or Admin PIN rollover for smart cards**   Leaving the default Admin key (for base CSP smart cards) or the default Admin PIN (for legacy smart cards) opens a lost smart card to compromise if the attacker has access to smart card management tools. Key diversification or Admin PIN rollover in ILM 2007 ensures that the PIN is changed from the default and changed each time an administrative function is performed on the smart card.

■ **Configure default Base Smart Card Settings in GPO**   Group Policy allows you to centralize smart card settings for all client computers where the GPO is applied.

Additional Information

■ Description of the software update for Base Smart Card Cryptographic Service Provider (*http://support.microsoft.com/kb/909520*)

■ Base Smart Card CSP Download (*http://www.microsoft.com/downloads/details.aspx?FamilyID=e8095fd5-c7e5-4bee-9577-2ea6b45b41c6*)

■ "Smart Card Minidriver Certification Requirements—For Windows Base CSP and Smart Card KSP" (*http://www.microsoft.com/whdc/device/input/smartcard/sc-minidriver_certreqs.mspx*)

■ "Windows Vista Smart Card Infrastructure" (*http://www.microsoft.com/downloads/details.aspx?FamilyID=ac201438-3317-44d3-9638-07625fe397b9&displaylang=en*)

■ Microsoft Official Curriculum, Course 2821: "Designing and Managing a Windows Public Key Infrastructure" (*http://www.microsoft.com/traincert/syllabi/2821afinal.asp*)

■ "The Smart Card Deployment Cookbook" (*http://www.microsoft.com/technet/Security/topics/smrtcard/smrtcdcb/default.mspx*)

■ "The Smart Card Cryptographic Service Provider Cookbook" (*http://msdn.microsoft.com/library/en-us/dnscard/html/smartcardcspcook.asp*)

■ Smart Cards Mini-Drivers with the Designed for Windows Certification (*http://test.catalog.update.microsoft.com/v7/site/Search.aspx?q=umdf*)

■ 227873: "Smart Card Removal Options in Windows 2000"

■ 248753: "Description of PKINIT Version Implemented in Kerberos in Windows 2000"

■ 257480: "Certificate Enrollment Using Smart Cards"

■ 259880: "Configuring a VPN to Use Extensible Authentication Protocol (EAP)"

- 281245: "Guidelines for Enabling Smart Card Logon with Third-Party Certification Authorities"

- 295663: "How To: Import a Third-Party Certificate into the NTAuth Store"

- 313490: "How To: Enroll a Certificate on Behalf of Another for Smart Card Users"

- 313629: "Custom Smartcard Template Is Not Available on the Smart Card Enrollment"

- 326474: "How To: Troubleshoot VPN with Extensible Authentication Protocol (EAP)"

- 830579: "Terminal Services Client that Is Using a Smart Card Cannot Connect to the Terminal Server"

- 832026: "'Local Policy of This System Requires You to Logon Using a Smart Card' Message Appears When You Try to Log On to the Server"

- 834875: "Update for the 'Interactive Logon: Require Smart Card' Security Setting in Windows XP"

Note The last 12 articles in the above list can be accessed through the Microsoft Knowledge Base. Go to *http://support.microsoft.com*, and enter the article number in the Search The Knowledge Base text box.

Chapter 22
Secure E-Mail

Many organizations use e-mail as a method of communication between employees and external customers. By default, Internet e-mail is sent without any encryption, exposing the e-mail content to any users that are able to capture the packets as they traverse the network.

This chapter looks at the public key infrastructure (PKI) requirements for protecting e-mail with cryptographic measures.

Securing E-Mail

Two different methods can be implemented to secure e-mail:

- **Securing the content of e-mail messages** The content of e-mail messages is secured by implementing Secure/Multipurpose Internet Mail Extensions (S/MIME).

> **Note** The design details of S/MIME version 3 are defined in RFC 2633, "S/MIME Version 3 Message Specification," available at *http://www.ietf.org/rfc/rfc2633.txt*.

- **Securing data as it is transmitted between the mail client and the mail server** The data stream is protected by implementing Secure Sockets Layer (SSL) or Transport Layer Security (TLS) to provide validation of the mail server's identity and encryption of the data transmitted between the mail server and the mail client.

The sections that follow provide more specific information on how the two methods work to protect e-mail messaging.

Secure/Multipurpose Internet Mail Extensions (S/MIME)

S/MIME extensions allow e-mail programs to provide both digital signing and encryption services for e-mail delivery. S/MIME is an extension to MIME that allows digital data to be sent using text-based e-mail.

E-Mail Digital Signing Process

E-mail digital signing uses the key pair of the sender so that the recipient can verify the authenticity of the message. (See Figure 22-1.) The process for e-mail signing is the same process used for general digital signing except that the original text is the e-mail message.

Note   The use of MIME allows the digital signing of e-mail messages. MIME converts binary attachments to text-based extensions in the e-mail message. The S/MIME encryption is represented as an additional MIME in the e-mail message.

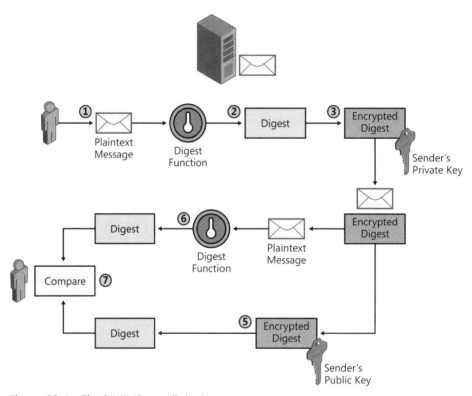

Figure 22-1   The S/MIME e-mail signing process

1. The sender creates an e-mail message.

2. The sender's e-mail client runs a hash algorithm against the plaintext message to create a message digest.

3. The digest is encrypted using the sender's e-mail signing private key.

4. The plaintext e-mail message and the encrypted digest are sent to the recipient.

Note   When using digital signing, no encryption is applied to the plaintext e-mail message. The e-mail message can be modified in transit, but modification invalidates the encrypted digest sent with the message.

5. The recipient decrypts the encrypted digest by using the sender's e-mail signing public key. Usually, the signing certificate, which contains the sender's public key, is included with the signed data.

> **Note**   If the sender has an e-mail encryption certificate, the e-mail encryption and e-mail signing certificates are typically included in the sent message.

6. The recipient runs the same hash algorithm used by the sender to create his or her own digest of the e-mail message. This digest is created against the plaintext e-mail message received from the originator.

7. The two digests are compared. If the digests differ, the message or digest has been modified during transmission, and the recipient is notified that the signature is invalid.

E-Mail Encryption Process

E-mail encryption uses the e-mail encryption key pair of the recipient of the e-mail message. When e-mail encryption is performed, the process shown in Figure 22-2 takes place.

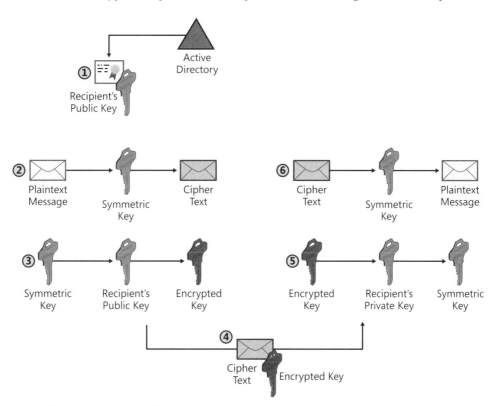

Figure 22-2   E-mail encryption process

1. The sender retrieves the recipient's e-mail encryption public key from Active Directory Domain Services (AD DS) or some other directory, such as their e-mail contact list, and extracts the public key from the certificate.

2. The sender generates a symmetric key and uses this key to encrypt the original plaintext e-mail message.

3. The symmetric key is encrypted with the recipient's public key to prevent the symmetric key from being intercepted during transmission.

4. The encrypted symmetric key and encrypted e-mail message are sent to the intended recipient.

5. The recipient uses his or her private key to decrypt the encrypted symmetric key.

6. The encrypted e-mail message is decrypted with the symmetric key, which results in the recipient viewing the original plaintext e-mail message.

E-Mail Encryption Fallacies

The most common mistake I see with customers is the belief that possessing an e-mail encryption certificate means that you can send encrypted e-mail to anyone in your address book. Actually, if you look at the details of how e-mail encryption works, the exact opposite is true.

Possessing an e-mail certificate means that maybe, just maybe, someone out there can send *you* an encrypted e-mail message. That is, only if they can find access to or retrieve your e-mail encryption certificate from some directory.

SSL for Internet Protocols

In addition to digitally signing and encrypting e-mail messages, you can increase the security of authentication and data transmission for several Request for Comments (RFC) e-mail protocols. These RFC-based protocols include:

- **Post Office Protocol version 3 (POP3)**   Used to retrieve e-mail messages from the user's Inbox on an e-mail server.

- **Internet Message Access Protocol (IMAP4)**   Used to retrieve any messages stored on an e-mail server. This includes messages in the user's Inbox and other message boxes on the e-mail server, including Drafts, Sent Items, and Public Folders.

- **Simple Mail Transfer Protocol (SMTP)**   Used to send e-mail messages to e-mail recipients.

- **Network News Transfer Protocol (NNTP)**   NNTP is used to download and post newsgroup messages from newsgroup servers.

More Info   For relevant RFCs related to implementing Transport Layer Security (TLS) with these RFC-based protocols, see "Additional Information" at the end of this chapter.

 Important   Although the RFCs reference TLS rather than SSL, the TLS RFC—RFC 4346, "The Transport Layer Security (TLS) Protocol Version 1.1"—describes compatibility between TLS and SSL version 3. It is an RFC-based client decision whether to refer to the security mechanism as TLS or SSL.

All these RFC-based protocols use plaintext when transmitting data between the RFC-based client and the back-end server. If an attacker were to capture the data stream with a network sniffer, the attacker could read all contents of the data exchanged between the client and the server.

By implementing SSL, you can protect the RFC-based protocols that are used to send and receive e-mail from a server running Microsoft Exchange 2000 Server, Microsoft Exchange Server 2003, or Microsoft Exchange Server 2007. SSL encrypts the data between the e-mail client and the server. When SSL is implemented, the server accepts connections on the SSL port rather than on the standard port.

Table 22-1 shows the protocols that SSL can protect and lists the default and SSL-protected ports.

Table 22-1   SSL Ports for E-Mail Protocols

Protocol	Default port	SSL port
POP3	TCP 110	TCP 995
IMAP4	TCP 143	TCP 993
SMTP	TCP 25	TCP 25 or TCP port 465
NNTP	TCP 119	TCP 563

To enable SSL on Exchange Server, the computer running Exchange Server must have a certificate installed that includes the Server Authentication Enhanced Key Usage (EKU) object identifier (OID), such as a certificate based on the Web Server certificate template. Only a single Web Server certificate is required for Exchange Server; the same Web Server certificate is used for each of the protocols as long as the subject of the certificate matches the Domain Name System (DNS) name used by e-mail clients to connect to the server.

Installing the Web Server Certificate

1. Log on to the computer running Exchange Server as an Exchange administrator.

2. From the Start menu, point to All Programs, point to Microsoft Exchange, and then click System Manager.

3. In the console tree, expand Servers, expand *ComputerName* (where *ComputerName* is the name of the computer running Exchange Server), expand Protocols, expand *RFCProtocol* (where *RFCProtocol* is the name of the RFC-based protocol, such as IMAP4 or POP3), right-click Default *RFCProtocol* Virtual Server, and then click Properties.

4. In the Default *RFCProtocol* Virtual Server Properties dialog box, on the Access tab, click Certificate.

5. In the Web Server Certificate Wizard, click Next.

6. On the Server Certificate page, click Create a New Certificate, and then click Next.

> **Note**   If you already have a Web Server certificate installed on the Web server, you can choose the Assign An Existing Certificate option.

7. On the Delayed Or Immediate Request page, click Send The Request Immediately To An Online Certification Authority, and then click Next.

> **Note**   This assumes that you are requesting the certificate from an enterprise CA, not from a standalone CA. If you are submitting the request to a standalone CA or commercial CA, you must save the request to a request file.

8. On the Name And Security Settings page, accept the default name and bit length, and then click Next.

9. On the Organization page, type the organization name and organizational unit (OU) name, and then click Next.

10. On the Your Site's Common Name page, type the DNS name used to connect to the e-mail server, and then click Next.

11. On the Geographical Information page, type the Country, State/Province, and City/Locality for the e-mail server, and then click Next.

12. On the Choose A Certification Authority page, select an available enterprise certification authority (CA) from the drop-down list, and then click Next.

13. On the Certificate Request Submission page, verify the details of the certificate request, and then click Next.

14. On the Completing The Web Server Certificate Wizard page, click Finish.

Enabling SSL for an RFC-Based Protocol

Once the Web server certificate is installed, the following procedure will enable SSL for an RFC-based protocol.

1. Ensure that you are still viewing the Default *RFCProtocol* Virtual Server Properties dialog box.

2. In the Default *RFCProtocol* Virtual Server Properties dialog box, on the Access tab, click Communication.

3. In the Security dialog box, select the Require Secure Channel and the Require 128-Bit Encryption check boxes, and then click OK.

4. In the Default *RFCProtocol* Virtual Server Properties dialog box, click OK.

> **Warning**   The enabling of SSL on a computer running Exchange Server will likely require modification of the organization's firewall to allow communications to the computer running Exchange Server from the Internet to the SSL listening ports. In addition, the firewall can close or deny access to the non-SSL ports for the RFC-based protocols.

Enabling SSL in the E-Mail Applications

Once you have enabled SSL on the computer running Exchange Server, you must enable SSL in your organization's e-mail client software. The e-mail client software must be modified to use the SSL ports rather than the non-SSL ports. For example, Figure 22-3 shows how Microsoft Office Outlook 2003 is configured to enable SSL for both IMAP4 and SMTP.

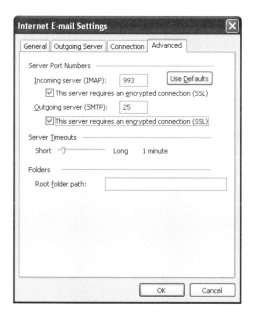

Figure 22-3   Enabling SSL for IMAP4 and SMTP in Outlook 2003

> **Note**   The actual configuration steps to enable SSL are dependent on the specific e-mail application software used by your organization. For details on how to enable SSL, review the Help files and documentation provided with the e-mail application.

Choosing Certification Authorities

When your organization chooses to implement secure e-mail using S/MIME, the first decision that must be made is where to acquire the S/MIME certificates. Your organization can choose to acquire the certificates from a commercial CA or issue the certificates from a private CA.

Choosing Commercial CAs

An organization will choose to obtain a user's S/MIME certificates from a commercial CA when their users send the majority of their S/MIME-protected e-mail messages to people outside the organization. Using a certificate issued by a commercial provider, such as VeriSign, that is trusted by most organizations increases the probability that a user outside the organization will trust a digital signature created with the certificate issued by the commercial CA. The drawback is that the organization must purchase each S/MIME certificate issued to its employees.

> **Note**   Alternatively, an organization can choose to purchase a subordinate CA certificate from a commercial organization. The commercial organization will then appear as the root CA in the CA hierarchy when an e-mail certificate is validated by another organization. An example of this type of service is included in Chosen Security's TC Root Signing program (*http://www.chosensecurity.com/products/tc_rootsigning.htm*) and CyberTrust's OmniRoot program (*http://www.cybertrust.com/solutions/ssl_certificates/omniroot/*). If you choose to create a subordinate CA below a commercial root CA, you must ensure that the Authority Information Access (AIA) and CRL Distribution Point (CDP) URLs included in the certificates issued by the subordinate CA are available on the Internet for certificate validation purposes.

Choosing Private CAs

An organization will choose to issue certificates from a private CA when the majority of the e-mail secured with S/MIME is exchanged between users of the organization. Because all the users exchanging S/MIME e-mail trust the same trusted root CA, all digital signing and encryption operations are trusted. There are no additional costs for issuing the private S/MIME certificates to an organization's employees because the certificate infrastructure is owned and managed by the organization. In addition, methods such as autoenrollment can be implemented to aid in the distribution of the S/MIME certificates.

Using Multiple Profiles

There are cases where a user can acquire two different sets of S/MIME certificates: one set for internal use and one set for external use. If the user is using Outlook, the user can create two separate profiles for sending e-mail:

- The first profile specifies that the internally issued certificates be used for all digital signing and encryption options.

- The second profile specifies that the commercially issued certificate be used for all digital signing and encryption options.

Both profiles access the same Microsoft Exchange Server mailbox, but each specifies a different certificate combination for S/MIME transactions.

Choosing Certificate Templates

If your organization chooses to deploy its own certificates for secure e-mail, the first decision that the organization must make is whether to use the same certificate for both signing and encryption operations or to issue two separate certificates: one for digital signing and one for encryption.

The advantage of a single certificate is that the user has to manage only a single certificate for all e-mail operations. The disadvantage is that if your organization implements key archival of the e-mail certificate, it is possible that another person could gain access to the signing private key associated with the e-mail certificate.

Note   For details on enabling key archival at a certification authority (CA) and the security issues of archiving private keys used for digital signing, review Chapter 18, "Archiving Encryption Keys."

The advantage of issuing separate certificates for signing and encryption operations is that by delegating encryption operations to one certificate, you can safely archive the encryption certificate without fear of signing impersonations. The private key associated with the e-mail signing certificate is not archived; only the private key for encryption is archived.

A Combined Signing and Encryption Template

If you implement a single certificate for e-mail, it is recommended to create a version 2 certificate template based on either the Exchange User or Exchange Signature Only certificate template.

Note   Outlook 2007 supports Cryptography Next Generation (CNG) for e-mail signing and encryption. You can consider creating a version 3 certificate template as long as you are using Outlook 2007 or another e-mail client that supports CNG algorithms. Ensure that your recipients also support CNG algorithms; otherwise, you will have to choose weaker CryptoAPI algorithms.

When you create the custom version 2 certificate template, use these recommendations for each tab:

- **General**   Ensure that you publish the certificate in AD DS to allow other users to send encrypted e-mail to the user referenced in the certificate. You can use your organization's naming conventions for the certificate template and set the validity period and renewal period based on the technical requirements of the organization.

- **Request Handling**   Change the Purpose of the certificate to Signature and Encryption to allow both digital signing and encryption. You can also enable the following options based on the requirements of your organization:

  - **Key Archival**   Key archival stores an encrypted copy of the e-mail certificate's private key in the CA database.

  - **Private Key Protection**   Enabling the option to Prompt The User During Enrollment And Require User Input When The Private Key Is Used ensures that the user can assign a password, separate from their logon password, that protects the user's private key.

Note   Alternatively, consider changing the cryptographic service provider (CSP) for the certificate template to a smart card CSP. This provides two-factor protection of the e-mail certificate's private key and portability of the credentials. Key archival is supported as long as the CSP supports the **WIN_CRYPT_ENABLE** flag.

- **Subject Name**   Enable populating the subject from information stored in AD DS. For S/MIME purposes, the certificate's subject must include the user's e-mail address in either the Subject field or the Subject Alternative Name extension.

Important   If the user account associated with the user requesting the certificate does not have a value in the *E-mail-Addresses* attribute, the certificate request will fail. The requesting user accounts must have the *E-mail-Addresses* attribute populated.

- **Security**   A custom universal or global group that contains all users that will perform S/MIME digital signing and encryption must be assigned the Read, Enroll, and

Autoenroll permissions. This permission combination will allow deployment of the certificate to users with computers running Windows XP by using autoenrollment.

> **Note** No modifications are required for the Issuance Requirements, Superseded Templates, and Extensions tabs.

Dual Certificates for E-Mail

Because of the risks of archiving the private key associated with an S/MIME signing certificate, many organizations choose to implement separate certificates for e-mail signing and encryption. Deploying separate certificates ensures that only the private key associated with the e-mail encryption certificate is archived.

> **Note** As with the single-purpose e-mail certificate, consider using smart cards to protect the dual certificates rather than implementing strong private key protection. Smart cards provide strong protection of the private key and better credential portability.

E-Mail Signing Certificate Template

If you implement a separate certificate template for e-mail signing, it is recommended that you duplicate the Exchange Signature Only certificate template. When you separate the e-mail signing and e-mail encryption certificates, you can choose to deploy the e-mail signing certificate on a smart card. If you choose to deploy the certificate on a smart card, when you duplicate the Exchange Signature Only certificate template, you must make the same changes recommended for the combination e-mail signing and encryption certificate. The only differences in the settings are on the General and Request Handling tabs.

General Tab On the General tab, it is recommended to *not* select the Publish Certificate In Active Directory check box. A user does not have to retrieve the user's certificate to verify the signature on an e-mail message, because the certificate is included in the message payload.

Request Handling Tab On the Request Handling tab, the recommended settings when you deploy the certificate on a smart card are:

- Purpose: Signature and Smart Card Logon
- Prompt The User During Enrollment: Enabled
- CSP: The smart card CSP associated with your organization's selected smart card vendor

If you choose to deploy the e-mail signing certificate as a certificate stored in the user's profile, the following settings are recommended for the Request Handling tab:

- Purpose: Signature

- Allow Private Key To Be Exported: If your organization allows export of the e-mail signing private key, enable this option. Conversely, if your organization does not allow export of the e-mail signing private key, disable this option.

- Prompt The User During Enrollment And Require User Input When The Private Key Is Used: Enabled

- CSP: Microsoft Enhanced Cryptographic Provider v1.0

Strong Private Key Protection

When you enable strong private key protection, the user is prompted during the enrollment process to enable medium or high security on the certificate's private key.

- If the user selects *medium*, the user is prompted each and every time the private key associated with the certificate is accessed. The user must click an OK button to acknowledge that the private key is being accessed.

- If the user selects *high*, the user is prompted to input a password each and every time the private key associated with the certificate is accessed. The user must type the password in order to access the private key.

> **Warning**   If the user forgets the password required to access the private key, all access to the private key is lost. Unless the private key is archived at the CA, there is no method of recovering the existing private key.

Although it is possible to enforce the requirement that the user must select high protection for all private keys, by enabling the "System Cryptography: Use FIPS Compliant Algorithms For Encryption, Hashing, And Signing" policy setting, this Group Policy Object (GPO) or local policy setting cannot be enabled if the organization deploys applications such as Encrypting File System (EFS) or wireless authentication. Applications such as EFS and wireless authentication do not expose an interface for the user to provide the password protecting the private key, which causes the applications to silently fail.

E-Mail Encryption Certificate Template

When you implement a separate certificate for e-mail encryption, it is recommended that you duplicate the Exchange User certificate template. The separate e-mail encryption certificate allows you to enable key archival for the encryption certificate. Because key archival is not supported for smart card certificates, you must store the certificate in the user's personal store.

When you duplicate the Exchange User certificate template, you must make the same changes recommended for the combination e-mail signing and encryption certificate. The only difference is the settings on the General tab and the Request Handling tab.

On the General tab, ensure that you select the Publish Certificate In Active Directory check box so that other users can retrieve the user's certificate from the global catalog when sending encrypted e-mail to the user.

On the Request Handling tab, the recommended settings when you deploy the certificate on a smart card are:

- Purpose: Encryption
- Archive Subject's Encryption Private Key: Enabled
- Include Symmetric Algorithms Allowed By The Subject: Enabled
- Prompt The User During Enrollment: Enabled
- CSP: The smart card CSP associated with your organization's selected smart card vendor

If you deploy a software-based certificate for e-mail encryption, use these guidelines for the Request Handling tab:

- Purpose: Encryption
- Archive Subject's Encryption Private Key: Enabled
- Include Symmetric Algorithms Allowed By The Subject: Enabled
- Allow Private Key To Be Exported: Enabled

> **Note**   You have to allow the export of the private key only if any of the users have computer running Microsoft Windows 2000 or earlier. This check box does not have to be selected if only Windows XP or Windows 2003 clients are deployed because key archival can take place without enabling the export option.

- Prompt The User During Enrollment And Require User Input When The Private Key Is Used: Enabled
- CSP: Microsoft Enhanced Cryptographic Provider v1.0

Choosing Deployment Methods

The deployment model that you choose will depend on whether you have deployed software-based or smart card–based e-mail certificates.

Software-Based Certificate Deployment

Whether you have chosen to deploy a single e-mail certificate or to implement separate e-mail signing and encryption certificates, it is recommended to enable autoenrollment for the deployed certificate templates.

Autoenrollment allows the automated enrollment of the e-mail certificates to all users that have a computer running Windows XP that is a member of the domain.

> **Important**   Automated enrollment requires the user's input if you enable a smart card for the signing certificate or implement strong private key protection for the certificates.

If your network includes Windows 2000 or earlier clients, you cannot use the Windows Server 2003 native autoenrollment methods. Instead, you must choose from the following methods to deploy the custom certificates:

- **Web Enrollment**   A user with membership in a global or universal group assigned the Read and Enroll permissions can enroll both version 2 certificates by using the Certificate Services Web Enrollment pages.

- **Scripted enrollment of the e-mail encryption certificate**   A user can run the enroll.vbs script provided on the companion CD to automate the request of the e-mail encryption certificate. The user must run the script at a command prompt by using the following syntax:

```
cscript enroll.vbs /ca "issuingca.example.com\Example Corporation Issuing CA" /certtype
EmailEncrypt /keyl 1024 /csp enhanced /archive /export
```

> **Note**   This command line assumes that the name of the CA you are submitting the request to is named "issuingca.example.com\Example Corporation Issuing CA" and that the certificate template is named EmailEncrypt. If you are running the command on a Windows 2000 client, you must run both the **/archive** and **/export** options. You do not require the **/export** option on a Windows XP or later client.

- **Scripted enrollment of the e-mail signing certificate**   A user can run the enroll.vbs script provided on the companion CD to automate the request of the e-mail signing certificate. The user must run the script at a command prompt by using following syntax:

```
cscript enroll.vbs /ca "issuingca.example.com\Example Corporation Issuing CA" /certtype
EmailSign /keyl 1024 /csp enhanced
```

> **Note**   This command line assumes that the name of the CA you are submitting the request to is named "issuingca.example.com\Example Corporation Issuing CA" and that the certificate template is named EmailSign.

No matter which deployment model you choose for software-based certificates, consider using Credential Roaming Service (discussed in Chapter 15, "Issuing Certificates,") to allow a user's certificates to roam between client computers. This ensures that the users have access to the same e-mail signing and e-mail encryption certificates when they log on to different domain-member computers.

Smart Card–Based Certificate Deployment

When you deploy e-mail certificates on smart cards, it is recommended to use a registration authority such as Microsoft Identity Lifecycle Manager (ILM) 2007 to deploy the certificates. A registration authority allows you to define life-cycle management workflows that ensure that the smart card and its certificates are managed with a high assurance level.

 Note Details on deploying certificates with ILM 2007 are discussed in Chapter 17, "Identity Lifecycle Manager 2007 Certificate Management," and Chapter 21, "Deploying Smart Cards."

Enabling Secure E-Mail

Once you have successfully deployed the certificates to the users, each user must configure his or her e-mail application to use the e-mail certificates for S/MIME protection. The following sections detail how to enable S/MIME security in:

- Microsoft Office Outlook
- Outlook Web Access (OWA)

 Note S/MIME is available only in the OWA provided with Exchange Server 2003 and Exchange Server 2007. Previous versions of OWA do not provide support for S/MIME protection.

Enabling Outlook

Outlook 2003 and Outlook 2007 automatically use available e-mail signing and encryption certificates if the certificates exist in the user's profile.

Outlook 2003

If you are running Outlook 2003, you can verify the existence of the certificates and configure the encryption and signing algorithms by using the following procedure:

1. Open Outlook.
2. On the Tools menu, click Options.
3. In the Options dialog box, on the Security tab, click Settings.

4. In the Change Security Settings dialog box (see Figure 22-4), ensure that the following settings are configured:

Figure 22-4   Configuring S/MIME settings in Outlook 2003

❑   Cryptography Format: S/MIME

❑   Default Security Settings For This Cryptographic Message Format: Enabled

❑   Default Security Settings For All Cryptographic Messages: Enabled

❑   Hash Algorithm: SHA1 or MD5, but SHA1 is recommended.

❑   Encryption Algorithm: 3DES, RC2 (128-bit), RC2 (64-bit), DES, or RC2 (40-bit), but 3DES is recommended.

❑   Send These Certificates With Signed Messages: Enabled

> **Note**   For a review of the strengths and weaknesses of each hash and encryption algorithm, see Chapter 1, "Cryptography Basics."

5. In the Change Security Settings dialog box, click OK.

6. In the Options dialog box, click OK.

Outlook 2007

If you are running Outlook 2007, you can verify the existence of the certificates and specify the encryption and signing algorithms by using the following procedure:

1. Open Outlook.

2. On the Tools menu, click Trust Center.

3. In the Trust Center dialog box, click E-mail Security.

4. In the Change Security Settings dialog box (see Figure 22-5), ensure that the following settings are configured:

Figure 22-5   Configuring S/MIME settings in Outlook 2007

❑   Cryptography Format: S/MIME

❑   Default Security Settings For This Cryptographic Message Format: Enabled

❑   Default Security Settings For All Cryptographic Messages: Enabled

❑   Hash Algorithm: SHA512, SHA384, SHA256, SHA1 or MD5, but SHA1 or higher is recommended.

❑   Encryption Algorithm: AES (256-bit), AES (192-bit), 3DES, AES (128-bit), RC2 (128-bit), RC2 (64-bit), DES, or RC2 (40-bit), but AES (128-bit) or higher is recommended.

❑   Send These Certificates With Signed Messages: Enabled

Note   For a review of the strengths and weaknesses of each hash and encryption algorithm, see Chapter 1.

5. In the Change Security Settings dialog box, click OK.

6. In the Trust Center dialog box, click OK.

Enabling S/MIME in OWA

To allow S/MIME usage in OWA, you must install the S/MIME Microsoft ActiveX control at the client computer. The S/MIME ActiveX control enables using S/MIME for both signing and encrypting e-mail messages.

> **Important**   Only a local administrator or member of the local Power Users group can install the ActiveX control. Once the control is installed, all users can use it. In addition, the ActiveX control requires Microsoft Internet Explorer 6.0, Windows Internet Explorer 7.0 or later running on Windows 2000 or later.

To install the S/MIME ActiveX control:

1. Log on to the computer as a member of the local Administrators or Power Users group.

2. Open Internet Explorer.

3. In Internet Explorer, open the URL *http://ExchangeServer/exchange* (where *Exchange-Server* is the DNS name of the computer running Exchange Server 2003 hosting the user's mailbox).

4. When prompted, type the user name and password for accessing your mailbox.

5. In Outlook Web Access, in the Navigation Pane, click Options.

6. On the Options page, under E-Mail Security, click Download.

7. In the File Download dialog box, click Open.

8. If any security warnings appear, click Yes to install the ActiveX control.

Sending Secure E-Mail

Once you have enabled S/MIME in the e-mail package, the decision to send secure e-mail is made for every message sent by the e-mail participant.

For example, Figure 22-6 shows a message window in Outlook 2007 that is enabled for both digital signing and e-mail encryption.

By selecting the Digitally Sign button and the Encrypt button, the sender can decide whether to implement signing, encryption, or both encryption and signing for the outbound e-mail message. In addition, the user can select the defaults to enable within the e-mail client for S/MIME e-mail.

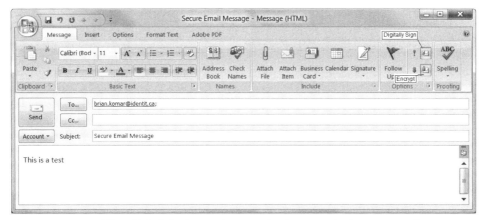

Figure 22-6 Enabling digital signing and encryption in an Outlook 2007 e-mail message

Note Although Figure 22-6 shows the Outlook 2007 client, similar buttons for enabling digital signing and encryption exist in Outlook 2003 and OWA.

Important To send encrypted e-mail to a recipient, the sender must have access to the recipient's public key. In an AD DS environment, the sender retrieves the certificate from the global catalog. The certificate is added to the *userCertificate* attribute of the user account during the enrollment process by selecting the Publish Certificate In Active Directory check box in the e-mail encryption certificate template. The *userCertificate* attribute is replicated to the global catalog. For nondomain members, the users can exchange encryption certificates by sending signed e-mail messages and then creating a contact object for the other user. The properties of the contact object include the signing and encryption certificates.

Case Study: Adventure Works

You manage the network for Adventure Works, a travel agency in New York that specializes in radical vacation trips. The organization implements the CA hierarchy shown in Figure 22-7.

To provide increased trust of the certificates issued by the Adventure Works Issuing CA, Adventure Works has purchased a subordinate CA certificate from VeriSign. The VeriSign root CA certificate is included in the packaged list of trusted root CAs distributed by Microsoft with the Windows operating system, increasing the trust in the certificates issued by the Adventure Works Issuing CA.

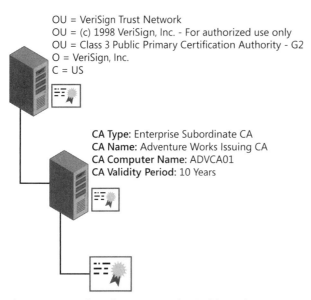

OU = VeriSign Trust Network
OU = (c) 1998 VeriSign, Inc. - For authorized use only
OU = Class 3 Public Primary Certification Authority - G2
O = VeriSign, Inc.
C = US

CA Type: Enterprise Subordinate CA
CA Name: Adventure Works Issuing CA
CA Computer Name: ADVCA01
CA Validity Period: 10 Years

Figure 22-7   The Adventure Works CA hierarchy

Scenario

Adventure Works implements Exchange Server 2003 in a single domain forest named
adventure-works.com. The computer running Exchange Server, ADVEXCH01, provides e-mail
services to all employees of Adventure Works and is also used to send and receive e-mail over
the Internet. All client computers use Outlook 2007 to connect to the mail server

All servers on the network are running Windows Server 2008 Enterprise, and the
client computers are running Windows Vista. The latest service packs are installed and
security updates are applied to all client computers on a weekly basis.

Recently, the IT, human resources, and legal departments drafted security policies for the
Adventure Works network. The following security policies are related to e-mail:

■ Any e-mail messages containing proposed or confirmed flight itineraries to customers
   must be signed to provide confidence to the customers that the contents are valid and
   did originate from the Adventure Works travel consultant.

■ Any e-mail messages containing customer confidential information, such as passport
   numbers, credit card numbers, and bank account information, must be encrypted.
   In addition, any e-mail messages containing classified data must be encrypted when
   sent to employees

■ The private keys associated with encryption certificates must be archived at the issuing
   CA to allow recovery of the private key in the event of computer failure, computer
   rebuild, profile deletion, or corruption of the private key. All key recovery must require
   the participation of at least two employees to prevent unauthorized access to a user's
   encryption key.

- The private keys associated with the signing certificate must never be archived to ensure that two users do not have access to the same signing certificate.

- E-mail signing and encryption private keys must be protected by a password. The password must be typed each and every time the private key is accessed.

In addition to enforcing the security policies defined for Adventure Works, the secure e-mail project must also meet the following design requirements:

- Several of the agents participate in a job-sharing program. When an agent comes into the office, there is no guarantee that he or she will sit at the same computer, so e-mail certificates must be portable.

- Some of the agents have laptop computers and connect to the mail server, ADVEXCH01, from remote locations. Secure access to their e-mail as well as the ability to use S/MIME for signing and encrypting e-mail must be provided.

Case Study Questions

1. Based on the security policies related to e-mail usage, how many e-mail certificates must be distributed to each user?

2. What certificate(s) must be published to Active Directory Domain Services (AD DS) to enable the sending of encrypted e-mail between employees of Adventure Works?

3. Will the current CA infrastructure allow the e-mail signing and encryption certificates to be recognized by the customers of Adventure Works?

4. What method would you use to deploy the e-mail certificate(s) to the Adventure Works users? What certificate template settings are required to allow this method of enrollment?

5. One of the travel agents is able to open his encrypted e-mail only at one of the available agent computers. When he attempts to open his encrypted e-mail at the other computers, the attempt fails. What can you do to ensure that the travel agent can open the encrypted e-mail at any of the travel agent computers?

6. How do you propose to enforce the security policy that requires two or more people to be involved in the recovery?

7. How do you enforce the requirement that users must provide a password to access the private keys associated with the e-mail signing of any e-mail encryption certificates?

8. If you had the budget, how could you further increase the security of the e-mail signing and e-mail encryption certificates?

9. What must a travel agent do to allow a customer to send an encrypted e-mail message?

10. What solution can be used to allow remote travel agents to securely access their e-mail and use S/MIME to protect the e-mail messages without enabling an additional e-mail client?

11. One of the travel agents has forgotten the password used to protect the e-mail encryption certificate and can no longer read her encrypted e-mail. What must you do to allow the travel agent to access the encrypted e-mail?

12. When performing the testing of your e-mail solution, you are told that customers are complaining that their e-mail applications are reporting that the digital signatures are failing. You look at the certificate and find the following URLs in the CDP extension:

    ❑ LDAP:///CN=Adventure Works Issuing CA,CN=ADVCA01,CN=CDP,CN=Public Key Services,CN=Services,CN=Configuration,DC=travelworks,DC=com

    ❑ http://advca01/certenroll/Adventure%%20Works%%20%%20Issuing%%20CA.crl

    What is causing the certificate validation to fail? What must you do to fix the problem?

Best Practices

■ **Issue separate certificates for e-mail signing and encryption.**   Using separate certificates allows your organization to archive the private keys of e-mail encryption certificates yet not archive the private keys for e-mail signing certificates. If you use a single certificate for both signing and encryption, there is a possibility of identity theft. Finally, implementing separate signing and encryption e-mail certificates allows an organization to restrict a user to performing only e-mail encryption or e-mail signing. If the organization wants to implement only e-mail signing, they can issue a certificate that enables only e-mail signing.

■ **Use strong private key protection for e-mail signing and encryption certificates when using software-based CSPs.**   Strong private key protection provides additional security for certificates stored in a user's profile. Every time the private key of the certificate is accessed, the user must provide a password. This strong private key protection prevents an administrator who resets the user's password from gaining access to the e-mail certificate private keys.

■ **Use smart card–based CSPs to provide the strongest private key protection and certificate roaming.**   Smart cards provide two-factor protection of the e-mail certificates and allow portability of the certificate and private keys between computers.

■ **Provide key archival for e-mail encryption certificates.**   Key archival allows the user's private key to be recovered in the event that the private key is deleted or corrupted. Retrieving the private key allows the user to gain access to e-mail previously encrypted with the public key of the key pair.

■ **Use autoenrollment or scripted enrollment to distribute e-mail certificates to users.** Automated enrollment ensures that each user obtains the required certificates for e-mail with minimal user actions. If you enable strong private key protection, the user will be prompted to provide the password used to protect the private key.

■ **Ensure that AIA and CDP URLs are accessible from both the private network and the Internet.**   If you send signed e-mail or receive encrypted e-mail, you must ensure that at least one AIA and CDP URL are accessible from the private network or from the Internet to allow certificate validation to succeed.

Additional Information

- Microsoft Official Curriculum, Course 2821: "Designing and Managing a Windows Public Key Infrastructure" (*http://www.microsoft.com/traincert/syllabi/2821afinal.asp*)

- "Key Archival and Recovery in Windows Server 2008" (*http://www.microsoft.com/downloads/details.aspx?FamilyID=b280e420-7cd8-4fd0-94a8-c91035b7b23b&displaylang=en*)

- "Exchange Server 2003 Message Security Guide" (*http://www.microsoft.com/technet/prodtechnol/exchange/2003/library/exmessec.mspx*)

- "TechNet Webcast: Message Security, Compliance, and Message Protection with Exchange Server 2007 (Level 200)" (*http://msevents.microsoft.com/CUI/WebCastEventDetails.aspx?culture=en-US&EventID=1032309159&CountryCode=US*)

- "Overview of Cryptography in Outlook 2003" (*http://go.microsoft.com/fwlink/?LinkId=17808*)

- "Administering Cryptography in Outlook 2007" (*http://technet2.microsoft.com/Office/en-us/library/40aeecab-c39f-4635-8b25-1adda35ca93c1033.mspx?mfr=true*)

- "Configuring and Troubleshooting Certificate Services Client–Credential Roaming" (*http://www.microsoft.com/technet/security/guidance/cryptographyetc/client-credential-roaming/terminology-assumptions.mspx*)

- "Quick Start Guide for S/MIME in Exchange Server 2003" (*http://www.microsoft.com/downloads/details.aspx?FamilyId=F2D49F68-9E36-414B-906B-13C7C075E1B1&displaylang=en*)

- RFC 2595–"Using TLS with IMAP, POP3, and ACAP" (*http://www.ietf.org/rfc/rfc2595.txt*)

- RFC 2633–"S/MIME Version 3 Message Specification" (*http://www.ietf.org/rfc/rfc2633.txt*)

- RFC 3207–"SMTP Service Extension for Secure SMTP over Transport Layer Security" (*http://www.ietf.org/rfc/rfc3207.txt*)

- RFC 4346–"The Transport Layer Security (TLS) Protocol Version 1.1" (*http://www.ietf.org/rfc/rfc4346.txt*)

- 823568: "How To: Configure Exchange Server 2003 OWA to Use S/MIME"

Note The last article in the above list can be accessed through the Microsoft Knowledge Base. Go to *http://support.microsoft.com*, and enter the article number in the Search The Knowledge Base text box.

Chapter 23

Virtual Private Networking

Virtual private networking allows users to connect to corporate resources from off-site locations, such as a home office or hotel room. This chapter discusses the certificate deployment required to implement client-to-gateway virtual private network (VPN) solutions.

> **Note** It is also possible to deploy gateway-to-gateway VPN solutions that join two offices over a public network such as the Internet. The certificates required for these connections are similar to the client-to-gateway scenarios and are not discussed in this chapter. Resources for more information on deploying gateway-to-gateway solutions are listed in "Additional Information" later in this chapter.

Certificate Deployment for VPN

When planning certificate deployment for VPN solutions, the main criteria in determining certificate requirements are the tunneling protocol and the user authentication protocol used with the tunneling protocol.

Point-to-Point Tunneling Protocol (PPTP)

Point-to-Point Tunneling Protocol (PPTP) encapsulates the Point-to-Point Protocol (PPP) datagrams in a modified version of Generic Routing Encapsulation (GRE). (See Figure 23-1.)

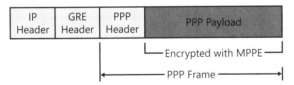

Figure 23-1 PPTP packet structure

In addition to encapsulating the PPP data within a GRE header, PPTP also maintains a Transmission Control Protocol (TCP) connection between the client and the server where the client connects to TCP port 1723 at the VPN server for management of the tunnel. To protect the data transmitted in the PPTP packets, Microsoft Point-to Point Encryption (MPPE) is used to encrypt the PPTP data.

PPTP does not require any certificates for the VPN client computer or the VPN server that the VPN client computer connects to. MPPE does not use certificates for the encryption of the data exchanged between the two computers.

VPN Authentication Options

When a user connects to the network through a VPN connection, the user must provide his or her credential information to the VPN server to authenticate with the network. The following protocols are available for user authentication when you implement a VPN solution:

- **Password Authentication Protocol (PAP)**   Transmits user credentials to the remote access server as plaintext, offering no protection against interception of the user's account and password.

- **Challenge Handshake Authentication Protocol (CHAP)**   Provides a stronger form of authentication by sending the password and a challenge to the server after passing the two items through the Message Digest 5 (MD5) hashing algorithm. When the authentication server receives the authentication attempt, the authentication server retrieves the user's password from Active Directory Domain Services (AD DS) and then performs the same MD5 hash against the challenge and password. If the results match, the user is authenticated. The use of the server's challenge protects the authentication attempt against replay attacks.

> **Warning**   CHAP authentication requires that the user's password be stored in a reversibly encrypted format in AD DS. This weakens password security and requires stronger physical security of the domain controller.

- **Microsoft Challenge Handshake Authentication Protocol (MS-CHAP)**   MS-CHAP differs from CHAP in that it creates the challenge response by passing the challenge and the user's password through the Message Digest v4 (MD4) hashing algorithm. MS-CHAP then uses MPPE to encrypt all data transmitted between the remote access client and the remote access server. MS-CHAP does not require that the user's password be stored in reversible encryption in AD DS.

- **Microsoft Challenge Handshake Authentication Protocol Version 2 (MS-CHAPv2)**   Requires the authentication of both the remote access client and the remote access server for a successful authentication attempt. In addition, MS-CHAPv2 implements stronger data encryption keys and uses different encryption keys for sending data than the encryption keys used for receiving data.

- **Extensible Authentication Protocol (EAP)**   Provides extensions to PPP connection authentication. These extensions allow advanced authentication methods, such as two-factor authentication, Kerberos, one-time passwords, or certificates. One of the extensions that EAP can use is Transport Layer Security (TLS). EAP-TLS uses the handshake protocol in TLS. The client and server use digital certificates to authenticate each other. The client generates a pre-master secret key by encrypting a random number with the server's public key and then sends the encrypted

> pre-master secret key to the server. The server then decrypts the pre-master
> secret key by using its private key, and both the client and the server then use the
> pre-master secret key to generate the same session key.
>
> Although a VPN connection can use any of the authentication protocols listed here, it
> is recommended to use only MS-CHAPv2 or Extensible Authentication Protocol–
> Transport Layer Security (EAP-TLS) authentication when allowing VPN connectivity
> to your network. Only these authentication methods provide strong protection of the
> credentials and mutual authentication of both the remote client and the authentication
> server.

PPTP requires certificates only if EAP-TLS authentication is enforced for VPN connections.
When EAP-TLS authentication is required, two certificates are required:

- **User certificate**   Used at the VPN server to authenticate the user account. The
  certificate must:

  - ❏ Be issued by a CA whose certificate is included in the NTAuth object in AD DS.

  - ❏ Be issued by a CA that chains to a root CA certificate trusted by both the VPN
    client computers and the authenticating server.

  - ❏ Include the Client Authentication Enhanced Key Usage (EKU) object identifier
    (OID).

  - ❏ Pass all certificate validity checks, including a revocation check.

  - ❏ Include the user principal name (UPN) of the user in the subject alternative name
    extension or be explicitly mapped to a user account in AD DS.

> **Note**   Optionally, a custom application policy OID can be added to the user certificate
> to indicate that the certificate is used for the organization's VPN solution. By including
> the custom application policy OID, an organization can implement a remote access
> policy profile that requires the custom application policy OID in the presented certificate.

- **Authenticating server certificate**   Used at the authenticating server. If the VPN server
  implements Windows authentication, the computer certificate must be installed at the
  VPN server. If the VPN server implements Remote Authentication Dial-In User Service
  (RADIUS) authentication, the computer certificate must be installed at the RADIUS
  server. The certificate must:

  - ❏ Be issued by a CA that chains to a root CA certificate trusted by both the VPN
    client computers and the authenticating server.

  - ❏ Include the Server Authentication application policy OID.

Layer Two Tunneling Protocol (L2TP) with Internet Protocol Security

Layer Two Tunneling Protocol (L2TP) combines the strengths of PPTP and Cisco's Layer Two Forwarding (L2F). When using L2TP, the original PPP data is encapsulated in an L2TP header, and then the combined PPP data and L2TP header is encapsulated in a User Datagram Protocol (UDP) header connecting to UDP port 1701 at both the client and the server. (See Figure 23-2.)

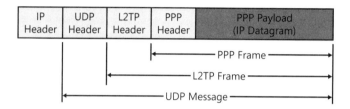

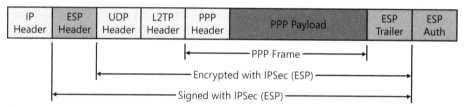

Figure 23-2   L2TP packet structure

L2TP does not have a built-in encryption mechanism like PPTP. To provide encryption for L2TP communications, Internet Protocol security (IPsec) with Encapsulating Security Payload (ESP) is used. As shown in Figure 23-2, IPsec provides both signing and encryption protection to the encapsulated L2TP data.

> **Note**   The specifics of how L2TP uses IPsec to protect L2TP data are described in RFC 3193, "Securing L2TP Using IPsec," available at *http://www.ietf.org/rfc/rfc3193.txt*. The combination of L2TP and IPsec is known as L2TP/IPsec.

When you implement L2TP/IPsec for a VPN solution, you require a minimum of two certificates for IPsec endpoint authentication:

- **VPN Server certificate**   Used at the VPN computer to provide authentication for the IPsec security association established between the VPN server and the VPN client computer. The certificate must:
  - ❑ Be issued by a CA that chains to the same trusted root as the certificate issued to the client computer.
  - ❑ Include the VPN server's Domain Name System (DNS) name in the certificate's subject or subject alternative name.

❑ Optionally include the IP security Internet Key Exchange (IKE) Intermediate application policy OID. If the IKE Intermediate application policy OID is not included, the certificate *must* include the Client Authentication application policy OID.

■ **Client Computer certificate**   Used at the VPN computer to provide authentication for the IPsec security association established between the VPN server and the VPN client computer. The certificate must:

❑ Be issued by a CA that chains to the same trusted root as the certificate issued to the client computer.

❑ Include the IP security IKE intermediate application policy OID.

❑ Include a DNS name in the certificate's subject or subject alternative name.

Note   Only Microsoft Windows 2000 and later include native L2TP/IPsec VPN capabilities. Windows 98, Windows Millennium Edition, and Windows NT 4.0 Professional clients must have the Microsoft L2TP/IPsec VPN Client for Windows 98, Windows Millennium Edition, and Windows NT 4.0 Workstation installed. Resources for more information on this add-on client are listed in "Additional Information" later in this chapter.

Caution   It is possible to deploy L2TP/IPsec without using VPN server and client computer certificates. Knowledge Base Articles 324258 and 281555, both titled "How To: Configure a Preshared Key for Use with Layer 2 Tunneling Protocol" (available at *http://support.microsoft.com*), describe how to deploy L2TP/IPsec without certificates. Although it is possible to use a shared secret for IPsec, deployment in this manner is not recommended. When deploying a client to a VPN server solution, the compromise of a single client computer would require changing the shared secret pass phrase at every client computer connecting to the network and at every VPN server.

You also require certificates for the authenticating server and the VPN user if you implement EAP-TLS authentication. The same authentication certificates are required for L2TP/IPsec as for PPTP.

Secure Sockets Tunneling Protocol (SSTP)

Secure Sockets Tunneling Protocol (SSTP) is a new tunneling protocol introduced in Windows Server 2008 and available only to Windows Vista SP1 and Windows Server 2008 clients.

SSTP was developed to allow VPN clients to connect to remote VPN servers through firewall, Network Address Translators (NATs), and Web proxies that prevent the passing PPTP or L2TP/IPsec traffic. SSTP accomplishes this by encapsulating PPP traffic over the secure sockets layer (SSL) channel of the Hypertext Transfer Protocol Secure (HTTPS) protocol. As shown in Figure 23-3, the tunneled IPv4 or IPv6 packet is encapsulated with a PPP header and an SSTP header. The combined SSTP header, PPP header, and Internet Protocol (IP) packet is encrypted by the SSL session.

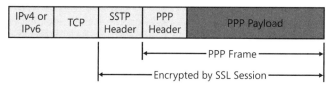

Figure 23-3   SSTP packet structure

To complete the packet, a TCP header and either an IPv4 or IPv6 header is added. These headers can be translated as the packet passes through firewall and NAT devices without changing the encrypted SSL data.

To deploy an SSTP tunnel, you require a server certificate installed on the SSTP server. The server certificate must:

- Be issued by a CA that chains to a trusted root certificate on the client computer.

- Include the Server Authentication Enhanced Key Usage (EKU).

- Have a subject name that matches the DNS name used by the VPN client to connect to the VPN server.

You also require certificates for the authenticating server and the VPN user if you implement EAP-TLS authentication. The same authentication certificates are required for SSTP as for PPTP and L2TP/IPsec.

Certificate Template Design

The number of certificate templates that you design for VPN access will depend on the tunneling protocol and authentication protocols used in your solution. The sections that follow detail the certificate template requirements for each component of the VPN solution.

User Authentication

The user authentication certificate must include the Client Authentication OID in the EKU. For the VPN user authentication, you implement either a private key and certificate stored in the user's profile or a certificate stored on a smart card.

If you choose to deploy a certificate on a Smart Card certificate for VPN authentication, consider duplicating the version 1 Smart Card Login certificate template. Make the following modifications to the new version 2 certificate template:

- Modify the certificate template to use the specific smart card cryptographic service provider (CSP) required by your organization's smart cards.

- Consider adding a custom application policy to the certificate template named *Organization* VPN User. When you define the application policy, ensure that you assign the application policy an OID from your organization's assigned OID arc.

> **Note**   You can increase the VPN connection's security by requiring that the user certificate include the *Organization* VPN User application policy OID in addition to the required Client Authentication OID. This prevents users from using other certificates that have the Client Authentication application policy OID and restricting VPN access to holders of the custom certificate.

- Assign Read, Enroll, and Autoenroll permissions to a custom universal or global group that contains all user accounts that will connect to the network through a VPN. This allows autoenrollment to automate distribution of certificates to users.

> **Note**   If users have computers running Windows 2000, they can still enroll the certificate by using the Certificate Services Web Enrollment pages or a custom enrollment script.

If you choose to deploy a user authentication certificate using a software-based CSP, consider duplicating the Authenticated Session certificate template. Make the following modifications to the new version 2 certificate template:

- Assign Read, Enroll, and Autoenroll permissions to a custom universal or global group that contains all user accounts that will connect to the network through a VPN. This allows autoenrollment to automate distribution of certificates to users. If users have computers running Windows 2000, they can still enroll the certificate by using the Certificate Services Web Enrollment pages or a custom enrollment script.

- Optionally, add a custom application policy to the certificate template named **Organization** **VPN User**. When you define the application policy, ensure that you assign the application policy an OID from your organization's assigned OID arc.

Server Authentication

For server authentication, it is recommended to deploy the default RAS and IAS Server certificate template. This certificate template implements the required Server Authentication application policy OID and is intended for deployment at remote access and RADIUS servers.

> **Note**   Remember that the decision of where to deploy the RAS and IAS Server certificate depends on the authentication method implemented at the VPN server. If you implement Windows authentication, the RAS and IAS Server certificate must be issued to the VPN Server. If you implement RADIUS authentication, the RAS and IAS Server certificate must be issued to the RADIUS server.

The only modification required for the RAS and IAS Server certificate template is to assign the RAS and IAS Servers domain local group Read, Enroll, and Autoenroll permissions. If multiple domains exist in the forest, you must create a custom global group in each and assign each domain's custom global group Read, Enroll, and Autoenroll permissions.

> **Note**   You must also ensure that all RADIUS server computer accounts are added to each domain's RAS and IAS Servers domain local group. This group membership allows the RADIUS server to view the Dial-In properties of the user's object.

IPsec Endpoint Authentication

For IPsec endpoint authentication, the certificate template that you deploy depends on whether the computer is a member of the forest. If the computer is a member of the forest, you can use the IPsec certificate template. This certificate template can be deployed using Automatic Certificate Request Settings in Group Policy to all domain member computers.

Because the subject information for a computer certificate is based on the computer account information stored in AD DS, this certificate template cannot be deployed to nonforest members. If a computer is a member of another forest or is a member of a workgroup, you can deploy the IPsec (offline request) certificate template. The only difference between the IPsec and the IPsec (offline request) certificate templates is that the IPsec (offline request) certificate template allows the certificate requestor to provide the subject information in the certificate request. This allows VPN users to provide the DNS name of their home computer in the certificate request.

The permissions of the IPsec (offline request) certificate template must be modified to allow a custom universal or global group the Read and Enroll permissions. The custom group must contain all VPN user accounts. The only way to deploy the certificate to nondomain joined machines is through the Certificate Services Web Enrollment pages, Microsoft Identity Lifecycle Manager (ILM) 2007 workflows, or custom scripting solutions.

> **Important**   If the home computer does not have access to the corporate network without the IPsec (offline request) certificate being installed, the user might have to request the certificate from an office computer, export the certificate and private key to a floppy disk, and install the certificate and private key at the home computer. The export file must contain the entire certificate chain.

SSTP Endpoint Authentication

When you use SSTP as the tunneling protocol, the VPN server must have a certificate with the Server Authentication object identifier (OID) in the Enhanced Key Usage (EKU) extension installed to authenticate the server during the TLS negotiation. The default Web Server certificate template is sufficient for the SSTP endpoint authentication. The template allows you to provide the DNS name that is used to connect to the VPN server for the subject of the certificate, and it contains the Server Authentication EKU OID.

Deploying a VPN Solution

The procedure for deploying a VPN solution, as documented in the following sections, is based on the network architecture shown in Figure 23-4.

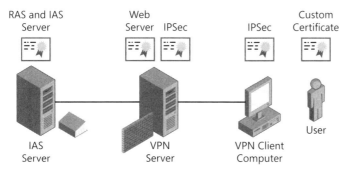

Figure 23-4   VPN certificate deployment

This network architecture assumes that the VPN client will connect to the network using an L2TP/IPsec tunnel and use EAP-TLS for user authentication, or utilize SSTP with EAP-TLS authentication. This requires that the following certificates be deployed before you start the actual network configuration:

- RADIUS server: A RAS and IAS Server certificate

- VPN Server: An IPsec certificate and a Web Server certificate

- VPN Client Computer: An IPsec or an IPsec (offline request) certificate

- User: A custom version 2 certificate template with the Client Authentication and the *Organization* VPN User application policy OIDs

Network Policy Server Configuration

Network Policy Server (NPS) provides RADIUS services in Windows Server 2008. To implement the strongest form of security, the Windows Server 2008 NPS service should be used. NPS allows inspection of the presented user certificate for a specific EKU or certificate policy OID.

Note   The ability to designate required application policy OID is also available in Windows Server 2003 Internet Authentication Service (IAS).

The configuration of NPS is composed of five steps:

■ Install the RADIUS server.

■ Add the RADIUS server to the RAS and IAS Servers group.

■ Define RADIUS clients.

■ Define the VPN access policy.

■ Enable logging at the RADIUS server.

Note   Deploying NPS on a domain controller, rather than on a member server, is recommended because it ensures that all communications between NPS and the domain controller are local procedure calls and not communications transmitted over the network.

Install the RADIUS Server

In Windows Server 2008, Internet Authentication Services no longer exists. Instead, the RADIUS features are deployed as a component of Network Policy Server (NPS). To install NPS on Windows Server 2008 use the following procedure:

1. Log on as a member of the local Administrators group.

2. From Administrative Tools, open Server Manager.

3. In the details pane, in the Roles Summary section, click Add Roles.

4. If the Before You Begin page appears, select the Skip This Page By Default check box, and then click Next.

5. On the Select Server Roles page, select the Network Policy And Access Services check box, and then click Next.

6. On the Network Policy And Access Services page, click Next.

7. On the Select Role Services page, click Network Policy Server, and then click Next.

8. On the Confirm Installation Selections page, click Install.

9. If prompted, insert the Windows Server 2008, Standard or Enterprise Edition, DVD in the DVD-ROM drive.

10. On the Installation Results page, ensure that the installation is successful, and then click Close.

Add the RADIUS Server to Each Domain's RAS and IAS Servers Group

Once you install NPS, you must add the RADIUS server's computer account to the RAS and IAS Servers group in each domain in the forest. Membership in the RAS and IAS Servers group allows the RADIUS server's computer account to read the user's Dial-in Properties in that specific domain.

1. Ensure that you are logged on as a member of the Domain Admins group.

2. From Administrative Tools, open Active Directory Users And Computers.

3. Ensure that you are connected to the domain where the RADIUS server's computer account exists.

4. In the console tree, expand the domain, and then click Users.

5. In the details pane, double-click the RAS and IAS Servers group.

6. In the RAS And IAS Servers Properties dialog box, on the Members tab, click Add.

7. In the Select Users, Contacts, Computers, Or Groups dialog box, click Object Types.

8. In the Object Types dialog box, ensure that the Computers check box is selected, and then click OK.

9. In the Select Users, Contacts, Computers, Or Groups dialog box, in the Enter The Object Names To Select box, type *ComputerName* (where *ComputerName* is the NetBIOS name of the computer hosting IAS), and then click Check Names.

10. Ensure that the correct computer name appears, and then click OK.

11. In the RAS And IAS Servers Properties dialog box, click OK.

12. Repeat for each domain in the forest.

13. Close Active Directory Users And Computers.

14. Restart the computer hosting the RADIUS service to use the new group membership.

Define RADIUS clients

To define the RADIUS clients, the VPN server's IP address must be known and added as a RADIUS client at the IAS server.

To define a RADIUS client at the IAS server, do the following:

1. From Administrative Tools, open Network Policy Server.

2. In the console tree, expand RADIUS Clients And Servers, right-click RADIUS Clients, and then click New RADIUS Client.

3. On the New Radius Client page, set the following options:

   ❑ Select the Enable The RADIUS Client check box.

   ❑ Provide a friendly name for the VPN Server.

   ❑ Provide the IP address of the VPN server.

   ❑ In the Vendor Name drop-down list: Select RADIUS Standard.

❏ In the Shared Secret section, choose between manually typing and confirming or generating a shared secret.

❏ Choose whether to require the Message-Authenticator attribute in access request messages.

❏ Specify whether the VPN is Network Access Protection (NAP) capable.

4. Click Finish.

5. Repeat this process for every VPN server that uses the RADIUS server for authentication.

Define the VPN Access Policy

Once you've defined the RADIUS clients, you must define the remote access policy for VPN access. This remote access policy will allow smart card users to authenticate with the network.

The following process creates and configures the VPN user remote access policy:

1. From Administrative Tools, open Network Policy Server.

2. In the console tree, select NPS (Local).

3. In the details pane, in the Standard Configuration section, select RADIUS Server For Dial-Up Or VPN Connections, and then click Configure VPN Or Dial-Up.

4. On the Select Dial-Up Or Virtual Private Network Connections Type page, click Virtual Private Network (VPN) Connections, name the policy **VPN Users**, and then click Next.

5. On the Specify Dial-Up Or VPN Server page, you can add any additional RADIUS clients (including the individual VPN server in the case of a VPN network access policy), and then click Next.

6. On the Configure Authentication Methods page, enable Extensible Authentication Protocol, in the Type drop-down list, select Microsoft Smart Card Or Other Certificate, and then click Configure.

7. In the Smart Card Or Other Certificate Properties dialog box, in the Certificate Issued To drop-down list, select the certificate issued to *ComputerName@DomainName* (where *ComputerName* is the computer account name of the RADIUS server and *DomainName* is the DNS name of the RADIUS server's domain), and then click OK.

8. On the Configure Authentication Methods page, disable all other authentication methods, and then click Next.

9. On the Specify User Groups page, click Add.

10. In the Select Group dialog box, add each domain's Domain Users group, and then click OK.

> **Note**   Alternatively, you can create a custom group containing only authorized VPN users. Consider using the same group used to assign permissions to the custom VPN User Authentication certificate template.

11. On the Specify User Groups page, click Next.

12. On the Specify IP Filters page, you can optionally configure IPv4 or IPv6 input and output filters, and then click Next.

13. On the Completing New Dial-Up Or Virtual Private Network Connections And RADIUS clients page, click Finish.

14. In the console tree, expand Policies, and then click Network Policies.

15. In the details pane, double-click VPN Users.

16. On the Settings tab, in the RADIUS Attributes section, select Vendor Specific, and then click Add.

17. In the Add Vendor Specific Attribute dialog box, select Allowed-Certificate-OID, and then click Add.

18. In the Attribute Information dialog box, click Add.

19. In the Attribute Information dialog box, in the Attribute value box, type **CustomOID** (where *CustomOID* is the custom *Organization* VPN User application policy OID defined by your organization to identify approved VPN users), and then click OK.

> **Tip**   You can copy the application OID by viewing the object identifiers in the Certificate Templates console (certtmpl.msc).

20. In the Attribute Information dialog box, click OK.

21. In the Add Vendor Specific Attribute dialog box, click Close.

22. In the VPN Users dialog box, on the Settings tab, in the Routing And Remote Access section, click Encryption.

23. In the details pane, deselect all check boxes except Strongest Encryption (MPPE 128-Bit), and then click OK.

Enable Logging at the RADIUS Server

The last procedure required in the Network Policy Server console is to enable logging for all RADIUS authentication and accounting events. Logging enables you to audit all authentication attempts submitted to the RADIUS server. Use the following procedure:

1. In the console tree, click Accounting.

2. In the details pane, double-click Configure Local File Logging.

3. In the Local File Logging Properties dialog box, on the Settings tab, enable logging for:

   ❑ Accounting requests

   ❑ Authentication requests

   ❑ Periodic accounting status

   ❑ Periodic authentication status

4. In the Settings tab, click Apply.

5. In the Local File Logging Properties dialog box, on the Log File tab, set the following options:

   ❑ Format: IAS

   ❑ Create A New Log File: Daily

   ❑ When Disk Is Full Delete Older Log Files: Enabled

6. In the Local File Logging dialog box, click OK.

7. Close the Network Policy Server console.

 Note   Alternatively, you can configure NPS to log all information into a SQL database. For details on enabling logging to a SQL database, view the Help files in the Network Policy Server console.

VPN Server Configuration

Once the RADIUS server is installed and configured, you can install the VPN servers. Each VPN server requires installation and configuration of Routing and Remote Access.

With Windows Server 2008, the first task is to install the Remote Access Service. Use the following procedure to install the Routing and Remote Access role service:

1. From Administrative Tools, open Server Manager.

2. In the console tree, select Roles.

3. In the details pane, in the Roles Summary section, click Add Roles.

4. If the Before You Begin page appears, select the Skip This Page By Default check box, and then click Next.

5. On the Select Server Roles page, select the Network Policy And Access Services check box, and then click Next.

6. On the Network Policy And Access Services page, click Next.

7. On the Select Role Services page, click Routing And Remote Access Services, and then click Next.

> **Note**   This enables both the Remote Access Service and the Routing role services.

8. On the Confirm Installation Selections page, click Install.

9. If prompted, insert the Windows Server 2008, Standard or Enterprise editions, DVD in the DVD-ROM drive.

10. On the Installation Results page, ensure that the installation is successful, and then click Close.

Once the Routing and Remote Access Services role service is installed, you can enable VPN connectivity. Use the following procedure to accomplish this:

1. From Administrative Tools, open Routing And Remote Access.

2. In the console tree, right-click *VPNServer* (where *VPNServer* is the name of the VPN server computer), and then click Configure And Enable Routing And Remote Access.

3. In the Routing And Remote Access Server Setup Wizard, click Next.

4. On the Configuration page, click Remote Access (Dial-Up or VPN), and then click Next.

5. On the Remote Access page, click VPN, and then click Next.

6. On the VPN Connection page, in the Network Interfaces list, select the network interface connected to the Internet, ensure that the Enable Security On The Selected Interface By Setting Up Static Packet Filters check box is selected, and then click Next.

7. On the IP Address Assignment page, click Automatically, and then click Next.

> **Note**   This procedure assumes that a DHCP server exists on the private network for the assignment of addresses to VPN clients.

8. On the Managing Multiple Remote Access Servers page, click Yes, Set Up This Server To Work With A RADIUS Server, and then click Next.

9. On the RADIUS Server Selection page, provide the following information, and then click Next.

    ❑ Primary RADIUS Server: **The *DNSName* or *IP address* of the RADIUS server**

    ❑ Alternate RADIUS Server: **The *DNSName* or *IP address* of a second RADIUS server**

    ❑ Shared Secret: **The shared secret defined at the RADIUS server for the RADIUS client**

10. On the Completing The Routing And Remote Access Server Setup Wizard page, click Finish.

11. In the Routing And Remote Access dialog box, click OK to accept that you must configure the DHCP Relay Agent at the VPN server with the IP address of the DHCP server.

12. In the console tree, expand *ComputerName* (local), expand IIPv4, right-click DHCP Relay Agent, and then click Properties.

13. In the DHCP Relay Agent Properties dialog box, in the Server Address box, type the IP address of the DCHP server on the internal network, click Add, and then click OK.

> **Note**   If there are multiple DHCP servers, add the IP address of each DHCP server in the DHCP Relay Agent Properties dialog box.

Create a VPN Client Connection

Once the back-end infrastructure is established, the user can create a VPN connection at the client computer. This book will show only how to manually create the VPN connection object.

The Connection Manager is a custom dialer that integrates with Windows operating systems from Windows 98 and later. The Connection Manager can be configured to manage all aspects of dial-up and VPN connections in a corporate environment, reducing the configuration required at the VPN client computers.

> **Note**   You can standardize the client VPN connection creation by using the Connection Manager Administration Kit (CMAK) that is included with Windows Server 2008. For details on creating CMAK packages, see the "Step-by-Step Guide for Creating and Testing Connection Manager Profiles in a Test Lab" white paper at *http://www.microsoft.com/downloads/ details.aspx?FamilyID=93fd20e7-e73a-43f6-96ec-7bcc7527709b&DisplayLang=en*.

Creating a Client Connection in Windows XP

To create a client VPN connection in Windows XP, you must set up the new VPN connection in the Network Connections window, using the following procedure:

1. From the Start menu, point to Control Panel, right-click Network Connections, and then click Open.

2. In the Network Connections window, click Create A New Connection.

3. In the New Connection Wizard, click Next.

4. On the Network Connection Type page, click Connect To The Network At My Workplace, and then click Next.

5. On the Network Connection page, click Virtual Private Network Connection, and then click Next.

6. On the Connection Name page, in the Company Name box, type the name of your company, and then click Next.

7. On the Public Network page, if you are on a network attached to the Internet, click Do Not Dial The Initial Connection, or if you dial an initial Internet connection such as a dial-up connection, click Automatically Dial This Initial Connection, and then click Next.

8. On the VPN Server Selection page, type the DNS name or IP address of the VPN Server's external interface, and then click Next.

9. On the Smart Card page, if you are using a smart card for authentication, click Use My Smart Card; otherwise click Do Not Use My Smart Card, and then click Next.

10. On the Connection Availability page, click Anyone's Use, and then click Next.

11. On the Completing The New Connection Wizard page, click Add A Shortcut To This Connection To My Desktop, and then click Finish.

Creating a Client Connection in Windows Vista

To create a client VPN connection in Windows Vista, you must set up the new VPN connection in the Network and Sharing Center window, using the following procedure:

1. From the Start menu, point to Control Panel, and then click Network And Sharing Center.

2. In the Network And Sharing Center window, click Set Up A Connection Or Network.

3. On the Choose A Connection Option page, click Connect To A Workplace, and then click Next.

4. If the Do You Want To Use A Connection That You Already Have appears, click No, Create A New Connection, and then click Next.

5. On the How Do You Want To Connect? page, click Use My Internet Connection (VPN).

6. On the Type The Internet Address To Connect To page (see Figure 23-5), provide the following information, and then click Create.

   ❑ Internet Address: **The DNS name you are connecting to.**

   ❑ Destination Name: **A logical name for the VPN connection.**

   ❑ Use A Smart Card: **Indicates whether a smart card is used for user authentication.**

   ❑ Allow Other People To Use This Connection: **Makes the VPN connection available for Windows logon.**

   ❑ Don't Connect Now, Just Set It Up So I Can Connect Later: **Allows you to define the VPN connection without establishing a connection to the VPN server.**

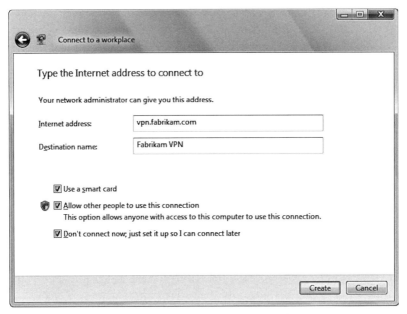

Figure 23-5   Configuring the Windows Vista VPN Settings

7. On the Connection Is Ready To Use page, click Close.

Once you have created the connection, you can edit the connection if you want to specify the specific tunneling protocol you wish to use. The default behavior is to try PPTP first. If PPTP fails, the client then tries L2TP. Finally, if that fails, the client then tries SSTP.

> **Note**   If SSTP is successful, a reconnection attempt tries SSTP first. If SSTP fails on the reconnection attempt, the client returns to trying PPTP first, and then L2TP.

To designate a specific tunneling protocol, use the following procedure:

1. From the Start menu, point to Control Panel, and then click Network And Sharing Center.

2. In the Network And Sharing Center window, click Manage Network Connections.

3. In the Network Connections window, right-click the connection you created, and then click Properties.

4. If User Account Control is enabled, click Continue.

5. In the VPN Connection Properties dialog box, on the Networking tab, in the Type Of VPN drop-down list, select Automatic, PPTP VPN, L2TP IPsec VPN, or Secure Socket Tunneling Protocol (SSTP), and then click OK.

6. Close the Network Connections window.

Connecting to the VPN

Once you have created the VPN connection, you can connect to the network. The user interface presented to the user will depend on whether you are using EAP-TLS authentication or MS-CHAPv2 authentication. If you are using a smart card for authentication, you must type the personal identification number (PIN) for the smart card to authenticate. If you are using MS-CHAPv2 authentication, you must type your user account name, password, and domain to connect to the network.

Case Study: Lucerne Publishing

You are the network manager for Lucerne Publishing. Lucerne Publishing has several acquisition editors who work remotely from their home offices and require access to resources on the corporate network.

Scenario

To allow VPN access, you propose implementing a VPN server, running Windows Server 2003 Enterprise Edition at each of the major offices, as shown in Figure 23-6.

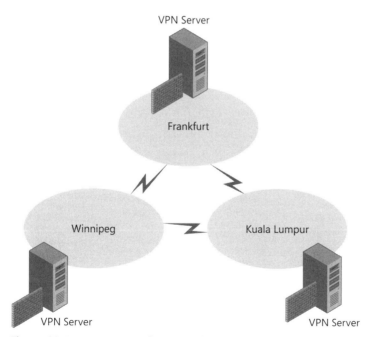

Figure 23-6   VPN server placement for Lucerne Publishing

To facilitate the issuance of certificates, Lucerne Publishing has implemented a two-tier CA hierarchy, as shown in Figure 23-7.

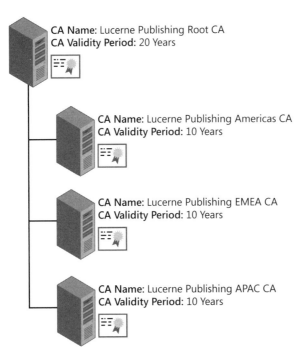

CA Name: Lucerne Publishing Root CA
CA Validity Period: 20 Years

CA Name: Lucerne Publishing Americas CA
CA Validity Period: 10 Years

CA Name: Lucerne Publishing EMEA CA
CA Validity Period: 10 Years

CA Name: Lucerne Publishing APAC CA
CA Validity Period: 10 Years

Figure 23-7   The Lucerne Publishing CA hierarchy

The following design requirements have been identified for VPN deployment:

- The VPN servers are configured with two network interfaces, one attached to the corporate network and one attached to the Internet, allowing connections to the VPN server. The VPN servers are configured so that the servers will accept only L2TP/IPsec connections from the VPN clients. Any attempts to communicate with the VPN servers with protocols other than L2TP/IPsec will fail.

- Lucerne Publishing employees will use a mix of computers running Windows XP and Windows Vista when they connect to the corporate network.

- Lucerne Publishing plans to use L2TP/IPsec for all VPN communications between the remote employees and the corporate network.

- In addition, all authentication initially will be performed by the users typing their user account and password. In the future, Lucerne Publishing plans to change the authentication to require smart cards.

- All connections between the VPN clients and the VPN servers must enforce mutual authentication.

- To prevent access to the network if a virus attack occurs, management wants the ability to immediately shut down all VPN access to the network at any given time.

- Many of the acquisition editors' computers are not members of the forest. Methods must be developed to provide certificates for the VPN connection to these editors.

Case Study Questions

1. What authentication protocol must be enforced for VPN communications to satisfy the initial authentication requirements?

2. What certificates are required for the initial VPN solution? Provide your answers in the following table.

Principal	Certificate
VPN user	
VPN client computer	
RADIUS server	
VPN server	

3. What authentication protocol must be enforced for VPN communications to satisfy the modified authentication requirements to enforce smart card authentication?

4. What certificates are required for the modified VPN solution that uses smart cards? Provide your answers in the following table.

Principal	Certificate
VPN user	
VPN client computer	
RADIUS server	
VPN server	

5. How would Lucerne Publishing ensure centralized remote access policy application and enable the ability to immediately shut down all VPN access?

6. What certificate template(s) are required for the L2TP/IPsec tunnel? What CA should you publish the certificates at?

7. What method could you use to deploy the IPsec certificates to forest member computers?

8. What method could you use to deploy the IPsec certificates to nonforest member computers?

9. When Lucerne Publishing switches to using Smart Card certificates, how can the Smart Card certificate template be modified to further restrict VPN access to the network?

10. What certificate(s) would you deploy at the VPN server when using RADIUS authentication?

11. If some users are having problems connecting using the L2TP/IPsec VPN because of firewalls at customer sites, what other tunneling protocol could be implemented? Are there any client restrictions with this tunneling protocol?

Best Practices

- **Allow only MS-CHAPv2 or EAP-TLS authentication for remote access clients.**   Only MS-CHAPv2 and EAP-TLS allow mutual authentication between VPN client and authentication server. In addition, MS-CHAPv2 and EAP-TLS provide the strongest protection for a user's credential information.

- **Allow only strong encryption for remote access clients.**   Ensure that the remote access policy enforces the strongest form of encryption to ensure that connections use 128-bit MPPE for PPTP connections, Advanced Encryption Standard (AES) for L2TP/IPsec connections, or 128-bit SSL for SSTP connections for encryption.

- **Create separate remote access policies for VPN access.**   Do not try to create an all-in-one remote access policy for VPN and dial-up connections. Create separate remote access policies for each application, and ensure that the policy conditions do not overlap.

> **Important**   If the policy conditions overlap, you must order the remote access policies so that the desired policy is applied to the correct users. For example, if you have one remote access policy applied to Domain Admins and another applied to Domain Users, you must place the remote access policy applied to Domain Admins higher in the remote access policy policy listing. This ensures that an administrator, who is a member of both Domain Admins and Domain Users, has the Domain Admins policy applied to his or her connection.

- **Deploy IPsec certificates to all VPN servers and clients if deploying L2TP/IPsec.**   Create a version 2 certificate template based on the IPsec certificate template to enable autoenrollment of the certificates to client computers running Windows Vista and Windows XP.

- **Implement RADIUS for all remote access authentication and accounting.**   RADIUS allows centralized administration of all remote access policy and collection of VPN connection activity logs. Also, configure both primary and secondary RADIUS servers for all VPN devices so that VPN connectivity still succeeds if a single RADIUS server fails.

- **Deploy RAS and IAS Server certificates to all RADIUS servers.**   If you use Windows Server 2008 NPS servers, you can deploy the RAS and IAS Server certificates by using autoenrollment. This server certificate is required for EAP-TLS mutual authentication.

- **Deploy a Web Server certificate to the SSTP VPN Server.**   The Web Server certificate allows you to provide a custom subject name, matching the DNS name used by the clients to connect to the VPN server.

- **Do not use preshared keys for IPsec authentication; use only certificate-based authentication.**   Although it is possible to configure L2TP/IPsec to use preshared keys for authentication, the risks are high. If a single laptop is compromised, an attacker could gain access to the preshared key and use the preshared key from other computers to connect to the corporate network.

- **Use smart cards for user certificate–based authentication to provide the strongest protection of user credentials.**   A smart card provides additional security by applying two-factor protection. An attacker must gain access to both the smart card and the PIN to access the network.

- **Implement a custom application policy OID in the user authentication certificates, and require the existence of the application policy OID in the remote access policy.**   The implementation of a custom application policy OID increases security by requiring the authentication certificate to contain the application policy OID. Use of a custom application policy OID limits authentication only to the designated certificate.

Additional Information

- "Deploying Virtual Private Networks with Microsoft Windows Server 2003" (*http://www.microsoft.com/mspress/books/5519.asp*)

- "Virtual Private Networking with Windows Server 2003: Overview" (*http://www.microsoft.com/windowsserver2003/techinfo/overview/vpnover.mspx*)

- "Virtual Private Networking with Windows Server 2003: Deploying Remote Access VPNs" (*http://www.microsoft.com/technet/treeview/default.asp?url=/technet/prodtechnol/windowsserver2003/deploy/confeat/vpndeplr.asp*)

- "Virtual Private Networking with Windows Server 2003: An Example Deployment" (*http://www.microsoft.com/technet/treeview/default.asp?url=/technet/prodtechnol/windowsserver2003/deploy/confeat/vpnexamp.asp*)

- "Step-by-Step Guide for Setting Up VPN-Based Remote Access in a Test Lab" (*http://www.microsoft.com/technet/prodtechnol/windowsserver2003/deploy/confeat/rmotevpn.asp?frame=true*)

- "Step-by-Step Guide for Creating and Testing Connection Manager Profiles in a Test Lab" (*http://www.microsoft.com/downloads/details.aspx?FamilyID=93fd20e7-e73a-43f6-96ec-7bcc7527709b&DisplayLang=en*)

- "Microsoft L2TP/IPSec VPN Client for Windows 98, Windows Millennium Edition, and Windows NT 4.0 Workstation" (*http://www.microsoft.com/windows2000/server/evaluation/news/bulletins/l2tpclient.asp*)

- "Microsoft Internet Authentication Services Web Portal" (*http://www.microsoft.com/windowsserver2003/technologies/ias/default.mspx*)

- RFC 2637–"Point-to-Point Tunneling Protocol (PPTP)" (*http://www.ietf.org/rfc/rfc2637.txt*)

- RFC 2661–"Layer Two Tunneling Protocol 'L2TP'" (*http://www.ietf.org/rfc/rfc2661.txt*)

- RFC 3193–"Securing L2TP Using IPsec" (*http://www.ietf.org/rfc/rfc3193.txt*)

- "Screencast: Deploying SSTP Remote Access" (*http://www.microsoft.com/downloads/details.aspx?FamilyID=fc4d7d3f-0376-45bf-9544-ec35329a2fc1&DisplayLang=en*)

■ "Step-by-Step Guide: Deploying SSTP Remote Access" (*http://download.microsoft.com/download/b/1/0/b106fc39-936c-4857-a6ea-3fb9d1f37063/Deploying%20SSTP%20Remote%20Access%20Step%20by%20Step%20Guide.doc*)

■ "Step-by-Step Guide: Demonstrate VPN NAP Enforcement in a Test Lab" (*http://www.microsoft.com/downloads/details.aspx?familyid=729bba00-55ad-4199-b441-378cc3d900a7&displaylang=en*)

■ Routing and Remote Access Blog (*http://blogs.technet.com/rrasblog/default.aspx*)

■ "The Cable Guy: Secure Socket Tunneling Protocol" (*http://www.microsoft.com/technet/technetmag/issues/2007/06/CableGuy/default.aspx*)

■ 248711: "Mutual Authentication Methods Supported for L2TP/IPSec"

■ 248750: "Description of the IPSec Policy Created for L2TP/IPSec"

■ 281555: "How To: Configure a Preshared Key for Use with Layer Two Tunneling Protocol Connections in Windows XP"

■ 314831: "Basic L2TP/IPSec Troubleshooting in Windows XP"

■ 324258: "How To: Configure a Preshared Key for Use with Layer 2 Tunneling Protocol Connections in Windows Server 2003"

■ 324915: "Description of the Microsoft L2TP/IPSec Virtual Private Networking"

■ 816573: "How To: Configure a VPN Server to Act as a Router in Windows Server 2003"

Note   The last seven articles in the above list can be accessed through the Microsoft Knowledge Base. Go to *http://support.microsoft.com*, and enter the article number in the Search The Knowledge Base text box.

Chapter 24
Wireless Networking

Many organizations are deploying wireless networks. Wireless networking allows users to easily move around the office, between their desks, to another employee's desk, or to meeting rooms while still maintaining network connectivity.

Although wireless networking makes it easy for employees to connect to the corporate network, it also makes it easier for an attacker to connect to the network if proper security is not implemented.

This chapter looks at how a public key infrastructure (PKI) can be used to increase your wireless network's security by requiring certificate-based authentication for wireless network access.

Threats Introduced by Wireless Networking

When an organization implements a wireless network, several threats are introduced that do not exist in a wired network environment, including the following:

- **Accidental connections to the wireless network** People might not realize that their computers may automatically connect to the organization's wireless network. This can lead to the computer being connected to the network without appropriate security measures, implementing the Windows Firewall or deploying a host-based intrusion detection system, making the computer a target for attackers. These visiting computers can then be used as launch points to attack the network.

> **Note** If a wireless network is detected, the default behavior of Windows XP is to connect automatically to any available wireless network.

- **Inspection of data** As data is sent from the computer over the wireless network, it might be possible for user credentials or other confidential data to be captured by an unauthorized person connected to the wireless network.

- **Data modification** If attackers can gain access to the wireless network, it might be possible for them to implement a man-in-the-middle attack whereby legitimate packets are intercepted and modified as they are transmitted from source to destination. Likewise, false packets can be transmitted from attackers who are impersonating valid users.

- **Rogue wireless access points (WAPs)**   Users can easily connect a WAP to the network and start using the WAP to connect to the corporate network, and the rogue WAP can prevent users from connecting to an authorized WAP.

- **Unauthorized network connections**   With a wireless network, an attacker can gain access to the network without entering the physical premises. You cannot easily stop the transmission of packets beyond the walls of your building. The distance the transmissions reach is entirely dependent upon the strength of the WAPs you deploy.

Protecting Wireless Communications

When you implement a wireless network, you must develop a plan for securing the network to reduce the likelihood of the threats mentioned in the previous section. Some of the more common methods of protecting a wireless network are mentioned in the sections that follow.

MAC Filtering

One of the most basic ways of protecting a wireless network is to implement media access control (MAC) filtering. At the WAP, you can configure which MAC addresses (the low-level firmware addresses of a wireless card) are allowed to connect to the WAP. Although this sounds like an ideal, easy way to secure a wireless network, consider the following issues:

- **It is easy to spoof an approved MAC address.**   Software, such as SMAC, allows you to modify your wireless card's MAC to an approved MAC address manually.

> **Note**   You can read more information on the SMAC at *http://www.klcconsulting.net/ smac/default.htm?v=readme11.*

- **MAC filtering is difficult to manage.**   Each MAC address must be managed manually at the WAP. If you have a large number of wireless computers, the addition and deletion of MAC addresses at the WAP is a labor-intensive, time-consuming process.

- **MAC filtering authenticates only the computer, not the user.**   If attackers steal a laptop or use a laptop included in the approved MAC listing, they can access the network.

- **The size of the approved MAC list is limited.**   In large environments, you might not be able to input all approved MAC addresses.

Wired Equivalent Privacy

Wired Equivalent Privacy (WEP) is one method of providing encryption services to wireless networking. When a wireless connection enables WEP, the wireless network interface card (NIC) encrypts each data packet transmitted on the network using the RC4 stream cipher algorithm. The WAP then decrypts the data packets upon receipt.

Warning   Wireless encryption encrypts the data only between the wireless client and the WAP. Once the data is on the wired network, no encryption is applied unless the wireless client applies other encryption technologies, such as virtual private networking (VPN) or Internet Protocol security (IPsec).

WEP requires that both the wireless client and WAP share a 40-bit or a 64-bit symmetric encryption key. When WEP is implemented alone, the wireless client and WAP must configure the encryption key manually. If 802.1x authentication (as described later in this chapter) is implemented, the encryption key is configured only at the WAP and is securely transmitted to the wireless client.

Note   Some hardware vendors also provide support for a 128-bit WEP key.

The symmetric encryption key is concatenated to a randomly generated 24-bit initialization vector (IV). The IV lengthens the lifetime of the symmetric key because of the random generation of the IV. A new IV is used for each frame transmitted between the wireless client and the WAP.

The problem with WEP is that a brute force attack can be executed successfully in a very short period of time. The weakness in WEP's implementation is two-fold.

- **The symmetric encryption key is rarely changed.**   Once an organization sets a WEP key, it typically does not change. This is especially true if both the wireless client and the WAP must input the key manually.

- **The IV is only 24 bits and is reused over time.**   When WEP is deployed on a large network, an IV is reused about every hour. An application such as AirSnort can capture frames over a period of time and determine what the WEP key is based on by identifying frames that use the same IV.

Note   For a detailed analysis of the weaknesses in WEP, please see the article, "Security of the WEP Algorithm," available at *http://www.isaac.cs.berkeley.edu/isaac/wep-faq.html*.

Wi-Fi Protected Access (WPA) and WPA2

Wi-Fi Protected Access (WPA) is an encryption method developed by the Wi-Fi Alliance to address the security issues found in WEP. The following major enhancements are included in WPA:

- **Increased data encryption**   WPA implements Temporal Key Integrity Protocol (TKIP), which uses a per-packet key mixing function, a message integrity check (known as MIC or **Michael**), and an extended IV with rules on sequencing. In addition, WPA implements a re-keying mechanism so that the same key is not used for long periods of time.

- **Support for personal and enterprise deployments**   WPA can be deployed either with the use of a pre-shared key at the WAP and the client (known as WPA-Personal), or with Remote Authentication Dial-In User Service (RADIUS) or some other authentication server on the network (known as WPA-Enterprise).

- **Dependency on 802.1x authentication for WPA-Enterprise**   WPA-Enterprise requires 802.1x authentication to ensure that only authorized users or computers are allowed connectivity to the wireless network. 802.1x authentication also ensures mutual authentication so that a wireless client does not connect to a rogue network instead of the corporate network.

IEEE 802.11i, also referred to as WPA2, is a security specification for wireless security standards. WPA2 adds secure fast handoffs, secure deauthentication, secure disassociation with WAPs, and strong forms of encryption from the Advanced Encryption Standard (AES).

To ensure compatibility with the WPA2 standard, the Wi-Fi Alliance has introduced the *Wi-Fi Certified* product certification that certifies wireless equipment as being compatible with WPA2. The entire goal of the Wi-Fi Certified program is to enforce mandatory security features of WPA2 that were previously optional for products that supported WPA.

802.1x Authentication Types

A Windows Server 2008 PKI provides the necessary certificates for 802.1x authentication for wireless and wired networks. When a user or computer performs 802.1x authentication, the following two authentication types are available:

- Extensible Authentication Protocol using Transport Layer Security (EAP-TLS)
- Protected Extensible Authentication Protocol (PEAP)

 Note   There are several wireless local access network (WLAN) security solutions similar to PEAP and EAP-TLS. For example, Cisco's Light EAP (LEAP) and Funk Software's Tunneled Transport Layer Security (EAP-TTLS) provide security comparable to PEAP or EAP-TLS, but they are vendor-specific, locking your organization into specific vendor solutions.

EAP-TLS Authentication

EAP-TLS is a certificate-based authentication method that provides mutual authentication between the user or computer and the Remote Authentication Dial-In User Service (RADIUS) server when implemented for a wireless networking solution. To implement EAP-TLS authentication, the following certificates are required:

- **Client Computer or User**   The client end of the wireless connection must have a certificate with the Client Authentication Enhanced Key Usage (EKU) object identifier (OID). This certificate proves the identity of the client computer or the user account.

■ **Server** The server end of the wireless connection must have a certificate with the Server Authentication EKU OID. This certificate proves the RADIUS server's identity to all connecting wireless clients.

> **Note** No certificate is required for the WAP when implementing 802.1x authentication. The role of the WAP is to translate EAP messages sent from the client to the WAP into RADIUS messages sent from the WAP to the RADIUS server, and vice versa.

PEAP Authentication

PEAP authentication allows the transmission of other EAP types within a TLS-secured channel. When PEAP is used, the user must type in a user account and a password that is sent to the RADIUS server. The user's identity is proven through knowledge of a user account and password, which are protected by using Microsoft Challenge Handshake Authentication Protocol version 2 (MS-CHAPv2). The RADIUS server still requires a certificate with the Server Authentication EKU OID to prove its identity and to protect the user's password as it is transmitted to the server, but no certificate is required for the user.

How 802.1x Authentication Works

802.1x authentication allows an organization to require users and computers to authenticate with the network before they are allowed full network access. The process includes enforcing mutual authentication of the client computer or user account with a RADIUS server. The process shown in Figure 24-1 takes place when a wireless client attempts to connect to a wireless network requiring 802.1x authentication.

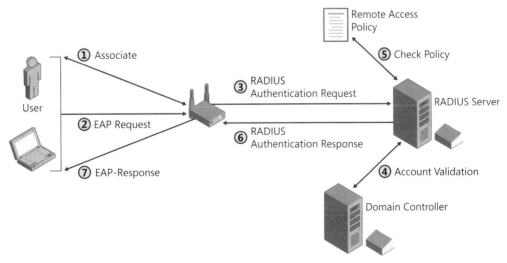

Figure 24-1 The 802.1x authentication process

1. The computer attempts to associate with the WAP, which responds that the user or computer must provide EAP authentication.

2. The computer or user passes its credentials to the WAP.

   ❏ If using EAP-TLS authentication, a signed request is submitted to the WAP, proving that the user or computer has access to the private key associated with the Client Authentication certificate.

   ❏ If using PEAP authentication, users must type their user account and password combination in an authentication dialog box.

3. The WAP translates EAP authentication packets into RADIUS authentication packets and forwards the authentication packets to the RADIUS server.

> **Note**   The WAP is simply an intermediary for the authentication process, translating EAP request messages into RADIUS request messages and translating RADIUS response messages into EAP response messages.

4. The RADIUS server contacts a domain controller to either validate the user account and the password combination or to use the user principal name (UPN) in the certificate's Subject Alternative Name to map the certificate to a user account in Active Directory Domain Services (AD DS).

5. The RADIUS server determines if the identified user or computer is granted access to the network based on the RADIUS server's configured remote access policies.

6. The RADIUS server sends a RADIUS authentication success or failure message to the WAP.

7. The WAP sends an EAP success or failure message to the wireless client.

   If the client is authorized, the user or computer exchanges encryption keys with the WAP. The encryption keys are used by the client and the WAP, allowing the client internal network connectivity. If the client is not authorized, no network connectivity is allowed.

Planning Certificate for 802.1x Authentication

To use 802.1x authentication, you must deploy to the RADIUS server, at minimum, a certificate with the Server Authentication EKU OID. If you are implementing EAP-TLS authentication, you must also deploy a computer certificate or a user certificate, or both to all wireless client computers.

Computer Certificates for RADIUS Servers

For RADIUS servers, it is recommended to deploy the default RAS and IAS Server certificate template. This certificate template implements the required certificate settings for the Microsoft RADIUS server—Network Policy Server (NPS):

■ The certificate template contains the required Server Authentication EKU OID.

- The certificate template populates both the Subject and the Subject Alternate Name extensions.

The only modification required is to change permissions on the certificate template. The strategy is dependent on the number of domains in your forest.

- If your forest consists of a single domain, perform the following steps:

    a. Add the RADIUS server's computer account to the default RAS and IAS Servers group.

    b. Modify the RAS and IAS Server certificate template permissions to assign the RAS and IAS Servers group Read, Enroll, and Autoenroll permissions.

- If your forest has two or more domains, perform the following steps:

    a. Create a custom universal group in one of the domains, for example, **pki-RADIUS-U**.

    b. Create custom global groups in each domain in the forest, for example, **pki-RADIUS-G.**

    c. Add the RADIUS server's computer account to the local domain's pki-RADIUS-G group.

    d. Add each domain's pki-RADIUS-G group to the pki-RADIUS-U group.

    e. Assign the pki-RADIUS-U group Read, Enroll, and Autoenroll permissions on the RAS and IAS Server certificate template.

Note Still add the RADIUS server's computer account to the *each* domain's RAS and IAS Servers domain local group. This group membership allows the RADIUS server to read the dial-in properties of users in that specific domain.

Why Not Use the RAS and IAS Servers Group?

You must modify the default certificate template permissions on the RAS and IAS Servers group in a multiple domain scenario because of the scope of the RAS and IAS Servers group. An issuing CA in any domain other than the forest root domain will not recognize the domain local group in the discretionary access control list (DACL) of the certificate template. Only computers in the same domain will recognize a domain local group.

Remember that certificate templates should use only universal groups and global groups for permission assignments in a multiple-domain forest.

User Certificates for Clients

If EAP-TLS authentication is implemented, a user must provide a certificate for authentication. To enhance the wireless network's security, you should implement a custom version 2 certificate template based on the Authenticated Session certificate template.

Two modifications can be implemented for the RADIUS user certificates.

- The first modification is to change the permissions on the custom certificate template. You must assign Read, Enroll, and Autoenroll permissions to a custom universal or global group that contains all user accounts that connect to the wireless network. This allows autoenrollment to automate distribution of certificates to users on computers running Windows XP or later. If users have computers running Microsoft Windows 2000, they can still enroll the certificate by using a custom enrollment script or the Certificate Services Web Enrollment pages.

- The second modification is to add a custom application policy OID named **Company-Name Wireless User** in the certificate template. The custom OID serves two purposes. First, it allows you to identify the custom certificate template in an enrollment script for users at computers running Windows 2000. Second, you can configure a network access policy to accept only authentication certificates with the custom application policy OID. For details on implementing a custom application policy OID, see Chapter 12, "Designing Certificate Templates."

Computer Certificates for Clients

If a computer is a member of a domain in the forest, installing a computer certificate allows the computer to connect to the network before a user logs on to the computer. This enables the application of the following:

- Computer Group Policy Objects (GPOs)
- User GPOs
- Logon scripts configured within a user-assigned GPO

If the computer is not issued a certificate, users log on to the computer with cached credentials. Only after the logon process is complete do users gain access to their Client Authentication certificates, permitting them to connect to the corporate network.

The Workstation Authentication or Computer certificate template can be used to provide the client computer a certificate with the Client Authentication application policy OID. A universal or global group containing the computer account must be assigned Read, Enroll, and Autoenroll permissions for the Workstation Authentication certificate or Read and Enroll permissions for the Computer certificate.

Deploying Certificates to Users and Computers

The following sections provide recommendations for deploying the necessary certificates for 802.1x authentication for wireless networks.

RADIUS Server

When implementing 802.1x authentication, it is recommended to use Windows Server 2008 Network Policy Server (NPS) as the RADIUS server. The implementation of computer running Windows Server 2008 allows you to restrict certificate-based authentication to certificates with a designated OID in the certificate, such as a custom application policy OID.

To enable autoenrollment of the RAS and IAS Server certificates:

- Ensure that the RADIUS server's computer account has membership in a custom universal or global group assigned Read, Enroll, and Autoenroll permissions for the RAS and IAS Server certificate template.

- Ensure that the RAS and IAS Server certificate template does not require user input for autoenrollment.

- Ensure that the RAS and IAS Server certificate template is available for enrollment on one or more Windows Server 2008 Enterprise enterprise certification authorities (CAs).

- Ensure that the RADIUS server's computer account is in an organizational unit (OU) where the Autoenrollment Settings Group Policy setting for computers is applied.

> **Note** Alternatively, a user who is assigned Read and Enroll permissions, who is a member of the local Administrators group at the RADIUS server, can manually enroll a RAS and IAS Server certificate.

Client Computers

Client computers require a certificate for 802.1x authentication only if the computer is a member of the forest. If not, a computer certificate does not associate with any computer account in AD DS.

The method used to deploy the computer certificate depends upon whether you are deploying the Computer version 1 certificate template or the Workstation Authentication version 2 certificate template.

If you are deploying to computers running Windows 2000, you can deploy the Computer version 1 certificate template by adding the Computer certificate template to the Automatic Certificate Request Settings Group Policy setting. The GPO with the Automatic Certificate Request Settings defined must be linked to the OU where the computer account exists.

If you are deploying to computers running Windows XP or later, you can deploy the Workstation Authentication version 2 certificate template by using Autoenrollment Settings. As with the RADIUS certificate template, the computer account must belong to a custom universal or global group assigned Read, Enroll, and Autoenroll permissions; the Workstation Authentication certificate template must allow autoenrollment without user input; and the GPO enabling Autoenrollment Settings for computers must be linked to the OU where the computer account exists.

Users

To connect to a wireless network, a user must acquire a certificate based on the custom version 2 certificate template discussed earlier in this chapter. To minimize the risks involved with deploying certificates, it is recommended to use autoenrollment for computers running Windows XP or later and scripted enrollment for computers running Windows 2000.

To enable certificate autoenrollment for the user certificate template for computers running Windows XP or later, you must do the following:

1. Modify the permissions of the custom certificate template to assign Read, Enroll, and Autoenroll permissions to a custom global or universal group containing all wireless users.

2. Modify the custom certificate template to not require user input during the enrollment process. By not requiring user input, certificates are issued to the user invisibly.

3. Ensure that the custom version 2 certificate template is available at one or more enterprise CAs for enrollment.

4. Enable the Autoenrollment Settings Group Policy setting at the OU or domain containing all wireless user accounts.

To enable scripted enrollment for users on Windows 2000 clients, you can use the enroll.vbs script discussed in Chapter 15, "Issuing Certificates." The enroll.vbs script can be used in a logon script to allow automated certificate enrollment for users with computers running Windows 2000.

Assuming that you have implemented an *Organization* wireless User application policy OID in the Wireless User certificate template and that the OID assigned is 1.3.6.1.4.1.311.509.4.2.1, you can use the following code in your logon script to enroll the Wireless User certificate:

```
cscript enroll.vbs /certtype wirelessuser /keyl 1024 /csp enhanced /app_policy
1.3.6.1.5.5.7.3.2 /app_policy 1.3.6.1.4.1.311.509.4.2.1 /fn "Wireless User"
```

This command enrolls the certificate template named *wirelessuser* with a key length of 1,024 bits using the Microsoft Enhanced Cryptographic Service Provider v1.0. In addition, the certificate is requested only if the user does not have an existing certificate with the Client Authentication (1.3.6.1.5.5.7.3.2) and *Organization* Wireless User (1.3.6.1.4.1.311.509.4.2.1) application policy OIDs. Finally, the certificate is assigned the friendly name of Wireless User when placed in the user's certificate store.

> **Note**   Alternatively, you can use manual enrollment for the Wireless User certificate template. A user with a computer running Windows XP or later can use the Certificates Microsoft Management Console (MMC) console or the Certificate Services Web Enrollment pages. A user with a computer running Windows 2000 can use only the Certificate Services Web Enrollment pages.

Implementing 802.1x Authentication

To implement 802.1x authentication, you must configure the RADIUS server and the WAP to implement RADIUS.

Configuring the RADIUS Server

In a Microsoft network, Network Protection Services (NPS) provides RADIUS capabilities on the network. To deploy NPS for wireless networking, you must do the following:

- Install the RADIUS server.
- Add the RADIUS server to the RAS and IAS Servers group.
- Define the RADIUS clients.
- Define a Wireless Computer network access policy.
- Define a Wireless User network access policy.

Install the RADIUS Server

In Windows Server 2008, Internet Authentication Services no longer exists. Instead, the RADIUS features are deployed as a component of Network Policy Server (NPS). To install NPS on the computer running Windows Server 2008, use the following procedure:

1. Log on as a member of the local Administrators group.
2. From Administrative Tools, open Server Manager.
3. In the details pane, in the Roles Summary section, click Add Roles.
4. If the Before You Begin page appears, select the Skip This Page By Default check box, and then click Next.
5. On the Select Server Roles page, select the Network Policy And Access Services check box, and then click Next.

6. On the Network Policy And Access Services page, click Next.

7. On the Select Role Services page, click Network Policy Server, and then click Next.

8. On the Confirm Installation Selections page, click Install.

9. If prompted, insert the Windows Server 2008 Standard or Windows Server 2008 Enterprise DVD in the DVD-ROM drive.

10. On the Installation Results page, ensure that the installation is successful, and then click Close.

Add the RADIUS Server to Each Domain's RAS and IAS Servers Group

After you install NPS, you must add the RADIUS server's computer account to the RAS and IAS Servers group in each domain in the forest. Membership in the RAS and IAS Servers group allows the RADIUS server's computer account to read the users Dial-In Properties in that specific domain.

1. Ensure that you are logged on as a member of the Domain Admins group.

2. From Administrative Tools, open Active Directory Users And Computers.

3. Ensure that you are connected to the domain where the RADIUS server's computer account exists.

4. In the console tree, expand the domain, and then click Users.

5. In the details pane, double-click the RAS and IAS Servers group.

6. In the RAS and IAS Servers Properties dialog box, on the Members tab, click Add.

7. In the Select Users, Contacts, Computers, Or Groups dialog box, click Object Types.

8. In the Object Types dialog box, ensure that the Computers check box is selected, and then click OK.

9. In the Select Users, Contacts, Computers, Or Groups dialog box, in the Enter The Object Names To Select box, type *ComputerName* (where *ComputerName* is the NetBIOS name of the computer hosting IAS), and then click Check Names.

10. Ensure that the correct computer name appears, and then click OK.

11. In the RAS And IAS Servers Properties dialog box, click OK.

12. Repeat for each domain in the forest.

13. Close Active Directory Users And Computers.

14. Restart the computer hosting the RADIUS service to use the new group membership.

Define RADIUS Clients

Each WAP that forwards authentication requests to the RADIUS server must be added as the WAP's known client list. The WAP's Internet Protocol (IP) address as well as a RADIUS secret or password, must be defined.

To define a RADIUS client at the IAS server, do the following:

1. From Administrative Tools, open Network Policy Server.

2. In the console tree, expand RADIUS Clients And Servers, right-click RADIUS Clients, and then click New RADIUS Client.

3. On the New RADIUS Client page (see Figure 24-2), enable the following options:

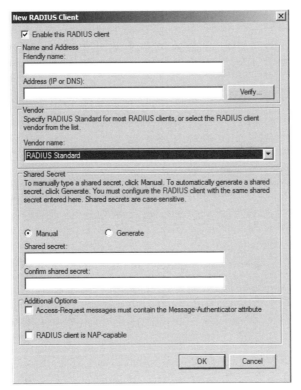

Figure 24-2   Adding a New RADIUS Client

  ❑ Select the Enable This RADIUS Client check box

  ❑ Provide a friendly name for the WAP.

  ❑ Provide the IP address of the WAP.

  ❑ In the Vendor Name drop-down list, select the vendor of the WAP.

> **Tip**   If the hardware vendor is not available in the list, choose the standard RADIUS option.

❏ In the Shared Secret section, choose between manually typing and confirming or generating a shared secret.

> **Tip**   If you choose the generated secret, you may have to reduce the length of the secret because some WAPs will not be able to support the long secret that is generated.

❏ Choose whether to require the Message-Authenticator attribute in access-request messages.

❏ Specify whether the WAP is Network Access Protection (NAP) capable.

4. Click Finish.

5. Repeat this process for every WAP that uses the RADIUS server for 802.1x authentication.

> **Note**   Microsoft's RADIUS server does not support the use of the "Any" designation. Each WAP must be manually defined as a RADIUS client at the IAS server.

Define a Network Access Policy for Wireless Computers

Once you designate all RADIUS clients, you must define a remote access policy for computer accounts. This remote access policy allows wireless computers to connect initially for logon and GPO download.

Use the following process to create and configure a remote access policy for computer authentication:

1. From Administrative Tools, open Network Policy Server.

2. In the console tree, select NPS (Local).

3. In the details pane, in the Standard Configuration section, select RADIUS Server For 802.1x Wireless Or Wired Connections, and then click Configure 802.1x.

4. On the Select 802.1x Connections Type page, click Secure Wireless Connections, name the policy **Wireless Computers**, and then click Next.

5. On the Specify 802.1x Switches page, you can add any additional RADIUS clients (the WAPs in the case of a wireless network access policy), and then click Next.

6. On the Configure An Authentication Method page, in the Type drop-down list, select Microsoft Smart Card Or Other Certificate, and then click Configure.

7. In the Smart Card Or Other Certificate Properties dialog box, in the Certificate Issued To drop-down list, select the certificate issued to *ComputerName@DomainName* (where *ComputerName* is the computer account name of the RADIUS server, and *DomainName* is the DNS name of the RADIUS server's domain), and then click OK.

8. On the Configure An Authentication Method page, click Next.

9. On the Specify User Groups page, click Add.

10. In the Select Group dialog box, add each domain's Domain Computers group, and then click OK.

> **Note** Alternatively, you can create a custom group containing only authorized wireless computers.

11. On the Specify User Groups page, click Next.

12. On the Configure A Virtual LAN (VLAN) page, you can optionally configure VLAN information, and then click Next.

13. On the Completing New IEEE 802.1x Secured Wired And Wireless Connections And RADIUS Clients page, click Finish.

14. In the console tree, expand Policies, and then click Network Policies.

15. In the details pane, double-click Wireless Computers.

16. On the Conditions tab, select NAS Port Type, and then click Edit.

17. In the NAS Port Type dialog box, in the Other section, clear the Wireless-Other check box, and then click OK.

18. On the Constraints tab, select Authentication Methods.

19. In the details pane, clear the following check boxes:

    ❑ Microsoft Encrypted Authentication Version 2 (MS-CHAP-v2)

    ❑ Microsoft Encrypted Authentication (MS-CHAP)

20. On the Settings tab, click Encryption.

21. In the details pane, clear all check boxes except Strongest Encryption (MPPE 128-bit), and then click OK.

> **Note** The same configuration changes are also made to the Network Policies version of the Wireless Computers policy.

Define the Wireless User Remote Access Policy

When enabling 802.1x authentication, you must configure a separate network policy for wireless users. Although similar, the main difference in the two policies is that the user remote access policy requires the custom *Organization* Wireless User OID in the user's certificate.

The following process creates and configures the user remote access policy:

1. From Administrative Tools, open Network Policy Server.

2. In the console tree, select NPS (Local).

3. In the details pane, in the Standard Configuration section, select RADIUS Server For 802.1x Wireless Or Wired Connections, and then click Configure 802.1x.

4. On the Select 802.1x Connections Type page, click Secure Wireless Connections, name the policy Wireless Users, and then click Next.

5. On the Specify 802.1x Switches page, you can add any additional RADIUS clients (the WAPs in the case of a wireless network access policy), and then click Next.

6. On the Configure An Authentication Method page, in the Type drop-down list, select Microsoft Smart Card Or Other Certificate, and then click Configure.

7. In the Smart Card Or Other Certificate Properties dialog box, in the Certificate Issued To drop-down list, select the certificate issued to *ComputerName@DomainName* (where *ComputerName* is the computer account name of the RADIUS server and *DomainName* is the DNS name of the RADIUS server's domain), and then click OK.

8. On the Configure An Authentication Method page, click Next.

9. On the Specify User Groups page, click Add.

10. In the Select Group dialog box, add each domain's Domain Users group, and then click OK.

> **Note**   Alternatively, you can create a custom group containing only authorized wireless users. Consider using the same group used to assign permissions to the custom Wireless User Authentication certificate template.

11. On the Specify User Groups page, click Next.

12. On the Configure A Virtual LAN (VLAN) page, you can optionally configure VLAN information, and then click Next.

13. On the Completing New IEEE 802.1x Secured Wired And Wireless Connections And RADIUS Clients page, click Finish.

14. In the console tree, expand Policies, and then click Network Policies.

15. In the details pane, double-click Wireless Users.

16. On the Conditions tab, select NAS Port Type, and then click Edit.

17. In the NAS Port Type dialog box, in the Other section, clear the Wireless-Other check box, and click OK.

18. On the Constraints tab, select Authentication Methods.

19. In the details pane, clear the following check boxes:

    ❑ Microsoft Encrypted Authentication Version 2 (MS-CHAP-v2)

    ❑ Microsoft Encrypted Authentication (MS-CHAP)

20. On the Settings tab, click Vendor Specific, and then click Add.

21. In the Add Vendor Specific Attribute dialog box, in the Attributes list, select Allowed-Certificate-OID, and then click Add.

22. In the Attribute Information dialog box, click Add.

23. In the Attribute Information dialog box, in the Attribute Value box, type **1.3.6.1.4.1.311.509.4.2.1** (or the custom OID deployed in your Wireless User certificate template), and then click OK.

24. In the Attribute Information dialog box, click OK.

25. In the Add Vendor Specific Attribute dialog box, click Close.

26. On the Settings tab, click Encryption.

27. In the details pane, clear all check boxes except Strongest Encryption (MPPE 128-bit), and then click OK.

Configuring the Wireless Access Point

WAP configuration is dependent on the WAP vendor's requirements and management interfaces. Rather than provide the details for a single vendor, ensure that you configure the following settings at your WAP:

1. Configure the WAP to implement RADIUS authentication by doing the following:

    a. Add the IP address of the IAS server for RADIUS authentication.

    b. Input the RADIUS secret for the IAS server.

    c. Specify the RADIUS listening port used by the IAS server (UDP port 1812).

2. Configure the WAP to implement RADIUS accounting by doing the following:

    a. Add the IP address of the IAS server for RADIUS accounting.

    b. Input the RADIUS secret for the IAS server.

    c. Specify the RADIUS listening port used by the IAS server (UDP port 1813).

> **Important**   The WAP must support RADIUS authentication. If the WAP does not sup-
> port RADIUS authentication, you cannot implement 802.1x authentication for your net-
> work when using that WAP.

Connecting to the Wireless Network

Once the infrastructure installation is complete, the wireless clients can connect to the
wireless network by using 802.1x authentication. The procedure varies depending on
whether you are using Windows XP or Windows Vista on the client computer.

Windows XP Wireless Connections

To connect a Windows XP client to the wireless network, the following procedure is required:

1. Open the Network Connections window.

2. Right-click your wireless adapter icon, and then click Properties.

3. In the Properties Of The Wireless Adapter dialog box, on the Wireless Networks tab, in
    the Preferred Networks section, choose the Service Set Identifier (SSID) of the wireless
    network, and then click Properties.

4. In the SSID Properties dialog box, on the Association tab, configure the following settings.

Option	WEP	WPA2
Network Authentication	Open	WPA2 or WPA2-PSK
Data Encryption	WEP	TKIP or AES
The Key Is Provided For Me Automatically	Enabled	Enabled

5. In the SSID Properties dialog box, on the Authentication tab, configure the following
    settings.

Option	WEP	WPA2
Enable 802.1x Authentication For The Network	Enabled	Enabled
EAP Type	Smart Card or other Certificate	Smart Card or other Certificate
Authenticate As Computer When Computer Information Is Available	Enabled if computer is a member of the forest	Enabled if computer is a member of the forest

6. In the SSID Properties dialog box, on the Authentication tab, click Properties.

7. In the Smart Card Or Other Certificate Properties dialog box (shown in Figure 24-3), enable the following options as needed:

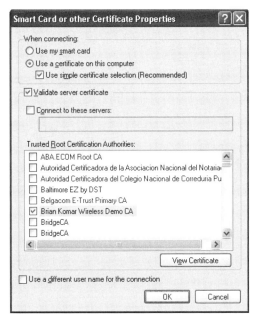

Figure 24-3 Configuring Windows XP certificate settings for EAP-TLS authentication

❏ **Use My Smart Card**   Enable if using a smart card certificate.

❏ **Use A Certificate On This Computer**   Enable if using a certificate stored in the user's certificate store.

❏ **Use Simple Certificate Selection (Recommended)**   Enable if the certificate's subject is the same as the user's logon name.

> **Warning**   Do not enable simple certificate selection if the computer is from a different forest or workgroup. By not enabling simple certificate selection, the user can choose the certificate for authentication manually.

❏ **Validate Server Certificate**   Enable this option to require mutual authentication. The client validates the RADIUS server's certificate and ensures that it chains to the root CA certificate designated in the Trusted Root Certification Authorities store in the local client machines.

❏ **Use A Different User Name For The Connection**   Enable this option only if the computer is not a member of the forest. This allows the user to choose a certificate that does not contain his or her current user name.

Windows Vista Wireless Connections

To connect a Windows Vista client to the wireless network, the following procedure is required:

1. From the Start menu, click Connect To.

2. In the Connect To A Network dialog box, click Set Up A Connection Or Network.

3. On the Choose A Connection Option page, click Manually Connect To A Wireless Network, and then click Next.

4. On the Choose A Wireless Adapter page, choose your wireless network adapter from the drop-down list, and then click Next.

5. On the Enter Information For the Wireless Network You Want To Add page (see Figure 24-4), type the Service Set Identifier (SSID) of the wireless network, select the Security type (WPA2-Enterprise, WPA-Enterprise, or WEP), Encryption Type (AES or TKIP, if using WPA or WPA2), and whether to start the connection automatically, and then click Next.

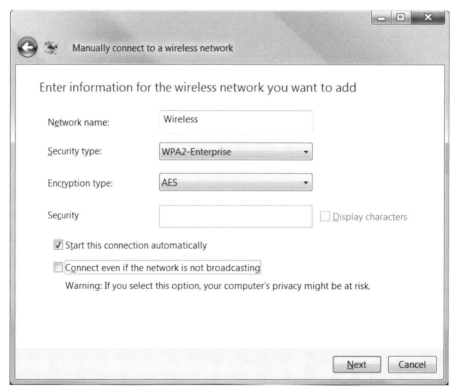

Figure 24-4   Configuring wireless settings for a Windows Vista client

6. On the Successfully Added *ConnectionName page*, click Change Connection Settings.

7. In the *ConnectionName* Wireless Network Properties dialog box, on the Security page, in the Choose A Network Authentication Method drop-down list, select Smart Card Or Other Certificate, and then click Settings.

8. On the Smart Card Or Other Certificate Properties dialog box (see Figure 24-5), enable the following options as needed, and then click OK:

Figure 24-5   Configuring Windows Vista certificate settings for EAP-TLS authentication

- ❏ **Use My Smart Card**   Enable if using a smart card certificate.

- ❏ **Use A Certificate On This Computer**   Enable if using a certificate stored in the user's certificate store.

- ❏ **Use Simple Certificate Selection (Recommended)**   Enable if the certificate's subject is the same as the user's logon name.

> **Warning**   Do not enable simple certificate selection if the computer is from a different forest or workgroup. By not enabling simple certificate selection, the user can choose the certificate for authentication manually.

❑ **Validate Server Certificate**   Enable this option to require mutual authentication. The client validates the RADIUS server's certificate and ensures that it chains to the root CA certificate designated in the Trusted Root Certification Authorities store in the local client machines.

❑ **Trusted Root Certification Authorities**   Designate the specific root CA that must be the root trust point in the server's certificate chain.

❑ **Use A Different User Name For The Connection**   Enable this option only if the computer is not a member of the forest. This allows the user to choose a certificate that does not contain his or her current user name.

9. In the *ConnectionName* Wireless Network Properties dialog box, click OK.

10. On the Successfully Added *ConnectionName* dialog box, click Close.

Using Group Policy to Enforce Correct Wireless Client Configuration

Group Policy can be used to ensure that wireless networking settings are configured correctly for EAP-TLS authentication (for 802.1x authentication). The GPO not only ensures that the connection is correctly configured, it ensures that clients will connect only to the preferred network when working at the office.

The GPO is applied to computer accounts and should be linked to either the domain or to the OU where wireless computer accounts are located. A wireless network policy allows an organization to do the following:

■ Enforce 802.1x authentication.

■ Restrict wireless connectivity to WAPs, not allowing ad hoc connections.

> **Note**   An *ad hoc wireless network* is configured directly between two wireless clients rather than clients connecting to a WAP connected to the corporate network. Many attackers use ad hoc networks to gain access to a wireless computer. Disabling ad hoc connections provides protection against this form of attack.

■ Enable Windows to configure wireless network settings automatically.

■ Provide preferred network SSIDs and prevent connections to non-preferred networks.

■ Enforce the use of WEP or WPA encryption.

■ Specify which form of EAP authentication is required: PEAP or EAP-TLS.

■ Specify whether computer authentication, user authentication, or a combination of both is required for connectivity to the wireless network.

■ Enforce mutual authentication by validating the RADIUS server's certificate.

> **Note**   Windows Server 2008 now supports a similar GPO for Wired Network connections, allowing you to define the specific requirements for connecting to a Wired network with 802.1x authentication.

Case Study: Margie's Travel

You manage the network for Margie's Travel, a travel agency in Seattle, Washington. The network implements a single enterprise root CA for its PKI as shown in Figure 24-6.

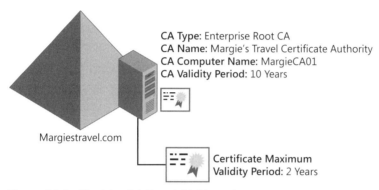

CA Type: Enterprise Root CA
CA Name: Margie's Travel Certificate Authority
CA Computer Name: MargieCA01
CA Validity Period: 10 Years

Margiestravel.com

Certificate Maximum Validity Period: 2 Years

Figure 24-6   The Margie's Travel CA hierarchy

Scenario

Margie's Travel is a new travel agency that has changed locations each year as the business has expanded. Because of the high costs involved in rewiring the new office each time that Margie's Travel changes locations, you are considering implementing wireless networking to reduce the costs associated with pulling twisted pair cabling to each desk in the office.

The servers shown in Figure 24-7 are currently deployed on the network.

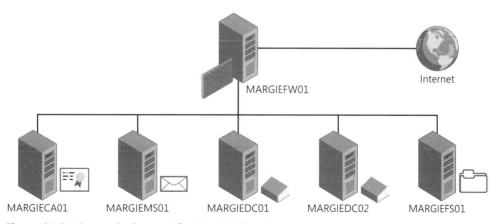

Internet

MARGIEFW01

MARGIECA01   MARGIEMS01   MARGIEDC01   MARGIEDC02   MARGIEFS01

Figure 24-7   Server deployment for Margie's Travel

You have gathered the following requirements for implementing wireless networking:

- Six servers provide the network infrastructure for the Margie's Travel network. All servers are members of the margiestravel.com domain. The six servers are:

  - ❏ **MARGIEFW01**   The computer running Microsoft Internet Security and Acceleration (ISA) Server providing firewall and proxy services.

  - ❏ **MARGIEMS01**   The computer running Microsoft Exchange Server 2007 providing e-mail services for the network.

  - ❏ **MARGIECA01**   The Windows Server 2008 enterprise root CA for the network providing certificates to all users and computers on the network.

  - ❏ **MARGIEDC01**   The first Windows Server 2008 domain controller for the margiestravel.com domain. This domain controller also provides DNS and Dynamic Host Configuration Protocol (DHCP) services for the network.

  - ❏ **MARGIEDC02**   The second Windows Server 2008 domain controller for the margiestravel.com domain. This domain controller provides DNS services for the network.

  - ❏ **MARGIEFS01**   The file server for the network. All customer records and accounting information are stored on this server. In addition, Internet Information Services (IIS) is installed on the server and hosts the corporate intranet Web site.

- The file server on the network contains confidential client information, such as credit card numbers and passport numbers. Unauthorized access to the networks must be prevented to protect access to this confidential information. Only company-owned computers must be allowed to connect to the network.

- Although several of the travel agents have laptop computers, several of the agents work only at the office and use desktop computers when connecting to the network.

- All client computers and notebooks run Windows Vista Enterprise with the latest service pack. All computers and notebooks are members of the margiestravel.com domain.

- All desktops and computers have wireless cards that support 802.11n. The latest updates are installed for all wireless cards.

- All servers are stored in a server room at the back of the office. The servers have 100 megabit per second (Mbps)–Ethernet cards.

- Because of the size of the current location, at least three wireless access points are required to provide sufficient coverage for all areas of the office.

Case Study Questions

1. What network infrastructure service required for wireless network is missing from the Margie's Travel network? On which server(s) would you install the missing service?

2. When you purchase the wireless access points for the networks, what features are required to satisfy the design requirements?

3. What certificate(s) are required on the wireless access points?

4. What certificate(s) are required at each desktop or notebook computer?

5. What certificate(s) are required for each user of the network?

6. What other certificate(s) are required for the wireless network deployment?

7. How many remote access policies are required for the wireless deployment?

8. How can you ensure that each desktop and notebook computer is correctly configured for connectivity to the wireless network?

9. What additional measures can be taken to ensure that only Margie's Travel users can connect to the wireless network?

Best Practices

■   **Implement the strongest form of wireless encryption available on your WAPs.**   Any form of encryption is better than no encryption. Even though WEP has known weaknesses, it is still better to enable WEP than to have no encryption at all if your WAP does not support WPA or WPA2. If you do implement WEP, ensure that you regularly modify the WEP key to protect against attacks against the WEP key.

■   **Implement only WAPs that support 802.1x authentication.**   802.1x authentication decreases some of the weaknesses associated with WEP encryption. 802.1x ensures that only authenticated clients (computers and users) can connect to the wireless network, and it provides automated distribution of the encryption keys.

■   **Implement PEAP or EAP-TLS for authenticating all wireless clients.**   Both authentication methods provide strong protection of the user's credentials. In addition, EAP-TLS and PEAP ensure that the computers or users mutually authenticate with a RADIUS server when they connect to the wireless network.

■   **Deploy certificates using autoenrollment or scripted enrollment for domain members.**   Automating the deployment of certificates ensures that all users and computers obtain the necessary certificates for wireless networking. Automated deployment reduces the chance of user error during the enrollment process.

■   **Use Group Policy to define Wireless Networking settings.**   Group Policy can ensure that computers running Windows XP or later are correctly configured when connecting to a wireless network. Group Policy eliminates user error when configuring the wireless networking connection.

Additional Information

- "Deploying Secure 802.11 Wireless Networks with Microsoft Windows" (*http://www.microsoft.com/mspress/books/6749.asp*)

- "802.11 WEP: Concepts and Vulnerability" (*http://www.wi-fiplanet.com/tutorials/article.php/1368661*)

- "Configuring Wireless Settings Using Windows Server 2008 Group Policy" (*http://www.microsoft.com/technet/community/columns/cableguy/cg0703.mspx*)

- "Designing and Deploying Wireless LAN Connectivity for the Microsoft Corporate Network" (*http://www.microsoft.com/technet/prodtechnol/winxppro/deploy/wlandply.mspx*)

- "Enterprise Deployment of Secure 802.11 Networks Using Microsoft Windows" (*http://www.microsoft.com/technet/prodtechnol/winxppro/deploy/ed80211.mspx*)

- "Enterprise Deployment of Secure Wired Networks Using Microsoft Windows" (*http://www.microsoft.com/downloads/details.aspx?FamilyID=05951071-6b20-4cef-9939-47c397ffd3dd&displaylang=en*)

- "Enterprise Solutions for Wireless LAN Security" (*http://www.wi-fi.org/OpenSection/pdf/Whitepaper_Wi-Fi_Enterprise2-6-03.pdf*)

- "Microsoft 802.1x Authentication Client for Windows 2000" (*http://www.microsoft.com/windows2000/server/evaluation/news/bulletins/8021xclient.asp*)

- "Securing Wireless LANs—A Windows Server 2003 Certificate Services Solution" (*http://www.microsoft.com/technet/security/prodtech/win2003/pkiwire/swlan.mspx*)

- "Obtaining and Installing a VeriSign WLAN Server Certificate for PEAP-MS-CHAP v2 Wireless Authentication" (*http://download.microsoft.com/download/9/f/d/9fd73f17-2fdf-4409-b2d2-31437c7f29f3/WLANCertEnroll.doc*)

- "Security of the WEP Algorithm" (*http://www.isaac.cs.berkeley.edu/isaac/wep-faq.html*)

- "Step-by-Step Guide for Setting Up Secure Wireless Access in a Test Lab" (*http://www.microsoft.com/downloads/details.aspx?FamilyID=0f7fa9a2-e113-415b-b2a9-b6a3d64c48f5&DisplayLang=en*)

- "Troubleshooting Windows XP IEEE 802.11 Wireless Access" (*http://www.microsoft.com/technet/prodtechnol/winxppro/maintain/wifitrbl.mspx*)

- Wi-Fi Alliance (*http://www.weca.net/OpenSection/index.asp*)

- "Wi-Fi Protected Access" (*http://www.weca.net/OpenSection/protected_access.asp*)

- "Wi-Fi Protected Access (WPA) Overview" (*http://www.microsoft.com/technet/community/columns/cableguy/cg0303.mspx*)

- "Windows Server 2008 Deployment Kit: Deploying a Wireless LAN" (*http://www.microsoft.com/technet/prodtechnol/windowsserver2003/proddocs/deployguide/dnsbm_wir_overview.asp?frame=true*)

- "Windows XP Wireless Deployment Technology and Component Overview" (*http://www.microsoft.com/technet/prodtechnol/winxppro/maintain/wificomp.mspx*)

- "Windows XP Support Patch for Wi-Fi Protected Access" (*http://microsoft.com/downloads/details.aspx?FamilyId=009D8425-CE2B-47A4-ABEC-274845DC9E91&displaylang=en*)

- SMAC tool (*http://www.klcconsulting.net/smac/default.htm?v=readme11*)

- "Wi-Fi Protected Access 2 (WPA2) Overview" (*http://technet.microsoft.com/en-us/library/bb878054.aspx*)

- "Wireless Networking in Windows Vista" (*http://microsoft.com/downloads/details.aspx?familyid=eb958617-b3d3-42cf-a434-87ad81259fc6&displaylang=en*)

- "Windows Vista Wireless Networking Evaluation Guide" (*http://go.microsoft.com/fwlink/?linkid=79943*)

- "Troubleshooting Windows Vista 802.11 Wireless Connections" (*http://technet2.microsoft.com/windowsvista/en/library/3ed3d027-5ae8-4cb0-ade5-0a7c446cd4f71033.mspx?mfr=true*)

- "New Networking Features in Windows Server 2008 and Windows Vista" (*http://www.microsoft.com/technet/network/evaluate/new_network.mspx*)

- "Connecting to Wireless Networks with Windows Vista" (*http://www.microsoft.com/technet/community/columns/cableguy/cg0406.mspx*)

- "IEEE 802.11 Wireless LAN Security with Microsoft Windows" (*http://support.microsoft.com/kb/927865*)

- "Implementing Security for Wireless Networks" (*http://msevents.microsoft.com/cui/webcasteventdetails.aspx?culture=en-us&eventid=1032280061&countrycode=us*)

- "How Microsoft IT Secures Wireless Networks at Microsoft" (*http://msevents.microsoft.com/cui/webcasteventdetails.aspx?eventid=1032273396&eventcategory=5&culture=en-us&countrycode=us*)

- "Configuring Windows XP IEEE 802.11 Wireless Networks for the Home and Small Business" (*http://microsoft.com/technet/network/wifi/wifisoho.mspx*)

- "Wireless Group Policy Settings for Windows Vista" (*http://microsoft.com/technet/technetmag/issues/2007/04/cableguy/default.aspx*)

- 313664: "Using 802.1x Authentication on Computers Running Windows 2000"

- 318710: "How To: Support Wireless Connections in Windows 2000"

- 815485: "Overview of the WPA Wireless Security Update in Windows XP"

- 816589: "How To: Support Wireless Connections That Use EAP-TLS Authentication in Windows Server 2008"

- 837911: "Windows for Wireless and Wired Networks"

Note   The last five articles in the above list can be accessed through the Microsoft Knowledge Base. Go to *http://support.micrososft.com*, and enter the article number in the Search The Knowledge Base text box.

Chapter 25

Document and Code Signing

Code signing allows users and computers to trust software published on a public network, such as the Internet. When you connect to the Internet, you can download device drivers for your computer's operating system, ActiveX controls, or Java applets for advanced Web content. The question remains: How do you know the link provides you with the content it suggests and is not a virus or an attack against your computer?

Likewise, document signing helps you trust the content of a document. The signature helps prove who created and signed the document and that the content of the document remains unchanged.

As long as you trust the certificate used to sign the software or document—including all certificate trust validation described in Chapter 11, "Certificate Validation"—you should feel comfortable installing the signed software or accepting the contents of the signed document.

 Note   Microsoft's solution for code signing is known as Authenticode, which applies an industry-standard signature to code developed with Microsoft tools.

How Code Signing Works

Code signing adds a digital signature to executable files (.exe), dynamic link libraries (.dll), ActiveX controls (.ocx), Microsoft Visual Basic documents (.vbd), Cabinet files (.cab), Java Archive files (.jar), Windows Installer files (.msi or .msp), driver files (.sys), and scripts.

 Note   Normally, it is sufficient to sign only the .cab file in which your components are packaged. However, if you intend to distribute the individual .ocx, .exe, .vbd, or .dll files without packaging them in a .cab file, you should sign the individual components.

The digital signature protects a user who accesses the software in the following two ways:

- The digital signature identifies the publisher of the software, allowing you to make an informed choice of whether to allow or prevent software installation.

- The digital signature allows you to determine whether the software has been modified between the time the code was signed and the time you decide to install the software.

Applications that are aware of code signing can be configured to choose how to interact with software that is signed or not signed. For example, in Windows Internet Explorer, you can define how to interact with ActiveX controls for each security zone, as shown in Figure 25-1.

Figure 25-1   Defining ActiveX and Authenticode settings for a Windows Internet Explorer security zone

Per security zone, you can specify how Internet Explorer interacts with potentially dangerous Internet content. For each setting, you can choose to enable the content, disable the content, or prompt each time the user interacts with the specified type of content.

Warning   Although code signing itself cannot guarantee that signed code is safe to run, it is a mechanism to inform users of who the software publisher is, allow the user to choose to trust (or not trust) the publisher, and know whether or not the code has been modified since it was originally signed.

How Document Signing Works

Like code signing, document signing applies a digital signature to the document object. The digital signature:

- Verifies the identity of the user that signed the document. Typically, this is either the last person to edit the document before distribution or the person that verifies that the content represents the views of the organization distributing the document.

- Allows a recipient to verify that content of the document was not modified after the digital signature was applied to the document.

Certification of Signing Certificates

The effectiveness of code signing and document signing is only as good as the level of trust in the certificate used to sign the application. The process used to certify the application for the Code Signing or Document Signing certificate varies depending upon whether the certificate is obtained from a commercial or an internal source.

> **Note**   Because of the importance of a Code Signing certificate, you should store the Code Signing certificate and private key on a two-factor device, such as a smart card, to provide stronger protection of the Code Signing certificate's private key.

Commercial Certification of Code Signing Certificates

When Code Signing certificates are obtained from a commercial entity, the type of certificate is referred to as a Software Publishing Certificate (SPC). To enroll this form of certificate, the requestor must meet the following criteria defined by the commercial certificate provider:

- **Identification**   Requestors must submit their names, addresses, and other information that proves their identities to the commercial provider. The identification process might also require a face-to-face interview.

- **The pledge**   Requestors must assure that they will not distribute software that they know, or should have known, contains viruses or would otherwise harm a user's computer or code. The assurance can be provided in writing or by agreeing to a statement posted on the commercial provider's enrollment Web site.

> **Note**   Code signing does not ensure that the code does not introduce security risks to an organization. For information and recommendations for writing secure applications, see *Writing Secure Code, Second Edition*, by Michael Howard and David LeBlanc (Microsoft Press, 2002).

- **Dun and Bradstreet Rating**   A requestor's organization must have financial standing in the business community. Typically, this is indicated by a Dun and Bradstreet rating. If an organization does not have a Dun and Bradstreet rating, it must apply for a rating before a Code Signing certificate is issued by the commercial organization.

There are different strategies for acquiring a Code Signing certificate:

- **Acquire a single certificate for the entire organization.**   This method ensures that all code signing passes through a central approval mechanism. Some organizations actually test the application in a certification forest before it is signed to ensure that the application causes no damage.

- **Acquire a certificate on a divisional basis.**   In decentralized organizations, different divisions or departments might have the responsibility of signing the applications that they develop. In this case, the certificate's subject might also include departmental information.

- **Acquire certificates on an individual basis.**   In some organizations, every developer is responsible for the code that he or she develops. By implementing Code Signing certificates for each developer, an organization can determine who created or modified a piece of code or determine if the code was changed after the developer signed the code.

In most cases, the certificate's subject is typically the name of the software publisher's organization rather than the individual who requests the certificate. Using the organization name in the subject of the certificate is recommended because the person is signing the application on behalf of the company.

> **Note**   The only exception occurs when certificates are issued to each individual developer. If each developer has his or her own Code Signing certificate, the Subject or Subject Alternative Name should indicate the identity of the developer.

Corporate Certification of Code Signing and Document Signing Certificates

If an application is used only within an organization, the organization can choose to issue its own Code Signing certificates. In this case, similar measures should be taken to validate the certificate requestor's identity.

It is recommended to issue certificates using a medium or high assurance registration model. Both the medium and high assurance registration policies involve a registration authority validating the requestor's identity before the certificate is issued. In addition, permissions on the Code Signing certificate template can be restricted to limit which groups are assigned Read and Enroll permissions for the certificate template.

> **Note**   A registration authority such as Microsoft Identity Lifecycle Manager (ILM) 2007 Certificate Management (discussed in Chapter 17, "Identity Lifecycle Manager 2007 Certificate Management") allows you enforce the requirement that all validation of the requestor's identity is performed *before* a certificate is issued to the requestor.

When a Code Signing or Document Signing certificate issued by the corporate CA hierarchy is used, the signature is recognized only by client computers that trust the CA hierarchy's root CA. Typically, this includes only computers that are members of the local forest.

Note   It is possible to trust the Code Signing certificate of another organization. Possible methods include implementing a subordinate CA below a commercial root CA or by using qualified subordination to trust only Code Signing certificates issued by a partner's CA hierarchy.

Planning Deployment of Signing Certificates

The deployment of Code Signing and Document Signing certificates within an organization involves designing the Code Signing certificate template and planning how to deploy the certificates to the developers who perform the code signing operations.

Important   If you are signing applications or code that will be used by people outside of your organization, it is recommended to obtain the Code Signing or Document Signing certificate from a commercial vendor, such as VeriSign.

Certificate Template Design

You can use different certificate templates for Code Signing and Document Signing certificates. The following sections provide recommendations on deploying separate certificates for code signing and document signing.

Code Signing

When deploying a Code Signing certificate, you can use the default Code Signing certificate template or develop a custom certificate template.

■ Choose the default Code Signing certificate template if your organization allows the Code Signing certificate to exist on the hard disk of the code signer's computer. The default certificate template uses the Microsoft Enhanced Cryptographic Provider v 1.0.

■ Create a custom version 2 certificate template if you wish to require certificate manager approval before the certificate is issued.

■ Create a custom version 2 certificate template if you wish to deploy the Code Signing certificate on a two-factor device, such as a smart card.

■ Create a custom version 2 certificate template if you wish to add an entry to the Certificate Policies extension indicating what measures were taken to validate the certificate's subject at certificate enrollment.

■ Whether using a version 1 or version 2 certificate template, ensure that the permissions of the certificate template are modified so that only the required users have Read and Enroll permissions for the Code Signing certificate template.

- Consider creating a custom user account in Active Directory Domain Services (AD DS) that requests the Code Signing certificate. Ensure that the user account's Common Name is the organization's name rather than the user's. This ensures that the certificate's subject is the name of the organization, which again increases trust in the signed application. Alternatively, you can implement a custom certificate template that allows the certificate requestor to provide the subject information rather than gathering it from AD DS.

Document Signing

When deploying a Document Signing certificate, it is recommended to create a custom version 2 certificate template based on the Code Signing certificate template. The modifications required include:

- Change the cryptographic service provider (CSP) if you wish to deploy the certificate on a smart card.

> **Tip** You must install the smart card CSP on the workstation where you edit the certificate template to have the CSP available for selection.

- Consider requiring certificate manager approval before the certificate is issued.

- Remove the code signing application policy. Code signing is not a required application policy OID for document signing.

- Add the document signing application policy, The document signing application policy OID ensures that the certificate can be used to sign documents but not be used for other authentication attempts.

- Add a custom issuance policy OID that describes the registration model used to issue the certificate. The issuance policy OID should reference an assurance level described in your organization's certificate policy.

- Consider creating a custom user account in Active Directory that requests the Code Signing certificate. Ensure that the user account's Common Name is the organization's name rather than the user's. This ensures that the certificate's subject is the name of the organization, which again increases trust in the signed application. Alternatively, you can implement a custom certificate template that allows the certificate requestor to provide the subject information rather than gathering it from AD DS.

Planning Enrollment Methods

The enrollment method you choose depends upon whether or not your organization requires CA certificate manager approval for issuance.

- If the Code Signing or Document Signing certificate is protected by a smart card cryptographic service provider (CSP), ensure that the person who obtains the Code

Signing or Document Signing certificate is issued a smart card and a smart card reader before the enrollment process commences.

■ If the Code Signing or Document Signing certificate may be acquired without certificate manager approval, the certificate can be enrolled using any enrollment method. This includes the Certificate Enrollment Wizard or the Certificate Services Web Enrollment pages.

■ If the Code Signing or Document Signing certificate requires certificate manager approval, the recommendation depends on the operating system used to perform the certificate request:

    ❏ **Windows XP or earlier clients**   Use the Certificate Services Web Enrollment pages to allow the requestor to view the status of the pending certificate request and complete the enrollment when the certificate is issued by the certificate manager.

    ❏ **Windows Vista**   Use the Certificates MMC console to initiate *and* complete a pending certificate request.

■ It is not recommended to implement autoenrollment for a Code Signing or Document Signing certificates. Because of the trust put in a code signing or document signing signature, the process should be initiated by the requestor.

■ If ILM 2007 certificate management is deployed, consider creating separate profile templates for code signing and document signing.

    ❏ Define an enroll policy that enforces the assurance level asserted in the certificate.

    ❏ Require data collection items that enforce the validation requirements defined in the certificate policy.

    ❏ Defined management policies for the entire life cycle of the Code Signing or Document Signing certificate.

Time Stamping Considerations

When you sign code or a document, the signature applied to the code or document will eventually fail validation. This can occur when:

■ The certificate used to perform the signing expires.

■ The certificate used to perform the signing is revoked.

Rather than re-signing the document or code when the original certificate is no longer valid, a time stamp service may be used to allow the signature to remain valid beyond the validity period of the original certificate. Time stamping establishes:

■ The exact time that the signing operation occurred.

■ That the certificate was valid at the time the signing operation occurred.

> **Note**   The time stamp effectively extends the validity of the signed object beyond the expiration date of the certificate.

A time stamp service can be an Internet-provided service or a hardware device such as nCipher's Time Stamp Server. Whatever solution you choose must be a trusted source of time information. If the time information source is not protected, an attacker could change the time on the time stamp service to apply a time stamp at an earlier time.

Performing Code Signing

The process of performing the code signing can begin once the Code Signing certificate is issued to the requestor.

Gathering the Required Tools

The Microsoft Windows Software Development Kit Update for Windows Vista includes a code signing tool (SignTool.exe) that enables code signing of any application. SignTool includes the following options:

- **sign**   Digitally signs the application at a command prompt.
- **signwizard**   Uses the signing wizard to digitally sign the application (recommended).
- **timestamp**   Applies a time stamp to a previously digitally signed application.
- **verify**   Verifies a digitally signed application.

> **Note**   When you run SignTool with options, you simply type **signtool (option)**. For example, to use the digitally signing wizard, you would type **signtool signwizard**.

- **Makecert.exe**   This tool creates a self-signed X.509 certificate for testing purposes only.

> **Important**   It is recommended to issue the Code Signing certificate from an enterprise CA by creating a version 2 certificate template based on the Code Signing certificate template rather than to test with self-signed certificates.

- **Cert2spc.exe**   Creates an SPC for testing purposes only. Again, it is recommended to issue the SPC certificate from the internal CA hierarchy rather than generate a self-signed certificate.
- **MakeCTL.exe**   Creates a certificate trust list to allow trust of certificates issued by foreign CA hierarchies.

- **CertMgr.exe**   Manages certificates, certificate trust lists (CTLs), and certificate revocation lists (CRLs) for the local user.

- **SetReg.exe**   Sets registry keys that control certificate verification.

The person tasked with code signing for your organization should download the Microsoft Windows Software Development Kit Update for Windows Vista from *http://www.microsoft.com/downloads/details.aspx?familyid=4377f86d-c913-4b5c-b87e-ef72e5b4e065&displaylang=en* and extract these tools to a folder on the computer where code signing is performed.

Using SignTool.exe

The following process allows you to sign an application by using the SignTool.exe utility:

1. Log on to a computer with the account that was issued the Code Signing certificate.

> **Note**   This example assumes that the Code Signing certificate and the associated private key are stored on a Schlumberger smart card. If the Code Signing certificate is stored in the local profile, you must perform the code signing procedure at the same computer where you requested the Code Signing certificate or where you imported the Code Signing certificate and private key.

2. Ensure that you have previously acquired a Code Signing certificate.

3. Copy the SignTool.exe executable file and the application file to sign into a folder on the current workstation.

4. Run **Signcode.exe signwizard**.

5. On the Welcome To The Digital Signature Wizard page, click Next.

6. On the File Selection page, in the File Name box, type the full path to the file that you wish to sign, and then click Next.

> **Note**   The location of the file does not matter during the signing process. The file can be copied to any location for the code signing process.

7. On the Signing Options page, click Custom, and then click Next.

8. On the Signature Certificate page, click Select From Store.

9. In the Select Certificate dialog box, select your Code Signing certificate, and then click OK.

10. On the Signature Certificate page, verify the certificate content information to ensure that it is the correct Code Signing certificate and that the intended purpose is code signing. Click Next.

11. On the Data Description page, in the Description box, type a description of the signed file, and then click Next.

12. On the Time Stamping page, select the Add A Timestamp To The Data check box, type the URL to your time stamp server or services, and then click Next.

> **Note**   You can skip time stamping at this time and apply a time stamp at a later time by running SignTool Timestamp.

13. On the Completing The Digital Signature Wizard page, click Finish.

14. If you are using a smart card CSP, such as the Schlumberger Cryptographic Service Provider, in the Confirm Smart Card PIN dialog box, in the PIN box, type the personal identification number (PIN) for the smart card, and then click OK.

15. In the Digital Signature Wizard message box, click OK.

This process results in the addition of a digital signature to the application file. The application file can now be verified as a signed file by other applications.

Visual Basic for Applications Projects

Within a Microsoft Office application, your organization might have created Microsoft Visual Basic for Applications (VBA) projects. By applying a digital signature to these VBA projects, your organization can increase the macro security level to high, as shown in Figure 25-2. By adding a digital signature, you can prevent the execution of any nonsigned macros through Group Policy, providing better protection to your Microsoft Office users.

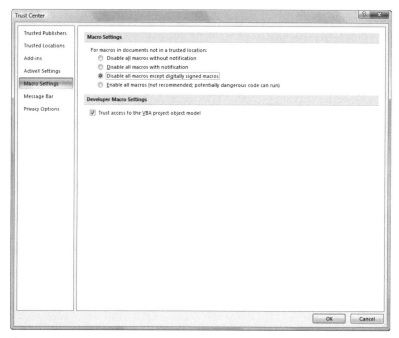

Figure 25-2   Restricting macro settings in the Microsoft Office Trust Center

To code sign your VBA macro project in Microsoft Office 2007, follow these steps:

1. Open the Microsoft Office document containing the macro project you want to sign.

> **Note**   The same series of steps works for any Microsoft application that implements the Visual Basic Editor.

2. Click the Microsoft Office Button, and then click *ProgramName* Options (for example, Word Options).

3. In the *ProgramName* Options dialog box, click Popular, and then ensure that the Show Developer Tab In The Ribbon check box is selected.

4. On the Developer tab, click Visual Basic.

5. In Project Explorer, select the project you want to sign.

6. On the Tools menu, click Digital Signature.

7. In the Digital Signature dialog box, click Choose to select your Code Signing certificate.

8. In the Select Certificate dialog box, select the Code Signing certificate you want to use, and then click OK.

> **Note**   You might have to view the certificate to choose the certificate with the code signing (1.3.6.1.5.5.7.3.3) OID in the Enhanced Key Usage extension.

9. In the Digital Signature dialog box, verify that the selected Code Signing certificate is recognized, and then click OK.

10. Close the Microsoft Visual Basic window.

Performing Document Signing

Document signing is becoming more prevalent in today's office. Documents are signed to:

- **Prove the source of the document**   The Document Signing certificate contains information about the organization of the signer.

- **Determine if the contents of the document are modified**   The digital signature helps determine if the content is changed in any way.

The method of signing a document depends greatly on the application used to create the document. The following sections describe applying a digital signature to Microsoft Office 2007 documents and Adobe Acrobat Portable Document Format (PDF) documents.

Microsoft Office 2007 Documents

To digitally sign a Microsoft Office 2007 document, you must first acquire a Document Signing certificate (described earlier in this chapter). Once you have acquired the certificate, the following procedure will apply a digital signature to the document.

1. Ensure that you have saved the document and that all content in the document is final.

> **Note**   Accepted formats for the file include all document and template versions from Office 97 through Office 2007 and XML format documents.

2. Click the Microsoft Office button, point to Prepare, and then click Add A Digital Signature.

3. If the Microsoft Office *ProgramName* dialog box appears, click OK to accept the introduction to digital signing.

4. In the Sign dialog box (see Figure 25-3), click Change to select a specific certificate.

Figure 25-3   Signing a Microsoft Office Document

5. In the Select Certificate dialog box, select your Document Signing certificate, and then click OK.

6. In the Sign dialog box, provide a purpose for signing the document, and then click Sign.

> **Important**   The purpose asserts your organization's reason for signing the document. In some cases, it is critical that the purpose is provided to meet legal or policy obligations.

7. If the Document Signing certificate is stored on a smart card, in the Smart Card PIN dialog box, type the PIN to the smart card, and then click OK.

8. In the Signature Confirmation message box, ensure that the signature was successfully saved, and then click OK.

Adobe PDF Documents

Many organizations use Adobe PDF documents to provide information to their customers or to partners. As with a Microsoft Office document, a digital signature can be applied to an Adobe PDF document to protect against modification and to prove the source of the document.

Adobe provides a way for you to sign documents but allow a user to fill in forms or apply further digital signatures (as part of a workflow or multiple-signature document). This method is known as *certifying* a document.

 Important Only the original signer can certify a document. Once an initial signature is applied, only the permitted changes specified by the certifying signer are allowed.

To apply a certifying signature to an Adobe PDF document, use the following procedure:

1. Open the pre-created PDF document in Adobe Acrobat.

2. From the Advanced menu, point to Sign & Certify, and then click Certify With Visible Signature.

3. If the Save As Certified Document dialog box appears, click OK.

4. The Adobe Acrobat dialog box appears describing how to create a signature field. Click OK.

5. Use your mouse to drag a box to designate the location of the certifying signature in the document.

6. In the Certify Document dialog box (see Figure 25-4), designate the Digital ID (the certificate used to digitally sign the PDF file), the appearance of the certifying signature in the document, and the changes permitted in the document after signing.

   The choices of allowed changes include:

   ❏ No changes allowed

   ❏ Form fill-in and digital signatures

   ❏ Annotations, form fill-in, and digital signatures

   Once the permitted changes are configured, click Sign.

7. If the Document Signing certificate is stored on a smart card, in the Smart Card PIN dialog box, type the PIN to the smart card, and then click OK.

8. In the Save As dialog box, provide a file name for the signed PDF file, and then click
    Save.

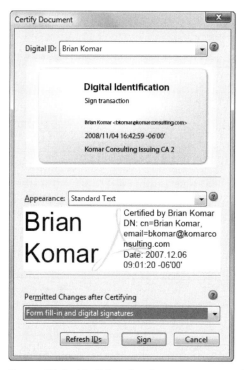

Figure 25-4   Verifying the signature on a certified PDF document

The digital signature appears in the document in the location specified in step 5. If Adobe
Acrobat is configured to use a Time Stamp Server, the date and time included in the
signature is provided by the Time Stamp Server. If not designated, the local computer's date
and time are used.

Verifying the Signature

Once a digital signature is applied to an application, a user that loads the application will want
to validate the application's signature.

Internet Explorer

In Internet Explorer, when you elect to install an application, a Security Warning dialog box
appears, as shown in Figure 25-5, indicating that the installation control is digitally signed.

Figure 25-5   Verifying the signature on an application in Windows Internet Explorer

In this case, Adobe Flash Player 9 is signed by Adobe Systems Incorporated. If you click the Adobe Systems Incorporated link, the signature details (see Figure 25-6) are displayed.

Figure 25-6   Viewing the details of the digital signature

As shown in Figure 25-6, the signature was applied on Monday, December 3, 2007 at 6:39:19 PM, and the VeriSign Time Stamp Server was used to apply a time stamp to the application.

If you choose to trust the application, you can click the Install button to proceed with the installation. Likewise, if you do not trust the entity that signed the application, you can click Don't Install to prevent installation.

Validating Signed Code

If an application is not used in a Web environment, you can still validate the code signing signature applied to the application file by running **Signtool verify**.

Signtool verify validates the signature and signing certificate used to sign the application. To verify the signature, use the following process:

1. Copy the Signtool.exe file and the digitally signed application file to a folder on the local computer.

2. Open a command prompt.

3. At the command prompt, type **Signtool verify /v** *filename* (where *filename* is the name of the signed application file).

4. The command will provide verbose output on the validity of the signed file to the command prompt window. The output contains all certificates in the certificate chain, and validation on whether the root CA is trusted. This combination of information allows you to validate the signing certificate.

> **Note** You can also view the signing certificate by clicking the More Info button in the dialog box.

5. If you trust the signature, you can click Yes.

6. The output in the command prompt will show that the validation succeeded.

Microsoft Office Documents

To verify a signature in a Microsoft Office document, use the following procedure:

1. Open the signed document in the Microsoft Office 2007 application used to create the document.

2. Click the Microsoft Office button, point to Prepare, and then click View Signatures.

3. In the Signatures bar (to the right of the document), you will see a list of all signatures applied to the document.

4. Click the drop-down list for a specific signature, and then click Signature Details.

5. In the Signature Details dialog box (see Figure 25-7), ensure that the signature is valid, and then click Close.

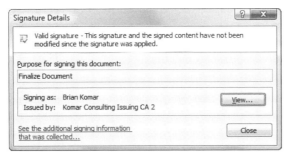

Figure 25-7   Viewing the details of the Microsoft Office digital signature

PDF Documents

In Adobe Acrobat or Adobe Reader, you can view the validity of the signature when viewing the PDF file. If you right-click the signature in the file and then click Validate Signature, you will see a dialog box reporting on the status of the signature. The status includes details on:

■ Whether the document was modified since it was certified.

■ Whether the signer's identity is known (included in the list of trusted identities).

■ Whether a time stamp server was used to set the date/time on the signature.

Case Study: Lucerne Publishing

Lucerne Publishing is a global publishing company with a two-tier CA hierarchy. Mike Danseglio manages the development team at Lucerne Publishing.

Scenario

Over the past year, Lucerne Publishing has been hit by several macro viruses. The primary cause of the virus outbreaks is users opening unauthorized macros in Microsoft Office documents. To restrict the macros that may be executed, you decide to start digitally signing all VBA projects created by your development team.

In addition, Internet Explorer settings must be locked down to prevent the downloading and installation of unsigned ActiveX controls at organization computers. Several financial applications within Lucerne Publishing are Web-based and use ActiveX controls to increase the Web page functionality. By digitally signing these ActiveX controls, Lucerne Publishing can restrict interaction with unsigned ActiveX controls in the default security settings of Internet Explorer.

During the information-gathering stage, you identify the following requirements for the Code Signing certificate:

- The subject of the certificate must contain the company name, not the name of the programmer who signs the certificate.

- The Code Signing certificate must be stored on a Microsoft Smart Card Base CSP smart card.

- All code signing must be performed by Mike Danseglio, manager of the Application Development department.

- All Code Signing certificate requests and renewals must be approved by a certificate manager designated by Lucerne Publishing.

- The Code Signing certificate must be valid for three years.

- The Code Signing certificate must have a minimum key length of 1,024 bits.

Case Study Questions

1. Does the Code Signing certificate template satisfy the design requirements? What must you do to meet the design requirements?

2. In the following table, define the settings on the General tab to satisfy the design requirements for your custom Code Signing certificate template.

Attribute	Your recommended design
Template display name	
Template name	
Validity period	
Publish certificate in Active Directory	
Do not automatically reenroll if a duplicate certificate exists in Active Directory	

3. What CSP must be enabled on the Request Handling tab to satisfy the design requirements for the custom Code Signing certificate template?

4. How must you configure the settings on the Subject Name tab to satisfy the design requirements?

5. In the following table, define the settings on the Issuance Requirements tab to satisfy the design requirements for the custom Code Signing certificate template.

Attribute	Your recommended design
CA certificate manager approval	
This number of authorized signatures	
Require the following for reenrollment	

Best Practices

- **Configure the Unsigned Driver Installation Group Policy setting to either warn or prevent installation of unsigned device drivers.**   This setting ensures either that the local administrator is aware that an unsigned driver is implemented, or it prevents the installation of unsigned drivers in the local operating system.

- **Use a commercially issued Code Signing or Document Signing certificate for publicly distributed applications.**   If the application you sign is intended for public use, acquire the Code Signing or Document Signing certificate from a commercial CA, such as VeriSign. This certificate increases the assurance in the signed application because the signing certificate chains to a root CA trusted by most organizations.

- **Use a corporate-issued Code Signing or Document Signing certificate for internal applications.**   There is no need to acquire a Code Signing or Document Signing certificate from a commercial organization for internal applications. All computers within the organization trust the local CA hierarchy's root CA.

- **Increase the protection of the Code Signing or Document Signing certificate's private key by using a smart card CSP.**   A smart card CSP provides higher protection of the Code Signing certificate's private key by storing the private key on a two-factor hardware device.

- **Create a custom version 2 certificate template based on the Code Signing or Document Signing certificate that requires certificate manager approval.**   This measure increases the assurance of the Code Signing or Document Signing certificate and allows stronger identity validation of the Code Signing certificate requestor.

> **Note**   Alternatively, use a registration authority to enforce the validation of the requestor's identity before the certificate is issued.

- **Implement code signing for all macros implemented in Microsoft Office applications.**   This practice allows an organization to increase the macro security level to prevent the execution of nonsigned macros, thereby protecting an organization from attacks based on Visual Basic macros.

- **Implement code signing for all ActiveX controls developed by your organization.**   This practice allows you to increase the ActiveX security settings within Internet Explorer, blocking the execution of unsigned ActiveX controls.

- **Outsource a Time Stamping Service.**   The outsourcer provides a date and time stamp to the code signing process, allowing signature-event recognition if the signing certificate is later revoked. As long as the time stamp is a date or time *before* the revocation date, the signature is still considered valid.

■ **Use the organization name as the subject of the Code Signing certificate.**   This associates the Code Signing certificate with the organization rather than an individual. You can accomplish this by creating a custom user in AD DS or by allowing the subject to be manually input by the certificate requestor.

Additional Information

■ Microsoft Official Curriculum, Course 2821: "Designing and Managing a Windows Public Key Infrastructure" (*http://www.microsoft.com/traincert/syllabi/2821afinal.asp*)

■ *Writing Secure Code, Second Edition*, by Michael Howard and David LeBlanc (Microsoft Press, 2002)

■ "Microsoft Windows Software Development Kit Update for Windows Vista" (*http://www.microsoft.com/downloads/details.aspx?familyid=4377f86d-c913-4b5c-b87e-ef72e5b4e065&displaylang=en*)

■ "Introduction to Code Signing" (*http://msdn.microsoft.com/workshop/security/authcode/intro_authenticode.asp*)

■ "Frequently Asked Questions About Authenticode" (*http://msdn.microsoft.com/library/en-us/dnauth/html/signfaq.asp*)

■ "Microsoft Technet: 5-Minute Security Advisor—Signing Office Objects" (*http://www.microsoft.com/technet/community/columns/5min/5min-402.mspx*)

■ "ActiveX Controls and Office Security" (*http://www.microsoft.com/office/ork/2003/seven/ch23/SecA05.htm*)

■ "Digital Signature Resources for Adobe Acrobat" (*http://www.adobe.com/security/digsig.html*)

■ "Details on Digital Signatures" (*http://office.microsoft.com/en-us/infopath/HP010967151033.aspx?pid=CH011097171033*)

■ "nCipher Time Stamp Server" (*http://www.ncipher.com/timestamping.html*)

Chapter 26
Deploying Certificates to Domain Controllers

One of the most common types of certificates deployed in a Microsoft Windows networking environment is domain controller (also referred to a Kerberos Distribution Center or KDC) certificates. The KDC certificates are used by domain controllers for:

- Authenticating the domain controllers when a user logs on to the network with a smart card.

- Securing queries by Lightweight Directory Access Protocol (LDAP) clients when a user queries Active Directory Domain Services (AD DS) using an LDAP Secure Sockets Layer (LDAPS)–protected connection.

- Securing Simple Mail Transfer Protocol (SMTP) replication traffic between AD DS sites.

Changes in Domain Controller Certificates

Windows Server 2008 includes four different domain controller certificate templates. The following sections describe:

- The history of the domain controller certificate choices.

- Implementing strong KDC validation.

- How a Windows Server 2008 domain controller selects its certificate.

History of Domain Controller Certificates

The Domain Controller certificate template was introduced in Microsoft Windows 2000 enterprise certification authorities (CAs) for two purposes:

- Providing a server authentication certificate to domain controllers for smart card authentication

- Secure e-mail replication between domain controllers in different domains

Table 26-1 outlines the specific attributes of a certificate based on the Domain Controller certificate template.

Table 26-1   Domain Controller Certificate Template Attributes

Attribute	Domain controller
Subject	CN=*Fully Qualified Domain Name (FQDN)*
Enhanced Key Usage	Client Authentication (1.3.6.1.5.5.7.3.2)
	Server Authentication (1.3.6.1.5.5.7.3.1)
Subject Alternative Name	Other Name:
	1.3.6.1.4.1.311.25.1=*GUID*
	DNS Name=*FQDN*

Note   Some organizations use the Domain Controller certificate template to enable other platforms to securely query AD DS using Secure Lightweight Directory Access Protocol (LDAP/S). The LDAP tools connect to TCP port 636 on the domain controller, securing the connection by using the domain controller's certificate.

In Windows Server 2003, two new version 2 certificate templates were created to separate domain controller authentication from securing e-mail replication.

- **Domain Controller Authentication**   Enables authentication of the domain controller during smart card logon. Also used to secure LDAP/S connections to domain controllers.

- **Directory Email Replication**   Enables encryption of replication traffic between domain controllers when Simple Mail Transfer Protocol (SMTP) is used as the replication protocol.

In both cases, the version 2 certificate templates are configured to supersede the Domain Controller certificate template. This configuration setting ensures that certificates based on the Domain Controller certificate template are replaced with certificates based on both the Domain Controller and the Directory Email Replication certificate templates.

Table 26-2 outlines the specific attributes of the Domain Controller Authentication and Directory Email Replication certificate templates.

Table 26-2   Windows Server 2003 Domain Controller Certificate Templates

Attribute	Domain Controller Authentication	Directory Email Replication
Subject	Empty	Empty
Enhanced Key Usage	Client Authentication (1.3.6.1.5.5.7.3.2)	Directory Service Email Replication (1.3.6.1.4.1.311.21.19)
	Server Authentication (1.3.6.1.5.5.7.3.1)	
	Smart Card Logon (1.3.6.1.4.1.311.20.2.2)	

Table 26-2   Windows Server 2003 Domain Controller Certificate Templates

Attribute	Domain Controller Authentication	Directory Email Replication
Subject Alternative Name	DNS Name=*FQDN*	Other Name:
		1.3.6.1.4.1.311.25.1=*GUID*
		DNS Name=*FQDN*

> **Note**   The biggest change in the certificate template design is implementing a blank subject name for both certificate templates. Instead, the FQDN is stored in the Subject Alternative Name (SAN) extension. The SAN allows longer FQDNs than the Subject (which is limited to 64 characters).

Windows Server 2008 introduces a new certificate template called Kerberos Authentication. The new certificate template is intended to replace the Domain Controller Authentication certificate template. The main change is changing the name recorded in the SAN from the FQDN to the domain name of the domain controller. The change helps in several ways:

- The domain-joined client can verify that it is connecting to a domain controller for the specified domain by validating that the domain name recorded in the SAN is the desired domain.

- LDAP/S clients can connect to *any* domain controller in the domain. Previously, the LDAP/S clients had to connect to a specific domain controller and provide *its* FQDN in the connection string.

Table 26-3 provides details on the attributes in a Kerberos Authentication certificate.

Table 26-3   Kerberos Authentication Certificate Details

Attribute	Kerberos Authentication
Subject	Empty
Enhanced Key Usage	Client Authentication (1.3.6.1.5.5.7.3.2)
	Server Authentication (1.3.6.1.5.5.7.3.1)
	Smart Card Logon (1.3.6.1.4.1.311.20.2.2)
	KDC Authentication (1.3.6.1.5.2.3.5)
Subject Alternate Name	DNS Name=*FQDN-domainname*
	DNS Name=*NetBIOS-Domain-Name*

Enforcing Strong KDC Validation

If you have deployed a Kerberos Authentication certificate to your domain controllers, you can enforce strong Kerberos Distribution Center (KDC) validation for computers running Windows Vista and Windows Server 2008. To enable strong KDC validation, you must

configure the HKEY_LOCAL_MACHINE\SYSTEM\CurrentControlSet\Control\Lsa\
Kerberos\Parameters\kdcvalidation registry value at all clients and servers.

- **0**: Disable strong KDC validation
- **2**: Enable strong KDC validation

If strong KDC validation is enabled, the client will require the presence of the KDC Authentication (1.3.6.1.5.2.3.5) object identifier (OID) in the Enhanced Key Usage (EKU) extension and the matching domain name in the subject alternate name of the domain controller's certificate.

> **Note**   For more details on implementing strong KDC validation, see section 3.2.4 of RFC 4556, "Public Key Cryptography for Initial Authentication in Kerberos (PKINIT)," available at *http://www.ietf.org/rfc/rfc4556.txt.*

Windows Server 2008 Domain Controller Certificate Selection

If a Windows Server 2008 domain controller has multiple domain controller certificates installed, the following rules are implemented to select which certificate is used by the server during a client authentication attempt:

1.   The domain controller will use a Kerberos Authentication certificate from the local machine store. The certificate is identified by the verifying the OID of the certificate template and confirming that the KDC Authentication OID (1.3.6.1.5.2.3.5) exists in the EKU extension. The selected certificate is used for Public Key Initialization (PKINIT) authentication attempts.

2.   If no Kerberos Authentication certificate exists, the domain controller searches its local machine store for a Domain Controller Authentication certificate. The certificate is identified by the existence of the Smart Card Logon OID (1.3.6.1.4.1.311.20.2.2) in the EKU extension. The selected certificate is used for PKINIT authentication attempts.

3.   If no Domain Controller Authentication certificate template is found, the domain controller will search its local machine store for a Domain Controller certificate. If found, this certificate is used for authentication connections. The selected certificate is used for PKINIT authentication attempts.

4.   If no matching certificates are found, PKINIT authentication is disabled on this domain controller.

> **Note**   The same selection process is used when a client attempts an LDAP/S connection to a domain controller.

Deploying Domain Controller Certificates

The method of deploying domain controller certificates is a dependency on the operating system version of the domain controllers and the operating system version of the CA.

Table 26-4 shows which certificate templates are deployed to domain controllers based on the operating system of the domain controller and the operating system of the issuing CA.

Table 26-4   Domain Controller Certificate Template Matrix

		Certification Authority Version		
		Windows 2000 Server	Windows Server 2003	Windows Server 2008
Domain Controller Version	Windows 2000 Server	Domain Controller	Domain Controller	Domain Controller
	Windows Server 2003	Domain Controller	Domain Controller or Domain Controller Authentication and Directory Email Encryption	Kerberos Authentication
	Windows Server 2008	Domain Controller	Domain Controller or Domain Controller Authentication and Directory Email Encryption	Kerberos Authentication

The method used to deploy the certificate templates depends entirely on the version of the certificate template.

Automatic Certificate Request Settings

Automatic Certificate Request Settings is used to deploy the version 1 Domain Controller certificates to domain controllers in the forest. Although not explicitly designated as a certificate template in the Automatic Certificate Request Settings (ACRS) Group Policy Object (GPO), domain controllers are hard-coded to automatically request a certificate based on the Domain Controller certificate if it is available at an issuing CA.

Note   Windows 2000 domain controllers can use *only* version 1 certificate templates and enroll only the Domain Controller certificate template by using ACRS.

Autoenrollment

Autoenrollment Settings is used to automatically deploy the Domain Controller Authentication, Directory Email Replication, and Kerberos Authentication certificates to domain controllers running Windows Server 2003 and Windows Server 2008.

To ensure that autoenrollment takes place, ensure that the Default Domain Controller Policy for each domain enables autoenrollment. As shown in Figure 26-1, you must enable the Certificate Services Client – Autoenrollment Properties settings for computer objects.

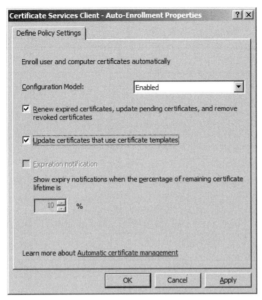

Figure 26-1   Enabling autoenrollment of computer certificates

By enabling autoenrollment settings, you ensure that Domain Controller Authentication, Directory Email Replication, or Kerberos Authentication certificates are automatically deployed to all domain controllers.

Note   If multiple domains exist in the forest, ensure that each domain's Default Domain Controllers GPO enforces autoenrollment settings.

Third-Party CAs or CAs in Other Forests

You do not have to deploy Microsoft CAs in a forest to deploy certificates for domain controllers. For example, if your organization has two forests (as shown in Figure 26-2), you can manually request and issue domain controller certificates to the three domain controllers in the extranet.fabrikam.com forest from the CA hierarchy in the internal.fabrikam.com forest.

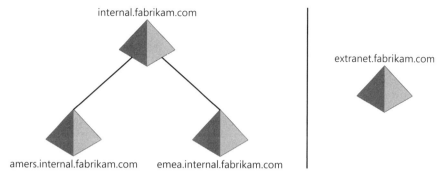

Figure 26-2   A network deployment with two forests: internal.fabrikam.com and extranet.fabrikam.com

For this example, assume that the CA hierarchy shown in Figure 26-3 is the CA hierarchy deployed in the internal.fabrikam.com forest.

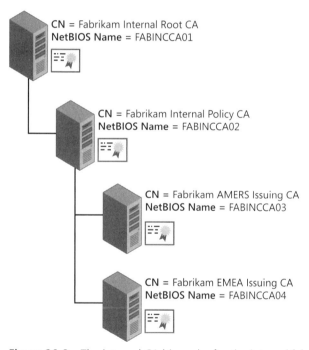

Figure 26-3   The internal CA hierarchy for the internal.fabrikam.com forest

The deployment of domain controller certificates in the extranet.fabrikam.com forest is accomplished by completing the following steps:

1.   Define the root CA from the internal.fabrikam.com forest (CN=Fabrikam Internal Root CA) as a trusted root CA in the extranet.fabrikam.com forest.

2.   Add the subordinate CAs for the internal.fabrikam.com forest as intermediate CAs in the extranet.fabrikam.com forest. This includes the policy CA and both issuing CAs.

3.   Add the issuing CAs from the internal.fabrikam.com forest to the NTAuth store in the extranet.fabrikam.com forest. This includes both the Fabrikam AMERS Issuing CA and the Fabrikam EMEA Issuing CA.

4.   Configure the issuing CAs in the internal.fabrikam.com forest to accept a SAN extension in a certificate request.

5.   Create the domain controller certificate requests at each domain controller in the extranet.fabrikam.com forest. A separate request must be generated for each domain controller in the forest.

6.   Submit the request to the issuing CA in the internal.fabrikam.com forest.

Note   The following procedures can also be used to request domain controller certificates from a commercial provider or from a third-party certification authority.

Add the Internal Root CA as a Trusted Root CA

You must designate the internal root CA as a trusted root CA in the extranet.fabrikam.com forest. The easiest way to do this is to use the **certutil–dspublish** command. Assuming that the default naming was used for the root CA certificate, the command would be:

```
certutil –dspublish –f "fabincca01_Fabrikam Internal Root CA.crt" RootCA
```

The command will add the Fabrikam Internal Root CA as a trusted root CA for all extranet forest members.

Add the Subordinate CA Certificates

To allow complete trust of the certificate chain, you must add the subordinate CA certificates as intermediate CAs in the extranet forest. This requires that you run the following three **certutil –dspublish commands:**

```
certutil –dspublish –f "fabincca02_Fabrikam Internal Policy CA.crt" SubCA
certutil –dspublish –f "fabincca03_Fabrikam AMERS Issuing CA.crt" SubCA
certutil –dspublish –f "fabincca04_Fabrikam EMEA Issuing CA.crt" SubCA
```

The commands will ensure that all extranet forest members will recognize all CA certificates in the internal CA hierarchy.

Define NTAuth Certificates

To allow certificates issued by the two internal issuing CAs to be used for smart card authentication, the CA certificates must be added to the NTAuth store in the extranet.fabrikam.com forest. Again, the **certutil –dspublish** command is used to add the two issuing CAs to the NTAuth store.

```
certutil –dspublish –f "fabincca03_Fabrikam AMERS Issuing CA.crt" NTAuth
certutil –dspublish –f "fabincca04_Fabrikam EMEA Issuing CA.crt" NTAuth
```

Enable the SAN Extension for Certificate Requests

By default, a CA running Windows Server 2008 ignores SAN entries included in a certificate request. A certificate is issued based on the request but does not include the defined entries for the SAN extension.

You can enable the CA to issue certificates that include SAN entries defined in a certificate request by running the following commands at each issuing CA.

```
certutil -setreg policy\EditFlags +EDITF_ATTRIBUTESUBJECTALTNAME2
net stop certsvc && net start certsvc
```

Note   In our example, these commands must be executed at both the Fabrikam AMERS Issuing CA and at the Fabrikam EMEA Issuing CA. You can verify the setting at a later time by running **certutil -getreg policy\EditFlags**.

Creating the Certificate Requests

With Windows Server 2008, you can no longer request machine certificates directly from the Web Enrollment Web pages. You must now create the request file using the Certreq.exe utility and then submit the request to the issuing CA.

The following process describes how to generate the certificate request for the domain controllers in the extranet.fabrikam.com forest:

1. Log on to the domain controller as a member of the local Administrators group.

2. Create an .inf file that specifies the settings for the certificate request. For example, the .inf file for the dc1.extranet.fabrikam.com would look like this:

```
[Version]
Signature="$Windows NT$"

[NewRequest]
Subject = "CN=dc1.extranet.fabrikam.com"
EncipherOnly = FALSE
Exportable = FALSE
KeyLength = 1024
KeySpec = 1
KeyUsage = 0xA0
MachineKeySet = True
ProviderName = "Microsoft RSA SChannel Cryptographic Provider"
ProviderType = 12
RequestType = CMC
```

```
[RequestAttributes]
CertificateTemplate = KerberosAuthentication
SAN="dns=dc1.extranet.fabrikam.com&dns=extranet"
```

3. Save the file as DCRequest.inf.

4. Open a command prompt.

5. At the command prompt, type **certreq −new DCRequest.inf DCRequest.req**, and then press Enter.

> **Note**   This creates a Cryptographic Message Syntax (CMC) request (as designated in the .inf file) and also generates the public and private key in the local machine store of the domain controller.

6. Copy the request file to external media, and then move the external media to a computer that is a member of the internal.fabrikam.com forest.

7. Ensure that you are logged on as a user with Read and Enroll permissions for the Kerberos Authentication certificate template.

8. Open a command prompt.

9. At the command prompt, type the following command to submit the request to the Fabrikam AMERS Issuing CA, and then press Enter:

```
certreq -submit -config
"fabincca03.amers.internal.fabrikam.com\Fabrikam AMERS Issuing CA1"
DCRequest.req DCRequest.cer
```

> **Note**   If you run the **certreq** command at the Fabrikam AMERS Issuing CA, you can omit the **-config "fabincca03.amers.internal.fabrikam.com\Fabrikam AMERS Issuing CA1"** part of the command.

10. Copy the resulting DCRequest.cer file to the external media.

11. Copy the DCRequest.cer file to the local file system of the domain controller (dc1.extranet.fabrikam.com).

12. Open a command prompt.

13. At the command prompt, type **certreq -accept DCRequest.cer**, and then press Enter.

This command installs the certificate into the local machine store and ties the certificate to the key pair that was initiated in step 5 of this procedure.

Managing Domain Controller Certificates

When you have deployed domain controller certificates in your forest, there are times when you may need to manage the certificates. The management may include:

- Verifying the existence of domain controller certificates.

- Replacing existing domain controller certificates.

- Removing all existing domain controller certificates.

Verifying Existing Certificates

You can use the **certutil –dcinfo** command to validate each domain controller's issued certificates. The command will return information for each domain controller in the current domain. First, the output will show you the root cert.

```
0: DC

*** Testing DC[0]: DC1
** Enterprise Root Certificates for DC DC1
Certificate 0:
Serial Number: 4d9fb0b6f75f539a45f8066766a15f4e
Issuer: CN=Fabrikam Corporate Root CA, O=Fabrikam Inc., C=US
NotBefore: 11/4/2007 5:10 PM
NotAfter: 11/4/2027 5:20 PM
Subject: CN=Fabrikam Corporate Root CA, O=Fabrikam Inc., C=US
CA Version: V0.0
Signature matches Public Key
Root Certificate: Subject matches Issuer
Cert Hash(sha1): 99 45 4f a7 0e 4c 85 56 be 0b 53 e7 e1 63 8b ab 1b 6e 3a 2a
```

Then, the output will show you all active KDC certificates for the domain controller. In the following output, the domain controller named DC1 has two certificates that can be used as KDC certificates: one Domain Controller certificate and one Kerberos Authentication certificate.

```
** KDC Certificates for DC DC1
Certificate 0:
Serial Number: 6182a6ba000000000004
Issuer: CN=Fabrikam Clustered Issuing CA, O=Fabrikam Inc., C=US
NotBefore: 12/16/2007 1:41 PM
NotAfter: 12/15/2008 1:41 PM
Subject: CN=DC$@fabrikam.com
Certificate Template Name (Certificate Type): DomainController
Non-root Certificate
Template: DomainController, Domain Controller
Cert Hash(sha1): 8c 7c ea 4a f8 d3 b5 d4 75 b0 f6 c4 51 31 da c0 cc e4 33 ec

Certificate 1:
Serial Number: 19e9a0cb00000000000a
Issuer: CN=Fabrikam Corporate Issuing CA, O=Fabrikam Inc., C=US
```

```
NotBefore: 12/25/2007 1:23 PM
NotAfter: 12/24/2008 1:23 PM
Subject: EMPTY (DNS Name=fabrikam.com, DNS Name=FABRIKAM)
Non-root Certificate
Template: KerberosAuthentication, Kerberos Authentication
Cert Hash(sha1): 89 b8 7c d3 0f bb 4a d0 9a c6 b7 ae 9d ee 61 a2 8d fe 6f 31


2 KDC certs for DC


CertUtil: -DCInfo command completed successfully.
```

If you have more than one domain, you must connect to a domain controller in each domain as a member of the Domain Admins group and run the **certutil** command for that domain.

> **Note**   You can go further with the command by typing **certutil –dcinfo –verify**. The command will then include validating the full chain for each domain controller certificate.

Replacing Existing Certificates

If the validation of the certificates shows that some of the certificates are "bad"—chaining to a nontrusted root, issued by a decommissioned CA, expired, or revoked—you can replace the "bad" certificates by running the **certutil –dcinfo –DeleteBad** command. The command validates all the KDC certificates issued to domain controllers in the current domain. If any certificates fail validation, they are removed from the specific domain controller. Once removed, autoenrollment will replace the KDC certificate with a valid certificate (if required).

Removing All Existing Certificates

In some cases, you may want to replace *all* domain controller certificates. For example, if you previously purchased domain controller certificates from a commercial provider, you may wish to replace the third-party party domain controller certificates with certificates issued by your internal CA hierarchy.

In this case, you can run **certutil –dcinfo deleteall**. All previously issued KDC certificates are removed from the domain controllers in the current domain. ACRS and autoenrollment will replace the domain controller certificates with those available at the issuing CAs.

Case Study: Consolidated Messenger

Consolidated Messenger, a package delivery contractor in Arizona, recently hired Ken Kwok as their new network administrator. Ken discovered that the previous network administrator had deployed a Windows Server 2003 based enterprise root CA for certificate distribution.

Ken has designed a new two-tiered CA hierarchy with an offline root CA as shown in Figure 26-4.

Figure 26-4   The proposed Consolidated Messenger CA hierarchy

Deployment Progress

The deployment of the new CA hierarchy included:

- Upgrading all client computers to Windows Vista from Windows 2000 Professional and Windows XP. Thus far, all of the computers running Windows 2000 have been replaced with new computers running Windows Vista Enterprise, but the Windows XP upgrades are not yet completed.

- Upgrading all five domain controllers in the consolidatedmessenger.com domain to Windows Server 2008. The upgrade was completed two months ago.

- Removing the previous enterprise root CA from the network by reinstalling the operating system and redeploying the server as the new offline root CA.

Case Study Questions

1. Ken has been tasked with deploying smart cards for authentication. The smart card authentication is failing. Do you have any idea why the authentication attempts are failing?

2. On inspection, Ken discoverers that the five domain controllers have not obtained KDC certificates from the new CA hierarchy. What is the easiest way for Ken to remove all previously issued KDC certificates from the domain controllers?

3. What certificate template should Ken make available at the Tucson and Scottsdale CAs for the domain controllers?

4. Ken wants to enable strong KDC authentication on the network. Are there any deployment blockers in the current environment?

5. Once all computers running Windows XP are upgraded to Windows Vista, how would Ken enforce strong KDC authentication?

Best Practices

■ **Use ACRS and Autoenrollment Settings to deploy domain controller certificates.**   ACRS and Autoenrollment Settings allow automated deployment of KDC certificates to all domain controllers in the forest.

■ **Manage domain controller certificates by using the certutil –dcinfo command options**   Certutil –dcinfo provides multiple command options for managing KDC certificates. You can verify all installed certificates by running **certutil –dcinfo**. You can validate the deployed KDC certificates by running **certutil –dcinfo verify**.

■ **Move toward replacing existing Domain Controller and Domain Controller Authentication certificates with Kerberos Authentication certificates.**   Kerberos Authentication certificates assert the domain's identity, rather than the individual domain controller's identity, better associating the certificate with the domain.

■ **Enable strong KDC validation only when all clients and servers are upgraded to Windows Vista and Windows Server 2008.**   Strong KDC validation is not supported by Windows XP, Windows Server 2003, and other earlier Microsoft operating systems.

■ **Generate custom domain controller certificate requests only if you do not have an existing Microsoft public key infrastructure (PKI) in your environment.**   Autoenrollment provides lifetime management of the domain controller certificates. If you generate custom requests, you must manually renew and replace the domain controller certificates through their certificate life cycle.

Additional Information

■ "Windows Server 2003 Advanced Certificate Enrollment and Management" (*http://www.microsoft.com/technet/prodtechnol/windowsserver2003/technologies/security/advcert.mspx*)

■ "Active Directory Certificate Server Enhancements in Windows Server Code Name 'Longhorn'" (*http://www.microsoft.com/downloads/details.aspx?FamilyID=9bf17231-d832-4ff9-8fb8-0539ba21ab95&DisplayLang=en*)

■ "Certificate Autoenrollment in Windows Server 2003" (*http://www.microsoft.com/technet/prodtechnol/windowsserver2003/technologies/security/autoenro.mspx*)

■ "Processing Domain Controller Certificates" (*http://technet2.microsoft.com/WindowsServer/en/library/d08181ca-4fac-1ca7-8171 b66e9e65606e1033.mspx?mfr=true*)

■ RFC 4556–"Public Key Cryptography for Initial Authentication in Kerberos (PKINIT)" (*http://www.ietf.org/rfc/rfc4556.txt*)

- 275528: "Windows Server 2003 Does Not Use the DNS Name as Certificate Subject"

- 281245: "Guidelines for Enabling Smart Card Logon with Third-Party Certification Authorities"

- 291010: "Requirements for Domain Controller Certificates from a Third-Party CA"

- 296975: "Unable to Connect to a Domain Controller by Using LDAP Connection over SSL"

- 555151: "How to Remove Manually Enterprise Windows Certificate Authority from Windows 2000/2003 Domain"

- 814662: "Windows Server 2003 Does Not Use the DNS Name as Certificate Subject"

- 931351: "How to Add a Subject Alternative Name to a Secure LDAP Certificate"

- 932834: "You May Be Unable to Connect to a Windows Server 2003-Based Domain Controller by Using LDAP Over an SSL Connection.

- 939088: "You Receive a Key Distribution Center 'Event ID: 20' Event Message on a Windows Server 2003–Based Domain Controller"

 Note   The last nine articles in the above list can be accessed through the Microsoft Knowledge Base. Go to *http://support.microsoft.com*, and enter the article number in the Search The Knowledge Base text box.

Chapter 27

Network Device Enrollment Service

Network Device Enrollment Service (NDES) implements the Simple Certificate Enrollment Protocol (SCEP) for Cisco devices and other devices that are SCEP compliant. Windows Server 2008 implements NDES as one of the Active Directory Certificate Services role services.

The service is implemented as an Internet Server Application Programming Interface (ISAPI) that requires the installation of Internet Information Services (IIS) on the same server. To protect the service, NDES runs in its own application pool named SCEP.

> **Important**   NDES is available only on Windows Server 2008 Enterprise and Windows Server 2008 Datacenter.

History of NDES and Microsoft PKI

NDES is not the first implementation of SCEP for Microsoft certification authorities (CAs). SCEP has previously been implemented as an add-on service for both Microsoft Windows Server 2000 and Windows Server 2003. NDES is the first native implementation of SCEP for a Microsoft CA.

SCEP (defined in an Internet Draft), utilizes both PKCS #7 and PKCS #10 data objects to automatically distribute certificates to devices that do not have accounts in the CA directory in a scalable manner.

> **Note**   SCEP is described in an Internet Draft (the current version is draft-nourse-scep-16.txt). The draft is not intended for a standards track. Rather, it is provided for historical information and describes the inner workings of SCEP.

There are several changes in features in NDES that were not available in previous Microsoft implementations of SCEP:

- **Designate Certificate Templates**   Previous versions of SCEP did not allow you to configure certificate templates for each request type.
- **Certificate Renewal**   NDES now supports renewing the service certificates.

■ **More secure default settings**   NDES changes the default settings to more secure values. For example, a password is now required by default for SCEP requests. Also, the maximum number of passwords was reduced from 100 to 5.

■ **Allow SCEP to be installed on a computer other than a CA**   Previous versions of Microsoft SCEP required that the SCEP service be installed on an existing CA.

■ **New default signing algorithm**   Previous versions of Microsoft SCEP used Message Digest 5 (MD5) as the default hash algorithm. NDES now uses Secure Hash Algorithm 1 (SHA1) as the default but allows you to revert to MD5 through a registry change.

■ **Virtual Directory configuration**   NDES implements two separate virtual directories, allowing the SCEP administration Web site to be protected with Secure Sockets Layer (SSL) encryption.

■ **Service credentials**   NDES can now run with a dedicated service account or the Network Service account rather than using the Local System account.

■ **Request size limit**   NDES limits the request size to 64 kilobytes (KB) to prevent buffer overflow attacks.

Simple Certificate Enrollment Protocol Enroll Process

SCEP allows the automated enrollment of certificates to network devices when the network devices do not have accounts in Active Directory Domain Services (AD DS). SCEP delivers the certificate in a secure manner through the user of a registration authority (RA).

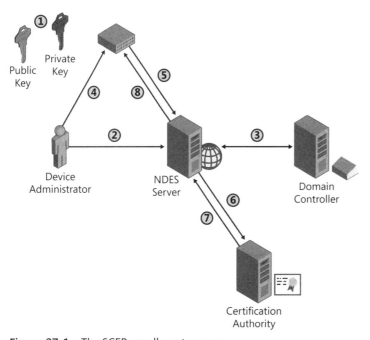

Figure 27-1   The SCEP enrollment process

The SCEP enrollment process (shown in Figure 27-1) involves eight distinct steps:

- **The network device generates a Rivest Shamir Adleman (RSA) public-private key pair.** The device generates an RSA public-private key pair and specifies whether the key is enabled for signing and signature verification, decryption and encryption, or both signing and encryption.

> **Note**   In Cisco IOS 12.4 and above, you can configure the key usage by running the **usage** command. To generate a key-pair for Internet Protocol security (IPsec), run the command **usage ike**; to generate a client authentication key pair, run the command **usage ssl-client**; and to generate a server authentication key pair, run the command **usage ssl-server**. You can create a multi-use key pair by combining usages on the same command line. For example, to generate a certificate for both client and server authentication, you would run the command *usage ssl-client*, ssl-server.

- **The device administrator must obtain an enrollment challenge password from the NDES server.**   This is accomplished by connecting to the *https://ServerName/certsrv/mscep_admin* URL, as shown in Figure 27-2.

Figure 27-2   Generating an enrollment challenge password

> **Important**   The enrollment challenge password is good for only 60 minutes. After 60 minutes pass, the challenge password is no longer valid.

- **The NDES server determines if the device administrator is able to request certificates on behalf of the network device.**   If the NDES server is an enterprise CA, the CA must have Read and Enroll permissions for all three configured certificate templates configured in the HKEY_LOCAL_MACHINE\Software\Microsoft\Cryptography\MSCEP registry key:
  - ❏ If the key usage of the requested key pair is signature only (0x80), the certificate template specified in the SigningTemplate registry value is used.

❑   If the key usage of the requested key pair is encryption only (0x20), the certificate template specified in the EncryptionTemplate registry value is used.

❑   If the key usage of the requested key pair is for signature and encryption (0xa0), the certificate template specified in the GeneralPurposeTemplate registry value is used.

> **Note**   If the CA is a standalone CA, the device administrator must be a member of the CA Administrators group.

■   **The device administrator must configure the network device to trust the organization's public key infrastructure (PKI).**   The actual procedure will depend on how many tiers exist in your organization's PKI.

> **Tip**   A great example on how to configure trust for a multi-tiered CA hierarchy is available at *http://www.cisco.com/en/US/products/sw/iosswrel/ps1839/ products_feature_guide09186a0080214a5d.html#wp1027265*. The document provides details on designating trust for the root CA and for subordinate CAs to allow trust of certificates issued by the internal CA hierarchy.

■   **The device manager submits a certificate request to the NDES server.**   The request is a PKCS #7 request that contains the required information for the network device. This includes:

❑   The subject name for the certificate.

❑   The enrollment challenge password (if provided to the device administrator in step 2 of this procedure).

❑   The key usage of the request's key pair. The key usage will determine whether the request is for a signing certificate, encryption certificate (0x80), or a combination signing and encryption certificate (0xa0).

> **Note**   If no key usage information is provided, the NDES server will treat the request as a request for a combination signing and encryption certificate and set the key usage value to 0xa0.

■   **The NDES server sends the certificate enrollment request to the CA.**   The NDES service performs several tasks before sending the enrollment request to the CA. The NDES service:

a.   Verifies that the enrollment request contains a valid enrollment challenge password.

b.   Determines which certificate template to include in the request. If the key usage in the request is 0x20, the template name identified in the SignatureTemplate registry key is designated. If the key usage in the request is 0x80, the template name identified in the EncryptionTemplate registry key is designated. Finally, if the key usage in the request is 0xa0, the template name identified in the GeneralPurpose-Template registry key is designated.

> **Note**   If the registry values are not specified in the HKEY_LOCAL_MACHINE\ Software\Microsoft\Cryptography\MSCEP registry key, then the IPsec (Offline Request) certificate template is designated.

c.   Creates the enrollment request.

d.   Signs the enrollment request with the service enrollment agent signing certificate.

e.   Submits the request to the CA by calling iCertReqest::Submit.

■   **The CA will issue the certificate based on the requested certificate template.**   Typically, the certificate is issued immediately. The only exception is if the designated certificate template enables the CA Certificate Manager Approval option on the certificate template's Issuance Requirements tab.

> **Note**   If the CA is a standalone CA, the default behavior is to pend all certificate requests until a user who has been assigned the Issue and Manage Certificate permission approves the request.

■   **The network device receives the issued certificate and associates it with the previously generated key pair.**

> **Note**   If the request was pended because of the CA being a standalone CA or the requested certificate template requiring certificate manager approval, the device administrator must send another request to the NDES server to receive the status of the requested certificate. If the certificate has been issued by the CA, the certificate is returned to the device and installed on the device.

Implementing an NDES Server

The implementation of an NDES server requires any machine that is capable of running Internet Information Services (IIS) that can communicate with a CA by using Distributed Component Object Model (DCOM) communications.

The following sections will walk through the installation and configuration of an NDES deployment for the network shown in Figure 27-3.

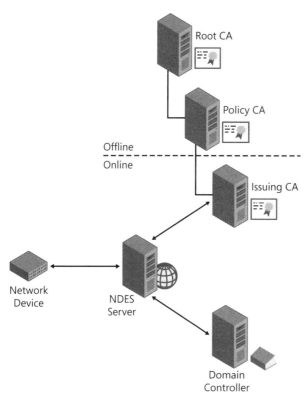

Figure 27-3   A sample NDES server deployment

This deployment follows best practices for a PKI deployment in that rather than installing the NDES role service on the CA, the role service is implemented on a separate server. The issuing CA of the three-tiered CA hierarchy is an enterprise subordinate CA, allowing the use of certificate template permissions to restrict who can request certificates for network devices.

Permission Requirements

To deploy NDES in the configuration shown previously in Figure 27-3, three user roles must be defined prior to installation. Each role will perform specific tasks during the installation and operation of the NDES server and require permission assignments specific to those tasks.

- **Service Administrator**   The service administrator is the user who will install and configure the Network Device Enrollment Service at the NDES server. To perform these tasks, the service administrator requires the following permission assignments:

  - ❑ The service administrator must be a member of the local Administrators group to allow the installation and configuration of the NDES role service.

❑ The service administrator account must belong to a group assigned Read and Enroll permissions on the Exchange Enrollment Agent (Offline Request) and CEP Encryption certificate templates.

❑ The service administrator must be assigned the Manage CA permission at the issuing CA to allow them to enable and disable certificate templates

❑ The service administrator must be assigned permissions to modify the certificate templates used by the network devices.

■ **Service Account**   The SCEP service account provides the credentials used by the SCEP service. The SCEP service account must:

❑ Be a member of the IIS_USRS group in the local account database of the NDES server.

❑ Be assigned the Request Certificates permission at the issuing CA.

❑ Be assigned the Read and Enroll permissions for the designated signing, encryption, and signing and encryption certificate templates.

> **Important**   The service account must be created *before* you start the installation and configuration of the NDES server.

■ **Device Administrator**   The device administrator manages the network devices and requests the enrollment challenge password from the NDES server. The device administrator must be assigned the Read and Enroll permissions for the designated signing, encryption, and signing and encryption certificate templates.

CA Requirements

Before you can install the NDES server, you must ensure that the required certificate templates are available at the designated CA. The following certificate templates must be made available for enrollment at the designated CA *before* you install the NDES server:

■ **Exchange Enrollment Agent (Offline Request)**   The NDES server uses this certificate to sign the certificate requests submitted by the network devices. The certificate includes the Certificate Request Agent Enhanced Key Usage (EKU) object identifier (OID) which allows the NDES server to create certificates with another device's name in the subject.

■ **CEP Encryption**   The CEP Encryption certificate is used for key exchange. The network device uses the certificate to encrypt all communications with the NDES server including transmitting the enrollment challenge password. The CEP Encryption certificate also includes the Certificate Request Agent EKU, which allows the NDES server to place the network device's name in the certificate's subject.

The permissions of both certificate templates must be modified to assign the Service Administrator user account, or a group containing the Service Administrator user account, the Read and Enroll permissions.

In addition to the two required certificate templates, you must also publish the three certificate templates designated in the HKEY_LOCAL_MACHINE\Software\Microsoft\Cryptography\ MSCEP registry key.

- **SigningTemplate**   A certificate that is configured with the Signature purpose on the Request Handling tab of the certificate template. The certificate is typically used for authentication purposes.

- **EncryptionTemplate**   A certificate that is configured with the Encryption purpose on the Request Handling tab. The certificate is typically used for encrypting data.

- **GeneralPurposeTemplate**   A certificate that is configured with the Signature And Encryption purpose on the Request Handling tab. The certificate allows both authentication and encryption.

> **Important**   If you do not designate the certificate templates in the HKEY_LOCAL_MACHINE\ Software\Microsoft\Cryptography\MSCEP registry key, then NDES will default to issuing the IPsec (Offline Request) certificate template, which can be used for signing or encrypting data.

Create the Service Account

Another task that must be performed *before* you install the NDES role service is to create the service account. The service account will be used as the identity for NDES and is typically a domain account.

Once you create the account and assign it a complex, non-expiring password, you must:

- Add the service account to the local IIS_USRS group.

- Assign the service account Read and Enroll permissions on the three network device certificate templates designated in the three registry values for NDES: SigningTemplate, EncryptionTemplate, and GeneralPurposeTemplate.

- Assign the service account the Read and Request Certificates permission at the CA that issues certificates based on the three certificate templates.

Installing the NDES Server

Once you have completed the prerequisites, you can now install the NDES role service by using the following procedure:

1. Ensure that you are logged on as a member of the local Administrators group.

2. From Administrative Tools, open Server Manager.

3. In the Roles Summary section, click Add Roles.

4. On the Select Server Roles page, select Active Directory Certificate Services, and then click Next.

5. On the Introduction To Active Directory Certificate Services page, click Next.

6. On the Select Role Services page, enable only the Network Device Enrollment Service option.

7. In the Add Roles Wizard dialog box, you will be notified that you must add the Web Server (IIS) role services. Click Add Required Role Services.

8. On the Select Role Services dialog box, click Next.

9. On the Specify User Account page, click Specify User Account (Recommended), and then click Select User.

10. In the Windows Security dialog box, type the user name and password for the service account created prior to installation, and then click OK.

11. On the Specify User Account page, ensure that the designated service account correctly appears, and then click Next.

12. On the Specify CA For Network Device Enrollment Service page, click Browse.

13. In the Select Certification Authority dialog box, select the designated CA, and then click OK.

14. On the Specify CA For Network Device Enrollment Service page, ensure that the configuration name for the CA appears, and then click Next.

15. On the Specify Registration Authority Information page (see Figure 27-4), provide the subject name information for the registration authority certificate, and then click Next.

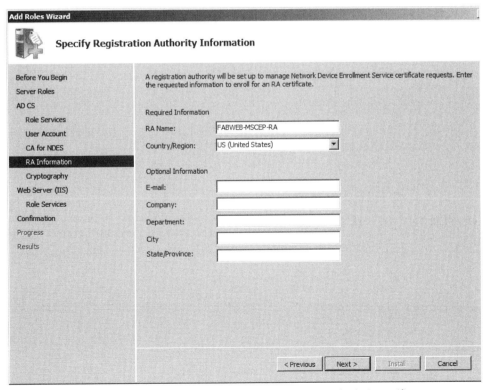

Figure 27-4   Providing the subject name for the registration authority's certificate

16. On the Configure Cryptography For Registration Authority page, you can specify a custom cryptographic service provider (CSP) and key length for both the signing certificate and the encryption certificate. After specifying the values, click Next.

> **Important**   Although you *can* modify the default values, it is recommended to leave the default cryptographic settings for the registration authority (RA) certificates. You *cannot* choose a Cryptography Next Generation (CNG) CSP for the RA certificates.

17. On the Web Server (IIS) page, click Next.

18. On the Select Role Services page, accept the recommended IIS settings, and then click Next.

19. On the Confirm Installation Selections page, click Install.

20. On the Installation Results page, click Close.

21. Close Server Manager.

> **Note**   After you install the NDES service role, consider implementing SSL protection for the NDES Administration Web portal (*https://ServerName/certsrv/mscep_admin*).

Configuring NDES

Once you have installed NDES on the server, there are post-installation procedures that can be performed. These procedures include:

- Modifying the registry to change the default behavior and options for the service.
- Enabling logging for the service.
- Backing up critical registry keys and certificates.

Modifying the Registry

You can change the default behavior and settings for NDES by modifying the registry values in the HKEY_LOCAL_MACHINE\Software\Microsoft\Cryptography\MSCEP registry key. Table 27-1 shows the available configuration options for NDES.

Table 27-1   NDES Configuration Options

Value	Default value	Usage
EnforcePassword\ EnforcePassword (DWORD)	1	0 = Passwords are not enforced. 1 = SCEP requires a password for enrollment requests.
SignatureTemplate (String)	IPSECIntermediateOffline	The certificate template used for device enrollment requests with a Key Usage of 0x20.

Table 27-1   NDES Configuration Options

Value	Default value	Usage
EncryptionTemplate (String)	IPSECIntermediateOffline	The certificate template used for device enrollment requests with a Key Usage of 0x80.
GeneralPurpose-Template (String)	IPSECIntermediateOffline	The certificate template used for device enrollment requests with a Key Usage of 0xa0.
CAType\CAType (DWORD)	Based on setup	Designates the type of CA used for certificate request. 1 = Enterprise 0 = Standalone
CAInfo\Configuration (String)	Based on setup	If the CA is not installed on the same computer as the service, this registry key must be set with the CA information in the format of *CADNSName\CAName*.
Refresh\RefreshPeriod (Binary)	7	The number of days that pending requests will be kept in the service cache.
CacheRequest\CacheRequest (DWORD)	20	The number of minutes that an issued certificate will be kept in the service cache.
CertsinMyStore\CertsInMyStore (DWORD)	1	1 = The service will look for its certificates in the computer "My" store. 0 = The service will look for its certificates in the computer "CEP" store.
PasswordMax\PasswordMax (DWORD)	5	The maximum number of available passwords.
PasswordVDir\PasswordVDir (String)	MSCEP_Admin	This is the name of the virtual directory that can be used for password requests. If set, SCEP will accept password requests only from the defined virtual directory. If the value is empty or not set, SCEP will accept password requests retrieved from any virtual directory.
PasswordValidity\PasswordValidity (DWORD)	60	The number of minutes a password is valid.
PasswordLength\PasswordLength (DWORD)	8	The Unicode character length of a password.
HashAlgorithm\HashAlgorithm (String)	SHA1	Specifies the hash algorithm the service will use when constructing the request to the CA.

Tip Many of the registry values in Table 27-1 require that you first create a new subkey below the HKEY_LOCAL_MACHINE\Software\Microsoft\Cryptography\MSCEP. For example, to designate a password validity period of 120 minutes, you must first create a new subkey named PasswordValidity, and then in the PasswordValidity key, create a DWORD named PasswordValidity with a decimal value of 120.

 On the CD The file mscep.reg, found on the accompanying CD, defines the default values for all NDES default settings. You can modify the file and apply your preferred settings.

Once all necessary registry entries have been configured, you must restart the IIS Service on the NDES server.

Enabling Logging

If issues are encountered when requesting certificates from the NDES server, you can enable trace logging for the service. The log file (Mscep.log) is stored in the NDES service account's profile.

To enable logging, use the following procedure:

1. Log on as the service account designated for the NDES service. This creates the user profile folder structure required to save the Mscep.log file.

2. Log off the service account.

3. Log on as a member of the local Administrators group.

4. Open a command prompt.

5. At the command prompt, type **certutil −setreg debug 0xffffffe3**, and then press Enter.

6. At the command prompt, type **iisreset /restart,** and then press Enter.

7. Ensure that the output of the command indicates that the service successfully restarted.

Once you have enabled logging, you can attempt to perform the task that caused the failure you are investigating. When the error occurs, you can now investigate the output in the C:\Users*NDESServiceAccount*\mscep.log file.

Backup and Restoration

To restore the NDES server in the event of server failure, two components must be backed up to allow restoration of the previous configuration. These components are:

- **Registry Settings** To restore the configuration settings of the NDES server, export the HKEY_LOCAL_MACHINE\Software\Microsoft\Cryptography\MSCEP registry key.

- **Certificates** To allow processing of previously submitted requests, but not completed requests, you must restore the original signing and encryption certificates. You can back up these certificates by exporting the certificates based on the CEP Encryption and Exchange Enrollment Agent (Offline Request) certificate templates from the local machine certificate store.

Case Study: Lucerne Publishing

Lucerne Publishing has recently acquired Litware, Inc. Litware, Inc. used Cisco VPN 3000 concentrators to allow virtual private network (VPN) access to the network. You have been tasked with configuring the Litware, Inc. clients to use the Lucerne Publishing PKI.

You must configure the Cisco VPN 3000 clients to utilize certificates from the Litware Publishing PKI. Figure 27-5 shows the Lucerne Publishing's CA hierarchy.

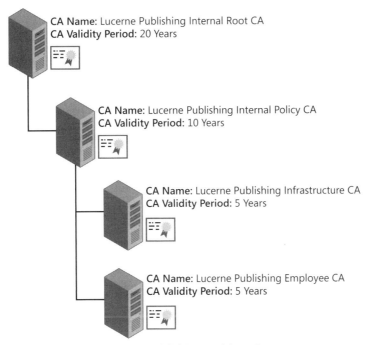

CA Name: Lucerne Publishing Internal Root CA
CA Validity Period: 20 Years

CA Name: Lucerne Publishing Internal Policy CA
CA Validity Period: 10 Years

CA Name: Lucerne Publishing Infrastructure CA
CA Validity Period: 5 Years

CA Name: Lucerne Publishing Employee CA
CA Validity Period: 5 Years

Figure 27-5   The Lucerne Publishing CA hierarchy

Requirements

The following requirements must be satisfied when you implement certificates to the Cisco VPN 3000 concentrators:

- Certificates must be issued to the VPN 3000 concentrators using SCEP.

- All certificates for the VPN 3000 concentrators must be issued by the Lucerne Publishing Infrastructure CA.

- Custom certificates must be issued to the VPN 3000 concentrators. The designated certificate templates are:

  ❏ **CiscoSigning** Used for certificates requiring the digital signing key usage

  ❏ **CiscoEncryption** Used for certificates requiring the encryption key usage

  ❏ **CiscoCombo** Used for certificates requiring the combined signing and encryption key usage

- A custom service account must be implemented for the NDES service. The account is named Lucerne\s-NDESService.

Case Study Questions

1. How many certificates must be imported into the Cisco VPN 3000 concentrators to allow them to trust certificates from the Lucerne Publishing CA hierarchy?

2. What accounts will require permissions on the three custom certificate templates? What permissions are required?

3. What group memberships are required for the Lucerne\S-NDESService account?

4. Assuming that the CiscoSigning, CiscoEncryption, and CiscoCombo certificate templates are available for enrollment at the Lucerne Publishing Infrastructure CA, are there any additional certificate templates that must be available for the NDES server? If so, what are they?

5. Lucerne Publishing wishes to utilize Suite B algorithms wherever possible. Can NDES be configured to use SHA 256-bit hashes?

6. What registry values must be modified to enable the three custom certificate templates?

7. If the Lucerne Publishing Employee CA was accidentally selected during the installation of the NDES role service, how would you change the CA used by the NDES server?

Best Practices

- **Enable SSL for the NDES administrator site.** SSL protection ensures that the enrollment challenge password is protected against inspection attacks when the network device connects to the MSCEP_Admin Web site.

- **Enable delegated enrollment agent restrictions on the RA certificate.** Windows Server 2008 allows you to restrict the enrollment agent certificate to request only the configured device certificate templates. By default, an enrollment agent can request certificates for anyone using any certificate template.

- **Create extended validity period device certificates.** The default IPsec (Offline Request) certificate template has only a one-year validity period. If you define custom signing, encryption, or general purpose certificate templates, consider creating a version 2 certificate template with a two-year validity period. A longer validity period reduces the management overhead for requesting device certificates.

- **Disable the NDES service when not in use.**   Stopping the NDES service ensures that unauthorized certificates will not be issued. Stopping the service also ensures that all data, such as all passwords that were not used by network devices, is cleared from the service cache.

- **Use the Security Configuration wizard to lock down the server.**   The Security Configuration wizard will provide you with recommendations on locking down IIS and any other services installed on the NDES server.

- **Implement Role Separation.**   Separate accounts should be deployed for service administrators and the device administrators. This prevents a single person from configuring the NDES server and requesting certificates for network devices.

Additional Information

- "Cisco Systems' Simple Certificate Enrollment Protocol (SCEP)" (*http://www.ietf.org/internet-drafts/draft-nourse-scep-16.txt*)

- "Simple Certificate Enrollment Protocol (SCEP) Add-on for Certificate Services" (*http://www.microsoft.com/downloads/details.aspx?familyid=9f306763-d036-41d8-8860-1636411b2d01&displaylang=en*)

- "Enrolling for Certificates from a Cisco Router" (*http://www.tburke.net/info/reskittools/topics/mscep_enrolling.htm*)

- "Configuring the Cisco VPN 3000 Concentrator 4.1 to Get a Digital Certificate Using SCEP" (*http://www.cisco.com/warp/public/471/vpn3k_scep.html*)

- "How to Configure Cisco PIX or IOS Router to Work with Microsoft Certification Authority (CA) Server for IPsec VPN" (*http://icmp92.com/Microsoft_CA_Cisco_setup.pdf*)

- "Multiple-Tier CA Hierarchy" (*http://www.cisco.com/en/US/products/sw/iosswrel/ps1839/products_feature_guide09186a0080214a5d.html*)

- "AD CS: Network Device Enrollment Service" (*http://technet2.microsoft.com/windowsserver2008/en/library/569cd0df-3aa4-4dd7-88b8-227e9e3c012b1033.mspx?mfr=true*)

- 249125: "Using Certificates for Windows 2000 and Cisco IOS VPN Interoperation"

> **Note**   The last article in the above list can be accessed through the Microsoft Knowledge Base. Go to *http://support.microsoft.com*, and enter the article number in the Search The Knowledge Base text box.

Appendix
Case Study Questions and Answers

Chapter 1: Cryptography Basics

1. Based on the encryption algorithms discussed in the "Default Encryption Algorithms" section of the white paper, does EFS use symmetric or asymmetric encryption?

   EFS uses symmetric encryption for actual data encryption. The File Encryption Key (FEK) can use DESX, 3DES, or AES encryption algorithms. In addition, the RSA asymmetric algorithm is used to encrypt the FEK for retrieval.

2. What encryption algorithm is used to encrypt EFS data on a workstation running Windows 2000?

   Windows 2000 uses the DESX algorithm to encrypt EFS data.

3. What encryption algorithms can be used to encrypt EFS data on Windows XP?

   Windows XP SP1 supports the DESX, 3DES, and AES-256 encryption algorithms.

4. How does the application of Windows XP SP1 affect EFS encryption?

   The application of Windows XP SP1 replaces the use of DESX for EFS encryption to AES with a 256-bit key.

5. What Group Policy setting enables use of 3DES and AES encryption algorithms?

   You must enable the "System cryptography: Use FIPS-compliant algorithms for encryption" Group Policy setting in Computer configuration\Windows settings\Security settings\Local Policies\Security Options.

6. What asymmetric encryption algorithm is used to protect the FEK in EFS?

   EFS uses the RSA asymmetric algorithm to protect the FEK in EFS.

7. A developer in your organization has a laptop with a dual boot configuration of Microsoft Windows 2000 Professional and Windows XP Professional. Both operating systems have the latest service packs and security updates. The user's Outlook data file is encrypted, and the same EFS key pair is used in both operating systems to provide access to the Outlook data file.

   This morning, your developer was unable to access the Outlook data file when working in Windows 2000, but you are still able to create new encrypted files. Fearing that the

Outlook data file was corrupt, she started Windows XP and was able to access the data file. What is the probable cause of this problem?

Group Policy is enabling System cryptography. Use FIPS-compliant algorithms for encryption of the Group Policy setting for the Windows XP computer account. The Outlook data file is being encrypted with 256-bit AES encryption, which cannot be decrypted by Windows 2000 Professional because Windows 2000 supports only DESX encryption.

8. A project manager has read an article on Cryptography Next Generation and asks whether he can use AES-GMAC as the encryption algorithm for his EFS-encrypted files. What is the minimum operating system that he needs to run to support AES-GMAC?

   AES-GMAC is supported only on Windows Vista SP1 or on Windows Server 2008.

9. Does EFS support the use of AES-GMAC for EFS encryption? What support does EFS provide for CNG algorithms and certificates that use CNG algorithms?

   No, EFS does not support the use of AES-GMAC for EFS encryption. Only CNG algorithms that are also supported by CryptoAPI can be used for EFS encryption. The project manager can use a certificate that utilizes CNG algorithms but cannot use CNG-only algorithms to protect his or her EFS encrypted data.

Chapter 2: Primer to PKI

1. What version is the certificate?

   The certificate is an X.509 version 3 certificate. You can verify this by viewing the Version field on the Details tab.

2. What is the name of the issuing CA?

   The name of the issuing CA is CN=adatumCA,DC=adatum,DC=msft. You can verify this by viewing the Issuer field on the Details tab.

3. What is the subject name of the certificate?

   The subject name of the certificate is CN = SCUser1, OU = Module09. OU = Labs, DC = adatum, DC = msft. You can verify this by viewing the Issuer field on the Details tab.

4. Are any other names included in the certificate for the subject?

   The Subject Alternative Name extension contains an additional name for the subject. The name is a user principal name, SCUser1@ADATUM.msft.

5. What is the length of the public key associated with the certificate?

   The public key length is 1,024 bits. You can verify this by viewing the Public Key field on the Details tab.

6. What other X.509 extensions are included in the sample certificate?

    On the Details tab, the following X.509 version 3 extensions are included: Key Usage, Application Policies, Certificate Policies, Enhanced Key Usage, Subject Key Identifier, Authority Key Identifier, CRL Distribution Points, Authority Information Access, and Subject Alternative Name.

7. What extensions must you inspect to determine what forms of revocation checking are supported by the CA that issued the X.509 certificate?

    You must inspect both the Authority Information Access and CRL Distribution Point extensions to determine what forms of revocation checking are supported by the CA that issued the X.509 certificate. If the CA supports OCSP, the URL of the OCSP Responder is included in the Authority Information Access extension. If the CA supports CRLs, the URLs for CRL Distribution Points are included in the CRL Distribution Point extension.

8. What forms of revocation checking are supported by the CA that issued the X.509 certificate?

    The CA supports only CRLs. The Authority Information Access extension does not contain any URLs referencing an OCSP responder.

9. Where is the CRL published when revocation checking is performed against the certificate?

    On the Details tab, two URLs are included in the CRL Distribution Points extension indicating where the CRL is published: *ldap://CN=adatumCA,CN=VANCOUVER, CN=CDP,CN=Public%20Key%20Services,CN=Services,CN=Configuration,DC=adatum, DC=msft?certificateRevocationList?base?objectClass=cRLDistributionPoint* and *http://vancouver.adatum.msft/CertEnroll/adatumCA.crl.*

Chapter 3: Policies and PKI

1. What is the relationship between a CPS, certificate policy, and security policy?

    A security policy defines an organization's security standards. The contents of an organization's security policy provides the input to the definition of a certificate policy. The certificate policy defines how a PKI will enforce the organization's security policies. Finally, the certification practice statement defines the operating rules for the PKI in the enforcement of any defined certificate policies.

2. In what document would you define the methods used to identify the new hires when they start with Fabrikam?

    The methods of identifying the subject of a certificate are defined in a certificate policy. The certificate policy will define the exact measures, such as different types of ID, required to validate the subject's identity before issuing a certificate.

3. Will the identification validation requirements for existing employees differ from those implemented for new employees of Fabrikam?

    Not necessarily. The answer depends on what measures are taken by the organization to identify employees when they are originally hired by the company. For example, if similar measures were taken before providing employees with photo ID cards, the employees could just show their existing employee card as an equivalent form of identification rather than show all the identification required for new employees.

4. The high turnover of employees must be addressed in the CPS. Specifically, what sections must be updated to define the measures taken when an employee is terminated or resigns from Fabrikam?

    The sections of the CPS that define the revocation policies of the organization are "Identification and Authentication," which is where you define how requests for revocation are submitted to a revocation authority, and "Certificate Life-Cycle Operational Requirements," which is where you define the circumstances under which a certificate is revoked (such as termination or resignation). Although it is tempting to consider as an option, the "Certificate, CRL, and OCSP Profiles" section is related to the format of CRLs, not the actual revocation of certificates.

5. You are considering modeling your certificate policies after the United States FBCA certificate policy. What certificate class would best match your deployment of smart cards?

    The FBCA High Assurance certificate. The FBCA High Assurance certificate describes certificates stored on two-factor authentication devices, such as smart cards.

Chapter 4: Preparing an Active Directory Environment

Answer the following questions based on the Tailspin Toys scenario.

1. Is there a minimum service pack level required at each domain controller before applying the Windows Server 2008 schema modifications?

    No. There is no minimum service pack requirement for applying the Windows Server 2008 schema modifications when the domain is already running the Windows Server 2003 or Windows Servers 2003 R2 schema.

2. At what computer will you run adprep/forestprep? What group membership(s) is/are required?

    adprep/forestprep must be run at Corp\ROOTDC02, the schema operation master by a member of the Schema Admins group, Enterprise Admins, and Domain Admins group.

3. What computer(s) will you use to run adprep/domainprep/gpprep? What group membership(s) is/are required? Is this command required to deploy Windows Server 2008 certification authorities?

adprep /domainprep /gpprep must be run at the infrastructure master at each domain in the forest. In this example, the command must be run at Corp\ROOTDC01 by a member of Corp\Domain Admins group, at Amers\NADC01 by a member of the Amers\Domain Admins group, at Emea\EUDC02 by a member of the Emea\Domain Admins group, at WingtipToys\WTDC02 by a member of the WingtipToys\Domain Admins group, and at Apac\APDC02 by a member of the Apac\Domain Admins group. This command is not technically required to deploy Windows Server 2008 certification authorities, but it is commonly performed at this time so that the domain upgrade is complete, allowing the deployment of Windows Server 2008 domain controllers.

4. What is causing the issuing CA to record the "Certificate Services could not publish a Certificate for request #" error for the certificate issued to Sidsel Øby?

   The issuing CA that issued the certificate to Sidsel Øby is not a member of the EMEA\Cert Publishers group. Only members of the EMEA\Cert Publishers group can write information to the Sidsel.Øby userCertificate attribute.

5. What configuration change is required to remove the error condition?

   The Cert Publishers group in each domain must contain all CA computer accounts. Currently, the CAs are a member of only their own domain's Cert Publishers group.

6. Assuming no changes have been made to the default scope for each domain's Cert Publishers group, record in the following table the expected scope for each domain's Cert Publishers group.

Domain	Scope of Cert Publishers group
corp.tailspintoys.msft	Global group
amers.corp.tailspintoys.msft	Global group
emea.corp.tailspintoys.msft	Domain Local group
wingtiptoys.msft	Domain Local group
apac.wingtiptoys.msft	Domain Local group

7. Write a script to convert any Cert Publishers groups from global to domain local groups. The script must contain only the Cert Publishers groups that are *not* already domain local groups.

```
Set grp = GetObject("LDAP://CN=Cert
Publishers,CN=Users,DC=corp,DC=tailspintoys,DC=msft")
grp.Put "groupType","-2147483640"
grp.SetInfo
grp.Put "groupType","-2147483644"
grp.SetInfo
Set grp = GetObject("LDAP://CN=Cert
Publishers,CN=Users,DC=amers,DC=corp,DC=tailspintoys,DC=msft")
grp.Put "groupType","-2147483640"
grp.SetInfo
grp.Put "groupType","-2147483644"
grp.SetInfo
```

8. Write a script to correctly populate each domain's Cert Publishers group with all CA computer accounts in the forest.

```
' Populate the Corp domain Cert Publishers group
Set grp = GetObject("LDAP://
CN=Cert Publishers,CN=Users,DC=corp, ,DC=tailspintoys,DC=msft")
grp.SetInfogrp.add ("LDAP://CN=AMERSCA01,CN=Computers,DC=amers,DC=corp,
DC=tailspintoys,DC=msft") grp.SetInfogrp.add ("LDAP://
CN=EMEACA01,CN=Computers,DC=emea,DC=corp,
DC=tailspintoys,DC=msft") grp.SetInfogrp.add ("LDAP://
CN=WINGCA01,CN=Computers,DC=wingtiptoys,DC=msft") grp.SetInfo
' Populate the Amers domain Cert Publishers group
Set grp = GetObject("LDAP://
CN=Cert Publishers,CN=Users,DC=amers,DC=corp,DC=tailspintoys,DC=msft")
grp.SetInfogrp.add ("LDAP://CN=EMEACA01,CN=Computers,DC=emea,DC=corp,
DC=tailspintoys,DC=msft") grp.SetInfogrp.add ("LDAP://
CN=WINGCA01,CN=Computers,DC=wingtiptoys,DC=msft") grp.SetInfo
' Populate the Emea domain Cert Publishers group
Set grp = GetObject("LDAP://
CN=Cert Publishers,CN=Users,DC=emea,DC=corp,DC=tailspintoys,DC=msft")
grp.SetInfogrp.add ("LDAP://CN=AMERSCA01,CN=Computers,DC=amers,DC=corp,
DC=tailspintoys,DC=msft") grp.SetInfogrp.add ("LDAP://
CN=WINGCA01,CN=Computers,DC=wingtiptoys,DC=msft") grp.SetInfo
' Populate the WingtipToys domain Cert Publishers group
Set grp = GetObject("LDAP://CN=Cert Publishers,CN=Users,DC=wingtiptoys,DC=msft")
grp.SetInfogrp.add ("LDAP://CN=AMERSCA01,CN=Computers,DC=amers,DC=corp,
DC=tailspintoys,DC=msft") grp.SetInfogrp.add ("LDAP://
CN=EMEACA01,CN=Computers,DC=emea,DC=corp,
DC=tailspintoys,DC=msft") grp.SetInfo
' Populate the APAC domain Cert Publishers group
Set grp = GetObject("LDAP://
CN=Cert Publishers,CN=Users,DC=apac,DC=wingtiptoys,DC=msft")
grp.SetInfogrp.add ("LDAP://CN=AMERSCA01,CN=Computers,DC=amers,DC=corp,
DC=tailspintoys,DC=msft") grp.SetInfogrp.add ("LDAP://
CN=EMEACA01,CN=Computers,DC=emea,DC=corp,
DC=tailspintoys,DC=msft") grp.SetInfogrp.add ("LDAP://
CN=WINGCA01,CN=Computers,DC=wingtiptoys,DC=msft") grp.SetInfo
```

Chapter 5: Designing a Certification Authority Hierarchy

1. How many tiers are required in the Fabrikam CA hierarchy?

    At least two levels are required in the CA hierarchy. The best answer is three, because there is a need for multiple policy CAs in the CA hierarchy.

2. What additional security measures are required for all CAs?

    All CAs must implement hardware security modules (HSMs) to protect each CA's key pair from theft and tampering.

3. Are there any external requirements for the CA hierarchy?

    Yes. The corporate Web site must use a certificate that is trusted by all customers. In addition, Europe and Asia have privacy laws that require the implementation of a separate policy CA in those regions.

4. Is role separation required in your CA hierarchy design? If so, how do you implement it?

    Yes. Role separation is required to manage the CAs. A local administration team in each regional office will manage the CAs.

5. How many policy CAs are required for the CA hierarchy?

    Two: A policy CA for the Americas and another policy CA for Europe and Asia.

6. What CA hierarchy design best fits the organization's requirements?

    a. A design based on certificate use

    b. A design based on geography

    c. A design based on company departments

    d. A design based on a combination of certificate use and geography

    The answer is b. The CA hierarchy must be based on geography to allow decentralized administration and provide high availability of certificate templates to all regions.

7. If offline CAs are implemented at the first and second levels of the CA hierarchy, where will you locate the offline CAs?

    The offline root and the offline policy CA for North America and South America should be located at the corporate office in Atlanta. No differentiation is provided between the Frankfurt and Singapore sites, so the policy CA for Europe and Asia can be placed at either site.

8. In what domain will the root CA's computer account exist?

    None. The offline root CA must have a workgroup membership rather than a domain membership. If the offline root CA were a member of a domain, the CA must be connected to the domain periodically to keep the computer account active.

9. In what domain will you place policy CA computer accounts?

    None. Offline policy CAs must have a workgroup membership rather than a domain membership to allow the computer to never be connected to the network.

10. In what domain will you place issuing CA computer accounts?

    Place the issuing CAs in their regional domains. This allows easier delegation of administration when implementing Common Criteria role separation. Do not place the computers in the forest root domain, because no administrative accounts (other than the default accounts) exist in that domain.

11. Based on the requirements presented in this case study, draw your proposed CA hierarchy for Fabrikam, Inc.

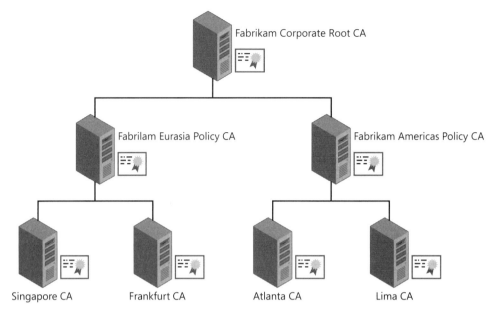

12. Assuming that your design resulted in a three-tier CA hierarchy and the maximum validity period of a certificate issued to users, computers, services, or network devices is five years, what is the validity period of the root CA certificates, the policy CA certificate(s), and the issuing CA certificates?

If the maximum validity period for issued certificates is five years, the validity period for the issuing CAs must be double that value, or 10 years. Likewise, the policy CA validity period would be doubled to a value of 20 years, and the validity period of the root CA would be 40 years. If your company is unsure about using a CA certificate's key pair for this extended period, lesser values can be defined, as long as the CA's certificate is renewed before the validity period of the CA certificate constrains the validity period of the certificates issued by that CA.

Chapter 6: Implementing a CA Hierarchy

The questions for this case study are divided into sections related to configuration of the Fabrikam Corporate Root CA, the Fabrikam Corporate Policy CA, and the Fabrikam Corporate Issuing CA.

Fabrikam Corporate Root CA

Answer the following questions relating to configuration of the Fabrikam Corporate Root CA based on the information provided in the design requirements:

1. How do you define the key length of 2,048 bits for the root CA during installation of the root CA?

The key length must be entered when you add the Certificate Services role in Server Manager.

2. How do you ensure that the key length will remain 2,048 bits when the root CA's certificate is renewed?

    In the CAPolicy.inf file, in the [certsrv_server] section, you must add the entry renewalkeylength=2048.

3. What entries are required in the CAPolicy.inf file to define the required base CRL and delta CRL publication intervals?

    [certsrv_server]

    CRLPeriod = months

    CRLPeriodUnits = 6

    CRLDeltaPeriod = days

    CRLDeltaPeriodUnits = 0

    Alternatively, you could define the CRLPeriod value as weeks and the CRLPeriod-Units as 26, as long as the overall period is equivalent to six months.

4. How would you suppress the inclusion of an AIA and CDP extension in the root CA certificate on Windows Server 2008 Standard Edition?

    Nothing needs to be defined. The default behavior suppresses the AIA and CDP extensions in a root CA certificate.

5. After configuring the CAPolicy.inf file, you note that none of the settings are applied to the root CA when you install Certificate Services. You check and find that the file is located in the c:\temp folder. Why did the installation not apply the settings in the CAPolicy.inf file?

    The CAPolicy.inf file must exist in the %Windir% folder. If the file is not in the %Windir% folder, the settings are not applied.

6. How do you configure the root CA to issue subordinate CA certificates with a lifetime of 10 years?

    You must run a post-installation batch file that contains the lines:

    certutil -setreg CA\ValidityPeriodUnits 10

    certutil -setreg CA\ValidityPeriod "Years"

7. How do you define the location in Configuration naming context for publishing the root CA certificate and CRL to AD DS? (Assume that the forest root domain is the same as shown previously in Figure 6-1.)

    certutil -setreg CA\DSConfigDN CN=Configuration,DC=Fabrikam,DC=com.

8. What command is required to define the AIA publication URLs for the certificates issued by the root CA?

    certutil -setreg CA\CACertPublicationURLs "1:%windir%\system32\CertSrv\CertEnroll\%%1_%%3%%4.crt\n2:ldap:///CN=%%7,CN=AIA,CN=Public Key Services,CN=Services,%%6%%11\n2:http://www.fabrikam.com/CertData/%%1_%%3%%4.crt"

9. What command is required to define the CDP publication URLs for the certificates issued by the root CA?

    certutil -setreg CA\CRLPublicationURLs "1:%windir%\system32\CertSrv\CertEnroll\%%3%%8%%9.crl\ \n10:ldap:///CN=%%7%%8,CN=%%2,CN=CDP,CN=Public Key Services,CN=Services,%%6%%10 n2: http://www.fabrikam.com/CertData/%%3%%8%%9.crl "

Fabrikam Corporate Policy CA

Answer the following questions relating to configuration of the Fabrikam Corporate Policy CA based on the information provided in the design requirements:

1. On the first attempt to install the policy CA, you receive the error that the CA is unable to determine the revocation status for the policy CA certificate. What must you do to ensure that the policy CA recognizes the root CA certificate as a trusted root certificate and can determine the revocation status for the policy CA certificate?

    You must publish the root CA certificate and CRL in the local computer store of the policy CA.

2. What command do you use to add the root CA certificate as a trusted root CA certificate on the Fabrikam Corporate Policy CA, assuming that the name of the root CA certificate is FABINCCA01_Fabrikam Corporate Root CA.crt?

    certutil -addstore -f Root FABINCCA01_Fabrikam Corporate Root CA.crt

3. What command do you use to allow the policy CA to access the root CA CRL, assuming that the name of the root CA certificate is Fabrikam Corporate Root CA.crl?

    certutil -addstore -f Root Fabrikam Corporate Root CA.crl

4. How do you configure the CAPolicy.inf file on the policy CA to include the CPS and related OID?

    You add the following lines to the CAPolicy.inf file, stored in the %Windir% of the policy CA:

    [PolicyStatementExtension]
    Policies = FabrikamPolicy

    [FabrikamPolicy]

OID = 1.3.6.1.4.1.311.509.4.1

URL = http://www.fabrikam.com/CPS/Fabrikampolicy.asp

Fabrikam Corporate Issuing CA

Answer the following questions relating to configuration of the Fabrikam Corporate Policy CA based on the information provided in the design requirements:

1. What commands do you use to ensure that the root CA and policy CA certificates are automatically added to the local machine store of all Windows 2000, Windows XP, and Windows Server 2003 domain members?

   certutil −dspublish −f FABINCCA01_Fabrikam Corporate Root CA.crt RootCA
   certutil −dspublish −f FABINCCA02_Fabrikam Corporate Policy CA.crt SubCA

2. What commands do you use to ensure that the root CA and policy CA CRLs are automatically added to the local machine store of all Windows 2000, Windows XP, and Windows Server 2003 domain members?

   certutil −dspublish −f Fabrikam Corporate Root CA.crl
   certutil −dspublish −f Fabrikam Corporate Policy CA.crl

3. On the first attempt to install the issuing CA, you receive the error that the CA is unable to determine the revocation status for the policy CA certificate. Assuming that you have successfully published the root and policy CA information to AD DS, what must you do to ensure that the issuing CA can determine the revocation status for the issuing CA certificate?

   You must ensure that the root and policy CA information is downloaded to the computer. Run gpupdate /target:machine /force, wait 90 minutes for automatic application of Group Policy, or reboot the computer to download the certificates and CRLs to the local computer.

4. What are the minimum components of the World Wide Web Service required to install the Certificate Services Web Enrollment pages?

   Active Server Pages and World Wide Web Service.

5. What commands are required at the issuing CA to publish the base CRL daily and the delta CRL every eight hours?

   Certutil -setreg CA\CRLPeriodUnits 1

   Certutil -setreg CA\CRLPeriod "Days"

   Certutil -setreg CA\CRLDeltaPeriodUnits 8

   Certutil -setreg CA\CRLDeltaPeriod "Hours"

Chapter 7: Upgrading Your Existing Microsoft PKI

The questions for this case study are divided into sections related to configuration of the Humongous Insurance Internal Root CA, the Humongous Insurance Internal Policy CA, and the Humongous Insurance Internal Issuing CAs.

Humongous Insurance Internal Root CA

Answer the following questions relating to configuration of the Humongous Insurance Internal Root CA based on the information provided in the design requirements:

1. Can you upgrade the root CA directly to Windows Server 2008?

   No. The root CA must first be upgraded to Windows Server 2003 before you can upgrade to Windows Server 2008.

2. How would you change the root CA's key length to 2,048 bits from the current 4,096 bits?

   In the CAPolicy.inf file, in the %Windir% folder, you must add the entry renewalkeylength=2048 in the [certsrv_server] section. You must then renew the CA certificate designating a new key pair.

3. How would you configure the root CA certificate to include a discrete signature? Is any additional configuration required to include discrete signatures in all subordinate CA certificates issued by the root CA?

   To include a discrete signature in the root CA certificate, you must include the line DiscreteSignatureAlgorithm=1 in the [certsrv_server] section of the CA's CAPolicy.inf file. Once the file is edited, you must renew the root CA certificate to add the discrete signature.

   To include a discrete signature in all certificates issued by the root CA, you must run the command certutil -setreg ca\csp\DiscreteSignatureAlgorithm 1, and then restart Certificate Services.

4. How would you change the root CA's hash algorithm from MD5 to SHA1?

   First, you must identify the CSP used by the root CA by running certutil −getreg ca\csp\Provider. Then you must determine if the current CSP supports SHA1 by running certutil -v −csplist and ensuring that SHA1 is reported as a supported protocol. If SHA1 is supported, you would then add the values assigned to Algorithm Class, Algorithm Type, and Algorithm Sub-id (typically this is 0x8004) and run certutil -setreg ca\csp\HashAlgorithm 0x8004. After executing the command, you must restart Certificate Services.

Humongous Insurance Internal Policy CA

Answer the following questions relating to configuration of the Humongous Insurance Internal Policy CA based on the information provided in the design requirements:

1. To save money, Humongous Insurance would like change the policy CA to Standard Edition rather than continue to use Enterprise Edition. Is this possible in an upgrade scenario?

   No. If you examine Table 7-1, you cannot upgrade Windows Server 2003 Standard Edition to Windows Server 2008 Enterprise Edition.

2. If you can upgrade to Standard Edition, what would be the process?

   You cannot upgrade from Windows Server 2003 Standard Edition to Windows Server 2008 Enterprise Edition.

3. If you cannot change to Standard Edition doing an upgrade-in-place, what are your other options?

   You could install a new Policy CA running on Windows Server 2008 Standard Edition. The server must use a unique CA name and NetBIOS name. The existing issuing CAs (or new issuing CAs) must be installed as subordinates below the new policy CA.

Humongous Insurance Internal Issuing CAs

Answer the following questions relating to configuration of the Humongous Insurance Internal Issuing CAs based on the information provided in the design requirements:

1. Can you perform an in-place upgrade to migrate the current issuing CAs from the 32-bit platform to the 64-bit platform?

   No, you cannot change the platform for an issuing CA using an in-place upgrade.

2. If you cannot upgrade in place to 64-bit Windows, what process would you use to change the issuing CAs in the hierarchy to 64-bit Windows?

   You would have to deploy a parallel migration. Both the 64-bit CAs and the 32-bit CAs would remain on the network.

3. What measures could you take to reduce the amount of time you must support both the 32-bit and 64-bit issuing CA?

   You would ensure that no certificate templates are published at the 32-bit issuing CAs. This prevents the issuing CAs from issuing any additional certificates after the 64-bit CAs are deployed. The 64-bit CAs must host all certificate templates previously hosted by the 32- bit CAs.

4. What PKI management tasks must be maintained throughout the remaining lifetime of the 32-bit issuing CAs?

    The 32-bit issuing CA must continue to publish updated base CRLs and delta CRLs until the last issued certificate expires.

5. In the worst case scenario, how long would you have to maintain both the 32-bit and 64-bit CAs?

    The 32-bit CAs must be maintained for a maximum of two years (the maximum validity period of issued certificates).

6. What measures can you take to further reduce the period for maintaining the 32-bit CAs?

    This period can be greatly reduced by revoking the currently issued certificates and issuing new certificates from the 64-bit CAs.

Chapter 8: Verifying and Monitoring Your Microsoft PKI

CA Hierarchy Verification Questions

1. Based on the PKI Health Tool display shown previously in Figure 8-9, which CA is incorrectly configured?

    The error icon indicates that the error condition exists for the Fabrikam Corporate Root CA.

2. Figure 8-10 shows the details for the Fabrikam Corporate Root CA. Is the problem with an AIA or a CDP URL?

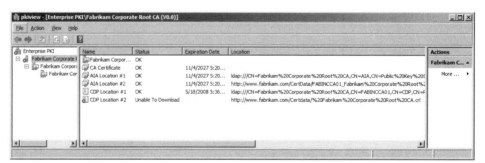

Figure 8-10   The PKI Health Tool details for the Fabrikam Corporate Root CA

    CDP Location #2 reports an Unable To Download status.

3. What is wrong with the HTTP CDP URL?

    The URL for the HTTP location was incorrectly recorded. The CA CRL name was preceded with a %20 character (a space).

4. Will this error prevent revocation checking from working for the Fabrikam CA hierarchy?

   It can cause errors if the LDAP URL is unavailable or fails for any reason. If the LDAP URL is valid and available, revocation checking will operate successfully.

5. What CA must be reconfigured to fix the error?

   The HTTP URL must be reconfigured at the root CA to fix the error.

6. Assume that the root CA computer's post-configuration file contains the following line. What is wrong with the syntax of the line?

   ```
   certutil -setreg CA\CRLPublicationURLs
   "1:%windir%\system32\CertSrv\CertEnroll\%%3%%8%%9.crl \n10:ldap:///
   CN=%%7%%8,CN=%%2,CN=CDP,CN=Public Key Services,CN=Services,
   %%6%%10\n2:http://www.fabrikam.com/CertData/  %%3%%8%%9.crl "
   ```

   The line contains an extra space in front of %%3%%8%%9.crl. This causes the %20 character to appear before Fabrikam Corporate Root CA.crl in the PKI Health Tool for the HTTP URL for the CDP extension.

7. After the error is fixed, is there any further reconfiguration required?

   Yes, you must redeploy both the Fabrikam Corporate Policy CA and the Fabrikam Corporate Issuing CA once you fix the configuration error.

Monitoring Questions

1. Can you use the Active Directory Certificate Services Management Pack with a third-party monitoring package?

   No. The Active Directory Certificate Services management pack only works with Systems Center Operations Manager 2007.

2. How would you report on operational issues every day at 07:00 and 19:00?

   You would create a scheduled task that takes place at 07:00 and 19:00.

3. What command would you execute to provide all monitoring tests and send the e-mail notification to PKIAdmins@fabrikam.com?

   Cscript camonitor.vbs /CAAlive /CACertOK /CACRLOK /KRAOK /SMTP / SMTPServer:mail.fabrikam.com /SMTPTo:PKIAdmins@fabrikam.com.

4. Are there any requirements for the SMTP Server designated in the monitoring scheduled task?

   Yes. The SMTP server must allow anonymous relay.

5. The Fabrikam Corporate Issuing CA's auditing configuration matches the settings defined previously in Figure 8-7, but none of the events described previously in

Table 8-3 are reported in the Windows Security log. You know there are configuration issues, but no errors are reported. Why?

You must enable Success and Failure auditing for Object Access events at the issuing CA. You can use either Local Security Policy or a Group Policy object (GPO) linked to the OU where the CA computer account exists in Active Directory.

6. One morning your third-party monitoring software indicates that an Event ID 30 was recorded by the CAMonitor.vbs script at the Fabrikam Corporate Issuing CA. The CA is no longer able to issue custom EFS encryption certificates. What must be done to fix the problem?

One of the KRA certificates designated at the Fabrikam Corporate Issuing CA has expired. The certificate must be replaced with a new certificate that is time valid.

7. A code-signing certificate issued last week was supposed to be valid for three years, but is only valid for two years and five months. If you look back at the Fabrikam Corporate Issuing CA's application log, what event should you find that explains why the certificate is issued with a truncated validity period?

The issuing CA's application log should have a report that a CA Certificate remaining validity period is less than half its lifetime event (event ID 12) when the CA certificate's remaining validity period reached 30 months or two and a half years. Remember that a CA cannot issue a certificate with a validity period longer than the remaining validity period of the CA's certificate.

Chapter 9: Securing a CA Hierarchy

1. If you were to script the configuration of auditing settings for the offline CAs, what command would you include in the script to meet the auditing requirements?

certutil −setreg CA\Auditfilter 127

2. What command is required to meet the audit setting requirements for the online CAs?

certutil −setreg CA\Auditfilter 126

3. Can you meet the security requirements for the CA hierarchy by implementing either a software-based CSP or a smart-card CSP? Why or why not?

No to both. The security policies of the organization require that all CA private key material is protected with FIPS 140-2 level 3 protection; this is only possible by implementing HSMs.

4. Can you use dedicated HSMs at each CA in the hierarchy and meet the design requirements? What are the drawbacks to this approach if it is possible?

Yes. You can deploy a dedicated HSM at each of the six CAs in the proposed CA hierarchy. The only drawback is the cost of purchasing six dedicated HSMs rather than using network-attached HSMs for the online CAs.

5. Can you use network-attached HSMs at each CA in the CA hierarchy and meet the design requirements? What are the drawbacks to this approach if it is possible?

    No. The City Power and Light security policies do not allow any network connectivity for offline CAs, and this excludes the implementation of network-attached HSMs for the offline CAs.

6. If you wanted to implement network-attached HSMs for the issuing CAs in the CA hierarchy, how many network-attached HSMs would you recommend to City Power and Light?

    Two network-attached HSMs are required to meet the design requirement to prevent a single point of failure. By deploying a network-attached HSM at both the Atlanta and La Jolla locations, you can configure each issuing CA to communicate with both the local and the remote network-attached HSM.

Chapter 10: Certificate Revocation

1. Management has defined the following circumstances when a certificate must be revoked. Complete the following table to provide recommendations on what revocation reason should be applied if a certificate is revoked under matching circumstances.

Revocation Circumstance	Revocation Reason Applied
An employee voluntarily resigns.	Change of affiliation
An employee is terminated.	Change of affiliation
A computer is stolen.	Key compromise
A Certification Authority is compromised.	CA compromise
A smart card or other two-factor device is lost or misplaced.	Key compromise
A certificate template is updated, requiring redeployment of certificates.	Superseded

2. What revocation checking method would you use for the offline CAs in the CA hierarchy?

    The offline CAs must use CRL checking. The OCSP Responder cannot communicate with an offline CA for revocation checking purposes.

3. Can you configure the issuing CAs to only use OCSP, or must you provide both OCSP and CRL support for revocation checking?

    You must implement both OCSP and CRL support on the issuing CAs. The reasons are two-fold: The Windows Server 2003 Web servers only support CRL checking for the certificate-based authentication, and the Online Responder determines revocation information by inspecting CRLs.

4. What certificate template would you use for OCSP Response Signing?

    The Windows Server 2008 enterprise CAs can issue certificates based on the default OCSP Response Signing version 3 certificate template.

5. How many revocation configurations must be defined for the Fabrikam network?

    Two. One for each of the issuing CAs.

6. Assume that you have created a three-node Online Responder array to process the OCSP requests. Where would you define the revocation configuration?

    You would define the revocation configuration at the array controller. The revocation configuration is then replicated to all array members from the array controller.

7. For the purposes of disaster recovery, how would you back up the Online Responder configuration?

    The responder configuration can be backed up for disaster recovery by performing a system state backup at the array controller.

Chapter 11: Certificate Validation

1. What URLs do you include in the Northwind Traders root CA certificate for the AIA and CDP extensions?

    None. The best practice is to create a root CA certificate without AIA and CDP extensions so that revocation checking is not performed on root CA certificates.

2. Are there any network design issues that prevent you from implementing an LDAP URL as the first URL in the list of available URLs for CA certificates and CRLs?

    Yes. The default format of the LDAP URL is not accessible by Windows servers that are not members of the forest. The format is also not accessible by BSD UNIX servers. You would have to include the DNS name of the LDAP server in the URL for it to be accessible to nondomain members or UNIX computers.

3. What form of URL should you implement as the first URL in CDP and AIA URL listings?

    To allow access by nondomain members, you should implement an HTTP URL as the first URL in both the AIA and CDP URL listings.

4. What protocol, by default, provides redundancy and high availability in an Active Directory environment?

    LDAP URLs reference the configuration naming context. The configuration naming context is available on every domain controller in the forest.

Troubleshooting Exercise

This exercise allows you to investigate a CAPI2 diagnostics log to determine why an error message is returned to a client when they connect to a Web server.

1. Ensure you are logged on at a computer running Windows Vista or Windows Server 2008 as a member of the local Administrators group.

2. From Administrative Tools, open Event Viewer.

3. From the Action menu, click section, and then click Open Saved Log.

4. Open CD:\XXXX\Chap11CaseStudy.evtx.

5. In the Open Saved Log dialog box, accept the default name, and then click OK.

Now that you have the event log open, answer the following questions based on the log entries.

1. What is the reason for the Verify Chain Policy error event?

   The error reports that the certificate's CN name does not match the passed value. The URL typed was ocsp.fabrikam.com, and the subject of the SSL certificate is www.fabrikam.com.

2. What object information is included in the X509 Objects event located between the two error events?

   The X509 objects event contains details on all processed objects. This includes four certificates (the three CA certificates and the Web site certificate) and four CRLs (the three base CRLs and the issuing CA's delta CRL).

3. Was revocation and CA certificate information downloaded from URLs or retrieved from cache?

   All CRLs and CA certificates were retrieved from cache. This is evident through the CryptRetrieveObjectByUrlCache events in the log.

Chapter 12: Designing Certificate Templates

1. What MMC console do you use to perform certificate template management?

   The Certificate Templates (certtmpl.msc) console.

2. Does the default Code Signing certificate template meet the design requirements?

   No. The Code Signing certificate template has a one-year validity period and does not implement any issuance requirements.

3. Can you modify the default Code Signing certificate template? If not, what would you do?

   No. The Code Signing certificate template is a version 1 certificate template. You must duplicate the existing Code Signing certificate template to create a custom version 2 certificate template.

4. Should you create a version 2 or a version 3 certificate template?

    You should create a version 2 certificate template. Windows XP and Windows Server 2003 do not recognize the use of CNG algorithms.

5. In the following table, define the settings on the General tab to meet the design requirements for your custom code-signing certificate template.

Attribute	Your recommended design
Template display name	Any valid name
Template name	Any valid name with no spaces
Validity period	Four years
Publish certificate in Active Directory	Disabled
Do not automatically re-enroll if a duplicate certificate exists in Active Directory	Disabled
For automatic renewal of smart card certificates, use the existing key if a new key cannot be created	Disabled

6. In the following table, define the settings on the Request Handling tab to meet the design requirements for the custom code-signing certificate template.

Attribute	Your recommended design
Purpose	Signature
Allow private key to be exported	Disabled
Minimum key size	1,024
Do the following when the subject is enrolled and when the private key associated with this certificate is used	Prompt the user during enrollment
CSPs	Only enable the Microsoft Base Smart Card Crypto Provider

7. In the following table, define the settings on the Issuance Requirements tab to meet the design requirements for the custom code-signing certificate template.

Attribute	Your recommended design
CA certificate manager approval	Enabled
This number of authorized signatures	Disabled
Require the following for reenrollment	Valid existing certificate

8. How must you configure the settings on the Superseded Templates tab to ensure that all certificates a CA issues for code signing use the version 2 certificate template?

    Add the Code Signing certificate template to the Superseded Templates tab.

9. What permission assignment modifications are required for the custom code signing certificate?

You must assign Read and Enroll permissions to the Code Signing group. To meet the design requirements, you also must remove the Enroll permission assignment for the Domain Admins and Enterprise Admins groups.

Chapter 13: Role Separation

1. The backup software implemented by Tailspin Toys uses a centralized backup services account. When reviewing the event logs, the backup operator notices that the backup fails every night on the two issuing CAs. On inspecting the event logs further, the backup software reports that the failed backup item is the System State backup. What is the likely cause of the error?

   The backup services account is assigned two or more of the Common Criteria roles. Typically, the issue is that the account is a member of the local Administrators group. This group is assigned both the backup privilege and the auditing privilege.

2. When inspecting the security permission assignments at the Tailspin Toys Infrastructure CA, you accidentally assign the CA Administrator group the Issue and Manage Certificates permission. When you try and fix the permissions assignment error, you find that access is denied. What must be done to fix the issue?

   A local administrator must first disable the CA\EnableRoleSeparation registry entry. Once role separation is disabled, the local administrator can fix the permissions assignment. Once the assignment is fixed, the local administrator should reenable the CA\EnableRoleSeparation registry entry.

3. The certificate for the Tailspin Toys Employee CA is reaching the halfway point of its validity period and must be renewed. You are logged on to the CA as a CA Administrator but all attempts to renew the CA certificate fail. Who must perform the renewal of the CA certificate?

   A local administrator must perform the CA certificate renewal. Only a local administrator has the necessary access to the local machine store to generate or access the CA key pair and generate the certificate request. If role separation is enabled, it must be disabled for the renewal process.

4. The Tailspin Toys Employee CA implements key archival for both Encrypting File System (EFS) certificates and e-mail encryption certificates. The security policy of your organization requires that all key recovery operations be performed by at least two employees. If you are assigned the Key Recovery Agent role, what Common Criteria role can you not hold, because this would break the security policy for key recovery?

   You cannot hold the Certificate Manager role. In the key recovery process, a Certificate Manager extracts the encrypted private key from the CA database, and then the Key Recovery Agent decrypts the encrypted private key.

5. Tailspin Toys implements several version 1 certificate templates at the Tailspin Toys Infrastructure CA. You have delegated the task of managing certificate templates to Andy, a member of the IT security team. Andy is able to create new version 2 and

version 3 certificate templates but is unable to modify the permissions for any of the version 1 certificate templates deployed at the Tailspin Toys Infrastructure CA. Why is Andy unable to modify the version 1 certificate templates?

Andy, or a group in which Andy has membership, was delegated permission at both the Certificate Templates and the OID container. Andy (or a group in which Andy has membership) was not assigned permissions on the existing certificate templates. This prevents him from modifying the permissions on the version 1 certificate templates.

6. Tailspin Toys wishes to deploy a new enterprise subordinate CA named Tailspin Toys Contractor CA to issue certificates to contractors and vendors working on-site. When you attempt to install the enterprise CA, the options for both enterprise root CA and enterprise subordinate CA are unavailable. What group memberships are required to install an enterprise CA?

You must be a member of the Enterprise Admins group to install an enterprise CA. Only Enterprise Admins have the necessary permissions to create objects in the Configuration naming context when a new enterprise CA is installed.

7. You have enabled auditing at all issuing CAs in the CA hierarchy. Today, you received a call from the audit department indicating that no events related to Certificate Services exist in the Windows Security log. You view the properties of each CA and find that the auditing is configured at each CA, as shown in Figure 13-3.

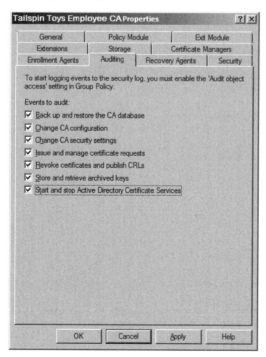

Figure 13-3   Auditing settings defined at the Tailspin Toys Employee CA

Why are there no audit entries related to Certificate Services?

The CA does not have success and failure auditing enabled for Object Access. The auditing must be enabled either in the local security policy or in a Group Policy Object linked to the organizational unit where the CA's computer account exists in AD DS.

Chapter 14: Planning and Implementing Disaster Recovery

1. When you perform the installation of the replacement root CA computer, can you use the default installation folder for Windows Server 2008?

   No. The original CA was installed in the folder C:\winnt. The replacement computer must use the same folder for installation.

2. Can you assign the replacement CA computer the NetBIOS name FABINCCA01A to designate this as the second instance of the root CA computer? Why or why not?

   No. You cannot change the name of the computer when you replace the CA computer hardware. The CRL Distribution Point (CDP) in AD DS includes the CA computer name in the publication path.

3. Which registry key should you back up on the original CA computer to reduce the replacement CA computer configuration?

   HKEY_LOCAL_MACHINE\System\CurrentControlSet\Services\CertSvc\ Configuration*CAName*, where *CAName* is the logical name of the CA.

4. What type of backup should you perform on the original root CA computer before you start the installation of the replacement CA computer—a system state backup or a manual backup?

   Assuming that the replacement hardware has advanced greatly in the last five years, it's most likely that you would perform a manual backup of the CA database and log files. Because of hardware differences, a system state backup can result in the failure of the replacement computer.

5. What software must be installed on the replacement CA computer before you start the installation of Certificate Services? Why?

   The HSM support software must be installed on the replacement CA computer to allow the replacement computer to communicate with the HSM and access the certificate and key material on the HSM.

6. How does this installation of Certificate Services differ from the original installation of Certificate Services?

   You must choose to use an existing certificate by choosing the HSM's CSP and the certificate with the original name of the CA computer.

7. Once the installation of Certificate Services is complete, what must be done to allow the CA to recognize the certificates issued by the CA on the previous computer?

    Assuming that you performed a manual backup before replacing the hardware, you must restore the CA database and log files to the original locations using the Certificate Services Restore Wizard.

8. What should be done to the original hardware before it is returned to the leasing company?

    The hard drives from the original hardware should be erased and degaussed to ensure that no data can be accessed from the original hardware. The use of the HSM reduces the risks because the private key material never existed on the hard drive— only on the HSM.

9. Do you have to republish the root CA certificate in AD DS once the hardware replacement is complete?

    No. The replacement CA is still using the same certificate and private key. There is no need to republish the same certificate.

Chapter 15: Issuing Certificates

1. Assume that a custom version 2 certificate template is created for code signing that requires CA certificate manager approval. What enrollment method should you use for deploying the custom code-signing certificates to the three members of the Quality Assurance team if you perform the request from a Windows XP client computer?

    The Certificate Services Web Enrollment site method is recommended because the Web site implements cookies to allow the Windows XP user to return and complete a pending certificate request.

2. If the user had a Windows Vista client, are other options available for enrollment?

    Yes, the Windows Vista Certificates console allows the initiation and completion of pending certificate requests. In fact, the enrollment can be initiated using the Web Enrollment pages and completed using the Certificate Enrollment wizard.

3. Assume that a custom version 2 certificate template is created for EFS certificates. What options must be enabled in the certificate template to permit autoenrollment for all users in the Lucerne Publishing forest?

    The certificate template must assign all users Read, Enroll, and Autoenroll permissions.

4. Where must you configure Group Policy to enable autoenrollment of the custom EFS certificate to all users in the LucernePublish.msft domain?

    You must configure a GPO linked to the LucernePublish.msft domain that selects all Autoenrollment Settings check boxes in User Configuration\Windows Settings\Security Settings\Public Key Policies\Autoenrollment Settings.

5. Does autoenrollment deploy custom EFS certificates to all users of laptops running Windows 2000, Windows XP, and Windows Vista? Why or why not?

    No. Autoenrollment Settings deploy custom EFS certificates only to users with Windows XP or Windows Vista laptops.

6. What method of enrollment allows EFS certificates to be deployed to users of laptops running Windows 2000 without user intervention?

    Lucerne Publishing can develop a Microsoft Visual Basic script that utilizes the Certificate Enrollment Control to submit a request for the custom EFS certificate. To provide automation, this script can be executed at logon to automate the distribution of the custom EFS certificate.

7. Assume that the default EFS Recovery Agent certificate template is modified so that only the two EFS recovery agents are assigned Read and Enroll permissions for the certificate template. What enrollment method(s) can they use to acquire their EFS Recovery Agent certificates?

    The agents can use any manual enrollment method, such as the Certificates MMC console focused on the current user or the Certificate Services Web Enrollment pages, to request their EFS Recovery Agent certificates.

8. Assuming that the default IPsec certificate is used for the IPsec tunnel mode project, do you use ACRS or Autoenrollment Settings to automate the deployment of IPsec certificates to computers running Windows Server 2008 at the corporate office?

    You must use ACRS to deploy the IPsec certificates. The IPsec certificate is a version 1 certificate that can be deployed only by using ACRS.

9. What must be done to the IPsec certificate template and the Automatic Certificate Request Settings Group Policy setting to enable automatic enrollment of the IPsec certificates by computers running Windows Server 2008?

    The permissions on the IPsec certificate template must enable Read and Enroll permissions for a group that contains the Windows Server 2003 computer accounts. A Group Policy that enables the Computer Configuration\Windows Settings\Security Settings\Public Key Policies\Automatic Certificate Request Settings GPO with the IPsec certificate template must be linked to the OU containing the Windows Server 2008 computer accounts.

10. What must be done to the IPsec certificate template and the Autoenrollment Settings Group Policy setting to enable automatic enrollment of the IPsec certificates by computers running Windows Server 2008?

    The IPsec certificate must be duplicated to create a custom version 2 certificate template. The permissions on the custom IPsec certificate template must enable Read, Enroll, and Autoenroll permissions for a group that contains the Windows Server 2003 computer accounts. Finally, the Autoenrollment Settings Group Policy must

be linked to an OU containing the computer accounts and enable all options in Computer Configuration\Windows Settings\Security Settings\Public Key Policies\Autoenrollment Settings.

11. How do you deploy IPsec certificates to the third-party VPN devices at the remote offices?

    A PKCS #10 request file can be created at each third-party VPN device and submitted to an enterprise CA by using the Certificate Services Web Enrollment pages.

Chapter 16: Creating Trust Between Organizations

1. Which CA in the production hierarchy must be issued the Cross Certification Authority certificate to satisfy the design requirements?

    It must be issued to The Phone Company South CA. If you issue the Cross Certification Authority certificate to The Phone Company Policy CA, certificates could be trusted from The Phone Company Policy CA and its two subordinate CAs: The Phone Company North CA and The Phone Company South CA, subject to any defined basic constraints.

2. What CA must be used to issue the Cross Certification Authority certificate on the test network to satisfy the design requirements?

    The Cross Certification Authority certificate can be issued by either The Phone Company Test North CA or The Phone Company Test South CA. Both CAs are enterprise CAs, and there are no restrictions on which issuing CA must be used. It is easier to work with two CAs at the same location (Barcelona), so this example uses The Phone Company Test South CA.

3. If the Cross Certification Authority certificate is issued to the The Phone Company Policy CA, what lines must be included in the Policy.inf file to recognize certificates issued by the The Phone Company South CA?

    [BasicConstraintsExtension]

    PathLength = 1

4. If the Cross Certification Authority certificate is issued to the The Phone Company South CA, what lines must be included in the Policy.inf file to recognize certificates issued by the The Phone Company South CA?

    [BasicConstraintsExtension]

    PathLength = 0

5. What name constraints are required in the Policy.inf file to limit permitted certificates to the single certificate issued to the software development manager?

    [NameConstraintsExtension]

    Include = NameConstraintsPermitted

Critical = true

[NameConstraintsPermitted]

DirectoryName = "CN=The Phone Company,OU=PKI Roles,DC=ad,DC=thephonecompany,DC=msft"

6. What application policy entries are required in the Policy.inf file to limit the certificates to only code-signing certificates?

[ApplicationPolicyStatementExtension]

Policies = AppCodeSignPolicy

Critical = false

[AppCodeSignPolicy]

OID = 11.3.6.1.5.5.7.3.3 ; Code Signing

7. Assuming that the Cross Certification Authority certificate is issued by the The Phone Company Test South CA to the The Phone Company South CA, how does the certificate chain for the manager's certificate look when viewed on a computer running Windows XP in the certification forest?

    The Phone Company Test Root CA => The Phone Company Test Policy CA => The Phone Company Test South CA => The Phone Company South CA => The Phone Company

8. Assuming that the Cross Certification Authority certificate is issued by the The Phone Company Test South CA to the The Phone Company South CA, how does the certificate chain for the manager's certificate look when viewed on a computer running Windows Vista in the production forest?

    The Phone Company Root CA => The Phone Company Policy CA =>The Phone Company

Chapter 17: Identity Lifecycle Manager 2007 Certificate Management

1. Does the proposed enrollment workflow enforce the defined certificate policy for enrollment?

    No. There is no data collection enforced in the workflow. The medium assurance certificate policy requires that the registration authority record data from a form of national or state photo identification.

2. How would you modify the enrollment workflow to meet the defined certificate policy?

Add data collection of form of identification. The data must be recorded by the certificate manager and be recorded in an encrypted state in the CLM database.

3. In Table 17-9, define the permission assignments required to perform the enroll policy workflow.

Table 17-9   Enroll Policy Permissions

Location	Permission assignment requirements
Service connection point	Assign the Contoso\CertMgrs group _____ and _____ permissions.
	Assign the Contoso\CertMgrs group Read and CLM Request Enroll permissions.
User or Group	Assign the Contoso\CertMgrs group _____ and _____ Permissions on the Contoso\KRAs group.
	Assign the Contoso\CertMgrs group Read and CLM Request Enroll Permissions on the Contoso\KRAs group.
Profile Template	Assign the _____ group and the _____ group _____ and _____ permissions on the Key Recovery Agent profile template.
	Assign the Contoso\CertMgrs group and the Contoso\ KRAs group Read and CLM Enroll permissions on the Key Recovery Agent profile template.
Certificate Template	Assign the _____ group _____ and _____ permissions on the Key Recovery Agent certificate template.
	Assign the Contoso\KRAs group Read and Enroll permissions on the Key Recovery Agent certificate template.

4. Are there any issues with the defined renewal workflow?

Yes. You cannot perform manager data collection when the renewal is initiated by the Certificate Lifecycle Manager Service.

5. Are there any issues with the proposed renewal request workflow? What must be done to fix the workflow?

Yes. You cannot have the Certificate Lifecycle Manager Service record data collection. You must remove the data collection item or have the data collection performed by the certificate subscriber.

6. Is it possible to send one one-time password to the subscriber and a second one-time password to the manager?

Yes. This is a common way of increasing the assurance level of a certificate. The subscriber must meet with his or her manager to obtain the second one-time password.

7. How many one-time passwords must be entered by the subscriber to complete the renewal request?

Two. The subscriber must input the one-time password sent by e-mail to his or her manager and the one-time password sent by e-mail to his or her account.

Chapter 18: Archiving Encryption Keys

1. At what CAs in the CA hierarchy must you enable key archival? How many key recovery agents must be defined at each CA?

    Key archival must be enabled at each of the regional issuing CAs. At each regional CA, you must define two key recovery agents: one at the corporate head office in Chicago and one at the regional office where the issuing CA is located.

2. What operating system must be installed on the issuing CAs to allow key archival?

    The issuing CAs must be running Windows Server 2008 Enterprise or Windows Server 2008 Datacenter to enable key archival.

3. Can you combine the key recovery agent role with the roles of CA administrator, certificate manager, auditor, or backup operator? Why or why not?

    You can combine the key recovery agent role with any of the Common Criteria roles, because the key recovery agent is not a Common Criteria role.

    What Common Criteria role is blocked from being a key recovery agent because of the design requirements?

    The key recovery agent cannot be assigned the certificate manager role. The design requirement specifying two individuals for all key recovery operations excludes this combination of roles.

4. What certificate template must be available to allow secure transmission of the requestor's private key to the issuing CA?

    The CA Exchange certificate provides the encryption of the requestor's private key as it is transmitted from the requesting computer to the issuing CA.

    What **certutil** command is used by a certificate manager to extract the encrypted BLOB from the CA database?

    The certutil –getkey command allows the certificate manager to extract the encrypted BLOB from the CA database.

    What **certutil** command is used by a key recovery agent to decrypt the PKCS #12 file within the encrypted BLOB file?

    The certutil –recoverkey command allows the key recovery agent to extract the PKCS #12 file from the encrypted BLOB file.

    What risk is there to allowing the key recovery agent to send the PKCS #12 file and password to the user in the same e-mail message?

    If attackers gain access to the message, they have the ability to import the PKCS #12 file into their profile.

5. What risk is there to archiving a certificate template with the purpose of Signature and Encryption?

If a certificate has the purpose of Signature and Encryption, the certificate can be used for both digital signing and encryption. The digital signing purpose can lead to impersonation if the private key is recovered from the CA database.

6. If ILM 2007 Certificate Management was used to recover the EFS and S/MIME certificates, what account would act as the certificate manager in the key recovery process?

The CLMAgent agent account is assigned the Issue and Manage Certificate permission at the CA, allowing the CLMAgent account to act as the certificate manager in the key recovery process.

7. If ILM 2007 Certificate Management was used to recover the EFS and S/MIME certificates, what account would act as the key recovery agent in the key recovery process?

The CLMKRAgent agent account is designated as a key recovery agent at the CA, allowing the CLMKRAgent account to act as the key recovery agent in the process.

8. Assuming that ILM 2007 will only use certificates issued by the Lucerne Publishing Americas CA, how many Key Recovery Agent certificates would be designated at the Americas CA? How many recovery agents must be used for each archival operation?

Three Key Recovery Agent certificate templates must be designated at the Lucerne Publishing Americas CA: the central recovery agent, the Americas recovery agent, and the clmKRAgent recovery agent. The CA must be configured to require that all three certificates are used for each archival operation.

9. What risk is there to archiving a certificate template with the purpose of Signature and Encryption?

If a certificate has the purpose of Signature and Encryption, the certificate can be used for both digital signing and encryption. The digital signing purpose can lead to impersonation if the private key is recovered from the CA database.

10. If ILM 2007 Certificate Management were used to recover the EFS and S/MIME certificates, what account would act as the certificate manager in the key recovery process?

The CLMAgent agent account is assigned the Issue and Manage Certificate permission at the CA, allowing the CLMAgent account to act as the certificate manager in the key recovery process.

11. If ILM 2007 Certificate Management were used to recover the EFS and S/MIME certificates, what account would act as the Key Recovery Agent in the key recovery process?

The CLMKRAgent agent account is designated as a key recovery agent at the CA, allowing the CLMKRAgent account to act as the key recovery agent in the process.

12. Assuming that ILM 2007 will only use certificates issued by the Lucerne Publishing Americas CA, how many Key Recovery Agent certificates would be designated at the Americas CA? How many recovery agents must be used for each archival operation.

Three Key Recovery Agent certificate templates must be designated at the Lucerne Publishing Americas CA: the central recovery agent, the Americas recovery agent, and the clmKRAgent recovery agent. The CA must be configured to require that all 3 certificates are used for each archival operation.

Chapter 19: Implementing SSL Encryption for Web Servers

1. Which CA should issue the Web Server certificate for the customer billing system Web site?

   The customer billing system requires a Web Server certificate from a commercial CA so that there is greater trust in the customer billing system Web site. By using a commercial CA, more customers trust the root CA certificate of the Web Server certificate's certificate chain.

2. Which CA should issue the Web Server certificate for the employee benefits Web site?

   The Web Server certificates for the employee benefits Web site can be issued by any of the three issuing CA's in The Phone Company's CA hierarchy.

3. Where should the Web Server certificate(s) be deployed for the customer billing system Web site?

   For the customer billing system Web site, the Web Server certificate must be installed on the DALTXIIS01 computer.

4. Where should the Web Server certificate(s) be deployed for the employee benefits Web site?

   For the employee benefits Web site, a separate Web Server certificate must be installed at each computer in the cluster: DALTXIIS02, AMSNLIIS01, and TORONIIS01.

5. How do you implement certificate mapping for the customer billing Web site?

   Certificate mapping should be deployed by using Active Directory mapping. The same certificate mappings are required at any of the three Web servers.

6. If you perform an implicit certificate mapping, what form of name must be included in the Subject or the Subject Alternative Name extension of the user certificate? Does the Smart Card User certificate template satisfy this condition?

   The Subject Alternative Name must include the user's UPN in the certificate's Subject Alternative Name extension. The Smart Card User certificate does meet this requirement, as the user's UPN is also required in the certificate to support smart card login.

7. What subject is required for the Web Server certificate for the customer billing system Web site?

    The subject of the customer billing system Web site's certificate must be *www.thephone-company.com*.

8. What subjects are required for the Web Server certificate for the employee benefits Web site?

    The subject of the three employee benefits Web site's certificates must be *benefits.thephone-company.com*. You can deploy the same Web Server certificate and private key at each Web server or deploy individual certificates and private keys at each Web server.

Chapter 20: Encrypting File System

1. Does the default EFS Recovery Agent certificate template satisfy the design requirements for the Lucerne Publishing EFS project?

    Yes. There are no specific design requirements for the enrollment of the EFS Recovery Agent certificate template. By assigning permissions so that only members of the internal audit department have Read and Enroll permissions, the enrollment is restricted to approved users.

2. Does the default Key Recovery Agent certificate template satisfy the design requirements for the Lucerne Publishing EFS project?

    Yes. There are no specific design requirements for the enrollment of the Key Recovery Agent certificate template. By default, members of the Enterprise Admins group have Read and Enroll permissions for the Key Recovery Agent certificate template.

3. Do the design requirements allow the EFS Recovery Agent and Key Recovery Agent certificate templates to be published only at the Lucerne Publishing Americas CA?

    Yes. It does not matter which issuing CA in the CA hierarchy publishes these certificate templates. As long as the issued certificates chain to the Lucerne Publishing Root CA certificate, they are recognized at all locations in the Lucerne Publishing network.

4. Does Andy's proposed solution meet the design requirements for designation of key recovery agents in the forest?

    No. The design requirements demand that key archival and recovery are enabled only at the Lucerne Publishing Americas CA. To meet the requirements, the key recovery agents from each region should be designated as key recovery agents at the Lucerne Publishing Americas CA. The proposed solution designates only a single key recovery agent at each region's CA, enabling key archival at all issuing CAs, not just the Lucerne Publishing Americas CA.

5. Is EFS encryption disabled for all computers running Windows XP not in the OU named OU=Notebooks,OU=Computer Accounts,DC=lucernepublish,DC=msft?

   No. The configured GPO resorts to using the locally defined EFS recovery agent. To prevent encryption at the computers running Windows 2000, an empty Encrypting File System policy must be defined. The application of no Encrypting File System policy results in the use of the EFS encryption settings defined in the local security policy.

6. Does Andy's proposed design disable EFS encryption for computer accounts of computers running Windows XP and Windows Vista not in the OU named OU=Notebooks,OU=Computer Accounts,DC=lucernepublish,DC=msft?

   No. The design does not disable EFS encryption for any computers running Windows XP. To disable EFS encryption for computers running Windows XP and Windows Vista, clear the Allow Users To Encrypt Files Using Encrypting File System (EFS) check box on the property sheet of the Encrypting File System Group Policy setting (for Windows XP) or select the Don't Allow option for Windows Vista.

7. Does the Lucerne Publishing EFS certificate template allow for autoenrollment by Windows Vista users?

   Yes. The certificate template correctly enables Read, Enroll, and Autoenroll permissions for the Lucerne Publishing EFS certificate template.

8. Does the proposed EFS Autoenrollment GPO enable autoenrollment of the Lucerne Publishing EFS certificate template by users with computers running Windows XP?

   No. The EFS Autoenrollment GPO must be applied to the OU where the user accounts, not the computer accounts, exist. The EFS Autoenrollment GPO must also be modified to enable autoenrollment for user accounts, not computer accounts. Because no user OUs are defined, you can define the GPO at the Lucernepublish.com domain, but limit Read, Enroll, and Autoenroll permissions to members of a custom universal or global group.

Chapter 21: Deploying Smart Cards

1. Can you use the default Enrollment Agent certificate template to satisfy the design requirements for City Power and Light? Why or why not?

   No. The default template is a software certificate template and does not require certificate manager approval.

2. If you create a custom certificate template for the enrollment agent, how do you enforce the requirement that only Andy receives a custom Enrollment Agent certificate?

   You can modify permissions so that only Andy has Read and Enroll permissions for the custom Enrollment Agent certificate. In addition, it is the responsibility of the

certificate manager to issue the certificate only to Andy. If another user requests the custom Enrollment Agent certificate, the request should be denied.

3. How do you enforce the Atlanta certificate manager's authorization of the Enrollment Agent certificate issued to Andy?

You can enforce the authorization by enabling the Require CA Certificate Manager Approval option on the Issuance Requirements tab of the custom Enrollment Agent certificate template. Even better, you could use ILM 2007 certificate management to define a workflow that requires data collection.

4. Can you use the default Smart Card User certificate template for the administrative smart cards?

No. The default Smart Card User certificate template enables secure e-mail. The smart card must be used only for smart card authentication.

5. Do you have to use a custom certificate template to meet the design goals of City Power and Light?

No. You can use the default Smart Card Logon certificate template.

6. How do you limit enrollment of the smart card certificate template to Andy?

You must modify the permissions of the Smart Card Logon certificate template so that only Andy has Read and Enroll permissions for the certificate template.

7. Assuming that the administrators can log on from both servers and desktop workstations spread among any OU in the forest, how do you enforce smart cards for interactive logon for the Administrator accounts?

You must modify the individual user accounts to enable the Smart Card Is Required For Interactive Logon option.

8. How do you enforce smart card authentication for remote access connections by the administrative staff?

You must define a remote access policy at the Network Policy Server that requires EAP-TLS authentication.

9. If a project implements smart cards for regular user accounts, can the administrators use the same smart card for their user certificates?

Yes. The administrators have computers running Windows Vista. Windows Vista supports multiple smart card authentication certificates on a smart card. With Windows Vista the default authentication certificate does not have to be in the default slot on the smart card.

10. Can you implement Elliptical Curve Cryptography (ECC) in a custom version 3 certificate template for the administrators?

No. ECC is not supported for smart card logon.

11. What tool would Andy use for enrolling the user smart card certificates?

   Andy must use the Certificate MMC console. The Windows Server 2008 CA no longer uses Web enrollment pages for smart card enrollment.

Chapter 22: Secure E-Mail

1. Based on the security policies related to e-mail usage, how many e-mail certificates must be distributed to each user?

   Each user must be issued two e-mail certificates: one for e-mail signing and one for e-mail encryption.

2. What certificate(s) must be published to Active Directory Domain Services (AD DS) to enable the sending of encrypted e-mail between employees of Adventure Works?

   The encryption certificate must be published into the *userCertificate* attribute of the recipient's user account in AD DS to allow a sender to obtain the recipient's public key from the global catalog.

3. Will the current CA infrastructure allow the e-mail signing and encryption certificates to be recognized by the customers of Adventure Works?

   Yes, as long as the customer has not removed the VeriSign Class 3 Public Primary Certification Authority from the trusted root store (of client machines).

4. What method would you use to deploy the e-mail certificate(s) to the Adventure Works users? What certificate template settings are required to allow this method of enrollment?

   You can use autoenrollment settings to enable autoenrollment of the two certificate templates. The two certificate templates must enable the Read, Enroll, and Autoenroll permissions for all users that will receive the certificates.

5. One of the travel agents is able to open his encrypted e-mail only at one of the available agent computers. When he attempts to open his encrypted e-mail at the other computers, the attempt fails. What can you do to ensure that the travel agent can open the encrypted e-mail at any of the travel agent computers?

   You must implement a roaming profile for each travel agent user account so that the user's certificate store is downloaded to each computer that he or she works at. The current computer must be used when the roaming profile is enabled, so that the roaming profile is updated with the certificates in the Current User store.

6. How do you propose to enforce the security policy that requires two or more people to be involved in the recovery?

   The Adventure Works Issuing CA must ensure that different people hold the key recovery agent and certificate manager roles. Separating the two roles ensures that two people are involved in every key recovery operation.

7. How do you enforce the requirement that users must provide a password to access the private keys associated with the e-mail signing of any e-mail encryption certificates?

    The certificate templates for both e-mail signing and e-mail encryption must enable the Prompt The User During Enrollment And Require User Input When The Private Key Is Used option.

8. If you had the budget, how could you further increase the security of the e-mail signing and e-mail encryption certificates?

    Rather than protecting the user's e-mail certificates with a software-based CSP, you could protect the smart cards with a smart card–based CSP. A smart card CSP provides two-factor protection of the e-mail certificates.

9. What must a travel agent do to allow a customer to send an encrypted e-mail message?

    To send the travel agent an encrypted e-mail message, the customer must access the travel agent's encryption public key. This can be accomplished by the travel agent sending the customer a signed e-mail message or by creating an externally available Lightweight Directory Access Protocol (LDAP) directory for customers to retrieve the travel agent's encryption certificate.

10. What solution can be used to allow remote travel agents to securely access their e-mail and use S/MIME to protect the e-mail messages without enabling an additional e-mail client?

    Because Travel Works uses Microsoft Exchange Server 2003 and Outlook 2003, the company can implement remote procedure call (RPC) over Hypertext Transfer Protocol Secure (HTTPS) to enable secure client access to mail services from the Outlook client. There is no need to implement an RFC-based e-mail protocol such as POP3 or IMAP4.

11. One of the travel agents has forgotten the password used to protect the e-mail encryption certificate and can no longer read her encrypted e-mail. What must you do to allow the travel agent to access the encrypted e-mail?

    You must delete the existing certificate and private key from the user's certificate store and recover the private key from the CA database. When you import the certificate, the user can choose a new password for the encryption certificate's private key.

12. When performing the testing of your e-mail solution, you are told that customers are complaining that their e-mail applications are reporting that the digital signatures are failing. You look at the certificate and find the following URLs in the CDP extension:

    ❑ *LDAP:///CN=Adventure Works Issuing CA,CN=ADVCA01,CN=CDP,CN=Public Key Services,CN=Services,CN=Configuration,DC=travelworks,DC=com*

    ❑ *http://advca01/certenroll/Adventure%%20Works%%20%%20Issuing%%20CA.crl*

What is causing the certificate validation to fail? What must you do to fix the problem?

None of the CDP URLs are available from the Internet. The customer computers are unable to retrieve a valid CRL for the Adventure Works Issuing CA. You must add an Internet-accessible URL to the CDP extension, and then revoke and reissue the e-mail encryption and signing certificates so that they include the correct URLs in the CDP extension.

Chapter 23: Virtual Private Networking

1. What authentication protocol must be enforced for VPN communications to satisfy the initial authentication requirements?

   MS-CHAPv2 must be enforced for the initial authentication requirements. MS-CHAPv2 provides the ability to type the user name and password for authentication and enforce mutual authentication between the VPN user and the RADIUS server.

2. What certificates are required for the initial VPN solution? Provide your answers in the following table.

Principal	Certificate
VPN user	No certificates required
VPN client computer	IPsec certificate
RADIUS server	No certificate required
VPN server	IPsec certificate

3. What authentication protocol must be enforced for VPN communications to satisfy the modified authentication requirements to enforce smart card authentication?

   EAP-TLS must be enforced for the initial authentication requirements. EAP-TLS enforces mutual authentication between the VPN user and the RADIUS server and can be configured to require smart card authentication.

4. What certificates are required for the modified VPN solution that uses smart cards? Provide your answers in the following table.

Principal	Certificate
VPN user	Smart Card User or Smart Card Logon certificate
VPN client computer	IPsec certificate
RADIUS server	RAS and IAS Server certificate
VPN server	IPsec certificate

5. How would Lucerne Publishing ensure centralized remote access policy application and enable the ability to immediately shut down all VPN access?

   Lucerne Publishing must implement RADIUS authentication by installing Network Policy Server on at least two computers.

6. What certificate template(s) are required for the L2TP/IPsec tunnel? What CA should you publish the certificates at?

   You must publish the IPsec and IPsec (offline request) certificate templates. The certificate templates must be published at each of the three issuing CAs: Lucerne Publishing Americas CA, Lucerne Publishing EMEA CA, and Lucerne Publishing APAC CA.

7. What method could you use to deploy the IPsec certificates to forest member computers?

   You could deploy the IPsec certificates to forest members by using Automatic Certificate Request Settings.

8. What method could you use to deploy the IPsec certificates to nonforest member computers?

   You could have users request the IPsec (offline request) certificate template and save the issued certificate and private key to a floppy disk. The certificate could then be imported on their home computers.

9. When Lucerne Publishing switches to using Smart Card certificates, how can the Smart Card certificate template be modified to further restrict VPN access to the network?

   A custom version 2 certificate template can be created that implements a custom application policy OID. The RADIUS server can then be configured to require the custom application policy OID in the certificate to allow access to the network.

10. What certificate(s) would you deploy at the VPN server when using RADIUS authentication?

    You would require only the IPsec certificate template at the VPN server.

11. If some users are having problems connecting using the L2TP/IPsec VPN because of firewalls at customer sites, what other tunneling protocol could be implemented? Are there any client restrictions with this tunneling protocol?

    SSTP uses SSL to create a tunnel that can pass through firewall devices. SSTP is limited to Windows Vista clients with Service Pack 1 installed.

Chapter 24: Wireless Networking

1. What network infrastructure service required for wireless network is missing from the Margie's Travel network? On which server(s) would you install the missing service?

   There are no RADIUS servers on the network. You must install the Network Policy Server (NPS) on at least two computers to ensure redundancy. The most logical choice is to deploy NPS on the two domain controllers.

2. When you purchase the wireless access points for the networks, what features are required to satisfy the design requirements?

    The wireless access points must support RADIUS authentication. Ideally, the wireless access points should support WPA to ensure the strongest level of encryption.

3. What certificate(s) are required on the wireless access points?

    No certificates are required on the wireless access points. The wireless access points simply translate EAP authentication request packets to RADIUS authentication request packets and RADIUS authentication responses to EAP authentication responses.

4. What certificate(s) are required at each desktop or notebook computer?

    Each computer or notebook must have a certificate that includes the Client Authentication application policy OID.

5. What certificate(s) are required for each user of the network?

    Each user must have a certificate that includes the Client Authentication application policy OID.

6. What other certificate(s) are required for the wireless network deployment?

    The two NPS servers must have certificates that include the Server Authentication application policy OID. For example, the RAS and IAS Server certificate provides this application policy OID.

7. How many remote access policies are required for the wireless deployment?

    Two remote access policies are required: one for computer authentication and one for user authentication.

8. How can you ensure that each desktop and notebook computer is correctly configured for connectivity to the wireless network?

    You can use Group Policy to ensure that the correct wireless security settings are applied to all domain members.

9. What additional measures can be taken to ensure that only Margie's Travel users can connect to the wireless network?

    The user certificates can include a custom application policy OID that uniquely identifies the certificates as approved wireless certificates. The remote access policies can include remote access profile settings requiring the existence of the custom application policy OID for a successful connection.

Chapter 25: Document and Code Signing

1. Does the Code Signing certificate template satisfy the design requirements? What must you do to satisfy the design requirements?

   No. The Code Signing certificate template has a one-year validity period and does not implement any issuance requirements. You must create a custom version 2 certificate template based on the Code Signing certificate template.

2. In the following table, define the settings on the General tab to satisfy the design requirements for your custom Code Signing certificate template.

Attribute	Your recommended design
Template display name	**Any valid name**
Template name	**Any valid name (no spaces allowed)**
Validity period	**3 years**
Publish certificate in Active Directory	**Disabled**
Do not automatically reenroll if a duplicate certificate exists in Active Directory	**Disabled**

3. What CSP must be enabled on the Request Handling tab to satisfy the design requirements for the custom Code Signing certificate template?

   The Microsoft Base Smart Card CSP must be enabled in the custom Code Signing certificate template. All other CSPs should be disabled.

4. How must you configure the settings on the Subject Name tab to satisfy the design requirements?

   You must allow the requestor to supply the subject in the request. This allows Mike Danseglio to provide Lucerne Publishing as the subject of the custom Code Signing certificate.

5. In the following table, define the settings on the Issuance Requirements tab to satisfy the design requirements for the custom Code Signing certificate template.

Attribute	Your recommended design
CA certificate manager approval	**Enabled**
This number of authorized signatures	**Disabled**
Require the following for reenrollment	**Same criteria as for enrollment**

Chapter 26: Deploying Certificates to Domain Controllers

1. Ken has been tasked with deploying smart cards for authentication. The smart card authentication is failing. Do you have any idea why the authentication attempts are failing?

   The smart card authentication attempts are failing because the domain controllers have KDC certificates from the previous CA hierarchy.

2. On inspection, Ken discoverers that the five domain controllers have not obtained KDC certificates from the new CA hierarchy. What is the easiest way for Ken to remove all previously issued KDC certificates from the domain controllers?

   Ken must run certutil –dcinfo deleteall to replace all existing KDC certificates. The command will delete all certificates that were previously issued to domain controllers.

3. What certificate template should Ken make available at the Tucson and Scottsdale CAs for the domain controllers?

   Ken should publish the Kerberos Authentication certificate template at both the Consolidated Messenger Tucson CA and the Consolidated Messenger Scottsdale CA.

4. Ken wants to enable strong KDC authentication on the network. Are there any deployment blockers in the current environment?

   Yes. Strong KDC authentication requires Windows Vista clients and Windows Server 2008 domain controllers. Ken cannot deploy strong KDC authentication until all of the computers running Windows XP are upgraded or replaced with computers running Windows Vista.

5. Once all computers running Windows XP are upgraded to Windows Vista, how would Ken enforce strong KDC authentication?

   Ken must change the HKEY_LOCAL_MACHINE\SYSTEM\CurrentControlSet\ Control\Lsa\Kerberos\Parameters\kdcvalidation registry key on all Windows Vista clients and Windows Server 2008 domain controllers to a value of 2.

Chapter 27: Network Device Enrollment Service

1. How many certificates must be imported into the Cisco VPN 3000 concentrators to allow them to trust certificates from the Lucerne Publishing CA hierarchy?

   The root CA, policy CA, and infrastructure CA certificates must be imported into each Cisco VPN 3000 device to allow certificate trust.

2. What accounts will require permissions on the three custom certificate templates? What permissions are required?

   The NDES Service account (Lucerne\s-NDESService) and the device manager account group must be assigned Read and Enroll permissions on all three of the certificate templates.

3. What group memberships are required for the Lucerne\S-NDESService account?

   The NDES Service account (Lucerne\s-NDESService) must be a member of the local IIS_USRS group.

4. Assuming that the CiscoSigning, CiscoEncryption, and CiscoCombo certificate templates are available for enrollment at the Lucerne Publishing Infrastructure CA, are there any additional certificate templates that must be available for the NDES server? If so, what are they?

    Yes, additional certificate templates are required. The CEP Encryption and Computer Enrollment Agent (Offline Request) certificate templates must be available for the installation of the NDES role service.

5. Lucerne Publishing wishes to utilize Suite B algorithms wherever possible. Can NDES be configured to use SHA 256-bit hashes?

    No. NDES cannot use Cryptography Next Generation (CNG) algorithms and CSPs. You can use only SHA1 or MD5 for hash algorithms.

6. What registry values must be modified to enable the three custom certificate templates?

    Three separate registry values in the HKEY_LOCAL_MACHINE\Software\ Microsoft\Cryptography\MSCEP key must be configured to enable the three custom certificate templates. The SignatureTemplate value must be changed to CiscoSigning, the EncryptionTemplate must be changed to CiscoEncryption, and the GeneralPurposeTemplate must be changed to CiscoCombo.

7. If the Lucerne Publishing Employee CA was accidentally selected during the installation of the NDES role service, how would you change the CA used by the NDES server?

    You can change the CA used by the NDES service by editing the HKEY_LOCAL_ MACHINE\Software\Microsoft\Cryptography\MSCEP\CAInfo\Configuration String value to the configuration string for the Lucerne Publishing Infrastructure CA.

Index

A

About the Author

Brian Komar is the President and co-founder of IdentIT Inc., a consulting firm specializing in identity integration and network security solutions. Together with Paul Adare, Brian's business partner, IdentIT Inc. delivers PKI and identity integration consulting engagements for Microsoft's customers.

Brian has written several books related to computer security during the past few years, including the *Microsoft Windows Security Resource Kit, MCSE Training Kit: Designing Microsoft Windows 2000 Network Security*, and *Firewalls for Dummies*. In addition to writing books, Brian has written three white papers related to PKI for Microsoft: "Implementing and Administering Certificate Templates in Windows Server 2003," "Troubleshooting Certificate Status and Revocation," and "Planning and Implementing Cross-Certification and Qualified Subordination Using Windows Server 2003," and he developed course 2821, *Designing and Managing a Windows Public Key Infrastructure*, the Microsoft Official Curriculum course on PKI. Brian is also a frequent speaker at IT industry conferences such as Microsoft Tech Ed, Windows Connections, and Microsoft IT Forum. Brian specializes in sessions that look under the hood at security and discuss practical implementation of security based on experiences from the field.

In his spare time (which isn't much), Brian likes to play volleyball, hike with his wife Krista, and play golf.

If you wish to contact Brian, you can reach him at brian.komar@identit.ca.

What do you think of this book?

We want to hear from you!

Do you have a few minutes to participate in a brief online survey?

Microsoft is interested in hearing your feedback so we can continually improve our books and learning resources for you.

To participate in our survey, please visit:

www.microsoft.com/learning/booksurvey/

...and enter this book's ISBN-10 or ISBN-13 number (located above barcode on back cover*). As a thank-you to survey participants in the United States and Canada, each month we'll randomly select five respondents to win one of five $100 gift certificates from a leading online merchant. At the conclusion of the survey, you can enter the drawing by providing your e-mail address, which will be used for prize notification only.

Thanks in advance for your input. Your opinion counts!

* Where to find the ISBN on back cover

ISBN-13: 000-0-0000-0000-0
ISBN-10: 0-0000-0000-0

0 000000 000000

Example only. Each book has unique ISBN.

Microsoft®
Press

No purchase necessary. Void where prohibited. Open only to residents of the 50 United States (includes District of Columbia) and Canada (void in Quebec). For official rules and entry dates see:

www.microsoft.com/learning/booksurvey/